Life and Letters of Janet Erskine Stuart, Superior General of the Society of the Sacred Heart, 1857-1914

Janet Stuart

LIFE AND LETTERS OF

JANET ERSKINE STUART

SUPERIOR GENERAL OF THE SOCIETY
OF THE SACRED HEART

1857 to 1914

BY

MAUD MONAHAN

WITH AN INTRODUCTION BY
HIS EMINENCE CARDINAL BOURNE
ARCHBISHOP OF WESTMINSTER

WITH ILLUSTRATIONS

LONGMANS, GREEN AND CO.
55 FIFTH AVENUE, NEW YORK
LONDON, TORONTO
BOMBAY, CALCUTTA AND MADRAS

1922

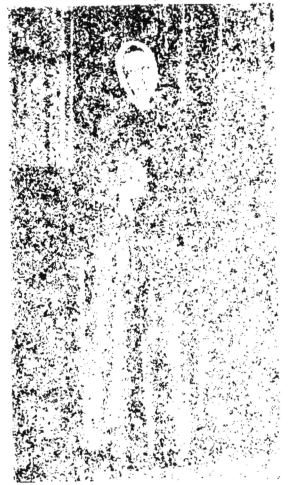

LIFE AND LETTERS OF
JANET ERSKINE STUART
SUPERIOR GENERAL OF THE SOCIETY
OF THE SACRED HEART
1857 to 1914

BY

MAUD MONAHAN

WITH AN INTRODUCTION BY

HIS EMINENCE CARDINAL BOURNE
ARCHBISHOP OF WESTMINSTER

WITH ILLUSTRATIONS

LONGMANS, GREEN AND CO.
55 FIFTH AVENUE, NEW YORK
LONDON, TORONTO
BOMBAY, CALCUTTA AND MADRAS
1922

Made in Great Britain

NIHIL OBSTAT

F. THOMAS BERGH, O.S.B.

Censor Deputatus

IMPRIMATUR

EDM. CAN. SURMONT

Vic. Gen.

Westmonasterii
die 9 Maii, 1922

INTRODUCTION

In the ordinary Providence of God each human life, even of those holding high public position in Church or State, exercises but a restricted and usually transient effect on the lives of others. Within a limited circle and for a few brief years the power flowing from such a life is felt. It grows gradually weaker and in the end ceases to be operative. When, therefore, a life clearly transcends the normal average of human influence, it is of great importance to succeeding generations that the lessons which it taught, and continues to teach, should be set forth in as full detail as may be possible.

In recent years God manifestly willed that the veil, which habitually shrouds from observation the marvellous supernatural existences of Carmel, should be lifted in the case of the little Sister Thérèse, to give to the world fresh joy and courage in the knowledge of high sanctity and close union with God, attained by such simple and childlike means.

No less, as it seems to me, is it necessary that the passage through this life of Mother Stuart, both in its purely natural and in its supernatural aspects, should be known not only in the religious family of which she became for too short a space the chief authority, but to all who care to follow and study God's dealings with His creatures.

It is indeed a very wonderful history. Of Scottish race, the youngest daughter of a clergyman of the Established Church of England, deprived of a mother's care and love in babyhood, losing apparently in girlhood any living faith, Janet Stuart was destined to become the Mother General of an institute of world-wide extent; to attain an intensity of religious faith and purpose, and to live a life of intimate union with God, such as have not often been surpassed;

and to exercise a Mother's spiritual sway over innumerable souls, both within and beyond the direct influence of the Society of the Sacred Heart.

No such life can ever be fully told. The record of it, to which I gratefully offer these few words of preface, ample and admirable though it be, leaves many things unsaid: some because they are too precious and too intimate, many others because there must be a limit to such telling, a vast multitude because they are in their fullness known to God alone. But, nevertheless, we have through this Life the privilege of knowing, in outline at least, the development of the mind, character, and heart of Janet Erskine Stuart, the gift of whose friendship is to so many of us one of the great possessions of our lives. And I may, perhaps, be allowed to single out as worthy of special attention some few characteristic features which stand out before me in special prominence, either as I read the story of her life or as I recall it in my memory of those days in which it was granted me to receive her friendship and to enjoy her confidence.

The history of her girlhood is of extreme significance and importance at the present day, for it sets before us a mental stage probably much more common than many people suppose, and often not understood by Catholics, especially in the continental countries. It is a condition of mind which must very often exist in those brought up outside the Catholic Church. I believe it also to occur among others who, bred into a traditional Catholicity, and even prepared for and admitted to the Sacraments, have yet never really assimilated and made their own the truth of the Catholic faith. Passing through the dimly conceived mysteries of life and death in childhood, faced by the shock of mental development in adolescence, without guide, or with one that may not be trustworthy, they are confronted by a veil of mist which for a time obscures all real conception of God or His dealings with mankind. They are called, they may call themselves, Agnostics. Are they really so? Their hearts and minds remain, in many cases, firm in the pursuit of truth, of beauty, of honour, of purity, and of high ideals. May we not say that instinctively, though they seem to know it not, their lives are striving after God?

May we not hope that, when by His grace the sun of His enlightenment shall scatter this veil of mist, they will give themselves wholeheartedly to His service? Janet Stuart, who was not spared this darkness and uncertainty, came forth from it to attain great sanctity and to be the Mother General of the Society of the Sacred Heart. She had learnt, as she was often to teach in the future, that *all* our past is, under God, to be never an obstacle, but always a help and preparation for the work that He gives us to undertake.

Then I would dwell upon her quite extraordinary power of uplifting others : of making them understand their own powers and the consequent responsibility of exerting those powers to the utmost ; of causing them to realise that there is no ground for discouragement in past faults and failures, but only new reason for fresh endeavour, with solid ground of hope for success. No one who knew her but would bear testimony to this exceptional gift which has made so many souls for ever her grateful debtors.

In a long intercourse with those entitled to write or to speak on spiritual things I have never known anyone who realised, as Mother Stuart did, the essential separate individuality of each soul in its service of God, nor one who respected more sacredly than she did that God-given individuality. Often souls are led to model themselves too minutely upon some exemplar—either the founder or foundress of the institute to which they belong, or the master or mistress who has trained them in God's service, or a spiritual guide, or some purely human tradition. The result has been constraint, much suffering, sterile uniformity, ultimate impotence, final decay. And individual existences, with their special gifts and powers, have been sacrificed all the time. Mother Stuart with a saintly boldness insisted upon God's rights in the individual soul, and upon the rights of the individual soul in God. She would not have her sisters or her daughters aim at being mere copies even of their own Blessed Foundress. For this outspoken teaching, arrived at after long experience, and after much painful striving in ways and methods which, by God's guidance, she had long outgrown, an immense debt of gratitude is due to Mother Stuart from those who cherish the liberty of the sons of God. After all our Divine Master is alone our true model, and as in His teaching so in His example it is *multifariam multisque modis* that He is pleased to live again as generation succeeds generation on this earth. While rules, and institutes, and methods will always have their own intrinsic and necessary use, they must ever remain but means, and never usurp the place of the one essential end, the union of the individual soul with God. Mother Stuart grasped and taught this truth with a clearness that I have never found surpassed elsewhere.

There are many other things upon which one would be glad to dwell, but it must be left to each reader to take and to choose from the rich harvest of teaching that the pages of this Life unfold. As the book is closed with deep thankfulness for all that is taught upon its pages, every reader will ask, ' Why did such an existence, so rich in experience, so full of promise, to human foresight so urgently needed, come to an end so soon ? ' In one of her letters Mother Stuart wrote : ' My head is full of plans and dreams of what might be done, but I must be patient : people are not ready yet.' It is, no doubt, God's Will that those whom He calls to govern should have their heads full of plans and dreams. It is not always His Will that these should be carried out. And when she wrote those words her working life was nearly at an end. We have no right to know God's purpose, but can we faintly discern it in the death of Mother Stuart at the comparatively early age of fifty-seven, in the first days of the Great War ? There are two reasons that, as I look back, seem to satisfy me when I try to explain to myself the opportuneness of a death which, when it occurred, seemed to baffle all human reasons or expectation.

I see, in the first place, God's great and special goodness to His well-tried and utterly devoted servant. By the summer of 1914 Mother Stuart was physically wholly exhausted. Who can contemplate what the moral agony of the prolonged war would have meant to her intensely sensitive nature, with her religious family made up of members from all the belligerent nations and set in their very midst ? God in His mercy had compassion upon His handmaid; and, even in the keenness of their loss, her daughters and friends are grateful to Him.

Secondly, in 1922 we see, as we could not see in 1914, that her real work was done. By her repeated journeyings she had visited practically all the houses of the Society of the Sacred Heart. By example, by precept, by sympathy, by individual intercourse, she thus held them, and the various nationalities of which they are composed, united in a mutual knowledge and understanding which had never been more urgently needed. Thus in her death she passed on to her children a bond of union and affection strong enough to withstand and to overcome all the disintegrating forces and misunderstandings which even in religious hearts are too often the almost inevitable outcome of universal war. Could she have given them a more welcome, a more necessary legacy? Have we not also, as we read her Life, solid reason to believe that already she has power to help her religious children and her friends such as would not yet have belonged to her had God allowed her continued sojourning in their midst?

We have reason to bless God for the life of Mother Stuart. To those who knew her, no written record is needed to recall her memory. She will ever be a strong and holy influence in their lives. But they are glad to dwell upon their memories of her and to have them enhanced by a fuller and wider knowledge of details and events beyond their own experience. To those, however, who did not know her personally, and to the generations that will succeed our own, this living picture of a very great and saintly personality will, I feel convinced, be a treasure-house of high aspiration, generous endeavour, and great achievement—things surely of extreme moment to the future of the Catholic Church in England, of which in these modern days the late Mother General of the Society of the Sacred Heart will ever be one of the great glories and possessions.

FRANCIS CARDINAL BOURNE,

Archbishop of Westminster.

Whit-Sunday, June 4, 1922.

CONTENTS

LIST OF ILLUSTRATIONS

JANET ERSKINE STUART

CHAPTER I

FAMILY AND CHILDHOOD

1857 *to* 1870

'So you will ride at ease over the breakers of this mortal life, and not care too much what befalls you—not from carelessness, but from the soaring gladness of heavenly love.'—*From a letter, J. Stuart.*

'THERE is no poem in the world like a man's life . . . however little it may be marked with what we call adventure.' These words of Father Faber find a vivid realisation in the life of Janet Erskine Stuart.

She was born on November 11, 1857, in the Rutlandshire village of Cottesmore. Her father, the Hon. and Rev. Andrew Stuart, was Rector of the parish.

The family traces its descent from Walter, High Steward of Scotland in the reign of David I, 1177 ; and, in even more remote times, there figure in their annals the Thanes of Lochaber and the Banquo of *Macbeth*. The witches' prophecy, that from Banquo should descend a line of kings, began to be fulfilled when Robert, the sixth in descent from Walter the Steward, became King of Scotland in 1370, on the death of his uncle, David Bruce. It is from the third son of this Robert, the Earl of Fife and Menteith, created Duke of Albany in 1398 ' with great pomp and religious ceremony,' that the Stuarts of Castle Stuart are lineally descended.[1]

The name figures in all the great events of the times. They fought in the Holy Land, were the founders of great abbeys, as Paisley—an offshoot from Cluny—which Walter the Steward established in his own lands, and endowed magnificently, ' to

[1] See *Genealogical and Historical Sketch of the Stuarts of Castlestuart in Ireland*, by the Hon. and Rev. Andrew Stuart, Rector of Cottesmore (Blackwood), from which all details of the family history have been taken.

B

the honour of God and the Blessed Virgin Mary'; and in less peaceful spirit they raided the Border and were heroes at Bannockburn and Flodden.

For generations they were in the full light of the King's favour. Titles and position were showered upon them. Two Dukes of Albany ruled Scotland in succession, as regents, during the long captivity in England of their royal cousin, James I. On his release in 1423 the fortunes of the family waned. Almost the first act of the liberated monarch was to imprison the Regent Albany along with his heir Walter. They were executed at Stirling in 1424, ostensibly on the charge of high treason, and property and titles were confiscated to the Crown.

Several grandsons of the Regent, children of Walter, escaped to Ireland; while the youngest, an infant at the time, found refuge with his mother in Scotland. He was known later as Walter Stuart of Morphie, and, as his elder brothers eventually died without issue, the claims of the family centred in his descendants. For the marriage of his mother, Janet Erskine, with the heir of Albany, a dispensation had been necessary. The document in which Pope Martin V granted it is preserved in the Vatican archives. It attests that 'the Holy Father being humbly supplicated on the part of his dear son Walter Stuart and his dear daughter Janet Erskine, has authorised the marriage,' the suppliants being within a forbidden degree of kindred.

In the reign of James II the exiles returned to Scotland, and were once more received into the royal favour. The head of the house was created Lord Avondale, a title exchanged for that of Ochiltree in 1534.

But the times were troublous, and after many vicissitudes the third Lord Ochiltree alienated his Scottish title and possessions, and the family passed, for the second time, into Ireland in 1610, where they had become possessed of a large grant of forfeited lands in Tyrone.

Here they received but scant welcome, and 'were obliged to erect a strong bawn of limestone against the natives.' This laid the foundation of a castle and village, now the market town of Stewartstown. Later on Stuart Hall was built on the Lower Eary, and is the home of the family to-day.

In 1618 the King, 'solicitous for the preservation of the fallen family in something of its former dignity,' created Andrew 'late Lord Ochiltree, Lord Stewart, Baron of Castle Stuart.'

Two centuries later the Baronetcy of Castle Stuart was raised to an Earldom. Robert, the second Earl, had three sons, of whom the youngest, Andrew, was Rector of Cottesmore.

Canon Stuart, as he became later on, was twice married. By his first wife, Catherine, daughter of Viscount Powerscourt, he had seven children, the eldest surviving son of whom succeeded to the Earldom in 1914.[1] The first Mrs. Stuart died in December 1845, and some three years later, in April 1849, Canon Stuart married Mary Penelope Noel. By this marriage he had six children, three sons and three daughters, of whom Janet was the youngest. 'The thirteenth of the family has good opportunities of acquiring a habit of looking up,' she wrote in 1909. 'I think I have a good deal of capacity for appreciation and admiration, and if one can call it so—power of worship.'

Her mother's family was of Norman origin, and came over to England in the train of the Conqueror. It is said to be still represented in Normandy in the 'de Nouel' family. In the reigns of Henry VIII, Edward VI, and Mary, we find the Noels sheriffs for Rutlandshire, and representatives of the county in Parliament. Edward Noel, Viscount Campden, and his son Baptist were faithful adherents of Charles I. Charles II rewarded the fidelity of the family by creating the next peer Earl Gainsborough. The title lapsed in 1798, through the failure of male heirs, but the estates passed to Gerard Noel Edwards, the son of the last Earl's sister. By his marriage with Diana, Lady Barham, whose father was at the head of the Admiralty when Trafalgar was fought, Gerard Noel had fourteen children, of whom the eldest became the first Earl of Gainsborough of the second creation, and the ninth son, Leland, became Vicar of Exton. He married Mary Foljambe of Osberton Hall, Notts. It was the second child of this marriage, Mary Penelope, who married Andrew Stuart in 1849.

Of the twelve children who had preceded Janet in the rectory nursery only seven were living in 1857: four of the first family, Theodosia, John, Richard, and William, and three of her own brothers and sisters, Horace, Beatrice, and Douglas. It was in a happy home circle that the fair-haired, blue-eyed child opened her eyes on a world which she was to find so full of wonder, and began that life which she afterwards described as 'an adventurous journey of faith and love with God in the dark.'

Wonderful gifts were showered on her cradle. Gifts of

[1] He died in 1921.

mind and heart and character. She was trusted with 'the eye that sees visions, the heart that kindles at them, the voice to word them for the inspiration of others.' [1]   Ruler, poet, mystic, saint—all was to be possible to her.   But none suspected these secrets of the future, when, gathered in the old village church, they thanked God for the new life begun among them.

The first phase of the journey was spent at Cottesmore. 'God gives us the home of our childhood, and it is one of our sweetest memories,' she wrote in later years.

Cottesmore is one of those quiet old-world Midland villages, full of charm, that are found in the hills and woods round Oakham. Its church is among the most beautiful in Rutland, the oldest portions date from Norman times, the twelfth century. The rectory, a grey stone building, with high-pitched gables and mullioned windows, stands close to it, its walls overgrown with lichens and ivy.

The scenery of Rutland,[2] though not grand, has a beauty all its own, and is typically English, with rich meadow-lands, bordered by hedgerows, overgrown with flowers, and dotted with stately trees; and densely wooded districts, the remains of the great forests of former days, still recalled in the names of the country round about.   In the north and west there is a circle of low, flat-topped hills forming a link with the central highlands. They are clothed from base to summit with magnificent trees and luxuriant evergreens. To the east the hills slope down to join the 'low fen lands so full of mystery.' Probably nowhere within so small a space can so much beauty and so great a variety of scenery be found.

Blue flowers are characteristic of the little county. In spring, the woods are carpeted with blue-bells, so thickly that 'the deep azure gives a distinct colour to the landscape,' while in summer the bright blue of the flax lights up the hill sides. Countless wild flowers, among which quaint orchis predominate, find their home in its woods and fields, and 'make Rutland a garden of delights, a paradise for children and lovers of flowers.'

All the country is given up to farming, corn-growing, cattle-breeding,[3] and the villagers, it is said, still keep the manners of their forefathers. The quiet and stillness of nature brood over the little land and make it a happy home for birds.

---

[1] The Most Rev. Alban Goodier, S.J., Archbishop of Bombay.

[2] See *Leicestershire and Rutland*, by A. Harvey and V. B. Crowther-Beynon (Methuen) ; also *Rutland*, by G. Phillips, editor of *Rutland Magazine and County Historical Record* (Cambridge: University Press).

[3] 1915.

Nightingales sing in every wood, wild duck live in its waters, tits and rare bee-eaters make their nests in its hedges. ' No long walk outside a little village, and the silence is only broken by the hum of insects.' An ideal country for fox-hunting, it owns one of the greatest packs of England—the Cottesmore.

Perhaps it was because of these varied charms that the Anglo-Saxon kings bestowed Rutland, as a dowry, on their queens !

It seems not without significance, in the light of later events, and it certainly was not without its influence on her character, that the first twenty-one years of Janet's life were passed in these surroundings ; for though there were visits to Scotland, Ireland, and Germany, ' home ' to her meant the rectory at Cottesmore, with its full life, its happy gathering of brothers and sisters, and the peace and joy of living in a ' place where everyone loved.'

Among these brothers and sisters one, at least, destined to a special place in Janet's life, must have more than a passing mention.

Theodosia, or ' Dody,' the eldest sister, was a singularly attractive person. From her extant letters there appears to have been a great similarity between her and her youngest sister.

True and unassuming in all relationships, singularly modest in her estimate of herself, she was a centre of love in the home circle. A keen sense of humour saved her from the exaggerations into which her ardent nature might have led her. Long before her due time she won that reverence which is generally given to age and experience, without losing the endearing qualities of youth.

She had, as she expressed it, a ' darling best friend,' to whom she poured out all her thoughts, in a weekly correspondence, extending over many years. This was Lady Victoria Noel,[1] the youngest daughter of the Earl of Gainsborough. The two girls were almost of the same age. They had many tastes in common, and Exton Park, the seat of the Gainsboroughs, at a distance of only two miles from Cottesmore, became like a second home to Theodosia Stuart.

' It is exceedingly pleasant having a dear friend, it helps one on one's way very often,' she wrote. In her letters she speaks of home joys and sorrows, of her work in the village

---

[1] Afterwards Lady Victoria Buxton. See her Life, by G. W. E. Russell (Longmans).

school, of her Sunday classes, of the gossip of the county, and of her hopes and ambitions. They give a living picture, and a most attractive one, of the home at Cottesmore.

While Dody gave herself heart and soul to all she did, she was preparing herself for some greater work, which she trusted God would one day give her.

On January 4, 1859, Mrs. Stuart died. Her last words were to entrust her little children to the care of their sister, who was henceforth to be a mother to them. In the following letter we see the spirit in which she entered on her new life.

Cottesmore : February 1859.

I have had so little time for letter writing since we came back that I have not before been able to answer your last.

It was so painful being here at first. When we came back the desolate feeling was hard to bear. The house so empty without that bright dear face, that gave it its life and attraction. But the goodness of God ! It is so wonderful. He sends something to alleviate the trials most felt, and I do feel what . . . love He has shown in leaving with us those four darling children [Horace, Beatrice, Douglas, and Janet, aged nine, seven, five, and one]. They are so comforting, and though my responsibility is great I feel so thankful to God that He has thus laid it upon me. . . . I cannot help loving what He has given me to do . . . for she left it to me . . . and her last words are constantly a help. . . . I did not know how much I loved her till she was taken away. . . .

The people here are all so sympathising. One feels and sees more and more how much she was loved. But though it is comforting to see this, it is very painful visiting them, for you know how they think the greatest comfort to those in sorrow is to talk a great deal about it. . . .

Young though she was—she was barely twenty—she entered on her new duties with a mind and character matured and softened by suffering, and by long habit of serious thought. So well did she fill the mother's place to the four children, that their childhood was a singularly happy one. From this time on, news of their sayings and doings finds a natural place in her weekly letters.

The children are well. Baby has been rather unwell, but seems all right again. Douglas announced to me the other day that he never intended to marry, but always to help Papa and me. He has taken a poetical turn lately, and requested me to read him ' Evangeline,' which he enjoys immensely.

Photo: Dolby Bros., Stamford.

THE RECTORY, COTTESMORE

And a little later :

My children sing so nicely now. We practise every Thursday evening, before beginning the Bible lesson. I should so like you to hear them sing ' The Better Land.' They are so fond of it, and really sing it with much feeling and softness. Poor Baby has had a dreadful cold. I was quite frightened about her one night, but she has been better to-day. . . .

The ' Baby ' Janet was barely fourteen months old when the great shadow fell upon her life. In her own childish way she realised the loss, and though the memory faded, the thought and love of her mother were enshrined in her mind. ' My shyness and reserve,' she said later, ' were that of a mother-less child.' The nurses often took her to visit the grave in the churchyard close by the house, and the strange, bewildering idea of death took possession of her.

I think [she wrote] I came to the age of reason early, for I remember thinking seriously on the subject of death, at three years old. My brother Douglas, aged six, who was my great resource for theological questions, had explained to me what death meant, and exhorted me to prepare for it. I neither liked nor believed the prospect, and asked if no one could escape. He said that Enoch and Elias had been exempt, and I made up my mind that I should be the third exception.

The nursery at Cottesmore was ruled over by Swiss nurses and nursery governesses, so that the children learnt French as they learnt to speak. One of these gives us a picture of the child in these early days.

Mademoiselle Janet était une enfant très facile, toujours bonne, gentille et aimable. Je ne me souviens pas de l'avoir jamais vue fâchée ou de mauvaise humeur. Elle apprenait facilement et a su lire le français de bonne heure. Nous nous sommes très attachées l'une à l'autre, elle faisait tout ce qu'elle pouvait pour me faire plaisir : elle était très pratique et aimait toujours être occupée ; ainsi après la promenade, c'est elle qui pliait et mettait de côté les effets, et le matin pendant que je la coiffais elle voulait toujours faire quelque chose pour moi, lire, par exemple, ou même découdre quelque chose : elle aimait beaucoup s'occuper des autres pour leur faire plaisir ou pour rendre service et ne pensait pas à elle-même. Elle avait un caractère très décidé et ferme.

Gentle, loving, unselfish, always occupied, firm and decided in character—time only deepened the lines of this picture. But

she would not perhaps have accepted the statement that she
was 'never angry,' made by one who took charge of her only
in her sixth year. 'I remember well,' she said, speaking of
her first nurse, 'the thrill of delight with which I crunched up
and tore off the frill of my nurse's cap, in anger at being refused
some coveted joy.'

At Dody's knees the children learnt their first lessons from
the Bible, and one of these made the deepest impression on
Janet. She herself tells the story:

It was on the subject of death that my faith, such as it was,
received its first shock, when I was six years old. Having
heard of the resurrection of Lazarus, and that miracles equal to
that could be worked by faith and prayer, I resolved to raise
my mother from the dead, and escaped from my nurse into the
churchyard to perform the miracle. Having prayed with all
my might, I shouted as loud as I could: 'Mama, come forth,'
without the slightest doubt I should see the grave open at once.
The disappointment was very great and left a seed of doubt
in my mind that bore fruit later.

The constant evenness of disposition, of which her nurse
wrote, was not a mere natural gift, but the result of deliberate
choice; for the gentle, unobtrusive child had already turned
her mind to things seemingly beyond her years.

One thought [she writes] at this age, six, stands out as a
landmark for me. I saw my brother and sister, a little older
than myself, one day fighting like two cocks, with scarlet faces.
I did not think it wrong, but it gave me a great contempt for
such outbursts, and I made a resolution, that come what might,
I would never lose my self-control like that. With one or two
exceptions, I kept the resolution, but it would have been better
for me to have broken it a hundred times, for it extended
gradually to all exhibitions of feeling, and I went in for being
a stoic, except with my father, to whom, as he afterwards told
me, I gave everything except my confidence.

This was indeed true. She poured out upon her father all
the love of her deep, strong nature, and he returned it fully.
She was his Benjamin, his favourite child, and, as she grew
older, his constant companion, sharing in all his interests and,
as she could, helping him. There was no jealousy among her
brothers and sisters at this special love. They recognised it
indeed, but understood and approved of it. For Janet was
never self-assertive. Others might mark her out for favour

and love, as was the case throughout her life, but it often caused her more pain than joy ; for in her own mind, and by her own choice, she was but one among the many.

Canon Stuart, 'tall Andrew,' has been described as 'a gentleman of the old school,' conscientious, upright, honourable, very charitable to the poor, and somewhat stern. Very gifted, and a man of many interests, all the time he could spare from his parish duties he gave to farming, gardening, and writing. A man of keen humour, he loved a good story, of which he had an inexhaustible number.

His first family had been brought up in stern, even Spartan fashion. But to his younger children, and especially to Janet, the shy, somewhat cold man gave more than a father's love.

' I had an old-fashioned, ceremonious home training,' she said later. 'Are homes more ceremonious if there is no mother ? ' Every evening the children gathered round their father to say good-night, and as the day had been, so was the warmth of the embrace. If ' very good,' his arms were round them, and they might hug him with all their might. If the report was only ' good,' a kiss upon the forehead was all that was allowed ; while the sad class of the ' naughty ' were only admitted to kiss his hand. This was a punishment keenly felt by Janet. ' A parent's momentary coldness,' she wrote, ' reaches further into the sensitive soul of a child than the loudest expostulations of lesser authorities.' High-spirited children, full of life, and enjoying great liberty, scrapes were not of infrequent occurrence, and the foreign nurses were often bewildered at the escapades in which the young ladies joined. ' But it is not ladylike,' they would expostulate. To which the elder sister would quickly reply : ' If I do it, it becomes ladylike,' reasoning to which they were at a loss to find an answer.

Attached to the Cottesmore living were some ninety acres or more of glebe land, and this Canon Stuart farmed himself. He was keenly interested in agricultural work, and an excellent judge of horses and cattle. A very early riser, he usually set out on an inspection of the farm before breakfast, with Janet by his side. So early were they, that a neighbouring farmer's wife related how she used to see ' the rector and the little lady ' pass before she was about, though she prided herself on ' being betimes.'

The child stood by while her father talked with the farm hands and inspected the animals. Nothing was lost on her ; not only did she get to know the various breeds of cattle, and

varieties of corn, but she became an expert judge in these
matters. Later on, when she saw a horse, or was questioned
about the worth of an animal, her father expected her to give
its good or bad points without hesitating. Those who know
say she was rarely mistaken, and the knowledge gained thus
early was never lost.

This intercourse with the country people gave her a great
admiration for farmers, 'strange, silent, observant, reliable
people, who know their own business to perfection,' she wrote
later, and her childish admiration led to the desire to imitate.
She would be a farmer too, and live as they did. And so she
would gravely ask for tea without milk, and for cheese, fare
which these friends seemed unaccountably to prefer.

The farmers, on their side, delighted in the child's visits,
and, as she grew older, they more than once consulted her about
their affairs, even writing to her when she was away from home
to tell of some 'heifer of no note' to be got rid of ; of some
cow of special breed to be secured ; or to give her details about
the year's crops. 'She's a great loss to the agricultural world,'
said a farmer, when he heard she had left Cottesmore.

In the case of most children these walks would have been
merely chances of play and fun, but to Janet they were a serious
matter, and finding nothing in her home library from which
she could learn a farmer's business, she began, at the age of
nine, to save from her little supply of pocket-money, that she
might take in an agricultural journal. So earnest was she in
her study that before long her father entrusted her with his
farming accounts, and for many years she followed up every
detail about the property.

It was in these early days that she began to gather that
store of quaint images and observations which seemed so
marvellous in later years, and gave such a touch of life and
humour to all her conversation. Her memory enabled her to
reproduce anything once heard, and her power of attention to
detail let nothing escape her.

A donkey and two ponies were the cherished possessions of
the Cottesmore children, and her first riding lessons were given
to Janet by her brothers in the rectory fields. The child knew
no fear. Indeed, she confessed later on that physical fear was
unknown to her, and she soon became a splendid horsewoman.
She also learnt to drive, and while still a little girl was, to her
delight, trusted with the reins.

The instinct of the sportsman showed itself early, and she

AGED 6 (1863)

learnt much, as she said herself, among dogs and horses. Her love for animals was very great. 'It was remarkable,' writes one of her brothers, 'how they appeared to know and recognise this trait in her character. It was as if by some magnetic influence she was able to convey to them her affection, in a manner unattainable by others, so that her influence over them was quite remarkable, the more so as it was established by the *gentlest and most imperceptible outward action and means.*' This power she shared with another brother, whose influence over horses she described as almost uncanny.[1]

It was to these brothers that she went for help and guidance in her childish troubles, and they fully returned the love and admiration of their ' Antigone,' as they called her. With the remembrance of these home joys still fresh in her heart, she wrote, long years after : ' God never established a more beautiful relationship, I think, than that between brother and sister, some of His best creations are brothers, and brothers are *des êtres manqués* without sisters ; there are such moments of life together, in all that is said and all that is unsaid.'

Lessons gave her no trouble. She learnt French as a baby, and a German governess was established at Cottesmore when Janet was only six. From that time, for some ten years, German and French governesses reigned successively in the schoolroom. Tradition says that she only ' struck ' on two occasions ; both were characteristic : once, when a governess, with too strong a passion for symmetry, insisted that all the books should be covered with brown paper. Books were even then her friends, and their individual covers had an attraction all their own, as every lover of a library knows. The second rebellion was in face of the endeavour to make her study Otto's German Grammar. It seemed to her such a tame, lifeless way to learn a language. But however willing to learn, the child was too full of life for lessons not to be irksome to her, and it was from the depths of her own experience that she wrote, ' the funereal tolling of a bell for lessons made a dark background, against which the rapture of release for play shone out with a

---

[1] This was Richard, who in later years went to Australia. There, it is said, ' two things distinguished him, his generosity, especially to the poor, and his amazing power over horses.' It is still remembered (1921) how he accepted the challenge of a certain Mr. X., the owner of an unmanageable horse, who had laid a wager of £25 that no one in Queensland could ride it. Mr. Stuart did so at once, and with perfect ease, the animal submitting to him completely. The £25 was handed over to the hospital kept by the Sisters of Mercy.

brilliancy which more than made up for it.' She loved
Saturdays, for 'they meant rest and peace, and always disliked Mondays, for all the lessons had to be begun over again.'

Sundays were, then and always, delightful days to her, with
an atmosphere of heaven. She never could bear that anything
should be allowed to spoil the brightness of that day for children.

Nous jouissions beaucoup [writes the old Swiss maid] avec
sa sœur, du Dimanche après-midi et soir, où l'on me plaçait
dans le fauteuil de notre grande chambre, et ces demoiselles,
perchées chacune sur un bras du fauteuil, nous chantions
ensemble des cantiques, ou bien nous parlions des choses du
Seigneur. C'est un souvenir encore bien doux.

But better than all books of delight 'she loved,' she wrote,
when still a little girl, 'the whole country with its fields and
trees and hedges and gardens. It is like one great book, in
which we can learn more than from all the learned books in
the world, and yet we need not be very learned ourselves to read
it.' These were her real playthings; toys, and especially dolls,
never attracted her, except for the chance they offered of having
a funeral, always a favourite game.

All the children had gardens of their own and were expected
to look after them. For a time, however, Janet looked down
on garden flowers, so great was her love for wild ones. Some
of her happiest moments, she said, were spent alone, in the woods
and fields, picking wild flowers. Many years later, recalling
these days of childhood, she was to write:

God has set over man many tutors and governors, uncertifi-
cated indeed, but supremely efficient, and if man does not lend
a willing ear to them, and a heart to their discipline, he may
reach distinction as a marvel of academical success, but he is
not educated. Wordsworth gives us the clue to this larger
education in the lines from 'Brougham Castle':

> ' His daily teachers had been woods and rills,
>   The silence that is in the starry sky,
>   The sleep that is among the lonely hills.'

These in their songs and in their silences first take in hand
the child . . . . These give him the hearing ear, the seeing eye,
the large horizon of solitude, and the quiet of mind which must
underlie all true greatness of thought and action.

There is something wanting in education where a child has
not had its share of this teaching, and the heat and stress of

human life has been round it from the beginning, never leaving it the leisure to be rapt in silence and alone. . . . However full of activity life may be, when pressing duties crowd upon us, something beyond is needed to make it perfect, some halls of space and avenues of leisure in the soul ; some stately distances of manner, and high porticoes of silence ; some long reverent approaches to the interior mansion where God and His angels condescend to walk, these are inherited from the early, silent, leisurely years—the woods and rills of the poem.

In this larger education Janet had her full share, and in this spirit she took possession of the world around her, and her child's soul, ' hushed in wonder, was very near to God.'

CHAPTER II

WONDERLAND. THE FIRST CALL

1870 *to* 1878

> ' How poor a life is in which there is not thirst. Craving and longing, and the restlessness which goes with them are a sort of consolation in themselves, and a hint of likeness with Him ; and it is craving and longing, more than anything else, which makes the difference between one's good and bad days. The greatest trouble is to be without them.'
>
> *From ' Notes of a Meditation,' J. Stuart.*

FROM fourteen to twenty-one is the wonderland of our life, the age of our mysticism, the years of ideals. We are then the discoverers of our own lives. Our world is new every day. Either we are sailing towards new shores, daring mariners in search of the unknown, and day by day the horizon dips lower and our stars rise higher, or we are explorers by land, and new wonders reveal themselves on each day's march. Some of us go by sea and others by land all through our lives. We do not love the glories of these years less, now that we can look back and see that some of them were clouds and some were mirages of the desert. They did their work, and they were the band of yellow, clear gold in our lives. We would not be without a day of them. In those years each morning brought its message ' Onward,' each evening asked ' Whither ? ' and the morning answered ' Onward again.' [1]

This ' wonderland ' was now opening for Janet, and in these few lines she gives a picture of her own life from thirteen to twenty-one. ' When I was twelve years old,' she told her sister, ' I began to think, and I was happy ever after.'

She turned her thoughts to many things, self-discipline among others. She was still a little girl when she forced herself to go into the big village church, alone, in the dark, just because she was afraid. She persevered till the fear was controlled. She would be master in her own soul. So again, when, absorbed in an interesting book, she felt the desire to finish it

---

[1] Essay on Colour, in *Essays and Papers*, 1888–1910, J. Stuart.

begin to rise strong within, she would get up, and putting the
book upon the table, deliberately walk near it till the unruly
movement was quelled.

It was about the same time that the gentle, shy girl said
that 'firmness' was the quality she admired most in a woman.

But into the midst of this happy child-life there came a
great awakening. She described it as 'my first movement
towards conversion—a negative one.' One evening when Janet
was thirteen, she was sitting alone with her brother Douglas in
the schoolroom. Brother and sister were working in silence,
when Douglas looked up from the book he was reading :

'Aristotle says every rational being must have a *telos*.
What is yours ?' When he had explained that a *telos* was
a last end, I had to confess that I did not know, and so had he.
But it seemed to me to be a very serious thing, to be thirteen
years old, and not to know my last end. I made up my mind
that it must be found. The search lasted seven years, and was
one of the happiest times of my life. It began by my examin-
ing the grounds of my faith, and they all melted away.[1]

Her mind gradually became conscious of its resources. And
she set out on her adventurous journey, feeling, searching for
light and beauty and truth. She began to realise that life
was full of unanswered questions and deep mysteries. She
observed, reflected, and studied other people, thinking to herself :
'Do you know ? Do you understand ? Can you explain ? ' But
she never ventured to express what was passing in her own mind.
The loneliness of spirit from which she suffered all her life began
even at this early age. It was partly due to the want of a mother's
love, and partly to the loss at this time of her eldest sister's
special care ; for when Janet was about fourteen, Dody became
an invalid, and though she still ruled the little household, and
was still the loved centre of the whole, the children were thrown
very much on their own resources and left to their governesses.
'If Dody had lived, that wave of agnosticism would never have
swept over my life,' wrote Janet in later years; 'nor,' added her
brother Douglas, 'would Janet have left home.' But now she
had to wrestle alone with the great problems opening before her.

---

[1] The account of her conversion given in this and the following
chapters is taken from a paper which she wrote at Mother Digby's request
during her noviceship in 1883. The greater part of it has already been
printed in the *Memoirs of Father Gallwey, S.J.*, in the chapter dealing
with converts. This book was published in 1913 by Messrs. Burns and
Oates, by whose courtesy the whole letter of Mother Stuart's is here
reproduced.

Her loneliness was probably also the penalty of her gifted nature—

> Making a poet out of a man :
> The true gods sigh for the cost and pain—
> For the reed which grows never more again
>   As a reed with the reeds in the river.

It was the loneliness of the artistic temperament, which finds mysteries everywhere. And above all, it came from that ' home-longing ' for God, the true keynote of her life. ' Thou hast made us for Thyself, O God, and our heart is restless, till it rests in Thee ' : true of every human soul ; but God, like man, has His friendships with His creatures, and coveting, more especially, the love of some human hearts, He plants in them a stronger yearning for Himself.

As to the loneliness [she wrote long years after], I think it is a sort of thing that almost belongs to human life, and certainly to all that is best in it ; it is a sort of home-longing for God, and nothing else will satisfy it. . . . He is the home of the soul. But heaven is coming, life is a moment, and then the loneliness will be over.

There were, she said in later years, three clearly marked stages in her life, three stages in the growth of the spirit, and each was heralded by a call from God. The first call came now ' thro' the mountains, mist, and ocean.'

In the first stage, I sought God everywhere in His creatures. He seemed to me to be in the heart of creation, drawing all things to Himself. This idea gave me my first living knowledge of Him.

God's Fatherhood was very real to her then, before she began to doubt the truth of her religion.

She revelled in nature and art, and lived in a dream-world of light and beauty. Nature spoke to her, and sang to her, awakening song in her inmost being, and opening out the loveliest horizons.

The ' call of the wild ' with all its fascination was very strong, and as she said herself, speaking of these years, ' her spirit strayed like a vagabond among God's creatures.' As a girl, her father allowed her to roam alone miles from home. In these solitary walks she loved to stand listening to silence, believing that words would frame in answer to unspoken

questions. She watched the play of light and shade and colour
in the woods, and it gave her the sense of the unseen pressing
on her. She heard the undertones of nature, and had strange
fears of the unknown and the unseen, but yet was drawn to
all that was invisible, longing to find the mystery at the heart
of things. Sights and sounds seemed to her full of symbol.
She loved unknown and unexpected paths. ' By-ways whose
terminus is often nothing at all . . . where the mysteries call
us onward, and the shy nightingales sing, and the stress of life
is lifted off, and the ticking of time is still . . . where life seems
larger, because of silence and calm, where the soul may be invaded and taken captive, unresisting, by the powers of the world
to come. . . .' Written in 1909, these words give some insight
into this period of her life.

Colour, beauty of form and of scenery drew her soul out
of itself, and she found her way, instinctively, to what was
best in art and music. They spoke to her, each with its own
message, and with a thrill that, even in those early days, went
very deep. Greek art especially delighted her. Its proportion and restraint appealed to her perfectly balanced nature.
' Nothing too much, appeared to me as an ideal canon of art,
even in girlhood. But it seemed far too tame, as a principle
of conduct, till many years later.' Even as a little girl of ten
or eleven the beauty of the Greek myths had taken hold of her.
About that time a playfellow of the Cottesmore children had
a narrow escape from drowning. ' He floated,' wrote Janet,
' for he could not swim, and his head was kept up by waterlilies, which seemed to me such an ideal and wonderful life-
saving apparatus for a beautiful boy as he was. I thought it
was like a Greek myth.'

But ' young, vigorous, full-grown life needs room to expand
in action, it needs the clash of thought with other minds, it
needs conflict and adversity, experience, humiliations and stripes,
efforts intense and long-sustained even unto weariness, to bring
its powers to maturity. There are lessons in all this for life,
and they are beyond the language of the woods and rills.' In
this second education Janet was now to begin to have her share.

When she was about fourteen, a remarkable woman came
to Cottesmore as German governess. The daughter of a well-
known Protestant theologian, Fräulein Rinz von Bürger was
a brilliant woman, and Janet became deeply attached to her.
Under the influence of this lady, the children's interest in
Germany and German thought developed. It was shortly after

c

the Franco-German war, and in one of their visits to Kissingen,
where they went for their father's health, they planned all walks
and expeditions with one object, to get a glimpse of Bismarck,
then in the town. Their efforts were at length rewarded by
one good look, and even by a recognition on the part of the
prince.

Of far greater importance than this passing hero-worship
was the influence of the books which Fräulein Rinz brought
with her to Cottesmore. These she lent freely to Janet, who,
with their help, made her way through the intricacies of German
schools of thought. For a time the fascination of Goethe held
her fast, and she hoped to find in him an answer to all her
questions.

Her own religion having failed her,

I tried [she says] to bring up systems of my own, chiefly
from German books which my governess brought into the house.
I would not let anyone know I was doing so. I used to study
at night, waiting till my sister was asleep, and then getting up
and sitting under the table that the light might not wake her.
My belief went through many phases. I never completely gave
up the belief in the existence of God, a word of Spinoza's held
me to that, to the effect that, if God were not, then thought could
conceive something greater than that which exists, which would
be impossible. It is ontologism, of course, but it was more than
good enough to hold me at the moment. At twenty I reached
a point that was more agnosticism than anything else. I had
left off praying and seemed stuck fast.

In some notes of meditation written more than thirty years
later, when God's presence had become her living joy and the
central fact in her life, she said :

I look back to the time when the longing that there should
be a God persuaded me that He must really be ; very imperfect
reasoning . . . but enough for me at the time, and a great joy
that the thought of Him should be its own proof of His being
to me ; that was like the satisfaction of the thirst of one's life.

During these years of inward stress and spiritual adventure,
the happy outward life went on as before. Only with ad-
vancing years came keener joys and more strenuous duties.
' Sixteen was the nicest time of my life,' and the search for
truth and God, far from causing a strain of sadness or of
gloom, was an unending interest and delight.

AGED 14 (1871)

No one could live with Janet Stuart and not realise that she was unlike others ; unlike in some wonderful power of attractiveness. But her superiority of mind and gifts never weighed on those about her.

The impression left by her early life [writes her eldest brother] was that of a staunch and true friend, and of a clear, calm, candid spirit, exercising a wise and practical judgment in an unobtrusive manner about the affairs of life ; looking always with a serene and cheerful spirit on the bright side of things, and not without a touch of humour of a distinct kind, with which the darker side, when unavoidable, was contemplated without fear.

Her special friendship with her brother Horace dates from this period, and began in a trifling incident. A large party was walking home one evening from a gathering at some neighbouring house. It was very dark, and Horace, aged twenty-one, fell into a deep ditch. The others were much amused, and instead of offering any assistance laughed at him unmercifully, to the young man's mortification. But Janet did all she could to help him out, and cheered him up the remainder of the way, all splashed with mud and dripping from the unwelcome plunge. From that time the two were fast friends, and for years she wrote to him every week, when they were apart. Brother and sister had many gifts in common, both were good musicians. Janet had a very sweet voice, and at this time delighted in German songs, Horace singing with her or accompanying her ; a good office which she in her turn performed for him.

A frequent visitor at the rectory at Cottesmore, during her childhood and girlhood, was Edward Thring. ' No one,' she said in after years, ' was more welcome. We children loved him almost as our own father.' This affection based on childhood's intuition of true worth gave place later to unbounded admiration, as she realised something of the magnificent faith and courage of the man. Not a few of his ideals became those of her maturer life.

The years from 1853 to 1878 saw the rise, threatened annihilation and wonderful resurrection of his school at Uppingham. Like many hundreds of that generation she fell ' under the spell of his strangely stimulating and inspiring personality ' ; and the ideas of the work of education as an enthralling interest, and of the schoolmaster as a true hero, took root in her mind.

And so, while her interest in the farmers and their affairs

was as keen as ever, it began to extend itself to their children, and the Cottesmore school became the object of her great solicitude. She visited it as frequently as she could. On week-days, lessons, farm duties, and various calls of home kept her very busy, but Sundays were all her own. In the mornings she taught in the usual Sunday school. This was a great pleasure, far surpassed however by the joys of the afternoon, when she was free, with her father's full approval, to organise matters as she chose. Every second week she had three successive classes at two o'clock, three o'clock, and four o'clock, for the older children of the village. One of these, known as the Young Men's Class, thought a great deal of itself. A still surviving member, one of the seven sons of the Cottesmore schoolmaster, who themselves all became schoolmasters, writes :

I first knew Miss Janet as the teacher of the Young Men's Class at Cottesmore, and as I was preparing for the teaching profession, she took special interest in my career, she also having studied school method and organisation. She lent me various text-books on the subject, which contained her own copious notes. Her lessons for the class were evidently prepared with the greatest pains. She was a frequent visitor at the village school, making the older children her chief care, observing and studying the methods employed. She had a vigorous personality, overflowing with health and spirits, entering thoroughly into every duty she undertook, obtaining respect and attention from all her pupils, upon whom her influence left a lasting impression for good.

On alternate Sundays she walked across the fields to Barrow, a hamlet a mile or so away, where she had brought a little Sunday school into being. After a happy hour with all the children she could gather round her, she played the harmonium at the service which her father held, and then walked home with him.

The love of teaching was an inborn taste, and it was not only at Cottesmore that Janet helped the schoolmaster. In her frequent visits to Scotland she made friends with an old Scotch teacher, of whom she speaks in her book, written many years later, on the Education of Catholic Girls. ' He urged his scholars on by his personal enthusiasm for knowledge. Having no assistant, his own personality was the soul of the school. The boys had the best of it, lassies were not deemed worthy of the classics, and the classics were everything to him.' But though he more than once expressed to her his opinion that 'lassies be mostly daft,' he accepted help from his visitor and gladly gave her a class to teach.

On one of these visits to Scotland she made a special expedition to Anwoth, 'fair Anwoth by the Solway,' for 'Emmanuel's Land'[1] was already very dear to her, and she insisted on seeing the place which had inspired Rutherford with love so great that

> E'en from the verge of heaven
> I drop for thee a tear.

The serious duties of her life never hindered her from sharing to the full in her brothers' amusements. She rode and boated and fished with them, and excelled in all these sports. 'She was a great walker over the moors,' was a gamekeeper's comment, as she often went out with the guns. While later the Donegal fishermen declared ' she was a grand lady,' for she could row a boat as well as they.

And so the years of her girlhood passed away.

A great sorrow was preparing to cast its shadow on the happy home. In 1878 Dody died at Bournemouth, where she had spent the last few months of her life. They had been full of suffering. But her letters speak more of the troubles of others than of her own. She seems indeed to have attained the realisation of her youthful desire, and to have wholly forgotten self. In the last extant letter to her ' darling Vic,' she says :

Perhaps when the weather is bright and I can get out in the air, it may please God to strengthen me ; it is all in His hands, whichever way it turns out, and I can leave it, though at the same time one cannot help hoping that if it is His will this state of things may not go on very long. How good He is to come to His children just when they need Him.

And a little later to her aunt, Lady Gainsborough, she said :

I do have some blessed comfort in feeling the presence of our dear Lord, it is so good of Him.

This appears to have been her last letter. She died on the morning of February 23.

This sorrow affected Janet deeply. Brought face to face with one of life's problems, she shrank from it in a way that

---

[1] This poem, known generally as ' The Last Words of S. R. ' or by its first line, ' The sands of Time are sinking,' is the work of A. R. Cousin, who composed it from passages chosen from Rutherford's letters.

seemed inexplicable to all. She, who was so brave, so resolute, so self-possessed, could not bring herself to go alone into the room where Dody lay dead. The mystery of life had been solved for one she loved, but what was the solution ? For Janet there was as yet no key, and death had great terrors for her. ' Some of my fear of death has gone,' she was to write more than twenty years later.

It has been said that souls further the growth of character and spiritual life, in those they love, more from heaven than they could do, or did, on earth. And it would seem that Dody still watched over her sister, for scarcely was she dead than the answer Janet sought to all her doubts was put before her eyes.

Onward [she writes in the Essay on Colour already quoted] means change, and our coming of age brings us up with a shock against the real. Wonderland is earth, and earth is green, and questioning becomes imperious for an answer, and we know that ' whither ? ' ought to be changed for ' where ? ' and that the ideal must take shape and show itself forth as something that is. And we want above all things to *do* and not only to discover ; to stamp the mark of our individuality on something.

And so it was with her own life.

I had passed through many stages of thought and wrestled with many problems—free will, heredity, matter and form, and even predestination. For a time I was almost pagan at heart in my devotion to the classics, and even for a brief space I was in sympathy with the Manichees, because of the solution they seemed to promise of some of life's problems.

So, and no otherwise [she wrote years afterwards], is the record of our various growths ; formative influences from without, meeting responsive possibilities from within, and the word of growing life is ' surrender, co-operate, wait, trust.'

After girlhood, she was to find that great realities lay hidden in her early dreams, and that her kinship with nature had led her to that strong consciousness of God's presence which later formed the basis of her life. Her love of truth and beauty, and the contemplative mind had led her to God. She had sought Him in nature, art, philosophies, until now she stood at the parting of the ways. Then He revealed Himself.

CHAPTER III

' When we had been caught between Pharaoh and his host behind
and the Red Sea before us, what was the answer that came clanging
from heaven to our wail of distress ? "Why criest thou to me ? "
" Speak to the children of Israel to *go forward*." Yes, into the impossible,
into the Red Sea, to be drowned, against all hope and reason. Yes,
into the impossible, *solvitur ambulando*, and in the end the sea did open
up and everything went through.'

From paper on ' Three Maxims for the Spiritual Life,' J. Stuart.

IN 1866 the old Earl of Gainsborough died and Exton passed to
his heir.

The second Earl had become a Catholic with all his family.
Intimacy, therefore, was no longer encouraged between the
children at Cottesmore and their cousins, for Canon Stuart and
his family were Low Church Anglicans, and Mr. Leland Noel,
his father-in-law, held the same views.

There were two sisters in the new family circle at Exton,
Lady Constance and Lady Edith Noel. The former married
Sir Henry Bellingham and died in 1891, the latter became a
Sister of Charity in 1878.

As they grew older, the cousins, though not intimate, met
from time to time, as complete separation was naturally
impossible.

Soon after Dody's death, Lady Edith Noel lent Archbishop
Ullathorne's ' Ecclesiastical Discourses ' to Horace Stuart. The
book fell into the hands of his youngest sister. ' I opened
on a passage concerning faith and unbelief,' she writes. ' The
Archbishop illustrated it by describing an old picture of
St. Francis of Assisi in an ecstasy, in the corner of which is a
toad ; parallels, he said, of faith and unbelief. I was struck at the
thought that I was occupying the place of the toad, and the
grand contempt of authority and faith, for the spirit of unbelief
made an impression on me. I asked the owner of the book to

let me keep it, to read it through—and I was invited to stay
with her.' The permission to do so was granted readily. 'We
had a long talk on the first day,' continues Janet, in her account
of her conversion, 'and it came upon me like a flash of lightning,
that it might be in the Catholic Church that I should find the
" last end " and the truth, about whose very existence I was
doubting.' It was a 'system' which, as a result of her surroundings, had not seemed to her, so far, worth while examin-
ing. The desire of truth was so strong, however, that she
would leave no stone unturned in her search for it. She asked
for books and was given the penny Catechism. 'I spent the
night reading it,' continues the narrative. 'The first answer
gave me the explanation of my " last end," and it came home
with a conviction that never left room for doubt afterwards.'

'The next day I was given Cardinal Manning's " Grounds
for Faith," and the " Memorare," which came as another flash
of light upon me, and was my first prayer for months, and for
long afterwards my only one.'

Writing to an intimate friend, in 1909, she recalled these
memories : ' Did I ever tell you how Our Lady first came into
my life ? It was by the Memorare . . . it took me off my feet
at once, for it was so daring a statement that I thought it could
not have lived if it had been a lie, and I said it constantly and
clung to it as the first definite something that seemed to come
authentically after my seven years of groping in the dark.'

After this, visits to Exton became more frequent, and Janet
got all she wished in the way of Catholic books. In the autumn
of 1878 Edith Noel entered the noviceship at Carlisle Place,
leaving her cousin engrossed in her arduous search. In the
month of November or early in December of the same year,
another friend was brought across her path.

I was staying at Exton [writes Mrs. Ross, a daughter of Sir
John Ross of Bladensburg] when one afternoon the Belling-
hams told me that Janet Stuart was coming to dinner, and that
they wanted me to talk to her. 'She is very much interested
in religious questions.' The two sisters arrived in due time
with their brother Douglas. Janet looked older than Beatrice,
who was very tall, like her father. The younger sister was
smaller. She was not exactly pretty, but had a beautiful
countenance, a broad high forehead, and blue eyes full of light,
with such a sweet, deep, straight expression, a very firm mouth,
and bright colour. Her smile was wonderful, it lit up her whole
face, and attracted one to her immediately. After dinner,

when the ladies had returned to the drawing-room, I sat down
beside her, and we began to talk. The conversation soon
turned on religion, and we became so engrossed that we spent
the whole evening talking. Beatrice and Douglas looked at
us from time to time, wondering what we could have found to
talk about.

The next day Janet rode about in the hope of meeting this
new friend and continuing a conversation, which she had found
full of interest, but they only met at a hunt breakfast, and for
a few moments at Cottesmore Rectory. On both occasions
conversation was impossible. Before leaving Mrs. Ross invited
Janet to come and see her in town, promising in the meantime
to do anything she could for her by correspondence.

The beginning of 1879 saw the Stuarts in London on a visit
to their cousin, Mrs. Kinnaird. Janet had not forgotten the
invitation, and, a few days after her arrival, found her way to
Curzon Street. What followed can best be told in her own words.[1]

By reading and correspondence I had come gradually nearer
to the Church—very reluctantly—for the grief it would be to
my father, and the idea of having to put a curb on my freedom of thought, made me most anxious to find a way out of
it. But it was useless. One day my friend said to me : ' Would
you like to see a Jesuit ? I could arrange it.' I jumped at
the idea, the name of Jesuit made me tingle with interest and
expectation. I thought all Catholic priests were oracles of
wisdom, but that, through contempt for my youth and ignorance,
they would not speak of what they knew. But a Jesuit would
surely explain things, if there were an appointment made on
purpose, and he would know all that could be known about
everything.

So one January afternoon in 1879, Janet went to Curzon
Street with her Swiss maid, Charlotte, to meet the Jesuit.

When Father Gallwey arrived, it was not the Jesuit of fiction
who walked into the room, but simply Father Gallwey, with his
great expanse of head, and the vision in his eyes, and his kind
smile, and his quick shuffle, and his reassuring abruptness of
speech. His coat collar was turned up, and his gown, his fisherman's coat, girt up underneath, as was his custom to wear it
when he came out in a hurry. There was nothing alarming or
mysterious about him. He held my hand a moment, and looked
me very straight in the eyes : ' Well, Miss Stuart, I've often

[1] See note on page 15.

heard of you,' he said, and I was too ready for anything even
to know that I was surprised. Father Gallwey made everything seem natural and inevitable, and it was a great blessing
to be able to skip the preface of the interview. There was no
question of ' how to begin.' ' Shall I leave you alone ? ' said
my hostess, fresh from the terrors of a lady who was afraid to
face a Jesuit by herself ! I gratefully accepted, and saw with
still greater gratitude that Father Gallwey would conduct the
interview. This was a novelty, and most helpful, for I was
mortally shy. Father Gallwey put me in an arm-chair, and
sat down beside me. He began to ask preliminary questions,
and I to answer them, feeling that it was the most natural and
the most unnatural thing that had ever happened. I felt like
Alice in Wonderland, and as if I had never been so young in all
my life. ' How old was I ? ' Father Gallwey wanted to know.
Just twenty-one. ' That's all right,' said Father Gallwey,
rubbing his hands. I wondered why, but it seemed to give him
satisfaction. ' Had I a father and mother living ? ' Only my
father, my mother had died before I could remember. ' Poor
child,' said Father Gallwey. He asked a few more questions,
and it touched and astonished me greatly that he seemed to
care about things in a way that made ' father ' quite a natural
title in speaking to him.

Then he came to the point. Where was I as to religious
belief ? I explained that I was just at the cross-roads,
having understood that there were only two alternatives, submission to the Catholic Church, or no fixed belief at all. ' What
had I read ? ' I had read the Bible and Hooker, and mostly,
of late, German authors, in whose obscurities, far beyond my
understanding, I had hoped to come upon the truth. ' All that
is very good,' said Father Gallwey. And then I had read
Archbishop Ullathorne, and the Catholic Church had started up
before my mind as a possible solution of my difficulties. Then
Father Gallwey began, from the cross-roads where I was, and
taking his stand on the existence of God, worked on to show
the Church as the Divine Teacher, and the only authentic
witness to the truth. I could not help seeing it, and recognising
the voice ' which spoke with authority, and not as the Scribes
and Pharisees.' I was very much struck by all he said in support
of the living authority on earth, and still more by the intense
interest he showed as to whether I should believe or not in
the Church. He stayed an hour, and went away with ' God
bless you, it would be a million pities if you should be lost.'
I did not understand what it meant ' to be lost,' but felt grateful
that he hoped it would not happen to me. My hostess escorted
Father Gallwey downstairs, and came back beaming. ' He says
you are sure to come right,' she said ingenuously, ' because

you don't come back to the same point once it has been answered.' This was anything but joyful news to me, for 'come right' had not the same meaning in my mind as in hers.

The Swiss maid who was waiting in the hall was immensely shocked to see who had been her young mistress' visitor, and reproached her respectfully for her rashness, as they returned to South Audley Street.

I told my father [continues the narrative] of the interview, and that I was thinking seriously of entering the Catholic Church. He was greatly grieved, and begged me not to meet Father Gallwey again. I promised that I would not do so for the moment, but I reserved my liberty as to correspondence. To please my father, and in the genuine hope that there might still be another answer to my difficulties, I read everything that was sent me by Protestant friends, and I saw everyone they begged me to see, even apostate Catholics.

Janet had some doubts as to the wisdom of this conduct, and wrote to Father Gallwey, at the same time submitting several difficulties. His answer is the only letter we possess of this period of their correspondence.

January 26th, 1879.

As I am leaving town to-morrow, for a week, I write . . . to assure you that I do not in any way blame you for the course you have taken. You do right to act according to your conscience. As far as I have seen, I think that Our Lord is helping you, and that you are acting very sincerely, and I have every hope that all will end well.

It is rather hard for you at present to take in the doctrine of the Real Presence, but the day will come when it will be the joy of your life. It is like the sun in the firmament of the Catholic Church. All the great holiness of martyrs and virgins is inspired by the close union permitted to us through the Blessed Sacrament.

You may remember, moreover, His words in St. John vi.: 'He that eateth My Flesh and drinketh My Blood hath everlasting life, and I will raise him up in the last day.'

When Our Lord became man His intention was, not merely to sanctify and glorify the one body and soul, to which He joined Himself, but, by uniting Himself with each individual, to sanctify and glorify each. Hence in the Ephesians v. you will see that St. Paul speaks of Christian marriage as founded on the idea of the Incarnation, and compares the union of Christ and His Church to the union of marriage. All this will be quite intelligible and most consoling later.

Old Lady Kinnaird, the mother-in-law of the cousin with
whom the Stuarts were staying, determined to see what she
could do to save her young friend, to whom she was much
attached. She sent accordingly for Janet, and ' establishing
me at a table with the Bible between us, chased me through it.
She asked for text after text, reference after reference ; fortunately I never hesitated, but was able to give all to her satisfaction. She shut the book with a sigh of relief : " Well, my
dear, it is impossible for a girl, who knows her Bible as you do,
to go to Rome." I replied, however, that I saw no alternative.
" Well, my dear, you will perish," she said, as she brought the
interview to an end.'

I was sent down to the country by my father, who remained
in town, to undergo a cure of controversial reading and discussion. But nothing touched my position in any way, since
the choice for me lay, not between the Protestant sects and
the Church—for Protestantism, as a religion, had been already
dead some years for me—but between the Church and agnosticism.
The work was only a labour and weariness, and before long my
mind was made up, and I wrote the decision to my father,
and came up to town. It was a very great sorrow to him, and
he told me that if this decision was final I must leave home,
but in the meantime we should go to Cromer for a fortnight,
to give us both time to think. Cromer was full of Quakers, a
serene and quiet atmosphere, and in those days there was no
priest nearer than Norwich. I was told of this decision at
six o'clock in the morning, and we were to go at ten. ' Then,'
I said, ' I will go and get Father Gallwey to receive me into the
Church first.' But Father Gallwey refused. ' No,' he said,
' I am not afraid for you. Go down to Cromer, and let your
father have every chance.' It was a great astonishment to
my relations when I came back saying that Father Gallwey
had refused my request. We then went down to Cromer.
Here my father made his last attempt to keep me back from the
Church. He asked me to write for him a full statement of my
position, and my reasons for being a Catholic. I did so, and some
days afterwards he told me that he had sent it to Mr. Gladstone
(knowing that I had a great veneration—almost a hero-worship
for him), asking him to give me an interview.

Mr. Gladstone was then in his seventieth year, the ' annus
mirabilis ' [1] of his life, as Lord Morley calls it. But his fifty years
of Parliamentary struggle had not dimmed his ' innermost

[1] Morley's *Gladstone*, in three volumes, 1903, vol. ii., p. 597 ; see also
vol. i., p. 197, and vol. iii., p. 88., for this description.

ideals' nor confined his field of interests. Their universality was amazing, as was also the depth of the attention which he devoted to them. A breath of other-worldliness was felt in all he said or wrote, and made it natural for those in trouble to turn for help to the busiest statesman in Europe. Whatever qualifications he might seem to lack, a minute and careful attention to the question was never wanting, and this irrespective of the personality of his client—known or unknown— he respected all alike.

He answered very kindly [continues the manuscript] that he had so often been drawn over the harrows of the Roman controversy that he had little hope of success, but was willing to try, so we went up to London and the interview took place. Mr. Gladstone took the line of loyalty to the Church of one's baptism ; that the Anglican Church was a branch that had not cut itself off, but was undergoing persecution from the Roman branch ; that it was a case to devote oneself to a dangerous cause and hold on till better times, when unity would come back, etc. But it did not appeal to me, for I saw only one authority that explicitly claimed the teaching power and used it, and the 'church of my baptism' had never awakened my loyalty, so that my intention was not changed by the conversation, though it gave me a certain shiver to read the solemn warning that Mr. Gladstone wrote me the next day, on the 'grave sin of moral suicide' that I was committing, and I did not like putting my head under the yoke. He said my mistake was to want a philosophy as well as a religion. The idea of mental and moral deterioration rankled, and it vexed my soul. Mr. Gladstone had written that he noticed it in all his friends who were received into the Roman Church.

A day or two after this interview, Janet went to Curzon Street and explained to her friend that she must see Father Gallwey again, for unless he could remove certain doubts and trouble of mind, which had been aroused by the visit to Mr. Gladstone, she could not become a Catholic. They went at once to Mount Street.

I said to Father Gallwey : ' Supposing I don't find my mind satisfied, once I have been received into the Church, I shall have put my neck in a noose quite unnecessarily.' Father Gallwey was sympathetic, and entertained the idea seriously. After a moment he said thoughtfully : ' I really don't see that you will be so much worse off than you are now, you will only have to go a stage further on and seek the truth elsewhere.'

This was far more reassuring to me than any discourse of the blessedness of the faith, and the impossibility of being dissatisfied when one was once in possession of it.

After some further conversation she returned to her friend saying that Father Gallwey had reassured and satisfied her, and that she would receive instruction and become a Catholic. Mrs. Ross begged her to come at once and stay with her, but Janet very rightly refused, she would not leave her father or sister as long as it was possible to be with them. The two friends met frequently however. One evening, having separated about ten o'clock, they arranged to meet next day. On returning from early Mass at Farm Street, Mrs. Ross found Janet waiting for her. She explained that on reaching the hotel the evening before, her father had told her that he was going to Ireland the next morning, where they would spend some time at his nephew's place, Stuart Hall, in Tyrone, and he begged her to accompany him. The poor father hoped that by a flight from London he might yet save his dearest child from a step which he dreaded for his own sake and hers. His friends had assured him that he was only facilitating her design by remaining in town. But it was not to be. Janet answered that it was impossible, she was completely convinced of the necessity of the step she was taking, and she could not leave London till she had been received into the Church. Very sorrowfully her father acquiesced. To both it was a heart-rending separation, and Janet never alluded to it. It was the price she had to pay for the gift of faith.

What her father's love had been to her can be read, perhaps, through the words of a meditation written thirty years later.

'Father, into Thy hands.' The overwhelming affection. Is it because it is less usual or because it seems more simply human that the word 'affection' here says more to me than the word 'love' for the Father? It seems to go down to the very deepest springs of one's life. . . . Father is the very dearest word to me for God, because of all that it implies, and I know all the aspects of the human relationship which stand for so much when one turns them to God, and it is such an immovable name, and helps me to understand resignation, surrender, submission, trust, all those great simple acts that seem to take one's whole being up to God.

She never lived with her father and sister again. Canon Stuart thought that he, as Rector of a parish, ought not to allow a Roman Catholic to live in his house, especially one whose influence was so great among his people. His course of action was determined by a straightforward, conscientious desire to do right. He suffered cruelly from it, for his love for his child was in no way lessened by her action. He wrote to her constantly, saw her whenever he could; from time to time she visited Cottesmore, staying for the purpose at Exton; and he provided generously for all her wants. It was with his full approval that her half-brother William, who had a living in the North of England, eagerly offered a home to his sister. All her brothers would gladly have done the same, for they took her part in the contest, considering that she had the right to exercise her ' private judgment,' and to follow her conscience, knowing her as they did, and knowing that it was no sudden resolve, but the outcome of years of patient study and research.

'But I could not bear to lose her,' writes Mrs. Ross; 'I had prayed so hard for a friend, and God had sent me *one*, as He alone could have done. I persuaded her to stay with me. The gain was indeed all on my side.'

A few days later, on the eve of the First Friday, March 6, 1879, Janet Stuart was received into the Church. The ceremony took place at the Altar of the Sacred Heart in Farm Street. ' I have always thought,' she said, ' that this was my real baptism, for a doubt upon matters of faith has never crossed my mind since.' The next day, the 7th, she made her first Communion. Her Confirmation was delayed for some two months by her own desire, for it seemed for a time as if her favourite brother, Horace, were about to follow her example, and she cherished the hope of being confirmed with him. He was in the Admiralty, and, living in London, was able to be the constant companion of his sister. He took the keenest interest in all she did, accompanying her to Mass and Benediction. But as he still delayed, she was confirmed in April by Dr. Weathers, Bishop of Amycla, auxiliary to Archbishop Manning. Her brother never became a Catholic.

The first phase of the long search was ended, God and truth and beauty had been found as one.

CHAPTER IV

1879 *to* 1882

> ' So you are standing at the covert side, and you cannot tell which
> way the hounds will break covert ! But when they do, then may you
> have a line of country before you which will make you forget all the
> beauty and the glory of your woodlands and pastures, and gallop till
> you are spent.'—*From a letter, J. Stuart.*

A NEW chapter in Janet Stuart's life was now opening. ' From
twenty-one to twenty-eight are our humanist years,' she wrote
in the Essay on Colour already quoted, 'exuberant in action,
and still glowing with the imagery of our golden age. Years,
when we are gathering experience, and learning the inexorable
conclusions of our incircumspect premises.'

The three and a half years following her reception into the
Church were spent, she said, in ' trying to serve two masters.'
She gave the day to fishing and hunting, and often the greater
part of the night to prayer and study, to fit herself for the life
she meant to lead. But what was it to be ? As yet she hardly
knew.

In London I was a little more pious, and visited the University Hospital, and a big Workhouse pretty regularly. Father
Gallwey piloted me with consummate tact, like a born fisherman,
never letting me feel the line till I turned my head to him, at
the same time never letting go, and sometimes hinting that I
was born for greater things than horses or fish. He never smiled
upon my plan of going out to teach Catechism to the Kaffirs,
or of taking a village school. But he would never say explicitly
that he leaned towards anything else, and he made every move
come from me. I had vague thoughts of religious life, and a
sort of conviction that I should be a nun some day, but it
always seemed not to be thought of at the moment.

The outward story of these years can be told briefly. The first
few months were spent in London. In July 1879 she went for

a short visit to Exton, and from there re-visited her own home,
and the villages, farms, woods, and fields, which held so large
a part in her heart, and had been the silent witnesses of her
soul's adventure.   The joy of seeing all again was damped by
the knowledge that her action was not understood by those
whom she loved best.   Standing there among familiar scenes
she realised her own words : ' Yesterday has gone, let it go
utterly ; even the manna, even the sweetness, even the light
of yesterday.   It did its work, its work is done . . . it was a
stepping stone, safe for a moment, then engulfed and the floods
rolled over it.'

After a few days spent with her cousins, she returned to
London, and then went over to Ireland, staying first at Ros-
trevor, before going on to Dunlewy House for the grouse
shooting.   It was a wild, out-of-the-way place, thirty Irish
miles from Strabane, the nearest station at the time.   The
property lay at the foot of Mount Errigal, on the shores of Lake
Nacung, and all round the house rose the purple-clad hills of
North-West Donegal.

There was much game in the neighbourhood, and excellent
salmon fishing.   Janet soon became an expert in this art, and
studied the ways of salmon with keen interest, the leaps between
the lakes especially delighted her.   ' I knew she was good at
fishing,' said Cardinal Logue, many years later—she made his
acquaintance about this time—' but I never knew she had so
much in her head.'

It had been with considerable unwillingness that Janet had
gone to Ireland.   She knew very little of the country or people,
and what she had seen at Stuart Hall had not attracted her.
But, as is so often the case, this first stay in the heart of the
country changed her thoughts.

Long excursions were undertaken among the mountains,
either in company with the guns, or alone in search of wild
flowers.   A favourite expedition was to Horn Head, where she
would stand gazing in delight at the great roll of the Atlantic
waves.   About two miles from Dunlewy was a little chapel
dedicated to the Sacred Heart, and there she went for daily
Mass.

The winter was spent in London, going down for the day,
or sometimes for a night or two, to Leighton Buzzard, where
her friends had a small hunting-box, and kept their horses.
Here Janet was in her element.   Though she had lived in the
heart of the hunting country, she had never hunted as a girl.

D

Absolutely fearless on horseback, she was stopped by nothing. She got many a bad fall, but always escaped unhurt. Her horses, one especially, knew her so well that they responded to every word or touch ; and once, when she had been thrown in jumping a ditch, and the terrified animal was about to bolt, her voice stopped him instantaneously, and he stood perfectly still, trembling violently, until she was able to creep out to rejoin and reassure him. ' Oh I the thrilling breathlessness,' she once exclaimed, ' of seeing the flash of four shining hoofs over one's head, as one extricates oneself from a muddy ditch.'

I rather hoped you would not get through your first season with the hounds without coming off [she wrote to a friend with similar tastes, long after her own hunting days were over]. Did you not feel rather naïve' coming down on the off side and so simply, it made me laugh to think how much you must have enjoyed it, and of the consternation of the groom ; it was good that the falling was so soft! Did your father mind much ? I am sure the groom was proud in his soul that his lady was down and up again so lightly and liked it. I want to hear about the hunting . . . and one hundred and fifty other things when you come . . .

[And again] : X. tells me that you have lamed your hunter ' in the same way as last time,' but I hope that it is not quite so bad as it sounds, for the last one was ' foundered,' wasn't he ? and had to be shot, out of consideration for his age and to save him from an inglorious end. This cannot have happened [now] or you would have sent me a telegram, or I should have seen it in the obituary of *The Times* ! So I believe it is something much less tragic. But I suppose it has stopped your hunting for the moment. And when one has been thrown out in a run, one goes home in a meditative mood, at great leisure.

All the attention she had once bestowed on farmers and their affairs she now turned on hunting and huntsmen, and a new store of type and picture was gathered in her memory, to reappear in all their freshness in the Essays and papers written many years later.

Oh I this is something like hunting [she wrote], the scent breast high, the hounds running so that you could cover them with a table-cloth—the big bullfinches frowning at you, making you take your heart in both hands and trust to Providence for what may be on the other side, and the broad vale before without a covert within miles.

Describing some of her friends with quaint humour in hunting terms, she said : ' So and so reminds me sometimes of that foreigner of distinction on his first introduction to English bullfinches, and an English big jumper : " My horse, he jump, *but I remain*." And X., about whom there comes to my mind a cruel but true description I once heard, of a relative of ——, " the hardest, and straightest, and worst rider in the hunt : no one gets so many falls, no one is so often engaged in the barbed wire, no one so rarely sees the hounds, but—no one better enjoys the sport." ' And her advice on the matter was summed up in a certain amusing paper : ' Ride fast at water, slow at timber. . . . 'Ware wheat always. 'Ware hounds also, don't ride the pack—don't ride the lambs—and above all, scrambling, galloping, jumping, muddy, steaming, tired, *somehow*—be in at the death.'

In the summer of 1880 she went abroad, visiting Paris, Dresden, Munich, and Oberammergau, for it was the year of the Passion Play. ' I did not care for it,' she wrote, ' it spoilt my meditation on the Passion for long afterwards.' The party then went on to Zurich and Interlaken ; several weeks were spent in Switzerland, where her delight in scenery was fully satisfied. A short stay was made in Berlin, and they then returned to England by Brussels. After spending a few days at Exton, she went on to Dunlewy for the shooting, and returned to London for the winter. It was spent much as the previous one, and the following summer saw Janet back in Ireland ; this time she organised a Sunday school, and the children became devoted to her.

The wonderful power of influence which she possessed, showed itself more day by day. It was a persuasive, rather than an aggressive influence. As it had been among horses, so now it was among people ; ' by the gentlest and most imperceptible of means' she led while seeming to follow. ' Shortly after she came to live with me,' wrote her friend, ' I found I did all she desired, and yet she never seemed to consider herself at all, but was always trying to help and please everyone, and to carry out their smallest wishes.'

Disturbances among the Donegal peasantry were very frequent during these years, and more than once the tenants refused their rents to the agent. But when Janet went down among them, and visited each house on the property, they willingly gave her what they had just refused to another. ' She was so affectionate and loving, so thoughtful and helpful, so full

of fun and merriment, that no one could resist her. We all felt
that she was called to something great, and dreaded the thought
of losing her.'

A few letters which Father Gallwey wrote to her during this
period have been preserved. They give a glimpse of her outward life, and still more of the strenuous inner life. Many
passages in them, seen in the light of fulfilment, appear now
to have been prophetic. Speaking of her intercourse with him
after her reception into the Church, she wrote :

> He devoted himself to keep in touch by writing or talking,
> to open out new points of view, to warn before bad turnings in
> the road, and to answer all possible and impossible questions.
> He was extraordinarily gentle in his suggestions and remon-
> strances, he ' begged as a personal favour ' that one would do
> this or that, and made it seem as if one put him under an
> obligation if one followed his advice. He waited three years
> patiently before he brought me to the point of making a retreat,
> proposing it every year, but never insisting and expressing
> himself as so grateful when at length the invitation was accepted.
> . . . He was very gentle with youthful dreams, but the light he
> turned on them by the wonderful ' Rules of the Second Week '
> dispelled their illusions more effectually than active opposition
> or severe criticism.

Letters from Father Gallwey

July 7th, 1881.

I cannot tell you how much your letters and your papers
comfort me. . . . I wish I was sure of seeing your handwriting
oftener. Each paper and each letter suggest so much to me I
would like to say to you.

Your paper on ' *accende lumen sensibus* ' and your enjoyment
of nature made me wish so much to take you through St. Ignatius'
Exercises. I think you would learn there how far you may go
and when to stop, and you will find many of your own ideas
confirmed, and you would have them put into order and presented
as a complete system. I hope that before long I may have the
consolation of helping my dear child in Christ through a retreat.
It would help you forward wonderfully. . . .

With regard to your last note and your sighing after freedom,
I need scarcely tell you that I have been all this time grudging
you to your present work and wishing that the hour of your
emancipation might come.

I know not, as yet, whether I shall be allowed to give the
retreat at Roehampton. If I am I hope you will make an effort
to make it, and meanwhile I beg of you as a great kindness to

write very often and tell me what Our Lord is doing in your soul, and all your thoughts.

July 21st, 1881.

Your letters make me so much wish that you were nearer that we might talk over matters. The Spiritual Exercises will be to you of incalculable value.

With regard to abstinence from the use of creatures, it does not go on indefinitely. What ordinarily happens is that as soon as you show your fidelity to your Creator by saying from your heart ' I do not wish to use any creature unless You wish me to do so,' He at once speaks in return, and tells you, either that He does want you to use creatures or that He prefers you to reserve all your energies for His Passion or His Blessed Sacrament ; as your personal love for Our Lord grows, creatures will lose their natural power over you, but you will acquire a new power far more entrancing. I tell you again, for your comfort and encouragement, that every letter you send me pleases me more and more. I see so clearly how Our Blessed Lord is drawing you to Himself. Write as often as you can without interfering with other duties.

May I try to get one of your papers printed in ' Catholic Progress ' ? When you come to make the Spiritual Exercises you will find that writing these papers has been an excellent preparation for them. So many questions have been started in your mind the answers to which will be found in the Exercises. I cannot in a letter say a tenth part of what your letters suggest to me.

One word about your double life. The day will come when Our Lord will take entire possession of His child, and then for His sake you will find yourself compelled to speak of Him to others in order to help others whom He loves. He will say to you as to St. Peter, ' Lovest thou Me ? ' and when you answer, ' Yes, Lord ; Thou knowest that I love Thee,' He will rejoin, ' Then feed my lambs and save for Me the lost sheep.'

Again I say I wish you were here, but till you are near do not tire of writing, and may Our Lord bless you every hour.

Mount Street, August 5th, 1881.

. . . You say that you want to form habits for the future— to live, as it were, watching and waiting—to have your trunk packed up for a better life. Holy David writes in the 118th Psalm, ' I carry my soul in my hands ' to watch it, to see that it is clean, and to be ready to say at any moment: ' Father, into Thy hands I commend my spirit.'

Will you, at moments when you have leisure, look at the 118th Psalm in the Bible and (1) notice how much personal love for God animates every verse ? In all the verses after the first

three you meet with the words 'thy' or 'thee.' He loves
everything that comes from God. (2) Ask yourself as you read
each verse 'Can I adopt it ? ' and tell me some time what verses
you can adopt thoroughly and what you cannot. God bless
you.

Mount Street, August 9th, 1881.

One part of our compact must be that you do not over-tire
yourself in writing. I say this because I see that you are like
the willing horse, and that you might fatigue yourself too much.
Otherwise I would say write more and more. I often dread the
post lest it should bring me some worries, but letters such as
you send me are a thorough refreshment. I wish you more
and more grace when I read what you write. . . .

I will write some random thoughts suggested from letters
lately from you.

(1) Tell me when you write how much sleep you get and how
much time you give to prayer at night. I am very anxious that
you should become truly holy and useful to others. Therefore
I wish much to prevent any indiscretion that might injure
health.

(2) Offer yourself as you are doing to religious life, you are
well fitted for it, and becoming more and more so every day.

(3) While you are enjoying scenery often make use of the
Canticle *Benedicite*: 'All ye works of the Lord bless the Lord,'
and try to mean every verse, and apply all to the Passion of Christ
after you have thought sufficiently of the creature.

The mountains should bless the Lord because Our Lord
prayed on mountains and suffered on Calvary. The sea because
Our Lord so often sat in the boat, walked on the water. . . . All
the outer world is only a figure of the larger world of grace. . . .

(4) I have shown your last paper to an expert. He gives you
great encouragement and adds these suggestions. Avoid the
use of the form ' one ' thinks, etc., and shorten the sentences.

(5) What I meant when I asked you what Our Lord says to
you in prayer was this. If you keep a diary and watch what
goes on, you will often notice that to-day it seemed to be put
into my mind that suffering was the greatest blessing—or something else.

I have always been fond of small sheets of paper in order to
write short letters, but in future when I write to you I will take
a large sheet !

Mount Street, August 16th, 1881.

From your last note I see that you have been visited by a
fit of desolation. You may remember that I explained to you
St. Ignatius's rules regarding consolation and desolation.

You will find in the first twelve or thirteen verses of the
2nd Chapter of Ecclesiasticus (not Ecclesiastes) a very good

instruction how to act while the visitation lasts. It is a time
when God hides Himself but does not leave you. . . . Write
to me again and let me know how you get on. . . .

.. What you wrote of the effect of your Communion, and the
love of suffering growing in your soul, is all in the right direction.
Our Blessed Lord is guiding His child and drawing her to
Himself. May He continue to pour out His mercies more and
more. . . .

You are Scotch to some degree I believe, and your nation has
the name of being thrifty. Do not be stingy of your thoughts
and inspirations.

                                        September 6th, 1881.

With regard to your last note, it is very hard to impress on
the mind sufficiently that, do what we will, there must be change
of weather in our souls, just as much as in the outer world.
Desolation is as necessary as winter and as clouds—you would
never arrive at your destination without it. Job's description
of man's life is this : ' *Nunquam in eodem statu permanet.*' (Read
again Ecclesiasticus, ch. ii., 13 verses.) The conflict between
your supernatural principles and your natural tendencies is
essential for your future destiny. You remember the Apostle's
question, ' How shall he be crowned unless he shall fight ? '

You can best show your love for Jesus Christ your Lord and
your Spouse by fighting against self, that is your lower self.   In
reality you experience less of this struggle between grace and
nature than many do, you have great advantages, you have had
a good start. Your strong passion for scenery is a harmless one,
it can easily be sanctified.

Your work seems to me to rise into a higher region.   I
will explain my meaning. You remember the Canticle of the
Children, ' All ye works of the Lord, bless ye the Lord.' The
first obvious meaning of the words is a wish that all the works
of creation should move us to bless the Lord.   Creation is like a
large church organ which stands silent till the hand of some child
of God, like yourself, fills the great organ with some of the rushing
wind that came down on the day of Pentecost and makes all the
works of God speak His praises.

But this is only the first part of your work.

When we speak of the works of God which are to bless Our
Lord, we mean besides the sun and the moon, etc., all the works
done by Our Blessed Lord during His Life and Passion and in
the Blessed Eucharist.

This is a new world in which you must habitually live. When
Our Lord was on earth Himself, and stood looking at the waters
of Gennesareth, He was reading in them the history of His future
Church.   When He was near the olive trees on Mount Olivet He

was thinking of the oil of grace and gladness with which He would anoint you in the Sacraments. When He sees you now enjoying some scenery, He is saying to you *'Sursum corda '*—' I have better worlds ready for you.'

The day will come when the drops of Blood and drops of sweat and all the ignominies of the Passion will appear to you to have more attraction than the works of nature, and the wish of your heart will be to suffer for your beloved Lord and Spouse, Jesus Christ.

I will send you with this note your paper on ' Trifles ' which ought to have gone back long ago.

I have read with very great consolation your paper on ' Religious Life.' If I had my way, the convent where you live should be one situated in the midst of grand scenery, so that your heart might be always helped by it to rise heavenward. But as grace works, you will I think agree with the words of St. Dionysius that ' of all divine things the most divine is to co-operate with Our Lord for the salvation of souls.' He will say to you, as to St. Peter, ' If you love me, feed My lambs.' May He ever bless you more and more.

The paper here referred to by Father Gallwey was one written at his request, in which she had stated very fully her ideals of religious life. She described her efforts to find out where these ideals could be best realised. She spoke of visits to several convents, of her attraction to the Society of the Sacred Heart, because of its name, and of her fears that it did not do enough for the poor. Some months later, in the spring of 1882, Father Gallwey sent this paper to the Convent of the Sacred Heart at Roehampton. It bore no signature, but was, he said, written by one who was thinking of joining the Order. Reverend Mother Digby, the Superior of the House, and Mother Henrietta Kerr read it with a few other Mothers.

We were much struck by it [writes one of these]. . . . When I was alone with Reverend Mother Digby, she turned to me and said: ' Do you know, I believe that paper was written by Miss Stuart ? ' I asked why. She could not say, but was convinced that it was so. Miss Stuart's name was known to us, but nothing more. Once in 1879 she had accompanied Mrs. Ross when the latter came down for a meeting of the Children of Mary, and we had heard of her conversion.

But this is to anticipate. Two other letters remain of those written by Father Gallwey at this time. In the first he answers some questions on prayer which she had submitted to him.

September 20th, 1881.

I think that you need not be afraid of using your heart more in your intercourse with Our Lord. Spiritual writers caution us very strongly against over-straining the head, and I myself have seen very good persons brought to a lamentable state of helplessness by over-straining. . . . It stops all prayer and often leads to great discouragement. So that it is much better for you to seem to yourself to be a little idle than to do a lasting damage to your working powers. . . .

Tell me sometimes when you write whether you are attracted more at present to the invisible Trinity or the Humanity of Our Blessed Lord. I have before now shown you how the Canticle *Benedicite* can be applied either to God Our Father and Creator, or to Our Lord Jesus Christ. . . .

Try the effect of indulging your heart in prayer, and tell me the result. . . .

Fishing is an admirable exercise for your purpose; you are alone and you have a little distraction for your mind, though not much. I only wonder how, with your heart for creation, you can bring yourself to kill a fish. God bless you, your letters comfort me very much.

The last letter written at this time answers some questions on the spiritual life and ends with the words: ' I fear you are too [rash] on horseback. It would not be at all a proper finale for you to die out hunting. If the savages were to kill and eat you as a Christian I should not mind, but I do ambition for you some fate better than a huntress with broken bones.'

During these years Father Gallwey introduced a friend to her, with whom she found some spiritual kinship. When in London they took long walks together every afternoon, and Janet, who thought at first that all Catholics had the same intimate intercourse with God, spoke freely and simply of her meditations, hopes and inspirations. The first surrender, the first great plunge ' into the impossible,' had been rewarded by no little consolation. Referring to these things, she said one day in her own expressive language, drawing simile from her hunting experience: ' You never know what is on the other side of the hedge ; ' true at the beginning of her life she was to find it true to the end, as each trustful surrender on her part revealed more of God.

' Engrossed in delightful conversation,' writes this friend, ' we lost all count of time and place. I often saw her quite rapt and out of herself when speaking about God.'

In her solitary walks she did as she advised another many

years later, whose spiritual progress she had much at heart :
' Walking in town,' she wrote, ' you cannot read, but you can
pray, so let that be God's time . . . sometimes let your mind
rest quietly in the thought that God is with you, within, around,
above you, most intimately with you, and walk as you would
walk in recollected happiness by the side of Our Lord Himself.'

Another turning point in her life was now approaching.
Thoughts of religious life were taking deeper possession of her,
but the obstacles appeared insurmountable, and it seemed
neither right nor possible to inflict this further pain upon her
family. God had not as yet spoken the last word. ' She had,'
said the friend quoted above, ' a most wonderful heaven-sent
vocation.' The story is told very shortly in her own words :

One day, it was May 6, 1882, when I was walking up through
Regent's Park to the Helpers of the Holy Souls, I was thinking
of religious life and saying to Almighty God, ' O my God, I
should like it very much, but you see it is impossible to think
of it at present '—and then and there, standing by the side of a
bed of blue hyacinths—*factum est ad me verbum Domini* and
I saw it all.

When I went into the convent chapel, the Blessed Sacrament
was exposed, and the nun who was on the prie-dieu was replaced
by another as I came in. I asked as a sign that, if the ' word '
was from God, He would put me on the prie-dieu instead of the
nun who had just come, and almost immediately she left the
prie-dieu and came to beg me to take it, saying she felt too ill
to stay—so I did not doubt further.

Blue hyacinths remained to her for ever after the symbol
of a great revelation. They were a fitting one, for her mind
and soul and life were full of flowers and their fragrance. She
always kept this anniversary, and if possible liked to look at
blue hyacinths on that day, but 1882 had been a late year and
in May they were often out of flower.

Twenty-seven years later she wrote the story of the conversion of Saint Hyacintha Mariscotti in the form of a dialogue,
' Comfort for the Faint-hearted.' This celebrated penitent died
in the Convent of the Franciscan Regular Tertiaries at Viterbo
in 1640, where she had become a nun in obedience to her
father's will, but against her own wish. Her subsequent life
was a long struggle between her longing for the world and its
pleasures, and efforts more or less prolonged to be faithful to
her vows. After many falls, grace at last triumphed and the
seemingly dead root blossomed into flower. In one scene

Sister Paula, is speaking with the 'late-flowering Hyacintha.'
The picture brought back the memory of the May day when
standing by the late-flowering hyacinths God had made His
revelation, and she tells the story of her own vocation by the
mouth of Sister Paula—a fragment of soul history, poured out
in its abundance for those who could understand. The passage
is as follows :

Tell me about your call to religious life. Did you ever love
the world ? asks Hyacintha.
Perhaps.
Why did you leave it ?
Why ?
Yes, why ?
Because one day I understood.
You thought it all so wicked ?
No, they say it is. I never saw the wickedness. It was
not that.
So trifling ?
No, I suppose it is, but it did not come to me that way.
So fleeting ?
I didn't want it even if it could stay, even if it was very
good, as people are very, very good in the world.
Well, do go on, what was it ?
It was all gathered up into a light, and it was all in a
balance. What is this and what is that ?   The whole world
was on one side, all that was best in it, and God on the other,
and my heart told me ' If thou wilt have one, thou must give
the other.' I saw that all life was to be seeking and all death
to be finding.
And what do you seek ?
God. Who would seek anything else when they have felt
His presence ?

Janet let Father Gallwey know that she would make the
retreat he was to give in the following July at the Convent of
the Sacred Heart, Roehampton. ' He expressed himself as "so
grateful " when at length I accepted his invitation.'

It was her first retreat [writes Mrs. Ross], and I, knowing too
well what it would lead to, tried to prevent her from going.
' I love you very much,' she answered, ' but I love God more.'
So together we drove down to the convent on the afternoon of
July 22.

Father Gallwey had no doubt as to what the issue of the
retreat would be, and said to one of the nuns : ' Tell Mother

Digby that if Miss Stuart offers herself for the noviceship, she is not to be refused. Tell her, she is the most complete person I have ever met. After forty years of ministry in London, she will know what that means.'

So the retreat began, a strenuous eight days, for Father Gallwey was at his best and in all his vigour. ' I sat on a bench on the terrace at Roehampton during the retreat asking myself,' she wrote, ' Could I face the idea of never mounting a horse again—it was what cost me the most. Could I for God brace myself to accept life in thirty-three acres of ground ? ' She little foresaw then that the ' call ' would one day lead her to girdle the earth in her travels.

At the opening meditation of the Second Week, ' The Kingdom of Christ,' Janet was in extreme desolation. But she held on through the long hour praying with all her will, and in spite of the great darkness made the closing prayer, the offering to follow Christ the King.

' Scarcely had I finished it,' she said, ' when a flood of consolation filled my soul. The chapel and every room at Roehampton were flooded with light and echoed glory,'—prophetic words of the life that was about to open. ' I could scarcely wait,' she said later, ' for the 7th of September, the day on which I was to enter, and my longing to be near the convent was so great that in the fortnight I spent in London before entering I went down one night to sleep in the village to be nearer to the house and chapel.' Roehampton was ever to her the ' land of vision.' ' What a place it is,' she wrote in April 1914. ' There is life and light in everything and an atmosphere of God.'

On the seventh day of the retreat Miss Stuart asked to see Reverend Mother Digby, and offered herself very humbly for the Society of the Sacred Heart, hardly daring to hope, as she said, that she would receive a favourable answer, for then, as always, she was ' humble, and little and nothing at all in her own eyes.'

' With all my heart I bless you for it,' said Father Gallwey, when I told him of the final decision, and opening the book of Esther, he read the touching passages in which Mardochai speaks of himself as watching Esther from the time she went in and out as a ' little one.' ' And he walked every day before the court of the house in which the chosen virgins were kept, having a care for Esther's welfare, and desiring to know what would befall her.' ' That is what I have always felt for you from the beginning, and what I have done in your regard.' It was perfectly true, no other words than those of Scripture in his mouth could so well have expressed it.

On the last day of the retreat [writes Mrs. Ross], Janet came to my room and told me of her resolve to enter the Society of the Sacred Heart on the following September 8. We had a long talk about it, and cried over it, at least I did.

My chief recollection of that day, July 30, was the extreme desolation of Miss Stuart's friend [writes Mother X.]. She assured us that we did not know what we were doing, which was true, though not in the sense in which she meant it—for we had no idea then of the greatness of the gift that God gave that day to our Society.

'God has given many gifts to your Order, but never a greater one than Reverend Mother Stuart,' was the verdict, many years later, of one who knew and valued both her and the Society. 'She explained,' continues the narrator whose words we are quoting, 'that Miss Stuart had wretched health, and that religious life would certainly kill her.' Father Gallwey's anxieties were also great. 'Will they appreciate her?' he said, on more than one occasion.

The next day, the Feast of St. Ignatius, the two friends left Roehampton and went at once to Dunlewy. A fortnight was spent there visiting all the old haunts which neither was ever to see again, and Janet took up her favourite sport of salmon fishing. 'I could not bear to return here without you,' said her friend. 'You will never be asked to,' she answered, and so it happened. On leaving Donegal they went to Knock to visit the shrine of Our Lady, which Father Gallwey had much wished them to see. The priest of the place blessed them, and in doing so laid his hands on Janet's head, 'much to my horror,' she said, 'for I had covered my cap with fishing hooks.' They then returned to London, and Janet went down to stay at the rectory at Cottesmore for a few days. It was the first time since her conversion. Those who know how strong was her love for home can realise what the visit meant to her, and how great was the parting wrench. The worst, indeed, had been done three years before, but the last look at all she held so dear was not without its touch of keen anguish. There was a large family gathering in the old home, as two of her married brothers were there with their wives.

On September 6 she returned to London, and the next day

drove down to the convent. Another stage of her journey was accomplished.

Writing many years later to one undertaking the same adventure, she said :

> I know so well, remembering it as if it were yesterday, what the last weeks in the world are before one enters, intense living and intense dying all in one, so I pray every day that God will help you through that day, and unlock His own park gates to you before long ' with a gracious and festive countenance ' as the Church asks Our Lord to meet us when we are dying. . . . You are like the Captain of a ship in a fog-bank off Newfoundland, you don't quite know what may loom up out of the impenetrable fog. But . . . trust it all to God and He will see you through it.

AGED 24 (1882)

CHAPTER V

1882 to 1884

' One of the things which appeals to me particularly in ivory is the life-history which has gone before, when the great tusk was carried through the free range of forest and jungle in the joy of life and exuberance of strength. After which came death, a great renunciation, a great surrender of the soul, and then a new existence " in chastity, in knowledge, in long-suffering, in sweetness." '

From ' Four Classes of Souls,' J. Stuart, 1910.

REVEREND MOTHER DIGBY and the sub-mistress of novices received the new postulant. It was with mingled feelings of awe and joy that she stood at last within the shelter of those walls on which the light of God had seemed to linger ; no longer there as a visitor for a moment, but to stay as a child in her home. She was taken to the chapel of the Sacred Heart and kneeling before the altar made the offering of her life on the spot, where, thirty-three years later, she was to rest from her labours. Then rising she went to begin her new life in the noviceship : that life which ever remains a mystery and a rock of offence to the world. ' Can those outside ever understand it ? ' she makes Hereswitha ask in the Dialogue of St. Hilda. ' I think never. The sweets of God are so within that they can only be read from within. You can see two shining lights— austerity and peace—from the one you shrink, the other perhaps you would covet . . . But not at the price.'

The spirit in which she made her offering may be gathered from a letter written many years later to one of her novices :

The day of entering is a very wonderful one, I remember the feeling of every hour of it. . . . I think it is more like death than anything I can imagine, and in fact that is just what it is, the death of one's first life, and rather sharp agony ; but one knows that as far as soul and will and resolve go, it is the intensest

day of life, when they are put out to the full, and one simply
gives all and goes in for death or for life or whatever God chooses,
and that is better than any high spirits or excitement.

The second stage of life, of which she spoke in later years, was
now opening, ' a great surrender and renunciation seeking God
alone.' The call came to renounce her enjoyment of nature
and all that it entailed, and to use it as a means of opening wide
fields of abnegation. ' We know we have been privileged to
give up things for God that we could not have given up for anyone
else,' she wrote to a novice in whom a gift of flowers had awakened
a longing for the home they came from ; ' those things that are
good all through, with no bad in them. It is not the " wicked
world " that is best worth giving, but the good and glorious
world, solitude and deep woods and great silences, and, one may
add, hunting.' The only side, she said, on which the world
had appealed to her. ' I know how it must ache and the whole
machinery creak round you, but it is all part of the thing, it
would not be worth half so much without all that. . . .' And,
to explain her ready sympathy, she added : ' I remember exactly
the same thing happening to me when I was very young in the
noviceship, and a hamper of cowslips arrived.'

' There is,' says a spiritual writer, ' a time when the soul
lives in God, and a time when God lives in the soul. In the
first, which is the earlier stage, the soul watches itself for God,
it is occupied in restraining itself and accommodating itself to
Him. Later only it becomes God-possessed, and lives in the
hands of God.' It was through this first stage that Sister Stuart
had now to pass.

On November 13, 1882, the Feast of St. Stanislaus Kostka,
she took the habit. Father Gallwey performed the ceremony,
choosing for the text of his sermon the words from the Collect
of the Mass, ' *Festinemus* : we may make haste to enter into
everlasting rest, redeeming the time by earnest work,' and
developing them with illustrations from the book of Wisdom.

' He was very proud of his novice,' writes the sacristan at the
time, ' and I can still recall the look of satisfaction on his face
as, after the ceremony, he came with Reverend Mother Digby
and Sister Stuart down the sacristy corridor. The latter stood
back to let her elders pass, but he motioned her to go on in front,
saying : " Dust before the broom, Janet ; dust before the broom." '
He asked to have a copy of everything that came from her pen.
His chief solicitude was for her health. Father Gallwey was of

opinion that the noviceship was unnecessarily severe, that it aimed too much at repression, and that Sister Stuart would be allowed to do too much. On one occasion he kept the sub-mistress of novices a considerable time in earnest discussion, trying to find what he called a harmless form of particular examen. In the end even he could not find a subject which her fervour would not over-do.

The first weeks after the clothing were difficult ones. ' I remember them so well,' she wrote later to a novice with whom she feared all was not going well. ' I wonder whether you have gone under, as so often happens ; just as when one is learning to swim, the floundering and choking . . . has to come some time, and it often comes then. Mother Digby called me one day as she went out from the novices' recreation, and said : " Do you feel as if God's air would never blow upon you again ? " and I said " Yes." That was all the conversation, but her look said the rest, that she knew what it was like, and that it would come right.'

It has often been seen in the annals of the Church how saints are born of saints, ' selon une ineffable génération *ex Deo* ' ; [1] thus St. Paul, the child of the prayers of St. Stephen ; thus ' the succession of Holy Abbots—Saints—at Cluny, during two centuries, each of whom distinguished himself by the zeal with which he prepared his successor.' [1] In this way, in a very true sense, Mother Stuart may be called the child of the prayer and hope of Mother Digby.

Yet it needed but a short time for her to realise that in Mother Digby she had found an almost complete contrast.

Both, it is true, were born sportsmen, and had that instinct of the sportsman, which Mother Stuart regarded almost as a sixth sense. She used to say that one sportsman knew another all the world over, and she hinted that the underlying something that made the born sportsman was closely allied to, if not identical with, that which made a master of men.

Both were solitary within their own souls, one with the remoter solitude of the mountain peak, standing calm and im-movable beneath the blows of time, inspiring awe and admira-tion as well as the deepest love. The other bore the impress of that strange solitude of nature lying even at our feet, so near, yet never fathomed ; full of sunshine and joy, thrilling to every human interest, a home for the human heart. ' Human,' some-

[1] See *La Vie spirituelle et l'Oraison d'après la Sainte Ecriture et la Tradition monastique.* Solesmes, 1899.

E

one said, ' was the word that best described her.'   But human
with that touch of the divine which is so rare a beauty upon
earth.   She was never remote or afar off, but within reach of
every call for help and love.   In spite of these differences, a deep
and life-long affection sprang up between them, each recognised
in the other the gift of God, and to the end it remained more
that sacred love between mother and child, rather than the tie
of friendship based on intuitive understanding and sympathy.

Mother Digby had a marvellous power of penetration, and
a keen eye for discovering the gifts of God in those around her.
She was soon satisfied that in Sister Stuart the Society of the
Sacred Heart had a subject capable of the greatest things, and
she trained her accordingly.   ' Formez-les moi fortes et sur-
naturelles,' were Mother Goetz's words to Mother Digby as
she gave the novices into her hands, and this had been her
guiding star in dealing with them.   Was the result hard ?
Some, perhaps, found it so :   ' the austere practical training,'
as one described it ;   but the fact remains that none of those
who passed through the crucible would give up one day or
hour of that ' hard training ' and that happy life.   Sister Stuart
was to have her full share in all this, and Reverend Mother
Digby took her in a special way under her own care.

Reviewing her methods of training, Mother Stuart wrote
in 1912 [1] :

We would have done anything at her word, without even
thinking it strange.   All of a sudden would come a check,
' No, you are not able to do that,' some very small thing it
might be ;   and how I winced at the words until it became clear
that it was for the health of the soul that precaution was taken,
and that it was only another string of one's instrument that
she had selected to tune.   This never lasted long ;   she would
propose some inspiring impossibility to be made possible, and
one had the comfort of knowing one was not intended for les
invalides.   She would not let us loiter in the way of perfection, nor look a second time at something that grace asked
for.   She insisted on self-command, even in material things,
and exercised us on ladders, scaffoldings, and single planks at
any height.   ' Go up by those ladders to the bell turret, and
see how the world looks from there,' she said to two of us one
day, and we climbed to the bell turret at Roehampton.

A great, perhaps the greatest, source of penance and suffering to her at this time, and throughout much of her life, was her

---

[1] See *Mother Mabel Digby*, by A. Pollen (Murray, 1914).

shyness. Her natural inclination would have led her to remain always in the background. Writing of Mother Digby's action in her regard, she said : ' She [Mother Digby] would never admit shyness as a covert into which one might withdraw ; it was no excuse ! Shyness was not an apostolic virtue, it had to be given up. She would prepare and offer many occasions, excruciating to a shy person, for this exercise. " I don't expect to have to open this subject with you again," she said ; " you must be thoroughbred in everything ! " She would not admit that an opportunity had been lost, and should be merely regretted. I had to go back and begin afresh, which, of course, doubled the difficulty.' [1]

' It was not without some trouble,' writes a fellow novice, ' that Reverend Mother Digby succeeded in training Sister Stuart to disregard her tendency to be silent, to remain in the background, to wait for others to take the initiative. In the noviceship, at first, she scarcely talked at all in general assemblies ; and when she understood that she ought to, it cost her very much to raise her voice, nor did she always seize the moment when it came.' For long after she entered, as she herself confessed, recreations were a real trial.

In 1882 Mother Henrietta Kerr's life was drawing to a close, and partly for her sake, and partly for the example of her holiness, Mother Digby named the new novice her ' errand boy ' and secretary, and most of her leisure went in this employment. About the same time she became sub-secretary to Mother Digby, and was given a little room near hers. From this time on, for some twelve years, she was her constant companion. ' My first recollection of Mother Stuart is as a figure in the background, as a shadow of Reverend Mother Digby,' writes one who was then a child at school.

Her position in the noviceship was thus an unusual one. ' That it did not cause the slightest shadow of jealousy, speaks much for her holiness and tact,' writes the *surveillante* of the novices at the time. Her genuine love of common life was evident to all. ' Two traits stand out in my memory after all these years. The first was the eagerness of Sister Stuart, during any temporary absence of Mother Digby, to make up for lost chances of such good things as scullery work and other household occupations. As I was then *surveillante*, she necessarily applied to me for the gratification of her lowly ambitions. The second

[1] See *Mother Mabel Digby*, by A. Pollen (Murray, 1914).

was her life-long and deep gratitude for a reproof which it fell
to my lot to make to her. I always attributed to this her marked
affection for me and her continual reiteration of what she owed
me. In her very last letter from Ixelles in July 1914, she said :
" You know that ever since you were my *surveillante* in the
noviceship, and still more my Mistress of Studies, I have been
very sensitive to your approval, and the judgment you would
form of anything that I might produce ! You would be surprised if you knew how much I remember of things that you
said, even casually. What dear and happy days."

Long hours were spent by the novice in wood-carving,
plan-drawing, and gardening. This outdoor work was generally
shared by children, those whom, for some reason, Reverend
Mother Digby wished to befriend or reward.

During my school-life [writes one such child] I saw much of
Mother Stuart. I was constantly with her in the garden, planting and weeding under Mother Digby's direction. She taught
me to break in a pony, to handle a donkey. We fished together,
boated on the lake, botanised and hunted for birds' nests. These
hours stand out in my mind as the sunniest that could ever shed
happiness on a child's life. . . . I was very backward for my
age, at nine years old, and was unable to read. I was handed
over to her to be taught, if possible. I sighed at the prospect,
but very soon I found that ' my novice ' meant to take me both
seriously and hopefully, for instead of bringing a baby book
about the ' fat cat ' that ever ' sat upon the mat,' she handed
me her Bible. Our lessons were usually in the garden, that the
exuberance of my delight at my daily progress might find full
vent. Very soon I discovered that I could read, and, better
still, I found I had a friend who was always hopeful and always
patient, one whose friendship during thirty years knew no ebb
or flow.

In the second year of the noviceship, those who are destined
for teaching begin a preparatory course of studies. In September 1883 Sister Stuart took up these new duties. Her
previous training and education had been well suited to fit her
for the work before her. She was already competent to take the
master's chair. Such an idea was far from her mind. ' In those
early days,' writes a fellow novice, ' she seemed to think that
everyone knew a great deal, reflected much, and gave all they
had to God, like herself.' In this spirit of a disciple, she sat
again upon the class-room benches. ' I have,' writes the novices'
class-mistress, ' a uniform, whole-souled impression of rare gifts,

unusual culture and maturity, and withal most refreshing
childlike docility and openness of mind—a perfect type of the
man of " good-will " to whom peace has been granted from on
high, once and for ever.'

This was the outward impression. But the postulantship
and noviceship are a difficult time for all, and were specially so
for Janet Stuart. She used laughingly to compare her previous
life to that of Job's ' wild ass of the desert,' and say that ' sweet
reasonableness and every good came to her when she had the
grace to put her head in the collar.' And this she did thoroughly
and completely, following her own advice to another, ' to waste
no time in beginning.'

She had been studying the life of St. John Berchmans before
she entered, and had determined to make his motto, *minima sed
constans*, her own. It upheld her in the inevitable moments of
discouragement and depression when, as she wrote, ' there is the
feeling of weariness and " what's the use," when everything
seems so insignificant as not to be worth doing, and the most
excruciating thing of all is that there is nothing which can be
fairly called excruciating. One has to make a resolute act of
faith that God cares, and that the meaning of it all will come
out in the end, and so it does.' ' A temptation,' she said once,
' which every teacher knows, every priest knows, every monk,
every Bishop . . . and I have often thought the Pope must
know best of all, having to spend hours in the day giving audience
to people to whom he *dare* not say more than a platitude.'

Obedience was from the first the virtue round which her
ideals centred. As in her childhood, so now again she took
Our Lord's word literally : ' They that hear you, hear Me,'
and applied them not only to the Rule but to every authority
in the house. 'Orders for her must be worded carefully,'
said Reverend Mother Digby, ' for she will carry them out to
the letter,' as was proved on more than one occasion. To pass
through religious life without having broken a rule or disobeyed
a command was one of her earliest spiritual ambitions, and was
literally attained. '*Que dans votre obéissance n'apparaisse le
moindre signe de votre volonté*,' said Mother Digby, speaking
to her novices one day, and Sister Stuart realised the ideal to
perfection. The novice Mistress herself confessed that she was
more struck by this understanding of the virtue of obedience
than by all the rest, and she gave many opportunities of
practising it.

The change from the free out-door life told on her, and her

health appeared to suffer, so that for a time her Superior insisted
on rest even at the expense of prayer and Communion. ' The
only answer I ever received,' said Mother Digby, ' was a " Yes "
or " Thank you," never an Oh ! of regret or entreaty.' But though
she obeyed in each detail, her spirit chafed inwardly at this too
great solicitude.   In her wish to do as Saints had done, she had,
before entering, practised severe bodily austerities with blessed
fruit, as she herself testified later.   Father Gallwey had exercised
a controlling hand, it is true, but nevertheless she had had great
liberty and had used it.   Now the voice of obedience spoke and
many of her practices were stopped, and to her great mortification she was henceforth protected from herself. ' Why,' she
said once to Mother Digby, when curbed in her desire for corporal
penance, ' why do you take more care of my body than of my
soul ? '   ' You may have another Superior who can do for your
soul what I have left undone, but if I let you damage your
body it can't be repaired,' was the answer.

The remark most often made about her was : ' How mortified
she is ! ' and her description of a mortified person, though written
many years later, throws light on her own methods :

A mortified person knows how to wait, how to listen, how to
laisser tomber, how to mortify mortification itself when charity
or obedience requires it.
She is polite, for politeness is *l'art de se gêner soi-même afin
de ne point gêner les autres.*
She gives no clue to her likes and dislikes, but takes things
as they come.
Her voice is low—an excellent thing in women, and *a fortiori*
in a Religious.
Her ways are gentle, for her soul is in her hands.
She plays second fiddle excellently.
She is a miser of time—God's time.

A favourite penance of hers was to remain a considerable
time without changing position, and this she often advocated
in later years as a means of strengthening nerve and will.   This
was characteristic of her.   Mere negation never appealed to
her, it was too akin to death ; restraint and denial were to
set her powers free.

She often alluded to St. Aloysius's practice of securing some
discomfort in every act ; and ' oh ! blessed inconvenience ! '
one of her doctrines of later years, was a principle of hers from
the beginning.

The intensity and responsiveness of her nature called, as she said later, for restraint.   But this restraint itself was not without its dangers; dangers of exaggeration and wrong self-repression, of destroying the wheat along with the cockle.   It is undeniable that she leant towards great severity with self.   To become dead to her feelings was, as it had been in her childhood, one of her acknowledged aims.   ' To lead myself a dog's life seemed then the pledge of fervour ! '   As a friend expressed it in later years, ' she sought God among the ruins.'   She belonged, perhaps, for a time to what she described in a paper written in 1897 as the 'School of Jeremias.'   'There is a school among these powerful and original thinkers (novices, etc.) that cries destroy.
. . .   " The Lord said to me, Lo ! I have set thee this day over the nations . . . to root up and to pull down, and to waste and to destroy, and to build and to plant," that is, make a clean sweep of everything and start afresh on nothing ! '   An attitude of mind that leads inevitably to some mistakes, and Mother Stuart did not escape its consequences.

Her love of beauty made her value perfection of detail in all things.   In this spirit, and because with true humility, she held life and talents as a trust from God, she had cultivated every gift and power He had given her.   And with this ideal she stood upon the threshold of religious life.   Then it *seemed to her* that even this must go, that there was perhaps something inordinate in her desire for self-culture.   God seemed to hold out His hand, and in her childlike, trustful nature there could be no denying Him.   He might ask for what He liked, the costliest gift, He must have it.   ' Yes, you are right, it is useless to hold out against God,' she wrote many years later to an intimate friend, ' He keeps putting out His hand for just that particular tiny flower you are holding on to, and in the end one gives it with a holy, loving shame, which makes a beautiful little act of contrition, and then we are lower in our own eyes and dearer than before to Him. . . .'   But this was the discovery of her maturer mind.

In the early months of her noviceship [writes a fellow novice], this trial seemed at one moment almost beyond enduring. Sister Stuart imagined that she must change into another being. She fixed her eyes on a novice, utterly unlike herself, but who appeared to her to have attained the desired goal.   For a moment, perhaps, her path became obscured, and it was hidden from her eyes that what she needed was merely the perfecting

of her own nature and not the assuming of another. The
result was a painful struggle,

> ' If not without the blameless human tears,
> By eyes which slowly glaze and darken, shed
> Yet without questioning and fears. . . .'

For was not God her Father, and she knew a Father's love.
A love to be trusted, though its workings were not understood?
On December 27, 1882, when, at the end of a famous sermon
preached by Father John Morris, S.J., in the convent chapel on
the words, ' *Possumus !* Blessed be God, we can ! ' the choir
stood up ; Sister Stuart, who was in the tribune, was so much
overcome that she could not sing a note. Why, none of her
sisters knew. But the costly self-surrender had been made.
Years afterwards she gave her mistake as an example of the
delusions into which beginners are apt to fall.

Reverend Mother Digby never fully understood the difficulty
nor the magnitude of the sacrifice that had been contemplated.
Had she done so she would have been far from giving her
approval. As it was, however, true to her own principles, she
exercised her novice in renunciation in this line, that she might
come to account all intellectual attainments, and all work,
even that done for God, as nothing in comparison with the
knowledge of Jesus Christ. Sister Stuart responded perfectly,
but it was from the depths of her own experience that she said
to another later : ' I *am* glad that you have laid aside that restless
fear of deterioration of mind through want of intellectual work.
Nothing can deteriorate it if its willed tendency is towards God,
the light and the life of the mind.' For herself she began now
to realise that better than all knowledge and usefulness is ' a
little living act of faith, or hope, or charity, escaping even from
the trammels of words ; a little leaning of my spirit on God,
that carries it out and beyond itself to Him.' And as secretary
and companion of Reverend Mother Digby she ran messages,
waited for answers, made up parcels, wrote business letters,
spent long hours in the garden amusing little children, and doing
a thousand trifles as if these occupations were what she most
enjoyed. For some years these odds and ends of duties, with
which her energies had to be content, acted as a curb for what
was natural in her activity. ' How you must have wondered
if that was the work which you had come to do,' said a friend
in later years. ' Yes, that is perfectly true,' she answered,
' but it was training of another kind.'

This was the spirit in which she looked on the accidents by the way. All life was a school, and we were to be taught now by one set of circumstances, now by another. To those who in later years spoke of things being hard, she would often say, ' Yes, but it is the making of the pup.'

But, as so often the case when passing through an experience, at the time these things were hidden from her eyes. ' I fear,' she said one day, speaking to a friend to whom reference has already been made, ' I fear that I shall be a fraud, and not able to do anything' ; but the friend saw things differently, and reassured her. ' No, God wants to work in you by Himself.' It was indeed true. And long after her years of training were over, Reverend Mother Stuart still offered to God the willing sacrifice of her taste for reading and study, and her capacity for intellectual excellence in any branch in which she might have chosen to specialise.

But yet another sacrifice was to be made, the full import of which she did not at the moment realise.

We have seen how, even as a child, she had a love of solitude and meditation, combined, however, with an overflowing energy of action ; ' a characteristic,' it has been said, ' of people called to fulfil a great mission in life.' With her power of concentrated thought and her gift of intuition, she had the makings of a contemplative ; and, while knowing nothing of ' kinds of prayer,' with the realisation of God which came to her on her conversion, she had aspired to as close a union with Him as possible, even in this life. This was the ' purpose ' to which Father Gallwey alluded in one of his letters, where he spoke of ' fishing as an excellent occupation well suited to your purpose ' to be ' lovingly attentive to God.'

But, on the other hand, the activity of her memory and imagination and her great fertility of thought needed, at first, an outlet, even in the realms of prayer.

When Father Gallwey had undertaken her direction he had taught her the methods of discursive meditation ; the only method which can be taught and acquired in the same way as any science. Though a careful perusal of his letters shows that he in no way closed the door upon affective prayer, yet at the time the ' methods ' appear to have absorbed her energies. They came as a revelation, and to her ordered mind were for long a source of both intellectual and spiritual delight. She realised, perhaps vaguely it is true, that her simpler manner of prayer in which she had found both light and peace was not in keeping with

her new knowledge ; but, ever self-diffident and powerless, even
from childhood, to express her innermost thoughts and aspirations,
she at once silently interpreted God's call to surrender to mean
that she should 'crush this inner life of inspiration and the
contemplative mind.' This judgment was confirmed when, upon
entering the Society of the Sacred Heart, she found the same
methods of discursive meditation taught to all the novices as
the 'grammar of prayer,' 'the thing which was within the
reach of *all* '; and as a great means of impressing the truths of
religion on the minds of beginners. 'I thought I was the only
crazy person among the wise, who knew exactly what path they
were going by, and where it led to,' she said many years later,
speaking of her experiences in prayer.

At what seemed then the word of obedience, ' she chose the
beaten track and journeyed as a pilgrim to the vision of God.
Her mind, fresh from its dreams of gold, was put in fetters,
highly disciplined and checked, its lavish growth pruned, and
in the throes of renunciation, the life within grew deep and
strong.'

For the moment she was led in the path of renunciation in
a spirit typified by her choice of St. John the Baptist for her
patron ; the friend of the Bridegroom who was content to
stand aside and send others to keep company with Christ. Her
spiritual exercises were reduced to the minimum, she was sent
here and there, and deprived of leisure for recollection, for
Mother Digby's judgment coincided with that of Father Gallwey,
and she feared ' there was nothing that her novice's fervour
would not overdo.'

And so she had entered on the 'hard and narrow way.' 'And
be thou sure of this, no other can do for thee, that appointed
thee by God. . . . Not any light shall shine upon thy road
for other eyes. Thou hast thy way to go, thou hast thy life
to lead.' 'I think it is so for many souls in religion,' she said in
later life, ' certainly it has been so for me.'

These trials did not end with the noviceship ; but hope
upheld her, and she never faltered in her trust of God. ' I
knew He would carry me through ; we learn by experience and
by stripes. We are at school here and we must learn our lesson.'

It was but a stage, and in years to come God gradually gave
back the life renounced for His sake, transfigured with new depths
of understanding. She had given up for Him her joy in nature
and glorious scenery, and He was planning to show her the
beauty of the world before she died. She renounced her love

of reading and study, and He so arranged it that in later years, when she could in perfect safety be friends with both worlds, all that was best and beautiful found its way to her. She left the by-ways where her soul had met Him face to face in prayer, and travelled by the hard and painful highway, until He raised the veil again and led her to the more rarely trodden path where two worlds mingle.

All had been surrendered trustfully into His hands, and when the purification was accomplished He was to call her again and to show her she was crushing His best gift, His life in her; and because a desire to obey had been the mainspring of her action, she was to turn at once from the path which she had followed. All had been allowed for the sake of the hundreds she was one day to teach, and to them, remembering her own experience, she would say later : ' Beware of extremes, beware of inhuman efforts, of violent measures, of all that drives you off your balance.' And again : ' Don't attempt the impossible. . . . Take yourself as you are, whole, and do not try to live by one part alone and starve the other. Control, but do not kill. . . .' But this time was not yet.

There was a great gravity about her in these years, as of one ' who had set her face to that which is, not to that which might, could, or should be . . . if.' The keen sense of humour, the instinct for the funny side of things, was not so visible as later on, but it was all alive within. ' You are very grave, sister ; I hope your conscience is at peace,' said Monsignor Weld one day to her, when still a novice, and struggling to keep a fitting composure, she was trying to measure him for a soutane. Behind all was the sportsman's instinct of ' playing up to God,' of bearing scratches and tumbles to be in at the death ; the adventurous spirit, looking on all life as a journey, ' glorious in its faith and hope and adherence to what we don't understand ' ; and, above all, the true *pietas*, the child's love for her Father, and therefore the love for all He might choose to do with her. 'God is working His pattern beautifully ; it hurts Him when you think it is not coming right,' she said, encouraging another with her own brave spirit.

On the feast of St. Stanislaus, November 13, 1884, Sister Stuart took her first vows. ' It is such a day to begin,' she said later : ' a sort of heavenliness like the Assumption hangs about the feast of St. Stanislaus, and makes it unlike any other day.' When her sister novices asked her for a parting word on the eve of her retreat, she gave them, as a summing up of the two years that had passed : ' Better is one day in thy court above thousands.' She had realised, as she wrote later, that ' it is in the most trifling things of life that one may learn to practise that uncalculating love which rises naturally to the call of greater things when it comes.' And the hard things seen in retrospect seemed to her as ' the low door into the Church. Go through without looking,' she wrote to a novice, ' and take it all as being certain to lead you right, for it will. Saints have gone that way and thought nothing of it ; St. Stanislaus, and St. Aloysius, who must have had a fearfully hard battle, and others, moderns too.'

She had learnt to love what she described to another as ' the real inner spirit and life of it all : . . . the hold that the consecrated life takes of one's whole being, the way in which it makes people fling all that is in them down before God for service and homage first, and then for love, and count it as nothing ' ; and she added, ' Those get to it quickest who wear the harness from the beginning, and give themselves without looking back.' It was what she herself had done.

Father Gallwey again performed the ceremony. His sermon on the words, ' *Ubi est qui natus est, vidimus stellam et venimus adorare eum,*' was wholly addressed to Sister Stuart, and reiterated much of his former teaching.

Many years later in an essay, ' A Parable from Nature,' Mother Stuart summed up the work and issue of these years. Her words speak as no others could :

Rooted in the loose limestone, the freshly pruned vines stood hideous, twisted, hacked, almost done to death, without a vestige of beauty, or, apparently, a stir of life ; stripped of all former growth, with nothing to live upon, and the bare rock to hold to. Yet in these hacked stumps slept the soul of the vine, and a few days hence, after rain, it would bound into life. And out of that came grapes ; so and no otherwise. The vine said, ' Surrender yourself to the life, and trust ' ; and after that the novice saw that the very hacking and hewing contained answers to the problems of life.

Hard I may be the comment of some who read, but there is no ' service ' in the world, worth the name, for which the training is not severe. There is an apprenticeship to sanctity as to all else.

CHAPTER VI

1884 *to* 1889

' God does not ask a perfect work, but infinite desire.'

IN the Essay on Colour, written in December 1899 Mother Stuart said : ' From twenty-eight to thirty-five is the cool, clear, blue age of Dialectics. . . . Reason is taking the mastery in us. We are not pessimists from twenty-eight to thirty-five, but neither are we optimists. We have set our faces to that which *is.* . . . We are beginning to know, not to guess ; to judge, not to feel the answers to our questions. It is our scholastic age, and these are critical years in our formation. For if dialectics go too far, and the mind, instead of broadening and sinking down on its base in the real, grinds itself to a knife edge ; if we learn to cut and dissect our ideals and those of others ; if wary reason stops and sounds too dubiously the chasms over which feeling and imagination used to carry us in one flight, then the riper and richer years of our life are dwarfed.'

The period of life, which she thus describes, was opening for her when she left the noviceship and entered upon her new duties in the community and school at Roehampton. To the search for personal perfection she had now to add the special work for which her Order was set apart in the Church, ' *Puellarum mores confirmandae,*' as the Brief expresses it. And to this we may first turn.

Mother Stuart was pre-eminently an educator. Once when a conversation turned on the question : What we should have liked best to be in life, she answered unhesitatingly : ' A teacher,' and added, ' I should not have minded what I taught, so long as I could have caught someone, and taught them something.' And though her actual intercourse as a teacher, with children, was of short duration, yet it may be said with truth that she taught, and, above all, educated all her life.

'The question of education is best solved,' she wrote, 'by those who have the double love of knowledge and of children. These two affections mingled produce great educators.' And these two loves were deep in her own soul. All that was young appealed to her, all that was growing and struggling to the light ; and with the thoroughness that marked all that she did, she now began, or rather continued, that study of character on which she had set out when scarcely more than a child herself. The result was an intuition of the minds of children, which gave such value to her written works and such life and reality to her teaching.

Her general theories of education will be more fittingly considered in a later chapter. Here we shall look at her among the children.

Two months before the end of her noviceship, in September 1884, she had been given an English class. To this was now added other work. She taught Christian Doctrine and Arithmetic in the school, and was Directress of the Aloysian sodality, while in the community she supervised the studies of the young nuns, and became the class-mistress of the novices.

From the first she realised the ideals set forth in the Schools of the Sacred Heart, where the class is a little family, of which the mistress is not only the teacher, but the mother, to whom nothing that concerns the welfare of the children should be indifferent. Her interest in them was never limited to class hours. Speaking in later years on this subject, she said :

Our vigilance should be like that of a naturalist . . . full of love and reverence. . . . If a naturalist had an aviary and made his morning round, he could certainly tell at the end of it what birds were off their food, out of health, moping, quarrelling, etc. If he studied them in the open air he would be all alive as to each bird he met, to notice its ways, its condition, its plumage ; to catch the first note of new-comers in spring, to perceive the first general movements among the swallows preparing to go.

And writing of a young nun who had been given charge of the Junior School, she said :

A field of hidden devotedness was opened out by this appointment. She [X.] was astonished to find how much there was to be done for the body as well as the soul in the education of these small creatures of God ; how large a part in their training turned round material things ; and the endless self-abnegation that was required to deal with details while not losing sight of ends.

This was her school of patience. All her natural tastes and artistic gifts seemed to be thwarted and held in abeyance by the stress of everyday wear and tear.

Mother Stuart took our class, the third, in September 1884 [writes one who was then a child at school]. Her standard was very high, and she patiently tried to raise us to it. . . . She never found fault with us on the spur of the moment, sometimes waiting until the last few moments at the end of class, when the warning bell had rung, sometimes till the next day. Once she waited for a week, when the whole class had been in fault. . . . She often gave us questions to think over (our ages varied from twelve to fourteen), and she wished each one to write a very short answer, however crude. What I treasure up for life from her teaching, was the picture of the great heroes of Church History, particularly Saint Athanasius and Saint Thomas Aquinas. I have often thought that if I had temptations against the Faith, the remembrance of those great minds bowing to the teaching of the Church would dispel them, and I have longed to be able to produce the same impression on the children I taught.

Of all the lessons that she gave at this time, perhaps those in Christian Doctrine made the greatest impression on her hearers. ' I still cherish the memory of her lessons,' writes one ; ' those on the Sacraments stand out clearly in my mind. Confession, she impressed on us, should be a neat sacramental act, standing sacred and remote from all not immediately connected with it.' She tried to make the subject appear as something apart, something that escaped from the trammels of the schoolroom. Even her examination papers were set on different lines from those given in other classes.

She gave us at times one comprehensive question for the monthly examination, for example, to take the form of morning prayers given in our school manuals and find out all the dogmas or doctrines of the Church contained in it. Such questions opened our eyes to the treasures of faith and devotion lying at our very doors. Her criticisms of our work were short and to the point, and not without a sparkle of fun in them.

She read Scripture as no one else [writes another]. Two lessons especially stand out in my mind. One Sunday, the 18th after Pentecost, she worked out a wonderful lesson on the Mission of Moses, from the words of the Offertory in the Mass for the day. Another time she gave us a similar lesson on Job. What remained to me of these classes was an impression of her great knowledge of Scripture and of its living interest to her ; and the desire was awakened to attain to something similar.

From the first the children respected and loved her ; some instinct told them that here was true worth. ' She seemed to bring with her an atmosphere of peace ; and when I saw her waiting for us at the study-room door, I had to be quiet and speak gently,' writes one who was then in the exuberance of youthful spirits.

Swiftness and silence summed her up [writes another]. Sometimes she had charge of the study-room. There was nothing irksome in her ' surveillance,' yet she was unmistakably at attention, and on duty the whole time. I was supposed to be observant as a child, and my powers of observation focussed largely on my mistresses, and on Mother Stuart in particular. But here special scientific skill was called for, as she had such a peculiar gift of effacing herself. Her gifts never flashed ; she was, it seemed to me, little noticed and less spoken of, though, of course, I had a great idea of her learning since the days when she taught me to read. For a time, I was constantly in the infirmary, and busy as Mother Stuart was, she never missed a day coming to see me. She was very gentle and had the instinct of what would comfort or relieve. In summer she brought flowers from the garden, no two alike, and about each she had something of interest to tell. She handled them so reverently and tenderly. Under her teaching they became my friends, full of symbolic meaning, and I understood how it was that she could not bear us to pull flowers to pieces when studying them, but preferred that we should grow them.

As Mistress of the Aloysian sodality, Mother Stuart's influence over some of the younger children made itself felt.

For two years [continues the above writer] I had the privilege of being in her congregation of Saint Aloysius. We made a study of him with her, discussing his character and virtues, though we did not read his life. He was a strong man, was the dominant note struck, I think, and the terms ' strong ' and ' innocent ' came to be in my mind almost convertible. She had not, I think, great facility for speaking to children of our age, and we were a little in awe of her. However, in time she drew us out, and we talked simply with her. The word ' self-denial ' was often to the fore, and we acquired some good, strong elementary notions of it, as well as of the Christian spirit of bearing with good grace the small crosses of daily life.

What struck us all most was her great reverence for us. It

inspired us with a sense of our own dignity, and the spirit of her appeal was *noblesse oblige*. She seldom used the word 'humility.' It was not, as she explained in later years, 'a virtue children can understand—it seems to them a colourless, spiritless attitude of mind. 'It is better,' she said, 'to inspire them with the sense of their dignity, than of their unworthiness. Let humility take the form of frankness and love of truth, and let them realise that they must never descend from the high thoughts of the children of God.'

She seldom spoke to any of us privately, but made an exception once in my case. For some time I had been out of joint, so to speak, with the authorities. I had been seriously scolded, and deservedly so; my face was set and I would not yield. Mother Stuart called me ; in a few words she dismissed the various complaints against me, and then very gently, very lovingly, showed me the root-fault in my character. In a moment I melted, yielded, resolved. It was an epoch in my school life.

These extracts give a faithful if but summary picture of her as she was in the early days of her religious life. From the first she sought, as she herself expressed it later on, 'to give personal worth to each child ; worth of character, strength of principles, anchorage in faith.' Loving the children, and longing to fit them for their inheritance, (her dearest aim was even then to give saints to God,) yet she never overstepped the bounds of what could or should be asked of them. No dreams for her own perfection, no too eager strivings for the death of self, were allowed to cloud her vision in dealing with them. Childhood should be perfect childhood, as later she would seek in women perfect womanhood. Too true an artist not to recognise beauty under any form, and not to shrink from misplaced ornament, her strong common sense and innate gift of balance and proportion, made her, even in youth, ask and expect of others only what they could give.

Her interest was never confined to the better endowed, nor to the souls more gifted, seemingly, for sanctity. It may be said, on the contrary, that her special mission seems throughout her life to have been to the rank and file ; to raise and strengthen the average person, above all in religious life. Her joy was to find the vein of pure gold in the most unpromising ground, and in its existence she firmly believed. This, her life's work, was begun now in the school, where every child was looked upon as worthy of the best she had to give.

But while working thus for others, her own soul, ' our first and favourite pupil,' was not forgotten. Writing of what may

be called the period of childhood in the spiritual life, she said
some years later :

Simplicity is not a monopoly or even a property of the
twentieth century child; it has been relegated to the grandmothers. The spiritual child, the novice, does not lead the
simple life ; the extreme ardour of her pursuit of perfection, her
exuberant delight in well-doing ; her thirst for instruction so
far beyond her capacity for assimilating it—these and other
qualities, under an appearance of simplicity, conceal a machinery
so complex that few even among spiritual mechanics are capable
of understanding, and fewer still of appreciating or manipulat-
ing it.

In no order of things is adolescence a time of the simple life.
The youths and maidens in their intolerable years are intolerable
on account of their complexities, in proportion to their complexities ; creatures of fancy and day-dreams, spook-haunted,
unreasonable, visionary, illuminate . . . and this is true, in
proportion, of the spiritual youth and maiden. When we
recommend the simple life to them, it is quite useless, for it is
not understood.

These words find their application in this period of Mother
Stuart's life. She had, she said herself, ' a tendency to *filer
trop fin*, and so to lose freedom of spirit.'

Straight and true by nature, she nevertheless did not escape
a phase in which she was not quite herself.

It has been truly said that saints are not born perfect,
but become so. The human soul must win to its fulfilment by
struggle and endeavour, by choice, self-discipline, and deliberate
act. And since its perfection lies mostly in the future, it is
impossible to deny that its earlier acts of choice and effort will be
less perfect than the later. They will be deficient in that wisdom
and force which practice and habit and gathered grace will give.
A saint in the making is not admirable in all things.

Clear-sighted as she appeared, even now, for others, for what
concerned herself, Mother Stuart had yet to wait in the faith
that somehow all would be well, and all would explain itself.
She had, in fact, to find herself like every sea-going vessel.
No wise guidance, or experience gained by others, seems able to
replace this process. There is no escaping it for those who take
life seriously. Until the soul has found itself, the true person
does not stand revealed, but we see, now one side, now another,
as each power is tried and tested, and as the possible solutions
of life's difficulties are examined one by one. ' But when at last

the true *Ego* emerges, and rises to take command, then discord
ceases, harmony ensues, then comes the true expression, the
impress of subtle personal quality,' [1] on mind' and thought, and
will and act. Sometimes the process is shortened, sometimes
unduly prolonged, and some there are who, living on the surface,
seem to die undiscovered continents.

There is necessarily pain in the finding, for it seems largely
to consist in trying to beat spades into spears and squares into
circles, and in fitting all things into a mould. It is often only
after years of exhausting effort that the light dawns, that it is
still, as it was in the beginning, when ' God made everything . . .
upon earth after its kind,' and that *restez-vous* is the last word
of wisdom. This lesson had yet to be learnt by Sister Stuart,
and the letters which have come down to us of this period are
in many ways a great contrast to those of later life, though here
and there comes a momentary flash from the light behind.

During a few days' illness in the noviceship, she had asked
Mother Digby to allow one of the novices to visit her, to go over
the matter of the daily instruction on the Rule. Mother Digby
had assented, telling her to choose whom she would. She
accordingly sent for a novice, and from that day, with the
sanction of authority, a spiritual friendship and rivalry in the
pursuit of virtue sprang up between them. They prepared by
special practices for their favourite feasts of the year, they met
at times for spiritual conversation, and corresponded regularly,
when, a year or two after leaving the noviceship, they were no
longer in the same house. A study of the ' practices' undertaken
in the first year of the aspirantship shows how strenuous was the
inner life, and how persistent the effort after perfection. They
were generally prepared by Sister Stuart, and then submitted
for the approval of her companion, while they mutually communicated the results and the discoveries in the spiritual life
which their efforts had led to.

The first letter of this period speaks of a novena to be made
for the Feast of SS. Peter and Paul. Its title alone might have
frightened less ardent souls, and Mother Stuart's amused laugh
in later days in face of such a programme can be imagined.

' Novena to annihilate ourselves.'

I am doing a great work and I cannot come down to speak of
myself, to make plans for myself, to give way to myself, to flatter
myself, to spare myself, to notice myself, to comfort myself, etc.

[1] An Essay on ' Expression,' J. Stuart, 1904.

Some dozen feasts in the year were prepared for in this manner, subsequent letters show that these practices were renewed yearly, at least during the time of aspirantship.

In the course of the year 1887 this friendly intercourse took another form.   Sister X. left Roehampton, and Mother Stuart began an interchange of letters with her which ended only with her own death.

Roehampton: January 9th, 1888.

You asked me not to write until I had leisure.   I have enforced leisure now, but hope this is the last moment of it. . . . I succumbed to the mumps four days ago. . . .

I am beginning to think that self-contempt and self-forgetfulness are not two different degrees of the same virtue, of which one passes through one to get to the other, but two different forms in which the same virtue takes hold of different characters, and in which people do not change, but carry their own line through ; and I do not see that one is necessarily higher than the other. . . . I wonder if this is right.   What do you think ? . . . This is a very dull letter, but that is all you can expect. I have been thinking about a practice.   We are a long time without one until St. Thomas' novena.   There is not much time this year, but would not a novena for the Presentation be nice ?   Something on the *Nunc dimittis*.   For instance to go to one's work because God dismisses one from His *immediate presence* ; but to go ' *secundum verbum tuum,' in pace.*   But this is vague. Perhaps you have better lights, I have not at present.   When the Antrim peasantry are annoyed with one another for indistinct speech, they say : ' How can I tell your meaning by your mumping ? '   You might perhaps say this with truth, but you would not be so rude.

Roehampton: February 13th, 1888.

My Shrovetide letter intended to be very early in order to extract one from you if you had time, but this intention failed. . . . At present I am taking a ' wild canter,' as Mother Kerr used to say, on an old and favourite hobby, the third degree of obedience, submission of judgment, as the perfect holocaust, the perfect security, the most perfect among *media ad finem*, because it throws all the responsibility of one's actions on to Our Lord. . . . I have got a new composition of place for it, the storm on Tiberias, and Our Lord asleep on a pillow, yet watching and governing all. . . . [Pray] that my wild canter may be practical, and not theoretical only.

As to self-contempt, it was looking at it from the practical, not the theoretical side that I arrived at the conclusion, by inductive reasoning in fact.   Of course it was only a hypothesis, but so far I am becoming confirmed in it. . . .

Roehampton : June 26th, 1888.

. . . I have a question of yours unanswered for a long time.
It made me laugh to think that you should suppose I could have
a point of view about mysticism in the theological sense of the
word. It would be rather like a caterpillar having views on
comparative philology. But here is my position. I have the
greatest possible attraction for it in the theological sense, *e.g.*
as for St. John of the Cross. . . . But in the modern sense, in
which it is synonymous with vagueness, and what Germans call
subjectivity, I do not like it at all, that is all. You see we agree
in the main point. You did not admit a modern sense. . . .

1st July. A long gap! Many thanks for your note and
promise of prayers. I count on them. For though I do
not quite realise what two months hence will bring me to, yet
when I do, my heart goes down into my shoes and it takes
all my spirit of faith to bring it up again. . . . It is a great
disappointment that you are not coming now.

These last lines refer to the 'probation' preparatory to
profession, for which Sister Stuart had now been accepted. Her
aspirantship was nearly over. 'An aspirant's duty in the
community is to serve,' was a favourite saying of hers, and this
had been her attitude during these four years, always ready to
help and showing respect and deference to all around her.

And so she had gone on her way. In her own eyes nothing at
all, and yet very few years had passed before Sister Stuart, gentle,
unassuming, retiring as she was, had become one of the ruling
spirits at Roehampton. 'Janet will always rule,' said an old lady,
who knew her well some years before she entered. 'Wherever
she lives, and whether she wishes it or not, even if she is the
youngest in a house, she will lead.' And so it was, even in the
presence of so strong a personality as Reverend Mother Digby,
herself a ruler and leader, of whom it has been said, 'she ought
to have been a man.' She too yielded to that charm which none
could resist, and bowed, with true humility, before what she
recognised as a superior faculty of insight and an almost prophetic power of intuition, a woman's gift, which went so surely
and swiftly to the end. 'I was amazed,' said one, who could
read between the lines, 'on my return to Roehampton, after
an absence of some time, to find how completely Sister Stuart's
views and ideas (she was then only an aspirant or young
professed) were adopted by Reverend Mother Digby.' And this,
though her study of humility in its various forms had led her to
choose for herself the way of self-forgetfulness—a way which

she followed so successfully that self-effacement with her was the most simple, natural and attractive thing in the world.

In a paper on ' Highways and By-ways in the Spiritual Life,' written many years later, she describes, without explaining, this phenomenon—the hidden powers that really rule.

She begins by contrasting the two types of soul. ' Highways attain, by-ways attract. . . . Highways dictate, by-ways influence, highways are open, by-ways are subtle, . . .' and concludes : ' In the end by one of those contradictory effects, which seem to be native products of the earth, the highway— the imperious, masterful, commanding, positive highway—is a servant ; and the elusive, undetermined, silent, solitary by-way is a master ; and by it we go, not because we want to go to some foreseen end, but because we *must* go.' And so it was with her, now and all through her life. She never urged her views nor forced her wishes and ideas on anyone, and yet the one desire of all who met her was to follow them, for she possessed ' that indefinable quality which marks a man for moral leadership. It belongs to those who not only possess a faith, but are possessed by it. . . . Often without any specific act of will on their part they *find* themselves leaders, rather than make themselves leaders.'[1]

A *dies Domini* was about to dawn, and the eager spirit thirsting for truth and beauty and love and God, was to feel the heralding breeze that sweeps over the slumbering world, whispering of fair things to come ; she was to begin to be set free from the bands of childhood, and to be bidden ' go forth, proceed prosperously and reign.'

In September 1888 Sister Stuart reached the Mother House, then in Paris, in company with three English nuns, to begin the six months of second noviceship in preparation for her final vows.

Of her outward life during this period there is nothing to tell. Writing ten years later to one who had shared this time of grace with her, she said :

This is only a little note of most loving good wishes for our tenth anniversary. How full these ten years have been of graces for each one of us. How good God has been, and, alas ! how poorly we have responded. I ought to speak for myself, and in the singular number, for I hope and think the rest of our spiritual clan are faithfully and lovingly ' constant ' to the

[1] A. C. Benson, *Escape, and other Essays.*

resolutions and lights of that blessed time. We are the children of saints, what a grace to have been Reverend Mother Desoudin's probanists. Let us try to make an end of *le mélange de la vie* which is, as she says, what one so regrets at the hour of death.

The evening before the long retreat opened the aspirants sang *In manus tuas Domine* at the night recreation. ' It made an impression that I shall not forget,' wrote Mother Stuart. ' It was like a key-note to the retreat. My own private word was helpful all through, *Vocabis me et ego respondebo tibi.*'

She had trained herself so far with great severity. The light of her long retreat was, she said, ' moderation.' ' Grace seized me,' she wrote, ' and shook a little sense into me between the doors of the *Econoimat* and the *Salon des Evêques.*'

The great renunciation had been made and accepted, and in the coming years she came back gradually to creation, which was no longer to speak to her in symbols, but she was to see all things beautiful and lovely in God. The change was not to be accomplished in a moment or without pain. ' So and no other-wise is the record of our various growths . . . and the word of growing life is surrender : co-operate—wait—trust,' she wrote. Perhaps above all she waited. ' One of the great lights of my retreat was not to go before the Holy Ghost,' she said. And God led her in His own way, with all the long leisure of Eternity. Nine years were to pass before she was brought face to face with a guide who would lead her soul out into paths of confidence and joy ; and yet another nine before she could *rest* in the true home of her soul in prayer.

On February 12, 1889, she made her profession in the chapel of the Mother House, and the next day returned to Roehampton. Those around noticed but little change, for, as someone said, ' in outward behaviour, improvement was impossible.'

A larger field of work was opened out to her, as she was immediately named sub-mistress of novices, and took over the greater part of Reverend Mother Digby's work with them. She gladly resumed her old life, working under her Superior, and having no apparent desire but to carry out her wishes, asking only to live in hiddenness and retirement.

A few months after her profession a great sorrow befell her in the loss of her dearly loved father. He had been in failing health for some time, and had resigned his living at Cottesmore in 1888. As Rector for over forty years he had won the respect and love of all, and especially of the poor, to whom he had always been a true friend. He died at Smedley on September 19, 1889, and was buried in his old church, where so many he loved were already resting.

In a paper written in 1903, in which the ' way of viewing life ' is discussed by Newman, Windthorst, Patmore, etc., one fictitious character appears, ' A Gentleman of the Old School.' In describing him, Mother Stuart drew her inspiration from her own father.

He had lived . . . with full acceptation of the conditions of life . . . knowing neither crags nor chasms . . . never entering upon pathless wildernesses . . . a singularly tranquil career. . . . He took his day as it came, and all in the day's work. His manner of living was simple, direct, unperplexed . . . the life that one might envy if one did not know it to be impossible. It is a gift to some, but to others not allowed. Ruling life by a few first principles perfectly grasped, and the whole man held in silence before them, he sees one end—he sees one—or two— or three luminous peaks, and he makes for these leisurely and imperturbably. . . . His hands are quicker unto good than those of many a fretful spirit. . . .

Her seven years of training were now over ; God's work had been surely done. In a beautiful passage in the ' New Sintram ' she seems to reveal her own thoughts and feelings as she stood on the threshold of the new life, idealised with the passage of fifteen years, for it was written only in 1904.

My seven years are ended ! What grave lessons I have learned ! How nearly, often and often, I have unlearned them all, . . . To-night the deepest beat in my heart is gratitude. I am thankful that I was spared, thankful that I was guided, thankful, above all, that I was *controlled*. Now sometimes a sweetness and a sense of strength calmly invades my soul and lifts me up. Humility has grown dear to me, and striving for it makes me breathe deep breaths of solemn happiness. The wild songs have died out of my memory. I care no longer to find the words for them, and, instead of them, I hear great psalm tones rushing through the pine trees, echoing from the rocks in glorious music ; ' Glory be to the Father, and to the Son, and to the Holy Ghost.' This is the song that the voice of the torrents shouts forth to heaven, and the stars give it back to me on earth. . . . But this is not the end, this is only preparation ; my life is no longer my own, but God's. He who created me will lead me forth as it pleases Himself.

CHAPTER VII

MISTRESS OF NOVICES

1889 *to* 1911

' Ye are warrior maidens. Be ye watchful, temperate, indomitable, serene, and great-hearted; humble and fervent, intrepid and strong, so would I have you.'—*From ' Obiter Dicta Long Ago in England,' J. Stuart.*

HER apprenticeship was over, and now, as a master-craftsman, Mother Stuart was about to begin the great work of her life; teaching others to manage their own souls.

' We should take our soul,' she said once, ' as our first and favourite pupil; give it every advantage we can; . . . make it stand on its feet, make it elastic, make it adaptable to circumstances, free in its movements; that is to say, not held down to a groove, and not holding to anything.' All her training was directed to these ends.

That much had to be done to attain them may be gathered from her own words. Speaking on this subject many years later she said : ' We generally arrive at the threshold of religious life with our minds undisciplined; a virgin forest of things good and bad, in great confusion; with inert, undecided, inconsistent wills; shrinking from personal responsibility and with super-abundant emotions and impressions which we are but little able to control.'

It will be convenient here to study her in her relations with novices during the twenty-two years she was in touch, more or less direct, with them.

On her return from probation, as already said, she was named Sub-Mistress of Novices, an office which she held for three and a half years. In September 1892 Reverend Mother Digby finally made them over to her care, as she herself was no longer able for the work since a severe illness in 1890. Less than two years later, in August 1894, Reverend Mother Stuart succeeded Mother Digby as Superior at Roehampton, when the latter was

named Assistant General, but she still retained the office of
Novice Mistress, and continued to do so at intervals during the
seventeen years of her government of the English Vicariate.
Even when of necessity replaced by a Mistress of Novices for
the details of the work, she always remained in closest touch
with the novices, directing their spiritual education through
those who helped her.

At first she was simply the exponent and executant of
Reverend Mother Digby's ideals of training, and her own
characteristics as Mistress of Novices were scarcely apparent.
She identified herself so completely with the chief authority that
there seemed to be but one person. This transition stage was
of short duration ; before long, Mother Stuart's individual action
made itself felt. She realised, as she said later, ' that each should
give their own gift, however humble ; copies even of the best
models were deplorable.'

Those who lived under her in the noviceship after the first
year or two, and later in the community, felt her care to be
somewhat after the pattern of God's Providence for His creatures,
whom He has endowed with intelligence and with the responsibility of their destiny. It was large, trustful, loving, and un-
emotional. ' That most perfect care' which Saint Francis of
Sales describes as ' that which approaches nearest to the care
God has for us, which is a care full of tranquillity and quietness,
and which in its highest activity has still no emotion, and being
only one, yet condescends to make itself all to all things.'

She studied the portrait of the Mistress of Novices as set
forth in the Constitutions, and became the faithful exponent of
what was there set down.

Being to those under her, as far as in her lay, what Our Lord
was to His disciples, reproducing His humility, His charity, His
goodness, His sweetness, His patience . . . never surprised at
defects and imperfections . . . forming by example rather than
by precept . . . leading to God . . . by love and confidence
rather than by fear . . . proportioning her teaching and trials
to the character, strength, and measure of grace of each individual,
making them understand that only by renunciation and death
to self can they reach the goal, and ever helping them by all the
means that unwearied charity could suggest.

She brought to this work of Mistress of Novices the soul
of the sportsman and naturalist. Of her sportsman's instinct
we have already spoken. In an essay on the ' Hunting Field,'

a psychological study of various attitudes of mind towards the problems of life, she describes, in a little Miss Wilhelmina's first day out with the hounds, the spirit she looked for in her novices. It had something of the gay, adventurous, and dogged about it. ' We are not out riding for exercise, Sisters, we are hunting for sport's sake, hence these fences, bullfinches, five-barred gates, and even occasional rolls in the mud are all part of the day's sport.' Young, buoyant, full of life and fun, she entered with sympathy into all the spiritual enterprises of these beginners in religious life, but she expected them to take the initiative.

She seemed to have a special interest in, and sympathy for, novices whose line had been sport. Though five years before her death, in a letter to an intimate friend, speaking of her earliest recollections, she said : ' I cannot tell you the admiring envy I feel for those . . . whose earliest memories are of martyrs and saints and all the things of faith, and—perhaps you will laugh at this, but it is true—the admiration and envy for a life quite indifferent to horses and hunting . . . it seems to be for ever on another plane ! . . .' A postulant, accustomed to country life, and who loved riding better than anything, had a very hard struggle on entering. Mother Stuart's sympathy and patience were inexhaustible. She talked to her of her horses, sent her to break in a pony in the convent fields, and helped her in a thousand little ways. Sporting terms frequently escaped her when talking with the novices. ' You must be thorough-breds, Sisters.' ' Don't pull so hard at the bit, you wrench every muscle in my hand trying to rein you in.' And referring to the clothing of a very spirited postulant, she said : ' What break-neck riding we shall see when Sister X. is bitted and bridled.' Whilst to one who was overstrained, the advice was simply : ' Sit your saddle more loosely.' ' More luminous than any treatise on the spiritual life,' writes one whom she loved dearly, ' was this word of hers to me.' ' Don't let the sportsman die within you. Handle your rebellious nature as your father taught you to handle your Arab chestnut.'

' Be cautious,' she said once to one who asked her advice in dealing with a difficult character, ' you would understand had you ever seen a hunted stag turn at bay ' ; and then her spirit kindled as she described a stag hunt, and how once she had come up with the hounds as the stag turned : ' For two or three awful moments I was able to call the hounds off and hold them back till the huntsmen came up. We do not always kill the stag, and this one we let go. Do you understand ? '

A born naturalist, Mother Stuart had the keen eye, the reverent touch, and the tolerant outlook which goes with this type of character, and these qualities served her to good purpose. As later, on all those whom she tried to help, so now she brought to bear on the novices this observing eye and loving interest. Every line in the face, every movement was studied. The curve of the lip, the colour and intensity of focus of the eye, the habitual position of the head ; every shade of expression of countenance, the inflection of the voice, the articulation in speech, the precision of movement, the pose of the hand, the step and the bearing of the whole being were noted, and revealed to her the spirit and mind and character within. She gained, by these observations, a clearer knowledge of the inner being than the attempts at self-revelation usually gave.

Her penetrating look had nothing critical or abashing in it. Love and kindly sympathy beamed from her eyes, for she possessed largeness of heart as the sands of the sea-shore, and her verdict on human nature, given in the last year of her life, was ' very frail, *very lovable*, with wonderful possibilities of good.'

' Once when questioning her about a person, whose strange ways I could not fathom,' writes one who was, for a time, *surveillante* of novices under her, ' she said : " Study those shaggy eyebrows, the curve of that upper lip, the timid questioning of those eyes. It is the wild, shy nature of the sea-bird, but she carries within a heart as true as the rock on which she was bred." '

In addition to the resources of the sportsman and the naturalist, Mother Stuart owed much of her power of training to a long and patient psychological study of women. It was an essentially womanly perfection that she sought to develop. ' The strength of women,' she said, ' is in their character, their mission is civilisation in its widest and loftiest sense '; and again, ' In two things we must establish her fundamentally— quiet of mind, and firmness of will.'

To be well brought up spiritually was an ideal she put before her novices. ' *Viriliter age*,' she said one day in a conference, ' what is that ? Thoughtfully, great-heartedly, constantly. The heart and spirit that you make for yourselves in the noviceship will persist. . . . Strong or slack, enterprising or cowardly, persevering or fanciful. In the dawn of your religious life you can give something of that first freshness to your worship that belongs to a new creation.' There was to be no flinching before a difficulty, or making much of what was hard, and still less was there to be the pose of a victim. All was to be done light-heartedly, with a laugh, as if it did not hurt. ' Sing, even if there are tears in your heart,' she wrote ; and again, ' Be brave, and laugh at the funny things ; it will often save you from crying.'

Without belittling the struggles of noviceship days, she looked on it as simply ' silly ' to make tragedies out of them. ' Take your faults,' she wrote, ' with a matter-of-factness that would seem to you almost brutal. Pay no more attention to your moods than a reasonable person, with serious duties on hand, pays to the weather.'

The remark of a young novice : ' There is something wrong with me, but I don't know what it is. I think a game would make it better,' was met by Mother Stuart in the spirit in which it was said, and all the novices were turned out for a day to play and work in the garden. She commended the good sense of this novice in discerning the suitable remedy for her trouble. ' Some of us,' she said, ' bring out all our heavy artillery to meet an enemy that could be disposed of with a pea-shooter.'

Her counsels were always on the heroic side. ' Go win your spurs as the Black Prince,' she wrote to one, ' while I sit up in the windmill and watch from afar ! '   ' Do not be afraid, do not try to save yourselves,' she said, ' I want to find you in the van when there is anything hard or humiliating to be done ; if anything has gone wrong, go forward if you can and take the blame.'   ' How proud I am that God can already trust you with hard things.'   ' You would not be without one pang of this pain, would you ? '   ' You are not going to miss your chance of sanctity ? '   ' Give one steady look of Faith, Hope, and Love at your Crucifix, and then press forward. There may be more life in one such intense act of contemplation than in long campaigns of struggle. Here is your call to embrace the folly of the Cross.'   These are a few examples of words of encouragement, chosen at random from many hundred letters—words which made the hardest things seem desirable.

In moments, however, when the stress had grown too great, and one's unaided strength was insufficient, her quiet, strong, motherly reassurance and support came to the rescue. But she could never stoop to coax, or pet, or caress. She lifted one to regions of faith, generosity, and truth, and appealed directly to the highest supernatural instincts.

' However feeble or troubled my spirit might be at the

moment,' writes one of her children, 'I always left her room serene, with the deepened conviction in my heart that "all things are loss that I may gain Christ." '

The word 'development,' it has been said, best expresses the end towards which her training tended. She discerned the germ of promise and possibility in those she formed, and this led her to give a singularly individual training and care to each, thereby laying a tax on herself, far heavier, than a more general method would have called for. There was no one standard of excellence for all, no mould into which all were to be pressed ; each was asked to give her individual gift to God, and that gift should be the best that natural endowments and grace made possible.

In the words which she put into the mouth of the Benedictine Abbess of Whitby, St. Hilda, in an address which she supposes her to give to her young nuns, Mother Stuart epitomises much of her teaching in this matter. 'Trade with the gifts God has given you. Bend your mind to holy learning that you may escape the fretting moth of littleness of mind that would wear out your souls. Brace your wills to action that they may not be the sport of weak desires. Train your heart and lip to song which gives courage to the soul. Being buffeted by trials, learn to laugh ; being reproved, give thanks ; having failed, determine to succeed.' [1]

She reproached us sometimes [writes one of her former novices] with saying our *Sume Domine et suscipe* too soon and offering to God an empty, vague, inaccurate memory, a lazy, inert or dissipated mind ; a fickle will, the sport of every wind of impression and mood. And she would urge us to look to it that we made our offering worthy of our consecration to God, by the schooling and cultivation of all our powers. 'If not, you will heap up brushwood for your purgatorial flames.' And in answer to the question : 'What do you think is the most common fuel for the purgatory of nuns ?' she said : 'Human respect, earthly views, waste of will power, buried talents, neglected hopes, faded energies.'

With her the law of self-conquest became that of self-development, thus opening a new vein of penance and self-denial to many. One who had been her novice writes on this very point :

The second stage in her training of my soul was reached when she insisted on self-development. God, she said, must have the

---

[1] *Obiter Dicta Long Ago in England*, J. Stuart.

best possible service from us, and He will not get that unless
we perfect and develop to their utmost extent all the talents
entrusted to us.   When I revolted against what presented itself
as a life-long campaign of self-improvement, she said : ' Well,
my child, where is supreme mortification and self-abnegation to
be found in our life, if not in these things ? '   It was a revelation to me and a vast encouragement to know that she thought
it hard too.   And to the objection that this campaign of mental
development and activity might be an obstacle to growth in
prayer and interior life she always answered that the perfecting
of our natural faculties was the best preparation for prayer and
a life with God.

To those who only saw the obvious, the line of action she
thus took with some whom she trained in the noviceship, and
later on in her communities, seemed at times inexplicable,
acting as she did, not in view of usefulness *now*, or appearances,
or quick returns, but in view of destiny, of eternity, and of
some hidden possibilities of good which she alone had discerned,
and hoped to bring to fruitfulness ; a hope that was very often
fulfilled, and sometimes in a most wonderful way.

Having known her has changed my life [writes one of those
whom she helped].   She never hesitated to reveal to a soul what
she called once ' God's gold in the fungus cup.'   ' You are the
fungus cup, but the gold therein is God's and must be recognised
and used to the best for Him.'   I had come to her very raw
material indeed.   She began by studying me, and when at last
she found something of promise it was that upon which she
worked, always holding before my eyes the good I could do,
the heights to which even I could arrive.

She believed God had a work for each soul, which no other
could do for Him, and so she strove to help each soul to give
this unique service.

The unconventional was another characteristic of all Mother
Stuart's training.   A mystic and a genius, she had, as has been
said of another, ' what is given to both, a liberty of mind which
established conventions cannot contain.' [1]

She found lights on the spiritual life in ' Alice in Wonderland '
and ' Through the Looking Glass,' as also in Rudyard Kipling's
' The Day's Work ' and ' The Jungle Book.'   Later she read
' The Ship that Found Herself ' almost every year to her
community at the beginning of the school year.

Endless and unexpected were her applications of nursery

[1] See *St. Francis of Assisi*, by Father Cuthbert, O.S.F.C.   (Longmans.)

rhymes, and 'The Hunting of the Snark.' To a novice who was too shy to speak at recreation she said : ' Sister, you are like the beaver, who always collected but never subscribed.' To another, who made such extensive and complicated efforts for perfection that she was oblivious of the essentials of everyday life, she applied these lines :

He had forty-two boxes all carefully packed,
  With his name printed clearly on each,
But as he forgot just to mention the fact,
  They were all left behind on the beach.

Another, who had committed some fault, and then had been too much dejected when it was pointed out, received in answer to a note :

O how much better 'twould appear
To see you shed a humble tear,
And then to hear you meekly say,
I'll not do so another day.

' This is from the address to Sara, the classic of Mother S——'s youth.'

Of one novice, whose conduct shocked several people, as the boy Ribadeneira had shocked the ' grave fathers ' in Rome, Mother Stuart's only comment was : ' She is just momentarily wearied out in her tremendous efforts of well-doing.'

She was always inclined to see the comic rather than the tragic in the frailties of human nature, as when a postulant, seeing a cart in the convent yard, jumped upon it, and, regardless of the rule of enclosure, drove down the lane at Roehampton.

The gaiety of the novices amused her. ' Oh, just listen to the irrepressible hilarity of those novices,' she said one day. ' If you asked them what the joke was, I am sure not one of them could tell you. It is the *joie de vivre* in their whole-hearted service of God that alone explains it.'

A little note of farewell, which she wrote when setting out on some journey with Reverend Mother Digby, is suggestive of the manner of her care for her daughters.

Good-bye, my dear sisters, I commend
Your health to the Infirmarian,
Your permissions to Mother R.,
Your studies to Sister M,,
Your impressions to the winds,
And your souls to God.

She wished the novices' spirituality to be very simple and free from exaggeration, and she possessed the art of saying the right word, and of bringing down from high flights to the realities of things, for side by side with her spiritual gifts was a very strong common sense.

A novice who, lost in recollection, was unable to raise her eyes when she went to speak to Mother Stuart, was greeted by the words : ' Now drop St. John Berchmans, sister, and be yourself.' Another, fervent to an ecstatic degree, who had been reading the life of some saint, who attributed all calamities to his presence in a place, said in a tone of distress at the following recreation : ' I am afraid my humility is not great ; if the ceiling were to fall now, my first thought would never be that it was because I, a sinner, was present.' ' I think,' answered Mother Stuart, ' my first thought would be that the cows' hair in the plaster had not been long enough.' Another relates how she wrote a long and complicated letter on her spiritual state, such as only a novice could write, and expected back illuminating answers, but ' pray for sense ' was all she found written in pencil at the bottom of the page. ' It would have been better for so-and-so not to have entered,' said a novice, speaking of a postulant or novice who had left the Order. ' No,' said Mother Stuart quickly, ' it was better to try, perhaps that is *all* that God asked of her.'

Such things as scruples and other morbid tendencies of conscience, for the most part, died a natural death in the germ, from the very sunshine and open-air tone that Mother Stuart gave to the noviceship life.

' Though we never felt her hand heavy over us, yet it was a very firm one,' writes a novice of the early days under her rule. ' When a soul needed it, or was capable of bearing it, reprimands in public and plain speaking were not spared.' ' I did not do such a thing through human respect,' said a postulant. ' Why do you not call it cowardice ? ' was the quick reply. ' If you do not mean religious life seriously, with *all* it entails, better not to come at all,' she wrote to a would-be postulant who had questioned about some hard things she foresaw, and, adds the person in question, ' she kept this note of severity towards me during my religious life.' ' Far better,' she said to the novices, ' return to the world than lead a life of sleepy piety in religion.' But speaking of the harshness with which some saints are said to have tried their disciples, she often said : ' I admire, but I could not imitate.' And though her love for souls wrung

G

something of this from her from time to time, especially in her younger days, yet in acting thus she had to do violence to her own nature, and she suffered more in the infliction of the hard word than the recipient. ' Her reproofs in public were very rare,' writes one of her novices, ' but when given they were never forgotten. I remember one that fell to my share, but the sting which might have been left was changed into real sorrow and courage by the tender way she said " my dear child " at the end, for I felt the pain it had given her to make the necessary correction.' Her reproofs were constantly followed by some little special mark of confidence, some request to the delinquent. to help her, some unexpected word of approval.

What she feared, she often said, was not faults, but faults unacknowledged and unrepaired. About reparation she was very firm ; but once made, all was forgotten. Forgotten in reality as if it had never been. ' Can you believe in me again ? ' wrote one who feared to have grieved her. ' Yes, I can, quite easily. Only you must brace yourself up to take things with sweet reasonableness, for your own sake, and the children's whom you influence, and the honour of religion, and the great sweet love of God.' ' Can you forgive me ? ' asked one of her children. ' Oh so easily,' and the words were accompanied by a look of surprise, as she added : ' You are always my own dear child.'

' Never stop to look at yourself after a fall,' she wrote, ' there are sure to be falls. But when you have been so unfortunate and so foolish as to show pride and want of religious spirit, as soon as you come to your senses make the most humble and generous reparation that you can, in the fewest words and with no expression of discouragement, then go and do better.'

Mother Stuart had far less tolerance of negative faults, such as those she suggested, in a quotation given above, as forming fuel for purgatory, than for positive ones, however troublesome. Of these last, especially if they came from quick temper, exuberance of life and the like, she would stand a great deal. To one who lamented her too constant falls, she wrote :

Do not be ashamed of making the same resolution again and again. The thing to be ashamed of would be to leave off making it. We shall all be, to the end, tempted and tried and sometimes overcome, but that is the warfare of the whole Church militant, and if it were not a probation and a good hard one for the soldier of Christ, there would be no such thing as real holiness.

So don't mind it too much, go on bravely, that is one of the golden rules.

She had, as might have been expected, great sympathy with those who, in their desire for the perfect practice of obedience, did seeming follies. 'It takes time,' she used to say, 'to adjust our minds, practically, to the law of obedience'; but she had sooner a hundred times such follies in a novice than one failure in the principle of obedience.

Her explanations of the Rule and duties of religious life, given in the frequent instructions to the novices, were most beautiful and full of heavenly teaching, and all things seemed possible to those who listened to her.

In the noviceship [she said on one occasion], our inward life is in the making. We are forging the gates of self-control in the mind, which guard it. We are building its foundations, setting them on rock or sand. Laying down our principles, the things that we never question again. We are beginning its walls and supports, by the habits of our wills. . . . We are even furnishing the mansion of our souls by all the true and beautiful thoughts which we accumulate and make our own—by the things we are learning to love.

And again :

There ought to be a holy emulation and rivalry in the novice-ship, each one being determined to signalise herself in God's service. Rivalry in the service of each other ; who can serve the most. Rivalry in humility ; who can be last and least. Rivalry in mortification ; who can do with the least and worst things. In a noviceship where there are these rivalries in arms, the standard will be high. . . . Yet in a sense it is true that though all will run, one, or very few receive the prize. How many begin the life of perfection with great desires, how few become saints ! Why do so many stick fast in the commonplaces of life ? Very good people, but not saints. Is there one saint in each noviceship ?

When you are inclined to look about you [she told them], check yourselves, saying : ' No, some day my eyes shall see the King in His beauty, they shall see the land afar off.'

Speaking on the Feast of St. Stanislaus in 1899, she said : ' When the Society accepts us for our vows, she does not expect to receive pious persons, but spiritual persons ; not common-place good Religious, nor even merely dependable Religious, but souls strong in the strength of God in whom they rest.'

Another time she put clearly before them the meaning and scope of a vocation.

To say that you have a vocation means to say that you are called by God, not as a flock, but as individuals, ' by thy name, thou art Mine.' Each soul is brought from far or near by its own way. Each vocation has a story, it is the story of a spiritual life ; of a choice, an election, a consent ; then adventures, vicissitudes, perils, risks sometimes ; or a long waiting, acute crises and sudden turning points ; then an accomplishment, and realisation of promises. . . . Now the romance is over and the reality lies before us. What are we called to ?

Called to honour. Called to the highest task that can be laid on a human being, to share Our Lord's own life, and work for the glory of God and the salvation of souls. To be more than servants, to be apostles, friends, familiars of His household. Novices are on the threshold, happy disciples, studying the theory and the practice of what is to be carried out hereafter. . . .

Called to labour. In the kingdom of heaven honour and labour are inseparably bound together ; titles are real, not of courtesy, and they carry duties with them. The highest in honour are the hardest worked. . . . It is not a grievance to be hard worked, tired, it is an honour ; you may aspire to it, be proud of it, not want things to be made easy for you.

Called to hardship. There is no sense in your noviceship life unless it inures you to hardship. What did you come for ? To find a school of perfection, and in a school of perfection our self-love must meet with hardships. . . . For some it is in common life, for some in silence, for some in the constant mortification our life calls for, for some in material devotedness, for some in intellectual effort. Say to yourselves, ' that is what I came for, what I am determined to give to God ! '

But this whole-hearted sacrifice was to be accomplished with joy.

It is an arduous journey, a great undertaking, not a little or an easy thing. . . . Sing in every way you can. . . . God gave song, to give heart and courage and joy in life ; . . . if not with the voice, sing with the spirit and the understanding ; sing by words of courage and hope, praise and thankfulness. Call out to one another by high thoughts and spiritual ambitions, these are the songs of our country. . . .

The rivalries in the pursuit of virtue, spoken of above, were encouraged directly by practices in preparation for Feasts, and indirectly by her own example.

A certain practice of humility in the noviceship at one time, taught a lesson that was not forgotten, and among that generation at least an excuse when found fault with was an unheard-of thing.

Another time she directed all their energies towards the love and practice of poverty. She established a confraternity of Poverty in the noviceship, the members of which were to aim at loving privation, inconvenience, and all that detached them from creatures. She wrote a manual for their use, with a short Catechism on the practice of Poverty, and the 16th of each month a special feast was held to honour the ' Lady of St. Francis.'

Tell the novices [she wrote when absent in America] to pray that they may enter into the spirit of Our Lord's poverty and littleness, that He loved for their sakes, and to draw them after Him. . . . Let it be their one aim in 1899 to follow always more closely, more generously, and more gaily, making less and less of self, more and more of His service and glory.

Her teaching on poverty, mortification and obedience was very strong [writes one of her novices]. She heartily congratulated those who could secure for themselves the most inconvenient place or the most worn-out instrument for their household work. She taught us that the true spirit of Poverty is ' a doing without ' and the suffering of a ' blessed inconvenience ' without complaint.

Her own joy in the meanest and most common to which the Rule refers [writes another] was marked in all that touched herself. I remember once during a ladies' retreat standing behind someone who seemed to me to be choosing her broom and dustpan rather carefully. Quietly she lifted down the worst dustpan, the oldest broom, the shabbiest floor-cloth, and when she turned round I saw it was Reverend Mother going to help the novices in the housework.

This she always loved to do, and in the early days did so continually, but even when it was no longer possible, she reserved two or three privileges in these matters for herself. Each year as her retreat came round she replaced a novice or sister for the eight days, in washing plates and dishes in the scullery. And in the yearly retreats for ladies she always helped in the extra housework that their presence entailed. She generally chose some remote corridor where the novices were working. ' Being in charge of several rooms during a retreat,' writes a nun, ' I put up a notice for the novices, with all details as to the daily work to be done. The first morning, on going to take down the paper, I found Reverend Mother reading it. She said : " It is such a comfort to be told what to do." And every day of the retreat found her there at work ; she even went the long way down to the kitchen yard to fetch tea-leaves for sweeping, on the days I had marked.'

Fidelity in detail was another lesson which she inculcated wonderfully by example. She looked for perfection in the most material things. ' Study every door-handle,' she often said, ' that you may be perfect in silence and never disturb the intercourse of others with God.' ' All the years I lived with her,' writes a professed, ' I only once heard her make a slight noise, when the handle of the tribune door at Roehampton slipped in her hand. It was something so unusual that I have never forgotten it.'

Looking back across the years to those days, her figure stands out with all the attractiveness of sanctity, but sanctity clothed with ideal simplicity and with the freshness and fragrance of flowers in spring. The words of a spiritual writer on ' perfection of virtue ' find a very real application in her life. ' While everywhere visible,' he says, ' it yet appears so natural that it calls forth no astonishment, like those monuments in which the perfection of harmony has disguised the immensity.'

Many years have passed since those happy noviceship days under Mother Stuart [writes one of her children], days round which must ever cling the aroma of first consecration to God in the morning of life, and round which she flung a unique atmosphere. I can only compare them to a Scottish moor, with its wide expanse, courting all the winds of heaven. The purple glow of the hardy heath tipped with glory by the morning sun ; the bracing scent, dew-drenched, rising from a thousand heather bells. Such was life as inspired by her. For her message was ever of joy and hope unconquerable.

ROEHAMPTON

Photo : Russell, Wimbledon.

CHAPTER VIII

FIRST YEARS AS SUPERIOR

1894 *to circa* 1901

' Look if you wish to reap a harvest, but look thoughtfully, patiently,
watchfully, and know why you look.'
From ' *The Harvest of a Quiet Eye,' J. Stuart.*

ON March 28, 1894, Reverend Mother Lehon, who had been
Superior General since 1874, died. She had greatly appreciated
Mother Digby, and had valued the work she had done in England.
It was said that she had given a verbal promise not to withdraw
her from the English Vicariate during her lifetime, ' but when
I am dead, you must be prepared to lose her.' Many, therefore,
realised that this death which was a sorrow to the whole Society
was the prelude of a still more intimate one for all at Roehampton.

The Congregation for the election of the new Superior General
was to meet on July 18. ' During the intervening months,'
writes a member of the community, ' I was often with Mother
Digby. One day she said to me : " If I were taken away, whom
would you put as Superior here ? " My answer came unhesitatingly : " Mother Stuart." " Yes, that is my own thought,"
she replied, and we were silent, both she and I knew the hidden
treasure we possessed better than others, for Mother Stuart was
much with the novices, and scarcely known in the community,
except by the younger members.'

On July 13 Reverend Mother Digby left Roehampton, and
ten days later a telegram announced the election of Reverend
Mother de Sartorius : for a moment all breathed freely ; Mother
Digby might yet return ; her letters spoke of it as an assured
fact. But the last act of the Congregation was to choose the
Assistants General ; one new member was required for the
council ; the votes fell on Reverend Mother Digby. The news
reached Roehampton on August 14. It was a moment of intense
sorrow, and to none more than to Mother Stuart.

Two days later the Superior of the Australian Vicariate, Reverend Mother Vercruysse, arrived in England, bringing with her letters nominating the new Superior.

The ceremony of Mother Stuart's installation took place on the evening of August 17, the very day which, twenty-two years before, had witnessed a similar ordeal for Reverend Mother Digby. A letter was now read from her, in which she said that in giving Mother Stuart as Superior, she gave her ' second self,' and she added : ' St. Jane Frances de Chantal tells Our Lord that whichever string of the harp of her heart He may choose to touch, it will always give out the note of complete adhesion to His Holy Will, with no reserve or *but*.' Mother Stuart then entered the room and each one went up to kiss her hand in token of religious obedience. When all was over she left the community, saying : ' God will be all in all to us.' That evening she appeared calm as ever, and by a merciful dispensation of Providence the whole household, of over one hundred people, spent the next eight days in retreat.

' The night of her installation,' writes one of the councillors, ' I paid her an intimate little visit. At the end she kissed me, saying : " I will try to make you very happy." How well that promise was kept God alone knows.' This promise, made in words to one, was made in her heart to all her daughters. To give happiness is a god-like influence, and the power to do so was one of God's gifts to Mother Stuart. She spent herself in creating happiness around her. To live with her was to live in an atmosphere of love and trust ; all fear, all misunderstanding was banished, and Roehampton became more than ever an earthly paradise. Seventeen years were about to open of such full and happy life, that those who shared it thought that nothing could go beyond it, in labour, in sacrifice, in love, in joy ; and yet it was in its turn but the prelude to a still more strenuous though shorter period. From this time, it has been said, the aim of her life gradually solved itself in what she held as a ' mission to shed abroad the very bloom of virtue.' ' To be a joy-bearer and a joy-giver says everything,' she wrote, ' for in our life, if one is joyful, it means that one is faithfully living for God, and that *nothing else counts* ; and if one gives joy to others one is doing God's work ; with joy without and joy within, all is well. . . . I can conceive no higher way.'

At the moment, however, the nomination was an over-whelming blow to her. Rarely, perhaps, has there been found in a person the union of such great gifts as she possessed with such intense shyness and self-diffidence. The notes of a retreat made in the following year, 1895, speak plainly of this struggle of a lifetime.

'Help will never fail thee, till My power fails.' Count upon it as if I felt it, therefore no discouragement about my incapacities and miseries.

'When I sent you without purse and scrip and shoes did you want anything ? But they said : Nothing.'

Judge according to these lights, not as if *I must necessarily be wrong.*

The first seven years after Mother Stuart was named Superior correspond very nearly to the age of asceticism which she described as follows in the Essay on Colour already referred to :

'Thirty-five to forty-two, years of indigo hue. . . . If our dialectic years have only given depth to our blue, then we have the age of true asceticism, deep, responsible, austere, keen-eyed, daring in thought and strong in act, greatly illuminated from heaven.' They were years of transition leading to the time when, as she expressed it, 'you finally are what you are'; years full of life, expectation, and promise. Facts and observations were being stored in her mind to blossom forth in 'thought and theory and bold soaring speculation.' She was studying all around her, within and without her convent walls, 'feeling her way,' she said, and learning to judge in the light of the practical spirit, which she defined as 'sound sense applied from the lowest to the highest things in life.'

There are few events to relate of these years of preparation. The story of two long journeys, however, both epoch-making in her spiritual life, find their place in them.

For the first few months, with exquisite tact, she took the attitude of simply replacing Mother Digby, who might have been absent on a journey. Though when someone spoke regretfully of the loss, she answered at once : 'When we have made a sacrifice to God we must never go back on it.'

In January 1895 Reverend Mother Stuart was summoned to Paris for her first visit as Vicar ; she thus had the consolation of spending a few days with Mother Digby. In the following March, Mother Digby returned to England for some weeks, and Mother Stuart accompanied her on her visits to Brighton, Hammersmith, and Carlisle. A Convent of the Sacred Heart had long been asked for in Scotland, and as a good opening offered itself at this time to the Society, in Aberdeen, the two

Reverend Mothers went there on leaving Carlisle, to look for a house. Thus Mother Stuart's first foundation was in her native land. A special interest, moreover, attaches to it, for it was the means of restoring to Scotland the ancient devotion of the people to Our Lady of Good Succour. Long before the Reformation, a miraculous statue had been honoured under this title in Aberdeen. It had been removed to Brussels to escape desecration at the hands of the Reformers. An exact copy of the old statue was made and sent to the Scotch foundation ; from that day the devotion revived, and shrines to Our Lady of Good Succour have since been multiplied in the country. The opening of the new convent took place in November 1895. Writing of it a month later, Mother Stuart said : ' It will keep your heart warm, I am sure, to know that there is a house of the Sacred Heart in Scotland. I hope you will see it some day. Everyone who went there left a bit of their hearts in Aberdeen.'

But before that date the Society of the Sacred Heart had again to mourn the loss of its Superior General. After a short rule of nine months, on April 30, 1895, Mother de Sartorius was struck with her last illness. The sorrows and trials of her short generalate had been too much for her, and she died on the morning of her feast day, May 8. Another had been destined by God to face the storm now gathering in France, and threatening the Society with destruction.

Named Vicar General by the secret note of Mother de Sartorius, Mother Digby was elected Superior General on the following August 25, the Feast of the Immaculate Heart of Mary, by the unanimous vote of the assembled Vicars. Writing eleven years later to Mother Digby, Mother Stuart records her feelings at the moment :

Some people keep the day of the month, but for this particular anniversary I do the contrary and go by the feast : dear feast of the Immaculate Heart, on which were lived through the intensest and most blessed twelve minutes that could fall to human lot to record. [The time the work of the election took.] How often I have thought since of the characteristic of God's work that was on it, in the utter stillness and recollection of it all. It was like one of His own great works, like a work of creation, and a great anointing of His chosen one. It is a day on which one's heart is full of thanksgiving for the gift of the day, and for all the chain of graces that followed after it.

To strengthen, and above all to comfort her Superior General in the heavy crosses of her life, became from this time one of

Mother Stuart's dearest duties. The attachment between their souls, kindred in an overwhelming love for God, increased with years, and Mother Digby was the inspiration of some of Mother Stuart's most beautiful poems.

On her return from Paris, whither she had gone for the election, Mother Stuart continued her work as Vicar, visiting the houses of the Order in England and Ireland. Each year saw her at the Mother House for a week, to give an account of her stewardship.

In 1897 she paid her first visit to Rome. Reverend Mother Digby had been forbidden by the doctors to spend the winter in Paris, and the Trinità dei Monti had been chosen as a temporary Mother House, and thither Mother Stuart went in February for some five or six weeks. The letters from Rome spoke of her visits to the Basilicas, of her delight in seeing the treasures of art, and of an audience with Leo XIII. He was then, as he reminded Mother Digby, eighty-seven years of age. England was much in his mind, and English visitors were welcomed cordially. ' How gladly I would bring England back,' he said, referring to the long controversy on Anglican Orders which had just ended with the publication of the Bull *Apostolicæ Curæ*. Mother Stuart was to see him once again, four months before his death, in March 1903.

July 1897 saw the beginning of a friendship which was of great moment in her life. She had, it is said, a genius for friendship. It was a flower which grew in every path she trod, and through which her life was wonderfully enriched. On the Feast of the Visitation that year, the newly appointed Bishop of Southwark, Dr. Bourne, visited Roehampton for the first time in his official capacity. A few days later he returned for the distribution of prizes, and in August for his canonical visitation. Of that friendship it is not possible to say more than that it grew with the growth of years and only ended with her death.

In May 1898 she was again in Paris, for the Superior's retreat, and returned to Roehampton the bearer of a message which she made known to the community at the close of her conference for the Feast of SS. Peter and Paul, saying : ' I wanted to take this opportunity of telling you that our Mothers have allowed me the privilege of being with Mother General during the few months she will be in America.' For Reverend Mother Digby had decided to fulfil the wish of her heart, and visit the houses of the Society in the New World. Much as they rejoiced for her sake, and for Mother Digby, this news was a great blow to the community, for the four happy years which had gone by since Mother Stuart had taken up the reins of government had won all hearts to her, and they feared to lose her. But Reverend Mother Digby reassured them. ' Reverend Mother is only lent to me, she will come back to you,' she said on her arrival at Roehampton on August 6. A few days later, on August 11, the two Reverend Mothers left for America. An account of the journey will be given in a later chapter in the letters written by Mother Stuart from the various houses visited.

It is not often that we can follow so plainly the steps taken by God in the training and formation of a soul. These journeys in America were designed in His Providence (as she herself believed) to be the means of drawing her out of herself, and making her surmount her excessive shyness and diffidence, and learn to rest in confidence on God.

In the first journey she was still sheltered under the shadow of Mother Digby's presence, but the great responsibility thrown upon her, and the necessary intercourse with many hundreds of people, ' dragged off,' she said, ' my shyness bit by bit.' When the journey was half over she wrote from Mexico : ' There is a wonderful providential care over Mother General's journey. It must be the prayers, and I am getting so accustomed to it that I do not have " the shivers " any more at my responsibility to the Society for the care of her, but have a fixed conviction that whatever things may look like, they will turn out all right in the end.'

The lessons learnt were to be impressed yet more deeply. Less than two years after her return from North America, she set forth again on a missionary journey to visit the houses of the Order in the West Indies and South America, and this time in the position of authority. Later on, many other great journeys were to be undertaken, wholly for the good of others ; these first two were her apprenticeship, and for the building of her own soul, to prepare it for the work in store.

Before she set out on the first of these journeys, one of the great graces of Mother Stuart's life was given to her. It has been already alluded to.[1] A friend[2] was brought across her path who was destined to render great services to her in this earlier part of her pilgrimage.

A more complete account of this event will be found in a later chapter. Many friends crossed her path in later years—for God

[1] See chap. vi, p. 71.   [2] Father Daignault, S.J.

was generous to her in this as in all else—to help her as need arose, in different stages of her solitary journey—solitary, necessarily, as that of all Superiors ; but this guide of her earlier and in some ways most trying years was never forgotten.

Her letters to him give insight into the many interests of her life at this time. Foremost among them were the educational questions of the day in England and the work of God's Church in the world, especially on the foreign missions. ' Her sympathies were world-wide,' wrote a Jesuit missionary from Bulawayo, ' and she was promoting God's kingdom north, south, east and west.'   Her practical interest was shown by the foundation of a missionary school at Armagh, on which she built many hopes. ' It is a very deep joy to have that work, and seems like a realisation of old desires that for me personally can never come to anything ; but to be allowed to help in the preparation of those who will go on the foreign missions is the next best thing to going oneself, and must replace my old enthusiasm.'

Difficulties from within and without brought this venture to an untimely close in 1903. It was a great disappointment to her, but it is characteristic of her that no word as to the final failure of her enterprise is found in her letters. She did all that lay in her power and then literally left the success to God. She never complained of lack of co-operation or hindrances, placed by others, to her schemes. If they were her superiors, loyalty closed her lips ; if her subjects, a wonderful charity restrained her. When questioned once as to the cause of the non-fulfilment of a plan which it was known she had much at heart, she answered : ' It has fallen through because of a letter written by X., but she has no idea what she has done, she meant all for the best.'   She never doubted the essential goodness of the motives of others. ' She delighted,' says one who was her assistant for some years, ' in seeing her plans upset by unexpected events, saying that it gave her great comfort, and that she looked on such things as an assurance that God was watching over her stewardship, was securing the accomplishment of His will, and working out His own designs.   Whether she traced the secondary causes to the prayer of a child, to the imperfection of an individual, to obstacles arising from misunderstandings, or to interference of outside agencies, she was joyfully and graciously ready to recognise the indication of God's ruling hand, and to allow herself to be guided by it.'

The year 1899 brought a great joy to Mother Stuart, the consecration of the world to the Sacred Heart. ' It is the greatest act of my Pontificate,' said Leo XIII to the Bishop of Liège. Writing on the Feast of the Sacred Heart, three days before the ceremony, which was fixed for Sunday, June 11, Mother Stuart said :

Let us say together thank God that we have lived to see the whole world consecrated to the Sacred Heart by the Holy Father ; there never was so glorious a feast, and as you can imagine, we can hardly talk or think of anything else to-day but this great grace ; and with us all our old children must be among those who rejoice the most, [and you must] have a great desire to spread the sacred fire all round you of real devotion to the Sacred Heart.

In 1900 the Society of the Sacred Heart celebrated the centenary of its foundation. ' We are having a very busy autumn in all our houses preparing for the centenary, which will be kept on November 21, the hundredth anniversary of the first vows of our Venerable Mother,' wrote Mother Stuart ; ' there will be as much exterior festivity as each house can manage and as great spiritual rejoicing as each soul can command. It will be a day of great thanksgiving for what God has done for us in the past and is still doing.'

Two days after the feast, writing to Mother Digby, she said :

At last there is a reasonable possibility of writing quietly to you, and how I have been longing to do it. . . . Now I had better begin with the Bishop's [1] message.   He said just before he went, and quite ' off his own bat ' when I was on the terrace with him looking at the fireworks : ' Send my blessing to Mother General and tell her the day has gone off perfectly, and I think it is calculated to do a great deal of good.'   From that I go back to the beginning.   The triduum ended as perfectly as it began. . . . There were fifty-one staying in the house for it, and they had a royal time ; as Mother X. said, as soon as anyone crossed the threshold the spirit of joy came on them and carried them away. . . .

Tuesday evening we had a very delightful gathering with all the old ones present, a great crowd. . . . The tableau of the ' apotheosis ' was quite lovely, though Mother X. gently complained afterwards of the conduct of the cherubs who had surrounded our Venerable Mother in glory, how they had quarrelled, as the sons of Zebedee quarrelled with their *confrères* to be ' at the right and left ' in her glory, and had pulled each others' wings and pinched each others' legs ! the consequence was that,

[1] Cardinal Bourne, Archbishop of Westminster, then Bishop of Southwark.

flushed with conflict they looked perfectly lovely around and above and below her picture. . . . All through this *séance* we had the old old things sung by the school, Latin motets and French hymns that the oldest of the old children remembered in their youth ; they were quite delighted to hear them again.

The next days were all very happy and went without a hitch. . . . The sermon was most beautiful, especially the last part. I am going to ask Father Bampton's leave to print it for private circulation. There was one very touching passage about the Jesuit struggle—or rather the struggle of the Society of Jesus against Jansenism, ' a struggle in which the Society lost its own life ' (a fine thing to be able to say, was it not ?) and how the work of spreading devotion to the Sacred Heart dropped from its dead hand into the hand of ' another Society ' which was to carry it on (ours !) He is most impressed with the connection between the two Societies and their similarity. . . .

At two-thirty we had the little play, or rather ' Scenes from English Catholic Family Life a Hundred Years Ago ' (the Welds' life at Lulworth). It is being typed for you. Daisy Maxwell Scott was John Weld (later Father Weld, S.J.), and was perfectly charming with her deep voice and sweet boyish drawl. Winnie Gerard, as the little daughter, Catherine Weld, bewitched every one by her very simple acting, and Meta Johnston as Dean Milner was a great success, also Gertrude de Stacpoole as George III. . . . The Bishop spoke most beautifully of the Society at the end, saying he looked upon it as one of the greatest of the great graces that are special to Southwark, that he has in his diocese three convents of the Sacred Heart, etc. . . . Benediction followed, at which there was a most glorious new *Ecce Deus*, in which the choir flew like birds to preternaturally high notes, to the joy of Mgr. Croke Robinson, whose ' immensity ' was in his purple robes, melting away with devotion at the beauty of the counterpoint.

I forgot to tell you that the first thing the Bishop asked me when he came in was to give him a copy of your letter to the children, which Reverend Mother Moran had shown him. He said it had touched him so much that he would like to have a copy to keep. . . . We have had it translated into English for our own children, and printed, for they all clamoured for it. . . .

Writing at the same time to another friend she said :

We had a very happy week of centenary celebrations, before and after the 21st. . . . Father Bampton gave a preparatory triduum to a mixed assembly of the school, the community and seventy or eighty old pupils who were staying in the house or came down from London by day. He had penetrated himself with the Life of our Venerable Mother, and the triduum was simply perfect, for it appealed to all, from the youngest child to the oldest ' old pupil ' and Religious in the house, and left one in love with tribulation and with humility.

Her nomination as Superior had withdrawn Mother Stuart from direct intercourse with the children, but it had greatly increased her power of working for their good.

As she wrote to another :

It is worth ten times more for you to help the nuns than the children. In the case of the child, you help the individual at less cost to yourself too. In helping a nun you help the body corporate and all the children with whom she has to do, through her.

With this end in view, she began in the summer of 1898, just before setting out for America, the series of conferences on educational matters, which were continued, with a break of two years, until 1909. In all, there remain the detailed notes of some sixty-two lectures. They cover a wide field, touching not only on matters obviously connected with the life of a school : discipline, work, culture, method ; but we find such headings as ' On taking interest in the world,' ' Folly, " incurie " fickleness,' ' The management of our minds,' etc.

A large volume could also be filled with the notes of her spiritual conferences. Some three hundred in number, kept in the archives at Roehampton, were all, from 1898, written in her own hand ; and in addition to these were the many given in the other houses of the Vicariate. Written year by year for the recurring feast days, there are not two alike. They offer not only a treasure house of meditation, but also afford a clear picture of the development of her own mind. The spirit of St. Francis of Sales breathes through the later papers, and the growth in liberty of spirit and nearness to God is very evident.

In December 1899, when the customary retreat for the close of the year was to be made, instead of reading instructions to the community as had been done hitherto, Reverend Mother Stuart herself gave the three meditations for the day, and so great was the spiritual profit, that what she had consented to do for once with some diffidence, became an established custom. For twelve years December 31 was a day of spiritual delight for all, but for herself another burden had been taken up.

It was during these years, too, that she began that extensive correspondence which holds so large a place in her life. The letters which she described once as ' travellers' tales ' form but a small portion of it.

The great work of Mother Stuart in the world was that of her spiritual influence.   Brought into contact with many thousands of people during the thirty-three years of her religious life, there ever radiated from her a sense of the presence of God; she was to those in touch with her a living witness to the truths of faith.

It is in her spiritual letters, her letters of direction and friendship, given in the second part of the book, that this aspect of her life is most fully revealed.

These letters hardly touch on exterior events, hence their individuality; hence, too, the reason for separating them from the story of her life, in which, however, they hold an important place.   They treat of the mental and spiritual outlook of the people to whom they were addressed.   The difficulties dealt with in them are those which are the common lot of struggling humanity; difficulties of faith, of hope, of charity; worldliness invading the inner sanctuary; laziness and cowardice in the labour of life; sorrow, pain, weariness in well-doing, and above all discouragement.   Each group of letters will be found to have a unity of its own.   They will be of interest chiefly, perhaps, to those who realise what Mother Stuart wrote : ' The life of a soul is so great a thing, that one of those distilled acts of faith and acceptance, without any light or feeling, is of greater activity and of greater vitality in God's sight than the tramp of armies and the power of those who command them.'

CHAPTER IX

1898 *and* 1899

'Choisir l'emploi le moins en vue, la place la plus effacée, lui paraît tout naturel. Elle n'ambitionnait rien de ce qui distinguait, et, appelée à faire de grandes choses, elle y est allée enveloppée de modestie. Partout elle a cherché l'oubli, comme pendant la chaleur on cherche l'ombre, et elle s'y trouvait bien.'—*From ' Formation à l'humilité,' Anon.*

On August 11, 1898, Mother Stuart left Roehampton in company of Reverend Mother Digby, to begin the first of the many long voyages of her life.

When she left Roehampton, she left also the office of Superior, and became as far as possible, as she said herself, ' a private.' Delighted to be again in the position of a subject, ' she was so silent and retiring,' writes a contemporary memoir, ' that though we had many opportunities of meeting her, nothing remains in my memory.'

' She seemed much relieved,' writes one who also accompanied Mother Digby on this journey, ' when she was not brought forward, and when she could hide herself behind her Superior General, with whom she identified herself so completely as to have apparently no desire, view, or thought apart from her. Her tact and adaptability in varying and trying circumstances were truly marvellous. Her keen sense of humour gave much merriment to our conversations: she would enliven them by amusing stories, and sometimes by singing Irish songs. She always had an Italian book in hand and gave all free moments to this study.'

The letters written to members of her community enable us to follow her through the various stages of her journey.

The first are dated, ' On board the *Dominion*,' August 14 and 17, 1898. They record a meeting with whales and icebergs, but are otherwise wholly occupied with details destined to allay the anxiety of those who, with reason, dreaded the long journey for Mother Digby.

On August 20 the *Dominion* reached Montreal, and the travellers drove out to the Sault au Recollet ; the name suggestive of a mediæval legend. There on the banks of the St. Lawrence, seven miles from the city, is a convent of the Sacred Heart. The house is surrounded by beautiful woods which reach down to the river's edge, and here Mother Stuart took the young nuns for a long ramble, hunting for wild flowers. ' We came across a little clump of immortelles, white and pale green, hidden in the waving grass,' writes one there present ; ' they delighted her, and that quiet morning walk had its consequences. We, the Canadians, were ashamed of our neglect of our beautiful wild flowers, and set to work to study them. A new interest had arisen, as was so often the case, from a word from Mother Stuart.'

The next few weeks were spent in Canada, with a visit to Halifax and a ' dip down into the States ' to Rochester, on the south of Lake Ontario. The line to Rochester passed the Niagara Falls. ' We saw them beautifully,' wrote Mother Stuart, ' but I refer all inquiring friends to the guide book for descriptions, and to their own imaginations for impressions, remembering Mother de W.'s golden rule, "Facts not sentiments." ' Writing to the community from Montreal she said :

. . . If this catches to-morrow's mail, it will reach you just in time for the re-opening of classes to give you ' three cheers for the Will of God ' as Mother Smith said, when you weigh anchor and embark on another school year, which I hope God will bless specially for each one, and for each child. I can see the state of things as it will be when this reaches you, or at least on the 12th. Mother D. in the parlour like Daniel in the den of lions, and some one looking over the top of the stairs into the den like Evilmerodach, asking in a lamentable voice if no one can deliver her . . . and bring her to the . . . reunion on the edge of the volcano, and Sister E. hurrying after a new child with six note-books under her arm, and a pencil much reduced by hard usage and affliction, and I can hear her repeating the lines Sister X. likes so much :

' A moment I give to natural tears
    And then you shall join the class, my dear.
  To-day our theme is the astral spheres,
    To-morrow the Greek hexameter '—

and I can see Sister M. trying to carry impossible portmanteaus and breathing the words of the ' Imitation ' (which, by the way, are a very good ejaculation in times of distress), ' May Thy

grace, O Lord, make that possible to me which seems impossible
to me by nature,' and so on. I can see you all. Mother Smith
and Sister K. at the boxes, Mother T. at the helm, and everyone
so nice and good ! ' surpassing all understanding.' Very many
thanks for all letters, you do not know what pleasure they are,
and I do not mind how many repeat the same thing, for it is
always from a different point of view. . . .

Good-bye, or I shall miss the good mail to-day. A slim,
meek, but inexorable aspirant comes in at the same second
every day, twice a day, and stands over me with the post bag
in silence : it would dry up greater volumes of eloquence than
mine, and between the moral pressure and the edification of
her presence, I can only say good-bye, with love to all the
uncanonised elect upstairs, and the *uncivilised* elect below.

Leaving Montreal, a thirty-six hours' journey brought the
travellers to Halifax.

They arrived at midnight [writes Rev. Mother L., then
Superior of the house]; the next morning Mother Stuart was
in the chapel at a quarter-past five, and from that time, until
she left, she was the living personification of the Rule, the
first at every community exercise. . . . At recreation, and
indeed whenever Reverend Mother Digby was present, she
completely effaced herself. It was only when she drove with
some of us to our country house at Sherwood that we became
aware of the charm of her conversation, and her knowledge of
everything in nature. She showed a wonderful familiarity
with the trees, grasses, and wild flowers ; even the pebbles,
shells, and sea-weeds of the Bedford Basin appeared to be old
friends of hers. . . . I asked her one day if she would give
the Mistresses some conferences on studies ; she declined very
promptly, saying she could not think of such a thing. The idea
was evidently very distasteful to her, but when the same request
was made by Reverend Mother Digby, she answered : ' Certainly,
if you wish it,' and without the slightest protest or sign of
repugnance the conferences were given, they were followed
by a model lesson in history. At its close she said : ' You
will pardon my impertinence in giving a class in the presence
of those who know so much better than I,' her manner and tone
were too sincere to leave any doubt that she really believed
what she said. On leaving the house she asked the librarian
if she would lend her ' an old copy of Evangeline,' as she wished
to read the poem to Reverend Mother Digby when passing
through Annapolis, the land of Evangeline.'

The beauty of the scenery delighted Mother Stuart. ' You
were perfectly right about the country,' she wrote. ' Oh ! the

St. Lawrence ! The lakes and forests . . . through which we
came yesterday ! Such loveliness ! God has indeed done
wonderful things for it.'

In Chicago, which was reached in the beginning of October,
there were two houses of the Society to be visited. Writing from
these, Mother Stuart said :

. . . This is the eighth house and the beginning of the
Western Vicariate. Reverend Mother Burke is coming up on
Monday to see about the new property that is just bought,
and about Mother Duchesne's witnesses. The Holy Father
has allowed the Cause to be begun again, but in Rome, and all
the witnesses must be *transported*, to use the local word here.

We are getting so accustomed to the local words that we
hardly notice them now, and hear without the least shock that
the weather or the view are ' elegant '; that the community
' had an elegant time at the country house ' in the holidays,
or that a person is not ' equipped with the usual amount of mind.'
. . . Our Mother has met some very interesting people in the
houses lately. One at Detroit who was taken by Mother Cutts
to be presented to Mother Duchesne, and got her blessing;
there were three : she [Mother Duchesne] looked at them and
told them two would persevere, and so it happened; one at
Grosse Point who lived through the terrible outbreak of yellow
fever at New Orleans, when so many died . . . ; some who
were for a long time at the missions of the Pottawattamies and
speak of it like yesterday. These are delightful pictures of the
past. . .

Chicago : 5th October, 1898.

. . . Yesterday our Mother had the nicest reception she
has yet had. This house is almost the only one, I think, that
has a *demi-pensionnat* of boys. Of course they are quite
separate. . . . These heroes were drawn up in semi-circle, heels
rigidly together, heads erect, very tight knickerbockers, very
large white favours, spotless kid gloves. The one who had
to make the speech was very self-possessed, one of those nice
red-brown heads that no school is ever without at least one
specimen of. . . . [He] spoke with all the finished articulation
of a boy that knows the value of consonants, and with great
deliberation . . . he had so much sang-froid that he went
back to pick up an important gesture that he had forgotten,
it was meant to be a wave of the open hand, but space was
limited, and he hit the boy next him on the waistcoat, with a
little loss of oratorical effect. Then each boy came up to offer
his flowers, looking at our Mother General with a respect and
awe that I hardly thought young America capable of.

Chicago is a perfect Babylon, nearly two million people all in

a hurry, they suppress all possible connecting words and speak
in substantives . . . to save time. . . . One goes about repeating ' *Cœlestis urbs Jerusalem, beata pacis visio.*' You can
imagine no more complete contrast to Chicago than that. . . .

Since I have begun this we have been out to the new property
at Lake Forest, and have come over to West Taylor Street, which
is in the Jesuit parish; one feels the spiritual atmosphere at
once, it is delightful; they do splendid work. It is a parish
that has life in it spiritually; one thousand six hundred Communions sometimes on a great day, fifteen confessors constantly
'sitting,' as they say in Ireland, and on the First Fridays the
Fathers are giving Holy Communion almost without intermission
from five-thirty to eight A.M. Is not that glorious?

With Chicago, the last of the houses in the lake district had
been visited, and the next halt was at Cincinnati in Ohio.

Cincinnati: 16th October, 1898.

. . . Here, and at the second house of Chicago, they had,
what is very rare in the States, two Masses. . . . Reverend
Mother Burke always has two. She does what she likes with
a 'most unworldly' community of Franciscans, as she calls
them, who seem to be as tame as Brother Junipers with her,
only they cannot be out on any pretext beyond eight P.M. So it
will be a race with the train on Wednesday evening: if it is
in time there will be Benediction, if it is late the 'unworldly
Franciscan' must depart. If I do not write much from Maryville
you will know why. Reverend Mother Burke has 'declared
her intentions before all present' of her community; 'she is
going to take a holiday during the visit; when she is not with
our Mother General, she will be with Reverend Mother Stuart;
when she is not with her, she will be with Sister Gurdon, and
so on.'

Cincinnati is nice, and the grounds beautiful, quite like
an English park, with single trees, and nothing but grass, most
unprofitable, but really beautiful, and not a yard of level
ground. . . .

Still going west, Maryville, a short distance from St. Louis,
in Missouri, was visited, and for the next few weeks the travellers
found themselves in the scenes of the early days of the Society
in America. St. Louis, Fleurissant, St. Joseph, St. Charles, all
spoke of the laborious, suffering life of Mother Duchesne.

Maryville, St. Louis: 22nd October, 1898.

. . . I wrote last on the way to Maryville. We were delayed
a good while on the journey by a freight train that broke down

in front of us, having 'left the track,' as they politely express
it. It seems to be the most natural thing in the world. Our
passengers got out and perched in rows, like sparrows, on the
fence ' to await developments,' while the poor splintered trucks
were being got out of the way. This is an American story.
A new *employé* on the line was told that he must always telegraph
to head-quarters when an accident occurred, so the first time
a train ran off the lines he wired a full and detailed account to
his chief. He received by return a reprimand, it was much
too expensive to telegraph at such length, next time, please
say only what was necessary. Next day the train left the
track again; when all was right and it ·had gone on again, he
sent the following message: ' Off again, on again, away again,
Finnigan.'

The arrival was rather damped by the unexpectedly late
hour, it was nine-thirty instead of eight, and pouring rain. The
steps were very high . . . at the bottom stood Reverend Mother
Burke only, her umbrella so agitated by emotion that it seemed
more like a flag she was waving than a protection against the
rain. . . . The Franciscan had got a dispensation to wait, as the
Blessed Sacrament was exposed. . . .

23rd October, 1898.

. . . I wonder if you will sing ' Blest are the departed ' after
Benediction on All Saints' Day, between the canonised and
the uncanonised elect. My spirit will be there to hear it on
the chance of its being sung. The chapel is beautiful here,
especially when the evening sun pours through the saints in
the stained glass windows, and all the coloured light goes back
on a great Crucifix that is against the first pillar, my only regret
is that St. Augustine's brown face is not on that side to get
the western sun. . . . I asked one of the [Franciscan] Fathers
if he had in his Order any Causes of canonization going on at
present—he answered modestly ' Fifty-seven ' !

Maryville : October 29th, 1898.

. . . Our Mother General has met a number of people that
interested her by talking of the old times in Missouri and in
France. A dear old lady who received her E. de M. Medal
from our Mother Foundress in 1826 ; she has just kept the
sixty-ninth anniversary of her wedding, and has lent her medal
to have a cast taken. Our Mother has long been looking in
vain for the first E. de M. medal that was struck for the Congregation. . . . This old lady could tell the story of how it was struck.
Our Venerable Mother called all who were to receive it, and
made them choose the design for the medal and the words to
put round it ; this old lady was one, and ·remembers a certain
Rose de Joigny, whose suggestion was ' *Cor meum jungatur vobis,*'

and our Venerable Mother liked it best and adopted it. . . . She would give the medal only she wants to die with it, and she added so quaintly ' *cela ne presse pas.*'

Father Hill, whose books we have so often used, lectures here every week, at present on Ethics. He is getting old and has lost his realisation of time, and it is the prettiest thing in the world to see how the lecture is brought to a close. . . . The Mistress of Studies lets him run on for about five minutes beyond the time, then walks up very filially, and respectfully shuts the book on the table before him and says : ' That will do, Father, you have spoken enough.' He gives a ferocious look, a grunt, and jerks back his chair. They have two Christian Brothers who give admirable classes in Latin and Mathematics. The latter told me ' he was raised on Euclid.'

An entry in the house journal at Roehampton shows that, though absent, Mother Stuart was still working for her own community. Under the date of November 21 we read : ' Delightful reading to-day, Reverend Mother had sent an envelope full of conferences from Maryville, one to the community, one to the novices, and one to the sisters.' A special letter to the aspirants for their feast day was not forgotten in the midst of so much work.

St. Charles: 8th November, 1898.

. . . At the risk of being late for the 21st I have waited to write to you from St. Charles, and am glad that I did so, that good wishes may come to you straight from the tomb of our dear Mother Duchesne : I cannot describe to you how her presence seems to be constantly here with one, even in the chapel which she never saw, but especially in the old house, and above all in the little cell where she died, and which they have made into an oratory. . . . At the end of it hangs the painting of the death of St. Francis Regis that Mgr. Dubourg gave to Mother Duchesne in 1831. Under it are the table on which she used to write—the note-books in which she copied, with her own hand, the letters of our Venerable Mother Foundress— her Office Book, with many prayers and loose sheets of intentions in her own fine beautiful writing—her crucifix of first vows (which I shall kiss for you all, think how she loved it !)—a little Loreto bell, which she brought out to America with her—two statues that were sent to her . . . gilded and very extreme in French renaissance attitudes, but dear and venerable from their associations—and one of the dearest things of all, an old chair of which she renewed the seat herself with a bit of cord and buffalo hide, and on which she always sat.

Now if I can obtain for you by prayer in that oratory and

at her holy grave, that you may believe as she believed, and
hope as she hoped, and walk as she walked, so independently
of self and so straight to God, leaving behind such a treasure
of poverty and abnegation for our use and example, it will be a
blessed visit to St. Charles for my dear aspirants whom I ask
God daily to bless.

St. Charles: 8th November, 1898.

. . . St. Charles is perfectly delightful, if only they could
all see and love it too. . . . Yesterday we arrived at ten-thirty.
The carriage drew up at the little hermitage of N. D. del Pilar,
and all the community were assembled there. . . . In the
afternoon our Mother General went out and sat in the garden
with Reverend Mother Burke, Sister Gurdon and me, to read
Mgr. Baunard's epilogue to our Venerable Mother's life. It
was very hard to listen without distractions. One felt like
the housemaid when asked sharply ' What *are* you thinking of ? '
answering ' A great many things are passing through my 'ed,
Mum.'

On the way to St. Joseph:
12th and 13th November, 1898.

. . . We had such an expedition from St. Charles. Our
Mother asked leave from the Archbishop of St. Louis to go to
Fleurissant. He gave leave, but after all she did not go, . . . but
sent Reverend Mother Burke, Reverend Mother Kavanagh and
me. We set off early in the morning, in snow, to drive all the
way with a pair of rough black horses that keep their tails and
manes long for the funeral work of St. Charles. . . . We picked
our way down to the Missouri, and asked ourselves if it was a
ford, but it turned out to be a ferry, half a mile. There was an
antiquated ferry boat, but no man visible. It was a case of
' Call John the boatman, call, call again,' as the poor children
used to sing. The driver began to call, and we sat some time
listening to his monotonous ' Hey, John,' and had time to make
interior comments on the second verse of the round—' John is
a good man, he sleeps very sound, his bones are at rest, etc.'
The driver's virtues were of the passive rather than of the
active order, he would not get down for fear of the horses.
Mother Burke thought it was *pas convenable* for me to get
down and hold them in so fashionable a quarter! besides it
was ankle deep in mud. At last John emerged with his tin
coffee-mug (pannikins they call them here)—he had been break-
fasting below—and stoked up his rusty old furnaces when he
saw us. The carriage was driven on to the ferry boat, the
horses' noses touched one side and the back of the wheels the
other when the gate was shut behind us. The horses were
young and somewhat fresh; Reverend Mother Burke did not

like it and asked if they had ever been across before. ' They
often take these little trips,' said the driver, smoothing them
down proudly, but he took the precaution of outspanning
them . . . and standing at their heads, and so we steamed
slowly across the Missouri, thinking of Mother Duchesne and
the Sioux Indians who used to live on the bank opposite in her
time.

Then the ferry boat was tied up, the horses inspanned, and
when the gate was let down they plunged into the track on
the other side. Such a track! No attempt at a road, but
simply the mark of carts that had gone there, full of mud holes
into which we often plunged up to the horses' hocks and the axles
of the wheels, sometimes on one side, so that Reverend Mother
Kavanagh moved hastily from one side to the other to restore
equilibrium, the driver did the same, and one said to oneself
' Courage, my soul, half an inch more and we turn over.' It
would have been very soft falling into the rich black Missouri
mud, just like one of Buszard's wedding cakes in a liquid state.

It was through a sort of low wood with the river on one
side and skeleton sun-flowers seven or eight feet high killed
with frost all round. It must have been nearly eighteen miles,
and one realised what the walk must have been when Mother
Duchesne did it on Christmas Eve with that recalcitrant cow,
and lost her pockets in the snow. No doubt there was not
even a track then. We saw the Jesuit place at Fleurissant
in the distance, about half a mile off. Our own place was a
great disappointment. There is a glaring, new, red-brick
' Academy '; however we saw the dear old building, the tribune
into the old Jesuit Church, where she used to hear Mass. The
Sister of Mercy we had counted on seeing, who knew a great
deal about Mother Duchesne and our old times, had died a
few months before. So we returned as we came, only with a
much longer wait at the ferry, as there is only one boat and it
was on the other side. It was useless to call ' John the boatman ' across the Missouri. He came to us in the end, and the
driver thought his pair were steady enough by this time not
to be outspanned, but between the cold and the delight at
getting near home one of them began a bear dance, which the
driver thought infinitely clever and amusing, and Mother Burke
considered *très mal placée*. . . .

Here are the latest Americanisms. A very nice E. de M.
devoted to our Mother kept on calling her ' Mother,' forgetting
any titles, at last she said : ' I wish I could get your prefixes
right! Believe my heart is all right, it is only my mouth that
is wrong.' The same one said, speaking of the youth of her
nation, ' You see we are always in extremes, we have not ad-
justed ourselves yet.' This morning several ladies were there

to see our Mother off, and one after another was asking : ' Where
was James ? ' (the convent servant) who was to bring the handbags in a little cart, at last one said : ' I am really getting
uneasy about the grips (handbags), James has not materialised
yet ! '

St. Joseph, Mo. : 13th November, 1898.

. . . I was invited to a ' Literary ' at St. Louis. It was
conducted rather differently from ours, each child reads her
own essay, others take notes, and any of them may be called
on at the end to give their criticisms. They do this very simply
and nicely. They are also called on to give an account of any
literary book they have read in the month and their criticisms
on it. This is most amusing. They are not in the least shy
and talk very easily, and come out with their own original
ideas, frank, crude, American, and often thoughtful enough.
They would be quite willing to discuss any question that might
be suggested, but thought mine rather cruel. There is no
music.

Their speaking is much better than their writing (the contrary
of ours), so voluble indeed that at times we had to cry ' enough.'
How you would have laughed to hear ' The Deserted Village '
summarised and critically commented on by young America.
The Mistress of Studies made apologetic eyes at me if a remark
was particularly astonishing. . . .

The personal appearance of the children is most interesting
to me, for their dress is quite one hundred years behind their
very modern little persons.

The elder girls often wear white clear muslin dresses (they
wear white but not uniform) down to the ground with full
bodies and sleeves and short waists, their hair parted and
smoothed down each side of their faces, turned up at the back,
or in ringlets. They are exactly like daughters of the Vicar of
Wakefield. The little ones wear ringlets too, of which three
are drawn to the front and tied with bows of ribbon on the
temples, when a black-haired one and a red-haired one come up
side by side they are a perfect little pair of King Charles'
spaniels, especially as round bright eyes and turned up noses
abound.

St. Joseph, Mo. : 18th November, 1898.

. . . We are to leave at twelve-forty and get to Omaha at about
five. . . . I meant to tell you how pretty the Missouri birds are ;
there are very pretty blue jays, not with barred feathers like ours,
but bright turquoise blue wings, heads and tails, and dove-
coloured backs. There are cardinal birds, too, red all over and
crested, but a little disappointing in their plumage ; it is rather
a dull red, probably it is the wrong time of the year, but the

heads of the woodpeckers make up for it. They really wear the
'great Lord Cardinal's red hat.' They run up and down the
trees like furies, and when the sun comes on their scarlet heads
they are most beautiful ; but never a note of a robin to be
heard. I believe there are hardly any singing birds even in
spring : no cuckoos.

It was at Omaha that an instance occurred, still remembered,
of Mother Stuart's winning power. ' I was in the convent at
Omaha,' writes one, now a professed in the Society, ' when
Reverend Mother Digby made the visitation of that house.
She was to be with us on the Feast of the Presentation, November 21, and the aspirants had been looking forward to that
specially privileged Renovation of their vows. The day before
the feast the Bishop announced that he himself would say Mass
the next morning in our chapel, but when the ceremony of
Renovation was explained to him, he refused to allow it to be
performed according to our ceremonial, saying that it was
contrary to the rubrics. There was general distress over the
decision in our little community when we knew that every
effort to induce the Bishop to change his mind had failed. On
the morning of the Presentation, when he arrived at the convent
to make his preparation before Mass, still unchanged in his
decision, Reverend Mother Digby had the happy thought of
sending Mother Stuart to him. What passed we do not know,
but after a few minutes' conversation the Bishop consented to
everything, and later on referred more than once with great
admiration to what he described as the " persuasive power of
Mother Stuart's irresistible humility." '

From Omaha the travellers took the wonderful journey of
over two thousand miles through the Rockies to San Francisco.
Going by Denver, through the high passes of Leadville and
Tennessee, passing Salt Lake and the Sierra Nevada, they reached
the city house of San Francisco at the end of November. It
was to be among the few left standing in the great earthquake
some years later, but it had to be abandoned when the city was
rebuilt.

In the last spurs of the Rockies : November 28th, 1898.

. . . You see by the above that we came by Denver. I did
not tell you before lest you should be miserable at the idea
that our Mother might be snowed up here. . . . We left snow
and frost in the plains, the higher we went the less snow there
was. It was driving snow at Denver, and cleared up into a lovely
afternoon. . . . The scenery was most magnificent, especially

the ' Royal George,' and this morning we have had two beautiful
valleys.   We are getting near to Salt Lake City now.   We passed
two hundred miles south of the Yellowstone region near Ogden,
that was our nearest point to it. . . .

San Francisco: 1st December, 1898.

. . . The prayers were splendidly answered.   It seemed an
almost miraculous thing . . . after a journey of two thousand
one hundred and eighty-six miles to arrive at San Francisco
to the minute, so that we were at the house almost before they
had begun to expect us . . . all the previous days that train
had been regularly three or four hours late.   The President,
E. de M., with her husband, the Vice-President and other
' officers ' of the Congregation, with their respective husbands,
each with a carriage and pair, were at Oaklands and *se dis-
putaient*, even the members of our Mother General's party.
. . . We were dispersed in four carriages.   I saw Sister Richardson being struggled for as a prize between rival claimants.
The husbands ran about with the hand-luggage like railway
porters, and everyone's hands seemed full of orchids of marvellous
size and beauty.   Some are eight inches across.   The violets
are so enormous and the fairy roses so small that the violets pose
as the big flowers and the rose as the little flower ! . . .
   To return to [the] arrival.   All these carriages were driven
on to the ferry boat, and we went in them four miles across
the bay, horses behaving perfectly.   It was after the great
silence . . . so the Magnificat was reserved for the following
morning at Mass. . . . Such a *Magnificat* . . . they gave it
with the full power that God had given them, up and down
in variations and ' happy returns.'   I thought all was over, when
they started fresher than ever in an intricate fugue on the
word ' Abraham.'   It seemed impossible that it should ever
reach a solution.   I was divided between great thanksgiving
at having our Mother alive and praying on her prie-dieu, and
the hope that Abraham might soon rest in peace. . . . Arums
and heliotrope are in flower in the garden ; palm leaves twelve
feet long cut lavishly for decoration, also long stems of vine
with ripe grapes and autumn tinted leaves.

8th December, 1898.

. . . We have been to Menlo Park since I wrote, such a
beautiful place, and such a curious mixture.   The style of the
house (only one wing built) is taken from the old Californian
mission houses, more Spanish than anything else.   It will be
a quadrangle with open cloisters.   The property is timbered
with oaks, quite an English park ; the two ranges of mountains
are distinctly Californian, such beautiful shapes and such
changing shades of blue.   The birds are so pretty at Menlo :

flocks of wild canaries that come in parties as numerous as our
sparrow parties, to feed on the seeds of the marigold.   They
are not yellow all over, but more like our mule-canaries, and very
tiny; they can sing.   The great blue jays are beautiful too, but
they are always in family quarrels, and so less edifying to look at.
The Sunday silence there is something wonderful, absolutely
no sound but a distant cow-bell ; the days are so long and warm
that our Mother came out after Benediction to see the last of
the sunset over the hills. . . . We came back part of the way
by carriage . . . to see our place in the cemetery, then by the
Pacific shore and the seal rocks, and home through China-town.
What a place ! Could one ever forget those swarms of faces
that look out from cellars and doors and windows, all stamped
with such a deep sadness, and some with such hatred.   I only
saw one nice one, a little girl of about fourteen, with the wax-white
complexion and long neck that one sees in Chinese pictures,
and bright coloured trousers ; she was scudding along with her
eyes down, looking so sweet, a real lily among thorns.   There
are ten excellent Catholics out of a population of twenty-five
thousand Chinese. . . .
The Pacific gave one the impression of being less impression-
able than the Atlantic. . . . We could see the seals in the distance
coming up on the rocks and plunging back into the sea, but the
wind was against them, so we could not hear them bark.

Leaving San Francisco on December 13, a three days' journey
brought the travellers to Guadalajara, in Mexico, some distance
to the north-west of the capital.   When El Paso, the frontier
town, was passed, the religious habit had to be modified.   A ruse
which, while deceiving nobody, yet satisfied that strange thing,
the official conscience.   For Mexico is the home of the anomaly
which makes a man in his official capacity execrate and condemn
all Religious, but as father of a family insist on confiding his
children to their care.

In the Gila Desert : December 13th, 1898.
. . . I write from the *'terra deserta et invia et inaquosa'*
that you know, and it is curious that it is now covered with snow,
and no snow had fallen since the winter of '89, just when you
passed.   Perhaps you saw it in the same state with yuccas and
dracænas showing above the waste of snow.   It is quite true
that the sunsets and sunrises are most lovely, and the purple
and blues and pinks of the snow mountains quite indescribable ;
and one is set up in life for compositions of place of desert subjects,
as we have seen deserts of sand, deserts of scrub, brush and thorns,
deserts of snow and deserts of rocks.   The sun is beautifully
bright, and we have the window open, to the horror of the darkie,

who threatens us with pneumonia, and says we must have come from a very cold country to be able to stand it. . . .

Guadalajara : 21st December, 1898.

. . . There is so much that I should like to tell you about Mexico, but as there is not time for all I must begin with what is most present, the Mass and Communion in the Elementary School this morning. . . . When I went over, the Indian school was already in the chapel (about two hundred or more, many pure Indians, some of mixed race), the acolyte was waiting outside with crossed arms, crimson cassock, white embroidered cotta, olive face approaching to black; put to that a background of plumbago in full flower, a stray humming-bird or two flying about, a very broad flight of rough red-tiled steps and a deep blue sky, and you have a picture ! Then the priest arrived, also olive-coloured and gentle, wrapped in a big cloak, and the vesting began : the small acolyte was master of the situation, pinching the beautiful embroidered alb into judicious folds, shaking his head when they fell below his expectations, then flinging the girdle round the priest with the expertness of a hand that was learning to throw the lasso, and standing on tiptoe to launch the chasuble over his head, somewhat on the same principle. This nice child considered that respect consisted in nearness, not in distance, so he established himself almost under the chasuble to serve the Mass, gazing up fixedly into the priest's face (it reminded one of the picture of St. Peter Claver and his negro), and almost getting under his feet for the *Confiteor*. There were little asides between him and the patient padre from time to time.

The general Communion was very touching ; the boy was too young to go, but was in all his glory with the candle in one hand and the glass plate, instead of Communion cloth, in the other, and of course he stuck to the priest like a small limpet ; both had to lean over the Communion rails so far to reach some tiny children that it is a wonder the boy did not set the father on fire and himself too. About sixty went to Communion ; the rest were too small, their recollected faces as they came back were a sight one could never forget. That is a real mission school, and only two years old. They say it does a great deal of good in the town. . . .

They cultivate English here as assiduously as we work at French. Yesterday at the distribution of ribbons they spoke very nicely in English, and they sang ' Faith of our Fathers.' Nearly all the school sang it, down to an infant of four years old, who tried in vain to keep up, but only managed to come in at the word ' death ' with a very vigorous stamp of her foot at the end of each verse. . . .

Mexico, Guanajuato, and San Luis Potosi were next visited. While at the first house Mother Stuart went for a day or two to Puebla at the invitation of the Archbishop.

Archbishop's Palace, Puebla : 2nd January, 1899.

Look at the address and pity a poor orphan ! I am very glad our Mother did not come, it would have been very tiring for her. She sent Reverend Mother de L. and me down here to explore, as the Archbishop is keen for a foundation, a training college especially, as there is no Catholic one in the whole of Mexico. There are very few trains in the day, so we could not go and return and explore all in one day, and had to accept the Arch- bishop's offer to sleep in his palace. . . . As it had to be done, it brought a great deal that is interesting and picturesque with it.

Mgr. Amesquita, the Archbishop, is extremely kind, most extraordinarily like Mgr. Rouse in appearance, especially when one walks behind him. . . . He has a most beautiful palace, built in 1630, round a quadrangle, and looked a fitting proprietor of it when he stood at the top of his great staircase to receive us, waving off his venerable old physician, and with shadowy clergy flitting about him. We were taken to supper with him first, through long, long galleries, one full of all the portraits of all the departed Archbishops of Puebla. Happily, only one pale seminarist had supper with us, his one preoccupation was to keep the Archbishop's glass full of water. The Archbishop's dog was the fifth of the party ; he was under the table and had alter- nate mouthfuls with Mgr. Amesquita off the same fork, the dog's was always a large bit and the Archbishop's a small one, the natural consequence is that the dog is as fat as a sheep and the Archbishop as thin as a lath.

I think he is very tender-hearted. The Infant Jesus in his crib is tucked up in red eiderdown quilts, evidently a man's efforts at tucking up. Then he showed us his chapel, a little gem, in Spanish style, all white and gold, and then he took us himself to our rooms.

In Reverend Mother de L.'s he stopped to explain to her that it was the room in which the Empress Charlotte had slept, poor thing, when the Archbishop of Puebla entertained her and the Emperor. We walked on through long galleries again. ' *Mon Dieu ! nous sommes à une lieue de distance l'une de l'autre,*' murmured Reverend Mother de L., who did not much like the association with poor Empress Charlotte. But my room was even more thrilling.

The Archbishop turned round with a kind smile and said : ' Here is the room in which the unfortunate Emperor Maximilian slept.' There are no doors, all these rooms are galleries opening into each other, with curtains ; at each end are paintings which give

an appearance of great distance beyond, the drawing and perspective wonderful, but the painting bad. ' Is it not strangely
prophetic,' said the Archbishop, pointing these out, ' that
Maximilian's room should end in a prison, the Empress's in a
hospital of Sisters of Charity.' Reverend Mother de L. had
life-sized Sisters of Charity with patients on crutches and in
bandages ; and I had cadaverous prisoners, life-sized with chains,
guards, and dogs. With dim lights, and very thick carpets, so
that you could not hear a sound, and side doors in the walls that
do not appear to be doors at all, and open into long side galleries,
it is the most ghostly suite of rooms that I have seen for a long
time.

Reverend Mother de L. invited me to bring my mattress into
her room, but I could not resist the possible ghost of the Emperor,
for which, however, I waited in vain.

We had an early Mass in the Archbishop's chapel ; he found
us in possession when he came down and was evidently a little
indignant at finding no sign of a cleric about, so he went off to
arouse the archiepiscopal household, and it must have been
done with a certain paternal severity, to judge by the flutter in
which they all arrived, two such nice infants from the *petit
séminaire* with purple sashes like miniature prelates, and the
rest in order of agitation and dignity.

We breakfasted with him and the same pale seminarist,
another tiny one of eleven years old was brought in to be admired,
evidently a great friend of the Archbishop's, with bright squirrel
eyes, the dog looked jealous, but was appeased at seeing that the
Archbishop did not offer him the fork. Then we went to visit
three possible houses, too long to tell about. . . . I am sure
Mother Stonor will be disappointed that I cannot bring back a
thrilling story of a ghost. . . .

San Luis Potosi : 16th and 17th January, 1899.

. . . This will be the last letter from Mexico, I hope. . . .
New Orleans will seem no distance after Guadalajara and Mexico.
This is an interesting house, the old Carmelite monastery. They
found quantities of human skeletons and bones in one of the
quadrangles, and a benefactor (probably) who appears to have
been buried at a bad moment, for though his coffin was very
smart indeed, it was buried under the monks' store-room or
cellar. There are nice old paintings everywhere of Carmelite
fathers and mothers. In the refectory is one of Our Lord
bringing a fig to Saint Teresa in her refectory, and the nuns
looking a little scandalised. Holy Father Elias appears everywhere, both in statues and paintings. The study-room has
paintings all along one side, scenes from his life ; in another room
is the Transfiguration, where, of course, he shows to advantage :

I

his Easter Communion according to the pious belief of Carmel : and his crucifixion, still in the future.

The most surprising thing of all is to go into the side chapel of the Carmel, where during repairs all the saints are gathered together, all life-sized, nearly all dressed.

Holy Elias meets you at the door, waving his flaming torch and wearing the habit of Carmel ; beyond him is St. Simon Stock, also in his habit and pressing you to accept the scapular ; St. Mary Magdalen in deep mourning next to St. Joseph, who is in green and has put on the worst of his three wigs because of the dust. St. John the Baptist baffles all description. But there are two really beautiful figures among all these wonders, life-sized crucifixes : one is called ' The Christ of the afflicted,' and the other ' The Christ of the despairing ' ; the latter stands just inside the church door usually, to catch the big sinners, and they say it is never without someone praying. . . .

To-morrow, the 18th, we start on the first real stage homewards.

In the midst of all the work entailed by these journeys Mother Stuart's thoughts often turned to those she had left, and, as she could, she ' spent her Christmas ' with them. ' Mother T. read us the Christmas conference written for us by Reverend Mother ; it was on the text " I am the flower of the field and the lily of the valley," ' writes one of those at Roehampton. ' When it was over she took the community into Reverend Mother's room (it was Christmas Eve). On the table was a statue of the Holy Child, and for each one a letter from Reverend Mother. Some forty letters in all.'

Leaving Mexico in the middle of January, the next halt was in Louisiana, with its old French traditions. Grand Coteau and St. Michael were moreover connected with the early years of the Society of the Sacred Heart in America, and with the names of Mother Duchesne and Mother Hardey. In the solitude of Grand Coteau, where the name of the nearest station, ' Sunset,' suggests its remoteness and the beauty of the scenery, a longer pause was made on the journey, and Mother Stuart took advantage of it to make a retreat, which she refers to as epoch-making in letters to be given in a later chapter.

Grand Coteau : 25th January, 1899.

. . . This is a quiet visit for our Mother, the community not large, and no visitors in this beautiful solitude. It will be an ideal place for her retreat, she has a sunny gallery outside her room to walk in. Her windows look down a beautiful avenue of large pines, like the aisle of a church—on a group of cedars and the Jesuits' park-like property in the distance, solitary and pastoral-looking with a big herd of cows.

When the children are not at recreation, there is no sound to be heard except the birds (and they are rare to hear in America). The mocking-bird seems to sing at every hour of the day and night and the cardinals sit up quite late singing glees and choruses by moonlight, in a way that hardly befits their dignity. They are in beautiful plumage now, real cardinal colour, and there are many of them.

The old house is charming, but the traditions about the rooms disappointingly vague, except the little hole under the stairs where Mother Audé used to see the children, and the place in the garret where her bed stood. But still one knows that she and Mother Duchesne knew the handles of all those doors, and had their foot on each step of the stairs. . . .

Grand Coteau : 3rd February, 1899.

. . . It seems to me that I have told you nothing of this beautiful Grand Coteau. It is a solitude almost like that of the Swiss family Robinson, the wonder is that telegrams and letters ever reach at all, especially telegrams. There were three from Reverend Mother Mahony last week. First arrived the correction, then the explanation, and lastly the original telegram. There is no office except at Lafayette, thirteen miles away. Then the message is telephoned to Sunset, but as the operator is constantly absent, and when there is sometimes too cross or too dejected to send on the messages, it is a wonder that they ever arrive at all. Our Mother has visited the coloured school and went for a drive round the property afterwards. She saw the departure of the black children, a most curious sight. All through the school hours the building is surrounded by horses, mostly asleep, for there is nothing to eat. At three o'clock the children come out, and each family claims its horse and mounts, sometimes there are three or even four on the same horse, barebacked of course, except a few black aristocrats who have an antique saddle of the Mexican type. The first mounts and slides to the tail, and then the next; the foremost, of course, is just on the neck. The girls wear enormous sunbonnets : we have not been here long enough to get accustomed to find something black under a sunbonnet when one expects pink and white. The lane is most picturesque when it is full of these crowded mounts. . . .

Our Mother's drive was very curious in its way too. The carriage was a buggy, and she found it easier to get up in front than behind, so she sat by the coachman, ' Theodule,' who was got up in his best clothes and nearly ' choking with pride,' as Sister M. says ; then there was a pair of horses that did not match—

one was ours, one was the Jesuits'; ours was fat, theirs was lean—
and there was an outrider to open the gates, a little creole boy
'Felix,' a singularly graceful rider on a wonderfully canny colt,
both of them pictures of 'merit in rags' and both of them equally
unconscious of their own excellencies.   Did Mother T. see Mother
Duchesne's well in the woods about a mile from the house?
. . . the wooden frame is still round it, just as it was in her time,
and I suppose the surroundings have not changed a bit since she
used to draw water there.   It is full of minnows, so the water
must be good.   Theodule made devoted but ineffectual efforts
to catch one for Our Mother to take away *en souvenir* !
    The well is now just over the edge of our property and on
the Jesuits'. 'It is not two properties,' said Father Rector
graciously, 'it is one property under two administrations.' . . .
The moss is really wonderful.   It is called the 'Englishman's
shroud,' but I do not think Grand Coteau can be so unhealthy;
probably New Orleans is; it is the 'Irishman's grave,' you know.

    New Orleans and St. Michael were next visited.   The latter,
some distance from the city, on the banks of the Mississippi,
was the scene of the meeting of the first six Superiors of the
Society in America, in 1829, when they met to review the labours
of the preceding fifteen years.   It was a Council which was a
turning-point in the life of Mother Duchesne.

                          St. Michael : 10th February, 1899.
    . . . Here we are in a house full of holy memories. . . .
They have had a severe winter, such as they have scarcely ever
seen in Louisiana.   Yesterday we came down by the 'Memphis
Express' (imagine if all the Pharaohs could have seen it !).   It
is not supposed to stop here, but was 'flagged by courtesy' to
let [us] down. . . .

    Philadelphia, Eden Hall, Atlantic City, New York, Boston,
Elmhurst were next visited, but no letters from these houses
have been found.   By the end of March, Manhattanville
had been reached, and here there was a great gathering of Vicars,
Superiors, and Mistresses of Studies from Canada, the States,
and even from Australia. 'Each morning,' wrote one of those
present, 'we have a conference on the Studies given by Mother
Stuart.   You know all this means.   In the afternoon we meet
again from two to three, and this morning she gave us a specimen
class on philosophy.'
    Though the last of a great number of educational conferences
given during the nine months' journey, they are, as are all Mother
Stuart's writings, marked by freshness and originality.   Each

new experience brought with it new points of view, and her poetic gift, the gift of metaphor, seemed to give her an unending variety of expression.

There is a difference between these earlier conferences and those given in later life. Theories put forward in the beginnings of her religious life were dropped or changed as years saw the development of her mind and the widening of experience. ' You did not think as you do now, when I was a child at school,' said youth to her one day in the face of such a change ; ' you held another theory.' ' I was young then, I have learnt many things since,' she answered.

Writing from Manhattanville, she said :

. . . Although it is Holy Week I feel no scruple in beginning a letter to you, as all these ' latter-day times ' writing time has been so scanty. Things are quieting down now, the Mistresses of Studies have gone, and already sixteen Superiors have arrived for the retreat, in addition to the Vicars who were already here. Of course the more Superiors there are in the house, the fewer letters there are to write . . . the newly arrived Superiors are busy getting lost about the house, and the Mother Assistant equally busy finding them. . . .

7th April, /99.

. . . They are going to give our Mother some electrical apparatus for the Conflans Juniorate. A small induction coil and various other things, and to show what they could do with this apparatus, Reverend Mother Mahony got a Christian Brother (they have such splendid teachers in their colleges out here) to give a lecture. . . . It was most interesting to hear a real typical American teach, as interesting to me as his lecture, which was very good. His two subjects at the College are Electricity and Pedagogy—perhaps more kindred subjects than they look at first sight. He did not waste a single instant, speaking breathlessly, clearly, practically. If he stopped for a quarter of a minute to hook on a new wire, he begged us ' to converse among ourselves' that no time might be lost, and then, with a catch in his breath, said ' Ready' and was off again. He, as he said, ' invaded the kingdoms of magnetism, heat, and light ' all in an hour and a half. . . . I am sure he will be found some morning in a fit of nervous prostration. . . . Here is an extract from the *New York Herald* which made [us] laugh. ' Owing to the late frost there will be a famine of peaches in New Jersey, but the inhabitants will *manage to worry along somehow*, unless the applejack crop should also fail.' We are told by an American that peaches there are like potatoes in Ireland. . . .

' Much amusement was caused at recreations during this visit by " our characteristic modes of expression,"' writes one of the American Mothers, ' and one evening Mother Keller, the Mistress of Studies, gave a lesson in verse on the American idioms, which had specially amused or interested the visitors. On the eve of their departure Mother Stuart replied to her in the same vein.' The following extract may be quoted here :

To M. K., Professor of English at the University of Manhattanville.
Tell us truly, O Professor, how much progress we have made
Since you took in hand our higher education, and you said :
I will give you many phrases which each one shall *memorise*—
Many words as *grips* and *rubbers*, *trouble* and *materialise*.

But we learned the *cute* expressions till they now are all our
    own :
We *locate* ourselves at once in the places we have known,
And we love the speech *well spoken* ; and have even learned
    to say
To an unexpected summons, ' *We are coming right away*.'

The last letter from the States was dated from Kenwood, the house of noviceship.

. . . We have just arrived. . . . This morning we left Manhattanville. . . . Central Park was alive with lovely little grey squirrels with tails larger than their bodies, and we saw with delight the first snowdrops and daffodils. . . . Reverend Mother Margaret Moran is in joy untold, refreshing joy to look at. . . . She is next to our Mother in the stalls, and I am next to her, receiving all the electric shocks of her joy. She had the *Te Deum* sung, and shook the book under my eyes to make me look over and sing with her. . . . It is really delightful to see any one so happy. . . .

Mother Margaret Moran had been a novice of Mother Digby at Roehampton.

On April 29 the two Reverend Mothers left America and arrived at Roehampton on May 12. ' I have brought you back your Mother,' said Mother Digby to the assembled house, as the curtain fell on the last tableau of the *séance* of welcome.

CHAPTER X

'Try to do the one thing worth doing, abandon yourself to His care and His love, and let Him love you in His own way.'

From a letter, J. Stuart.

ON Reverend Mother Digby's departure for Paris a few days later, Mother Stuart resumed the quiet home life with her community. The real history of the next year and ten months was within—in the hearts and souls of her children. There she was silently, imperceptibly casting her bread upon the waters, to find it after many days. Her ideals, her teaching, her principles, were sinking deeper into the minds of those around her, transforming lives, and winning hearts to God.

But this peaceful life was not to be for long. On January 10, 1901, she received a letter from the Mother House nominating her Visitor of the houses of the Order in the West Indies and South America. Her answer was written the same day to Mother Digby :

The first line of your most dear letter told me that something was coming, so I took it down to St. Thomas of Canterbury's and read it *coram Domino*, with a very full heart ; so grateful, dearest Reverend Mother, to be allowed to be of the smallest service to the most dear Society ; too dazed at all the thoughts yet to take in more than *le stricte nécessaire*, and that *stricte nécessaire* is that I am most miserably insufficient and that God is more, and a thousand times more than sufficent, and that He will see it through, since it is His will through you to send me. So *in verbo tuo laxabo rete.*

I am not at all afraid of the travelling, dear Reverend Mother, and do not consider that the ocean is an unfriendly creature of God ; in fact I have no *physical* fears of it, only the moral and the spiritual, but for these I have the most absolute trust in the grace of obedience. I have no feeling or preference for one route rather than another, only if the Cordilleran route is available—I heard from Miss G. that it saved eight or ten days—the order would be reversed I suppose, and Buenos Ayres would come first instead of last, for February or March are the most open months over this way.

The most interesting date of all is the first one, which is not on the paper : When shall I see my Mother ? I can go to the ends of the earth when I have seen you and had your instructions and your blessing. . . .

I must write again when I have gathered my thoughts together ; this is only to tell you how lovingly and gratefully I take the work from your dear hand, asking you to bless it and promising to try by prayer and fidelity to make it fruitful. . . .

Writing to Father Daignault on January 29, she said :   ·

. . . Our Lord is quite determined to teach me the lesson of confidence and make me overcome my shyness before I die. Mother General is sending me to visit for her our houses in the West Indies and in South America. . . . I am to leave this on the 8th of February for Paris and sail about the 16th for Porto Rico. It is a great work, and I know I am quite unable for it of myself, but I have entire confidence in God's help and the grace of obedience. It will be a long journey of about six months. . . . I want your prayers and blessing more than ever, Father, and I know they will follow me. I don't analyse my feelings on the whole subject, *Deus providebit*. It must be His Will, for it certainly is not mine.

On January 24 a bell summoned the community to their common room, and with no little sorrow and surprise they heard of the coming separation. In her parting conference a few days later, speaking of conformity to God's Will, she reminded them that it should not be ' a half-reluctant acquiescence,' but as ' St. Francis of Sales' " certain incomparable act of resignation, which he made one morning having a little leisure." He does not say,' she added, ' what it was about, but it was one in which his will expanded and his courage rose, letting go the shadow to have the substance.' On February 7 Mother Stuart left Roehampton for Paris to begin her long and eventful journey, eventful in the inner life no less than in the outer.

The *Olinde Rodriguez*, in which she was to sail from Bordeaux, was not to leave till the 19th or 20th. A few days of the intervening time were to be spent at Joigny in Burgundy, the birthplace of Blessed Madeleine Sophie Barat. From there she began the series of letters which enable us to follow her on her pilgrimage.

Joigny : February 13th, 1901.

. . . I am thinking of and praying for everyone, and trying to look through everyone's eyes as well as my own. The subject of meditation that comes to one here as natural and on which I made mine this morning, was the text of Father Bampton's centenary sermon (twelve weeks ago to-day ! How little one knows what is coming !) ' Look to the rock . . . and the hole of the pit whence you were dug out.' Thinking of that in the *mansarde de Sophie* makes me pray for the lowliest possible thoughts of self, for us all, and most immense confidence in God's goodness for ourselves, for the Society, for all our future, and for our eternity.

The bricks and tiles and rafters and door-handles and walls all say the same thing of lowly beginnings and humble thoughts and hidden life. . . .

It is wonderful to see the tower of St. Thibault that one has studied so often in that nice page of the ' Illustrated Life.' That curious figure at the corner is St. Thibault himself mounted on a horse of questionable pedigree. They are repairing the tower, but there is no scaffolding, and we heard the Angelus ring on the same bell that rang for our Venerable Mother's Baptism, Confirmation, First Communion, and that called her to daily Mass. . . . Now I am off on a pilgrimage alone to the holy little attic. . . .

Paris : February (?), 1901.

. . . To finish the story of Joigny. During breakfast the town crier came, and after beating a great roll on his drum, invited all within hearing to a wild boar hunt in the forest. *Battue de sangliers demain à huit heures du matin*, giving details as to the meet, etc. It seems that anyone who likes can go, and wild boar must be pretty plentiful as they are not preserved. The servant who escorted us to the station and who was *né dans les bois*, explained all about it. If you meet a wild boar who is not wounded *il ne vous dira rien du tout*, but if he is wounded he makes apparently the most personal and unpleasant remarks. If you are lucky enough to kill the wild boar, he is all your own to do as you like with ; conversely if he kills you, you are all his own. The forest there is pretty wild, for quite lately a soldier was riding through and a wolf thinking he had some designs on herself and her cubs, rushed up behind him and sprang on the croup of the horse—an object lesson on self-occupation ; he did not know that she existed, still less that she had precious cubs ! She pulled the horse down and it bolted, and the man fought as best he could, but he was so mauled that he died in a few days. There must be plenty of wolves, for they only give twenty francs to anyone who kills a wolf, more if it happens to be the wife. This takes one back to the days of Edgar.

They have a special netted enclosure at Joigny to contain a *coq Anglais* and his family; they were said to show joy at my approach! They looked very nearly thoroughbred Golden Hamburgs: the cock is so very small and so very 'dominant' and lordly, for he even flies at the dog, that they call him 'Lord Roberts.' I forgot to tell you that at Joigny, over the Mairie, there is in large letters *République Française*, and underneath the arms of France and the Fleur de Lys. When attention was drawn to the inconsistency of this they said that 'it was not worth while changing—*cela change trop souvent.*'

I know we shall meet in thought to-morrow. We leave here at ten-fifteen A.M., arrive at Quadrille at about nine-thirty P.M. Leave on Tuesday morning the 19th to embark at eleven. They say the *Olinde Rodriguez* touches at St. Thomas, from where our first letters will be posted.

This is all the *itinerarium* I can make, as no dates can be fixed. All must depend on connections in the beginning. I spend ten days in each house, more in the larger houses. The time of travelling between one can make out fairly well from the guides. Thus four days from Havannah to Colon, and I think nine days beyond to Lima. The Andes are out of the question. . . .

The Spanish-American war, which had only ended in 1898, had disturbed communications in the West Indies, so much so that, when asked to arrange the journey, Cook's agent in London had replied: 'I can get Madame Stuart to Porto Rico, but I do not know how I shall get her out of it.' Events proved the truth of this forecast.

On the way to Bordeaux: 16th February, 1901.

. . . We are now in a *rapide* that does not hurry itself unduly. We are five: one to be dropped at Poitiers, one to take on to Bordeaux, my two companions and myself. I have a beautiful passport from Her Britannic Majesty's Ambassador Extraordinary and Plenipotentiary, requiring and requesting in her name (pronoun not yet changed) that everyone shall give me whatever aid and protection I may be in need of when travelling 'wherever I shall please' in South America. It reads like an 'obedience,' only without that beautiful ending '*attendant du Seigneur leur récompense.*' Anyhow it gives me the feeling of having all the power of the lion and the unicorn at my back. I have letters patent too, specially drawn up

for my visit, and sending me ' in the name of the Father and
of the Son and of the Holy Ghost.'   I have the Holy Father's[1]
blessing too: that kind Archbishop Costantini went from the
Villa to the Vatican to ask for it, and he said that the Pope was
so kind and so interested ; asked who was going, by what way
and ' by what seas,' to what houses, and sent his blessing to
the visitor, the companions, the journey, the inhabitants of
each house. . . . So I am indeed started *in viam pacis*. It
is so nice to think of that prayer said every day at Roehampton.
    We are passing Tours and have saluted St. Martin and the
Saints of his Order, and what we believe to be the *tours des
cloches* of Marmoutiers. . . .

            Quadrille (near Bordeaux) : February 18th, 1901.
    . . . I have found here one of our probation. . . . We
renewed recollections of probation and especially of Mère B.'s
direction in public, with Reverend Mother Desoudin's ' *Allons,
B., vous êtes toujours occupée de vous.*' ' *Enfin, ma Mère,
je n'ai qu'une âme, il faut bien que je la soigne.*' Did I tell
you that our Mother General drew St. Paul for me for the
journey; it was nice, and the *bouquet spirituel* is *Quis nos
separabit?* And certainly he had experience in travelling,
and he knew what it was to be left high and dry at Malta,
with his connections disorganised. . . . The ship is 4,900 tons.
I will tell you what she is like when I see her, and her manners
and customs at sea.

            On the way to Pauliac : February 19th, 1901.
    . . . This is like Baby Bedford's ' one more love ' with
which she announced a final hug. . . . The Baron de Bock
has been most kind and useful, for the slip-shod company had
never let us know that the station of departure for Pauliac was
changed at the last moment, or that there were so few passengers
that no special train would run. This was good news, for it
means clear decks ; if only there is a clerical element among the
few ! The last boat of the line carried off fourteen priests, S.J.
and others. . . .

            Beyond the Azores : Sunday, 24th February, 1901.
    . . . This is the beginning of the journal of our travels, and
when it reaches you [which it did on March 27] it will break
the first long silence, after which no other will be so long. . . .
Our journey began with a great disappointment—no Mass.
The priest had nothing. It is all the greater joy to think of
Father Kenny's novena of Masses. Our three priests dwindled
into one, the other two are Christian Brothers. . . . The boat
is old, the elder Christian Brother came back in her from Haiti

            [1] Pope Leo XIII.

twenty years ago, and I doubt if even then she was in her first
freshness, for they say only the old boats are put on this line.
She has only one funnel, and looks smaller than the Holyhead
boats, or about that size. She carries some antique rigging,
and when the wind was behind we put up a sail, a very small
one. . . . We give the mornings to silent work, the early afternoons to classes. Sister Santa Anna gives us each a Spanish
lesson, and I give them each an English lesson. The late afternoons go in spiritual exercises and needlework. We have a
nice moment on deck to see the stars and the phosphorescence
. . . and we finish with Office and preparation of meditation
in the ladies' saloon. The only living creatures seen so far
are sea-gulls and fat porpoises, who came jumping alongside
in schools. . . . We had a very bad day to begin with, but
now are all right, and can stand anything, I suppose, short of a
storm. . . .

Tuesday, 26th.—We are getting into more populous quarters
and have seen three ships. We get on but slowly. The *Olinde
Rodriguez* wastes a lot of time and energy rolling. We are
now about three hours in time behind you. I sometimes take
a turn at about seven-thirty, nearly ten-thirty with you, and
visit each head on its bolster, hoping to find it asleep, and pray
for it. And I often think of people who would like to share my
geographical emotions—being taken up into the trade winds, as
we shall be to-morrow, going to the very root of the Gulf Stream,
and seeing the Great Bear dip his tail in the sea. . . .

First Friday, March 1st.—We have been making our retreat
of the month on a grand scale, with everything except the
usual essentials ! . . . We had a distinct view of a battle between
two sperm whales. The tactics seemed very simple—one ran
away, the other ran after him with his mouth wide open; we
saw them bounding along, but did not see the end. . . .

In the harbour of St. Thomas, 5th March, 1901.—This is the
second number of the irregular-journal. . . . It is a great
delight to be at land though not on land. We sighted the
first lighthouse at three P.M. yesterday, a lonely thing on a low
island, miles from anything else. Then at sunset the Virgin
Islands came in sight and the sun set behind the ' Virgin Gorda ';
when the full moon rose we saw a whole procession of Virgins,
some tiny dots, others larger. I made out what I thought
was Mother Rumbold's old friend Tortola. . . . We reached
St. Thomas a little before midnight with fearful shrieks of our
fog-horn and rockets for the pilot, who never came until we
had threaded our way through the narrow way in. The smell
of the land, and the ' voice of the cock that crowed in the morn '
were very inspiring after a fortnight at sea, still more the sound
of the Redemptorist's Mass bell . . . .

The town and harbour are so pretty, wooded down to the water's edge, roads bordered with cocoa and real palms, and such a bright, pretty Danish town backed against the three hills. There was a heavy shower just as we came on deck, followed by the most lovely double rainbow, in the very middle of which my eye rested on the Red Ensign on a British steamer—I do not know of what line—which gave rise to many reflections, surrounded as it was by the double bow of hope.

They say it is quite unusual to have such a good passage in February, so that is what the prayers have done. . . . All the passengers have gone ashore during the coaling. The priest hoped to say Mass. . . . I saw in a book on Haiti that the average life of the French missionaries there is four years !—so many die in the first two years; so it is very touching to see his boyish enthusiasm for his mission, he is panting to get there.

To-morrow at eight A.M. we hope to land at Porto Rico. . . .

Enclosed with this ' journal ' were the notes of a conference for the Feast of St. Joseph to be read to her absent community.

The lesson in common to all the joys and sorrows of St. Joseph [she wrote] is that every life that is led very near God is a life in which great sorrows and great joys meet. There are not colourless lives in the inner sanctuary. . . . The joy follows the sorrow in each case as the flower breaks from the thorny branch, not the thorny branch from the flower. . . . There is a connection between the sorrow and the joy . . . they spring from the same root ; . . . this is a reason for looking with friendly eyes at sorrow : ' You are not only the forerunner, but the maker of future joy.'

Several other conferences were sent to Roehampton before her return; for Holy Thursday, the Month of May, Pentecost, the Feast of St. Aloysius, etc. A characteristic note was struck in that for Pentecost :

Only two loves can fill our souls—God and self. If self invades our faculties, there is room for nothing else ; if God takes possession, the whole world comes in with Him, but ordinated and subordinated to Him : His creatures, His dear ones, His Saints, His needy ones, His suffering members, His little ones. It is not they that keep Him out, it is we ourselves. . . . The proof of this is in the lives of the Apostles and the great apostolic Saints. . . . Had they less of God because every creature of God had a right to their love and service ?

Porto Rico : 7th March, 1901.

. . . We arrived here yesterday at eleven A.M., a very pretty arrival, but so slow ! The port is very difficult to navigate,

full of hidden rocks, and we took one and a half hours to get in.
The Red Ensign was floating over the same steamer that we saw
at St. Thomas yesterday.   A group of Children of Mary were on
the wharf, with bouquets—' *C'est une noce*,' said our passengers.
At last we landed in a tropical shower.   The joy of getting here
made up for all, for they had a most beautiful surprise ready
for us, Mass in the presence of the Blessed Sacrament exposed
. . . and Benediction immediately afterwards.   Was it not kind
of them to think of it and of the Bishop to allow it ?   The kind
priest had waited since eight A.M. when we were expected, and
would not be persuaded to give up and say his Mass. . . . There
is no means of getting away from Porto Rico until the 27th.
There is a Spanish tramp ship to-morrow, but it takes a fortnight to reach Havannah, calling at all the ports. . . .

March 13th, 1901.

. . . I am beginning my retreat to-night after a fruitless
effort to go yesterday. . . . A transport appeared at eleven A.M.
It was announced that it would leave at two or four P.M. for
Santiago (in Cuba), and we could have gone on by Cienfuegos, and
thence by land ; and we packed up with great jubilation, and I
gave conference, and said good-bye, and the carriage was at the
door, when word came from the colonel that the transport was
absolutely full, not a single place to be had !   The Bishop tried,
and all the ' high and mighty ' tried what they could do, but
it turned out to be a genuine impossibility.   The transport
was packed with negro soldiers, who are going to reinforce the
coasts of Cuba, where a rising is expected. . . . It was a great
disappointment, but of course it must be for the best, as we
made every possible effort to obtain a passage.   Now we have
decided to take a coasting steamer on the 23rd, she is named
Julia ; she will arrive at Havannah the 31st March or 1st April.
. . . It is all at sixes and sevens at this part of our journey. . . .

I have seen something of the suburbs and the country just
beyond, the flowers are too beautiful even now, though May
is the great time.   Imagine all our most cherished and delicate
hot-house things ramping about half wild like weeds ; things
that we should be sitting up at night with to keep them alive—
great scarlet hibiscus, of different sorts ; bouvardias, bougain-
villeas, rhynchospora, jasminoids, four times as big as any I
ever saw in a hot-house ; huge passion flowers, lilies and amaryllis
of all sorts, simply wild.

I do not speak of the groves and avenues of cocoa palm, or
the still more lovely royal palms seen above dark blue sea,
or the pretty carpeting of baby pineapples under them, or all
the other things that the geography books will enumerate.

I will tell you of something better still.   We got inside the

Carmelite convent, with the Bishop's leave, to see if it might do for us. One of our *affiliées* was the godmother at the clothing of the Superior, and had the privilege of coming in too. We were kept waiting a little at the door ; and evidently the community bell was rung, for, when it was opened, there was the whole community of fifteen waiting to receive us—the sweetest faces you could imagine, with the 'peace of God surpassing understanding ' in their eyes.

We began with the kiss of peace all round; then they took us over the house, except into the private cells. It was like being on another planet. They were so charming to talk to, and so entirely out of the ordinary everyday things of the world, so interested in seeing us, and so pleased to show us everything. . . . They have nice cloisters, and looked so beautiful in a group standing in them, in St. Teresa's own habit. I should have liked to stand and watch them instead of talking business. It was nice to think there are such people and such places in such a place as Porto Rico, but they want to leave and go to Spain. . . .

There are quantities of mules here, really beautiful mules— sixteen hands high. The Americans brought them in. The horses of the country are scarcely eleven hands high, but are said to be very strong ; they are ugly little atoms. Most of the work is done by beautiful bullocks, golden-tawny coloured, like very yellow Alderneys, with big horns and great soft eyes, with no trace of vice, but so slow. No wonder the Americans brought their cross-grained but hardy mules.

We saw an albatross fly across the harbour as we came in, quite close; such an ugly weird-looking bird. . . .

Porto Rico : 21st March, 1901.

. . . I am beginning to think that it is useless telling you plans beforehand, because the next letter is pretty sure to contradict them. If I miss the one monthly boat for Colon, I shall go to Vera Cruz to meet Reverend Mother de L. I have given up the coasting steamer *Julia*, and decided to take the Spanish Mail, which by the last telegram from the Canaries is hurrying up in very respectable time. . . . Once over the isthmus there will no longer be a real difficulty as to connections. We cannot see the sea, but we can see the semaphore station ; it puts up black balls and black parachutes when ships are seen coming, and then the flag of the nationality as soon as it can be discerned ; it was prematurely active to-day : three black balls and three parachutes were up together, one of them developed into your mail, the others were all of no use. . . .

I nearly made a mistake and stayed nine days in retreat, it was such a pity I found it out too soon. The kind people here, in honour of the eighth day, put the most beautiful flowers into my room, among them such a lovely Eucharist Lily, just shaking itself dry after a storm, a real Resurrection flower, so beautifully strong and large. They fling about delicate things with such prodigality, crotons of all colours, and caladiums of great beauty.

I had an ideal place for retreat, not three yards from the Tabernacle; the tiny sacristy opens into the tiny sanctuary, quite close to the altar; of course there are no windows, or rather, big windows, but no glass, so it is very noisy, but one gets accustomed to it. The *calle de la Cruz* is always full of people, mules, dogs and fighting cats. Then there are the street criers at it all day long : ' eggs and oil,' ' oil and eggs.' There appear to be an indefinite number of meals, and at all of these oil and eggs must be the *pièce de résistance*. . . . We have such lovely rainbows constantly here, it is tropically showery in honour of the equinox. The Mistress of Studies says *arco de iris* with profuse apologies for her language that has only such a pagan name for it. . . .

25th March, 1901.

. . . I have been considering, with great consolation, that the Annunciation is the feast of the ' impossible,' *quia non erit impossibile apud Deum omne verbum*, so I am asking many impossible things, according to the natural order and to human views, for us all. I am sure that Our Lord likes to be asked for such things on this day when He overstepped all the limits of possibility and credibility from a human point of view, and the omnipotent Word ' leaped down from His royal Throne ' in the silence of the night. . . .

Things look as bad as possible for getting away from Cuba. That will have to be a little addition to my impossibilities. . . .

At last the long-desired Spanish Mail arrived, and Mother Stuart set out for Cuba ; nearly two months had passed since she had left Roehampton, and but one of the twelve houses on her itinerary had been visited.

On board the Spanish Mail, *Isle de Pannay* :
Palm Sunday, 31st March 1901.

. . . I unite myself to your first Alleluias and to all the ceremonies of Holy Week, and the lamentations which I shall not hear sung this year, and I assist in spirit at all the Easter holidays, remembering last year's with their remarkable events.[1]

[1] The visit of Queen Victoria to the convent at Mount Anville, near Dublin.

We hope to arrive at Havannah to-morrow, but though a mail
boat, this is very slow.

It is a great contrast to the *Olinde Rodriguez*, very dignified,
very picturesque, rather dirty, ratty and cockroachy, but so
far we only have cockroaches, not rats in our cabin.   Everything
has an antiquated and grave look ; we are all painted in black
and gold.   The table stewards are all aged and have their
whiskers cut to uniform pattern, like very antique butlers
with us.   But it is the Captain that interests me, as particularly
typical, just the Spanish Captain of strong, ferocious type that
I imagine in the sixteenth century, when his people and ours
were deadly enemies on the high seas.

By way of a colourless remark, I said yesterday that this
was a lonely road that we were travelling on, we saw so little
shipping.   He laughed into his black beard and said : ' It is
well ; better none than enemies.'   I thought he was thinking
of the Stars and Stripes, and explained that I meant shipping
in general ; to which he answered : ' Every other barque is an
enemy.'   No doubt he meant from the point of view of com-
petition, but the ferocious smile and the words carried one back
three hundred years, and I could quite see him ordering the
passengers below and clearing the decks for a broadside from
Sir Francis Drake ; and in perspective behind one sees Queen
Elizabeth and Sir Walter Raleigh, not as solemn ghosts, but
as actualities ; and we are just going to pass the bay where
Columbus landed when he discovered Cuba, so one is all in
souvenirs of the past.

We have very devout sort of passengers, all pilgrims returning from Jerusalem and Rome, mostly Mexicans ; so you can
imagine the edification of their conversation.   We have Mass
every day and Communion whenever possible, and the Rosary
in the saloon every evening, led by the Chaplain, who kneels
at an improvised altar, his tonsure and his white officer's
jacket making such a contrast ; and a very mixed congregation
behind him, nearly all the passengers, except two Americans,
. . . a few officers, and as many of the stewards and seamen
as are off duty.   Two very sweet infants, Fernando and
Raphael, crawl about the floor and join inarticulate crowings
to our prayers.

We have three priests on board, but only the Chaplain says
Mass ; one of them . . . makes our thanksgiving aloud, the
other is very ill.

This morning, as everyone had to go to Mass, the oratory
was not large enough, and we were on deck, but on the second
deck, one side of which is occupied by the cows ; it was a real
Bethlehem, and they kept turning their yellow heads and great
eyes to look.   I hoped they would have gone down on their

K

knees at the Elevation, like St. Peter Canisius' herd of buffaloes.
There was a queer mixture of devoutness and indevoutness,
and being perfectly at home with God, especially when the
infant Raphaelite went on all-fours and, hopping frog fashion
up to the altar, having caught sight of the Chaplain whom he
loves, was just caught in time by one of the antique stewards
before he had reached the alb.

Monday, April 1st, 1901.

This morning the babies turned in for the Elevation by a
door close to the priest, and maintained a doubtful equilibrium
by clinging to the legs of the steward who was serving. It was
very pretty, for they might have come out of one of Hoffman's
pictures of children round Our Lord.

We have beautiful sunsets into the sea, when [the sun] plunges
down without cloud or haze straight into the water. It is
surprising how quickly it disappears, two minutes and thirty
seconds from the moment it touches the water till the last ray
has disappeared. . . . They say we shall see the remains of the
Maine when we go into the harbour. The Americans left it
there *ad perpetuam rei memoriam*. . . .

Havannah : Good Friday evening, April 5th, 1901.

. . . Yesterday during the night-watch, and to-day at
three o'clock . . . I asked Our Lord to overlook the difference of
time and look upon us all as present before Him at that hour
. . . *suscepit nos Dominus in sinum et cor suum*. . . . One
thing here was a great privilege. . . . I wore all day from
Thursday's Mass to the Mass of the Presanctified the key of
the Tabernacle : the Chaplain wears it during the Mass and
sends it to the Superior afterwards. It is worn outside on a
gold chain like a Bishop's pectoral cross. . . .

I have lost my heart to Reverend Mother Fesser for her likeness
to Mother Kerr. In face she is strangely like the photograph
on the bureau in Marie Immaculée, or rather what that would
have been like at sixty-four years old; so like in her ascetic
energy. She would have been dead years ago but for this.
She has the same dreadful choking fits of coughing ending in a
laugh and a joke, when one thinks she must be almost dead ;
and she leans on one's arm to walk with just the same light hand.
You feel as if it were all spirit and no body, or, like the holy
Bishop of Thessalonica who ' used his body only as a veil to
cover his soul, not for purposes of business.' Everyone thought
at one moment that she would be dead before I could get here.
But she is going about more every day, walked into the chapel
at midnight last night and again at six A.M., and seems none the
worse. What a wonderful thing mortification is, ' dying and
behold we live ' about ten times as much as other people. . . .

I have had X. here for two hours, presenting one vocation after another. It was a very severe two hours for me, as he speaks English, and the young lady with the vocation was always ' him ' and ' he,' and the ferocious father, who would not let her go, was ' she,' and occasionally both were ' it ' for a variety. And whenever he meant ' press ' he said ' pinch.' He did not think the time had come to ' pinch ' the ferocious father. It sounded a delicate and dangerous business at any time. I had all I could do to keep my face straight. . . .

I often wish I had an assortment of appreciative eyes in a box to bring them out now and then, according to their taste, for the things I see (the community's eyes, I mean) and return them to their owners with the views in them. We have a terrace, a flat roof, to walk on here, and on the vigil of Holy Thursday we went up to walk by the light of the Paschal full moon, the tropical full moon too, which is far brighter than ours. From the roof we see the port, a very pretty bay quite landlocked. The great fortress is just opposite to us, and the waves break against the foot of it, and not fifty yards from us is the Cathedral, so old and venerable, with a red-tiled, very wavy red-tiled roof, and a little dome, flat and low like a cock-chafer's back ; the moon on it was lovely. There, until two years ago, rested the bones of Columbus. The Cathedral is ' San Cristobal,' in honour of his patron, and between the Cathedral and the ' Morro ' fortress was all the port full of lights ; it is very full of shipping of all sorts. They have taken the bones of Columbus back to Spain now.

This afternoon the Children of Mary are coming, and to-morrow the Affiliées, and in the afternoon a congregation of coloured girls, and in the evening we go out to the Cerro, but come in again on Friday 12th, the night before we start. . . .

The difficulty of getting a passage from Cuba to Colon was, however, to be as great as that of getting one from Porto Rico to Cuba. ' I found myself,' she wrote, ' like a king on a chess-board in a very bad position ; it was check on every side.' And having tried for a passage by six different routes, she was finally obliged to go to New York. ' It seems simple enough looking at the map and sitting reflectively in the Old World to say: "How absurd to go to New York ! I should certainly not do so "—but when you have to work the matter in practice from the West Indies, and that since the war, it is a very different thing.'

Cerro, Havannah : 11th April, 1901.

. . . This letter will probably travel with us. . . . I am going to New York after all. . . . It is of course a much easier journey, and I shall see Reverend Mother Mahony, Mother Errington, and others. I am very glad. For once nature and grace meet.

This is such a place for vegetation. The royal palms are lovely beyond description. You gather handfuls of gardenias off a garden hedge, as we might gather monthly roses in June. And the tree-trunks are matted with our choicest orchids—cattleyas and odontoglossums—as ours are with ivy, or the old trees in Ireland with ferns. They tear them off as we tear off the ivy for the good of the tree. It looks an iniquity to a European eye. Then, as a rarity, they brought me a violet of which a beetle had eaten away a good part of the petals—Oh ! think of it !

Continued on board the *Mexico* off the coast of Florida, and carried gaily along by the Gulf Stream . . . in a beautiful new Ward Line steamer, not very big; but it is a pleasure to see a ship so smart and clean, and as a ship should be, after our two venerables, and going nearly twenty-two miles an hour now. . . . Poor dear *Olinde Rodriguez* used to do ten miles per hour, twelve if she bestirred herself very much. We left Havannah Saturday morning, and hope to be in New York Tuesday evening. . . .

Manhattanville.—The rest of the journey was too bad to write a word. Now we are here, and to me it is a great holiday, and the kindness of everyone is beyond description. . . .

                                    S.S. *Allianca*, 27th April, 1901.

. . . Each letter seems to begin in stranger surroundings : yesterday we passed in the latitude of ' where the lone Bermudas ride.' I saluted without seeing them, this distant outpost of the British flag. To-day I write in sight of what is believed to be the original San Salvador, Columbus' first landing place, now called ' Cat Island ' or ' Watling's Island.' What a drop down ! It makes a great impression on one to think that this is the land he first saw, and that he sailed over this very identical ocean space with the great joy of discovery in his heart. We are scarcely a mile from the land, and can see it perfectly.

These last two days we have a calm sea and every facility for travelling, with a little breeze behind us, and we are trying our best to make up time. I hope we may secure our connection at the isthmus, but my *voie* in this journey is to be held in doubt till the last minute. We lost nearly eighteen hours at the first, starting from New York ; the fog came down so thick that the pilot would not let us stir for hours, finally we crawled out, threading our way through a crowd of shipping, but when we got out to sea the fog was just as thick and the night

exceptionally dark, and at eleven P.M. we ran into a schooner.
It was her fault, not ours,—I believe it is the rule at sea to excuse
oneself, and I like to follow the local custom—for we were
going very slowly and blowing our steam-whistle every two
minutes. We felt a grating shock and the stopping of our
engines, and all the passengers, except ourselves, went out 'on
the war-path,' the more timid prepared for the worst. The
schooner struck us forward on the port side, and our cabin is
aft on the starboard side, so we heard and felt the least of it.
But as a matter of fact we do not go out on the 'war-path' at
night for anything that we hear, for the old *Olinde Rodriguez*
has so accustomed us to shocks and gratings and dead stops
and shoutings at night, from the constitutional infirmities of
her own old machinery, that we take all we hear as a matter
of course. Our crew saved all the crew of the steamer in boats,
and our Captain was so nice that he hung about all night trying
to tow the schooner, but the schooner said that she did not
want to be towed and meant to go down as soon as possible.
She would have been a nice handful to tow all the way to
Colon . . . we had to cut her adrift with her cargo of timber
and leave her a 'derelict' on the high seas, and I suppose she
has gone to the bottom by this time, or is drifting recklessly
about endangering other ships; in that case the U.S. Government
will have to send out and blow her up. We had the Captain
and his crew of eight on board with us until last night, such
a fine old sailor and so dignified in his trouble, he came to the
saloon followed like his shadow by a boyish and very respectful
young mate. . . .

Last night we met the *Washington*, a big sister of our
own line, and asked her if she would take our supercargo back
to New York, and she came up alongside in a very stately way,
and said she was delighted to oblige us, and carried off the
dignified old Captain and shipwrecked crew. . . . Another
detail of my *voie* of doubt until the last moment is as to
the connection with Reverend Mother de L. at Colon. She
wired from New Orleans, when I was at New York, asking if
she could get a passage on this steamer, but finally elected to
go as she had first planned. And I had a letter from her the
day I left saying it was because she doubted about her connection
at Port Limon, where she has to change steamers, but *un ami
dévoué de la maison* had assured her that it was all right and
the connection certain. I hope he is as accurate as he is devoted,
if so she will be at the landing-stage with Reverend Mother S.
to meet us, if not she will be high and dry at Port Limon, a
most distressful situation. . . . We have only about a dozen
passengers on board, besides ourselves, going to most outlandish
places, Guatemala, obscure parts of Honduras and Colombia,

etc. It gives one the feeling of being on such an out-of-the-way track and going to ' places in general ' rather than to any place in particular. . . .

I forgot to tell you that we had no serious damage from our collision, our taffrail was broken, some irons bent . . . we shall have an interesting semi-invalid look as we come into port to-morrow. . . .

Hospital del Cerro, Panama: 1st May, 1901.

. . . One more chance of writing to you before leaving for Lima, as our steamer is delayed a day or two and only leaves on the 3rd, so we have two days in Panama, and I can tell you all about everything.

First of all we arrived safely at Colon, and were met by a message from Reverend Mother de L., saying that she was at the Sisters of Charity's Hospital, waiting for what I decided to do, about going on at once or staying there a day or two.

The kind Sisters had sent a species of antediluvian buggy to meet us, with two of the smallest, leanest, and most ugly ponies I ever saw, a ' mulato ' *qui avait de l'esprit*, and a negro who had none.

They had some memorable days here last July, five hundred men held the town against two thousand five hundred. They carried off General Pinto to the Cathedral when it was all over to return thanks and congratulate him, and he unbuttoned his coat and showed a scapular of the Sacred Heart, and said ' It was that which saved us.' [1]

To return to Colon. I decided to come straight on here. But as there were some hours to wait, we went to join Reverend Mother de L. and Reverend Mother S. at the hospital : such a poor strange damp place, built on piles with the tide coming in under it. It was raining cats and dogs, chiefly dogs, a regular tropical downpour, and Colon looked about as miserable a place as you could see. But it all looked nice when the long-desired meeting . . . was accomplished. . . .

The rain cleared up and we had a beautiful afternoon for seeing the isthmus; cool and grey and with the sun vertical. . . . I had expected the isthmus to be sandy and rocky and all defaced by the old works of the canal, but instead of that the railway here is cut through a real virgin forest, and the latter part of it runs alongside of wooded glens with distant mountain views, just too big for Scotland and too small for California.

But that virgin forest ! That is what I should have loved all your eyes to see. There one can understand how people have cut their way foot by foot through such places : such lovely trees worthy of California, such creepers, and then open

---

[1] One of the ' events ' in the revolutionary movement of 1898–1902, at the end of which Panama, with the help of the United States, finally severed its connection with Colombia. Pinto was the Colombian general.

places with most delicate red and white lilies, big ones, and
stout arums in the swamps as thick as waterlilies in the streams
in July in Ireland.   How the sacristans would love to be turned
loose before the great feasts in these parts !

One thought of Reverend Mother du Rousier so much in
that passage.   I can quite imagine the place where she slipped
over the steep side of the glen and hung.

We got across in three hours and were met by a Sister of
Charity to whom we had telegraphed, asking to which of their
hospitals we should go, and they sent us up to this most
beautiful one on the hillside of Panama.   It was built at the
time of the canal works and consists of ever so many houses.
We are in No. 15, and there are some higher up ; pretty wooden
bungalows with verandahs all round.   All the most distinguished
or most contagious diseases have a house to themselves, for
instance consumption has a house, yellow fever has a house
(no one in it at present).   We went first to the Sisters' bungalow, which is quite separate, and we were taken into their
refectory where they were already at supper . . . it was strange
to see rows of cornettes behind the tables instead of us . . .
they are really very picturesque.   After [that] we were taken
a little walk up the hillside to our bungalow, where we are
entirely alone, which is most delightful.   We were given the
key to lock ourselves in, and told that it was all right if we
heard men's steps round the verandah at night ; it would only
be the police making their nightly prowl, but we might have
a negro told off as guard if we liked.   But we declined the negro
and satisfied ourselves with police protection.

Our bungalow has not been occupied, except by priests—
Religious passing through—for some time.   The last inhabitants
were *les petits Frères de Jésus* on their way to Mexico, it
sounds such a sweet little party of travellers. . . .   We go out
to Mass at five A.M. to the Sisters' chapel, which is downhill,
or to the strangers' chapel, which is above us. . . .   The Sisters
have an immense property, and a great part of it is wooded,
and they say there are deer and a few monkeys and small
tigers in the wood.   I do not believe these last are anything
more than tiger cats.   We have seen none of these animals,
only enormous butterflies, brilliant blue, scarlet and black,
bright yellow, etc.   The frogs are very pretty, their skin is like
black velvet, not the usual wet leather texture—with turquoise-
coloured spots and markings, and they are very small.   The
bats are large and are said to bite, they have not attacked
us.   The race of Panama mosquitoes is handsome and rather
ferocious.

So much for surroundings, and to-morrow after Mass and
Communion we shall be afloat again, not on the *Chile* but
the *Arequipa*.

CHAPTER XI

REVEREND MOTHER DU ROUSIER, the foundress of the houses in South America which Mother Stuart was about to visit, and to whom she refers in the last letter, had crossed the Isthmus in 1853 under the most trying circumstances. The railway had scarcely been begun. The greater part of the journey was accomplished in canoes and on mules. There was no road, but the track led through mountain torrents, through forests and valleys, along the edges of dangerous precipices, down one of which the mule of Reverend Mother du Rousier fell. She and her mount were saved almost by miracle. So many were her hairbreadth escapes, and so great the sufferings of the journey, that one of her companions remarked : ' Her mule appeared to have received an order from the devil to hinder the Chilian foundation ! ' The same distance was crossed by Mother Stuart in three hours, and after a few days at Panama she embarked on the *Arequipa* for Lima. Writing on May 9, 1901, she said :

. . . I wrote last from the hospital at Panama. The last evening we suddenly saw in the moonlight a crowd of cornettes, and there was the whole community of Sisters of Charity coming up to have recreation with us, and we all sat on the verandah together . . . very interesting to see another Religious Order, especially ' at play.' . . . They invited us to dinner in their refectory next day, the young ones stipulating that there should be talking. Of course we went and met there another guest, who dropped in unexpectedly from Buonaventura. This was a Sister of St. Joseph de Tarbes, and really a most interesting person to see ; I am delighted to have met her : she had travelled on the same boat with M. le Directeur, the Lazarist Father Visitor, whom the Sisters were expecting, and who was to give them their retreat ; he had been delayed three or four days, and there was no news of him, '*c'est la quaraniaine ou la guerre,*' they said : these incidents of the way are taken quite as a matter of course, and the retreat was put off in general. It reminded me of *premier prélude comme on voudra, second prélude comme on pourra.*

To return to the Sister of St. Joseph. She is seventy-two years old, and is travelling quite alone : she was twenty-five years Superior General of her Congregation, and when by their Rule they could no longer re-elect her, they made her Assistant General and named her Visitor of their houses in India, when she was sixty-five. Then last year they were sending out a colony of young Religious to Popayan, their furthest mission in Colombia, and the Superior General was a little unhappy about sending them alone, so this dear old lady volunteered to take them, and they named her Visitor of the houses here, to kill two birds with one stone. So she brought her colony and disembarked them at Buonaventura and from thence began a journey on horseback to their different houses, two days to this one, and three days to that one, and six days to another, finally twelve days on horseback to Popayan where she left her band and came back quite alone with a guide, ten or twelve days to the coast all on horseback. The last three days she had fever, and they even hesitated to take her on board at Buonaventura for fear they might be put in quarantine on her account. She said in such a matter of fact tone that she must write a line to her Sisters there before starting, *parce qu'elles languissent un peu, pensant que je suis morte en route.*

She was going to take the first steamer she could find for Caracas, and having visited the houses there, go thence to Europe. She regretted very much not being able to come to Peru with us to see her convents there *puisque je suis si près,* but the Superior General had seen them herself last year.

She has such a dear old face, wiry and weather-beaten like an old huntsman, and clear innocent eyes, but so shrewd, as if she had been looking after foxes all her life—(I do not mean that her daughters are foxes, they are obviously hounds)—and a mouth that looked as if it could keep the most frolicsome pack steady on its way to covert. . . .[1]

[1] The Religious here referred to was Lucie Bareille, in religion Mère Marie de l'Incarnation. She died in 1909. She came of a patriarchal family in the neighbourhood of Pau, in which the missionary spirit seems to have been an inheritance. Her brother, a priest of the Foreign Missionary Society, worked in India for many years, and was succeeded in his apostolate by a nephew ; while three nieces followed in the footsteps of Mère Marie, two devoting themselves to the Indian Mission, while the third died at a similar post in South America. The Order of St. Joseph of Tarbes, to which she belonged, was founded in 1843 in the village of Cantaous Hautes-Pyrénées, by a holy priest, l'Abbé Bazerque, in conjunction with the Vicar General of Tarbes, l'Abbé Laurence, and a young girl, Francine Gorré, in religion Mère Marie des Anges.

We have stopped at three ports since I wrote last, and are now at our fourth, which leaves one more before we reach Callao, Lima. We were a whole day at Guayaquil, which made me think much of Garcia Moreno, he must have known the port so well. Our crew is mostly composed of Ecuadorians, very short people, with gigantic chests and arms, very brown, with heads just like the pictures in the old editions of Jack the Giant-killer, before they took to making the giants like Teutonic demi-gods, which is very wrong on principle. They are very strong, very slow and very stolid, the people of Guayaquil were of course of this stamp. But now at the Peruvian ports it is quite different, they (the Peruvians) are active as monkeys and as gay as larks, more like Neapolitans than anything else and always laughing. We spend a great deal of time taking cargo on board and discharging it—tobacco, rice, fruit. This morning three great hampers fell into the sea and had to be fished out with great difficulty ; at one port we took about two hundred cows on board, they must have been half starved to prepare them for the journey, for they never uttered a sound or made any resistance when they were slung up in a waistcoat of sacking and hoisted up by the crane, except one or two indomitable old ladies—the Lady Desmonds of the herd—who still showed fight, otherwise each cow turned her head with a mild expression of ' good gracious ' and let herself be hoisted without a sound. Yesterday we took on three horses, who were much more alive to the situation and struggled a good deal. I wonder they did not blindfold them. They had great difficulty in reaching us, taking two hours to do quite a little distance from the pier, the barge was so heavy and the wind so strong. . . . We are due (at Lima) Saturday 10th, but we left Panama a day late.

There is a most beautiful comet which we watch on clear nights. I always wonder if you can see it . . . it is near Orion : anyhow, I do not send messages to you by anything so flighty and eccentric as a comet. . . .

Pacific Ocean, S.S. *Chile* : 23rd May, 1901.

We are coasting down the ports of Peru in a beautiful ship, but she is behaving like an omnibus, for we make fifteen stops on the way. Valparaiso is our sixteenth station, and they say it is very ugly all the way ! This is a calumny. The last part of our journey to Callao was beautiful. The Andes come right down to the coast, only the lowest and last spurs of them, of course, but line above line, one behind the other, and the smallest Andes are like the biggest of many other chains. It is like the one bunch of grapes of Ephraim and the vintage of Abiezer. . . .

25th (Anchored off Mollendo).— . . . Lima is a most delightful and interesting house, full of holy Jesuit memories, too long to write about . . . full also of memories of Mother Marcella Digby, whose congregation of dear poor Indian women I saw last Sunday. . . . One of them called out to me in the middle of the reunion, ' Best remembrance to the relation of Mother Marcella.'

I visited her grave, as it is in our property, the only property we have at Lima, as the house belongs to the Government. The cemetery is very beautiful, and they take great pride in it. Parts of it are full of monuments over family vaults . . . like an Italian Campo Santo in a rich quarter. Others are a real necropolis with streets built about ten or twelve feet high, and the coffins are put into cells, catacomb fashion, each street called after some saint. The children's part is under the patronage of St. Aloysius and St. Stanislaus. We have now a vault of our own, but Mother Marcella was first buried just under a Chinese.

There are numbers of Christian Chinese in Lima ; in the cemetery their epitaphs are both in Latin and Chinese. The entrance is very beautiful. There is a fine figure of the Angel of the Judgment, blowing the last trumpet ; this stands outside the cemetery, then a short avenue of royal palms, and the cemetery chapel, in the middle of which is a dead Christ in white marble. It is arranged so that each side of its base is an altar, so that on All Souls' Day four Masses go on at the same time. The figure of the dead Christ is most beautiful. The Chilians tried to take it away after the war, but happily they found it too heavy. On the other side of the chapel is a very broad walk arched all over with beautiful flowering creepers and much visited by humming-birds—and then all around the great city of the dead.

I had to go property-hunting a little outside Lima, so I saw something of its surroundings, among others the property of the Magdalena which used to be lent to us, and where Mother Marcella used to enjoy so much the solitude and the sea. This gave us the opportunity of walking over the *huacas*, or burying-places of the Indians, which are in its enclosure. They are very interesting, and one can still see quite well the cells where they were buried . . . everything of value—pottery, coins, arms, etc.—has been taken long ago.

There is a beautiful wood of old olive trees in the Magdalena property. They were planted for, or by, one of the Viceroys, to whom it belonged, and now in their old age they are very dignified and beautiful, all the more picturesque because of the cream-coloured, long-horned cattle who stared and snorted at us from among the trees, but fortunately did not charge.

Little passion flowers grow wild in that wood, and nasturtiums, as large as our garden ones, and probably quantities of other beautiful things in the season of flowers, but this is winter. It is like our best September weather, neither hot nor cold. . . .

The portress brought a message one morning that the ' Governor of such a place sends his compliments and a bull for the Altar Society.' I was unfortunately with the Rector of the Jesuits, and could not for the sake of the *convenances* say, ' Will Your Reverence wait a minute while I go to see the bull ? ' So I had to let him go, though he was at the-door. The sacristan, who has charge of the Altar Society, blinked with satisfaction when I told her (she is stout, calm, and charming, like Mother Martinez in the days of her youth) ; it seems she is accustomed to receive an occasional tribute of bulls from devout friends, for the Altar Society. Sometimes they are so ferocious that they cannot be brought into the city, but this one had been led in as far as our door. He was ordered off to the butchers, or to be sold for a bull fight—no one knew which ! And he would be worth only about two vestments . . . as bulls are plentiful !

They had a disturbance in Lima the night before we left. Everything was ready for a disturbance, as the election of the deputies was to come on this week, and the Government were hurrying on with the paving of the streets, as paving stones are favourite and rather formidable weapons in the hands of the mob. This disturbance was about that wretched play ' Electra ' that had made such trouble in Spain. . . . As soon as the audience came out of the theatre it was ' Down with the Jesuits '—in the post of honour, of course—' Down with the Religious,' ' Down with religion,' etc., and they began to break windows.

Fortunately our children had a *sortie* that day for my visit, so they were not in the dormitories. One heavy stone fell close beside a child's bed and covered it with broken glass. In the Normal School the infirmary windows were broken and the shutters smashed in. They are so accustomed to that sort of thing that the students sleeping in the infirmary got up and went into the inner cloister, where they waited until the disturbance had quieted down, and then went back to bed.

They did not think anything of it, but of course we made a fuss with the authorities the next day, and the Jesuits were up all night guarding their house and expecting a worse attack the next night ; but others said that the troops would be out . . . and there would be nothing.

I saw a young Jesuit Father who had been tied and dragged through the streets of Quito five years ago when the Rector was shot at their College of Riobamba. . . .

Arica (almost at the boundary line between Chile and Peru),
May 26th.— . . . We had the great consolation of having
Mass and Communion this morning, so our Feast of Pentecost
has been a very happy one. We got here at six-thirty and heard
that there was a Mass at nine. Such a pretty little church, and
well kept—a wonder for a country district here. So we went
off in a small boat, about a mile to shore, and the priest kindly
gave us Communion at the beginning of Mass, as we did not
want to risk the possibility of the *Chile* going off without us.
. . . There is a beautiful rock five hundred feet straight down,
with a sad memory, overshadowing Arica. One of the first
battles of the war [1] was here, and the Chilians caught the
Peruvians in a trap, and when they saw it was hopeless, a number
of young Peruvians threw themselves over the rock into the sea,
rather than be taken prisoners. . . . So far this journey has
been in very good weather, and since Pentecost the sea has
been like a lake. . . . I cannot fix exact dates for Chile, as
the fast trains only run three times a week. . . . They tell
me I am sure to be caught in the inundations in Chile. The
railway bridges are swept away by them, some every year, and
the check to traffic lasts about a month. . . .

Pacific Ocean, Port of Caldera. May 30th.— . . . We are
coming to the most outlandish places of all, for they say the
Chilian ports are served only by this Company, and that means
only one steamer a fortnight to send or receive letters, except
when the Transandine route is open, and that is not now.
However I am prepared for everything except to find the floods
out, and the bridges carried away, and a month's delay in the
provinces, as they call them, *i.e.* at Concepcion, Talca, or
Chillan. . . . The Biobio which runs past Concepcion is the
worst to deal with in a flood. I believe last year one of ours
was just *lancée au domestique* as the flood rose over the line,
and so got through to probation.

We have two or three ports more before Valparaiso, but
we hope in any case to reach it by the 1st June. The captain
will receive a wire here as to whether we are to call at Carrizal
for copper. I hope the copper may not be ready for us, then
we skip the port. We have a Peruvian crew this time, very
light-hearted and not very business-like. The captain and
officers are, of course, English, very smart officers . . . their
clipped sailor-like English accent speaking Spanish to their
men is very amusing to listen to. . . .

Valparaiso: June 2nd.
. . . We arrived yesterday . . . my hopes of leaving Chile
on July 16th were broken up before I had been here twenty-

[1] War between Chile, Bolivia, and Peru in 1879.

four hours, because the scarcity of trains made me lose twenty-eight hours at once . . . so now the earliest I can hope for is July 30th.

English is the rage here and in Lima, as in Porto Rico and Havannah. English, Scotch and Irish people here are called ' Gringoes.' I thought this was a Chilian form of ' Jingo,' but it seems not. The first English-speaking colony that came here was Scotch, and they were always singing the old Scotch song ' Green grow the rushes oh ! ' to solace their exile *super flumina Babylonis*, and hence ' Gringoes.'

It amuses me very much to find the Irish expression ' after ' so and so, quite ordinary in Spanish here, and in Peru : for instance a person is ' just after going out,' etc. Perhaps it is only South American, and not Spanish Spanish, that admits it. I often think that Sister Maunsell's eyes will grow round and haggard over my Spanish if I come back with a Porto Rico intonation, and a Cuban lisp, and Peruvian idioms and Chilian mannerisms and an Argentine burr on it.

Good-bye, dear Mother, if this reaches you on July 25th, I shall be at Santiago, the town house, and at Santiago Maestranza somewhere about the 13th or 14th, and afloat again on the 30th, if all goes well.

Llai-Llai, between Valparaiso and Santiago : June 8th, 1901.

. . . Writing moments were scarce at Valparaiso, so I take twenty minutes here to scribble, while passengers breakfast : the trains oblige us to spend Sunday at Santiago. . . . Valparaiso in itself is not very interesting, though prettily placed. Our houses of course are always interesting, and travelling by land after so much by sea is quite a novelty. Part of this journey is said to be very beautiful, so far it is only pretty, of course this is a bad moment of the year, mid-winter, and there is nothing in flower except eschscholtzias, of which the railway cuttings are full, almost aggressively bright for the season, like people that will insist on chirping cheerfully in face of general disaster, and I see the berries of mesembryanthemums in the distance. . . . I thought of you all on Corpus Christi, and of each event of our beautiful day, from the dear First Communicants to the great ' Blessed be God ' in the crowded chapel after the procession. . . . It must all have been lovely. . . .

The stay at Santiago was only for a day. Mother Stuart returned there for the visit in the middle of July. In a letter of June 9 she wrote : ' To-day I saw Don Ladislas Larrain, who pulled Reverend Mother du Rousier up, when the mule rolled over the precipice at the Isthmus of Panama.' On June 10 she was again *en route*—this time for Concepcion.

On the way to Concepcion.

. . . This is another step forward. Santiago is so nice with all its holy memories of Reverend Mother du Rousier, and her grave. The alley of orange trees she planted is now loaded with fruit, and her cocoa palms are bearing fruit for the first time.

One of the Mothers at Valparaiso gave me such a relic, Mother du Rousier's copy of the Constitutions, and another gave me a very nice photograph of her and a scolding she had received in Mother du Rousier's handwriting—and I should add, profited by, for she never needed another admonition on that subject.

It was a great pleasure to see novices again at Santiago. Of course I have seen a few lay-sister novices, but not the flying virgins of the choir. They looked very like ours, standing together like a herd of deer, shaking their antlers, and looking over each other's heads and shoulders. Like ours, too, in that when they had the whole empty chapel before them, they would go four in a bench intended for three, and were making hospitable attempts to squeeze in a fifth when their elders interfered, also like in their eagerness for a *bouquet spirituel* when I had not been five minutes with them. They are only fourteen and two postulants. . . .

Santiago itself is not so very interesting as a town, except that it is Santiago de Chile. The ways and dresses are a little like Mexico, but not so picturesque, nor have they the beautiful little Mexican horses. They very often drive three horses abreast. There is one driver in the usual place and a man rides postillion on the near horse, wearing a poncha . . . of rather bright tawny colour or brilliantly striped in red and blue, or spotted like a leopard skin. The horses have beautiful mouths. They are often ridden with only a bit of rope through their mouths, and yet they turn with a finger.

It is very pretty to see the bright colour of the farmers' ponchas when they are riding over their farms on black cobby horses, and also agricultural damsels, daughters of the soil, in bright skirts ' riding a-farming ' with picturesque papa, and sitting so nice and squarely on their primitive side-saddles. The farmers have immense herds of cattle, rather fine ones sometimes, but they do not take the pride that we do in having ' level herds.' Their gaunt spotted pigs are repulsively ugly, with no pedigree whatever, and backs like the Andes in miniature. What an unspiritual letter! but I write of what is under my eyes at the moment. We have the real Andes in the back-ground of our view all day, beautiful snow-peaks in the sun, and you are all on the other side of those Andes and beyond.

We passed Talca two hours ago, and a crowd of Children of Mary, Consolers of Mary, children of the poor school, came with kind messages and quantities of lovely flowers. When we were clear of the station we offered the flowers to two Dominican Fathers who are in the train, for their church : they were very glad to have them, and in their beautiful habit with their hands full of roses and camellias, they might have come out of one of Fra Angelico's pictures of Dominicans in glory. . . .

The rain is keeping off wonderfully, it must be the prayers; we have just passed the remains of the great bridge that was carried off last year, the trains still go over a temporary construction, and that is where our communications might easily be cut. . . .

We have had a small earthquake as a specimen of the country's productions; the rather prolonged underground thunder and then the sharp shock are very impressive, and make one feel that we are only ' tenants at will,' *i.e.* at God's Will of this lower world of ours.

Concepcion : June 11th, 1901.

. . . Our arrival here, as they would say in the Circulars,[1] had ' *un caractère tout particulier*,' after a lovely evening of watching the sunset on the Andes, their peaks in glory and their bases inky black. It made me think of ' light on the hill tops.' We were only an hour late, not much in these parts. I had been warned that the Bishop would send his favourite milk-white horses for us, but after making a mental note that I must write early to thank him, having vaguely wondered whether their tails would be plaited, I had dismissed the subject from my mind.

The crowd of ladies at the station has now become familiar, and I go through the Chilian embrace with its varying gradations of cordiality, with a fair amount of fortitude and gravity : but this time when I had extricated myself from the advance guard who came into the train, I saw before me an expanse of Roman purple, and a pectoral cross, two hands in Roman purple gloves and a big diamond : the heart of a Pontiff and a parent expanded to receive us ! There was a Canon to right of him and a Canon to left of him, a secretary and the ' famulus ' behind, and a crowd of ladies around. I gathered together hastily the list of ecclesiastical titles and filial sentiments : such mouthfuls as the titles are, you cannot get on with anything shorter than *Illustrissimo Señor* or *Su Illustrissimo*. He insisted on my going in the carriage with him, and one of the Canons and a lady : the other Canon and the President of the

---

[1] Yearly letters sent to the Convents of the Sacred Heart, recording matters of interest in connection with the Order.

E. de M. took Reverend Mother de L. ; Sister de L. was handed over to the secular powers, a whole Christian family took possession of her, and the other ecclesiastics followed up in the last carriage. I hoped it was only as far as our door, but he was determined to ' see the thing through,' and told me he was going to preside at the Magnificat. He stood by while all the first greetings with the community and children were gone through, and then we went to the chapel. . . . He came again to-day and sang Pontifical High Mass, and the Rector of the Salesians preached a very nice sermon. . . .

The Bishops of South America have a very singular privilege since the Latin-American Council, they wear the red *Cappa Magna*, like Cardinals, only it is differently carried. There are yards and yards of train, and a Canon wraps himself up in it like a Highlander in his plaid, only on the other shoulder, and walks along behind the Bishop : it has a most singular effect, but the privilege is much valued. . . .

Reverend Mother du Rousier's first novice is here, first Chilian novice, such a dear old relic. . . .

On the way to Chillan : 20th June, 1901.

. . . We are off again in *Viam pacis et prosperitatis* on the way from Concepcion to Chillan, a short run, we shall arrive in time for the First Vespers of St. Aloysius. . . . The prayers are something wonderful . . . such a winter has not been known in Chile for twenty-five years. Day after day the rain holds up, and we have had three bright days out of ten, almost unheard of at this time of the year at Concepcion. Consequently we are having a very easy journey to Chillan along the course of the wicked Biobio that loves to come out at this time of the year, flood the country and carry off the bridges, and now looks as retiring and unassuming as a second-class European river in a dry season. . . .

All Chile is in a state of excitement about the election. President Errazuriz's time is up on the 18th September (if he lives so long— he is dying). But the election of his successor takes place on Tuesday next, the 25th, there were mild riots in preparation every night at Concepcion. The Bishop ordered an extra general Communion and the Litany of the Saints every day in public. An imp of the Third Division made signs of distress to the mistress of discipline (they call her ' Vigilant General ' in Spanish ; so pretty, I think) the first day before it began ; when the Vig. Gen. went to her she asked anxiously : ' Mother, which candidate is it for ? ' ' For neither,' replied the Vig. Gen., with equal apropos and dignity, so I do not know what the creature prayed for. It was not a moment to enter into the depth and breadth of the question at stake.

L

The Bishop was true to his colours to the last, determined
to show his paternal affection for the Society. He said he would
come the last day, say Mass at six, give Holy Communion, and
take us in his carriage to the station, though it was too early
for the white horses! And so he did. . . .

There are quantities of Religious Orders in Concepcion. I
saw the Superiors of seven Orders of priests alone, of course
they all go about in their habits, and when they come in twos
they are so nice to each other. An Augustinian, dead black
all over, came with a *Mercedario*, whose habit was radiantly
and spotlessly white, and their little running exchange of mutual
courtesies was so pretty. . . .

Talca : 3rd July, 1901.

. . . Did I tell you of our arrival at Talca. I suppose I
am getting accustomed to be, not myself, but someone named
to go through the thing as proxy for our Mother General, so
that I can stand a good deal, though each time I think of what
the huntsman of the Cottesmore called out at a big fence :
' Come along, my lord, certain death on one side, and eternal
shame on the other ! '

The platform was packed with a solid crowd, in the middle
of which were five priests and the council of the Congregation
of Children of Mary ; the Congregation of Friends of the Sacred
Heart, and Consolers of Mary in their blue and red ribbons,
forming a double line like a cordon of police through the crowd,
and strewing rose leaves ! ! ! all the way to the carriage ! (White
horses !) To walk through this side by side with the Parish
Priest and an enormous bouquet in one's hands was indeed
like ' being a fool for Christ's sake ' ; Reverend Mother de L.
followed with the Rector of the Salesians, and Sister de L.,
as usual, fell a prey to a Christian family. The most exquisite
part of the situation is having to look as if one liked it.

The house is charming, with a real church, with a real
church bell, and a nave, and two aisles, and a beautiful statue
of Our Lady of Mount Carmel high up over the altar. All
this the gift of the late Parish Priest, who is buried in the
sanctuary. The rest of the house is also very nice, with open
galleries like cloisters and beautiful orange trees loaded with
fruit in the quadrangle. There are one hundred and sixty
children between the Boarding and Day Schools, and an Elementary School and numerous Congregations of the poor. . . .

But I must tell you of an expedition that we had to make
to a property of ours called the ' Colorado,' where the community
go sometimes for the holidays, or to ' convalesce,' as they say
in the States. It was given to us some years ago, and we built
a house there ; so of course I had to visit it. The natives did
all in their power to dissuade us on account of the state of the

roads, for the rains have begun, and as the soil is clay until one gets to the mountains, and the roads are only tracks, you can imagine what they are like.

It is forty-two miles from here, and they told us all possible stories of how carts and carriages stuck fast in the mud and the oxen died of their efforts to drag them out, etc. However, we counted on the prayers and decided to go, Reverend Mother de L. and I, taking Mother Jele, the assistant, and a lay-sister. . . .

We started at six-thirty A.M., with three horses abreast, an outrider leading a fourth horse, which was to be added as soon as we got outside the town, as four are not allowed within the city limits.

When we had gone about an hour's distance from Talca, the pole broke. I must say that I have never in my life seen mud before, even in Louisiana. The marvel is that the carriage held together at all. We waited in pelting rain, up to the hocks and axle-trees in the mud, till the mounted servant, 'Delfin,' had ridden on to a *hacienda* and borrowed another pole. The next thing was that the sister put the bread through the window—I mean she broke the window, but retained the bread. This was not much loss, except that it let in a good deal of rain. About twenty miles from here we came to a *hacienda* belonging to the family of some of our children, who had sent word that everything possible was to be done for us. So we waited there while the man went to the pastures and lassoed four fresh horses, and with these we started again, having four led horses besides and saddles. About a mile from this *hacienda* we stuck fast in the mud, and remained some time. After a delay and much useless plunging, we saw a very brilliant *poncha* in the distance, and a countryman came splashing through the mire to join us. He had been sent by the mistress general of the Elementary School to see if he could render service, and indeed he did.

We walked on for a bit to lighten the carriage, having fortunately shod ourselves in the strong leather shoes of some of our Sisters. The men harnessed on two more horses with their lassoes, and after a while the carriage came plunging after us, and we went on a long way successfully. The system of four horses abreast is bad, as the two outsiders must necessarily pull at an angle and lose a great deal of power. It was wonderful how we got on, for every now and then it seemed as if by all mechanical and physical laws we ought to have overturned. The Sister was a farmer's daughter, and knew every track of the mountains—we took to the mountains after an hour or so— and she gave useful advice to the men at intervals. . . . We made her precentor of the Rosary on account of her big voice,

as we were saying it in Spanish. So it was 'Hail Mary, full
of grace.' . . . 'Good gracious, man, with six horses you can
get out of it,' when we stuck in a bog. . . . ' Blessed art thou
amongst women ' . . . ' put on two postillions,' etc. We had
to make her shut her eyes in the end.

About ten miles from Colorado there was a mountain stream,
swollen by the floods to a river, about as wide as the lake at
Roehampton, and the current was so strong that the coachman
said he dared not try it even with six horses, for the carriage
must turn over. So stern duty made us take to the saddle-
horses, and we left the carriage at a shepherd's hut close by the
river. Reverend Mother de L. mounted on a big bay horse,
the sister had a strong and hideous chestnut, my share was
one like the little terra-cotta Mexican horses we have in the
museum—very light made, active as a cat, and with a perfect
mouth. Delfin's accoutrements were rather like those of that
Mexican horseman, only he wore the poncha instead of the
sarapé. We had black mackintosh ponchas and helmets,
borrowed from the cavalry at Talca, for possible emergencies;
we put them on over our habits, caps and veils. They were
excellent coverings. . . . When we were mounted, Mother
Jele confided to us that she could never mount a horse without
getting a vertige. This would never do crossing a swollen
river, so it was decided that she should get up en croupe behind
Delfin, and with her eyes shut be transported across! This
was successfully accomplished. In fact we all got across very
well, with the water breast-high on our horses. I watched
Reverend Mother de L. coming across, and did not know
whether it was more suggestive of Joan of Arc or the mounted
police. She has a very good seat on a horse:

We left Mother Jele in charge of the faithful Delfin and
another servant and pushed on with the sister to get the house
ready. The rain got heavier and heavier, and between that
and the hour, darkness came on before long and the track grew
more and more like a long lake.

Occasionally one subsided to the girths in a mud-hole; but
the horses were very clever in keeping their feet in the streams,
and jumped very steadily, for we had a little jumping to do,
not big obstacles; but for some occult reason they had in a few
places laid logs and brushwood right across the track, perhaps
to break the current. The horses jumped them standing with
water up to their hocks, which was really clever, and I think,
thanks to the prayers, the Angels must have been given a
special charge concerning us, for in spite of slips and stumbles
none of them lost their footing. Finally we arrived at the
Colorado, our lovely villa, twelve hours after departure from
Talca.

A shepherd and his wife are in charge of the house. The Sister went off to the kitchen to prepare some supper, and we to find beds and bedding, etc. We had to trust to Providence for it to be dry, or we should have sat up all night. Mother Jele's adventures are too long to write, too interesting to abridge, quite indescribable. I must tell you when I see you, but it can never be the same as hearing her tell them. We had her bed made and sent her straight into it . . . when she arrived, in spite of her assurance that she was very much alive.

Then Reverend Mother de L. and I sat down to dry ourselves over a brasier with wood cinders, while the Sister hung her things to dry in the kitchen. We had a good long talk of many holy things, and at last Reverend Mother suggested that we had better go to bed a little earlier as we had a long day behind and before us, and we found it was ten o'clock . . . so with some confusion and amusement we said night prayers and retired.

They had wanted to send a Chaplain with us, but I had declined. We breakfasted at six-thirty, and as soon as it was light made the visit of our property. It seemed quite a patriarchal visitation, to see the Society's flocks and herds, bees and vineyards. The rain had stopped, and the country is very lovely.

At eight-thirty we saddled up and started back. When we got to the ford where we had left the carriage, it turned out that the horses were off in the mountains and would have to be lassoed and brought in, so Reverend Mother de L. and I rode on to gain time. It was a beautiful ride of eight hours, and we had occasional heavy storms. The snowy chain of the Andes was very beautiful, and the nearer mountains were wooded up to the top. There were numbers of eagles about, solitaries of course, sometimes flying quite close to us, such beauties, and little partridges running among the acacia shrubs.

We telephoned from the *hacienda* half-way to Talca, as Reverend Mother de Bogaers had been in a great fright about us, and so about six miles from home we met a carriage with four fresh horses that she was sending for us. Our mounts were quite done up, so we were very glad of it, and as they were picked horses, as well as fresh, they took the hills at a gallop, Roscrea fashion, but in the state of the roads and the bridges, I do not know how the springs held out !

Anyhow, we got back in time to change clothes and get Benediction, and we were none the worse for the wettings, only poor Delfin is down with fever, but that belongs to Mother Jele's adventures. I am very glad to have seen the Colorado. . . . . We shall be five weeks nearer home when this reaches you. I hope it will not get lost. . . .

From Talca Reverend Mother Stuart went to Santiago, where she spent seventeen days. The next letter in the collection is dated :

S.S. *Oropessa*, Straits of Magellan : 4th August, 1901.

. . . Here we actually are ! or rather not actually but potentially in the Straits. We ought to be there, we are supposed to be there, we are bound to be there, but we are not yet there, but still in very rough water between a group of needle rocks called the ' Evangelists ' on the north, and another group called the ' Apostles ' on the south : or according to the less detailed charts, between Desolation Island and Cape Pilar. We have had three days bad weather, and yesterday were solemnly battened down, and the waves broke over us *ad libitum*. This has put us back a good deal, but they say one cannot expect anything else at this time of year. Now we shall be in smooth water for a day, and then we shall see what the Atlantic will do for us. They say it is much better than the Pacific at this time of year in these southern latitudes. How nice it will be to be at the same side of the world again and not at the back of God speed with the great ridge of the Andes between us. . . .

5th August.—We did get into the Straits at last at ten A.M. The Captain said it was because he could not pick up the light that he knocked about all night : he did not dare go too near the land, as he did not want ' to have us all in the water off Desolation Island,' and indeed I agree with his tastes, it would be a dreadful bit of coast for a shipwreck. . . . I saw the pretty little *Talca*, a sister ship of this, not a year old, a complete and pathetic wreck off Coronel, wrecked just a week before we passed. . . . We have the most careful Captain of the whole line, and with such a reputation that many people will not travel this way except with him, and this is his one hundred and fiftieth passage through the Straits of Magellan, so he knows the channels by heart.

It is wonderful to find myself here, anchored off the last Chilian Port, Punta Arenas, and with Tierra del Fuego the other side. We have seen no Patagonians yet, perhaps it is only in summer that their canoes come out in the narrows and swarm round the steamers with furs to sell. Now it is all in snow : by contrast, this day four weeks I hope to be near the equator. Orion was standing almost perpendicularly on his head this morning when I went out for meditation, his hunting-knife sticking straight up into the air, and the three kings were looking too foolish for words to a northern eye.

I cannot say too much of what the prayers did for the weather

in Chile, in that region and season of 'superabundant preci-
pitation,' as the guide books gracefully call the winter floods.
We were seventeen days in Santiago and had only one day's
rain, the rest all sunshine : bright Canadian sort of cold in the
mornings and a Roman sun at mid-day. The humming-birds
drop with the cold, either dead or ' spacheless,' sometimes they
revive in the warmth of the hand. When they pass one by,
with the flash of a red head and the gleam of a green waistcoat,
they make me think of the sudden flash of a happy thought
in a meditation that has gone flat.

We had a most beautiful sermon on the Feast of St. Mary
Magdalen from the Bishop of Ancud, the greatest orator they
have in Chile, and they pride themselves, rightly I believe, on
their ecclesiastical oratory. He is a great prelate, and they say
will be the next Archbishop of Santiago. At present he is the
devoted bridegroom of a somewhat unmanageable spouse, the
diocese of Ancud, which goes from a little below Concepcion to
the South Pole ! He has the whole of the Chilian part of Tierra
del Fuego, and whatever undiscovered land lies to the South.
He knows that he has three hundred inhabited islands, and does
not know how many besides, and so far he has scarcely any
priests who can speak or even understand the language or
languages. It is a heavy charge. He was just going off on his
Visitation to Tierra del Fuego, it will nearly all have to be done
in little boats or on foot, and as he is a gigantic prelate that will
be something like mission work in earnest, and the Confirmation
of the Patagonian babies a real labour of love. . . .

Now I am going to get the last variation on my Spanish, by
adding a little Argentine touch. . . .

The first smiles of the Atlantic were deceptive, we got into a
gale this side, but we are getting out of it and hope to get into
Montevideo to-morrow. . . .

Buenos Ayres : August 11th, 1901.

. . . This is very near Europe. Such is my reflection many
times a day and with great satisfaction, and I am saying to
myself many times also, ' the week after next.' Mother N.
used such a happy expression in one of her letters, that exactly
described what I often thought on sea, for on land there was not
time to think it, ' that those months on sea were paralysed.'
The time in Chile, no ! And now the end has come with a rush.

Miss G. came to meet us at Montevideo, with a deputation
of Montevidean ladies, who put me through some moments of
anguish, for they were very stout and stately, and would insist
on coming on board first, and then back with us down the
swinging staircase at the side of the steamer, into the bounding
steam launch, from there after a short transit, into a crazy
barge that was skipping alongside the river steamer to which

we were transferring ourselves, and one had to hop at a moment the waves were propitious across the water from one to the other, and first one and then another all but fell into the water, and what a fuss that would have made. . . .

In all our travels the fellow-passengers have left us perfectly quiet. Only in this last journey I made an acquaintance, for an old Scotsman came on board at Punta Arenas and when he saw my name on the passengers' list he came and claimed acquaintance on the ground of nationality, and wept, positively wept, over the murder of James IV, of which I had never heard such full details, and the broken heart of James V. It was an impossible grief to console. He played strathspeys and reels beautifully on the violin, and imitated the bagpipes to perfection, the drone in his throat and the air on the violin. . . .

S.S. Oravia : 28th August, 1901.

. . . This is, as the ballad singers say, ' for to make a beginning '; it will be ' for to conclude and make an end,' when we get off Lisbon, if the purser recommends to post there. . . .

We had to embark on the river steamer on the afternoon of the 25th [Feast of the Immaculate Heart of Mary], a day of great memories, having of course had Mass, the Archbishop's Mass, and Communion from him, and a good share of the Exposition. The Internuncio was coming for solemn Benediction, preceded by a sermon from a distinguished Jesuit, but I left before the function began, leaving Almagro in the quiet sunlight of Exposition.

You can imagine the happiness of finding on the *Oravia* three French Redemptorists and a secular priest . . . so there are four Masses every morning. . . . It is a great joy and makes all the difference in the world for these three weeks at sea. The days will crawl, of course, but not with such a creeping paralysis as in other sea journeys when there was no Mass or Communion.

There is a certain distinction in travelling by the *Oravia*. The Captain is a Royal Naval Reserve man, so we sail under the Blue Ensign instead of the Red. One feels all straightened up with respect under the Blue Ensign ; and as to the White ! I have seen it twice in these journeys : the *Phaeton* was at Callao when we came away, and another cruiser of ours, whose name I could not find out, was in the port of Montevideo when we arrived. . . .

September 8th, 1901.

. . . I got a most beautiful surprise yesterday at the Cape Verde Islands. I was buried in the study of the acts and decrees of the Plenary Latin-American Council of 1899, and had reached a touching note of how the *Eminentissimi* and *Reverendissimi* Fathers in Council had melted into tears of sweet devotion when they pronounced the Consecration to the Sacred Heart, when a shadow fell across my book : ' Madame Stuart,' and the Captain stood before me stiff and stately, holding out your letters. . . . I left the most Eminent and Reverend Fathers to dry their own tears of sweet devotion, or to have them dried by the students of the College *Pro Latinis,* who were allowed the privilege of shutting the doors and running messages for the Fathers in Council, and I spent a very happy quarter of an hour reading the contents, when an officer, neither stiff nor stately, came flying up the companion : ' Madame Stuart, I think ? ' bringing the novices' envelope and a letter from Mère le Bail. . . .

St. Vincent was all alive with niggers ; niggers to coal, niggers diving for sixpences, niggers selling bananas and shells, above all niggers screaming, yet for all that it seemed like a stepping-stone to Europe, with an interesting ' feel ' of being at the same time so near Africa. We only stayed four hours to take in three hundred tons of coal, and now we are labouring northward again against a head wind. . . . Probably we shall see Lisbon on Thursday . . . La Pallice, Sunday 15th, and if we catch the morning train, Paris Sunday evening, and Roehampton when !

Good-bye now . . . if there is anything worth saying I shall write from La Pallice, if not the next letter will be from Paris. . . . Meantime I shall see if the Eminent and Reverend Fathers' tears are dry. . . .

So ends the journal. A few days later the great lighthouse at St. Nazaire ' flashed to the wanderer " home," ' as she said in an essay, ' The Three Children in the Twentieth Century,' written soon after her return, for the community at Roehampton.

In a letter to Father Daignault she sums up the work of these months :

God's Providence has watched over these journeys wonderfully. I got into New York by the last boat before the quarantine began. I was prevented from taking a steamer on which I had set my heart, and saw her afterwards stuck fast in the sand banks at Guayaquil; another that I thought of taking had an outbreak of yellow fever on the trip, and was not received at all at the port I was bound for. . . . These, and numberless other things too long to write, have strengthened immensely my confidence in that dear Providence of God, and to tell you the truth, I think you will find me a good bit changed.

This journey has done me immense good, I hope, for my

soul, seeing so closely God's Fatherly care, being thrown entirely on my own resources, that is to say on His ; having to come out of myself and act and speak—in my imperfect Spanish— regardless of shyness, and also seeing the trials and difficulties of so many others, the good done, the virtues practised, all that has done me good. . . .

After a week spent in Paris to give an account of her mission, she returned to England on September 23rd. 'A few minutes before seven, we all went to the lodge,' runs the entry in the house journal. 'Reverend Mother arrived shortly after, she looked well and we were very happy. We went to the chapel and sang *In viam pacis*, it was a heavenly moment.' The next day her postponed feast was celebrated with great joy, and the result of seven months' work for poor churches was offered to her ; some eighty or ninety vestments, copes, altar linen, etc., etc. Her delight was great, for she was thus enabled to give help to some of the poorer missions in England—a work always dear to her. A few days later the children returned, and the old life was resumed.

For nine years, almost without a break, she devoted herself to training souls for God. Speaking of this time she called it her 'heroic age.' All the gifts, all the tastes, all that she had been and done in childhood and in early youth, all that had seemed to be stifled and wasted and cast aside on entering, sprang again to life and found, she said herself, the fullest outlet in religious life, 'in my own Order, which I love beyond words, and in which I am so completely satisfied.' There was about her at this time the serene confidence of one who had trusted and had not been disappointed, of one who had staked all on a great venture of faith and had found it a thousand times worth while.

Sportsman, lover of nature, poet, mystic, full of practical common sense, endowed with the keenest sense of humour, with gifts of heart as great as those of mind, clear-eyed and steady in her outlook on life, and withal the simplest, humblest, most lovable of God's saints, there were few souls with whom she could not find a point of sympathy and contact. And as the 'third stage' of her life, as she herself described it, now approached, 'she came back gradually to creation, and saw all things and people, beautiful again, but in God.'

These years saw, too, the formation of her deepest friend- ships. Writing in 1909, she explained her ideal on this subject :

'Complete trust, in which nothing else matters, because all is understood, is the only thing worth calling friendship. I have never been able to understand jealous friendships. It seems such a confession that the whole thing is a failure.'

Flashes of intuition showing her in symbol the treasures hidden in the souls of others, often formed the basis of these friendships.

Our highest friendships [she wrote] are staked on hazardous guesses, and silent understandings. By these I mean the friendships that are all of admiration and live in the ideal, not the prosy give and take of good offices, still less those that are exacting of affection, but the friendship in which our best self calls out, and the ideal other answers. 'How timely then a comrade's song comes floating on the mountain air,' even though we should not be able to catch the words, we are raised higher by what we have seen, by what we have guessed, and by what, in glowing consciousness, we believe to be there.

Soul touches soul [she wrote again], words and other contact are not necessary. Like ships that pass in the night, we have seen the lights and heard the voices. God allows the paths to cross, that sister souls may waken in each other the deeper springs that for the most part lie untouched.

Subsequent chapters will show her in the full exercise of these gifts, and reveal something of what it meant to have her for a friend.

CHAPTER XII

INNER LIFE

1894 *to circa* 1905

> ' But what puts us on our knees is the sight of a strong interior life
> within, and alien to, a strong outside activity : . . . when . . . is
> revealed a soul aloof from all these things . . . and in tone, not with
> the crabbed dialects of the class-room, nor with the fretful noises of
> courts and councils, but with the mountains, the firwoods, and the frozen
> stars of winter. This . . . through a width and depth of vision and a
> force of will, unable quite to submit to all these tyrannies.'
> From ' St. Bruno,' in ' Upon God's Holy Hills,' *by C. C. Martindale, S.J.*

HERE we must pause a moment in following the course of
events, and look at least, if full entrance is denied, towards
that closed garden, that inner sanctuary, ' the heart of your
heart, and soul of your soul,' as she herself described it.

What was the well-spring of her action, what the secret that
lay beyond the veil, the light that flooded all her life with joy?
To such questions no complete answer can ever be given.

The first record dealing with her spiritual life is concerned
with the period from 1894 to 1905. It is gathered from notes
of retreats, and from the pages of a correspondence with the
friend to whom reference has already been made,[1] and whom
she called ' the father of my soul.' This friendship began only
in 1898, so that for the first four years after Mother Stuart was
named Superior, a few short notes are the only clue we have
bearing directly on this inner life. Much, however, that she
could not, or did not, commit to letters may be gathered from
her writings. A more intimate knowledge of her is gained,
perhaps, from her poems and essays than from most direct
attempts at self-revelation.

The first note, already quoted, shows clearly the great
struggle of this period of her life. A struggle which few, if
any, realised. While her decisions and her words brought

---

[1] Father Daignault, S.J. See chap. vi, p. 71 and chap. viii, p. 92.

peace and a great sense of security to those around her, none
dreamt that she, meanwhile, was encouraging herself to decide
and act, and not to 'judge as if I must necessarily be wrong.'
'To trust,' in fact, as she wrote in an essay in 1903, 'to the
illative sense . . . the faculty of insight. . . . In the high
principles of human things, an almost prophetic intuition.
" So it is, or so it is not, I know not why, but so it is." . . .
A sense bearing swiftly and safely over the thin ice—too swiftly
to be engulfed ; the ice would not bear if the mind rested for
a moment, but the end is reached.'[1]

A woman's faculty, it has been called, and it was one of
which she had more than an ordinary share. It is perhaps
among such people that this painful feeling of insecurity is
most often found. With clearest vision they have grasped the
end, raised their palace of music ; then slow reason reasserts
itself in them, or in some cautious monitor, and what has been
seen as utter truth appears suddenly to be without foundation.

As the weight of responsibility grew upon her she turned
herself more and more to prayer. 'I have understood more
clearly,' she wrote in 1896, 'that all results and fruit in souls
must come from God alone. I wish above all to acquire interior
spirit and union with the Sacred Heart, therefore—apply myself
lovingly to prayer at all times. Give all stray moments to
prayer, even if it should seem to me desirable to think out
something, rather pray about it instead. "For your Father
knoweth that you have need of all these things." This praying
at all times will mean for me, *rester comme Madeleine aux
pieds de Jésus, tranquille, humiliée, attentive,* and when the time
comes for action pray that the wisdom, the strength, the sweetness of Our Lord may be given to me ; then follow without
anxiety what seems to be the inspiration of grace.'

The same thoughts were uppermost in the following year,
1897. 'There must be more prayer in my life. I will make
an hour's prayer instead of half an hour's in the afternoon, in
order to have more and better to give to others.'

For the remainder of her life this determination to spend
at least an hour before the Blessed Sacrament every afternoon
was faithfully adhered to, and those who came to her for counsel
were frequently urged to do the same.

Another note, but a most characteristic one, is struck in
1898. '*Sequere Me.* Follow in the spirit of the meditation of

---

[1] From *A Specimen of the Thoughts of 1903. The Reality and the Value
of the Illative Sense.* J. Stuart.

de regno, seeking in all things His Person and His Personal
service, the best I can give under the circumstances.   I
must lead a really Apostolic life, look always at the mission,
the means, the end, go without "impediments" of which self
is the greatest.   The thought of self, either in good or bad,
shall be a forbidden subject for me.'

To those who lived with her, this ideal appeared to have
been attained, but, looking ever from a higher standpoint, she
herself judged otherwise.   Many years later, commenting on
the words of Our Lord, ' Father, forgive them,' she wrote to
an intimate friend : ' The " self-oblivion of love " was what
caught and kept my attention.   I think it is the thing that one
longs for, and yet cannot attain.   God alone can give it, for
it is so different from self-repression ;   that is not even the
way to it. . . . To act as if one were oblivious of self, that is
elementary self-abnegation; but to live within oneself, with a
constant hush on one's self-movement, that is just where one
might spoil it all, by too great attention to repress it.   And
so it seems to come back to waiting and longing for it, to under-
·stand and to have it.'

But, as she wrote of another, ' God wished to take her
sailing out into the glory of His thoughts and love '; and she
needed the guiding, strengthening hand of friends in the difficulties attending such spiritual ventures, to help her on the
slippery ice and counsel her in the dark ways.   And just at
this moment one of these was brought across her path.[1]

In 1898, having written to the Provincial of the Jesuits to
ask for a Father for the community retreat, and having expressed
a wish that it should be given before her departure for North
America in August, she received an answer saying that no
Fathers were available for the date named, except one who
had just returned to England to beg and work for his mission.
He was quite unknown to her; but, armed with the Provincial's
permission, she wrote to make arrangements for the retreat.
The Father,[2] however, excused himself: he was not a suitable
person for nuns, he said ; he was only fit to preach to Jack
Tars, simple, downright souls.   The tone of the letter pleased
Mother Stuart, and she wrote again, saying that that was
exactly what she and her community needed and appreciated,
and so the retreat began.   She was not making it, and it might
have seemed as if it could have no great part in her life ; but

---

[1] Chap. viii, p. 92.   [2] Father Daignault.

it was especially for her that God, as she said, sent this director from the ends of the earth. She was won to confidence by his downright speech and manner, and evident insight into the things of God; and for years she sought his counsel in her letters, and wrote freely of all that concerned her own soul. Her resolutions of retreat were frequently submitted for his approbation. The value she set upon this friendship can be gathered from her own words : ' It is a grace,' she wrote, ' to feel the repose of being understood and of speaking without difficulty or *arrière pensée*, a unique grace in my life of shy solitude.' And again, in another letter : ' I can have *decem millia pedagogorum sed non multos patres*, and having one I shall profit to the full, if God gives me the chance.'

The following extracts have been taken from a paper which, written to him a few months later, appear to refer to this time.

I. I live in confidence because I have nothing else to live in. God is so good as to give me a steady and constant light on my sins, miseries, and foolishness, so that I live also in a state of shame and confusion : which is good, I suppose, in so far as it keeps me flat in the dust before God, and bad in that I let it paralyse me sometimes and make me exaggeratedly shy and diffident. My great battle is against shyness. Could this be the *one* thing that is an obstacle to one's gift of self to God ?

II. I get phases of this paralysis, but find it answers best to close my eyes and go on recklessly, feeling that things are so desperate that God must bring them right, because of His own great goodness.

I almost enjoy now this human despair, because it makes a solid foundation for hope, as there is no lower depth to reach. I think it is like what people say they feel in drowning: when the choking is over, it feels like sinking into nothing and drowning, but being resigned to drown, and hope remains.

. . . Realising responsibilities sometimes gives it to me. Of course councillors can only help us up to a certain point, then we must take the decision. I do it with great sinking of heart, but a determination not to look further, and a sort of confidence at the back that God will pull me through, and the thing decided also. He does this wonderfully and often. . . .

III. About exterior mortifications. When one is held very severely for this and allowed very little, how can one avoid losing the taste for them ? The giving up one's own will in the matter does not insure this, does it ? And how can one replace them as a means of obtaining spiritual light ? For they are this, are they not ?

The answers given she summarised shortly :

The state of shame and confusion is good, but let the sunshine of God's mercy and goodness and love penetrate your soul, vivify it, strengthen it, fill it with light and warmth. . . . Resist that sense of paralysis with all energy . . . it may prevent you doing for God and souls what He expects from you. . . . After taking the ordinary means to arrive at a right decision, act fearlessly, resting confidently on the special guidance which the Holy Ghost gives to those in authority. . . .

Make up for exterior mortification by greater interior mortification and closer union with God. . . .

Be careful not to judge too hastily, too severely . . . without shutting your eyes to defects and faults, have them *open to see all the good which is done and be ready to praise it.* . . .

Esto vir. I tell you in God's name that *all is right.* Now go ahead ! and God bless you.

These last words and the promise of a daily memento in his Mass were a constant source of comfort and support through life.

The friendship thus begun only ended with her death, and it was by no means one-sided : ' once her influence is felt,' he said many years later, ' it is for a life-time.'

But scarcely had the comfort and strength of this new friendship been given, than Mother Stuart was sent off for nine months to North America ; and before her return Father Daignault had set out once more for his distant mission. They met but rarely in the course of the next few years—a circumstance to which we owe the following letters.

Guadalajara, Mexico : December 24th, 1898.

. . . Spiritually I am somewhat battered and dusty ; you will say ' better to be dusty than drowned.' Since some intensely happy days at St. Charles with Mother Duchesne, I have been living in dust and ashes on the seven Penitential Psalms and fighting hard. I do not say much about myself, you tell me ; it is just for the reasons that you suggest—first, I hardly have time to think on that subject ; secondly, I am trying to keep things in their right order : (1) God, (2) neighbour, (3) self ; yet I have some notes of things that I hope to tell you if you are still there when we return, some touches of God's wonderful goodness, and some thoughts that have gone into the very soul of my soul and opened new horizons. These will have to wait. . . . A nun at Brighton sent me a few thoughts from the triduum you gave there. I was very glad of them, especially for the meditation on the Crucifixion. I am sorry to say I have no insight into the Christmas mysteries, more and more the Passion fills up the horizon of my prayers, and I am looking forward to the Octave of the Epiphany, after which I can go back to it. . . .

Mexico : January 3rd, 1899.

Your letter, so full of kindness as always, was an unexpected pleasure. Thank you very much for it, and for all your wishes for me in 1899. I shall be rich indeed. Thank you too for saying ' when I pray for you at Mass,' it is nice to hear it. . . . A remembrance in your Mass is a special grace for which I cannot thank you enough.

There is a wonderful providential care over Mother General's journey. It must be the prayers, and I am getting so accustomed to it, that I do not have ' the shivers ' any more at my responsibility to the Society for the care of her, but have a fixed conviction that whatever things may look like, they will turn out all right in the end. It has happened so often already. There are moments that are excellent for the exercise of confidence, you will be glad of this for me ! In fact in many ways this long journey is a good discipline for me ; for my rashness, impatience of form and ceremonies, and other vices of the same kind.

To go to another subject. When one is somewhat laboriously trying to pray, and a thought cuts clean across the current that one was following, without any relation to it, and filling one's soul with consolation, one may take it as coming from God, may one not ? . . . I know you prefer questions in concrete form, so here is an instance. We had a delightful night with the Blessed Sacrament exposed, to see the New Year in, and I took for my occupation *trahe me post Te, curremus*, etc. There came suddenly right across that (I do not mean like a voice, but like a flash of thought from the Blessed Sacrament), and if I may say so, almost playfully, ' What is thy petition, Esther, and what is thy request ? if it were the half of my kingdom it should be given thee.' I do not know if I was more filled with confusion or consolation ; it seemed to come from God, inviting to unlimited confidence and *hardiesse* in prayer—did it ?

And I ventured to ask for ' that certain part and fellowship with His Apostles and Martyrs ' that is prayed for in the Mass.

Grand Coteau, Louisiana : 4th Feb., 1899.

Reverend Mother General decided to stop here and make her retreat, so I took advantage of the opportunity and have made mine too. You will see the direction in which my thoughts have turned by the paper which I enclose, of course it can be torn up when you have read [it], as I have kept a copy—not

M

for the same purpose I hope as the priest that had his resolutions 'that had never been used quite fresh for the following year!' Anyhow you see I want to go out into the harvest-field like Ruth and glean after the reapers, and according to the advice you gave us last year, not only to 'love God and go ahead,' but to love my neighbour and go ahead. . . .

I have made a real and realistic meditation on hell for the first time in my life, and that ought to bear fruits of zeal for souls. I took it by contrast with heaven, the twenty-first chapter of the Apocalypse, point by point. No one but the 'enemy of human nature' to say 'they shall be my people and I will be their God.' No one but him to say 'I will be to him a father and he shall be to me a son.' Such a father and such a sonship. 'God will wipe away all tears from their eyes,' the enemy mocking at these tears. 'Behold, I make all things new,' the eternal weariness of hell. 'I will show thee the bride, the wife of the Lamb.' I will show thee what was meant for God, and is cut off from Him for ever, and so on. It is very awful, but I think profitable. . . .

[Paper enclosed.]   February, 1899.

'The harvest is indeed great, but the labourers are few. Pray ye therefore the Lord of the harvest that He send forth labourers into His harvest.'

One real labourer is worth ten mediocrities. I will try to excel in the things which seem to me to make the real labourer.

I. Fear. By motives of Faith to realise what is the loss of glory for God, the loss of souls, the loss of graces. This spur is necessary.

II. Love. *Fortis est ut mors dilectio.* Nothing can resist love. God Himself cannot resist it, neither can souls. To live without love is to vegetate in oneself. Love is itself an apostleship, and the condition of all apostleship, and the power of all apostleship. It makes everything possible.

Love is giving oneself with one's own hands to all, at all times, for the sake of the one loved. Love all so as to see the best in all. Love so much that I shall never believe anything to be impossible.

III. Prayer. Constant, intimate personal intercourse with God.

Do you approve of this? Is it *in vias rectas*? If so, please make the sign of the Cross over it for the grace of perseverance.

Now let me tell you what use I have made of the direction you were good enough to give me two months ago, and also thank you most gratefully for your letter of September 2nd, which was almost as great a surprise as the one that met me on the *Dominion*. . . .

I recognise the truth of what you told me, that I have a tendency to draw things too fine, and so lose freedom of spirit and concentration of energy on the one thing necessary; also the tendency to judge too quickly and severely, though I do not think I hold to those judgments when I reflect on them.

I have not been drowned once since I saw you! and hardly know myself, when I find firm ground under my feet, with no possibility of doubting. It is a great joy and I thank God with deep gratitude for putting my soul (as He did Himself, I think) into your hands. There is plenty of fighting of course, but I am trying, exactly as you say, to laugh at what would have drowned me a short time ago. It is difficult sometimes and my act of confidence often consists of 'I firmly hope because Father Daignault said it was all right.' This wandering life is not an obstacle to prayer so much as I expected, though the first effort to concentrate my attention is greater.

My particular examen which puts me back *comme Madeleine aux pieds de Jésus* is always a help, with flashes of very great joy in realising for a moment the mysteries in the thought of which I am trying to live. Sometimes the question arises: 'Of what use is this? It is nothing but activity of imagination delighting in its own exercise.' I answer it thus:

I. Even if it is so, better that it should be on these subjects than on others.

II. The thoughts that come to me thus are clear, simple, and joyous. You told me to open my soul to such thoughts and even to pray for them.

III. They leave me with greater desires for good, and better disposed for harder moments that may come afterwards, and so at all events they cannot be bad.

Now please do not think that I want an answer to all this, if it is all right; but I know that if I went off the *via recta* you would stretch out a hand to put me right. . . .

The following description of her, written by one who knew her well in her last years, is not without interest here, bearing as it does on what she calls 'this tendency in herself to judge hastily and severely.' He writes: 'The fineness of her nature, the completeness of her training, the sensitiveness of her tastes, the breadth of her horizon, the perfect balance of her judgment, produced in her a certain instinctive quickness for detecting faults and shortcomings, which would have made another critical and restive, but in her it was permitted no more than to sift the chaff from the wheat.' [1]

---

[1] Rev. Alban Goodier, S.J., Archbishop of Bombay.

A few weeks later she wrote again :

Providence, Rhode Island : 11th March, 1899.

. . . Let me finish with a word about my soul. It is doing day-labourer's work, breaking stones, and I am doggedly ' hoping against hope,' though seeing no reason for doing so except that I am told to. I had such a nice letter from you in New Orleans. It helps me very much, and I often read it over. For Lent my programme was not to miss a single opportunity for mortification that had not been actually forbidden by obedience. I wonder if you will think this is a fanciful way to help myself to it. I took it that the ashes received on Ash Wednesday were the raw material for forming a Crucifix for Good Friday, and that every act of mortification is to shape the ashes into the Crucifix—to give expression to the eyes, to the brow, etc. Is that a very childish idea ? It works well practically, but I wanted to carry it through without a miss, and I have had three so far ; it takes pretty constant attention.

Roehampton : 28th July, 1899.

. . . All the business is in the other letter. I thought I would put my soul affairs on another sheet, and in fact I am almost ashamed of writing about them at all to such a distance and where the pressure of work and the ' instant need of things ' must be so great ; yet you were good enough to allow me to write, and it is a hold upon one's soul to feel that one is held, and I know that you will always give me a place in your prayers. I had a Canadian summer, short and warm in the month of the Sacred Heart ; since then my enemies have been on the war-path again and I have had to fight. But things are not going badly on the whole. The tendency of good thoughts in June was to *simplify* everything. I know what you will think about this, and the thought that remains is that ' the law was our pedagogue to bring us to Christ,' and that perhaps I have made *too much of the pedagogue*; anyhow, that the one thing necessary is the personal service of a personal Master, and that I must pass more and more from the law to the life of His service.

I do not yet succeed in reasoning against overwhelming thoughts. It seems to me I might as well try to stop a run-away horse with a syllogism, but I fight and am not drowned; all that you have written to me helps me, and I try to express my thanks by grateful prayers. . . .

Roehampton : 7th September, 1899.

. . . This is not a letter that expects an answer, but only to express my most grateful thanks for yours of July 31st. . . . It was a great joy in more ways than one, and brought me light and help, as your letters always do. . . . God has been so good to me through you that I have a direction for life. . . .

Things have gone back now into their ordinary course, and the months in America are getting into perspective. As to the outside, they have taught me a great deal, made me feel older and more sure of things, not as if I had to feel my way so much. They have left me also a sense that life is hurrying on to its end, not with any particular thought of the nearness of death, but rather of the shortness of time and that one must work while it is day. . . .

Roehampton : Epiphany, 1900.

. . . This is too much of a missionary feast for me to let it close without wishing you a happy one. They sang ' How beautiful are the feet of them that preach the Gospel of peace ' after Benediction, which finished off worthily a good day for missionary prayer. I have spent all my meditation time with the Queen of Saba, whose daring search after wisdom fascinated me. If she had lived a few centuries later, what an intelligent disciple she would have been of the ' greater than Solomon.' . . .

Now I must tell you about my soul. As regards the active life, things have been better. . . . The contemplative life has not been so good the last few months. As one goes up the other goes down. This is of course not what ought to be, but what *is*. Holy people succeed *à mener de front* the two lives, but I do not. This is no doubt want of mortification. My balance always dips to one side or the other, not always to the same side. The year takes its colour from the retreat ; if that has turned mostly on intercourse with God this dominates in the year, perhaps somewhat to the detriment of action. If things have turned more on action during the retreat, prayer goes down a little during the year. It is nearly a year since my last retreat, and that is the retrospective view. I have had on the whole less consolation ; not that I have been without it : there are moments when I seem to have some insight into what the love of God means, and a great burst of music goes through my soul, gratitude and confidence and admiration, and a great deal besides, but the general prayer of every day has been harder. And I have had some bad moments, too, when thinking of my duties and responsibilities and how I accomplish them. I can best describe these as slipping on a *mer de glace*, with an encouraging ' Go ahead ! ' from your Reverence keeping me on my feet, and going. You will laugh at this, but you will understand what I mean.

At those moments there is nothing for it but to make up one's mind *not* to see and *not* to feel and *not* to ask questions, but to remember what one has been told, and keep on moving somehow, and somehow action seems to restore equilibrium after a time, or God comes to the rescue. My instinct would be to seek to recover light and balance by a great deal of corporal mortification, but since I entered religion I have never had my way in this. It is always a light and a comfort to know that you pray for me, and *au fond* I always believe that God is helping me, and that, as you told me, ' In God's name all is right.'

Roehampton : May 16th, 1900.

. . . What a delightful surprise at the beginning of my retreat to receive your letter of the 3rd April, bringing the blessing that always does me good and the assurance that you do not forget my soul. . . . Now let me say a few words about my retreat, please Father. I began it with very good dispositions as to confidence, but with a sort of weariness of the uncertainties and perplexities of life, and an impatience to tear the veil away and see how everything is to come straight, and God be glorified and proved right in the end, out of so much that seems to go wrong. I despise and disavow this weariness and impatience as a most unworthy and cowardly frame of mind, and with my will I am perfectly content to struggle on and take decisions, and do the best I can and wait for God. . . .

I will put on another sheet of paper my resolutions, and one or two stray thoughts that have occurred to me. If you think of it when you are good enough to write again, perhaps you will tell me if these thoughts and resolutions have your blessing and approval, and you will, as they say in Ireland, ' cut the sign of the Cross over them ' for me.

My spirituals are simplifying, and confidence in God grows steadily. I know you will be glad of this. . . .

[Paper enclosed.]   May, 1900.

    I. ' *Vocabitur Nomen ejus Admirabilis, Consiliarius.* . . . *Princeps Pacis.*' Take counsel of Him a moment before giving decisions.

    II. ' Son, leave thyself and thou shalt find Me.' *Stand without choice.* ('Imitation,' III. 37.)

    III. ' *Quis nos separabit ?* . . . *Tribulatio an angustia ?*' Therefore my soul always in peace, *why not ?*

Stray thoughts, are they true ?

What you take from the body you give to the soul, and what you give to the body you take from the soul (beyond necessaries).

You cannot go wrong in mortification if it is done with liberty of spirit. Too little produces repugnance for it. Too much leads to anxiety. Freedom of spirit shows the right balance in the matter.

Our Lord took the scourge to drive the buyers and sellers from the Temple. But He was ' ready for scourging,' *ego ad flagella paratus sum*,—not inflict anything as correction that one is not willing to bear ten times more of oneself, from love.

Tact in those called to the apostolic work is the perfect blending of the serpent and the dove—then it must be possible, since both are *commanded*.

Better from all points of view to ' mourn and be comforted ' than not to mourn and not to be comforted.

Suffering and sorrow, ' the mourning of the saints,' was never far removed from Mother Stuart's path, and were to grow with her growth in love for God and man. But the best of comfort was not withheld. ' In one moment God will give you such a heavenly visitation as will wipe out the suffering of years,' she said once, in a tone of conviction that betrayed experience, and her letters speak sometimes of such moments.

Roehampton : August 5th, 1900.

. . . I see by your letter that for the first time one of my letters to you has been lost ; for the account of the Queen's visit to Mount Anville has reached you, but you had not received a long letter I wrote by the same post. I could very easily have forgiven the postal authorities for losing the account of the Queen's visit, but I should have very much liked the letter to reach you, as it was written during my retreat, and it gave you an account of it, as well as of other things.

As to the retreat, the same thing as usual happened to me, the real help of the retreat came afterwards, and came especially in the realisation of the words ' in the world you shall have distress, but have confidence, etc.' So that I understood that distress is to be the normal of life and that *il faut s'y faire*. It is to be the matter of course, and when things are calm and go well for a moment that is not the normal, but only a breathing space. This simplifies one's point of view very much and detaches from many things. It was a very happy light to me because these three months have been very anxious ones, trying to save a beautiful young life from making shipwreck amongst dangers and temptations that seemed endless and diabolical. I never realised the devil's personal action before, it is very horrible to come in contact with it. I do not yet know which way this case will end, but some good has been effected. I understand how intolerable it must be for priests to see souls occupied with themselves and making account of their own difficulties, when there are so many souls in danger, to be prayed for or saved.

I am trying to do my best, and leave my own soul to the mercy of the Sacred Heart ; sometimes a whole ocean of joy sweeps through it, and the rest of the time it goes on as it can.

I have changed my particular examen and make it now on doing each action as if for the last time : this makes me accept responsibility, distress, uncertainty better, and keeps away impatience for the solution of things.

I had a lesson in it this week in the rather sudden death of my brother Horace . . . he got a sunstroke in bicycling and died in forty-eight hours, apparently unconscious, but Mgr. C. gave him conditional absolution, and he may have followed everything though unable to make any sign.

We were very specially united and I am very grateful that he has died before me or before I am moved from Roehampton, as he would not have liked either of these things. He died on the First Friday of the month, wearing the badge of the Sacred Heart and the brown scapular. I saw him three weeks ago to-day in perfect health, and planning to spend his holidays among the old cities of Italy, ending at Assisi. It makes the end of life seem very near.

Roehampton : 13th September, 1900.

. . . The after-lights of my retreat . . . continue to help me, and I think things are going fairly well spiritually. I have been so taken up with other people's troubles and difficulties, which seem to absorb all my prayers, that I don't seem to have followed up my own soul at all. I suppose this has its advantages. But I think the intimate study of Our Lord loses some what by that constant pressure of praying for others. This is off me a little lately, but the pressure of work is considerable ; this does not, however, or ought not to interfere with prayer.

My brother's death has made me live very much, if I may so say, on the edge of life, feeling how short it is, as if my hand were almost on the door which he has just passed through ; it is a help in one way, but I have to struggle against a feeling of unreality in it.

Roehampton : 2nd November, 1900.

I am not down in the depths, Father, by no means, and I don't think I am meant to *me faire à la détresse* within, and if it is only without, you won't mind such a trifle for me ! Or rather you would approve of my trying to pass into the ranks of those who ' rejoice in adversity, are restored by suffering and refreshed by sorrow,' as St. Gregory says. Sometimes I think that I am just beginning to understand this a little, certainly the last clause of it ; there are certainly some sorrows that are most refreshing and do one a great deal more good even than joys (or than most joys). Spiritual joys, however, are very refreshing too! Yesterday, the Feast of All Saints, was a very happy one in a realisation that everything here is so transitory, not worth troubling about, and that the joys and realities and glories of God's kingdom are really, *really* there, and will be shówn to us one day.

The Feast of All Saints was always a day of joy to Mother Stuart. 'I am spending All Saints at Seville,' she wrote in 1912. 'Many thoughts will meet at Roehampton, where it is one of the heavenliest days of the year.'

A change of tone in the above letter will not escape those who knew Mother Stuart well. She speaks here, as it were, with something of the voice of later years. The secret of the change may be partly traced to the books she was now reading. It was about 1900 that she first met with ' The Revelations of Divine Love of Juliana of Norwich,' and, strange as it may appear, it was only in this year that she began, by the advice of Cardinal Bourne, then Bishop of Southwark, to *study* the works of St. Francis of Sales. These were in their various ways epoch-making discoveries to her.

Roehampton: 30th November, 1900.
. . . This ought to reach you between Christmas and the New Year. . . . I beg a remembrance in your prayers that the New Year may be one of fidelity and progress, as I wish to make it. I am not at all satisfied with this one, but at all events some useful lessons have been learned, some of my fear of death has gone. I have learned more about confidence in God, but I am miles away from what I ought to be, with all the grace that I receive.

One grace of this year has been that I have learned to know and appreciate St. Francis of Sales. I am reading his works a good deal lately and am full of admiration for them. I used to think him just a little too sweet! but see now that this is just the perfect balance and the delicate completeness of his sanctity. The letters to persons in religion are my delight at present. I know you admire him too, you have often quoted him to me, and many things I read in his works are, I know, your views.

Roehampton : 14th January, 1901.
. . . Your letter of December 10th, such a kind and precious one, reached me last week. . . . When I think of all that you and your Fathers and the nuns suffer for God out there, I am ashamed of my own existence, and convinced that I do not

know the meaning, or even the spelling, of the Cross. Such thoughts at least are salutary, and do not come under the head of drowning thoughts that have to be overcome. These last wash up and down like a tide over me, but have not done much harm lately, I think. There was so much joy in the close of the year and beginning of the new century—the Holy Father's Encyclical, the night of Exposition of the Blessed Sacrament, and midnight Mass to usher it in. All that, and all those days were very full of joy. Of course there have been moments of anxiety and perplexity as to what was best to be done, etc., all that belongs to the undesirable part of Superior, but that is meant to be so, I suppose, and cannot and must not be otherwise.

S. Juan de Porto Rico : March, 1901.

Having finished my work here, which was consoling within, but suffering very much from the political crisis outside, I have gone into retreat. . . . It is a very out-of-the-way place to make a retreat. . . . However, God took pity on my strange position. . . . As to the retreat itself, I came to the conclusion that the best retreats I have made were those in which the resolutions turned on the inner life, and not those in which I made plans or resolves as to my exterior work.

St. Mary Magdalen has helped me again. I don't know if I am right, or whether it is presumption to think that her relationship with Our Lord, so intimate, so devoted, one of the beautiful friendships of His life, is the type of what He wishes and allows my inner life to be. And with her, the mainspring of everything was that she loved Him ; then the work arranged itself, circumstances dictated the way of the apostleship, and guided by His Heart she always had the intuition of what to do, without a preconceived plan, and *au jour le jour*. Of course my Rule and the various duties that are given to me shape my life in the main, but there is so much that each day must bring and that has to be decided day by day, as the need arises. I feel this more than ever at present, for the isolation is complete. With such long distances and very irregular posts I cannot count on receiving any instructions or answers to questions from Europe. God has cut me away from my anchorage and sent me out on the ocean, with Him alone for my Councillor, for the next few months. I have a young secretary with me, but no one of whom I could ask advice, so I must do the best I can, counting on God from day to day, and I feel that this is excellent for me, though to you I may own that it is at moments a little crushing, and I have had some bad moments already, but *never drowned*. And you will not think that I mean by the enclosed resolutions that I don't

intend to do my best with all human means at my disposal ;
or that I am going to decide by 'saying a pair of beads and
doing first what comes into my head.' No, I am really trying
to do my reasonable best, and counting absolutely on God for
results. . . .

You see God really means to make an end of my shyness,
for this is a very different thing to travelling with Mother
General two years ago, and that time I thought was pretty
good training for it ! However, it is much better, and I go
composedly through things that would have 'destroyed me
entirely' at that time. You will be glad of this. . . . If you
can write to Buenos Ayres I should be so grateful, and it would
be very kind if you would give me any news you can of yourself. In the meantime I pray and offer all your intentions
daily to the Heart of Our Lord, and whatever you suffer. . . .
I do not ask you to pray for me, having such confidence that
you do not forget me before God. . . . Do you like my
resolutions ?

Feast of St. Joseph, 1901.

The real life is within, the smallest part is that which
appears. My intercourse with Our Lord will be the chief thing
in my life, and He, not I, shall be its centre. 'Where a man
seeks himself, there he falls from love.' ('Imitation.')

Be with Him as St. Mary Magdalen, *tranquille*, *humilite*,
attentive.

Swift to hear, slow to speak.

Give to others what I receive from Him.

Give to others as He gave, when He made Himself 'all
things to all men,' sympathy to their joys ; tears, His tears,
to their sorrows ; service to their wants.

Believe in the strength He gives, and act on the belief. . . .
Leave myself to His care. *Deus providebit.*

One more letter written towards the end of the journey
spoke of change and growth, and here this record closes. For
the next few years Father Daignault was stationed in England.
Whatever intercourse there was, was carried on *viva voce*.
That it continued on some lines, we gather from the following
note written during her retreat more than four years later.
The lapse of time is felt in the spirit and wording of the paper.

Roehampton : 10th November, 1905.

I am getting to the end of my retreat, and I should like
to ask you to bless my resolutions. Last year's were a help
to me all through, and in spite of many failures it has been the
best year of my life spiritually.

This is the programme for this year.

I was struck with the thought of Our Lady taking counsel with God—*Virgo prudentissima, et Mater Boni Consilii*—so I put all under her protection.

I. Take counsel with God. His counsel is generally for what is most hidden ; sweetness and peace are its true notes ; ' secret as the ministries which ripen the corn and make the wild flowers perfect in form and hue, where no eye of man shall ever see them.'

II. ' Never to need or seek recreation out of Jesus.' ('St. Philip Neri.')

III. Do all common things *doucement et bellement* to please Him only and moderate my eagerness.

What do you think of these ? I like them in prospect very much. It remains to be seen how I can work them out in daily life.

Here she seems definitively to have taken her stand, and to come before us in this self-made picture, freed from all trammels of self, clothed in liberty of spirit, adorned with simplicity, radiant with confidence, refreshed by sorrow, loving and loved, breathing peace and joy around her, for in her now and henceforth was ' God's homeliest home and His endless dwelling.'

But this was not the end. As she wrote herself in this year : ' All is restored, all is well, but all is not finished.' The period ending had been but a stage and a prelude. Life's problems had begun to solve. Nature, art, and symbol took new meaning. God had His part in each, and she understood, she said, ' that to turn from them, or to crush their solicitings, would be to warp the fibre of the soul.'

She had begun to read the mystics, and this gave her the explanation of what God was doing and was about to do in her own soul. ' I knew then that it was good to wait in silence for the salvation of God.'

Speaking in after years of God's dealings with her at this time, she said : ' After I was made Superior, I heard God's call again ; this time it was to break with convention, to seek the liberty of children, and to live free in His house.' The light came gradually. An invitation to unlimited confidence, ' *hardiesse* in prayer,' was followed many months later by that other word : ' These laws are not for thee.'

But ' the break with convention was followed by a great void, such as sometimes comes after self-surrender,' and at first ' the new freedom touched on something like despair, in the misunderstandings it occasioned. God does not pledge Himself to flood us with consolations because we do His will,' she said, and added ' nor will He always make our way clear. The moment of the most complete gift of self is often one of agony in the seeming insecurity in which one finds oneself. . . . But gradually the gift of self was simplified for me, and came to consist in a greater lowness of soul and nearness to God, and life became a glorious opportunity to pour myself out in love.'

How wonderfully she took that opportunity her life is witness.

CHAPTER XIII

WORK FOR SOULS. THE WAY OF THE CROSS

'God loves souls above all things, and will do everything for their growth : just as in His love and lavishness He has covered the Himalayas with His brightest flowers, unseen by any eye but His, so He will expend Himself to give the souls of His Saints their most perfect finish.'

From a letter, J. Stuart.

'As grace works,' wrote Father Gallwey in 1881, 'you will, I think, agree with the words of Saint Dionysius that "of all divine things the most divine is to co-operate with Our Lord in the salvation of souls." He will say to you . . . "If you love Me, feed my lambs." '

But 'no redemption has been wrought but by the pain of one who loved,' and those who aspire to share in this divine labour must expect suffering as their daily bread.

The Heart of Our Lord is a thorn-crowned Heart ; those who read its secrets are first pierced by the thorns. Sometimes suffering looms large in a life and all eyes behold it. Sometimes it lies within, and 'under a smiling and sweet countenance is hid a heart of great anguish.'

And so it was in the life of Mother Stuart : she hid from all the things she suffered. But those who were brought into close contact with her could not doubt the world of suffering, as well as of mystery and of joy, that lay veiled behind her serenity of countenance.

Her very temperament exposed her to a larger share of suffering than falls to many people [writes the Archbishop of Bombay]. The aspirations and cravings of her soul— the sense of distance and aloneness that enclosed her for years —the constant giving with no apparent return, these things would sometimes overwhelm her, and often drove her into herself where none could follow, or out to the work of God, where she might hide from herself ; but never did they break down that evenness of temper and that devotedness of service which alone others were allowed to know.

Then again the hunger of her heart after God, the longing
to find Him in this world, and in every part of it and in every
individual, especially every priest and Religious, at times were
crushed with disappointment, till the tears were forced from
her very soul; yet those who failed her never knew, and her
own hope fed itself and revived in the mystery of God's dealings
with the world.

In like manner the ideals she held of what man should be,
of what the Church of God should be, of what she herself should
be, as a favoured child of her Father, filled her at times with
an overwhelming sense of failure. Once for a long period in
her latter days it was an agony bordering on despair. Yet all
this was kept God's secret and her own, and the hope never
faltered however darkened, and the courage never slackened,
and none ever saw the hand tremble that continued to do its
work.

That the joy outweighed the suffering of her life, those who
knew her also knew. Her own words give good ground for this
conviction.

'I thought so much between the last two bells at supper one
day that it would take a whole book to expand it! I wish I
could write that book! It would be on the Love of God in our
religious life and the title would be *Domine, Domine, quis
sustinebit?*'

And the words of one of her Eastertide poems suggest the
same truth:

> Though but a moment as they pass,
> Such priceless joy they leave behind,
> Nor years nor sorrows can efface
> That golden glory from the mind.

But though this was so, at the end of her life she confided
to one who had shared something of her secret: 'Now I know
what crucifixion of the heart is.'

In the stress and burden of work, which seemed at times
beyond what could be endured, she said: 'When my soul is
altogether weary and sighing for God, I just stop a moment and
say: "My God!" The "my" is like a bridge leading to Him.'

'Once,' writes a member of the community, 'I had to intrude
upon the privacy of her retreat. I came away overwhelmed by
the anguish I met. I took her hand; it was cold, like the hand
of the dying, and I felt a tremor through her whole being. She
bade me go and pray. Another time I came upon her in a

similar condition close to the Tabernacle in prayer.' Thus she
paid the price for the souls she so loved in God. ' But it seems
to me,' continues the above writer, ' that in later years she
so ruled her soul that she could say to all suffering of spirit
" thus far and no farther," and her advice to others was " Say
with the voice of faith : ' Peace be still,' and do not allow the
waters of anguish to overwhelm your soul." '

> Peace and the Cross are one for those that be
> Across its arms at rest, nor speak nor stir
> Save in the accents of unuttered prayer,
>   Thy Cross itself the light,

she wrote, and her life was a vivid illustration of her thought.

Her interests were never confined within her convent walls,
not even when, as Superior General, so many thousand Religious
and children looked to her for guidance and inspiration. The
former were always indeed her chief care and solicitude, and
for them she was truly ' the one who carries the burden.'

But beyond them lay another circle, ever widening in its
circumference ; it included all manner of people, for in all parts
of the world there were those who claimed her as a friend.
Bishops, priests, parents and relations of nuns and children ;
chance friends of an hour whom God brought across her path,
for all she had a solicitous love, for all she was in the truest sense
a friend to whom it seemed natural to turn in sorrow and in joy.

One of these friends, the Vicar General of Southwark,[1] writes :
' She had in a high degree what Newman has beautifully called
" solicitude of heart," for all those in whom she took an interest.
Their joys were her joys, their trials her trials ; she received
much trust and affection, it is true, but then she gave more
strength and comfort to others than she could ever receive from
them in return.'

To each friend, it has been said, she appeared to be wholly
theirs. But as a mother does most for a child who is in difficulty, or perhaps handicapped for life, so it was with Mother
Stuart. She had a special love for the burdened, the lowly, the
poor in every order. It was need not merit that attracted her.
' Of four very dear children,' writes one of the quartette, ' it was
the naughtiest that had the place nearest her heart.'

Beyond all other causes, this double love of God and of the
souls He loved became her crucifixion. It brought into her life

---

[1] From an appreciation by Monsignor Brown.

a strain of suffering such that those who watched her in earlier days feared would break her health, and it did indeed shorten her life. To console the 'Heart which had so suffered' was her desire; '*Tantus labor non sit cassus*' her prayer. 'I esteem it an inestimable favour,' she wrote in a little book of meditations not meant for other eyes, 'to receive one stripe, that it may not be inflicted on Him. . . . If I take it with patience, He will take content in it, and it will give Him no small comfort.'

To help a soul there was nothing she would not do. The number she befriended in trouble, encouraged to go from good to better, taught to understand and appreciate life, made to believe in her ideals, to love and know God better, is incalculable.

Once when the fall of a loved soul seemed imminent, and all hope was given up by those who had not reckoned with the force of a Mother's prayer, she spent the greater part of the night in the chapel at Roehampton, with two others. A few hours before the fatal deed was to be done, he who had threatened the destruction of this loved child was suddenly struck down and died in a short time, saying to one who had connived in his project : 'This is the hand of God, have nothing more to do in this matter.'

She often asked one or other of her community to help her in this divine work, especially those who were suffering. She would, as it were, beg for their sufferings for the soul in peril. On one such occasion she received a letter from a former child of the house, for whom much had been offered in prayer and penance. 'How is Mother X. ? ' it ran. 'I was troubled in my dreams by seeing her lying in great pain and offering all for me,' then followed resolutions to do better. The nun in question had died after a short illness, and her sufferings during it had been offered at Mother Stuart's prayer for the soul in question. The girl's letter was dated the day of the nun's death, but coming from a distance, reached England when all was long over.

Another time, when suffering greatly from her anxiety for the safety of a soul, after a sleepless night, towards morning Mother Stuart fell asleep, and in her dream Our Lord stood by her and revealed to her the future and the safety of this soul.

' Many a time,' writes one whose privilege it was to share her sorrows, ' when I witnessed her anguish of heart for one or other of the many souls she won to God, the words of the Bishop to St. Monica were my comfort : " A child of such prayers and tears cannot perish." '

It was not even necessary to have met her to enlist her help

N

and sympathy. During the short period of her Generalship, just three years, a friend whom she had never seen received no fewer than fourteen letters written by her own hand.

I felt [writes another] a great attraction for Reverend Mother Stuart, even though I had never had any personal intercourse with her. Her writings and all I had heard of her drew me to her irresistibly. Sorrows, too great, I thought, to confide to any human heart, had entered my life. An inspiration came to me one day that they were not too great for her; she surely could help and sympathise. So I wrote, and with all confidence told her of my many and great needs. Her answer came quickly, and with the intuition and sympathy of the saints I found she understood all. Her words and prayers changed me at once, and the whole aspect of my life. . . . I feel her influence is ever with me brightening the way . . . so hard until the touch of her spirit changed my weakness to courage.

Her love for and outlook on humanity were Christ-like, and led her, in imitation of her Master, to heights and depths where others could not follow; and hence at times came misinterpretations and doubts as to the wisdom of her line of action. She never held what is called a low view of human nature. Such a view would have been too uninspiring. Like Père Yves of Paris,[1] the great Capucin humanist, she would have said that to judge badly of human nature is to judge of the sun by its eclipse, of the flower when it is faded. And like the wise man whom he describes she ' easily persuaded herself of perfection in a creature, which bears the image of Infinite Goodness, and which is the object of His love, and had no eyes to see evil in a mystical body of which the Head was in possession of glory.' And so it came about more than once that she was, or seemed to be, mistaken, and that in a manner that seemed inexplicable to others who, loving less, saw clear as day. It was the weakness of her strength. She could not crush the bruised reed nor extinguish the faintliest glowing taper, or perhaps she felt : ' there is but one way to brow-beat this world . . . to go on trusting, namely, till faith move mountains.' And sometimes it did. But sometimes it fell out otherwise, and her love, to judge from human standpoint, was bestowed where it was but little merited. Her own sincerity was so great that she could not bring herself to believe in deceit in any on whom she was lavishing the truest love. She believed

---

[1] For this description see *L'Humanisme dévot*, H. Brémond (Blond et Gay, Paris).

also in the possibility of good in every soul, even the most unpromising. She would set no limits to the power of prayer. She believed in moments of grace revolutionising lives, moments after which things are as never before. She had, as she said of herself, ' hope beyond what the ordinary person thinks credible.'

In these moments of struggle for the spiritual life of some dear child, she carried charity to an heroic degree in the way she sacrificed her time, her inclinations, her whole self to the welfare of those in difficulty. ' Her whole manner of acting in such circumstances,' writes one who witnessed it, ' was a faithful reproduction of the tenderness of the Good Shepherd.'

' What struck me most in Mother Stuart,' writes one who lived with her for many years, ' was her intuition of good in men and things. The good in her seemed to go out spontaneously to the least and most hidden vestige of good in others, and so established a point of contact. . . . Not only did she go about doing good, but finding good there where few others would have suspected its existence. Not that she did not see the other side. She perceived clearly both light and shadow, but with ready understanding made. straight for the good. She met each soul at its highest level, and saw in it already what it might become. This explains her keen interest in every form of life, her wonderful, almost incomprehensible power of loving each soul with an individual personal love, not two of them alike ; an exclusive love, it would appear, and yet all-including, the nearest approach, so one should think, to what God's love is, who gives Himself whole and entire to every single soul.'

In a letter written towards the end of her life she explained this attitude of mind, this idealising of all around her.

I can't see an intermediate way of taking life for a thinking person ; once to admit mud into one's scheme, I mean once to look at it, would blind one's eyes for the stars, I mean in the religious life. And I believe that the more one idealises, the nearer one comes to the truth ; the only thing is to stop at nothing, to ' bear all things, believe all things, hope all things, and endure all things ' with a persuasion of faith that they will all work out for the very best. They are incomprehensible at first, but the thing is to trust them and let the magic work. . . .

Writing on the same point, the Archbishop of Bombay says : ' More than anything else, in her training of others, I noticed her absolute simplicity of vision ; with her, as with St John the Baptist, the motto was " Prepare ye the way of the Lord, make

straight His paths. Every valley shall be filled, and every
mountain and hill shall be brought low; and the crooked shall be
made straight, and the rough ways plain; and all flesh shall see
the salvation of God." This was her ideal, her aim, her plan of
campaign. She saw the end in view, perhaps far away in the
distance, for every soul; she saw the hills and valleys lying
between, and the crooked roads; but her own simplicity never
for a moment hesitated, and no mountain was too high to be
levelled, no valley too deep to be filled up; but she set to work
at once, doing what to others might have seemed impossible,
while to her the possibility of its being impossible never occurred.

' I think this utter simplicity sometimes caused her very great
pain. I recall two or three instances when she found a person
had failed her. . . . She thus had to endure the sorrow of
failure in the management of souls, as Our Lord had to endure it,
and as all the saints who have trained souls have endured it
from time to time after Him.'

At times, as was inevitable, ingratitude crossed her path.
' It is such a grace to meet with want of gratitude,' she wrote.
' It is good to have such an opportunity as with X., one's
best efforts pulled out of shape and "returned empty with
compliments and thanks," this helps you to understand Our
Lord better, for that is what He met with from people all His
life. It must never make us wither up and say " never again." '
She indeed never did, she was always ready to begin again, to
give a full and loving confidence; and one knew that it was no
mere external kindness, but that in her heart too all distrust was
banished. ' Strive every day,' she had written, 'for that spirit
of the Sacred Heart which is summed up in the words " nothing
but sweetness ever came out of His Heart " '; and her wish for
her own Society, written in her first circular letter as Superior
General, was literally fulfilled in her own person: ' May God
give to each a heart as clear as a diamond, too noble, too pure
to let itself be disturbed by petty misunderstandings, little
prejudices, mean and unworthy thoughts.'

No injury, no suffering, no provocation aroused in her in the
end even a passing resentment. To one who in a moment of
bitterness wrote her a letter deserving of reproach, she answered :
' Now I think it would be unworthy of you if I were to answer
all the other torments of thought, because they are so untrue. . . .
Are you not my own dear X. from the beginning, and do I
not love every detail about your life, and rejoice in it all; and do
you not know it and I too.' And in answer to another's letter

meriting reproof, she wrote : ' I was waiting, praying, hoping for a better letter. . . . I blame myself for having told you so quickly before you had time to rest. I am not in the least angry with you, only sad, and filled with anxiety for my dear child. . . . And only God knows how much I am praying for you.'

And so it was continuously : ' her heart was too rich to know suspicion, too sweet to hold resentment.'

Alluding to some sorrows and the consequent frustration of her hopes and plans, she said : ' I go to prayer and my soul comes out patient and ready to surrender all to Him.' And again : ' I am sure that God over-rules all the details of life, from the smallest to the greatest, with love and tenderness and Divine knowledge ; it would be against right thinking, as well as against love and trust, to say anything else except that it is all for the best and that good will come out of it.'

Once when she felt crushed by her burden, Our Lord stood by her in a dream, a jewel in His outstretched hand. ' He looked at me,' she said, ' and I knew what it all meant.'

Years of patient endurance and apparently fruitless effort left her still loving, still hopeful, still ready to excuse, to encourage, to uplift. She was almost hypersensitive at times lest the intolerant should quench the flickering flame of hope and effort in some poor child of nature. To one on whose fresh hopes and new beginnings an unthinking and unkindly hand had thrown the cold water of doubt and discouragement, she wrote, in answer to a cry of distress : ' Do not be troubled about all this. . . . Remember that God *allows* all things, and if He lets us be reminded of old follies, it is only to make us cling humbly and lovingly to Him. Don't let yourself get sore, or turmoiled, or " moidlered," or " upset " by what anyone may say, but go on your way simply to God. What is anything when you think of eternity, except a means to get there. . . . So laugh at everything, and go on in God's name.'

Meditating one day in 1909 on the ' Disciples of Our Lord,' she wrote afterwards, as a summing-up of her thoughts : ' He had given Himself so entirely to them that their failure did not disturb His affection for them. He looked beyond it.'

' She told me once,' writes one already quoted, ' that if the light and response came only on the death-bed, it was worth all she could do.' The hours she lavished on these children of her tears when other and apparently more important work pressed on her, seemed to her, as indeed they were, well spent.

She was at the disposal of all, to be used at their, not her, discretion ; inconvenience to herself was of no account, and due consideration was by no means always shown to her. This intercourse with her was remotely, it may be, but surely paving the way to better things ; sweetening and softening a nature, disposing it for God's hour. She felt it deeply if those who might have seconded her efforts were inclined to take the more utilitarian view ' What is the use ? ' With her all was a work of love, not merely of endurance, seeing as she did ' a god, though in the germ.'

She cast her seed into the ground, by inspiring souls with the love of the best and noblest, and then trusted to God's action, while she prayed and waited, it might be for years, confident that at least to God's hand and eye, if to no other, a harvest would some day be gathered.

But it was not only in moments of acute difficulty or danger that her Mother's love and endurance were tried. The heroicity of her hope and love shone even more perhaps in the unwearying efforts, sustained during long and uninterrupted years, to win souls to the practice of truer religious perfection. This was her work *par excellence*, as is fully demonstrated in innumerable letters.

' The life of a soul is the most interesting thing on earth to me,' she wrote in answer to a letter telling of a soul's ascensions ; ' the greatest thing in creation is the inward life of the soul, its acts of faith and hope and love and self-oblation, even the smallest.' To this absorbing interest she devoted all her energies.

Her desire was to train the souls confided to her for God, and then to let Him do what He would with them. For life or for death they would be ready to His hand. Those who lived with her know the joy that was hers in the souls of some whom she yielded up to God in death, a perfect work. ' Utility is not the thing at all,' she often said, ' but holiness.'

' What is Bede to become, Lady Abbess ? For what are you training him ? ' she makes Abbot Biscop question the Abbess Hilda, in a paper entitled ' *Obiter Dicta* Long Ago in England.' '' I train him for God, let God do with him what He wills.'' '' Have you no dreams or plans for this favourite son, Lady Abbess ? '' '' No dreams for anyone, Father Abbot, but that God should dispose of them. If God has work for Bede to do, and I train him for God, then God will find him ready to His hand when the time comes. I think Bede will be a teacher of men. I may be mistaken, but if God is better pleased that he should plough and sow the land and reap the harvest, provided he keep heavenliness of soul, what is it to His servant ? " '

She had [writes her assistant] a patient and intuitive genius in helping difficult people. ' Jewels God gives us to polish,' as she called them, speaking in later years to the Superiors of the Society. She studied them, made them her special care, seized upon their good points, made the most of them, and recognised every effort. She gave them work which interested them, and put into their lives as much happiness and love as she could, and from that led them on to face what would have seemed at one time impossible. She was not deterred by faults and defects, and while taking them into account, she never let them interfere with the hopes that she placed in the talents, ten, five, or even one, with which God meant His work to be done. She did not expect to reap where God had not sown, but she was sunshine to His harvest. . . . Though she helped people most efficaciously according to their needs, she did not carry them, nor relieve them of their own share of the work. . . . She insisted on the personal responsibility of each one to tend as far as possible to excellence in things mental, moral, and spiritual, and warned them against the danger of leaning overmuch on the kindness and helpfulness of those around them. . . . She held that of the two dangers—thinking too much or thinking too little, the latter is the most to be dreaded : ' Do not fear, take the risk,' was her advice, and when a soul came face to face with the great and unanswerable questions of life and destiny, she could say : ' I don't know any answer; let us fold our hands and say " I believe." I love these un- answerable questions ! They make God so great.' . . . When change of thought and views opened out new horizons she was ever ready with encouragement. ' Do not for a moment regret the favourite thoughts, friends of all your lifetime which are dropping off of themselves. This must be, it would be most regrettable if it did not happen ! You would have sterilised flowers that would last, but without life. The blossom must drop, that the fruit may follow. For any cherished thought that drops God will give you more and deeper truth ; this is the way in which God educates our minds, there is no question of starvation but of greater plenitude. Do not hesitate, do not falter, you will be carried through.'

Her heart was wrung by the sight of those souls in religion who, through want of proper teaching, feared to trust themselves entirely to God, and so cramped and warped their life with Him. This, she said, was one of her greatest sufferings during her last years, and gave her a longing to carry her message of freedom

and confidence everywhere. It grieved her that any should
think unworthy thoughts of God, or be afraid of Him. She felt
it as a personal sorrow, as one feels the dishonour or want of
affection shown to a loved friend. The spirit of Jansenism was
her special abhorrence, 'that heresy makes me more angry than
I can say,' she wrote.

There was nothing hard or frightening in her conception of
God. 'You make God a theologian,' said the Venerable Jean,
Abbot of Fontfiorde, 'but He calls Himself Infinite Mercy.'
That was Mother Stuart's way of looking at Him. 'I don't
feel worthy of any love of God,' said an anxious soul one day.
'But that is not it at all!' she answered. 'He loves because
He loves as mothers love babies. Bless you!'

The following letters, chosen among many, show how she
tried to bring this same cause of joy—'right thoughts of God'
—into other lives.

You have not right thoughts of God yet. Don't you know
that *of course* what He does is the rightest and most glorious
and splendid thing that can be. It must be so, even if it were
far more incomprehensible than it is. But even humanly, it
hurts to have one's face scratched by briars, yet how gladly
one puts up with it to be 'in at the death' or to get the blackberries! How much more, etc! . . .

The only possible contentment for our souls is in God, and
remember that to doubt or kick or repine or judge hardly of
God is to go back to the old fetish-worship which you have
given up. A God who could be anything but incomparably
sweet and loving is not *our own God*, but a terror dressed up
in our morbid minds. Think the best and sweetest thoughts and
believe them, but you can never reach half of what He is. . . .

. . . To end with the most interesting thing of all. Yes,
do be a saint, why not? What else is worth living for, caring
about; and every little thing in the day may help you on
towards it, if you will look at it on the right side as coming
to you from our dearest God, who is so *in* with us in our daily
troubles and duties, for whom nothing is too great or too small,
who is so understanding and loving to all our moods and aches
and longings, and asks only one thing, that we should take our
worries to Him to be comforted and our joys to be blessed,
and our tangles to be pulled out, and our choking gulps of trouble
to be quieted down; if you have Him in the details of your
life with you, all is well, and you can manage anything; the
only one thing to avoid is thinking hard and hateful and

unworthy thoughts of Him and misunderstanding Him. So
love Him and trust Him all you can, and let nothing take you
away from the keep of that strong castle, God the refuge of
His people.

. . . Don't forget . . . that God is your best and dearest
friend, that all you know that is good and lovely is pale and sallow
beside Him. He loves you dearly and cares for everything.

You cannot think how I wish that you could manage to let
go of those ' old, unhappy, far-off ' thoughts of God, and really
believe Him to be what you know He must be, and could not
help being, the whole sweetness of life, the whole power and
love of the world, and that you would give yourself into
His hands, by ' an incomparable act of resignation,' sure, so
sure that nothing you could dream of can come near to what
He is planning for you, and wants to give you if you will only
let Him.

He wants to take you sailing out into the glory of His thoughts
and love, and through sheer fright you cling to the rope and the
steps of the bathing machine. Father Niremberg would say
Go to,' and I say ' Let go,' and so does God. . . .

Happy feast, blessed Easter. May Our Lord look at you
with one of those surprises through the hedge by the road-side,
which, you say, is the manner of the heavenly visitation in
your soul, and may you look back at Him, straight into His
eyes, with love and trust beyond words—your *Paschale gaudium.*

Speaking of her action on souls, one of her children writes
as follows :

I find it difficult to express all that I owe to Reverend Mother
Stuart. Through her I not only gave up a position which
would have been full of danger and difficulty for me, but I also
became a Religious. I saw her for the first time in October 1903,
after a rough crossing during a stormy night, a picture of my
life at that time. And like Our Lord she stood on the shore
to receive me in the morning, at Roehampton. What a welcome
she gave me, though I had never seen her before. From the
first moment I was her child, as she often told me afterwards.
I had no thought of the possibility of a religious vocation.
For me there seemed to be but one way : to become an artist,
and thus realise the great desires and designs which my parents
had had upon this point. Mother Stuart knew all this. Our
first interviews always ran on music. But little by little another
note was touched, and then suddenly it dawned upon me that I
had to exchange my musical career for a religious one. When

I told her this, she asked me to put aside such thoughts, it was too soon. Only after many months of reflection, during which she was to me the kindest of mothers, did she receive me as a postulant. Of course there was many a difficulty, and many a bad moment after that, but she knew that when the waters rose too high help would always come from music, and she would then ask me to compose a fugue, or play to her.

Another writes :

Reverend Mother Stuart seemed to be the very channel of God's grace to souls, or her prayer its condition. It happened that I was cut off from all intercourse with her at a period of great anguish of spirit. . . . One night I dreamt that she came to me : ' What takes your soul straightest to God ? ' she asked. Power to speak failed me, so after a moment's pause she answered her own question : ' Adversity ; so courage, child, this trial is leading you to God.' I awoke with the sense of joy that her words brought me. . . . At that very hour she had received Holy Communion at Roehampton and had prayed for me. At another time, with the pressure of her hand on my head, came to me the revelation of suffering before me and the grace to embrace it.

On one of her many journeys she turned out of her way unexpectedly to visit a house not on her itinerary ; a unique occurrence, for she held strictly to all arrangements made for her journeys. One of her former daughters was there, and, it so happened, in great distress of soul. After a long talk, which proved a new point of departure for the latter, she said : ' Reverend Mother, I think God brought you here for me.' ' Yes,' she answered, ' I too was thinking that I know now why He sent me here.'

On another occasion she urged a person who was at a crisis in her spiritual life to surrender herself completely to God. Next day, when receiving Holy Communion, that advice was followed. An hour or two later she went to Mother Stuart, who greeted her with the words : ' I want to tell you how very happy I am that you have made your sacrifice, and so entirely. That is a new victory, a great step onward on the road of trust and surrender.' When asked how she knew, she answered : ' Our Lord has told me, and I am so happy.'

It was not only in the greater things of the spiritual life that God gave her a knowledge of the needs of others and sent her to their rescue. One day when she was writing a letter something impelled her to put down her pen and go to the

School Infirmary, though she believed there was no one there, as she had not heard that anyone was ill; opening the door of one of the rooms, however, she was greeted by a child with the words: 'O Reverend Mother, I have just been praying that you might come to me.'

Once in her last years at Roehampton, a member of her community, who knew the loftiness of her ideals, asked her if her work of training Religious had been a disappointment to her. Mother Stuart paused, put her face in her hands, as she did sometimes when thinking, then answered: 'There is perhaps less of the outward polish, the military discipline I looked for in my early days, but as to the inner sanctification, God's work in souls—oh, no; far from it. This has far outdone my earlier dreams and hopes.'

And thus it was that to the end the joy of her life outweighed its sorrows, weary and full of suffering as it often was to her. 'Do you like this postcard picture?' she wrote from Sydney on the last long journey of her life, enclosing a copy of Mantegna's 'Presentation in the Temple.' 'I love it. It is so wonderful to represent the First Begotten of the Father and of His Holy Mother *singing* on His entrance into the way of our mortal, weary, suffering life.'

That wonder she too had realised in her own life, and true to her teaching had gone on her 'pilgrim way, singing to God'; singing while there were tears in her heart.

CHAPTER XIV

CHARACTERISTICS

' Partly gift and partly virtue, happy disposition or precious training; sweet reasonableness inborn, or hardly-won unselfishness; sternness of schooling or native adaptability,—industry, training or genius—these have gone to make it up.'—From ' The Practical Spirit,' J. Stuart.

' JANET STUART! How well these spare dissyllables befit the character of her who bore these names !' wrote Monsignor Brown, Vicar General of Southwark. ' No one who knew her could ever think of her with a signature of many names, with what may be termed the flourish of an elaborate spelling.

' A woman of remarkable gifts of mind and heart, Mother Stuart, in many cases, would not impress people in the first stages of acquaintanceship. All her powers were so disciplined, so well under control, that a casual, unobservant visitor might easily come away without in any way realising the wonderful wealth of mental endowment that lay concealed under that calm and patient exterior.' [1]

' But the greatest good is done,' says an author on the spiritual life, ' by those who efface themselves. God comes and takes them, as it were, by the hand and accompanies them on their way.' In these words we find, perhaps, a key to Mother Stuart's power. Humility in its most attractive form was the groundwork of her life. And from this rare possession came that impress of restful peace, that free and pliant dependence on God's will, that wonderful power of pleasing, of being listened to, of being loved. It brought with it a deep understanding of the truths of faith, so clear that it seemed like vision, for to the lowly in mind is given the key ; a mysterious instinct which discovered all that was good, and made her appear to the less clear-sighted, extravagant in her esteem of others.

The years which followed her return from South America

[1] See note, p. 176.

were those which saw the complete development of all these powers, and brought her strong personality to its full height. She was then entering her forty-fifth year : ' the time—forty-two to forty-nine,' as she wrote in the Essay on Colour, ' when you finally are what you are . . . when life consists more of answers than of questions, more of appreciation than of criticism, more of the fruit than the flower, more room in the retrospect, more of the vision of the end.'

In a letter written during her homeward voyage, she had said : ' To tell you the truth, I think you will find me a good bit changed.' Whatever be the explanation of this change, the fact remains that Roehampton under her rule, during the years that followed, was an ideal home. An indefinable charm drew all hearts to Mother Stuart. There was in her something of that grace and delicacy of finish which we find in the great women saints. They stand out like the fairest jewels in the heavenly crown that adorns the Church. St. Agnes, St. Gertrude, St. Catherine, St. Teresa—there is music even in their names, a fragrance in their thought that has been denied to the more rugged splendour of others. They are as the flowers of the field among the stately forest trees. This touch of God Mother Stuart shares with them.

The simple conviction of her own lowliness made it impossible for her to be exacting with anyone. Gentleness and gratitude marked all her dealings with her neighbour, and none could resist her.

Charming everywhere, she was undoubtedly seen at her best in the heart of her own community. There she poured out her love without restraint, her gifts found their fullest play, and she was her truest self.

As a Superior [writes Monsignor Brown in the paper already referred to[1]] she had the splendid quality of justice of mind. How few are really just in their dealings with those under their authority. It is easy enough to be kind to persons congenial to us, even to be patient with their shortcomings ; but hard to be just all round. To be just means going against both predilections and prejudices, and everyone has them in greater or less degree. But she did it. She succeeded in being even-handed in her treatment of all. Perhaps she made her greatest demands of those who were dearest to her, of them she seemed to expect more and to exact more than from others ; and this very attitude of mind won her all the fuller service. It may

[1] See note, p. 176.

have been her method of turning natural preference into supernatural perfection; her way of transmuting weakness into strength.

She was a Mother to everyone in her house, and realised in herself the picture she drew of the perfect Superior: sensitively alive to the needs and joys and sorrows of each member of her community. The most womanly of women, her strength was in her love, and this thread of gold ran through all her life.

It was said of her by a priest who had known her intimately for many years, that her faith and hope and charity were perfect, and this was indeed true. It was these great theological virtues which stood out like shining lights in her life, throwing radiance round her and revealing God. She said of herself that from the day of her Baptism, on her reception into the Church, a doubt on matters of faith never crossed her mind. But that was not all. Her faith meant much more than that. She positively loved and gloried in the dark things of faith, as throwing her more completely and more blindly into the arms of God. She comes back upon this again and again in her writings. In the notes of a conference we read:

There are two lives: one, Moses, 'faithful as a servant in all his house.' Faithful in detail, perfectly obedient, perfectly contented, not wanting to see, not asking more than 'What shall I do in the present moment?' . . . But there is another way. 'Christ as a Son in His own house.' Not a faithful servant, but a child in His Father's house, daring to look and face the mysteries, daring to let the will and mind roam among them, accept them, because so sure of its love and trust, really glad and delighted, more than resigned to the darkness of God's secrets. One bears with the storms and the things that go wrong, the other loves them because they hide God's fruitful action. One would wish peace to the Church, and the other exults in her warfare. It is the life that someone has called *un magnifique vagabondage*, a magnificent beggary—nothing to live on, and living splendidly; nothing to walk on, and walking fearlessly. But to live that life we must make up our mind that the things that are going most right are those that seem most utterly wrong, and the prayers most magnificently answered will be those from which we seem to get nothing.

She loved thus to lean on God, to wait in perfect trust, when things were darkest; to believe His word when it seemed most impossible of fulfilment. Two of her favourite poems were

'A Grammarian's Funeral' and 'Rabbi Ben Ezra,' where Browning expresses these very thoughts.

So often [she wrote in 1914 to one of her friends] you are in a kicking, doubting, panic-stricken attitude, as if God were not God, and did not with tenderest Providence direct each detail of life for the best. Don't you believe this? Go on making acts of faith and absolute submission until you do— 'a self-surrender absolute' which will carry you beyond all doubts as to circumstances, or wishes that they should be otherwise than just as they are. God knows and loves. We cannot understand. If we could understand, all the best beauty of our life would wither away. It is glorious in its faith and hope and adherence to what we don't understand. May Our Lord give you light on this, and love for the adventurous journey of faith and hope with Him in the dark.

A little later, in answer to a letter which had seemed to question the ways of God, she said :

I do not like you to admit such a thing as a puzzle about God, because everything about Him must be ' of course ' to us. It is equally ' of course ' that we should not understand. That is part of the worship. It is faith to *know* without understanding, and real love to love what we do not understand, because it is love and faith and hope together. ' All shall be well.' Even to natural reason it seems so luminous that in the domain of our probation for heaven, suffering should be good and precious and lovely. I wish you would believe those ' fleeting lights ' which tell you that you could be a saint! It means an ' incomparable act of resignation ' here, now, to things as they are, for the love of God, and whenever you think of it again. It is a fundamental thing built on a rock, not a pious practice.

And returning to the subject again, she said :

You know your life is all right, you know it *now*, don't you? And you trust God utterly and don't mind things being weird and unaccountable, do you? Because you know that He knows all about it, and will make it all right in the end. All crooked things will go right, and the word will come into the riddle, and the key into the puzzle, and we shall be so delighted to think that it was right all along and that we trusted Him when things were darkest and most incomprehensible.

God designing His pattern and the weaver seeing only the wrong side as he worked, but trusting all to the designer, was a

symbol she liked, and in one of her earliest essays she took it
for her subject. She often referred to it in letters.

God is good, He is good to us all; do not let yourself be
dr-r-r-r-eary, for He is weaving His pattern beautifully, and it
hurts Him when you do not think it is coming out right, ' thou
shalt see it thyself that all manner of things shall be well.'

Almost her last conversation with her community at Roehampton, in July 1914, turned on this blind trust in God. Commenting on the words of the letter of St. Ignatius on Obedience,
where he speaks of ' that blind impulse which shows a will
desirous to obey,' she said that a blind impulse, blind obedience,
was not one that did not think, but one that sees and weighs
all difficulties and dangers and yet goes on, leaving all to God ;
hoping against hope that He will bring things through, counting
on Him to save all royally, if not now, later ; if not for me, yet
finally. ' For lo I Our God is able to save us from the furnace
of burning fire, but if He will not, yet, O King, we will not
worship thy gods.' One of the greatest acts of faith and hope
ever made, she said ; believing that God would come in and
bring a great deliverance.

Asked once which of the words spoken by Our Lord she would
best have liked to have had addressed to her, she answered :
' You are they who have continued with Me in temptation.'

Even more striking to the casual observer was the all-
embracing and yet detailed character of her love. Her charity
was so unfailing and so universal that, to explain it, many have
believed she made a vow never to refuse a kindness, little or
great, if it were any way possible to grant it.

This may have been so, but it is none the less true that she
was by nature, as has also been said of St. Francis of Sales,
presque trop bénigne.[1] So rare a fault, and so lovable, that
suffering humanity crowns it as a virtue. By instinct she would
always have yielded, and, like the great Bishop, self-conquest
in her often meant ' *de se résigner à la raideur, à la résistance.*'[1]
He too, when reproached one day by Père Binet for accepting
to preach every sermon he was asked for, answered : ' *Que
voulez-vous ? C'est mon humeur qui me porte à cette condescendance ; je trouve le mot non si rude au prochain que je n'ai
pas le courage de le prononcer lorsqu'on me demande quelque
chose de raisonnable.*'[1] Mother Stuart would, there is little

[1] See the chapter on St. Francis of Sales in *L'Humanisme dévot*,
H. Brémond (Blond et Gay, Paris).

doubt, have seen her own portrait in these words. She seemed to consider that her position, as Superior, entitled her to be a servant to all, and she carried out this office so beautifully that she made her service of others a joy to them as well as to herself. The labour it cost her was known only to God. A word taken from a letter seems to reveal the mainspring of her action : ' Remember,' she wrote, ' that others are the hedge, the gaps through which God looks at you are their eyes. This will make you very tender to them.'

Casual wishes expressed in her presence and perhaps scarcely adverted to again, were found fulfilled. A tone of regret in the voices of those she knew was enough, their unexpressed desire was satisfied. ' It had been one of the sorrows of my life,' writes one such person, ' that, owing to a variety of circumstances, I had not gone to the Mother House to make my profession. Mother Stuart knew of this, but it seemed a sorrow without a remedy ! And as years passed by it might have been supposed forgotten. But this was not so. Many years later, when she herself became Mother General, a most unexpected summons came for me to go to the Mother House. And in the course of happy days there, she gave me many tokens of her love as a remembrance.'

A constant companion of the last three years of her life, Mother le Bail, writes :

Elle avait une charité extraordinaire pour le prochain, au point de s'identifier aux peines, aux joies de chacune ; mais l'universalité prouve bien la liberté de son âme. Chacune aurait pu se croire unique, tant la Mère Stuart l'aidait, la soutenait, ne lui laissant, pour ainsi dire, rien à désirer, et aucune n'était négligée, quelle que fût l'ancienneté ou la nouveauté des relations. Il n'y avait pas de déceptions en se confiant en elle ! pas d'inégalité de tendresse. Au milieu du travail le plus important, du voyage le plus fatigant . . . elle répondait aux lettres confidentielles qu'elle avait reçues ; s'il s'agissait d'une âme, d'un secours à donner, tout le reste passait en second.

Dans plusieurs endroits elle a rencontré des découragées, brisées . . . Sa sollicitude alors était extrême ; elle multipliait les attentions délicates, rendait la joie au cœur et l'âme reprenait sa course dans la voie de la perfection. Sa condescendance pour les désirs qui lui étaient exprimés était sans limites, au point d'étonner parfois. Changements de maison, d'emplois étaient accordés quand elle y découvrait la possibilité d'un bien pour l'âme. . . .

She never feared to love too much, nor to show it, but was simply natural in her response to the love received. ' Why should not a child love her Mother ? ' she said. In her case the claim to that title was fully justified. One who had lived with her many years, and who felt deeply the pain of inevitable separation, said to her : ' Send me from time to time a " token " that things are as they have always been between us, anything will do.' Till her death the promise given was never forgotten. Sometimes it was a copy of her verses signed 'A token.' Another time a photograph of Mother Digby with the words, ' A token from me to you, all is well and God loves you ' ; again, a bit of wild thyme from a grassy bank in front of Cicero's villa.

There was in her soul something that made it impossible for her to suppose that any Religious could love selfishly and exclusively, or in such a way as to allow human affections to interfere with the sole rule of God. Claims of earth and heaven did not clash in the serene atmosphere where her soul dwelt in the last years of her life. Within her realm things divine and human had given the kiss of peace.

When occasion required she could speak severely, but rarely wrote severely, feeling, perhaps, that the written word could not be undone. ' Did I really write that ! How could I ! ' she exclaimed in genuine astonishment when shown a letter she had written twenty years before, and she tore it up quickly, saying : ' Forget it all.' More often her letters of reproof were full of love.

You know that your poor old Mother loves you very much. I am going to have just as frank a talk with you as if we were together. [Then followed the reproof, and the letter ended], ' do not be sad about it, only thoughtful and not afraid, and you will learn by the experience of it all.'

This gentle admonition was followed two days later by another letter, as though she feared the first might have made too painful an impression :

I want to write just one line after my hurried letter on Sunday, because I am so afraid that being run down and tired it may have ' upset ' you, to use Mother R.'s word. It seemed so roughly and bluntly said ; but you know all the loving sympathy that was behind it, and though it hurts for the moment you will say afterwards that it was a blessed experience. And this is now an excellent chance of taking a thing with your head and not with your heart. . . . God's blessing will be over all.

In a paper entitled ' A Witenagemot, or the Meeting of Seven Wise Men,' written in September 1903, Mother Stuart discusses the art and manner of viewing life; the final paragraphs give her own ideal.

They who know not say that the age of vision is past, but the Church knows, and those who have seen can know, that the enduring vision is given to those that love. They see beyond the grinding pressure of hard-featured toil the beauty of daily life, the glory of immortal souls ; they see hidden graces where the unloving eye sees only shattered nature; they see the foot-prints of God where others have lost His trace ; they say ' He is here—and here—and here,' and they can show Him to those who, like themselves, can see.

But the world cannot understand, and those that do not love cannot understand, ' their words seem to them as idle tales,' and themselves optimists, dreamers, enthusiasts. So it has ever been, yet they may not desist from loving and hoping and crying aloud; by the imperious force within them they must go on and sing their prophetic song and deliver their Gospel, for those who love are the Prophets and Apostles of the world, and the victory will be given to them in the end.

Love goes beyond goodness or action or reverence or duty, or even fortitude. It leaves behind it faith and hope, for it sees and grasps, and what it lays hold of in this world, that it lays down at the feet of God hereafter in His Kingdom.

Another characteristic of Mother Stuart was her power of work. ' All great men are great workers,' says Ruskin ; ' nothing concerning them is matter of more astonishment than the quantity they have accomplished in the given length of their lives.' This was markedly true of Mother Stuart ; she did enough to fill many lives, and yet all in such apparent peace and quiet, without hurry or distress.

There is probably no exaggeration in saying that she never wasted a minute; she was always working, and she had such command over her mind that she could concentrate at once on anything she wished to do.

One who was her secretary for some years, writes : ' Her use of time was marvellous. There was never a vacant moment, and all was arranged so methodically that no pause was necessary. During four years of incessant work I never knew her to mislay even for a time any important paper, or to leave any letter that required an answer without one, and this in spite of a heavy correspondence which grew year by year,' for to have seen her made one long to know her better and wish to go to her in sorrow and trouble, and so letters poured in from all sorts of people and from all parts of the world. Nearly all were answered by her own hand, and this not only when she was at home, but on her many long journeys.

Her letters had a wonderful freshness and charm about them. Monsignor Brown who had received many, writes :

Her style of speech was never diffuse, her mind was very concentrated, and this quality showed itself in terseness, direct-ness, and simplicity of language. Her written language is equally clear and concise. The book by her on the ' Education of Catholic Girls ' is an admirable example of luminous yet con-centrated writing. But it is perhaps in her private corre-spondence that her gifts reveal themselves most fully. She could write a long letter without a dull line, a trivial comment, a superfluous sentence. She had a quick eye for all the salient features of a town and its people, and a ready sympathy of imagination, if one may so style it, which enabled her to catch the point of view of strangers and foreigners. Letters from Rome, from Austria, Egypt, Japan, Australia, New Zealand and Canada contain vivid impressions of the varied types of character, of the influence of environment upon temperament, of the work of the Church in difficult surroundings—all seized in a brief visit, during which she was kept hard at work with a mass of absorbing business. Yet they betray no sign of haste, the penmanship careful and neat as usual, the sentences full and well balanced, the choice of words and illustrations as happy as if there were ample leisure for letter-writing, not a few moments snatched from the crowded hours of a long and arduous day. It was this gift of sympathetic writing that bound so many to her with the ties of lasting affection and friendship.[1]

She wrote letters with great rapidity. When seeing numbers of people in succession, she usually had an unfinished one before her, and would continue it in the moments between the inter-views—intervals no greater than the time required for opening and shutting a door. She read them with such attention that she had rarely to refer to them again. When giving work to her secretary, five minutes would suffice to give the answers to half a dozen important letters. So completely did she keep *au courant* of all the work she had on hand, that when she went away to visit the houses of the Vicariate, there were no apparent preparations for departure, everything was in perfect order.

[1] See note, p. 176.

pour out more before them — Could
He be insensible to this? Could
He be God and not be touched to
the heart by it. I think He would
be Moloch! But He is our own
God and knows that failing often
and blundering daily we are trying
to give Him of our best, and the
result is the best worship that earth
can give Him, the fullest music —
the most heavenly thought. The
more you pray and give yourself with clean
hands the better you will see, the
more you reason and struggle to see the
darker it grows.
    May He always bless you
        your devotedly in Him
                J. Stuart

FACSIMILE OF LETTER

Mother Stuart not only valued time for herself, but she had the greatest respect for other people's time. It never entered her head to keep anyone waiting, no matter whom. She went promptly to all visitors, and if an interview was one of business, she arranged all beforehand, saying: 'So and so is a busy man; we must not waste his time.' The business over, she was ever ready to listen to conversation, interesting or otherwise, and was always kind and sympathetic, and apparently never in a hurry. Writing on this point Monsignor Brown says:

> Some very talented people must display their gifts . . . all intercourse with duller or unappreciative minds is irksome and unwelcome; they need the extraneous support of listeners impressed by their powers. Not so Mother Stuart. Ready to discuss the commonplaces of life with those who sought her counsel and help, she never betrayed the least sign of the mental arrogance that sometimes unfortunately goes with great intellect. To her nothing that concerned the needs, especially the spiritual needs of others could be trivial. Life, as she knew, is a succession of minute incidents, of small doings, of little hopes and fears, so she could never be impatient of detail where the well-being of others was concerned. . . .[1]

Her invariable punctuality and her dislike of all slackness in this matter made the patience with which she bore remissness on this point the more remarkable. One day when she was visiting one of the convents in London, by some mistake of a messenger, the cab which should have taken her back to Roehampton in time for an important interview did not arrive. She only said: 'I was to have been back in time to meet an elderly lawyer on the doorstep,' and then without further comment continued her conversation with the community for fully half an hour. The next day she wrote to the Superior of the house:

> It was a very nice afternoon, and the sweet Providence of God ordained that the person who had an appointment with me was also half an hour late, so the cabman did the Will of God in blindness; a happy explanation of so many of the things of life that seem to go all wrong and in reality are the very things that ought to be.

One of her books was written in the hours she could get in the morning of one day each week. During the week she made notes here and there as thoughts struck her, and when the day

[1] See note, p. 176.

came she wrote, and invariably produced the chapter she had proposed to herself to write. A second book was written on her journey round the world, and only in the earlier sea-voyages of that journey; it was written, as someone expressed it, ' by an extraordinary economy of time and unexplainable control of surroundings.'

Not unfrequently people said : How easy it all is for her, with her great gifts of mind and will ! But her teaching was that there is no such thing as ready-made perfection in any order. Saint or hero, all have paid their price ; the more simply beautiful they appear to be, the greater, we may be sure, has been the cost. ' That God vouchsafes the best that He can give to the best that we can do,' was true certainly in the case of Mother Stuart.

While it might have been said of her, as it was of another, that ' toil was her native element,' [1] yet she understood sympathetically the shrinking of others in face of a similar programme. She appeared to know all the little subterfuges of the lazy, and was unsparing in her warfare against laziness of mind, which was, she thought, the great enemy for most people.

' Material devotedness never fails us,' she wrote, ' but how rare is the devotedness that will brace up its powers, and labour and chisel and polish until they are excellent. . . . There ought to be so many who are excellent, there are so few.'

While reverencing the self-sacrifice of manual work, she held that for many it was a refuge from work that was far harder, the development of their own minds, and their inner life. To make people think and develop their gifts was one of her great objectives. She often said that few had any idea how much they could do, and that we had within us undiscovered continents. ' Let no one think they are played out, there are indefinite possibilities in each one,' she wrote ; and again : ' Considering that we have often to do with persons of splendid capacity, and proprietors of great estates who have grown up with the conviction that they are paupers and paralytics, there is a great deal of preliminary work to be done,' she said, thus gently ridiculing the too common inclination of people to take refuge in their want of capacity as an excuse for not developing the untilled acres lying fallow in so many minds. She liked to quote the words of Professor Münsterberg to the students at Harvard : ' We think that our nerves are out of order when we are wanting in attention ; we think that we are anæmic when we are wanting in thoroughness ; we think that we are broken down

---

[1] Morley's *Gladstone*, vol. i, p. 186.

when we are not yet broken in ; we think we require a physician when what we really need is a schoolmaster of the old type.'

She disapproved of the theory that only the immediately useful should be sought and all the rest eliminated and discouraged as something dangerous in the spiritual life ! She always said that the spiritual classics which thunder against the dangers of learning were written for men, that for women the danger lay the other way, in a contented ignorance. She held as a result of her own observation, that intellectual and spiritual progress were closely allied; hence she encouraged all, from the youngest to the oldest, to learn all they could ; directly or indirectly it would be useful. ' There is great use in learning everything that you can learn,' she wrote to one who questioned her on this matter, ' languages, general information, points of view, experience—it is all good. . . . It is the quality of the being, especially the quality of the religious being, which is *you* . . . that matters.'

This was the subject-matter of one of her last papers, written in 1910, ' A Morality Play on the Story of Cock Robin.' Cock Robin, the ' fair mind,' is killed by a poisonous thought, ' What is the use ? ' shot by the utilitarian sparrow, who in the trial that follows explains his view that the proximately useful is the only desirable thing. ' Seek the thing that is immediately useful, eliminate the rest. Do not learn, do not consider, do not enquire. . . . Learn for your work, leave all else aside . . . and thus I save you from so much waste and the burden of unused learning.' But Conscience, the judge, answers him, that by this method the ' fair mind ' is cramped and crippled . . . and that God surely will contrive use for our learning ; moreover the holder of this theory can never have thought of the qualities of the person or of the beauty of gems polished to perfection.

She fully understood the need for rest and relaxation in holidays, but she held that rest did not mean idleness, but change ; change of occupation, more than change of place. The happiest holidays were those spent in the pursuit of some favourite hobby or study. In this spirit community holidays were to her a means of making progress, and in the places where her ideas were most fully entered into, if greater seriousness seemed to prevail, there was no lessening of the joy of life. ' Think and act seriously, labour humbly and vigorously . . . great grave acts of mind and will and effort, this God blesses,' she wrote on one of the little sheets on which she prepared her daily meditation. ' We must never try to escape the obligation of living at our best.' She asked this of others, but all saw it was what she herself did daily.

The home-life of the community under her was ideal. Summing up her wishes for it one day, she said : ' And my people shall sit in the beauty of peace and in the tabernacles of confidence and in wealthy rest ' ; and in a paper written in 1907, ' A Community Accomplishment,' she describes the atmosphere of that inner life. Its opening paragraphs run thus :

In community life the greatest acquirements are the virtues. First come the theological. . . . Then come the lesser virtues, *les petites vertus* of St. Francis of Sales, small but precious and charming things which he likens to wild thyme and other lowly aromatic plants growing at the foot of the Cross.

There are likewise arts in community life. The art of government, the art of teaching, the art of persuasion, the art of conversation. Of all our major arts perhaps it is the most precious and the one we should most earnestly cultivate, for artists in spiritual conversation are treasures in community, as painters of truths and mysteries, portrait painters of saints, ' genre painters ' of virtues, animal painters of the antics and frailties of fallen human nature, and so on. . . . Afterwards come the host of minor arts and minor artists, whose works enrich community life with many charms ; not only the minor painters and embroiderers, and musicians, and singers, and verse writers, and designers, and writers of script or black-letter, and illuminators, and costumers ; but the ingenious inquirers, the askers of conundrums, the people who intellectually suggest, even if they fall short in expression ; the people who make spiritual salmon flies, and then pass them to their neighbour, and all the brotherhood, Friars Minor, though not Franciscans, whose happy minor art is tact.

After greater and lesser virtues, major and minor arts, follow the accomplishments. . . . There are so many to choose from that it is almost embarrassing, but I have fixed my choice on the accomplishment of taking the last place. . . . The problem is sometimes to find it, and the accomplishment, in looking as if there had not been a problem at all. . . .

No school gossip, no ' shop ' was allowed within the closed doors of the community. There all met, not as schoolmistresses, but as friends, as fellow-travellers on the adventurous path of life.

Everyone was expected to contribute some share to the ' thought market of recreation,' as she called it.

This is one of the joys of community life [she wrote], the strongest, the sweetest, the most intimate thoughts of others are often flashed upon us unconsciously, or trustfully put into our hands, and we go away richer in mind and heart,' wondering in ourselves at that which has come to pass ' in these fleeting apparitions of Our Lord. I know this has also its comic side, when, as Mother N. says : ' You bring out your poor little thought, and all the microscopes of the community are turned upon it in the same moment.' But we can brave that for the sake of the eyes that look through the microscope, ' alive, alert, immortal,' and bringing light as often as they ask for it. It is a greater ordeal when they come out with their spectroscopes, and our simple little ray of white light is broken up by spectral analysis into seven distinct bands, each of which we must account for, though we never suspected its presence in the original light.

She was herself the centre and life of all, but she never absorbed the conversation, she rather followed the lead of any good thought. ' She was never one to do all the talking,' wrote Monsignor Brown ; ' if anything, she was inclined to be over-reticent, to let others express their views very fully, while she contented herself with an occasional remark which showed the bent of her mind or guided the conversation in another direction.' She listened most attentively to what was said, nothing escaped her. Often when the conversation was at its height, a timid voice would be raised to offer a thought or suggestion. It seemed to pass unnoticed, but invariably, in the first lull, Mother Stuart would turn to the speaker and repeat her observation, asking for or giving an explanation. So that no one was left outside or forgotten.

Plied with questions, asked for her opinion on innumerable matters of interest, she never gave an unconsidered answer. ' Too big a question to answer straight off,' she would say sometimes, and the conversation would continue on other lines ; but after a time she would turn to the questioner : ' I have thought over what you said, and I think this is the answer. . . .' And yet while thinking it out she had taken her share in all that was going on. Sometimes a day or two would elapse before the answer was given, but was it ever forgotten ?

In a paper written in 1903, Mother Stuart gives a picture of these recreations :

In community a young member makes a deep remark. It has cost her, we hope, days of thought, and perhaps minutes of anguish, before she uttered it in the best chosen words she could find. But at last there it is.· Then we know what happens. If the community is in full holiday force, this young and deep remark is playfully caught up by a professed and volleyed across the room to someone who is supposed to be like-minded. This one responds to the challenge and proceeds to explain the remark. Before the original speaker is able to make herself heard to protest that she never meant anything so wise, the original remark has been labelled, catalogued, indexed, and reported, reviewed, annotated, and prefaced and dedicated and edited in two or three editions, then translated into two or three languages, and summarised, or perhaps published in an abridged and expurgated edition for the special use of the young by Sister M. Then it has been scratched with a *nihil obstat* by the young professed, and received the *Imprimatur* of the old professed, and gone out into the world bearing at least ten more meanings than the one it originally bore, and the bewildered author recognises ' that every one of them is right.' For all the time the meaning has been coming out all round, if the thought has any real value, ' a future in it,' as we say, spreading out beyond the phrases and the words, and we are awed at moments by seeing that we have said more than we knew, and we can understand better about the

> Words made musical by poets dead
> In which the fullness of all sweetness lies
> Sweetening and gathering sweetness ever more. . . .

and how a poet may grow up to understand his own best lines with wonder how he wrote them, half comprehending.

Those with whom she lived will realise how true to life this picture is. There was nothing strained or unnatural in these conversations, no pious platitudes found place there ; whatever the subject, they were always full of interest, and were the spontaneous outcome of minds which had been trained to think and·to value thought. Few, if any, in the end, were passive receivers, but all contributed according to their measure, so that Mother Stuart could write to the community when she had left it : ' I have a Christmas present for you, it is what you like better than anything, an idea.'

One of the things of which Mother Stuart was most particular was this choice and right use of language to which she referred in the passage quoted above. To the last she was an indefatigable student of words, and tried to awaken those around her to their ' forgotten duties to language.' In an essay called

' A Specimen of the Thoughts of 1903,' she makes an avowal on this point which is of interest.

Here is my specimen thought. It opens with a renunciation of what I have often maintained—*confiteor*, it is good to begin with this. I have often said that your thought could be expressed in words if only you were attentive enough, or painstaking and laborious enough, or enlightened and educated enough, or provided with sufficiently good dictionaries to find them. I renounce and abandon this theory. ' Not in dialectics has it pleased the Lord to save His people,' said St. Ambrose centuries ago, and man cannot rescue his thought in words, any more than the Lord can save His people in logic. Language carries his thought, but too often must carry it as a bullock train in South Africa must carry a statesman, Cecil Rhodes, let us say, a precious life ; an unwieldy carriage sticking fast in the mud, breaking down at the fords, hopelessly stayed by the obstinacy of the team. The statesman is unworthily borne along, slowly and heavily. If he reaches his journey's end safely it is much ; if he is only exhausted and delayed, not shattered, it is all that he can hope for. [But the paper ends with the advice] : Never give up trying to express your meaning although you know that you never can. It is one of those efforts doomed to failure that are nevertheless some of the best things in life ; always nearer to your meaning, always better, but never there. . . . It is of these impossibilities that our best achievements are born.

' Each year the traditional holiday known as the '' Mothers' Holiday '' left a long track of light on our path, and was at the same time a revelation of what she was to her community, and what they were to her,' writes her assistant. ' She prepared every detail with the greatest care. It was all to be worthy of the community, and she spared herself no trouble. She usually chose in advance and wrote with her own hand some little word suitable to each one. The great event of the day was always the paper written for the occasion, usually in the form of a dialogue.' At the end of each, one wondered how she would find more to say ; but though she wrote one every year there was never any repetition. It seemed each time there was nothing left to wish for, so wonderfully did she picture the struggling life of the soul, with its ups and downs, its failures, its disappointments, its hopes and achievements, its weaknesses, contradictions and oddities. Nothing escaped her, and every picture was true to life.

With equal power she drew the ways and dealings of God

with each soul; so that, as someone said : these writings were more helpful than a retreat, better than any sermon, for they touched the innermost heart of things, answered unuttered questions, gave courage for enterprise, made all trouble seem worth while, all life worth living, and above all gave new and truer knowledge of God.

All that she wrote came from her own soul. But though she was most original in the treatment of a subject, she nearly always chose an old and well-known setting. Fairy tales and nursery rhymes were forced into the service; she felt, perhaps, as Chesterton says, ' that the fairy tales contain the deepest truth of the earth, the real record of men's feelings for things.' The last she had planned to write was a spiritual rendering of ' Beauty and the Beast,' which ' teaches the eternal and essential truth that until we love a thing in all its ugliness we cannot make it beautiful.' This she was unable to do, being called away by weightier business.

Among the most characteristic and delightful of those which she has left are : ' The Three Classes of Men : a Parable from Grammar '; ' A Witenagemot, or the Meeting of Seven Wise Men '; ' A New Sintram '; ' The Ugly Duckling '; ' Virgins Wise and Otherwise : a Modern Cinderella '; ' *Obiter Dicta* Long Ago in England '; ' Comfort for the Faint-hearted '; ' Who killed Cock Robin ? a Morality Play.'

Some of these have already been printed, but nothing was written for publication. She wrote all for those on whose love she counted, for minds into which she had looked and which had looked back into hers with trust. And this is the secret of much of their charm. There was no danger of being misunderstood, no need to speak half-truths. All were radiant with the light of what she called ' Eternal Thoughts,' in verses written in 1902 :

> And yet we need them more and more
>   The thoughts that live, the hopes that fire,
> Words that can bear the weight of life,
>   Truths that can satisfy desire.

Perhaps this study of her characteristics can best be closed by that which has been called ' the most far-reaching influence of her life,' her love of nature.

We have seen it in her childhood and youth, and seen too how she used it as a means of mortification. But it was a power that could not die. Its source was something too deep within her, and its effects were apparent at every moment of her life. To show the contact between the seen and unseen was part of her message, and some of her power lay in the knowledge of where symbol and reality meet, and in her gift of imparting this secret to others.

There was nothing forced nor sought after in this manner of interpreting nature, which gave such charm to all intercourse with her. To her the inner meaning was always visible, seen instantaneously ; more real, perhaps, than the outer image ; the lightest touch sufficed, with a word she could brush the veil aside and reveal for a breathless moment the underlying depths, ' the subtle relations which,' she said, ' were below the surfaces of so many things.' Her writings are full of such inward flashes, and in her conversation, too, they abounded. Advice, encouragement, and even reproof were all given in picturesque phrase full of meaning : ' I think God wants you to be a poppy in a wheat-field, not a violet in a wood.' ' You must grow like a tree, not like a mushroom.' ' Notice after cloudy weather that the sun has climbed still higher in the sky.' ' Remember, a seed of sorrow turns into a great tree of joy.'

' Joy's trumpeters ' was her name for daffodils, and a group of children in white frocks and veils dancing round these heralds of spring made her exclaim : ' See, a Fra Angelico has come to life ! ' ' Behold youth admiring hope,' she said one day as she gazed on a group of novices looking with upturned faces into the depths of pink cherry-blossom ; and ' Maturity contemplating strength,' she added, as she turned to the professed who stood with her under a group of oaks.

Spring came to her with fresh wonder each year. She sometimes walked the whole length of the property to greet the early snowdrops and crocuses, and she would offer a reward to the finder of the first aconite. ' Bulbs and books are a sore temptation to me,' she said. The discovery of a new fern or flower was a joy to her. The gardener at Roehampton, a Scotsman, said : ' I would think myself honoured, I would, to walk a hundred miles to find a British fern or flower that Madame Stuart didn't know.' He met her as one who shared his knowledge, and understood the secret of his art—a rare favour from a gardener.

She loved warm colouring in nature, clusters of jackmanni overhanging ivy-leaved geranium, the deep purple of hyacinths, the blue of gentian ; but the practical point of view, that of the farmer, was never forgotten. Poppies in the cornfield, and

buttercups in the meadow, gave her only a partial pleasure.
' Lovely to the eye, but for the land ! ' she would say.

Commenting on some papers sent to her by the children
at Roehampton after her election as Mother General, she wrote :
' I read every word of them with interest. They could not
understand this, but their fresh and youthful delight in lofty
things beyond their understanding, and their naïve outlook on
life, made them as gay a sight as a handful of buttercups out
of a May pasture ! quite delicious.'

Thanking a nun who sent her a box of flowers in 1913, she
said :

I was delighted to get the box of flowers and lovely totter
grass. I could have spent a long time shaking it. One day it
spent on my bureau, and then I told Sister Richardson to dry
it carefully for the winter with the sweet little immortelles. . . .

Totter grass for our trembling nature, dark pansies for our
deepest thoughts, immortelles for our blessed hopes ; that was
it, was it not ?

To the end wild flowers had her preference ; their characteristics were, she thought, ' truth, delicacy, and hardiness.' [1] ' In
the field flowers,' she wrote, ' there is what we call " the scent of
the wild," an aroma, something almost bitter, not luxurious ;
like the flavour of Alpine strawberries or the scent of heather. . . .
Wild flowers grow anywhere and everywhere, on hill or rock ;
they ask very little because they depend on God for everything,
just a little water, sun, soil, and very poor soil sometimes it is.
They ask for no care of man. Day by day, moment by moment,
the right thing is given to them.' [2] And when asked once for
a programme of life, she answered : ' You are all God's property,
and your life must be one wild bird's song of praise, one wild-
flower's face looking up to him. Do not try to be a garden
flower. I think He likes the wild flowers best, and I know that
I do ! '

Birds, too, had a large place in her affection : young robins
especially, who, as she put it, ' were not yet promoted to wear
the pink.' The song of their elders was ' the song of pure hope,'
she said. She protected the wild life on the property at Roehampton, and was delighted when waterfowl built on the ' lake,'
a piece of water not far from a road, made horrible for shy
creatures by the noise of modern traffic.

The grey squirrels who were denizens of the place, the owls

---

[1] Conference given at Malta, Christmas, 1912.   [2] *Ibid.*

who dwelt in a deserted chapel near by, the herons who sailed overhead morning and evening, and occasionally dropped to fish on their way to distant supper-pools by the Thames, king-fishers and wood-peckers who paid fleeting visits, all were watched and their advent remembered with pleasure.

Mother Stuart believed very strongly in the power of nature to form habits of mind invaluable in life, in particular quiet of mind, so essential to all progress. She said that many of the modern complaints of women could be lessened by hard work in the fields, and she advocated gardening as a remedy for unhinged nerves and hasty tempers.

It was not only in the realm of colour that her love for symbolic interpretation found play. Perhaps one of the most perfect examples is her description of the flame of a wax candle :

The form of its myrtle-leaf, its movements of exquisite balance and of impetuous striving, its tremulous response to the slightest air, the transparent blue of its base, the brilliancy of its apex, the determined hold it keeps on a sudden gust, the gaiety of its quick recovery, if it can recover itself, or the suddenness with which its wraith is extinguished by too strong a blast, a violent death but no surrender ; all these moods make it like a living thing, like the life of a brave spirit, the persistence of an heroic child, the evanescent glory of a short life.

To those to whom appeal through sound was of more force, she spoke in terms of music, and with wonderful accuracy of expression. ' I was often taken by surprise,' writes one, who was a trained musician, ' by the musical knowledge which she possessed by intuition. She constantly gave me work to do for her, and she was not easily pleased.'

Set your life to music [she wrote], and give Our Lord in the depths of your soul harmonies, melodies, that will be of the best. Now I think if you do not [overcome such a little fault] you would give Him a Chorale with one of the parts missing ; and if you let yourself think about disliking anyone . . . there will be one of the violins playing false in your orchestra ; and if thoughts of jealousy are allowed . . . then there is something gone wrong in the execution of your interior fugue. Do you see what I mean ? It must all be music for God, and you must sing in your soul Chorales, and Christmas Carols . . . and ' Glees,' nice things that will make Our Lord smile, that will be a real carrying out of the command *psallite sapienter*.

[And again] : You are so responsive to God's touch on your soul; it is an excellent disposition for prayer. Be a violin in the Artist's hand, do not try to find out what melody you are playing, but let Him draw it forth.

[And on another occasion] : Is not this influence on your soul like Bach's music ? I never get tired of his works ; they are so full of light and truth, so transparently sincere and full of deep joy.

The secret of this all-embracing love of nature we have in her own words :

We love beauty of scenery, of form, of art, of gifts of mind and talent . . . because God is there. We love earth because it is a parable to show forth heaven, but we do not hold to the parable when we can have the truth unveiled.

Such was Mother Stuart in the last years at Roehampton when the problem of her life had found its solution, and she had realised the truth of what she called ' the sober, hopeful, truthful promise, *solvitur ambulando* ; the maxim of the mixed life, and the verified utterance of all Christian experience ' ; and when, as she wrote in 1905 :

After years in Lebanon, under the cedars, the face had changed again, though it was still the same. At fifty (this you will recognise as my favourite thesis to an unbelieving world) the face ought to make quiet affirmations. Either the questions are answered, or it does not matter that they cannot be. The answer to so many questions is only ' wait ' ; and their victorious solution is ' trust.' And there is nothing so restful as the faces of ' fifty and over ' which tell of :

Imaginations calm and fair,
The memory like a cloudless air,
The conscience like a sea at rest.

CHAPTER XV

SOME EDUCATIONAL THEORIES

' It was said of a distinguished man (Fénelon), that he was a man of transition, and what he lost in distinctness, he gained in significance. . . . It is difficult to say exactly where we are, the one thing we are all agreed about educationally is that it is a period of transition.'

From ' An Age of Transition,' J. Stuart.

A GREAT deal might be written about Mother Stuart as an Educator. Perhaps enough has already been said to show how truly she deserved this title. To live with her, as was said of another, was in itself a liberal education. She was gifted for this work as few have been. Shortly after her election as Mother General, a Cardinal in Rome, speaking of her, expressed his opinion that there was no one like her alive at the time, then pausing for a moment he added : ' Perhaps there are two in the world.'

Her views and theories on educational matters can be very fully studied in her two books published in 1911 and 1914. Commenting on the first of these, ' The Education of Catholic Girls,' a leading, non-Catholic, American periodical wrote :

Despite the novelties of co-education and the attractions of public institutions of learning, convent education still has a charm and a power which all are free to admit. . . . In the training there received, the standard of true womanhood is the loftiest conception the world has ever known. . . . It is not surprising therefore that men and women of every shade of belief have chosen for their daughters a convent education.

' What do you think of " The Education of Catholic Girls " ? ' asked a friend of Mother Stuart of a Jesuit, whose opinion was of weight in the educational world. ' The mind of two men and a half,' was the spontaneous answer, as he passed hurriedly on.

She herself explained the purpose of her book in a few words of introduction. It was, she wrote, ' to present a point of view which owes something both to old and new, and to make

P

an appeal for the education of Catholic girls to have its distinguishing features recognised and fully developed in view of
ultimate rather than *immediate* results.'

That same wise compendium of the purpose of education is
found in her second book, ' The Society of the Sacred Heart,'
a character sketch of a Religious Order devoted to the education
of youth, where she says :

What stands by us in life is, after all, discipline of mind,
habits acquired, the power of steady, application, and such
knowledge of first principles as will enable new knowledge and
experience of any kind to find its right place and true proportion in what has been already acquired. . . . We must regret
that the aim in early years of education should be to reach
something accomplished, instead of something well prepared,
to which the analogies of all living organisms should have
directed us, as well as experience of children and their needs.

In a letter thanking for the gift of this book, Dr. Shanahan,
of the Catholic University of Washington, wrote :

Truly I think it sound and charming. I read it through
from title page to the blank leaf at the end, and looked at the
back of that to see if there was any more.

I must say to begin with, that the book was an answer to
a perplexity of mine. My first visit to E. filled me with the
idea that there was something special about that community.
I called it an atmosphere of joy, for lack of a better phrase, at
the time I noticed it. But now I understand its psychology,
pedagogy, and meaning. You have enlightened me by this
little book, exquisite in its frankness, delightful in its style,
charming in its informality of manner. . . .

Perhaps the deepest, keenest observation in it is that about
' untabulated . . . uncritical knowledge . . . the result of a
study that is enthusiastic and non-professional. . . . A study
of children more than of " the child." That let me into the
secrets of Mother Stuart's mind more than anything else she
said, save perhaps the remark on the following page (82) : ' For
such educators, their system is themselves.' How good and
how refreshing, how sensible, keen and true, this recognition
of non-professional knowledge, non-professional powers of mind
especially in these days of pedagogy, when knowledge about
teaching is supposed to make a teacher.

I copied several sentences down, just for their ring and
balance. The poise of the book, its serenity, and originality
make one wish that there were more like it. . . . But that
would be to have more Mother Stuarts. Her book was herself.

She wrote her own epitaph in the words ' For such educators, their system is themselves.'

. . . If these be its informing principles, spirit and ambitions, I understand your Order as never before. The Chapter on growth and development is noble. Keep your identity—yes ; but grow, grow into all the new things of education. Change your methods, your text-books, your traditions, anything and everything that is accidental, *passé*, outlived, outworn ; but keep your spirit intact, your true self, your distinct personality as an Order unchanged. Mother Stuart had the true vision : identity plus development.

' One does not often come across such a combination of heavenly wisdom and literary charm,' wrote another friend. ' *Le style c'est l'homme !* '

The years 1894 to 1911, during which Mother Stuart was Superior at Roehampton, were years of warfare in the educational world. The Boer War did much to awaken concern as to national deficiencies, and the efforts at reconstruction evolved, perhaps necessarily, at least temporary confusion. Many panaceas were offered from which the ' child ' of the future was to derive most consoling results. Those in whose hands was the welfare of the actual children had great need to keep a calm head, and the end well in view.

Looking back now over two decades, it would seem that the mistake then was the fundamental one so aptly described as ' a failure to define our end, a vague reaching out for a " beyond " in every order.' ' The Englishman,' says the writer quoted, ' does not know what he wants, he does not know what he has lost ; but he realises in a confused way that he *can never have wanted what he has got*. The best he can do is to put up with it.' [1]

Mother Stuart succeeded in so steering her course through the troubled waters of controversy, that without yielding anything of principle, she adopted what was necessary in the new ideas, and brought the school at Roehampton to an acknowledged supremacy in its own line. This was fully recognised in the inspections held by the Board of Education and other bodies.

' Education is the battlefield of the present day,' she wrote in 1899, ' and we have work on this battlefield, not accidentally but essentially.'

Her ideal of the work and influence of a true educator has been beautifully set forth in a paper, where, under the name of

[1] From an article on ' Town Housing,' which appeared in *The Times Literary Supplement*, May 20, 1920.

the 'Interpreter,' she draws a sketch of the trainer of youth. Too long to quote in its entirety, and spoilt, perhaps, in extracts, we shall give but one. Having spoken of the Interpreter's action in childhood and early youth, she continues :

But when slowly and in course of years reason rises and takes her royal seat upon her throne, not the first time which makes the child responsible, but the second time which makes him wise, then the Interpreter's great hour has come. Then let him gird himself to the task, and become all patience, all understanding, all sweetness to his charge. . . . Let him show himself indeed a master to the struggling mind that is coming into being. Let him show himself so true a master, that, as one has said, 'under the supposition of his displeasure no roses would seem worth plucking again.' Let him stand by in its moments of light to bid it ' ride on, go prosperously and reign'; but let him stand nearer still in the hours of darkness, when the untried spirit wearies in its efforts. Let him say to it that the hour of darkness is the true hour of incense . . . that the young mind may learn betimes to take its troubles to the Sanctuary ; and when he has taught that lesson, so that it can never be forgotten, then may he draw back and trust the soul to find and follow its master. . . .[1]

Such a teacher, each in their own setting, was, she conceived, a Vittorino da Feltre—a Thring of Uppingham. Of the work of the former she gives an attractive picture in the play, ' A School-master of the Renaissance, Vittorino da Feltre and his Friends,' written for the children at Roehampton in 1908.

Though no doctrinal or moral lesson is obtruded or even hinted at in the direct and simple progress of the piece, there is interfused throughout a sense of a deep motive conveying the author's impressive message to the hearts of teachers and scholars alike, to the one, of encouragement and of hope when all seems hopeless ; to the others, of life-long confidence and trust in those who have taught them the ways of virtue in their youth.[1]

Some further light may be thrown on her ideals from passages gathered from the yearly lectures on educational matters to which reference has been made in an earlier chapter.[3]

[1] From *The Three Children in the Twentieth Century*. By J. Stuart.
[2] From the Introduction to *A Schoolmaster of the Renaissance*. Father Roche, S.J.
[3] Chap. viii.

In the last of the series given in 1899, ' The reward of our work,' she drew a picture of her own method.

Our work [she said] is eminently a work of faith; in the natural order, the sowing of the seed is the best type. We have to begin by parting with something very precious, the seed, and putting it beyond our power, leaving it to the action of sun and frost and rain. . . . Those who have experience in sowing never despair of the harvest, they are not frightened by bad weather. . . . If they have sown good seed it will come up. . . . We may consider together some of the advice given in Holy Scripture to the sower.

(I.) ' Cast thy bread upon the running waters, for after a long time thou shalt find it again.' This figure applies especially to southern countries. The casting of the seed might seem a rash act, and so to us, it will often seem that we are casting our seed upon running waters; the children seem so light, so volatile, so forgetful, but let us cast it all the same, we may not find it again, but God will.

(II.) ' Sow beside all waters.' That is, think every mind and will is capable of something. If ever we give up anyone as hopeless we do great wrong. . . . .

(III.) ' In the morning sow thy seed, and in the evening let not thy hand cease, for thou knowest not which may rather spring up, this or that.' That is, sow at all times, something for now, something for later on.

(IV.) For the cautious: ' He that observeth the wind shall not sow, he that considereth the clouds shall never reap.' That is, do not wait for ideal circumstances, they will never come; nor for the best opportunities. Prayer will make every time and circumstance fruitful.

Writing later to a young nun, who found her work hampered by the difficulty of her surroundings, Mother Stuart said :

If you look to Sacred History, Church History, and even your own experience, which each year must add to, do you not see that God's work is *never* done in ideal conditions, *never* as we should have imagined or chosen, but that God's own saints, wherever they are, have fixed their eyes upon Him, and tried to work out a perfect will, His, and their own locked in His. You do not know, He knows; you do not understand, He understands; you cannot, He can; and the one thing He cares about is not that you should fill the school with children, but that you should ' work out a perfect will ' and be a saint; that is what you came for. ' Bernard, Bernard, wherefore camest thou thither ? ' Not to make a first-class boarding-school for Britons, but to be a saint.

To educate children was, she said, 'to fit citizens for the kingdom of heaven . . . to train them that they might so pass through things temporal that in the end they lose not things eternal.' But in her mind this 'passing through things temporal' was to be combined with making the fullest use of them, and living the fullest life.

'It is a useful question to ask ourselves : What is success in education ? ' she wrote in 1899, and answering, she emphasised a favourite theory :

Success to be worthy of the name must mean an end proposed and attained. . . . We bring up the children for the future, not for the present, not that we may enjoy the fruit of our work, but for others, for God, for the Church, for their parents, for their home life. Therefore we must have to do with things raw and unfinished, and unpolished. The children will come to us untaught, and leave us half-taught. We sketch a plan, but never see the crowning of the edifice.

So we must remember that it is better to begin a great work than to finish a small one . . . the work in the rough . . . may look ugly and yet be full of promise. . . . A piece of finished insignificance is no true success. . . .

Our education is not meant to turn the children out small and finished, but seriously begun on a wide basis. Therefore they must leave us with some self-knowledge, some energy, some purpose. . . . If they leave us without these three things they drift with the stream of life.

Speaking of the influence of the Mistress, she wrote :

The personal influence is great in proportion to her dependence, and powerful in proportion to her impersonality. This seems a paradox, the less personality the more influence ; but it is like one of those other paradoxes in the spiritual life— lose all to find all, die to live. . . . If we stand alone we shall feel the weakness of isolated action—littleness and variability.

Writing to one to whom this seemed a hard saying, she said :

Yes, I understand the struggle of it all, but you must remember that God's training is always done thus, 'just where it hurts most,' as Father Morris would say ; and if you lay down the price of your resentful thoughts, and the will that struggles for a free hand, God will bless your work and use you for His instrument of grace. Only at this price can it be. It has *always* been so. And when all rises up inside, think how God Incarnate allowed Himself to be taught by St. Joseph at Nazareth, step by step, the use of carpenters' tools. . . .

And again, speaking on the same point, she said :

Simplicity of aim makes it possible for us all, divergent as we are in views, characters, opinions, tastes, to concur in our great work, and to work as one person. Each brings her share, and often the strength of her co-operation is in what she keeps in reserve ; a great leverage is gained from that ; from the subordination of a strong will, the docility of a great mind, the power of restrained emotion in the loyalty of subordinate authorities, the abnegation of those who stand over the details, the sacrifice of gifts and tastes, the self-repression of perseverance, the moderation of personal fire in discipline, etc.

These all make the one person which is the Society, which educates its children all the world over with different nuances but with the same foundation.

' What nun has helped you ? ' asked a mother of her child during the holidays, struck with the improvement. ' It is not one nun, mother, but all the nuns,' came the answer, which greatly delighted Mother Stuart.

Each parent [she wrote again] has a right to ask us : ' What have *you* done *with* my child, *for* my child ; show me the trace of your influence in its mind, heart, conduct.' We can never answer : ' Was I the child's keeper ? ' All share the common responsibility.

Speaking of discipline, she said :

Our vigilance must be from love. The standard given to us is that of a mother, and her care is proverbial ; even God takes it as an illustration of His own.

A reason for our vigilance is the respect we owe to the children . . . the need to give them a habit of living before a witness, of living in public, which will make them at once fearless and responsible.

In a series on the teaching of Christian doctrine, she asks :

What do we want to teach ? and answers : The faith and practice of a Christian life.

(1) *Faith.*—As all is taught now by preference in the concrete, so all our teaching may and should centre round the Person of Christ, the living Church, the Vicar of Christ, and the whole heavenly system of sacrifice, prayer, and sacraments, which bring the things of eternity down among the things of our daily life. *Ecce tabernaculum Dei cum hominibus. . . .*

(2) *Practice.*—The Christian view of life which is expressed
by the fact that we are pilgrims and strangers; this keeps
hope in adversity, and in prosperity ' the hardness of a good
soldier of Jesus Christ '; and it takes the glory from earthly
things, for we know more, we have better. The surest *apology*
for our faith in these days of pessimism is an ardent radiant
hope, the sort of hope which is a true antecedent of possession.
. . . If we are possessed of that we can get it to take hold
of the minds of the children, and though much of the beauty
of their early piety may be battered away, that faith and hope
will remain as their sheet-anchor.

In classes of Christian doctrine especially she found her
opportunity of teaching ' Right thoughts of God.' ' The child
has a right to learn the best that it can know of God, since the
happiness of its life, not only in eternity, but even in time,
is bound up in that knowledge,' she wrote in the ' Education of
Catholic Girls.' She held that lessons in religion should appeal
at least as much to the heart as to the minds of children, for,
reasonable beings though we be, yet to the great mass of
men, when all has been said and done, and all arguments have
been called in review, the last word is spoken, the final solvent
of doubt is given by the heart. And what the heart knows is
probably never unlearnt.

So often explanations of faith are given and accepted as
religion, and yet no trust in God grows in those who are learning.
The root of faith is trust, but trust in a person, not in an argument.
There is no real religion in the mere acceptance of the explanation of doctrine. Religion is personal trust of a person, known
and loved. Arguments and controversy hold an honoured
place, but should not be allowed to usurp the field of religious
teaching. But neither should ' pious practices,' these without
solid foundation do not stand the stress of life.

Right thoughts of God [she wrote]. What idea should we
wish to give ? . . . Think out our highest ideals of all that is
most lovely and lovable, beautiful, tender, gracious, liberal,
strong, patient, constant, unwearying ; add all we like . . . tire
out our imagination ; and then say that is nothing to what
He is. . . .

Speak largely, trustfully and happily of God and bring out
that *nemo tam pater quam Deus.* Speak of the relationship
of Creator to creature, child to ' Our Father.' . . .

On the other hand there is a great want of understanding
of God's sovereignty and our dependence ; there are free and easy
ideas of God ; that man may question, and criticise, and call

God to account—a great deal of material blasphemy. The truth is overlooked that we are absolutely dependent and without a word to say for ourselves. God's marvellous meekness with His creatures makes man think he can take liberties. . . .

Some letters to a young mistress general illustrate her ideals and show how she trained those in contact with the children, and encouraged them in the inevitable difficulties of their work.

Remember the rule is community first, children second (self last, of course!). The danger of a young mistress general is to see all through the eyes of the children and not uphold the nuns. If you uphold them God will uphold you and them. . . .

. . . So the year has ended, and how unspeakably good God has been, you must be more than ever anchored in confidence. Troubles are sure to arise, but it won't be a first year again with all the special conditions that made this one such a big thing to face. And now in the holidays you will remake your soul, taking deep breaths of prayer and quiet thinking and learning. Your own soul is the first thing of your charge. You have seen that already, if it is well, all is well, for God is with you. It is a great trust from Him, all these young souls and the precious nuns, *His precious nuns.* . . .

. . . I think these awful moments of dire sadness and helplessness are the making of one afterwards. One touches the bottom and cries to God *De profundis*, and He never leaves one without help. But we know our own weakness better, and this is good for ourselves and others. . . .

. . . It is of no use asking oneself if one is fit to be what one is. If one answers ' Yes,' it does not amount to much ; if one says ' No,' it is depressing and apt to get ' panicky.' Better not look too much, act and pass on. If you have to regret, well *regret* and learn by experience, but learn always, and still more always hope. God will not leave you. And His best work is done just *thus* and through imperfect instruments. Do you know Mrs. Gatty's ' Imperfect Instruments ' in the ' Parables from Nature ' ? it is full of teaching. . . . If everyone was perfectly trained and formed and moderate and tactful, what would you do with life ! The work of administration is simply that, dealing with difficulties ; young relentless energy needs a great deal of taming, good for you again to have this work of moderating.

Returning to the same point, she wrote :

To have your staff young and easily held in check and very perfect in obedience and religious spirit . . . may be a hindrance to a greater good, because it makes a ' one man management,' which is apt to grow one-sided, and it is a less good thing for you . . . because when you can easily carry out your own views there is a danger of getting into ' so and no otherwise,' and you might not grow so much spiritually and in mind and character, and so God's work might be limited in a way.

Such were some of her theories, it only remains to give some personal touches and show her living her own ideals during her last years as Superior at Roehampton.

Every week she assisted at a criticism lesson in the school. These she looked forward to with genuine interest. When she wished to give special pleasure to any visitor, she would send for the mistress of studies and ask that a criticism lesson should be arranged, choosing the mistress herself, often with a laugh and the comment: ' She will give us most sport.' Mother Stuart was a most attentive listener. She studied the notes of each lesson most carefully, and expected all present to do the same. Her own comments were always written. Nothing escaped her, and there was generally a delightful summing-up of the lesson with a little word-picture of mistress and class. Whatever natural sting there might have been in such things, it was removed by the gentle humour and sympathy with which they were done. She never forgot to be gracious, and preferred that criticisms should be proffered as questions rather than as laws. As someone wrote of her, ' She´set forth the results of her experience and thought in gracious guise, and in an atmosphere of graciousness, which was as sweet as it was practical.' ' Sanity, gentle humour, and tranquil decision marked all her utterances.'

The charm of these things is lost in their separation from their surroundings, and the detailed·criticism of a lesson could have no interest. Commenting on a lesson in arithmetic, she wrote : ' The lesson tended to darken counsel by introducing too many difficulties at once . . . the manner I should call an ethical rather than a mathematical manner, hushed, impressive, deliberate ! X. lives on other planes than that on which walls are papered. It was Dominie Sampson in face of domestic problems.' And of a lesson which had delighted her, contrasting pagan and Christian literatures, having given the good points, she added : ' Weak—a little overpowering, but the better fault. Those of the class who had worked under us before held on very well, but it was like St. Philip by the chariot of Candace's Chancellor," the spirit of God snatched him away " ; in this case the charioteer sped away. The new ones dropped off, but in the last reading they were breathless. The lesson was informal but profoundly educational.' Another was described as ' a bouquet tied with a loose bow,' and so on. New imagery never failed her. With the certainty of such entertaining criticisms, these lessons, which could have been so wearisome, as none who know will deny, became one of the pleasures of the week, and the loss of one was a matter of regret to mistresses and children.

To read well aloud and to write good English were arts which Mother Stuart tried to foster. The latter was, she said, the best all-round test of general culture. Struck by the rarity of good reading in her visits to the classes, she proposed to the community to devote their energies to the cultivation of this art during one of the summer holidays. Reading-lessons, at which she herself presided, and in which she took part, were organised. Passages of prose and poetry were selected for each meeting, and all who cared to do so could enter the lists. One day she invited several mistresses to give their rendering of the ' Intimations of Immortality,' and after a detailed criticism of each reading she summed up the different versions as : facts, surprise, wonder, regret, tenderness, sadness, bitterness, and simplicity.

At the last meeting all were asked to read their own selection. Her choice fell on ' A Grammarian's Funeral,' which expressed, she said, the best spirit of the humanism of the Renaissance. Reviewing the work of these classes, she wrote :

Such a course gives—
(i) Some understanding of the importance of reading well aloud, and of what is important in it.
(ii) Courage to admit to our hearers that we have some feeling of sympathy with what we are reading. (A thing some appear to feel bound in honour to keep as a dark secret.)
(iii) Some realisation of the effects of good reading in developing things that have their springs very deep : self-control, patience, consideration for others, active thought for them, positively and negatively. We have to remember that we read for them, not for ourselves, and so must not put too much of our personal idiosyncrasies into our reading lest it may jar on them.
It teaches the necessity of consideration for our author and our audience and forgetfulness of ourselves.

As one great means of learning to read well is to listen to good reading, for several summers in succession she selected the best from Wordsworth, Tennyson, Dante, etc.—each year a

different poet—to be read aloud by one or other whom she considered the most capable interpreter. And it may be said that
in these matters she was difficult to please. For Wordsworth
she wanted the most understanding soul. For Tennyson the
most exquisite instrument—no jarring voice, nor any with the
least touch of dialect or unrefinement could be allowed to render
' In Memoriam.' For Dante, grasp of intellect, etc.

Reading in every sense held a very high place in Mother
Stuart's estimation. She held to it that all should read seriously ;
without that she considered, as indeed St. Bernard teaches,
that prayer was impossible, and conversation necessarily trivial.
She herself was in her earlier days an omnivorous reader. She
never read but the best ; but she confessed three years before her
death that she had ' just discovered how much she had lost by
not reading more slowly.'

Hearing that a new library was being established for the
community at Roehampton, she wrote :

Now this is an important message for them. I hear, and
I am delighted to hear, that there are new cupboards and spiritual
and liturgical and scriptural wealth at their disposal. But it
puts a responsibility on them to use it wisely, frugally, and to
spiritual advantage. They must take care not to get a habit
of tasting everything, dipping and flitting in a desultory way,
living in a spiritual picnic.

They must read like *poor* and *earnest* students. There are
certain millionaires with precious libraries, and certain book-
fanciers whose joy is to *have* books, and look at well-filled shelves.
And there are other people who are real lovers of books, not
fanciers, who know their books well and read them again and
again. . . . Each one ought to think out how she will use
these cupboards, safe-guarding herself from millionaire ways
and desultory habits of reading. . . . And especially let them
guard against rapid reading, which in spiritual books seems to
nourish a whole nest of little vices.

Writing about the same time on ' our duties to books,' she
said, among other things :

We should love them ; it is a mark of a good education to
hold a book well, and to turn its pages with care.

We should not give ourselves up wholly to the author, or
put all our trust in the written word, but use our own judgment
constantly. Examine, compare, learn from books, but do not
think that each one calls for some final decision on our part.

Rather use books according to the idea of the author. One

writes to suggest, another to convince ; another merely because he likes to, and so on. Do not take too seriously the conclusions arrived at by those whose only end was to arouse thought.

We should not read a book through unless it is of gold ; but we should learn to find the important chapters from the contents. We should learn to glance over, to skim, to analyse, to study thoroughly according to the weight of the book. We should know some books thoroughly, and be able to find our way easily in many others.

We should seek for the characteristic marks of style in the best authors. It is good manners in the world of books, as of life, not to make mistakes as to a name when meeting distinguished acquaintances.

We should never give up books for reviews.

Among books we should have our preferences, form a circle of friends ; one becomes like those one loves.

More than once during these years, to help in stress of work Mother Stuart became a class mistress, giving courses of lessons to the novices in 1908–1909, and in 1910 to some young nuns who had been sent to Roehampton for their studies.

The greater number of her lessons in both years were devoted to the teaching of English, as the fundamentally important subject. In the last notes which summed up her teaching to the novices, she wrote :

' Why have we spent so long upon the teaching of English in the short time at our disposal ? ' and she answered :

Because it is the fundamentally important subject to learn :

(i) As an instrument necessary for all else. For accurate expression in science and mathematics—for the true use of words, the gate to philosophical studies—for the beautiful use of words—literature is human thought and feeling beautifully expressed.

(ii) As a discipline of mind. To make us know what we think, what we mean, and what we mean to say. It clarifies our ideas like nothing else.

(iii) As a discipline of character. It is a help to truthfulness, to moderation, to patience (the quest of the right word), to self-control—' Prune thou thy words.'

(iv) As an artistic training, for the formation of taste, which is judgment exercised in the matter of beauty.

To learn what to admire, and what to condemn, is much, and also why to admire, and why to condemn.

Her lessons were prepared with the greatest care. ' Easy teaching is not good teaching,' she said. These classes might have been her chief occupation. ' Notes of lessons on principles of teaching for novices beginning their juniorate ' is the heading to the closely written pages of one of her note-books—no mere pencil notes. Exercises were given after each class, and carefully corrected by her own hand.

In answer to the question: ' How to keep in hand the direction of a lesson ?' we read :

There are two extremes in this matter, the extreme of rigidity and the extreme of discursiveness. One belongs to the disciplinarian without much culture, the other to the superficial mind or to the person very full of matter and eager to give it. . . . Driver or cultivator. Both kinds are necessary. Drivers for immediate results, examinations, etc. Cultivators for real development, to kindle true enthusiasm, reasonable enthusiasm for knowledge, truth, beauty. [And the practical conclusion given was] : Aim at the style of teaching in which you are likely to succeed. Develop a type, be *somebody* on the staff.

To acquire the art of questioning [she told them] was to cultivate a habit of clear expression of thought. One questions as one talks. Good questioning, like good exposition, is the outcome of habits of clear thought and precise expression. Here, as elsewhere, general life-habits dominate school-work.

Effective learning means arriving at new power [she said], and the consciousness of new power is one of the most stimulating things in life.

Speaking of the cultivation of the love of the beautiful in children, she explained that it tended to make them thoughtful, not childish, awakened the true human element in them and made them grow up. ' It has been suggested, that beauty gives to children what suffering gives to older people—something completed, accomplished in the best sense.'

In 1910 it was the good fortune of three young American nuns to have Mother Stuart for their class mistress. One of them writes as follows :

No detail was too small to escape her notice. The method of keeping a study journal, the division of time, the choice of books, the visits to the different classes—all was arranged . . . and she told us ' that she would reserve to herself the pleasure of giving us a weekly class in English composition.' We met in her room on Wednesday evenings, a subject was given to be developed in a paper of about five hundred words, and returned to her by five o'clock the following Tuesday. At the next meeting these papers were read aloud, and criticised first by us, then by her, and finally revised according to a scheme which she prepared each week.

A short plan had to be written at the head of each essay, however brief. Sometimes entire paragraphs were remodelled by her and handed to us with our next paper. After three of these meetings she was called to Rome! And we supposed our classes would be indefinitely postponed, but no, she left a written list of subjects. Each week we were to go at a fixed hour to hear the new title, write the essay and send it to Rome, and each week brought a set of corrected papers in return. This continued for nine weeks. She was quite merciless in the criticism of certain faults, such as exaggeration, inaccurate statements, phrases that had no thought behind them, meaningless adjectives, and above all what she called 'cheap writing,' a superficial, easy manner of handling a subject without having 'thought to a finish,' as she said once, apologising for giving an answer after very short notice.

She always gave us the reasons for her rejection of a word, and substituted others with a note of interrogation, submitting them to our approval.

These seventeen sets of papers which we each received, with their closely written marginal notes, their comments and suggestions, all leading up to a final word of appreciation, are a striking example of her method of training minds.

These were only works of 'supererogation,' nothing was dropped because of them. On the contrary, they were undertaken at the moment she had begun to write her book on the 'Education of Catholic Girls,' and when she was also giving her evidence in the Cause for Beatification of Mother Duchesne. And yet she always seemed to be at leisure for what was wanted. 'Gross forms of selfishness being disposed of,' she wrote once, 'I must have no moods, no fads, no claims. I must never be bored, never be offended, never be busy. To be busy is to be engaged in an occupation which makes it inconvenient to be disturbed.' Perhaps some of her secret lay in the perfect accomplishment of this programme.

CHAPTER XVI

LAST YEARS AT ROEHAMPTON

1902 *to* 1911

'Through change to God . . . remind them that in all my inevitable
changes and struggles and defeats you have the one and immutable,
that for which others are crying out and struggling often in vain.   You
have the better part, and in it you may well be, as you alone are in this
restless age . . . content.'—*From ' The Zeitgeist,'* 1901, *J. Stuart.* .

THE preceding chapters have shown Mother Stuart in her life's
work, and have revealed something of her spirit.   Here we shall
do little more than chronicle the chief outward events of this
period, from her return from America in 1902 to her nomination
as Vicar General in 1911.   These were very full years in every
sense.

In May 1902 Reverend Mother Digby came to England.   Her
visit lasted several weeks, and Mother Stuart accompanied her
as she went round the houses of the Vicariate.   Writing from
Hammersmith on June 3 she said :

I am going to answer your letter, but left it behind in a
hasty departure yesterday evening when I was sent for.   Our
Mother wished me to see the Cardinal [Cardinal Vaughan] with
her, but as my cab was delayed and he arrived half an hour
early . . . he got here first ; and when I walked in he and our
Mother were sitting on two of the smallest chairs, framed in
one of the beautiful windows with the garden behind them and
with an enormous bowl of peonies between them, they looked
as you can imagine I   When I had ' homaged ' the Cardinal,
as they say in the Midlands, and turned to kiss our Mother's
hand, he said with his eyes, as St. Augustine might, ' *unde hoc
animal Deus meus ?* ' and with his mouth, ' Where does she
come from ? . . . Then he remembered our last talk. . . .
Good-bye for to-day.   I shall answer when I rejoin your letter
to-morrow.   This is only recreation, *currente calamo.*

Another event of the year 1902 was the foundation of the
Roehampton Association for ' old children.'   The first meeting

took place on December 4, and Cardinal Bourne, then Bishop of Southwark, presided.

It had long been Mother Stuart's wish, echoed by all who had been at school at Roehampton, that the tie should be made a life-long one in some definite and recognised manner, extending beyond mere sentiment: 'a bond of fellowship unites us, give it the blessing of immortality.' She wished that all who had begun their life's adventure there should never cease to look on it as a home, a place to turn to for sympathy and help in joy and sorrow. The years which have elapsed since that December day have seen the steady development of this good work. The reports of its meetings bring consolation to members in all parts of the world. Even when she had left Roehampton, Mother Stuart still watched over the Association, criticising the style of the reports, and suggesting improvements ; for she wished that there as in all else excellence should be aimed at.

March 1903 found her on her way to Malta, *vià* Rome, where a house of the Society was about to be founded. It was at first proposed to attach it to the English Vicariate, but after various vicissitudes, and the foundation of two houses in Egypt, it became the nucleus of a self-supporting province, the smallest in the Society, but the most varied in its composition.

These were the years of the great exodus of Religious Orders from France. From the forty houses of the Order closed there, some three hundred Religious found their way to England. Beginnings were often difficult, and few knew a word of English, but Mother Stuart did all she could to smooth the path, studying the needs of each arrival individually, that she might, as far as possible, send them to places which would best suit them and where they would find work congenial to their aptitudes and even to their desires. No one came within the influence of her 'extraordinary charity,' as one described it, without a renewal of courage and joy.

After a short time she identified herself as completely with these new members of her family as with the old, and interested herself as deeply in their spiritual welfare as in that of those who had been with her from the beginning. One of them writes :

'When I was sent to Roehampton . . . I was very much afraid of Mother Stuart . . . I do not know what I expected. But before the end of my first walk with her she knew all my sorrows, my fright was gone for ever, and my trust and heart given for ever. Then little by little I went from wonder to wonder. I found that she really cared for everything, for

Q

progress and improvement in the smallest things, and I began to
understand more of what God must be, if His saints were so
good. She taught me everything, even correcting my written
points of meditation. Since I have known her, the spiritual
and intellectual and moral outlook has changed in my life, and
sometimes I believe I am changed myself.'

The following little note to another of these exiles, Madame
Marc, shows how quickly sympathy and friendship had been
established. She had been for a time at Roehampton, but the
need of an organist in another house obliged Mother Stuart to
part with her. She wrote :

La volonté de Dieu se manifeste que c'est à Wandsworth qu'il
désire voir cette année ' Marc son évangeliste.' Tant de fois j'ai
tâché de vous sauver ; tant de boucs j'ai offert en place de mon
Isaac ! Ils ne sont pas agréés. Voilà le dernier qui s'enfuit dans
le désert ! Il n'a jamais vu un orgue de près. Vous voilà
donc chère Sœur bien dans la volonté de Dieu, très regrettée à
Roehampton. . . . Courage ! C'est consolant de voir de près que
malgré nos combinaisons c'est Dieu qui dispose de nous. . . .
Au revoir, cher évangeliste, car nous habitons près de vous.

Many new houses were opened in England to meet the need of
the moment, some of a temporary character, as ' refuges,' others
to become the schools of the future. In this way a convent
was founded at Leamington, in what had been a boys' college.
Whether from like causes or not, the girls' school succeeded as
little as the boys', and has since been transferred to Tunbridge
Wells, a change which Mother Stuart desired but did not live
to see accomplished.

In July 1903, Goodrington House, Paignton, became a
Convent of the Sacred Heart. Beautifully situated on the
Devonshire coast, where the green and the red of the meadows
and cliffs gleam as emerald and ruby in a sapphire sea, the old
house had a history of its own. Its doors made from the wood
of Nelson's ships bore the marks of the bullets of Trafalgar.
Here a number of exiles, many already old, found an ideally
peaceful home. But the house had no future as a school, and
having only been accepted as a ' refuge ' died a natural death in
the course of time.

A more important move was made in December of the same
year, when the convent at Carlisle was closed and its inmates
transferred to Newcastle ; not a great distance, perhaps, but
a world away. The change was from the sleepiest old-world
town, looking west, to the keenly alive city facing east. At

first a pupil-teachers' centre and a day school were opened. In a short time, however, the second Training College of the Society in England was established there, a work which appealed very specially to Mother Stuart.

In 1904 Roehampton was in its turn recognised by the Board of Education as a ' Secondary Training College ' where members of the Order could qualify for their work as teachers. This arrangement was carried out successfully for several years, until further developments in the ever-varying schemes of education necessitated a readjustment.

In the summer of the same year a new convent was established in the Isle of Wight at Bonchurch, in a house where Mother Stuart had often stayed as a girl. In December St. Charles's College was opened in what had been a cherished foundation of Cardinal Manning for the Oblates of St. Charles. The staff and students were transferred from Wandsworth, and the old work took new life ; the seed sown in tears began to be reaped in joy.

The next year, 1905, saw a short-lived foundation at Blackheath. The house had been asked for as a pupil teachers' centre, and was closed when the system to which pupil-teachers belonged was for a time abolished.

All these foundations and changes gave a great deal of work to Mother Stuart, and necessitated frequent absences from the home life with her community in which she found all her joy. For one house founded, half a dozen had been visited. And to these journeys must be added the usual yearly visits to all the houses of the Vicariate, and the week or ten days spent at the Mother House in Paris or Brussels.

In 1904 a second visit to Paris was added to her year's itinerary, for in May of that year the Sixteenth General Congregation of the Society was held, the last on French soil. At its close Mother Stuart, writing to Roehampton, ended her letter with the words ' The Society is glorious, thank God for it.' Her return brought many visitors to Roehampton, for she was accompanied by the Vicars of North and South America and Australia. They had scarcely left when she was called to Armagh to take part in the festivities in honour of the opening of the Cathedral, built with the pence of the poor.

In the spring of 1906 a summons came to Mother Stuart to join Reverend Mother Digby in Spain. The plan fell through, however, and she wrote :

Welcome be the Holy Will of God, thank you for having told me so quickly. It would be absurd to pretend that it was

not a great disappointment, about which I must think with some
precaution ! But if God wishes it, it must be for the best, and
I shall return to the life of hope without immediate expectation
of fulfilment, until He is pleased to send me something better.
But I am for ever grateful to you for having thought of this
and planned such a joy.

In the summer of that year this hope of a meeting with
Mother Digby was realised, and she paid her last visit to the
Mother House in Paris. A year later it was transferred to Con-
flans, and in 1909 to Ixelles, Brussels. This proved, however,
no permanent resting-place, the events of 1914 necessitated a
further move, and the centre of the Society was established in
Rome. Writing on August 11, 1907, the day after the old
Mother House had been closed, Mother Stuart said :

With all the sorrow of it, I am grateful that it has not
dragged on longer. Most of us were in the chapel yesterday at
five, believing that it was the hour at which you would be
leaving that dear and holy Mother House. What a date
the feast of St. Lawrence will be for us now for evermore ;
it is a great feast and a fitting one for a great act. How we
pray that God may bless your coming in and going out of
Conflans. For, alas ! there is another going out a year hence,
we must fear, but it is a grace that Conflans is there for the
moment. . . .

Visits to the Mother House were always golden moments to
Mother Stuart. On June 5, 1906, she wrote in answer to an
invitation :

Just coming from the oral religious examinations in the
school I find what I have been longing for, my welcome summons
to Paris. Oh, dear Reverend Mother, how good you are; how
happy I am. . . . I have such a quantity of thankful and
happy thoughts in my head that I do not know what to do
with them.

And the following year, on a similar occasion, she said :

No words could tell you the joyful surprise with which I
read your letter this morning ! How dear and kind of you to
write it with your own authentic hand. . . . I am getting
L. on Thursday to give her a day's rest here, as she is not
a good traveller, and we shall come over with untold joy in
our hearts on Saturday. I can hardly believe it yet. To see
you is the greatest joy I have in the whole world.

And when the week was over and she was back at Roehampton, she wrote again :

It was only when I got back to work that I understood and felt how much this week of heaven had revived me in every way. It is good to go back to in thought, and to have had again to-day a precious reminder of it. I had imagined to myself that I should be long without seeing your writing, and I found your letter there on going to my room after Mass. All that from your dear hand ! How gratefully I thank you.

In 1906 there was a lull in outward events, and during the summer holidays Mother Stuart gathered all the communities of the London houses at Roehampton for one of those rare ' holidays ' for which all details had been planned by her with the greatest care. And in her paper ' *Obiter Dicta* Long Ago in England,' she put before them, in the mouth of St. Hilda of Whitby, her ideal of religious life, its dangers, trials, and privileges. Cædmon, Bede (as a child), John of Beverley, and Bennet Biscop come upon the scene, and the old story of the poet led to a discussion on the *Dies Domini* of the soul, ' when giving all for all, the world, and heaven and earth become its own.' When alone with her nuns, her monks having returned to their labours, St. Hilda sums up the lesson of their lives : ' Do you see that to love is to live, and to serve is to reign for ever ? And the lowly are highest, and the highest are lowliest ; that to yield is to command, and to be unknown is to be celebrated ; and that work that seems of little use comes nearest to the working of miracles ? '

It was perhaps one of the most beautiful of Mother Stuart's writings, and as always with the uttermost simplicity, not to say nullity of plot, there was combined a profound analysis of thought.

The year 1907 was a sorrowful one for the English Vicariate. For reasons connected with the general government of the Society, Reverend Mother Digby decided, with regret, to divide the Vicariate into two parts. Five houses were thus removed from the jurisdiction of Mother Stuart, to the great grief of all concerned. For all had sprung from the same centre, fed on the same traditions, and all looked to Roehampton as to a home. As a matter of fact it was but *la présence corporelle qui manquait* a great deal indeed, but the old loving intercourse by letter continued, and perhaps even increased.

At the beginning of 1908 the first house of the Society was

founded in Japan, and just one month earlier another had been opened at Bogotá. The former drew foundation stones from Australia and England, and even Bogotá demanded a tribute of four from Mother Stuart, as no schools were acceptable in South America unless English could be taught.

The following letters were written by her to the Japanese missionaries and received at Port Said and Tokyo.

17th January, 1908.

MY DEAR MOTHER . . . AND ALL THE OTHERS,—

We were quite delighted to get news of you which the pilot brought ashore, all our hearts are following after you to the Land of the Rising Sun, with many prayers and much thankfulness to God for the great grace He has given to you. Its very suddenness in the end has left us wondering and happy. It seemed just as it should be for so great a setting out. Father X. wept from genuine holy envy when Father Kenny told him that you had actually sailed. . . . Of all things encouraging after all, the one that will really carry you on and through everything, is the thought of Him in whose name you go, and how you are part of His Church on earth, never more in the History of the Church than now, on your way to foreign missions—the prize sighed for by so many and granted to so few.

8th February, 1908.

. . . Your two letters and p.c. from Port Said and Suez, and the enclosures arrived safely and gave the greatest delight to everyone. . . . I think you will like to see the accounts of the journey to Bogotá from the coast. [The Magdalena had been in one of her bad moods, and the railway had only been carried a few miles beyond the town, so the journey inland had been accomplished on steamboats which stuck fast in the sands, and on mules and ponies endowed, fortunately, with great climbing powers.] One could not imagine a greater contrast than the two missions that started so soon one after the other; both such real missions, yours so accessible, but the minds you have gone to so inaccessible at present, I suppose ; and the other so inaccessible to travel to, but everyone so eager to have them when they get there. Both will be doing God's work, and by the side of both we feel small and envious.

A month later, as Mother Stuart was presiding at a criticism lesson, word was brought to her that the old house at Fenham Hall, Newcastle, had been burnt to the ground. No lives had been lost, and the barely completed new wing had been saved, but the danger had been great, for the fire starting in the roof had spread so quickly that in a few hours the building had been

completely gutted. A telegram from the Mother House sent
Mother Stuart to the scene of the disaster. An entry in the
house journal at Roehampton says : ' The telegram came at
twelve-thirty. She was gone in half an hour.'

In March she went to Jette, near Brussels, for the opening
of the tomb of Venerable Mother Barat. A few days after her
return to Roehampton she wrote to Mother Digby :

The first idea that comes to one's mind is this : the dream
has vanished, and we have come back to this lower world of
reality ; but in reality, it is the other way. Those things were
the realities seen for an instant like the moment of the Transfiguration ; and now we have come back to things which are
not real, in the midst of which we walk by faith. . . . It was
very sorrowful to say good-bye to you . . . and to know so
little of all that is before you, except that suffering and the
Cross are never wanting. . . . I do not dare allow myself to
look into the future, not even so far as the days of the Beatification, but the more I think of it, the more I hope that you will
not attempt the journey to Rome at this time of year.

This advice, which was that of all the Assistants General,
was reluctantly followed by Mother Digby. May 24 found
Mother Stuart in Rome for the ceremony of Beatification,
when there was a great gathering of Religious and children of
the Sacred Heart to witness the realisation of the promise
et exaltavit humiles.

> She is among the Saints, and God in her
> Has crowned a creature's utter lowliness.

The joy of these days was marred by the absence of Mother
Digby, who had done so much for the triumph of the Cause.
' The joy of joys,' Mother Stuart had written to her some months
before, ' is to think of what it will be for you who knew and
loved our Mother Foundress and were formed by her, and have
worked for her Cause *usque ad defatigationem.* Then to see the
realisation and happy outcome of all that ! '

The following little note to a nun who was obliged to leave
England in her absence was written from Rome :

This is what a certain holy Mother used to call *une espièglerie
du bon Jésus !* I felt so sure that you would be there when
I came back, that I ought to have had a counter assurance to
the contrary, which would have been consistent with my usual
experience when feeling ' cock-sure.' However, nothing could

have happened otherwise even if I had foreseen it, so one must
say that it was God's will that it happened so. And I must say
good-bye from here with very full feelings, my dear . . . giving
you to God again and feeling sure that in every difficulty (and
they may be many) God will ever be with you to guide, and help,
and support you, and I cannot help a conviction, not cock-sure,
but modest enough to be true, that we shall meet again, even
before the great final reunion of the Society, when we shall be
together from all parts of the world and for evermore.

On June 3 Mother Stuart was again in England, and a few
days later the ceremonies to commemorate the Beatification
opened at Roehampton. When all was over she wrote to the
Mother House :

We are full of thankfulness for the way everything went off,
and the cordiality of everyone. I must say that all of ours,
nuns and children, were at their best and made everything a
success. On the first day, the master of ceremonies crawled
round to my stall during the sermon and begged me to come
and hear his latest inspiration, which turned out a most happy
one : a solemn veneration of the relic which had been a joy to
us on the altar all day. . . . I thought it most touching to see
row after row of priests, many so old and venerable, go up and
kiss that little scrap of her old veil.

The panegyrics in honour of the newly Beatified were preached
on the successive days by Father Goodier, the future Archbishop
of Bombay, Father Bernard Vaughan, and the Archbishop of
Westminster.

Writing again to Mother Digby on June 25, Mother Stuart
said :

Yesterday had a glow all over it, from the kind and most
precious lines which you wrote, and from your goodness in offering
your Communion for me. It is an immense grace to be prayed
for by any one, but especially by you . . . for God having
set you at the head of the Society will surely grant all that you
ask for us, especially for your Superiors Vicar, who form the
second circle round you, and in such close dependance on our
head and centre. What a lovely thing the Society is ! One
realises that more and more, and this year its beautiful build
and constitution seem to come out all the more in the light
that has fallen on us through the Beatification.

On September 9 of this same year, 1908, the Eucharistic
Congress opened in London. Mother Stuart had asked the

Committee to allow her to give hospitality to at least a dozen Bishops and their secretaries. The offer was accepted in a way that delighted her.

Last week was most beautiful here [she wrote] with so many Bishop's Masses, the house seemed to overflow with *la plénitude du sacerdoce*, and our dear old Cardinal [Cardinal Logue] was so happy. They all said they were, and they were a most manageable *pensionnat*.

And writing to another, she said :

Thank you so much for your kind thought and liberal loan and prompt reply. We held out very well up to six altars, but when we found we must furnish a seventh, our resources gave way. Cardinal Logue arrived this morning with the Bishop of Dromore who came as ' a delicious surprise ' as his name was on no list. It must have been a happy thought of the Cardinal's at the last moment. They arrived just as we were putting the veil on the head of the Brazilian postulant. The fresh incidents of each hour, by telegram, telephone, and arrivals in the flesh are most interesting, and it is a sight to see the affectionate foreigners throw themselves into each other's arms.

The Bishop of Lismore[1] (beloved of God and man, with the true lilt of Co. Cork in his voice) and the Cardinal are well matched in anecdote.

Other Bishops present in the house were Monsignor Zorn de Bulach, at the time auxiliary Bishop of Strassburg, whose friendship with Mother Stuart dated from this visit ; Dr. Hendrick, the Bishop of Cebu in the Philippines ; Monsignor Morelle, Bishop of St. Brieuc ; the Bishop of Mazara in Sicily, Monsignor Audino ; Dr. Foley from Detroit ; and the Bishop of Athabasca, Monsignor Grouard.

Writing to Mother Digby, Mother Stuart said :

We are filling up. Yesterday was a day of arrivals. . . . Just as we were putting the veil on Sister B.'s head, Cardinal Logue was announced with an unexpected Bishop, the Bishop of Dromore. We made room for him by translating the Bishop of Waterford to another see ! Then the arrivals went on at intervals during the day. The Bishops of Lismore, Dunedin, Detroit, in quick succession. . . . The Bishop of Cebu is very touching ; he has inserted the profession ring of his dead sister in his chain to carry his pectoral cross, he has brought the rochet you gave him, and sent it up to show me. . . . He and Cardinal Logue have made great friends. He opened the door

[1] Lismore, N.S.W., Australia.

just now when I was sitting with the Cardinal, and was greeted with ' Here comes the King of the Cannibal Islands.'   We have a dear and holy Bishop from Athabasca, his see is called Ibora, I suppose he is a titular Bishop.   I think he has charge of the North Pole !   The Bishop of the South Pole, San Carlos of Ancud, is with the Bishop of Southwark.   The Bishop of Athabasca started as soon as he received the Archbishop's invitation, that is to say in the end of July, and he reached Liverpool yesterday, having come by canoe, by cart, by a little trading steamer down the Slave Lake and the Athabasca river, then seven days and nights by rail to New York, and thence by Cunard.   He is a thoroughbred missionary Bishop, and has been forty-six years out there. . . .

At the end of the month the new chapel at the Training College, St. Charles's Square, was consecrated by the Archbishop of Westminster, and on the evening of the ceremony, after her return to Roehampton, Mother Stuart wrote to the Superior :

September 25th, 1908.

We were so polite we could not say good-bye !   So I must write one line to tell you what a heavenly day I spent.   Which of us there present can ever forget the morning's ceremony. I don't know what it was about the chapel that seemed so unspeakably touching, and like the New Jerusalem coming down from Heaven ' prepared as a Bride adorned for her husband,' there is a purity about the lines of the building, and a simplicity and a repose that are quite indescribable, and the whiteness which has only its own natural tints . . . make it almost alive.

My dear, tell it to them, impress it upon them that ' we shall all be there the day after to-morrow,' all who were here in the Jerusalem on earth to-day, and then we shall all be together, and it will be heavenly for evermore, a million times more than it was this morning, and that is saying a great deal.   Give my love to them all and tell them *Ambulate sancti Dei !*

In October Mother Stuart was in Ireland.   She reached Mount Anville in time to help one of her former novices to die.   And wrote a few days later to one of the Superiors in England :

. . . I do not know if you have had any details of Sister Wall's death, so I write in the train on chance.   I imagine you must have been in the noviceship together, at least when she was a postulant.   The day I arrived she was in the hall with the others, looking most dreadfully ill—the next day she was down in the school for a few minutes, and on Sunday she was at Mass.   Tuesday the doctor said she was very gravely ill, and we should be justified in giving her the last Sacraments, so we sent for the priest and she had them then and there, surprised but grateful to receive them. . . .

I am deeply grateful to God that she died when she did and as she did, and so grateful to have been with her, there is a great consolation in seeing one of one's novices safely off to God. It was the most leisurely departure that I have ever seen, for seventeen hours we were with her expecting her end at any time, but seeing that she might hold out indefinitely. For the last fourteen hours she gave no sign of consciousness, but she may have heard and followed all. It was a most wonderful night watch, a still warm night—a high moon and a mottled sky—most beautiful, and all those weird little noises of night that are nothing anywhere else, but in Ireland so full of significance, little tinklings and whistlings far away on the hills, little shrieks of birds and rattles of distant carts—and little barkings of dogs—and through all, the weary breathing exactly like a spent runner, for her heart and her lungs were so good that there was not a catch in her breath; it *simply failed*, and the change was so imperceptible that it was only looking back on two or three hours that one could see it. We thought she would not open her eyes again, but two or three hours before the end she did so—and looked as if she saw that—what is it ? which they do see before the end comes. Is it not wonderful the ending of our life in such silence and mystery ? We sent for the curate when he came for Mass to give her an absolution ; he rushed in very much *saisi*, not having known of her illness, and fled away to his Mass. And in the end she gasped her soul out as if she could run no more, but just dropped at the feet of her Maker after the race. And so shall we all in turn, but I think not many in such great leisure and so easily, and holding for so many hours such a numerous *levée* round her as she did. This line is not made for writing letters. I wonder if you will be able to read it. . . .

Mother Stuart often spoke of this last look of wonder seen in the eyes of the dying :

> Show what they saw
> With a smile as they died
> Whose love had been tried
> And was true.
>
> Where evermore
> To the exiles of years
> The vision appears
> Salve, oh salve at last !

she wrote in some verses dated 1900.

Several times in the course of these years she had been given this ' supreme consolation ' to see one or other of her friends and children ' safe home.' Of one who died after a short illness, she wrote :

It seemed to Mother M. that she was always just at the beginning, trying to be patient, to be devoted, to give way, to be obedient, to set her plans aside. And it seemed to her that she would have to fight for years. ' I think I shall live to be very old,' she often said, wondering if fighting would be the law of existence to the very end. Then to the great surprise of all, her own more than anyone else's, it seemed that God considered the work done, and in three days she was taken from us, without a fear or a murmur, or a regret or even a sign, but in a great silence and in full submission to the Will of God.

And of another, a very dear friend who died at the ends of the earth, in far-off Australia, barely three years after leaving the English Vicariate, she said :

The quality which struck me most in her character was consistency, and if it were represented by symbol, that symbol would be a straight line . . . she was true to the stock from which she sprung . . . and died ' free as a bird,' utterly happy, as she wrote to me but a few days before her death. But this finished work was the process of years, and not everyone knew the conflict through which such freedom was attained. . . . Her own spiritual way was not easy—long tracks of desert, and few oases were in the line of her soul's journey. In the end, and much more quickly than she had foreseen—leaving many hopes behind her, leaving us surprised, she had been made perfect in a comparatively short time—she has gone to God, having given with head and heart for His service, with great faith and fortitude, all that she had to give.

So she followed them all, watching with wonder and reverence the drama of life ; and as the years went on, one can gather from her conferences that death became more and more a home-going, a meeting, a beginning, the seal and crown of life. ' *Going* they went and wept casting their seed, but *coming* they shall come with joyfulness carrying their sheaves.' Life the going, death the coming, and neither one nor the other meant to be understood by us here and now.

The year 1909 was a less eventful one. Three letters written to the Superior at Brighton give glimpses into the daily life.

In July President Reyes of Colombia visited the convent there, and in answer to the Superior's invitation to be present for the occasion, Mother Stuart wrote :

No, I won't come down and see President Reyes ! I will come and see your own selves when he is out of the way.

Mother Leborne in the infirmary is a more tempting bait than the President in the reception room. . . .

The next letters were written while on visits to the houses at St. Charles's Square and Armagh.

Roehampton : June 1900.

. . . I have only come over here for the day from St. Charles, because there was a Missa Cantata at which the Elementary School sang, so I had to be here. They would not be helped by anyone, and sang even the Proper ; it was very nice to hear them picking their way through *tu cognovisti sessionem meam et resurrectionem meam*, and sailing safely across *Consubstantialem Patri* supported by the steady voices of little boys, so happily unconscious of all the controversy and suffering and shedding of blood enshrined in that word, and then pattering down in great glee through *Catholicam et Apostolicam Ecclesiam*. They enjoyed it immensely. . . .

Armagh : November 1909.

. . . The week here has been most delightful : the Quarant' Ore in this very devotional chapel, the praying crowds ; even our stalls filled with these wonderful people. They managed to defend mine for me to get in among them, but once in no one could get out, and how they prayed ! The Cardinal carried the Blessed Sacrament in both processions, and it was a devotion in itself to see him in the sanctuary through the Masses, beating his breast and kissing his beads at each decade, absorbed in his prayers. He was very charming when I saw him too.

They do such nice little *gracieusetés* here. The Vincentians gave a nine o'clock Mass as an extra. My favourite preacher was called in by special request, and preached the most fascinating sermon ; and in the evening the pipers came up. They have full dress costume of ancient pattern now, saffron kilts and linen tunics, and cloaks of many colours with the old Celtic brooches on the shoulders. They piped the weirdest marches, and then danced step-dances in the house, and then sat down round a simple spread of buns and apples. Such fine heads and good faces; one could imagine the same in the many-coloured cloaks round a banqueting board at Tara ; but when one of them called for grace to be said, and they all stood up and said it together with folded hands, it was Tara after the coming of St. Patrick.

Writing to another at the same time, she said :

On Sunday I was at Armagh, they got my favourite preacher for me at my request, and in the falling twilight, and that lovely chapel, he preached an exquisite little sermon on the old days and the old faith of Ireland, the rock altar stones now transported into churches, and the raths and fairy hills, and the spirits of departed ancestors who had not the happiness of Christian faith, but perhaps enjoy a natural beatitude round the old haunts ! It was weird and fascinating, though my neighbour went to sleep !

Mother Stuart had a special affection for the convent at Armagh. Writing on another occasion she said :

It is very lovely here, SS. Patrick and Benignus and Celsus and Malachy and Concord (that is Blessed Cornelius) seem to be in the air, and the venerable Oliver Plunkett is under discussion, and Dr. Crolly in white marble at the Cathedral door, and Dr. Dixon in the cemetery, and the Cardinal on the hill, so it is all very holy. . . .

Early in 1910 the serious illness of Reverend Mother Digby filled everyone with alarm. But in answer to the most fervent prayers, the shadow on the dial was moved back and fifteen months granted as a respite. It was a warning, but few if any understood it. For the moment Reverend Mother Digby had recovered ; it was enough, we so rarely dare anticipate sorrow.

On March 24 Mother Stuart received a letter from the Mother House, telling her she had been chosen to give evidence in the Cause of Beatification of Mother Duchesne. Part of her work in North America had been to collect this evidence. She was invited to pass through Brussels on her way to Rome, and while regretting a possibly long absence, this visit to Ixelles was, as she wrote, ' a greater joy than all the rest.'

The following letters were written during this stay at the Mother House:

Ixelles : March 30th, 1910.

. . . I will be very moderate in my statements and only say that Reverend Mother looks five years younger, you may consider it much more. . . . She is more herself than ever. It is like a dream and a miracle to hear her laugh, and to see how she thinks of everything, and takes the same living interest in everything as before. The Assistants General are blooming like the paradise of God in their joy at her recovery. They flow over with it and can talk of nothing else. In fact the whole house is given up to joy, Paschal joy, spiritual joy, and joy of the united family . . . and the Blessed Sacrament shines and glows down upon it all. . . .

Ixelles : March 31st, 1910.

. . . I am in the same ideal quarters as before, the house agents would call it a ' bijou residence ' in the suburbs of the *secrétariat.* I am sixty-four steps, that is about forty-two yards from the chapel door . . . and moreover I live in an *impasse,* so that the only drawback is that it is too nice. An incidental drawback is the uncertainty of tenure. I may have to go off to-morrow morning ; if not, then it will probably be on Monday. . . .

Ixelles : April 1st, 1910.

. . . We went to Jette this morning, that is Mère de V. . . . a nice Belgian probanist and I ; leaving at ten minutes to seven, we got there by cab, train and foot at a few minutes before eight, while the Blessed Sacrament was being exposed, so we had a quiet quarter of an hour at the shrine,[1] while the faithful were at breakfast. Then they made the Consecration of the First Friday, and it was beautiful to be kneeling at the shrine and hear the words she must so often have read before the Blessed Sacrament exposed. I saw all the people that it was *convenable* to see, but managed to get two good hours at the shrine, and you may be sure no one was forgotten. I prayed for all, the ill and the well, the wise and the unwise, the even and the odd, the uppish (not many) and the downish (a few), the inward and the outward (who shall compute their proportions), the good and the perfect, the less perfect and the unbegun. . . . This morning at five twenty-five A.M. I met our Mother at the cross-roads going to the chapel, it was like one of the early Easter apparitions. Good-bye, my next will be from Rome.

On April 4 she left for Rome ; the letters written from there will be given in another chapter.

No picture of Mother Stuart's life at Roehampton would be complete which did not speak of her loving care for those who were ill or suffering. In her own home when yet almost a child she had shown this womanly instinct, and her father spoke of her as the ' best of nurses.' ' How I grieve,' he wrote to her when she was a novice, and her tears fell fast upon the letter, ' that I can no longer share in those loving attentions you now pour forth on strangers.'

[1] The shrine of Blessed Mother Barat.

Many have known her in the exercise of this work of mercy.
She never failed to visit those who were ill, and there was ' always
a sense of leisure about her at these moments even if her stay
could be but short.' When absent she never forgot them, and
even in her last illness inquired daily for them. ' I sent her a
message once,' writes one who had much to suffer, ' that I would
accept distasteful things for her intentions. Her answer was
characteristic : ." Thank her, but tell her I would rather have a
few Hail Marys." '

You must be a babe and a lamb [she wrote to the same].
Don't fight against anything they want to do for you, even
against being made comfortable, for that is God's Will for the
moment, and all your perfection lies in being as gay and as
obedient as possible. You know what I would give to go up
those stairs and see you. You must think instead that your
poor Mother's spirit goes in and out many times a day. Always
blessing you and commending you to God.

Another writes :

I spent three months in the infirmary at Roehampton, and
I may say that it was there I really learned to know Mother
Stuart. In the beginning of this period there was an operation,
and when I woke it was to see her standing by me, Rosary in
hand, and there she remained the rest of the morning reading
or praying, and all the time silently attentive to my least movement or want. She did everything for me herself, but so simply,
graciously and sweetly that one forgot the Superior, seeing
only the love of a mother. . . . Then began a golden period,
two months of daily visits, each one a joy. At first only a
word of sympathy or comfort, so fearful was she to weary me.
But as strength returned she showed her idea of a convalescent's
life. She did not ask or even advise, but gently proposed little
mental enterprises, such as joining the community in essay
writing or answering questions, etc. When I left the infirmary
I had read several books, written three essays, and had learnt
to reflect daily on principles and teaching gathered from various
sources. . . . Sometimes coming in, she would find me in the
dark, and go off to get a light ; if the Sister had forgotten to
remove a tray she would say with genuine satisfaction : ' I am
going to relieve you of this,' and carry it off in a way that told
of her pleasure in these little opportunities of service. These
visits were the red letter moments of the day. They made
me forget pain and weariness, and when she left something of
heaven remained. If on very rare occasions she was prevented
from coming, she would send a message to show she had not
forgotten, and the next day would prolong her visit.

Quotations might be multiplied, but we have seen enough to realise how Mother Stuart guided and encouraged souls to live at their best : we may close this chapter with another picture, showing how she helped a dearly loved child to die.

The question was once put to her : ' Which would you prefer to be—a spoilt child of God to whom He can refuse nothing, or a valiant follower of Christ who can refuse Him nothing ? ' ' I should choose,' she wrote, ' to be the valiant follower of Christ, for I have found that God's refusals are among the greatest of His gifts. I believe very strongly that " God of whom is all Fatherhood in heaven and on earth," has, like His representatives among earthly fathers, souls who are sons, and souls who are daughters to Him. He chastises His sons " to bring them to glory," and pets His daughters to make them as " polished corners of the Temple," and it seems to me that the pair in question are a daughter and a son. After much consideration I elect to be a son.' And it appears that her love went out more to the souls whom she classed as sons ; among whom was Sister Violet Ashton Case.

She had never been very robust, and just two years after her profession, in the autumn of 1909, her strength seemed to fail, and she was sent down to Brighton. She gained nothing by the change, and a few days after her return the verdict was given by the doctors that there was no hope for her.

Reverend Mother Stuart loved her too dearly not to feel all that there was of human sorrow in the prospect of the parting. It was with tears that she broke the sorrowful news to her sister, and a little later she wrote the following letter to Sister Violet :

MY DEAR CHILD,—

These thoughts came to me about your great journey, and I thought I would write them, for I am afraid of not saying them quite steadily. Supposing that when you were small, say ten or twelve, you had been told you were going to Rome, alone ; much as you would have loved to go to Rome, yet the thought of picking your way across Europe by yourself would have given you a kind of *saisissement*, and you would have wondered how you would manage a hundred details of it—getting tickets, on sea, at the frontiers, among strangers, in long tunnels, not sure of the language, etc., etc., and yet all the time you would be glad to go. And then, if someone had said to you that you had not understood the message, that it was that you were to go to Rome alone with your Father—how the whole thing would have cleared up and become lovely, and to everything

R

that came into your mind you would answer : ' Father will
see about it.' It is *exactly* like that.   God will see to everything, everything, and you have only to *vous laisser faire*, leave
everything to His forethought and care, and think only of the
loveliness of it.   May He bless you always.

Some lines in a shaky hand tell how much of strength and
help was brought by this letter.   Some one urged Mother Stuart
to invoke the assistance of St. Gerard Majella, and she wrote :

Thank you so much for a most interesting letter . . . with
the precious relic of St. Gerard.   I took it straight up to Sister
Ashton Case and she has got it on, and—I am perfectly certain
that the wonder-working Saint *could* cure her in a minute, and
I need not tell you that it would be an untellable joy if he did—
but I think she has seen the harbour lights !   I don't think she
wants to stay, and although it aches most dreadfully to lose her,
I can't even say that I want it now, do you understand ?   There
is so much of her that is in heaven already that it would seem
to me almost too earthly.   There is my inmost thought about
it . . . and perhaps it will seem strange, but it would not if
you saw her.   Do you know this little Manual of St. Augustine
—I took one up to her and she can't let it go, she says there is
sunshine on the very pages and printed words of the book, and
so there is. . . .

A few days later she wrote to the same :

You know I was struck with remorse at not having risen
to the proposal about St. Gerard Majella, and we are in full cry
after him, and Sister Ashton Case is certainly better, lower
temperature, less burnt out with fever.   I am beginning to
think she may be given back to us, and wouldn't it be a joy,
though it seems just a little cruel to slam the door of the cage
just as the bird is getting away.   But she will be patient enough
to live on again if God wants it, with a doubly consecrated life.

At the end of the novena Sister Violet made a great rally and
for a short time there were hopes of saving her.   Reverend
Mother Stuart, who was at Brighton for a few days, wrote to
her :

It is a great happiness to everyone, but a most special one
to your old Mother who is so glad to see that God offers you
the chance of doing and bearing more for Him before you
go to your crown.   It is a new beginning of life, twice given,
twice consecrated, and now it must be God's more than ever—

il ne faut rien d'extraordinaire—soyez fidèle, the little things of religious life are the humble ' way ' to get there, and the great thoughts and the great love of the wayfarer are the *going* in it, so, doing the least things you must have your heart in the greatest, and there, with your mind and heart anchored in God, so happy and so very, very calm—that is where I dream for you that your new life will be. God will take care of the rest. May He bless you always. . . .

The improvement was only temporary, but Reverend Mother did not lose hope.

We must begin again at St. Gerard about you, my dear Son, when I come back [she wrote from Wandsworth], a preliminary triduum now and a great general novena as soon as I am back— not long now. Thank you for a dear letter just received— writing so good, bless you again.

Mother Stuart was a constant visitor in the infirmary. She would go up three or four times a day, taking with her each time something of interest—a flower, a poem, community essays ; or she would sit by the bed reading her own letters. She would talk while cutting the envelopes, or join in the ' family conversation ' with amusing stories of her own childhood. Every evening found her there for the night prayers, which she herself described as follows : ' Sister Violet liked in the last days to have a rambling kind of night prayer said beside her, made up of things she liked, with " I believe and I confess " as the basis, and a little hymn which she had taught to the Junior School, " Jesus, tender Shepherd, hear me," for the compline of her evening devotions, at the solemn hour of the day when night was coming.'

Another writes :

I was at Roehampton the Christmas that Sister Violet was so near death. She told me that no one could imagine what Reverend Mother Stuart was to her, the constant thought, the tiny attentions. ' I could not feel resigned for a long time to being away from Our Lord in the chapel,' she said, ' it seemed to me that it was doing harm to my soul, and when I told this to Reverend Mother, she quoted the words of St. Augustine about finding God in my own soul, and it came with such wonderful light, just as she herself must know it in her soul. I have been perfectly happy since, and feel no longer far away.'

One night, feeling very ill, she thought it might be the end, and was in trouble of mind, longing for Reverend Mother, but she did not think she ought to ask the Sister to ring for her, so she waited patiently. Suddenly the door opened and Mother Stuart stood by her. 'You wanted me,' she said; 'never hesitate to send for me,' she added, as Sister Violet explained her fears, 'you know how I love to come.'

She liked to hear reading aloud [writes Mother Stuart, speaking of those days], especially Bernard de Morlaix's 'Rhythm of the Celestial Country,' or anything that spoke of heaven, the Fatherhood of God, the presence of God, the life of grace and prayer. She had always said that the word 'contemplation' was full of wonder to her and even the utterance of the word seemed to open a whole world before her mind. Saint Augustine's Manual gave her great delight, 'even the pages, even the printed words are like sunlight on a path, *they all glow*,' she said, and she could not have given a better insight into her own view of spiritual things, so full of light and glow, so entirely tranquil and simple. 'Sunlight on a path,' said it all, and the path was half woodland, half garden, full of wonder, but never far from home.

Sent to Rome in the early spring of 1910 by Reverend Mother Digby on business connected with the cause of Venerable Mother Duchesne, Mother Stuart took her dear 'son' with her in spirit in all her journeyings.

Yesterday I prayed for you at Mater Admirabilis, and I remember and pray for my dear son every day, asking God for courage, patience, brightness (He gives them all!), and daily closer intimacy of friendship between you and Him. All these long months are a time of hidden graces and a great ploughing and sowing time; the wheat will be ripe in eternity, and it will be lovely; you can't imagine, but you can believe, and that is better—but however much you believe, it will be an overwhelming glory of surprise in the end. Tell me what you are reading when you write again, and may God bless you every day and hour. Everyone at the Mother House asked news of you, and prays for you—blessed young son!

A few days later she wrote again, in answer to a troubled letter:

My dear Child,—
    Our Lord has taken you out riding across country where the going was pretty rough, but trust Him, He knows what He is doing and you must have absolute confidence in Him whatever

you feel, and when you can do nothing else, shut your eyes and fall back upon the simple affirmation which contains all else, ' I believe in God the Father Almighty '; you need not say more, you need not *feel* even so much as that, but it is *true*, and the consequence of that truth is that ' all shall be well, and all shall be well, and thou shalt see it thyself that all manner of things shall be well.' Don't argue, don't fight inside, but just agree with God in will, though you do not see what He is going to do. It is very weak-minded of me to wish to be with you when your soul is in straits, because if I were necessary or useful I should be there, but now you are the Black Prince, hard-pressed but *winning your battle*, and I am sitting on the windmill, watching you win your spurs. Our Lord will never leave you alone. When He seems furthest He is quite near and full of sympathy, and knowing and understanding just what it feels like, having tasted of all these things Himself, fear, loneliness, weariness—questioning of what it is all to lead to—He knows it all, and His passing through it has left `the grace for you, and you will come out of it a more seasoned soldier of Christ, and understanding more of His love and suffering than before, and that is worth much, isn't it? I am glad you like ' St. Catherine of Ricci,' I liked it very much. God bless you, I shall pray *hard*.

Early in May it became evident that Sister Violet was sinking. On account of her partial recovery at Christmas leave was given for her to receive Extreme Unction a second time. Reverend Mother Stuart wrote from Rome :

It is a very great disappointment to me to hear that you have been less well again, instead of hearing that you were cured on Sunday as I had hoped. We must each day renew the offering of our dearest wishes to God, that He may sanctify, bless, grant them as His Will knows to be best for us. I hope there is sunshine in your soul all the same. When we all get to the other side and are together again (and how happy that will be—one can hardly think of it), some of the brightest things we shall look back upon will be the hours that seemed most grey and weary, when, without understanding what God wanted, we let ourselves be passive in His hands and asked Him to do what He wished. I think this is all He wants, the rest He must show us bit by bit, day by day ; and I know, my dearest child, that this *will* is yours, you want Him to do all exactly in His way and not in yours or mine. We can see so little, and He knows how to bring good out of everything. May Our Lord bless you and draw you very near to Himself and make you happy. . . .

A few days later Sister Violet wrote in answer :

. . . I would have liked to have written before to thank
you, but you will have heard of yesterday's ceremony. It was
heavenly, beyond words, ever so much more lovely the second
time, when there is nothing at all thrilling about it, but all
peaceful and blissful, and one knew exactly what was coming,
and then I had Communion too this time, and renewed my
Vows. You know how much I would have liked you to be
there, if it had been God's Will, but then it clearly wasn't.
Lilies came from home just half an hour before, they little
knew what they would be used for. I am ever so happy—
really—and I am ready for anything, I hope. I think life is
going away rather fast. It would be *such* a joy to see you
again, so great that I cannot afford to let myself think of it,
and I have given it up to Our Lord if He will have it, and He
knows what it means. I can only thank you again for all you
have done for me. I pray for your intentions every day of
my life. Please bless me and pray for me. Your grateful and
happy child. . . .

To Sister Violet's sister, Reverend Mother Stuart wrote a
few days later :

. . . God's ways are not what we should have chosen for
our precious Vi. She and we and your Father must all make
again our supreme act of resignation and walk on blindfolded to
whichever alternative God will grant us in His love and wisdom.
It is *costly* not to be with her in the hard days, and I know she
misses her old Mother's visits—again God knows best.

Sister Violet never spoke of her longing to see Reverend
Mother Stuart again before dying. She made whole-heartedly
the sacrifice of all desire, and God rewarded her by what Mother
Stuart called ' those precious forty days which God was good
ènough to grant me after I came back from Rome.'
Those forty days were filled with love and thoughtfulness.
The night prayers together had about them the hush of sunset.
The daily visits were moments of spiritual intimacy more deep
and wonderful than heretofore. There was no longer any
reticence on either side, Mother Stuart would answer Sister
Violet's questions about her own thoughts of life and death with
unhesitating simplicity. And all the time she was thinking of
those who were feeling most the agony of separation. ' Sister
Violet's room is always full of flowers and all its spiritual atmosphere is like flowers,' she wrote, ' and she, a tall white violet in

the centre of all. It is almost too beautiful, for she is so un-conscious of herself that she rather overwhelms one.'

Her letters to my Father were frequent [writes the dying nun's sister]. On the day before the end I found a note pinned on the outer door of the infirmary in Reverend Mother's writing, asking that no one should go in. Thinking that this injunction did not apply to me, but was only to hinder visitors from tiring our invalid, I went in and arranged flowers on the little altar. Then seeing only too well that a great change had come I went with my sorrow to Reverend Mother. She had wanted to tell me herself, and her grief was great. 'Could you not guess that it was just for you that I put up the notice.' On that Sunday evening, July 10th, Holy Communion was taken to Violet for the last time. At two o'clock the next morning I was summoned to the infirmary and found Reverend Mother there, praying aloud. From two to six we knelt, one on each side of the bed, praying and talking with the dear one, as she spoke in her childlike way of heaven. To all her questions Reverend Mother had a satisfying answer, messages for home, this or that detail of death 'to be left to God,' and when she spoke Sister Violet invariably said : ' Yes, Reverend Mother, it will be all right.'

Throughout that night Reverend Mother's tears fell fast upon the bed. She made no effort to check them, though now and then she looked across at me with a radiant smile as the quaint rambling talk of heaven went on. The constant ejaculation was ' I shall see, I shall see. How lovely, how glorious ! '

The things of earth were growing dark, but the light came more and more brightly from the other side [wrote Mother Stuart]. She went up to its threshold and we with her to the very end. She did not pass through the mysterious vestibule of unconsciousness, but went step by step full of wonder, and her death seemed only the last, deepest act of submission and resignation.

When Sister Violet had been carried after death to Our Lady's Chapel, Mother Stuart laid roses on her with reverent love. ' Come and see our *beata*,' she said to a Superior staying in the house, and added : ' The secretary has gone on a little while before.'

A few days later she wrote :

We have just buried dear Sister Violet . . . planted our white violet root in God's acre to come up again, and it was a very heavenly ceremony. Father Rector came himself to sing the High Mass, and there was sunshine, and the children in white massed in the cemetery, and the grave lined with cypress down to the bottom, so not at all gruesome to look at, and the *Benedictus* sung in the cemetery. The whole of the death was very heavenly. . . . I have had an electric bell put in my room for the use of the infirmary and I assure you when it goes off in the night, one understands about the midnight cry 'Behold, the Bridegroom cometh.' But she stayed on until eight-thirty, longing for the end and so completely herself, the most simple and informal departure that I ever saw.

Reverend Mother Stuart never forgot the anniversaries connected with this dear ' son.' Birthday, death-day, and other landmarks in that year of suffering are all alluded to in exquisite little notes from which the following is taken :

On the 11th we shall think together of Vi from early morning onward, and how we offered her to God and led her between us up to the very door, and then she left us behind to look after her, and love her in heaven and hope for the day of meeting again, as we have done ever since. She was one of the sweetest things God ever made, wasn't she ?

CHAPTER XVII

SOME FRIENDS OF MOTHER STUART

' The *elect* of all nations understand one another and are strangely alike.'—*From ' The Education of Catholic Girls,' J. Stuart.*

THE last years at Roehampton saw a great development in Mother Stuart's sphere of influence outside the limits of her Order. As she went through life, she had a message of sympathy and understanding for many whose call led by widely different paths. Many persons of the world sought her help and claimed her as a friend. Some of the greatest of these friendships were with bishops, priests, and nuns of other Religious Orders. Testimonies from all these sources have been gathered in the following pages.

As was to be expected, a number of her friends were girls standing, as she wrote, ' at the covert side, waiting to see which way the hounds would break covert.'

One of these writes :

I left Roehampton without knowing Mother Stuart. During the next five or six years, though frequently on visits to the convent, my intercourse with her was of the briefest. She was always kind, but left me to make the advance, and I was far too shy to do so ; besides, I had an inward conviction that should I make friends with her, her power over me would be such that I should not be my own mistress, and at that time I dearly loved my so-called liberty. I kept, therefore, at a safe distance from her, determined never to fall under her control. At last, however, a day came when I agreed to see her, though still inwardly resolved not to give myself away. I waited with some uneasiness at the cloister door leading into the garden, where the secretary left me, saying, Reverend Mother would be down in a moment. After an affectionate greeting, she took me out, and we went round the long walk almost in silence. I wished I had never asked for the interview. Then all of a sudden—was she praying for me ? —my stronghold yielded to the influence of her sweetness, and

I gave myself away. From that moment she was my friend. The walk continued for an hour, and was followed by many another, and a correspondence began between us. For amidst all her immense work, she thought it worth while to bestow much of her time on girls such as I, who, without any thought of religious vocation, were leading the usual home-life with its ordinary duties and pleasures.

No detail seemed too small to interest her. In every phase of life she was full of sympathy and understanding, and never shocked ; on the contrary, always encouraging and hopeful. Her personal love gave her words an untold power. She made family sorrows and joys her own, remembering anniversaries in a marvellous way, always sending some little token, or showing some thoughtful attention to give pleasure. A box of flowers from the country would delight her, and she would write thus :

'I cannot delay my best thanks for your dear thought of sending flowers from the home garden, and telling you how much I liked them ; so much that I had to send a few to X. to bring her the scent of the garden which she loved.'

Her invitation to me to make a retreat was not accepted for a considerable time. Referring to the matter, she wrote :

'A retreat seems such a formidable thing that I am not surprised you feel as if you could not make it or meditate ; but once you tried, you would find how one's mind and heart go out to the big truths that are really the basis of all our life, and how your thoughts, which are so often dissatisfied and restless, would come to anchor in these great realities. I am looking forward for you to the time, in spite of all the horrors and shivers and tossing of the head, like a colt on the grass, that will go before it.'

The following extracts show how she followed up the home-life.

Now I want a few lines very much to tell me what home-life looks like after the long absence, and if you have begun to read. What about *Marius the Epicurean* ? It is a book which will make you think. . . . Please never think that I should find anything 'stupid' that you told me about yourself, or that it would be a 'bother' to me. It would all be interesting, and I should like everything that would help me to know you better. I wish I had time to type a few things to send you for your extract book. If you have Browning at hand, see if you do not like 'Rabbi Ben Ezra,' but it wants reading over and over again to appreciate it fully. . . .

And again :

If you only knew how often I wanted to write! But I shall have to establish a custom of making no apologies, and counting on your forbearance, and writing when I can. Is that settled? Meanwhile I go on praying constantly for my X. and hoping that she keeps a brave heart, determined to live her life nobly, giving to God and to others ; not undervaluing God's good gifts to her or letting depression invade her mind and heart.

Is it not funny how different we are ; sometimes we have to say : ' Oh, do try and think a little less of yourself, and do not be so delighted with all you do ' ; and to other people, among whom there is X. : ' Do try and believe in the good that is in you and let it out.' I like your ' I's ' better than anything, the more the better when you write to me ; first what you do, then what you read, better still what you are thinking and dreaming and planning ; what you are down about, and what, in a rare and happy moment, you may be up about, and all the successes and non-successes. . . .

I do not believe that you could, or even should have a regularly fixed order of day. I hardly think it is possible, and quite agree with what St. Francis of Sales writes, that a gentleman's house should not be conducted like a monastery, nor, he would have added, ' a girl's life like a novice's.' But a few duties placed in an elastic sort of way, not rigidly tied by time, but faithfully done, can give a backbone and a whole shape to your life that will keep it from being frittered or sauntered away. . . .   Could you not say, for instance, I will do two hours' good reading . . . so much gardening ; so much for others, not necessarily the poor, but something to make others happy . . . and then God's portion of the day, a few minutes' reading of something spiritual, your rosary, the morning duties. What do you think of that ?   Shall you ever read this volume ?

In moments of depression or trouble her love and care redoubled. In one such time she wrote :

Yesterday's letter cannot remain without an answer, or you will imagine that I was very much astonished and much disappointed at the blackness and desperation of the moods that sweep over you sometimes. I am not in the least. It seems to me that I understand them so well, and can feel them with you : all the restlessness and the weariness of things as they are, and the wish to go to sleep for a year and find everything settled, even the wish that everything was over.

Do you know that there are very few people that feel so strongly and deeply as you do, and keep all hidden away within, who have not to go through a phase and moods like that before

they ' beat their music out.' I do not know any more than
you do what is the sphere that is to hold all your pent-up
energy and power of loving, but I do know the remedy for the
moment, such a hard one to take when one is in the thick of
the struggle—*hope* and *prayer* and *patience.* Believe that the
God who created you has wanted you for an end, a real living
purpose ; and work to fit yourself for it, but be patient and
strengthen your character and your soul in waiting. You
know, X., that with your capacity for loving there is nothing
to satisfy you but God. I don't mean being a nun, but
having God for your innermost friend, making your intercourse with Him the fountain of joy in your life ; it is the only
one that never fails, that will carry you through everything,
and raise your heart and mind above the struggles in which
we get so dusty and battered, to the holy and noble thoughts
and wishes in which all that is best in you will utterly rest and
be satisfied.

And again, a little later :

Many thanks for a nice full letter (there is never a page or
a line too long for me !), and a post-card in the train, when the
blues had come on badly, poor dear X. Yet do you know
that it is good for us, shy people like you and me, to have to
pull ourselves together and face things that we should gladly
run away from.

Shyness, like nerves, grows upon one and makes dreadful
ravages in our possibilities for good unless we fight it systemati-
cally. Now I am going to give you a bit of advice ; try to lose
sight of the charm of wit and beauty and dress, and see some
of the deeper charm of life, earnestness, helpfulness, sympathy,
service of others. Remember you have oceans to give, only if
you under-value it, you won't bring it out, and I assure you
people would be deeply grateful for it ; it is such a hungry, lonely
age. People, especially who have not the faith, are so miserably
lonely, feeling about for something to cheer and to guide them,
and often a word from a Catholic of kindness, or of sympathy
or understanding, goes a long way. Do not be too distrustful
of yourself, do go forward to meet people half-way, they are
perhaps just waiting for the help that you can give and longing
for it. . . .

To another girl friend in somewhat similar circumstances,
Mother Stuart wrote :

Don't think for a moment that it was waste of my time
to wander about with you, it was not. I have gone a long way
further towards knowing you, even in talking of things in

general, and please never think you need talk of anything in particular unless you want to. I like you to know that if you should want to, there is someone who cares to hear it, but I know as well as you do the agony of being inarticulate, so never force yourself with me. And never mind! God understands all we cannot say, and sends help in His own way. Don't forget that you promised to pray for me, I do for you every day.

To the same.

Yes, I do know about the hungry feeling that one wants something, impossible to say what ; . . . and I think it is one of the deepest things in us. Isn't it (although we do not call it that at the time) the thirst for God, because we know so well that nothing less will satisfy us ; and the problem of the way to get what we want, and the knowledge that we can only partially reach it in this life, is the aching part of it.

But I am sure that it is meant to be thus, if anything could satisfy us down here we should be very small and tame indeed, and that profound discontent is the best thing about us, if we find out the right use of it. It is the thirst for the strong living God which makes contemplatives, and the fire which makes apostles, and it is only when we use it badly that it turns back on ourselves and makes us really unhappy.

I hope and believe that you will never be really unhappy. To be friends with God is the deepest spring of joy, and you have that, so I can only wish that you may have it more and more.

To the same.

I was very glad to hear from you after a long pause, during which my thoughts had often wandered after you, and I see by your letter that it has not been quite smooth sailing. . . . I have prayed very hard ever since. The more one cares the less is it possible to say more in a prayer than a petition for courage and light, or light and courage, and my favourite prayer which goes into one word is ' *perduc*,' lead her through, right through, and straight through ; ' *perducat nos ad vitam æternam*,' that is final ; but on the way ' *perduc*,' lead her safe over the fences, safe through the brambles, and straight over the water-jumps of this mortal life. You are in it now . . . and I am sure often puzzled what is best and truest to do, and longing for clear light and a strong heart to follow it. I will pray daily for both.

To the same.

. . . When X. wrote to me of her intention, my first thought was for you. . . . Everyone cannot go in such a

straight undoubting flight to the goal of their lives, you must
not mind having a great deal to go through in finding the
answer to your own question. It has to be so. And whatever
it is . . . it will have to be a much harder way; you are made
so differently, but God will guide you as surely . . . though it
may be a longer way.

> I shall arrive ; what time, what circuit first
> I ask not . . .
> In some good time, His good time, I shall arrive.

Don't you like those lines, but your ' arriving ' must be something very different from Paracelsus' dream of things to
come. . . .

To the same.

What a nice letter you wrote me, I liked it very much. I
am glad to know that you don't mind—no—that you like to
be told things straight out, because when I get to know people
well, I begin to get ambitious for them, and if I care about
them I cannot bear to see them wasting gifts and talents, or
above all character and will ; that is a great deal about myself,
but you will understand it, and why I am glad that you give
me leave to be hard upon you. It is one of the best marks
of affection, I think, to be hard on people !

To the same.

. . . I am glad you don't like controversy, and hearing the
wrong side. Of course it is necessary that there should be
controversy and ' alarums and excursions ' as in Shakespeare's
stage (I wonder how they did it ?), just as it is necessary that
there should be bacteriologists and specialists of all sorts in
medicine ; but we who are in good health are saner and happier
without dabbling in these things, they seem to produce a mono-
mania-microbe on the brain, and that makes people unfit to
live with, when it concerns health, and unfit to live at all when
it concerns theology !

I don't believe that instant death is the greatest of all
sacrifices, and I agree with what I believe from your letter
that you think, that you can only be satisfied about your love
of God when you have put it to the proof of sacrifice. But
God must say His own word in His own time. We cannot
invent these things for ourselves, or do them *motu proprio*.
One of the hardest and most precious lessons is to wait for
God. So you are standing at the covert side, and you cannot
tell which way the hounds will break covert ! But when they
do, then may you have a line of country before you which will

make you forget all the beauty and the glory of your woodlands
and pastures, and gallop till you are spent.

That is a nice wish, isn't it ? but you will quite understand
it. . . .

To the same after a long silence.

. . . I am more glad than you can think to see your writing
again, though the dates were, like Prince Charlie's spelling,
'bewildering.' December 22nd for the first letter was not so
hard, but the second was dated February 30th, a day that has
never existed, I suppose, since the origin of the Julian calendar.
But I don't mind wrong dates, or even impossible ones, the
letter is the thing that matters. And I see you are in the very
thickest of the fray, inside—pulled both ways and strained
until endurance nearly snaps. And one can see so well how
it came about . . . and how it almost inevitably came ; and
in spite of your feeling that it has almost swept you off your
feet, and that perhaps you doubt if you will ever find a footing
again—perhaps after all you will see later that it was a grace
to be allowed to test your powers in this way, and see how
we have to hold hard on to God, and how weak we are alone.
Nobody can see just at this minute how it will end, but I have
such confidence in God's special love for you, and your true
love for Him, though it has all gone out of sight and sound and
feeling for the moment, that I cannot for a moment doubt
that all will be well, and best, and blessed in the end. I have
been praying very hard, for your silence seemed long, and I
shall go on, my very best. . . .

To the same.

. . . The main point is that you have to put your will into
the setting in order and drilling. You have willed wilfully in
old days, but that will goes with the 'first wind,' as soon as it
has to breast the hills, and you need to cultivate for yourself
(I mean *of* yourself and *by* yourself) the tougher kind of will
that does not flinch before difficulties and weariness. The
great thing and the hard thing is to stick to things when you
have outlived the first interest and not yet got the second which
comes with a sort of mastery.

I have so often watched that desperate moment, and seen
whereabouts it comes in people's undertakings, when the
difficulties grow as thick as blackberries. . . . Don't expect
ever to be able to say to yourself that you 'do something really
well,' for the more you see of anything that is worth doing,
the more you will feel that you are ever a beginner. Yet God
is yours, your own God ; He will not let you go, and He will

never disappoint you, and all you put into His hands will come
out right.

Another friend, to whom many letters were written, conceived the idea of making herself a pilgrim by ' proxy ' for
Mother Stuart, and in her name and for her intentions visited
many shrines and holy places in Europe. And when, in the
years of her generalate, long journeys were undertaken by
Mother Stuart, this faithful pilgrim arranged that Masses
should be said daily for her, to take the place of those of which
she was necessarily deprived while travelling.

Writing to her, thanking her for some service, Mother
Stuart said :

    . . . I am much more grateful for that great pilgrimage . . .
and for your promise of the daily, inestimable grace of Mass
during my journeys.

So now my pilgrim is at home again, and taking up the
daily cross. Our Lord knows how weary you often are in
carrying it . . . but it is His own Cross, and He has carried
it before you every step of the way, knowing that you would
follow, and walk in His footsteps and think lovingly of Him
as you do.

'There is nothing that makes me so grateful,' wrote Mother
Stuart to another friend, ' as to have Mass said for me ; please
thank Father G. for his.' And when this most acceptable
gift had been offered to her for the anniversary of her profession,
February 12th, she said : ' So many thanks for that magnificent
gift of four Masses for my profession ! One for each vow—
what a unique idea, M. ! '

Another very dear friend, whose intimate connection with
Mother Stuart began in 1895, writing in 1915 says :

I had only a ten minutes' talk with her, that day in 1895
at X., but what a ten minutes they were ; they changed my
life. I got to know her then, and her kindness never wearied
during all these years. Her letters to me were very frequent,
more and more so as the years went on. I sometimes had the
happiness of accompanying her on her journeys, and frequently
stayed at Roehampton. When there she would see me always
twice a day. Once it was my privilege to accompany her
from Rome to Paris, we were alone ; passing through the valley
of Susa I remember her standing with me by the window
pointing out and naming everything we passed—places, trees,
flowers, birds—she knew them all, and they all seemed to make
her so happy.

The following are a few among the many letters written to this friend. In one of the earliest of all Mother Stuart wrote: ' Your letters are never too long . . . nor can you write on any subject which interests me so much as yourself.'

That will not do at all! Why should you starve your soul just because you are hungry and cold; and shall you ever be more worthy [of Communion] by waiting? If the ' sense of unworthiness ' made you throw yourself humbly and blindly upon Our Lord, it would make you so welcome to Him, and draw you so near to His Heart, which is never so loving as when we come back like silly babies that have been naughty and say, ' I am sorry,' *lovingly* not bitterly.

Your letter gave me so much pleasure that I must write a line at once to thank you for it. You know what pleased me so much? The warmer and more intimate terms with Our Lord, the increase of pleasure in being before the Blessed Sacrament, ' the one mighty joy of those who have sorrow, till He comes.' It makes a great difference in spiritual life when joy is there, and it delights me too to find that you are beginning to understand how homely duties can be transfigured in His service.

Was it very heartless of me to laugh when I read your letter and your account of your spiritual shortcomings? If you went bounding along from victory to victory I should be far more unhappy about you; for humility is cheap at any price, and a few failures in trying to reach our ideal are the shortest way to humility.

In 1908, writing on Christmas Eve, she said :

. . . To-night at midnight Mass I shall think of you and beg God to bless you and take possession of you and give you especially a great gift of faith to supernaturalise all you do, and make you see the value of things which now seem useless and incomprehensible; just as the swaddling clothes and the Hidden Life and the long delays would seem to an earnest Modern Reformer, who would want ' not to beat about the bush but go straight at it ': that would be the view of common sense, and Faith sees over its head and beyond it to truer truths and higher ideals. So I commend you to the Divine Infant, that He may be your Prince of Peace and rule you as it pleases Him, and make a saint of you—for at present you are but a ' poor thing '! God bless the poor thing!

S

In the following year for the same feast she said :

What shall I wish you for Christmas ? I think the best
Christmas wish is that some holy and lovely thought may come
to your heart with your Christmas Communion, and make its
home with you and stay to strengthen you and help you to
' walk forty days and forty nights ' like the heavenly bread of
Elias. God only knows the bread to give His creatures, and
when He says one word it makes the impossible possible, and
the unlovely lovely, and the unmeaning become a revelation.
So that is my wish, my dear M. Do you know that my dear
secretary, Sister Violet Ashton Case, is dying ?—just as fast as
she can, and so beautifully. I know you will pray for her.

In a time of great sorrow and suffering she wrote :

Lent has brought you a great trial, a great cross, Our Lord's
own best gift ; and you must take it in blind faith that it is so :
you cannot realise it, for all the hard and harrowing details
will press upon your feelings, and shut out from them the inner
value of it all. You can do nothing but say, ' Not my will
but Thine be done,' the prayer of the Agony. What you can
do is to close your eyes and offer to Our Lord all that has come
already and all that is before you—for we cannot help fore-
seeing that there is a great deal. Indeed I will pray for you
and for X., that each day may bring its own strength and all
that is needed of grace and patience and wisdom and faith.
Our Lord will never fail you : you will always get strength
from His Passion—strength for two, for X. will lean on you
more than ever now. . . .

. . . I very often pray for you that this time of trial may
be a time of grace, in which much hidden work, of which you
know nothing, will be done by God Himself in your soul. Lend
yourself to the things as they pass . . . each is God's message
to you ; each call which interferes with your own wishes and
plans is a distinct call from God to give Him that ; the things
matter very little in themselves, but the gift of them matters,
and lives for ever and ever in the mind of Our Lord.

Why has it been on my mind and in my prayers that my
child and ' poor thing ' was ' in the blues ' or not well or very
much worried or something ? Is there anything on your mind,
troubling you, that I could share and at least pray for, if I could
do no more ? The First Friday coming without a letter confirmed me in this feeling ! So I will not put off another day
writing to ask. Life must in any case be very difficult at
present, and anxiety for X. does not tend to diminish. You

have been so long without a break that I often wonder how your health is keeping up.

There is a nun (Helper of the Holy Souls) going to E. on Tuesday with their Superior General to visit the house there. . . . If you were not so tired I should have asked you to go and see her (Mère de St. Paul), as she was an object of veneration and a great help to me in the old days,[1] the first specially holy nun I ever knew, and she is so near to God that I thought it would be a help to talk to her. I met her accidentally in the train the other day, coming back from Brussels, after twenty-eight years!

Your little talk on paper in the last hours of 1910 was most welcome. We were so happy as to have Exposition of the Blessed Sacrament all that night, and you may be sure my ' poor thing ' was not forgotten. I offered to Our Lord in your name all that the last year had been and all the unknown things of this year. We shall turn over page by page, and there will be written on each the will and word of God for us, and, at the head of each page that brings sorrow or trouble, ' My grace is sufficient for thee.'

You have experienced it more than you can measure in this year, which has been one of trial, and if, through human frailty and weariness, you have sometimes to bewail a ' short ' or sharp mood or tone of voice, you must get the benefit of it by humbling yourself at Our Lord's feet. Often there is nothing that brings us so close to Him, even sensibly sometimes, as a nice straightforward, childlike sorrow for faults, from which our affectionate trust in Him keeps all bitterness, sadness, or discouragement away. Make it a point of honour this year that no amount of falls or failures shall ever infuse an element of distance or distrust in your relation with God, or make you sing half a semitone flat in the song of your soul.   I will end with my favourite words which Our Lord said to dear Juliana of Norwich : ' All shall be well, and all shall be well, and thou shalt see it thyself that all manner of things shall be well.'

Mother Stuart had a great veneration for all whose lives were consecrated to God. To do anything for one of them was, she said, a privilege. ' To give joy to the least of God's children is to give joy to Him. But I always think,' she wrote, ' that what we do for nuns is most precious of all in His sight.' Among those with whom her work at times brought her into contact, one whom she very specially esteemed was Sister Mary

[1] Mère de St. Paul had been a friend to Mother Stuart in the years after her conversion.

of St. Philip. The magnificence of her lifelong labours in the cause of education has been recognised by all, but Mother Stuart's friendship, which dated from a visit to the Notre Dame Training College at Liverpool in October 1902, rested still more on her admiration for the personal qualities of this great Religious.

From another Order, that of The Poor Servants of the Mother of God, a very dear friend of Mother Stuart writes:

One received something from her, something indefinable of strength and joy, each time one visited her, because she herself was so full of God.   Yet she always made one feel that it was she who had received the joy.

She loved people, because God loved them, or because she wanted them to love Him, and she found that to love them herself was the best way to bring about this result.   She enjoyed people as God's gifts to her.

The last time we met, she looked so ill that I was startled almost to tears, but her welcoming words: 'What a joy!' and the sincerity of her pleasure, put her suffering almost out of sight.

The limits to her interests were only those of the Sacred Heart of Our Lord; hence her power of entering into little things as well as great, her wide-stretching circle of affection and helpfulness; the depth and sincerity of her understanding and sympathy in the sorrows and joys of others.   Her letters alone are multiplied instances of this.

'I have been praying specially for all details that would come and that you are dreading [she wrote to me], and I am quite certain that Our Lord has helped, and will help, you through every day and hour as it comes, and He will understand all the things that no one round you can understand, and feel with you the things that no one else can feel.   May He comfort you in them all. . . .

'We are still in spirit going up the Holy Stairs together, and still not getting to the top!   Life is meant to be full of all sorts of incomprehensible things, I believe, but "all shall be well, and all shall be well, and thou shalt see it thyself that all manner of things shall be well"; that is too grand an assurance to have come from anyone but Our Lord.'

Writing from Sydney in 1913, she said:

'You cannot think how glad I was to see your writing, for I think of you so often and of the many intentions in which we are both interested.   Your own special one is very often in my prayers, and as it lies even nearer to the Sacred Heart of Our Lord than to ours, we must keep a great hope about it, though there may not be the evident answer that one longs for. God has His own ways, and they lead our faith and hope by such intricate paths that one cannot help feeling that it is a joy to Him to feel that they *won't* be put down or put off, and that we *will* keep on hoping and believing. He could never let us hope or believe in vain.

'Dear Mother, let us keep together in our prayers, and may Our Lord bless us both. . . . Thank you for your enclosures. Those are dear lines of poor Digby Mackworth Dolben's, I think. It is one of my joys that our best English poetic talent of late years has been Catholic ; he may almost count, as in a few months he would have been received. Do you not delight in many of Mrs. Meynell's, for instance "A General Communion" and many others ?'

Another delight was her sense of humour, the quiet fun that would peep out in some discussion, or at the close of some business letter. Her power of interesting herself in many things, so practically, so sweetly and completely, may be illustrated by the way she helped me in a work connected with the establishment in England of the League of Prayer for Priests.[1] The greater number of the letters in connection with it were written after she had become Mother General.

Writing to me from Brussels, Mother Stuart said :

'Do you remember a bit of work which you set me to do, which I have never done ? When I criticised the *Manualetto delle Religiose Adoratrici* as too wordy and complicated for England, you very rightly suggested that I should propose some more acceptable form !

'Cardinal Mercier's letter, which I enclose, gave me the idea of something more simple and—British ! I think it is very beautiful by its unadorned directness, and must appeal to any Religious. His Eminence has sent a copy to every nun in his diocese.

'If something like this simple plan could be expanded into a permanent arrangement. . . . It seems to me that without much machinery one might arrive at the desirable result that there should not be in England an hour of the day or night, all the year round, in which there was not at least one nun praying for the Clergy.

'The great thing would be [to get] a letter from the Cardinal,[2]

[1] The organisation of the League is in the hands of The Private Secretary, Archbishop's House, Westminster.
[2] Cardinal Bourne.

and the signatures of all the Bishops. . . . Perhaps you will find an opportunity of laying it before his Eminence some day.'

Part of the Italian Manual had already been translated into English. This was sent to her to criticise. She answered :

' As you say criticise, I will do so. It does not seem to me that the exclamatory and highly-wrought style of devotion gets the best prayers out of us in England, and one feels that it is a translation in every sentence. But the only way to avoid this would be to re-write the Italian instead of translating it. The idea is such a great and good one that one would regret its being presented in England in a form so un-English. . . . I think that you would easily get something that would make more impression . . . by inspiring one of your own nuns, or one of the staff of the C.T.S. writers to put the whole into a native form. . . .'

When Bishop Butt had consented to write the Manual, she wrote :

' It was good of you to send me his pages. I am delighted with what he has written, entirely delighted, for it seems to me that the whole mind and spirit of the proposed Association is there, and it is so expressed that not one word could be cut out. This seems to me perfect, for an idea that has to make its way in England. . . . Let us pray hard that it may be cordially taken up. I should think it could hardly fail to awaken interest and sympathy.'

It is a grace to have known Mother Stuart upon earth, and a happiness to look forward to the meeting there where ' all manner of things shall be well.'

Among the most constant of her friends of many years was Monsignor Croke Robinson. A convert to the Catholic Church in 1872, he only became acquainted with Mother Stuart as preacher and lecturer in the Archdiocese of Westminster. He made no secret of the strength and comfort he derived from his visits to Roehampton. So much did he value them that they formed part of his programme of life. Every First Friday of the month was set apart for the purpose. When Mother Stuart left England for Belgium it was a great personal sorrow to him. The monthly visits were no longer possible. The distance to Brussels was no insurmountable obstacle, but her many long journeys entailed frequent absences from the Mother House at Ixelles. He readjusted his plans, however, to meet the new conditions, and arranged to go to Belgium from time to time for three or four days, during which he would say Mass at the convent, and spend a part of each morning with Mother Stuart. And this he did on more than one occasion. He died when she was in America, and nearing the end of her journey round the world, on April 17, 1914.

Her own death, which followed so shortly afterwards, was a sword of sorrow piercing many hearts, and revealing thoughts which perhaps in her lifetime few, if any, had conjectured. She was ' a friend, a confidante, an encouraging and stimulating influence in the many trials that occur in a life like mine,' wrote the Vicar General of an English diocese. Similar testimonies came from many quarters : from the Archdiocese of Armagh, where a priest who had known her for very many years wrote : ' She was my ideal of the valiant woman, such a worker for God, yet so womanly and tender and true. To me she was kind beyond measure, and her letters were events in my life. . . . I too have lost a Mother and a friend ' ; and from a poor and hard-worked mission in England another wrote : ' I owe Mother Stuart more than I can ever hope to repay. She was my fairy godmother always, and a dear friend to whom I told my troubles.'

Another priest, speaking of her, said : ' She was very human in her influence, and therefore very effective. St. Paul made himself all things to all men, she too had that gift of making herself all to each ; even people who only met her once thought that they were in a special way her friends.'

Among those who met her thus in the last years of her life, when she had reached the full stature of her sanctity, and whose esteem was none the less genuine by reason of its quick development, may be mentioned the Bishop of Nueva Caceres, in the Philippine Islands, Dr. MacGinley. He has recorded his impressions in the following lines :

My impressions of Mother Stuart were formed in a brief visit, but they are so deep and lasting as not readily to be effaced. And my memories of her, like those I cherish of Pius X, sweet and pleasant always, emit, now that both are dead, a gentle, sacred, mystic fragrance, redolescent of the eternal hills.

To these holy recollections a chapter is devoted in a volume I have written, not on paper, but on the enduring tablets of the heart. That record I have entitled ' Saints I have known,' and is my personal impression of the half-dozen souls of preeminent sanctity it is my privilege to number among my friends, or whom, at least, it has been my good fortune to have met.

All ' my saints ' differ among themselves in almost all the
circumstances of life ; they are of various races and tongues
and social conditions ; but in the life and character of all there
is a wonderful family likeness. They are all so thoroughly,
desperately humble, and all are so passionately in love with
poverty and obscurity ! Several had their longing for retirement
gratified, for their very existence is unknown beyond their own
narrow circle. Theirs are the short and simple annals of the poor.
. . . Others of ' my saints ' were dragged from the obscurity
they loved and set on a pinnacle to be seen of all men. Such
were Pio Decimo and Mother Stuart, who for the good of others
and the glory of God had to sacrifice their beloved retirement.
His transparent, deep, sincere, consistent humility was what
most impressed me on the three occasions I was privileged to
see and speak with His Holiness. And this same sterling
humility I recognised in Mother Stuart the moment I met her.
Instinctively, you know, when it rings true.

I went to Manhattanville to ask a favour of Mother General.
I had received a Sister from my native county of Donegal into
the Society of the Sacred Heart about Easter of 1906. Naturally
she was longing for the end of the eight years that separated her
from profession ; and she was hoping that I might be in America
to officiate at the ceremony. . . . Her superiors, however, had
judged it wise to postpone her profession, deeming her too
immature, ' too childish,' to be admitted as a professed Sister.
The cross was heavy, but accepted in a spirit of faith ; it proved
very salutary.

It was to intercede for the profession of this Sister that I
wended my way one day to Manhattanville ; not without trepidation and much misgiving. I had had, in many lands, some
experience of the majesty that hedges in great personages ; and
was anticipating now a dreary series of ante-chambers and long
delays. . . . I was returning from the chapel along the open
cloister, after lunch, when I met a nun who bowed as I approached.
I returned the bow, and was passing on, when Reverend Mother
Vicar whispered : ' This is Mother General.' So after all there
was to be no waiting for an audience ! Instead, she had come
herself to search for me. Because of this act of humility and
courtesy, so like that of Her who ' went with haste ' to do a
kindness, Mother Stuart's dignity suffered not at all in my
estimation. But she was all unconscious of having done anything unusual, as she led the way to the parlour.

I had no trepidation now in making known my request. And
to my delight I found it already granted ; for Mother General
had studied the case, and had decided on Sister X.'s profession
in November. She told me she was convinced that the Sister
was not childish but ' child-like ' ; ' and of such,' she said,

with her face all luminous with the light of faith, ' of such is the kingdom of heaven.'

Then she asked about Donegal ; and from the very wistful look in her eyes as she spoke, I knew she was evoking out of the past pleasant and holy memories. . . . Then, for a moment she fell into reverie, in which I am sure Errigal, and the Clady river and Bunbeg were pictured ; from that she roused herself with a sigh and a smile ; her face clouded as she spoke of Mexico, and her agony of worry about her daughters in that war-torn land. . . . When I rose to go, Mother General knelt for my blessing. As I gave it, I strongly felt that instead I should be kneeling for hers. It is consoling to recall that she promised to pray for me.

The visit had a pleasant and characteristic sequel. One day soon after, I think the very next day, Sister X. was high on a step-ladder cleaning some chandeliers. She was sad, for in a few days Mother General was to go, and with her all hope of an early profession, unless something should happen. It did ! Suddenly she heard someone at the door calling her. She looked, it was Mother General ! She tumbled rather than alighted from her perch. Mother Stuart raised her up and with a happy smile said : ' Sister, you are to be professed in November.' Whereupon Sister X. clapped her hands and jumped for joy ! Far from censuring this levity, Mother General laughed delighted, and then, as she turned the corner of the corridor, paused for a moment to wave her hand to the Sister she had made so happy. That gesture was a benediction and a caress. How like all this is to the ways of Him, who ' went about doing good,' and Who said, ' unless you become as little children you shall not enter into the kingdom of heaven. . . .'

When November came, Mother Stuart had gone to God ; but her wishes were faithfully carried out ; Sister X. was professed, and it was I that officiated at the ceremony. Thus was Mother Stuart beloved of God and man ; is it any wonder that her memory is in benediction ?

Of another ' kind and gracious friendship,' as Mother Stuart described it, it is allowed to give a more complete account. It has already been alluded to among the incidents of the Eucharistic Congress held in London. Speaking of it Monsignor Zorn de Bulach, Bishop of Erythrae, and for long Auxiliary Bishop of Strassburg, writes :

I first made the acquaintance of Mother Stuart during the Eucharistic Congress held in London in September 1908. I look on it as a special favour of Divine Providence that I received hospitality at Roehampton during those days.

Nothing at first sight betrayed either the dignity or the eminent intellectual superiority of Mother Stuart, so completely was she animated by the spirit of those words which our Divine Lord said of Himself : ' The Son of Man is not come to be served, but to serve.' Humble and obliging, she appeared to be every-where where help was needed, and yet was invariably calm in her activity.

The convent was crowded at the time with distinguished guests who had come from all parts of the world, so that I was far from being the only Bishop with whom she was occupied ; for that reason her solicitude for all that concerned me touched me the more deeply.

An expedition to Oxford detained me in England a day longer than the majority of the visitors ; and it was on the evening of this last day, when all but myself had left, that I learnt to know this eminent woman, and holy Religious, whom Our Lord, by a favour for which I shall never cease to bless His Divine Heart, had given me the consolation of meeting.

On my return to Alsace I sent Mother Stuart a book of which I had spoken to her, the Life of Madame Julie de Massow. On September 24th I received a letter of thanks. This letter opened the series of a precious correspondence which I have kept with the greatest care ; the last letter in it bears the date of July 27th, 1914.

These frequent letters, and our too rare meetings at Kientz-heim, Brussels, and Rome developed and strengthened the friendship begun at Roehampton.

A gracious tie had already bound me to the Society of the Sacred Heart, for my mother had been for many years a child of the convent at Metz, and had there acquired that strong foundation of faith and piety, and that spirit of self-sacrifice, which are characteristics of the training which Blessed Mother Barat has bequeathed to her daughters, and through them to the children educated by her Society. . . . My veneration for my own mother had always inspired me with gratitude towards the Order with which I considered myself connected. . . .

Mother Stuart responded to my feelings on this point, and took a deep interest in all that concerned me. Her great in-tellectual powers, her sure and straight judgment, and still more than these natural qualities, the clear and penetrating insight of her mind illuminated by faith, inspired me with the greatest confidence in her ; while she on her side received all my com-munications with inexhaustible charity and the most delicate sympathy.

' A Bishop's life is almost always a life of crosses,' as Mother Stuart said, and mine was no exception, but I found in her the support and consolation that a friendship drawn from the Heart of Our Lord gives. I know, too, that my sympathy and interest in the Society was not without its value in her eyes, as may be gathered from several letters, especially those of 1911, after her nomination as Superior General.

On July the 5th of that year, when still Vicar General, she wrote :

'May I thank you, my dear Lord, for your kind letter of June 5th, and the fervent and encouraging words which you were good enough to write to me on the new charge which had just been laid upon me. The remembrance of them has often been a consolation to me, and also the passages from St. Paul and the *Imitation of Christ* which Your Lordship pointed out. I wish I might realise them and catch from them the smallest spark of St. Paul's own zeal and charity.'

And again on the 13th of September of the same year she said :

' Your Lordship's thoughtful kindness touches me more than I can say, and I thank God for it as well as thanking you. Such kind and gracious friendship is His gift, and now that heavier responsibilities have fallen to my lot . . . it becomes all the more precious. I did indeed receive Your Lordship's very kind letter on the day of my election, and it was a very great comfort to me on that day which changed so much in my life. Up to the last I had hoped that this charge would not be given to me, but now that God has seen fit to lay it upon me I know that it would not be right to look back, and that I must take each day from His hand and His Heart just as He sends it. The thought of your Lordship's good wishes to me, the fact that you are pleased at my election, the conviction that I have your blessing and a remembrance in your prayers, all this gives me great consolation, and I thank Your Lordship again for it.'

In her last letter, written from Ixelles on July 27, 1914, she said, referring to several letters of mine which had met her at the various stations in her long journey round the world :

'When one is so far away from Europe, letters like those you are good enough to write to me have a double value and are a great comfort. You know it by your own experience, my Lord, that those who have charge of others, have, of necessity, a very solitary life, so that, as Keble writes :

"How timely then a (distant) voice
Comes floating on the mountain air,"

as it tells one that there are others among life's pilgrims who are
climbing up the same ascending paths ; and besides that, your
letters always bring a Bishop's blessing with them.'

Twice I had the consolation of meeting Mother Stuart in
the Convent at Kientzheim, in June 1912, and in the beginning
of October 1913, when she was setting out for her journey round
the world. At Brussels in January 1913, and in Rome in the
spring of that year, the same happiness fell to my lot. Intercourse with her drew one nearer to God, and each interview
which she was able to grant me in the midst of her numerous
occupations was in my eyes a real spiritual grace. My veneration
for her, and the immense importance of her life to her Society,
made me caution her on one occasion at Kientzheim against
overwork. . I was then Bishop Auxiliary and Vicar General
of the diocese of Strassburg, and I told her that I always urged
on ecclesiastical superiors the necessity of a division of labour ;
keep, I said, to yourself the work that you can do better than
others, and let them do the rest, this is not idleness but prudence.
It was on the same occasion that I told her that my love of
literature made me still a constant reader of our classics. Many
beautiful passages in them, lending themselves to a spiritual
interpretation, can become a prayer ; the very beauty of the
form facilitating its expression and making it rise with greater
depth of meaning to the God of all beauty. On both these
points I found she was in agreement with me, and in a letter
written from Liège on July 19, she came back on this subject
of the classics.

'May I tell you a little thing which was a real joy to me.
Speaking of your love of poetry and literary beauty, and saying
that you did not pass a day without going over some of the
·excellent beauties of your own classics, you let me see how
you turn the earthly to heavenly beauty, and sing the Songs
of Sion, by reading into the lines of the Mastersingers things
beyond what they thought or understood themselves. And
as this is a favourite practice of my own, it was a very great
contentment to me to find it justified by Your Lordship's
example.'

From the beginning of our friendship, Mother Stuart was
interested in what has been one of the chief endeavours of my
life. Living as I have done in a country where there were many
of those whom Leo XIII called with exquisite charity ' our
separated brethren,' I had always been struck by the fact that
numbers of these souls, in good faith and of good will, needed
but to know the truth to embrace it. But the difficulties actually
in the way of converts are neither small nor easily overcome,

and, as in all works of true zeal, prayer rather than direct action is the most powerful and frequently the deciding factor. The Life of a celebrated convert, Madame Julie de Massow, which I had sent to Mother Stuart, confirmed me in this idea, and encouraged me to take an active part in the Apostolate of Prayer already established for this purpose. Later, in the sanctuary of Saint Odile, the patron Saint of Alsace, I conceived the idea of making this Apostleship known throughout the world by means of the Eucharistic Congresses. This peaceful crusade of Prayer appealed to Mother Stuart, and she interested Reverend Mother Digby in the work. Writing on August 23, 1909, she said :

'I have asked Mother General to recommend to the prayer of all our religious houses in every country the intention which Your Lordship has so much at heart for the reunion of Christians. How happy it is, my Lord, to have an *idée fixe* which is so entirely in conformity with Our Lord's Sacred Heart, and its wishes for the salvation of the world. One cannot help feeling that such an idea must have been a gift from Our Lord Himself.'

When she knew that I was about to deliver a discourse on the subject at the Eucharistic Congress of Vienna, she wrote :

'I shall have special prayers for this intention, and on the 13th I shall try to be before the Blessed Sacrament to pray at the time that I think Your Lordship may be speaking. It is quite true, as you say, the simplest words go the furthest. And after all simplicity of discourse was Our Lord's own manner of teaching. And the subject is too great and intimate to be made into a work of oratory, it is meant for souls—an apostolic word—meant for the whole world.'

When she herself had become Mother General her co-operation was still more precious to me. Her joy was great indeed when Pius X approved the scheme of the Association by a papal rescript, dated December 4, 1912.

In a letter written from Point Grey, British Columbia, she spoke of her consolation in hearing that over nine thousand names had been inscribed in the register of the Association, kept in the Convent of Marie Reparatrice in Strassburg,[1] and she expressed her wish that I should have an indulgence attached to the prayer recommended to the Associates for daily recitation. ' It will,' she said, ' surely add much to the attention and devotion with which the leaflet is received, an indulgence like a Roman seal always arrests attention.' This desire of hers was

[1] Convent of Marie Réparatrice, 14 Rue Sainte Elizabeth, Strasbourg, Alsace.

accomplished to my great consolation, and in the years which have elapsed since that date, 1913, in spite of all the difficulties of the times, some thirty-one thousand names have been enrolled in the apostolate, gathered from all countries of the world.

Two more extracts from Mother Stuart's letters will show another side of our correspondence. On September 10, 1912, after a retreat made at Jette, she wrote to me :

'It has been a great grace to have eight days in complete solitude by the resting-place of Our Blessed Mother Foundress, and I had time to think of many things, in hopes of making my life more pleasing to God and more useful to my charge.

'Two things especially have struck me. . . . The way in which every one of us depends upon the others, so that the prayer of one well made is the good of all ; this is a great stimulus of effort, when one feels that others will benefit by it as well as oneself. The other was the great importance of habitual thought of holy things and of God, since our thoughts, although they pass into forgetfulness as far as our present consciousness goes, are yet deathless and incorruptible, as my author said.'

Writing to her on November 22, 1913, I sent her the beautiful antiphon of the Office of Saint Cæcilia : *Cæcilia famula tua, Domine, quasi apis tibi argumentosa deservit.* (Cæcilia, thy handmaid, serves Thee, O Lord, as a busy bee.) Mother Stuart's indefatigable activity made me often think of this comparison with the wise and industrious bee. Answering me from New Zealand she said :

'I must thank Your Lordship very gratefully for your letter of November 22, St. Cæcilia's day, with the Antiphon from her Office which has always given me devotion. I am glad to have it in your writing [her exquisite courtesy made her notice things which were scarcely worth while], and may I say that the whole of that letter was a great joy to me, it was forwarded and reached me in New Zealand, where one has the feeling of being at the outermost limit of the world of ordinary life.'

It was in the service of God that she had undertaken this long and wearisome journey, which was a source of much suffering to her. But walking in the footsteps of her beloved Master, she had always before her eyes the Holy Will of God ; had she chosen a motto it might well have been 'My meat is to do the Will of Him who sent me.'

And now this venerated Mother (to use a phrase of St. Francis of Sales, whose letters were her delight) 'tastes the sweet honey of the love of God in the true land of promise in paradise.'

This thought is a consolation in the sorrow of having lost her at an age which gave every reason for hoping that her Society would possess her for long years to come. More united now to the Sacred Heart and the Immaculate Heart of Mary than she was on earth, she watches over us and prays for us with still greater fervour, for, as Saint Paul says, ' Charity never falleth away.'

My ardent desire is that one day God will deign to glorify in this world this Religious who served Him with her whole heart, and my hope is that once again will be realised, for Reverend Mother Janet Stuart, the words of the most humble, but most holy of creatures, Mary Mother of God : ' He hath exalted the humble.'

CHAPTER XVIII

> ' This is only for odds and ends. The first, is it an odd or an end ?
> that your letters are always a bright spot in my post.'
>
> *From a letter, J. Stuart.*

MOTHER STUART hoped, if she did not expect, to be kept only
two or three weeks in Rome ; but nine weeks passed before the
business which had called her there was concluded.   During this
time she wrote the first chapters of her book on the Education
of Catholic Girls.   The following letters were all written to
Roehampton.

Before Spezzia : 5th April, 1910.

This will be written under difficulties which you know—
shaky trains, tunnelly ways, crowded carriages, and all the
inhabitants of this one seem to be lamenting that they have
been delayed by missing connections at Basle or Turin, so once
more God has looked after our journey for us; there was enough
snow on the ground to make us lose any connection.   I wonder
whether you will get my postcard posted at Alessandria I think.
It will tell you of all the kindness I met at Turin, fortunately
without being obliged to leave the train.   My companion Mother
V. Perrin, whom I dropped at Turin, had many interesting
things to tell us.   She was born and brought up at Cluny—
her own aunt's house had been the palace of the two (?) worldly
Priors.[1]   She had been in childhood a tame kitten at the Visitation at Paray-le-Monial, where her aunt was Superior, so she
frisked in and out of the enclosure and saw everything.   And
the Blessed Curé of Ars blessed her when she was three years
old, and said she must be a saint. . . .

Wednesday, Villa Lante, Rome.

This will have to be finished in a hurry, just to tell you that
I am here after a good journey.   The snow came to an end
after Turin, rain took its place, but there were stars when I got

[1] See *Life of St. Bernard*, Notre Dame Series, chap. vii, p. 69, for
Pons, one of the two alluded to.

to Rome at seven fifty-five, having left Brussels at seven-thirty (P.M. Monday), so it is just thirty-six hours straight through. I shall not be able to do it so well coming back, as through spite they arrange all the connections not to meet.

I cannot tell you how it will be here, but the Promoter of the Faith has sent word—(how can such an angel of kindness be called the Devil's advocate!) that he has special faculties from the Pope by which he by himself can constitute a Tribunal, and that perhaps he will use these faculties for me, so as to get me through more quickly than if they had to get together the complete Court. If he is alone he may come three times a week, otherwise the Court never sits more than twice.

Mère R. is here in full vigour, there are three hundred and twenty-six articles in the summary of the Ordinary Process, these are given to us to look through, and she says that she will have something to say on all except two or three, so I am glad I have the start of her. . . .

April 7th, 1910.

. . . This is only a small line as I have been writing round to Bishops to ask them to write postulatory letters for the Cause of Canonisation of our Blessed Mother. . . . A nice portress, weak in French, came up and announced ' une *femme* de Roehampton.' I went with some expectation and found two ' femmes,' K.M. and M.A. They have broken all the records of the celebrated four, in the things they have been privileged to see [allusion to four Roehampton children who had spent a year at the Trinità]. . . . Things have not begun to happen yet, but the Devil's Advocate may look in to-day to say what he is meditating and when we will begin. He was written to yesterday and usually answers a letter in person. Is that a pleasant or an unpleasant way? I am delighted to hear how the community search the Scriptures . . . I wonder how many have found the prayer of Jabes, a thing that has to be found accidentally!

Villa Lante : 9th April, 1910.

This is recreation. I am going to write a joint letter to thank for many individual ones. So far I have spent every spare moment in getting my evidence into shape, since I have seen the ' Articles ' of the Process. I was afraid of being caught napping by the Devil's Advocate, but the holy man is keeping close in covert and has not yet appeared. The Postulator of Pius IX's Cause flew in this morning to ask that Mother Filippani [1]

---

[1] She died in 1916. Her father, Count Filippani, was instrumental in effecting the escape of Pius IX from Rome in 1848. The family of Filippani was intimately connected with that of the Mastai.

T

should be got back from Albano to be ready for next week. It would seem easy enough to secure her from such a short distance. . . . I must go back a little and tell you that I came by the Mont Cenis route, that was through Paris, at Mons I saluted in spirit the ' stirring substance ' of Monsignor de Croy, at Compiègne the holy memory of Jeanne d'Arc; the railway line keeps rather outside the town, but before reaching it I could see the sort of causeway (chaussée) along which they rode that last light-hearted ride to reconnoitre the Burgundian camp, the ride that ended so tragically. And then there was St. Thomas of Canterbury to salute at Sens, and our Blessed Mother at Joigny for which a gleam of sunshine came out, and Domenico Savio in the Vale of Susa, but that was in the night, and Don Bosco at Turin, and Don Rua died two days after. R.I.P.

There are people here who do not vegetate physically or wither away as they grow old and infirm.

There is Reverend Mother Dedier who was supposed never to walk again after her accident, she was five weeks in bed, a year in her room, then she emerged, and by heroic determination proceeded to walk, now she conceals one crutch very privately under her arm and swings along at a considerable pace with scarcely a dip in her walk ! She has a white face and black eyes, and makes lace assiduously without spectacles.

There is Mother R., the one who loves adventures and meets with them. She is mortally afraid of taking des habitudes d'oisiveté, while waiting for the Commission of the Congregation of Rites, and she is panting to get back to her work in Mexico. She is seventy and most vigorously alive, most of us are half alive beside her. (Of course in her own way! I could not get her to look out one hundred texts in Scripture. I do not believe that the whole Congregation of Rites could.) She protests that she is overwhelmed at being a witness in the Cause, but we all feel sure that she loves it.

Then there is Mother T., aged forty, with a most singular form of arthritis or rheumatic gout. She suffers most terribly, but gets about with a crutch and a stick, and teaches a class in the elementary school all day, she has an ascendant phéno-ménal over them, except on occasional days when the arthritis locks her jaw, and then she has to give up, but is ' off again, on again, away again ' as soon as it unlocks. . . .

I must tell you of the last clothing here, alas ! it was the day before I arrived. There were vows too, and Cardinal Gennari officiated. They have a new Chaplain who is ' distraught ' with learning, just as we are distraught with ignorance. He undertook to pilot the Cardinal through the ceremony, and when His Eminence came down to the postulant the Chaplain presented the book at the page for the vows. ' *Figlia mia*,' began the Cardinal tenderly, ' what do you ask for, declare your intentions, etc.' The postulant no doubt had intentions, but was too well brought up to declare them, remembering that ' little girls that ask don't have,' so she kept a discreet silence, only after some seconds Reverend Mother was able to catch the Chaplain's eye and make a sign to him that he was off the right road. Then they went on with the ceremony, and 'at breakfast the Chaplain started the theory that the novice's things had not been blessed. ' I must bless them now,' said the Cardinal, ' let them be brought.' ' They are on the novice,' said Reverend Mother. ' Then let the novice be brought.' The novice came, and the ceremonial was brought and much holy water with which he aspersed her profusely as she knelt in the middle of the room. The Cardinal would not have drawn back from the incense, but Reverend Mother thought that it would be more than the little novice's gravity could stand to kneel and be incensed by a Cardinal, so she made the excuse that the fire in the thurible was out. . . .

The novices are just like other novices, full of ideas. I had to share their tribune for holy hour, as the chapel is not left open, and this seemed to them rather an adventure, and a good opportunity for corporal works of mercy at close quarters, for the tribune is tiny, so one brought a paraffin lamp and set it on a sloping prie-dieu desk to enlighten me. (I would not trust novices with paraffin lamps!) Another tried to squeeze a chair behind me which produced a dead-lock when the visitor[1] came round; another went away and had a long hunt and came back with a cushion for me to kneel upon! So it was well after nine-thirty when the dear kind things were able to settle down to their prayers. . . .

Rome is getting terribly modern, but its variegated smells still savour of the past, and must have been the same very far back—smells of spring growth, rain, hay-blossom, garlic, and the mysterious Roman smell (every capital has its own smell, I think). This always suggests to me imperial dust. The foundation of the smell is dryness and great ancestry!

This morning Reverend Mother and I started for the Trinità for Mass and Communion at Mater Admirabilis. . . . Meantime the Promoter of the Faith did not turn up, but the Postulator of the Cause of Pius IX came to say they want Mother Filippani to go on with her evidence. It had been interrupted because they wanted to hear a Bishop's evidence as he was very ill, and they said coolly ' lest he should escape.' So he has now either finished or escaped to the other world. There is a

[1] The Sister whose business it was to make the round of the house at nightfall.

complication! If the Commission is going to sit here to hear
Mother Filippani for Pius IX, nobody knows what will happen
about the Commission for Venerable Mother Duchesne.

One hears so many things, and I am beginning to think the
' formula for all cases is,' but it is the contrary. . . .

April 14th, 1910.

. . . Yesterday I had Mass at the Crypt of St. Peter's, that
was a great joy, and it is so small and so devout where the altar
is, that there is nothing left to be desired. The vice Rector
of the Scots was ill or he would have come himself, but he sent
his brother to say the Mass. . . . He also sent lovely white
roses for me to lay on the Stuart tombs to which we went down
afterwards. The sacristan says there are nearly always flowers
there, white roses in the season. . . . It is very pathetic to see
them there in the crypt among the Popes. The sarcophagi
of the Popes are very impressive, one could spend hours down
there, especially without the sacristan's stories (gruesome and
otherwise) about this and that Pope ; he suddenly broke into
English, laying his hand on the granite sarcophagus of Adrian IV,
' Eenglish Pop,' and said no more. . . .

The Rector of the Scots College has just been in for a long
talk. I told him my circumstances, and he said for my consolation : ' Ye'll wait.' . . .

April 15th, 1910.

. . . Now I must tell you about our audience yesterday and
begin at three-thirty when Reverend Mother kindly invited me
to go on with her before to walk round the Vatican gardens with
a private permit, so there was not a soul about except ourselves
and the gardeners, and they were few and far between, and old
and simple and friendly. In the Italian garden they have done
the Holy Father's[1] arms beautifully in clipped box, but that
is the only part that is well kept up, the rest is rather unkempt.
He does not care to spend money on it, but the broad walks
between trimmed hedges are very fine, and the woody paths
nice and wild, and the fountains lovely.

Real oaks, Teutonic oaks, look so strange in Rome, some of
them in full foliage already. We saw the new Lourdes grotto,
with a facsimile of the front of the basilica of Lourdes above it,
the Holy Father went for the inauguration. *Just* behind
Lourdes are Menelik's lions, in their cage, they were in a very
passive mood and stared hard, not avoiding the eye as other
cats do. The Holy Father does not care for them at all, and
their meat bill is monstrous besides their attendance, but he
keeps them lest if Menelik should hear that he has parted with
them, he would turn on the Franciscan missionaries, ' an eye

[1] Pius X.

for an eye, a tooth for a tooth, a Franciscan for a lion.' Such are the complimentary gifts of the semi-civilised.

We went in at five-fifteen to the Vatican and met the rest of our party and waited a few minutes, then were ushered in—six of us—to the Holy Father's study, and he stood up to greet us : such a vision, very much changed since my last sight of him two years ago. . . . He had been alone when we came in, and who can tell what sorrowful things he had been pondering over. He was not wearing a *zucchetto*, but a great crimson cap right down to his ears, like the portrait one knows so well of Julius II. And when one thinks who he is, and of the burden of the Church which he carries on his mind and soul, and sees the traces of that burden on him, it goes very deeply into one. He would not have his foot kissed, only his ring, and made us sit round him just as any bishop might have done. I was so close that I could see the brown spots in his eyes, and how he does look out of those eyes. . . . He talked about all sorts of things, and one saw that though the outer man is somewhat fainting away under the weight of his labour and troubles, the inner man is in no way following it. . . .

There are two things I put aside in my mind for our mental profit. Talking of Calabrian and Sicilian orphans, etc., he said that it was not intelligence that was wanting, and that intelligence was good and necessary for clergy, seminarists, religious, but what was most needed was education, training, culture, study. *There !* reflect please, all the more as I see this has not been put in the account of the audience. . . .

Yet another thing which struck me very much—his satisfaction at the renewal of field labour in the Campagna, and the spiritual profit that comes of the work of the clergy among this growing population, he said the word *labora* with a relish and a gesture that showed all it said to him . . . one felt the untiring, unconquerable mind and heart going on though the machine break down . . . thinking and planning to restore all things in Christ ; and one felt above all as a characteristic, the apostolic simplicity of the whole, the simplest bishop one can imagine could not beat, could scarcely reach him in simplicity or be more accessible, and his laugh is like a child's, that is the only likeness left to his episcopal *boyhood* as a Patriarch of Venice.

He has the Blessed Curé of Ars in bronze on one side of his desk, and loves him ; on the other side is Blessed Joan of Arc, but I could not see what the statuette was like . . . high up on the wall opposite to me was a portrait in oils of—you will never guess of whom : Menelik's lion when he was a cub, painted with such vehemence, that he seems to come right out of the picture and sit in front of it looking straight out, with his tail almost lashing. . . .

18th April, 1910.

I was glad to hear of the first swallows at Roehampton, there are flocks of swifts here. But my first swallow appeared this morning in the shape of the Promoter of the Faith—he passed through the parlour where I was talking to G. M., and I heard soon afterwards that it was ' himself ' and that he wished to see me. He only came to look round and to say kind things, and tell us once more that nothing could be changed about the Cardinal Vicar, and that he hoped the first session of the Commission here would be on Saturday, if not it would be on Monday, and after that he would arrange them as closely together as he could. What that means we shall find out in time. He gave me useful advice concerning the giving of evidence, which was very nice coming from the Counsel for the Defendant ! By way of adding something cheerful and encouraging, he said : ' You know these courts are composed of such experts, they have such a genius for inquiry that they make you say just the thing you did not expect ! '

Mère de Boisjourdan [1] was kind enough to make a great ado about my being kept waiting so long, he raised his eyes and hands to heaven and said that the Venerable Madre Duchesne would watch over England. ' *Mais ce n'est pas du tout la même chose,*' said Mother de Boisjourdan, with a blunt earnestness that did not notice the unspiritual aspect of her remark !

28th April, 1910.

. . . I must go back to tell you of the visit of the Cardinal Protector,[2] which was a great joy. As he has not been seen here for two months owing to influenza and relapses, I was afraid I should leave Rome without seeing him. But his first outing was to the Vatican, and his second, the following day, to come to us. He was announced when Reverend Mother and I were at adoration, we went down and found him slowly climbing up the great staircase and looking so pleased to be back. Reverend Mother introduced me as ' *la Madre Vicaria d'Inghilterra,*' and he astonished us both by saying without a moment's hesitation ' *Hé-é la Madre Stuart.*' Isn't it a wonderful memory for names at the age of eighty-two, and barely having seen one of so many at the Beatification time, and not for four years before that. They say he remembers the whole circle of Vicars and even what they said to him. . . .

Do you remember the tusks of Indian ivory that one used to see, with collars of very white filagree silver, if you imagine a petal of a scarlet geranium to fall upon this tusk you have the colouring of the Cardinal Protector's head, with the skull cap on it. . . . I was astonished at the fresh vigour of his mind,

[1] Died in 1918.   [2] Cardinal de Pietro died in 1914.

his memory for details, his living interest in everything, and
the thing which struck me most is the way he has got into the
Society's way of looking at things. . . . They say that he has
made such a study of the Constitutions that he knows them better
than most Mistresses of Novices. . . . Better than all is that
he is a great man of prayer, he never comes without making a
long visit to the Blessed Sacrament. . . . There is a point
on which I am entirely in accord with him, he likes not only
to be told that people have prayed for him, but also inquires
to whom they have prayed and what they have said. . . . He
has a great objection to being told that the whole Society prays
for him at its morning prayers, because he says that is like grace
before meals, a matter of routine which they may say without
attending to it, but he likes to be *really* prayed for.

April 30th, 1910.

. . . I had a second session yesterday and am promised
another on Tuesday. . . . I will tell you what I feel when I
watch this Commission at work : that I have never taken trouble
in my life, and do not even know how to take trouble about anything ! I assure you they make one ashamed of oneself, but they
are delightfully human, and laugh all together, so pleasantly.
While the notary is laboriously writing I have plenty of time
to observe the saintly Archbishop of Iconium, Mgr. Lazzareschi,[1] as he mostly has his eyes shut it is easy. I thought at
first the holy man was praying if not asleep, but I was soon
undeceived as to the sleeping, when he showed signs of having
attended minutely to everything ; he is seventy-five.

May 1st, 1910.

I told you the other day my impression of the Commission
and the trouble they take, and yesterday I had another example
confirming the preceding doctrine. Father H. P. came in, having
a holiday in honour of St. Catherine of Siena, and he told me
something of his work. From six forty-five A.M., after breakfast,
until twelve-fifteen, with one short break, perhaps half an hour to
say his Office in the courtyard, he is preparing his lecture, and
the results of these hours of preparation have to be given to
his students in forty-five minutes in the afternoon. Is not that
something to reflect upon ! Scripture is his subject, and his
students are thirty Dominicans of the flower of the Order, and
thirty Augustinians, equally the finest blossoms on their tree,
and all men in their fourth year of theology, ravenously keen
and as docile as lambs. . . . It was very nice to have the chance
of seeing the Dominican habit on St. Catherine's feast, and to
think how often she had looked at the same beautiful dress of

[1] Monsignor Lazzareschi died January 24, 1918.

the Blackfriars when she had occasion to scold or confess her
sins to her ' little father ' Raymond of Capua.

May 8th, 1910.

. . . They have Mass here in the noviceship on all Saturdays
in May. There is a very nice altar, on the predella of which
has been placed several times the throne for Gregory XVI
and Pius IX, when they paid surprise visits with only a few
minutes' notice. There was a special bell rung on those occasions like a fire bell. . . . Must it not have been thrilling to
receive thus what St. Catherine would call ' the sweet Christ
on earth ' !

The parish priest of the Vatican died last week, aged ninety-
two. It is an Augustinian by privilege who has this charge, and
he becomes the Pope's ordinary confessor (he sends to Venice
for a favourite Jesuit when he wants an ' extraordinary ') ; and,
curiously, the confessor of this ancient Augustinian was our
confessor, a conventual, and the dear old man did not like to
trouble him to go to the Vatican, so he used to drive over here
on the mornings that Padre Polesi was ' sitting ' and make his
confession in the carriage, as he could not have climbed the
great staircase.

The roses are a vision here at present. There are some that
are kindred to our ' China roses,' but of the better quality ; and
on some of the bushes there are more roses, I think, than leaves ;
but they have choice kinds also, very good hybrids. . . . They
shut out the sun from the chapel as much as possible—I suppose
it is necessary—but there is one crack they cannot shut, and in
the afternoon just one sunbeam comes through and lights upon
a most queenly arum lily, which is turned towards it, and it
becomes so dazzling in the rest of the half-light that one can just
look steadily at it and no more—and how much it says !

9th May, 1910.

. . . The first news of the King's[1] death came to me
telephoned from the Trinità, and I hardly believed it, thinking
it was from the newspaper criers, but . . . they telephoned for
me to the British Embassy, who would not tell till they heard
it was for a British subject, and then they said it was true. . . .
Yesterday we could see from here the flags at half-mast on
Castell Sant' Angelo, the Quirinal, the Law-courts ; and driving
to the Trinità every street had flags at half-mast and with
crêpe, and here and there one saw a Union Jack or British
Ensign. There is a great deal of sympathy, and the Holy Father
is very much distressed. I am sure he will pray.

---

[1] Edward VII.

What a moment for the King to die, with the Lords in the melting-pot and the Commons standing on end . . .

Some one asked if the Sessions of the Commission were interesting : it seemed to her they must be dull ! Will you tell them that of all the things I have lived through they are about the most interesting, perhaps because it is such a unique experience in one's life to be in one of the outer Courts of Law of the heavenly Jerusalem, to give testimony to the heroic virtues of one of our own Mothers[1]—and such a one, for she grows upon one more and more ! Then so much turns upon the precise meaning of words, and, though an amateur, I am a fancier of words. It is no small interest also to have a leisurely observation of Roman prelates, in a world which is peculiarly their own—this quite apart from the natural interest of their light-hearted ways, blended with extreme conscientiousness ; and [then there is] the sudden *détente* which comes with the conclusion of the Session, when the Notary, who has slaved at his pen all through, lets fly the neatest little shafts of fun at the Sub-promoter of the Faith—since he dare not attack bigger game— and the elect of God, the Bishops, tease each other gently.

It is true that it goes slowly, but to be dull—no, it is all choice.

Speaking of the many delays, in another letter she wrote :

I feel rather like a buttercup that has been licked up by a sacred Roman ox and is being ruminated at leisure ! . . .

May 10th, 1910.

. . . Indeed the King's death is a crushing blow, and most particularly at this moment. How hard we must pray. For I suppose things have rarely been so critical for the whole Empire and for the Constitution. I like the new King's little grave word about God in his first message. He must be crushed. . . . It is nice to see how the King was loved by all classes, and to think how his Catholic subjects will pray for him. They say the Holy Father is much distressed about it. A curious person told me yesterday (an Italian) that she had been to the Vatican shortly after the King had been to see the Pope, and she asked a group of *Monsignori* and *Camerieri* which they had liked best of the two sovereigns, the Emperor of Germany or Edward VII.[2] They answered that the Emperor was *molto bello* . . . *ma il* vero Signore *è il Rè d'Inghilterra* ; and I think that was what everyone felt about him, he was so unaffected, so simple and genial with all classes of his subjects. ' My people ' was the word I liked to read in his proclamations and

---

[1] Mother Philippine Duchesne.
[2] Both sovereigns visited Pope Leo XIII in 1903.

sayings; it is a huge thing to say when one thinks that it means about a quarter of the human race. . . .

May 13th, 1910.

. . . Whenever I go to a place which is reputed mild or hot, it turns out more vicious and cold than the memory of man can recall—as Louisiana, when the priest held the chalice to keep it from freezing, and the Mississippi came thundering down with ice which had not been seen for fifty years. Here I was on the look-out for something to match our frost between May 10-12 and May 17-22. We had for the first dates thirty-six hours of straight, cold, steady rain just like slate pencils. When we recovered what do you think we saw ? The hills snow-covered down to their skirts—not a powdering of snow, nor patches, but they stood solid, white and gleaming, like Alps. To-day we have a faint and feeble sun. . . .

I shall not be there [1] for the lovely Forty Hours ; my spirit will be in its stall at the procession, and my soul, I hope, under the feet of the *cortège* as it goes round the dear chapel. . . .

I laughed at you feeling that I am under detention, as a sort of prisoner, but it is quite true, as a matter of fact, with these censures hanging over me if I do not turn up promptly when wanted by the Court. I have thought sometimes of ' Alice through the Looking-Glass ' when the White Knight stuck fast in the extinguisher. ' I was stuck as fast as lightning.' ' But that's another kind of fastness,' said Alice. ' It was all kinds of fastnesses with me,' said the Knight. Indeed, if the whole thing were not so holy, and if it were not for the oath, I could write an ' Alice in Prelate-land ' which would be quite interesting.

May 14th, 1910.

. . . I think it was this day last year the first sod was cut, or rather the first gravel upturned, for the new building. How much has happened since . . . ending now with the King. You have reminded me of what I was trying to remember, about the date of the last time ' Our Lord fell in Our Lady's lap . . .'[2]; this time it is all England that has lost its head, more and more regretted each day, I fancy, as people begin to realise what a significant figure this *vero Signore* was in the Councils of Europe.

Now I must give you my latest news. The Commissioners were in great spirits yesterday, and during coffee, which precedes the Session, they all fell on the holy Mgr. Lazzareschi, and told him it was all his fault that the Roman populace is so unsettled, etc., etc. The holy man folded his hands and bent his head

---

[1] At Roehampton.   [2] *i.e.* Good Friday, on March 25.

and said : ' You are perfectly right ; I am capable of anything bad.' I feel sure he thinks so in all earnest. Many of the poor women in his quarter of Rome have the custom of making a vow to have a Mass said when they are in any fix. But they fulfil the vow by asking the saintly Archbishop to say it, and of course no honorarium is required or offered.

It is the age for beatifying, as Sister X. says, ' young men and old women.' I heard of another boy of only sixteen, who is on his way to Beatification. . . . Simply a blacksmith's apprentice, taken by a cruel uncle when his parents died. The uncle was a blacksmith, and made him work beyond his strength, and when the child could not lift the heavy iron weights that he ordered him to bring, the blacksmith used to beat him with an iron bar : in the end he was seriously injured and was taken to hospital and there died. His patience throughout was so heroic, and his death surrounded by so many miracles, that he is on his way to the Altars of the Church. Isn't it both heart-breaking and beautiful ? I am sure Almighty God has a cohort of these little heroic souls in the back streets of the world, and to encourage them all He will show what He thinks of one. The name, I think, is Muzio Sulpicio, and he died under the Pontificate of Pius IX. . . .

May 15th, 1910.

. . . The household raised a deafening cheer when Mère de Boisjourdan announced that she had drawn the fruit of Benignity ! She has it already in such abundance. When she could make herself heard she said that she had also drawn the Gift of Fortitude *cela tempérera la Bénignité.* We made up for a mild morning yesterday (Pentecost) by having five priests for Benediction, and a sermon afterwards from Père P. The holy man was already wrought up by the feast to such an exaltation of spirit that he came in with an open smile, and set out on his discourse on the level of fervour at which he might have been expected to end it. Of course he could not go higher ; there was nowhere higher to go, since he set out in heaven *Ascendit Deus in jubilatione,* but he was inexpressibly happy at the thought that we were all going there, and spoke with such astonishing rapidity that I often lost my Italian footing, and had to listen, as one listens to a nightingale's ' shattering cadences,' wondering at the finish of each note, and at his intonation, which ran up and down like arpeggios and seemed to have no limit. . . .

May 17th, 1910.

. . . Did I tell you that I had a *séance* or reception . . . in the elementary school here ? The children are very nice, and oh ! how self-possessed, and with an operatic timbre in their voices ! It gave one quite a jump when a creature of nine or ten began a solo with those flourishes and intonations and the perfect assurance of the stage! and yet it is simple in them.

Our Calabrian orphans go to the classes in the Elementary School, and their dark faces and fierce eyes show up quite startlingly among the little Romans. It is curious how often, comparatively speaking often, to what one expects, these latter are fair with blue eyes; one longs to know the family history and pedigree—some old Lombard or Gothic stock that crops out again. In Palermo, Reverend Mother tells me there are quantities, especially in our part of the town, and they are still locally called Normans; in fact they call every fair person a Norman. These Palermo people must be something of which we have scarcely an idea, from all I hear of them, but they have not so much *joie de vivre* as the Neapolitans.

May 20th, 1910.

. . . What a solemn day this is in England [the King's funeral]. The whole space of time which surrounds the King's death has something which shows the hand of God very clearly, *Manus Domini tetigit nos* as a nation, and because it is *Manus Domini* it must be good. For one thing it has united all in one feeling, except the veriest outcasts from all good feeling . . . for another, probably it will remove from our Statute Book the great blot [1] much sooner than it would have been otherwise ; for another, that the Constitution is on its feet still ; and in the truce who can know what further lights may come to the nation.

Altogether one is fully satisfied, because God has done it, and each one of us is grieved with the sorrow of a personal loss ; such a wonderful thing, yet so unmistakably true, and the hush over the evil tongues, which are usually so loud, is another touch of God's hand. . . .

On Sunday I am invited to the Trinità for the Feast.[2] One of my ideals of bliss is a great Church function with no responsibility for anything, except one's own devotion, and this will be extra great, because the Cardinal titular of the Church, the Cardinal of Lyons, will be there. . . . He is too old and feeble to sing the High Mass, but he will assist at the throne, no doubt pontifically, and the Benediction will also be on a scale proportioned to the Feast.

[1] This was done in August 1910, when the form of the declaration of the King's belief, required at his coronation, was altered, and all expressions hostile to the Catholic faith were removed. ' The duty of uttering the old formula at the beginning of his reign had been most repugnant to King Edward VII,' said Mr. Asquith, in moving the introduction of the Bill.

[2] Feast of the Blessed Trinity.

Our procession is said to start at five-thirty on Corpus Christi, but they say it never does start until five forty-five . . . so for a good part of the time we shall be in union. . . .   A Bishop will carry the Blessed Sacrament. . . . Santa Rufina is much more enterprising and invites a Cardinal, although they have no space to proceed in, but go round and round upon themselves melting with devotion.   At the Trinità of course it is done in great glory, with a Cardinal to carry the Blessed Sacrament, and the German College to sing, the so-called ' Lobsters.'   We have the Conventual Friars from the house of studies close by, and you have *haec minima Societas*, and I suppose Father Rector will officiate and all will be beautiful.

I can write about it now with a certain lightness of heart, knowing that my days are numbered. ⏌ It is a bad moment leaving Rome, but I have been away a long time from England.

May 23rd, 1910.

Yesterday was a great solemnity at the Trinità.   I was there from High Mass until after Benediction. . . .   The Choir was Caproni's from St. John Lateran's and the Mass was Caproni's, but he himself was not there, so they were a little out of hand.   And the unction of the spirit did not ooze upon the vocal chords at all . . . and I was, as I expected, more anchored than ever in my devotion to the singing of nuns and children when they sing their best, and are *in* the words that they sing. . . .

I love it when clear consecrated voices drop their words like blossoms of utterance on a stream of prayer and one feels that they are nothing to themselves, and all for the worship of God.   I must say, however, that I like the big bass voices just for Amens.   They make one think of the four apocalyptic animals who said ' Amen ' all together, and *c'est leur métier* !
. . .   The music I liked best in the whole day was when the children sang, *Jam sol recedit igneus*, at Vespers.   It came as a surprise for the Vespers were said, and only the hymn and the *Magnificat* sung, but it was very sweet and childlike, and all the Trinity words are so transcendent that the hymns came nicely *ex ore infantium.* . . .

A novice wrote me a delightful touch, written of the Roman Curia in the sixteenth century, ' Not even dog-days can change the slow earnestness of the procedure of the Roman Courts.' That is, quite perfect ' slow earnestness ' describes it exactly, and they are evidently exactly the same as they were then.

May 24th, 1910.

. . . Yesterday we made good way at the Session.   When they are in particularly high spirits they work all the better (and this is true of everyone, I think).   At all events they

were in great glow yesterday. I have discovered that one of
the Bishops understands a few words of English and have tried
in vain to get him to utter, by saluting him in that language.
He looks down at once like a very small boy refusing a fence
in his lessons, and says, ' I don't spick, I don't spick.' He is
a Canon of St. Peter's, and was up until twelve o'clock on
Wednesday night confessing the crowds that surged into the
churches in terror of being killed by the comet before morning.

In fact the comet has given a most successful Mission in
Rome.

There are very delightful moments (at the Sessions) sometimes when a theological point comes up. I love it, for they
get so hot at once and talk all together in the full strength of
their Roman voices, and gesticulate so splendidly, and the
Notary throws down his pen and joins in the fray, and nobody
can hear, of course, in the tumult, the very weak voice of the
saintly Mgr. Lazzareschi, and all of a sudden they come to
themselves and turn to him with most tender smiles and the
expression on their faces of ' dearest Father in God, what were
you trying to say ? ' and he says his little say, and laughs his
little inward laugh to himself, and then everything quiets down
and we go on again. It is lovely to listen to, especially as in
the middle of it one of them lets out a flash of real deep devotion,
and shows a little of what is hidden behind their light-hearted
manners. But after one of these *sorties* it is some time before
Don Francesco, as they affectionately call the Notary, can be
steadied down from his heart-breaking sighs and little irrepressible jokes under his breath.

They are as simple as, I will not say schoolboys, for that
race. is sometimes hard and wary, but boys in the golden age of
the nursery. . . .

Rome Terminus Station : May 27th, 1910.

. . . The title of this Chapter is ' Last days in Rome,' and
I am beginning it at the station awaiting departure for
Florence. . . . The Cardinal Protector came on the morning
of Our Blessed Mother's feast for Benediction. Fancy his
kindness in bringing me a big box of *Agnus Dei*, and what
touched me even more than his thinking of it and carrying it
himself up the great staircase was the evidence that he had
arranged and tied it up with his own venerable hands, from the
way in which the *Agnus Dei* were helplessly arranged and the
red ribbon twisted like a cart rope to get a grip of it, and a
very uncertain knot tied after an heroic pull. I wish I could
have kept it just as it was, but I could never have got back
the twist and the knot ! A ribbon smoothed out and neatly
tied seems so commonplace by comparison. . . .

Florence.—The carriage filled up so much that I could not go on writing. My would-be companion was stricken with a quinsy, so I am alone to-day and to-morrow as far as Bologna, where I am to meet the maiden all forlorn who has been entrusted to me, and without whom I might have fled to Brussels without a pause. It was a beautiful journey to-day as far as Cortona when a thunderstorm came and seems inclined to settle down for the afternoon. I shall have two Julys this year, as to flowers; they were exceedingly beautiful, there were fields of sainfoin, and beds of wild thyme, and patches of broom and sprinklings of cistus, and wreaths of wild roses and great crimson stains of poppies, and sometimes in the cuttings mesembryanthemum for variety. It is very interesting going through Tuscany and thinking of the past and all the fearful Guelf and Ghibelline feuds. If one is near enough one can see which side the castles were by the shape of the battlements. . . .

Between Basle and Strassburg. Midnight.—I have come considerably nearer since my last communication from Florence. This will only be posted in Brussels, but I begin now to save time. No adventures so far. At Bologna I dragged the maiden all forlorn from the arms of her weeping parents, and when she had dried her tears she became like St. Cuthbert's boy and ' never ceased expressing the thoughts of her mind ' . . . which gave me occasion for many reflections.

I heard that she was a novice tertiary of St. Dominic and . . . was obliged to explain that I, though unworthy, and not gifted with the star upon the brow, was at present *locum tenens* to our Holy Father St. Dominic, until one of his sons could gather up the threads at Ostend, and say what should be done, so I have sustained her with hard boiled eggs and good advice and hope to tow her into port successfully in a few hours.

Oh! but the scenery was lovely through the heart of Switzerland, the part that one usually passes in the night.

Sunday.—One word only to say that I have arrived and have seen. But as our Mother says she is sending me back at once, Tuesday, I add no more. Charing Cross five-twelve unless I write again.

On June 1 Reverend Mother Stuart reached Roehampton. The train arrived so early that, for the first time in her life, there was no one to welcome her at the door, ' and we found her standing outside the chapel as we came down for Benediction.' It was indeed a joyful surprise.

But her stay was not for long. On August 8 she was again at Ixelles, this time to take part in the General Congregation

which Mother Digby had summoned. She had little time for
letter-writing, as the work of the Congregation fully occupied her.

Ixelles : 12th August, 1910.

. . . I am going to begin a letter and go on with it as I
can. The triduum is going on. The Father Provincial is
distinctly nice, he has a strong face and Spanish eyes, which
might belong to ' one of our first Fathers '. . . . His doctrine
is plain, close, strong, condensed, no waste of words, and all
gilt-edged with rational optimism. I am glad to say our Mother
does not go to the instructions, but I take notes for her. I
have got a job—also gilt-edged—as it means seeing her every
day for business (as well as the precious time she gives me
during second Mass). When she looks straight up and smiles
at us all assembled she is *exactly* herself, and the smile takes
off the look of fatigue, and when she blesses us all together
it is inexpressibly strong and solemn. There is prayer in all
the house and throughout the Society to keep her up through
the labour of every day. One feels that the whole Society is
one heart and soul round her and animated by her.

Sunday.—This has stopped for forty-eight hours, but I could
not help it. To-morrow the perfect and glorious feast of the
Assumption ! I hope it will be a happy one for all. It is one
of the breathlessly beautiful feasts of the year, isn't it ; heaven
begun and earth nowhere. I hope you will have real Assumption
weather, the strong sun drinking up light clouds, and all the
distances blue with heat haze . . . and a lovely Office. Here
in the absence of the probation . . . it is pitched . . . low
out of compassion for the Vicars, we are not *la fraîcheur de
la Société*, though an old Sister called us that in 1895 when we
had octogenarian Vicars at the head of the procession. . . .

20th August, 1910.

. . . We are getting on very sedately. The work seems to
me crushing for our Mother . . . yesterday she looked quite
grey, she was so tired. . . .

Reverend Mother Nieuwland has been good enough to go
with me in the garden just now to show me the particular spot
where the Waterloo soldiers are. In one of the area gratings
is a shaft that one can see down about 30 feet, ' *mais ce n'est
rien,*' she said to the depth at which they are buried. There
were very deep hollows on the property when we bought it—
sand pits, beautiful pure sand—so probably it was a sand pit
and the dead were thrown in and easily covered. I am glad
to know where they are.

Cardinal Mercier has given up going to the Congress at
Montreal, because he is again giving himself (and straight on
end, I suppose, with a week-end break between), the *seven* clergy
retreats. Marvellous man !

Ixelles : 30th August, 1910.

Yesterday we were at Jette.   Too long to tell about to-day, only that it was holy and wholesome.   To-day the Cardinal [Mercier] is coming.   I am looking forward very much to seeing in the flesh (the minimum I believe) the prelate whom we venerate in the spirit.   To-morrow we go to the Rue du Grand Cerf, and to Lindthout ;   on Thursday the departures begin. . . .   We are going very early to stand on the threshold and wait for the Cardinal *avec un air convenable !*

On September 4 she returned to Roehampton.   October saw her in Ireland for the usual autumn visit, and in November she was back at Roehampton ; this time to stay for ' the longest unbroken period she had ever given us,' seven months.   It was the preparation for the end.   February and March, 1911, saw her at work on ' The Education of Catholic Girls,' which she finished on April 1.   As she said herself of those last months, as usual idealising all she loved, ' so much seemed to reach a perfect stage in its development that I often pray, " when it is most beautiful take it from me." '   She feared lest the beauty of God's work might enthral her more than God Himself, and she added that she loved to say to Him :

> Shouldst Thou try me
> With all supply me
> Nature desireth
> Or heart requireth.
> Whisper this counsel of love in my breast
> God is the greatest,
> The fairest, the sweetest,
> And of all treasures the noblest and best.

God heard her prayer and accepted her oblation of all she loved only too quickly.   On May 14 she left Roehampton to spend a few days at St. Charles's College.   On Tuesday, the 16th, a telegram from Brussels announced the fatal and altogether unexpected news that Reverend Mother Digby had been struck with paralysis ; everything was to be feared.   Mother Stuart returned at once to Roehampton, and the next few days dragged out in slow suspense.   Could she have followed the dictates of her heart she would have gone at once to Ixelles, but this was not to be till the sacrifice had been consummated.   On May 17 she wrote to the Superior at St. Charles's, from whom she had been obliged to part so unceremoniously.

. . . I wanted to write yesterday to tell you how happily my visit had begun and how sorry I was to have cut it short

U

like that, but it could not be otherwise. It was God's Will that it should be so, and a breathless waiting on His Will is all that can be in our souls at present. I am writing early and there is no news yet, our thoughts are all collected in one spot, and there is scarcely anything even to be said.

. . . Will you tell the students how sorry I was not to see them, the date of taking up the visit again must of course be quite indefinite now. At all events I am glad to have seen you and the Mothers. Strange that you should have had a wakeful and weighted spirit in the night. We will be united in prayer now and in quiet of mind, committing every wish and thought and trouble and difficulty to the Sacred Heart of Our Lord.

Letters from Ixelles succeeded each other, and hope—a faint hope—began to revive. A great wave of prayer swelled up round the throne of God, but this time it was to be unavailing.

Going into her room on the afternoon of Saturday, the 20th, Mother Stuart opened her Bible, to see, as she said, ' what God might have in store for us.' Her hand touched the first verse of the fourteenth chapter of Isaias, ' Her time is near at hand, and her days shall not be prolonged. For the Lord will have mercy on Jacob and will yet choose out of Israel.' She shut the book quickly, knowing that she had had her answer. A few moments later re-opening it she read: ' My flesh and my heart hath failed me, but God is the God of my heart and my portion ever more.' It was just half-past two, the hour, as she knew later, when Mother Digby entered on her agony.

Sunday, May 21, was a glorious spring day, such as seem to belong peculiarly to England, and Roehampton looked its loveliest, the trees in their spring dress, the may in full bloom and flowers everywhere. Writing to one of her friends she said :

Many thanks for the box of clematis, they came quite fresh and brave and stiff, not fallen or limp. And this is what we will be ourselves by the grace of God, though the great sorrow hangs over us, and is coming. We will hold up our heads and look to God still and offer Him the best gift which He has given us and now asks back. . . .

Everything appeared to go on as usual, though there was but one thought in every heart. After Vespers Mother Stuart took the aspirants for their usual Sunday walk in the garden. She had scarcely reached her room at two forty-five when a telegram was handed to her announcing that all was over, and telling her to proceed at once to Ixelles, ' for we have decided to bury Mother

THE CHAPEL AT ROEHAMPTON

1922

Digby at Roehampton,' it concluded. A bell summoned the
community to their common room, its first note had told the
dreaded truth.

At six o'clock a second telegram from Brussels asked Mother
Stuart to bring a companion with her, and that was all. She
again met the community for a farewell talk, and at seven-fifteen
left the house, saying ' Good-bye till Wednesday at the latest.'
Neither she nor any one there realised that the separation was
final. Perhaps, as some hold, such things are better so !

As she left the house she handed the assistant a little paper
on which were written her half-finished notes for the conference
for the coming feast of the Ascension. They had been written
with the shadow of the dreaded separation from Mother Digby
hanging over her, but to her community they spoke also another
thought.

' And while they looked steadfastly towards heaven, as He
went up, they said Alleluia.'

It is not Scripture but the word of the Church which tells
us that they said this. If we are to understand it literally, and
why not ? If they did say Alleluia at the moment of that
supreme separation it must have been by a very spontaneous
and perfect and uncontending spirit of faith, assenting to all,
affirming their faith, expressing the full assurance of their hope.

It was good that He should go, faith said it, because He had
said it Himself, ' it is expedient for you that I should go, for
if I go not the Paraclete will not come.' If they had continued
to enjoy His visible presence they would not have graces to the
full strength of their spiritual manhood. They would have
leaned upon the visible and audible, not sought the unseen and
lived by faith.

It was a splendid act of resignation, ' an incomparable act '
embracing so much, known and unknown, the actual vanishing
of the face they had loved, the prospect of the unknown warfare
before them ; the realisation of their own weakness was so
fresh in their minds.

It was a declaration of love, ' If you loved Me you would
rejoice that I go to My Father.' *Mon âme est heureuse*, a
joy learned in renunciation. . . .

The next morning brought a letter to Roehampton announcing
that Reverend Mother Stuart had been named Vicar General
by a secret note of Mother Digby.

A long chapter in her life had been closed, just thirty years
at Roehampton. She belonged henceforth to a wider world.

CHAPTER XIX

VICAR GENERAL. MAY TO AUGUST 1911

'Remember that whatever happens . . . you must say to yourself, according to circumstances, joyfully and thankfully, or humbly and submissively, or bravely, or if need be *defiantly* to the troubles within, " *This is part of the story*," and the story is God's love for you and yours for Him.'—*From a letter, J. Stuart.*

VERY early on the morning of May 22, 1911, Mother Stuart arrived at Ixelles. No word was spoken at the door, and after a silent greeting she went straight to the room where Reverend Mother Digby had been laid out. Kneeling down she kissed the hem of her habit, while tears streamed down her face. Then rising she went to the chapel for Mass, accompanied by Reverend Mother de Pichon. Having genuflected, she turned to ask where she should go. ' *Mais vous êtes Vicaire Générale,*' whispered Mother de Pichon in surprise, pointing to the vacant assistant's place. And so the fatal news was broken, and she realised that the hasty farewell to all she loved had been final.

' At seven-thirty, I was kneeling by Mother Digby,' writes one of the English probanists, ' when Reverend Mother came in, she stood by the bed gazing at the face of her beloved Mother, arranged the veil and flowers, giving all a touch that she only could give. There were traces of tears and a deep look of pain on her face, but at the same time a wonderful· expression of supernatural peace.' Her will and God's were wholly one, and in the Communion of that morning she had made what she so often recommended to those around her, ' an incomparable act of resignation to things as they are for the love of God.' In that lay all her sanctity and all her strength.

In the afternoon she gathered the English nuns round her to make them tell all they knew of the last days of Mother Digby. One said bluntly, ' But you will of course go back on Wednesday for the funeral.' ' So I thought,' she said, ' but it seems it is not the custom. Mother B., who came with me, will return in charge.' A little later the portress hastily entered Mother Stuart's room : ' American visitors, old children of the Sacred Heart, and their mother have arrived, asking for Mother Digby, to whom they have brought letters and messages from Manhattanville, I could not tell them what has happened.' 'No, I shall do so,' said Mother Stuart. The visitors were quite unknown to her. ' I am Mother Stuart from Roehampton, Mrs. H.; you do not know that you have come to a house of mourning. Mother General died yesterday.'

We were horrified [writes one of the daughters], and struck dumb by the look of pain on Mother Stuart's face. We tried to express our feelings but could not. Then she, with infinite tact and charm and quite forgetful of herself, became full of sympathy *for our distress*; she, who needed so much compassion, consoled us, and with her own heart so heavy, led us on to tell her of our plans, our friends, our interests and our sisters in the Society. I marvelled at her self-control. Having prayed with her by Mother Digby's side we took our leave. So gracious had been our reception that we left feeling we had conferred a pleasure on Mother Stuart !

That evening [writes the probanist already quoted] she came to the community room to have some rehearsal of the coming ceremonies. She stood at the end of the room between the venerable old Mothers, looking so young and solitary. Utterly forgetful of her own shyness and feelings, she quickly gave the necessary recommendations. During the next two days I often saw her kneeling motionless at the foot of Reverend Mother Digby's bed. But whenever children and others came in with rosaries with which to touch the hands, she would rise, take them and reverently lay them for a moment on the bed, then return them to their owners. . . . On Wednesday afternoon the whole household assembled on the terrace to await the departure for England. As the coffin was carried out, it passed close by Reverend Mother; she did not move. The procession passed slowly across the terrace between the long lines of nuns, while she stood alone, erect, on the top of the steps, her eyes following her beloved Mother, till all had passed beyond the great gates. With that last glimpse of the black plumes of the drivers over the high wall of our enclosure, a sacred past silently closed and a new life opened before her. She turned quickly and went straight to the chapel; a few minutes later I found her there, kneeling upright in her stall, tears pouring down her face, but still her look was full of grace and peace. The picture of her as she stood alone on the top of the steps will ever remain fresh in my mind, recalling the Mother of Sorrows on Calvary.

Her first letter to Roehampton bears the date of May 22 :

. . . You know the blow which fell upon me on my arrival, and which falls upon us all now. That hasty good-bye was for longer than we thought yesterday ; perhaps it was as well, *of course it was*, that we did not know it, since God willed it so. I know all our houses will in their charity pray for me that I may not do harm during these three months that a precious trust is in my hands. I will tell you about our Mother when I write more. The Mothers (Assistants General) looked to me at first one more broken than the other, but that was early in the morning.

The same day, in a letter to one of the community, she wrote :

This is God's Will. He understands all about everyone concerned ; loves us all and will Himself make up again the things that are broken as He our Creator only can do. . . .

Brussels : 23rd May, 1911.

. . . Your letter told me exactly what I expected ; how you were, as I knew you would be, quite forgetful of self and united with God's Will ; pray that I may be the same. . . .

Our Mother is each time more beautiful than when I first saw her. Then I thought the face was in a moment of suffering, now the triumphant repose grows hourly more beautiful, her mouth and eyes are firmly closed, she is ivory white. I have seen her in convalescence after illness look like that in sleep. I have put all the flowers on her myself (ours were the first), and kissed the hem of her habit for us all ; and I am sending you pictures which have touched her, and medals for the old children and anyone to whom you think fit to give them. The room is full of flowers now from the children and houses, mostly white lilies. She is in the little parlour close to the chapel, under St. Antony with the Holy Child, and the two Cardinals Protector.

Sister Richardson says she understood perfectly when she was spoken to in English ; sent us all her love and blessing. Sister Richardson said, ' Would you like Reverend Mother Stuart to be sent for ? ' She answered, ' We must not do anything extraordinary.' So she followed her own ritual of self-forgetfulness. When I go to pray beside her, I take all the United Kingdom with me . . . especially her own Roehampton ; and in looking back over all she taught us, the two things that each time come to my mind are truth and self-sacrifice, they are what her life spoke of.

The Assistants General are more kind to me than I can

say; but you can understand how one feels ashamed of one's existence in a position like this, and that its details as well as its *wholesale* are not to be described. To begin with a tiny one—to have to give one's blessing to these venerable Mothers ! A saint would give a holy kick and there would be a tearfully beautiful contest. Being no saint, and only a British subject, *I bless* like a lamb. After a little while I shall be able to laugh at the way in which it was broken to me, but it is still too bad to be thought of. . . . Do you think you could get some photographs, if only some snapshots, of the procession at the funeral and of the grave before it. I can see it in my mind but the Mothers cannot, and I think it would be a consolation to them. . . . I ask a prayer that the many new things which the dear Reverend Mothers Assistants General have to pour into my head may lodge properly in it.

May 24th, 1911.

. . . Mother B. will have a great deal to tell you, but no words can say what our Mother's departure was, only it was an untold comfort that Roehampton was at the other end of her journey. She will be amongst you all. Isn't it strange that she sends me away just as she comes back !

There were about twenty priests for the funeral, the Jesuits quite unmistakable. Our friend of the Eucharistic Congress, Mgr. le Doyen de St. Giles, sang the Mass, the auxiliary Bishop, Mgr. Legrève, gave the absolutions.

Mother B. will tell you what a bad accident the Cardinal [Mercier] had before Easter flying along in his motor seeking *le repos ailleurs*: a crazy woman whose mania is a desire to be killed under an automobile (such patients should not be at large), sprang up in front of the motor, the chauffeur pulled up so short of necessity that the car swerved and was wrecked. His Eminence went straight through the plate glass . . . many cuts about the head, but he is not diminished thereby and is still seeking *le repos ailleurs*.

May 31st, 1911.

MY DEAR MOTHERS AND SISTERS,—

Before May is quite out I want to thank everyone for their letters and their precious prayers. You know how I should like to thank each one in particular for what she wrote, but that is not possible, so you will accept a letter in common. Our sorrow and consolation are all in common, and I never knew how well I know you, for it seems to me now that I can enter into each one's particular thoughts beyond the letters and see what she is feeling and thinking. It is all given to God, isn't it, as our Mother taught us all her life how to do, and now more especially in her death. The charm of your letters about

the funeral was that each one told me some particular detail
which no one else mentioned, down to the detail of the white
butterfly among the flowers at the grave which only Father
Goodier [1] speaks of. I am glad this creature of God, my
favourite symbol of the resurrection, was not wanting to add
its touch of perfection. That funeral was all so perfect and so
exactly what I could have wished, that it will live in my mind
always as a most precious memory, as it will to everyone who
was there.

There are a few small things from here which you may not
have heard, and I have been treasuring them up for you. Sister
Richardson had been sent to lie down after a night watch, and
she longed to see our Mother's eyes once more, they were shut
from the beginning, so she prayed to Mother Duchesne ' do
let me see her eyes once more,' and she was called in after a
few minutes, and our Mother opened her eyes, she did not look
at Sister Richardson, but straight up. But Sister Richardson
had her wish. . . . Then do you know what was our Mother's
last spontaneous word—as far as we can make out—on Saturday
morning a few hours before her agony began ? It was Alleluia !
Isn't that something to carry in our hearts for evermore, it
was for that, as you will see, that I managed to get an Alleluia
into her mortuary card which you will soon have. I carried
her precious head when we placed her in the coffin, and it was
my privilege too to lower her veil over her face for the last
time, and would you believe it, I had to raise it again twice
for two blessed Thomases among her own, who came late, and
had a right to a last look ; it was a great consolation, for it seemed
as if she were looking back twice herself to say good-bye as she
went on her journey. She did not look more than forty, I think,
when we laid her in her coffin. You know those four intentions
that you were kindly recommending for me to St. Eustachius ?
I must say that one is gained now, because it was for her, and,
as Juliana of Norwich says with a touch of grim sweetness,
' It is better that man should be taken from pain than that
pain should be taken from man.'

The time to write this has been stolen. I must not steal
more. . . . Thank you again for all your letters and prayers
and everything, and God bless everyone. . . .

Writing to the Superior at Cairo, she said :

MINE DEAREST,—
    You wrote me a sweet letter and I must send a few lines
back to you. We stand at the turn of the road, looking into
the sunset where our Mother has disappeared, and knowing

[1] Father Goodier, S.J., Archbishop of Bombay.

nothing of the road before us. For you and me it is the last
vanishing of the great protection and guide of our religious
youth, and the precious traditions are more than ever our trust
and treasure. This is really the moment of which she has often
spoken to us as being such a critical one for the Society, when
all those who had known our Blessed Mother will have disappeared, gone on into the light and left us behind. But they
will not fail us, nor will He, only we must be so good!
not 'monsters.' How I shall love to see you again; but how
suddenly all has changed, just at a moment when the sentries
kept repeating ' All's well! ' Truly Our Lord came as He said
He would, the Bridegroom at midnight unannounced. We do
not grudge *Ma Mère* to Him, nor Him to her. It was fitting that
she should go to Him, and I am thankful that she went before
the Society could feel that she was on the decline. They say
that she was never so lost in God, and at the same time
so sweetly and liberally given to His creatures as these last
months, since her last retreat, which seems to have been
literally *confirmatum transformare*. . . . May He bless you and
me too. . . .

She was once more in what she had described the previous
year as ' ideal quarters . . . a bijou residence.' But under
very different conditions of tenure. Even to her at first the
work seemed overpowering; ' I can just manage to learn my
daily lesson,' she wrote. As far as possible her outward life was
exactly as before. No grief or anxiety was allowed to master
her, or enter within the sacred precincts of her inner fortress.
There peace reigned secure. Gradually the old living interest
in all around her reappeared in her letters. But though so
completely mistress of her feelings, she felt the suffering none
the less acutely.

Two months after her arrival in Ixelles a young professed,
who had been one of her dear ' sons,' passed through Brussels on
her way to the missions. ' My son, isn't this lovely! ' was her
greeting, and then she added: ' I am sending you to Roehampton
before sailing, you are going to see the dear ones again, and the
dear tomb! ' ' I passed many happy moments with her during
those days,' writes the person in question, ' but at my last visit
before leaving she could speak only with an effort, and in the
letter she sent back with me she wrote " Sister C. will bring
you my love and my blessing, you know all that that means
and how much you have of it already." With her eyes full of
tears, but still smiling, she blessed me as I left, saying, " Love is
life, is it not, my son ? " '

She liked to see the English probanists serving in the refectory,
' It is like old times to me to see you there,' she said. Once
only the cry escaped her ' Wouldn't God be good if it could all
be the same again after this . . . but it will never be so.' As
a rule, however, her principle was that once a sacrifice had been
made it should not even be regretted in thought. ' We must
not talk or think of such things,' she said to one who regretted
they were not both together at Roehampton.

To the sorrowing household at Ixelles she was, as one said,
' An angel of joy in the house, no one can know what she has
been to us. . . .'

Her own letters will tell the story of the next few months.

June 3rd.

. . . This morning I was correcting proofs and Sister
Richardson came in and saw the slips. She said, ' Mother General
was so happy about that book that she read it aloud to me ! '
She said, ' This is a great thing, Sister Richardson.' (Richardsonia
are unlike anything else for their directness ! but it was a joy
to hear this.)

June 4th.

. . . I am glad you have asked the Bishop [1] for Corpus
Christi. That day I hope to be at Jette, where there is a procession at three-thirty, and to make my pilgrimage to our Blessed
Mother's tomb. . . . Yesterday I had a rather dreadful experience, fancy having as Vicar General to give conference to all the
household . . . the niceness of it is that for two years they
have not heard any conference at all as Reverend Mother de
Pichon's voice can no longer be heard ; and our Mother gave
none for two years or more. I appreciated Sister Richardson's
approval . . . she prowled about a moment pretending to
bring the lamp, and then said : ' That was very nice, Reverend
Mother, I heard every word.' . . . I have written to Longman
thanking him for offering me such a tempting bit of work [to
write a book on Holy Communion] but saying that I could
not think of it at present, that Father Roche [2] would do it to
perfection if he could find the time. Good-bye. . . . I could
see you all sitting on the terrace and the herons flying by.

June 17th, 1911.

. . . Oh the crying and the whining for British subjects
in all parts of the world ! would that we had them. Reverend
Mother Rumbold . . . is the last to lift up her voice in a
supplication for British subjects for Heliopolis, everything

---

[1] Dr. Amigo, Bishop of Southwark.
[2] The book written by Father Roche, S.J., in answer to this request,
was *The House and Table of God* (Longmans).

depends on this! Santiago de Cuba must have English if it is to do any good, etc., etc. . . .

It was a great satisfaction to see in the photograph of the children that they walk on good principles (this is a marginal note of things to be said to you 'children's legs'). Photographs are great tell-tales, but they almost all would fit the diagram which I showed the community, a right-angled triangle, with the hypotenuse behind them, as they walk beautifully in Renaissance times in Italian pictures. I am making further researches into the walks of Religious!

We had a nice procession on Sunday, distinctly popular in its setting, a large group of maidens in violet veils carrying instruments of the Passion, a parade of the Promises of the Sacred Heart and of the Mysteries of the Rosary, etc. St. Mary Magdalen with alabaster vase and streaming hair. They say St. John Baptist was there, but I did not see him. He was *vêtu de percale* underneath the sheepskin which made him unduly stout. Mère G. said with a touch of malice that it was probably '*par une suprême convenance*' that he had the extra clothing and added with the same spice that he was the '*précurseur de l'Enfant Jésus de Prague*' whom I missed. Now I hope that it will be lovely to-morrow for the procession and that the First Communion will be, as it always is, happy and holy.

When it had been arranged that Mother Digby's final resting place should be in a vault in the chapel of the Sacred Heart at Roehampton, Mother Stuart wrote:

16th June, 1911.

. . . I have filled up the form which Mr. W. sent me from the Home Office; when the transfer is made a brass plate ought to be put on the coffin, Mary Josephine Mabel Digby, etc. The Home Office ask the reason for the transfer, I have put 'to give an exceptionally honourable burial.' When you get the order you will have to see about the vault; it will be just opposite to where Père Varin's slab is, I suppose, and her slab will be a match to his, we shall get the inscription from Rome. Strange that she should rest where St. Sabatia's relics were hidden so long, for which the old Bishop walked the cloister in purgatorial exercise for so many years. . . . Did I tell you that the community at Ostend made holy hour to watch the mail steamer, which carried her precious remains as it went out to sea? and, just when they lost sight of its lights in the distance, midnight tolled ushering in the feast of the Ascension.

22nd June, 1911.

. . . Many interruptions have prevented me from writing as I intended a good long letter, but you know, everyone knows, that my thoughts are not behindhand, but are often to be met

about the house. Perhaps certain ascetical writers would say
'too often,' but I do not think Our Lord would take their point
of view. In any case I wish everyone a golden day to-morrow,
with music in their souls and graces in their minds and wills,
an overflowing day of God's own giving [it was the feast of
the Sacred Heart]. All that has been taken from us by the
Will of God makes us more apt to receive those precious things
which He intends to give us. Père de Vos quoted a word of
St. Ignatius which always strikes me when I hear it, 'Few
suspect what God would do in their souls if only they would
let Him do it.' So we will all be wisely quiet and watch Him
at work. We are having a good (indeed excellent) triduum,
and it was curious and interesting to me to hear this morning
detail by detail the story of Père Chavanal which Father
G. told us last December with the 'Vow of Stability' on
the Mission and all—exactly as Father G. said it—only in
the setting of a Belgian mind instead of a Welsh harp, strung
to the uttermost. The Belgian mind is a wind instrument,
well nourished with a steady supply of air! Outside the
triduum I have no news ; souls have been added to my daily
bill of fare. . . .

July 5th, 1911.

. . . Next Sunday will be the half-way day, exactly seven
weeks backwards to Our Mother's death, and seven weeks
forward to the Immaculate Heart of Mary [the day appointed
for the election]. The line which we have so often heard from
the sixth class at examinations goes through my mind from time
to time, ' " Gallop ! " gasped Joris, " for Aix is in sight ! " ' But
it is not good to think too much of it. . . . What is good to
think about and to see is Reverend Mother Borget, aged eighty-
four. I am lost in admiration of her vigour and her courage. She
gave us a small alarm on Sunday and consented to go to bed
for half an evening. But as soon as she was there and the
pressure of work off her, her gaiety and fervour of spirit had free
play and soared up like a lark or the spirit of Father C.
in the morning at meditation, and she talked to me in a way
that was simply delightful about her life and the early days
of her aspirantship, so hard and so happy. She has thriven
on the hard things, and lived so straight and so simply through
them, and now in her old age, although she would be delighted
to die, yet she still finds life supremely worth living, not a huge
task to be got through ! I sent for the doctor, they were well
matched: he wanted a little rest, she wanted a little freedom,
and the end was 'c'est plus facile, Monsieur, d'enchaîner un
lion que de m'enchaîner,' with which he quite agreed, and now
the lion is at large again, better than ever. . . .[1]

---

[1] Reverend Mother Borget died at the age of ninety-two in 1919.

July 19th, 1911.

. . . We had the procession of the Blessed Sacrament at Lindthout on Sunday, it was the village procession. . . . The children had done nice carpets in sand and flowers at intervals, all along the route, they had been allowed to go out in groups at five A.M. to buy flowers, and got bath-fulls, single carnations and bright things of all sorts. There were two hundred or more blind men and boys walking four abreast holding each other by the arm, and the two outsiders were held by a deaf and dumb man, such an Institute! all marshalled by Brothers 'so-called of Mercy.' . . . Of course the poor blind men plunged and pounded through the carpet patterns, but it could not be helped. St. Henry, patron of the Parish, was carried on a *brancard*, but his holy spouse St. Kunegundis, being alive, walked on foot with four maidens to carry her train. St. Aloysius walked with pages whom in life he could not have tolerated at his heels! The Holy Child walked in pink robe with flaxen wig and hand upraised in blessing surrounded by seven doctors of the Church in brilliant colours, keeping his eye on the master of ceremonies of his *cortège*, a young priest who walked backwards in a cotta before him, without a shade of amusement on his face.

We fell in behind the Blessed Sacrament when all this had passed, and as they left our property at the opposite entrance we fell out, and the devout rabble behind streamed past us. I am sure I counted eight women, perhaps more, who must have been six feet high or over.

The property at Lindthout is charming, beautifully laid out, with many choice trees and shrubs, but also, what is choicer, so many wild flowers. The choicest sight of all to me was a handful of the Junior School running like hares by themselves without an escort . . . the children looked so happy and natural. . . .

26th July, 1911.

. . . Our little Spaniard died on Monday evening, a beautiful death, curiously like St. John Berchmans, with the same three dearest things always in her hands, the same little moments of temptation and struggle, the same singular obedience and thoughtful courtesy for everyone. The Chaplain went in to give her an absolution, and she said as he went away, '*Monsieur l'Abbé, je vais au ciel et je verrai votre chère Maman!*' that was exactly what he had called her in his telegram to me announcing her death, which was a terrible grief to him. So he fled out of the room in tears saying, '*C'est un ange.*' Another time we got dear old Monsieur Gyts, aged eighty odd, to give her another, as no one else was within reach. She said very seriously to me afterwards, '*C'est bien un saint prêtre, ma Mère, mais* (with great astonishment) *savez-vous que je l'ai vu verser une larme.'* We are going to have her Requiem now. . . .

30th July, 1911.

. . . Will you tell the community that I have seen the explanation in a book [Welton's 'Psychology of Education,' p. 398, etc.] of what I have so long noticed and regretted, that people so often think that observation is acquired by indiscriminate looking at things, and so they look and look and are like Pharaoh's lean cattle, not a bit better. He puts it that observation is the elimination of the obvious. There is a great deal in that which I recommend to their consideration for themselves and others.

August 4th, 1911.

. . . Will someone tell me more about Father Lancisius' four words ' don't, do, dare, desire,' which commend themselves very much to me. . . . Please tell the community how much I will pray for the retreat and follow each soul on the track that I know it, hoping that each one will come out confirmed in faith and hope and joyfully resolved to give the best to God.

Writing later to another Superior she said :

. . . Your community retreat must be in mid-ocean now. I think of all the retreatants and think that God sends each one, directly or indirectly, what her soul needs ; God, who feeds the young ravens who cry to Him ; and if He feeds these hideous young wretches, how much more our precious nuns ! His precious nuns.

The retreat season is wonderful, house after house. And at the end, at the harvest home, the laden waggons pass me with a cheer, and many hold out their sheaves for my admiration, and I cheer back as well as I can, which obliges me to be short to-day. . . .

. 20th August, 1911.

. . . This is the gracious message from Cardinal Mercier's letter about my book. ' Ce matin même je reçois votre beau volume " The Education of Catholic Girls " et vous suis très reconnaissant de cette aimable attention de votre part. Je lis très peu, je n'en trouve plus de loisir. Mais ce volume je le lirai, parce que, d'une part, je suis très peu au courant de ce qui concerne l'éducation de la jeune fille, et d'autre part, j'ai confiance que ce que vous dites n'est pas copié de livres étrangers, mais dicté par votre expérience. Puis-je en retour

vous offrir l'hommage de la traduction anglaise de quelques
Conférences à mes Séminaristes ? '

Isn't it kind ? *Le repos ailleurs* has now flitted before
him to the solitude of Beuron Abbey, where he is going to
'*trouver la solitude, et s'il plaît à Dieu travailler à la rédaction
d'une retraite que j'ai prêchée au clergé.*' . . .

We have all the Vicars in but four now. The community
and we shall part company on Monday. Mère G. takes
charge of them. The triduum begins on Wednesday evening
and the election is on Sunday at nine-thirty.

23rd. . . . We have the Provincial of Lyons for our
triduum, he has a Lyons accent, the Lyons manner, the Lyons
smile (a study in smiles). What he says is very good. . . . He
is a great big Father, which I like better than a little shadowy
person going about like a disembodied spirit. But these are
details. It is time for prayer.

On August 25, two days before the election of the Superior
General, Mother Stuart wrote as follows to Father Daignault,
the friend who had guided her earlier years : [1]

. . . Your kind letter of the 27th June has been much too
long unanswered, yet I was so grateful for it. . . . For the
last three months I have lived as I could from day to day, and
consequently many things have got into arrears. . . . Now
I see with joy the end of my term of office approaching, for
on Sunday 27th, two days hence, our election takes place.
Personally speaking, I cannot regret these months because
they have taught me as nothing else could do, many things
which it is good to know ; what a cross the general charge
is, and how certainly all those bearing and surrounding it must,
as the *Imitation* says, ' lead a dying life ' ; and also what a
great thing religious perfection is, either in the individual or
in the body ; and how much the tone of each house depends
on the personal holiness of the Superior ; and how tenderly
God watches over all, down to the least détails, and averts
disaster by the slightest touch of His hand, changes circumstances ever so slightly, which makes all things take another
turn and saves from dangers unknown at the time. It does
undoubtedly increase one's confidence in God and one's recourse
to prayer, to see these hidden forces at work. So I am thankful
for the lesson, but so thankful also to have reached the last
page.

It may appear difficult to understand that Mother Stuart
really believed that ' her term of office was over.' But though

---

[1] See chap. xii, p. 156.

to the eyes of all she was manifestly fitted to be Superior General, she was convinced for many reasons that an English woman would not be chosen for the second time to fill this post.

The following letter was written to Roehampton by one of the Vicars [1] then at Ixelles.

. . . She [Reverend Mother] is just her own dear self, so sweet and humble, doing or rather leaving nothing undone that her present position requires, yet never going beyond, full of gentle deference for the Assistants General . . . helping all, and making all believe it is they who help her. . . . She is the first in the chapel, never misses Office or a community exercise, and presides in the community room at night prayers, although there are only half a dozen people there. I think she is fairly well, although she looks very thin, and much paler than I am accustomed to see her. She does not get out much. . . . The Reverend Mothers are dropping in, Reverend Mother goes to meet them all. They kiss her hand, she is too humble not to let them do it ; she makes me think of Our Lord, ' I am in the midst of you as one that serves.' . . . She is all peace and self-forgetfulness. . . .

On August 27 Mother Stuart was elected Superior General, as all, except herself, had foreseen. The first telegram of congratulation was received from Roehampton : it re-echoed her own last words there, and the last word of Mother Digby. Whatever hearts felt at this consummation of their sacrifice, the telegram only said ' Alleluia.'

In the afternoon of the same day Reverend Mother Rumbold again wrote to Roehampton :

August 27th, 1911.

. . . It is about two o'clock. Office is just over, and I came to my room to write to Cairo, but, somehow, I think it must be the Holy Spirit that entices me to scribble to Roehampton. . . . The wire will have told you that the Vicariate's sacrifice is consummated and that the Society has the best and dearest we could give at its head. These days have been great days in every way. I wonder how Reverend Mother has lived through them, and yet she has been her own self all along, no rush, no hurry, but everything done and not an iota omitted. I saw her twice since writing. She spoke beautifully to the Mothers assembled, on the solitude that should as it were surround us during these days, the heart of the Society in suffering, the soul of the Society in prayer.

I have been running about too to the Assistants General :

[1] Reverend Mother Rumbold, who died at Roehampton on September 21, 1921.

day by day they understand better what God has given to them in Reverend Mother. Reverend Mother Borget says she is an '*Âme d'élite,*' and that no one can imagine how exquisitely tactful she has been during these three months. Reverend Mother Nerincx, after speaking of her gifts, added '*et puis elle est sainte.*' Reverend Mother de L. could not sufficiently impress on me what she thought of Reverend Mother's union with Our Lord. Another, in speaking of her, said, '*C'est une création divine.*' I tell you all these little odds and ends, knowing my letter is going to loving hearts who need no one to tell them what Reverend Mother is, and has been, ever since God gave her to us.

Just after the opening of the Council I said to her, ' It was a hard day to-day.' ' Yes, it was rather bad, wasn't it,' she said ; ' but it is over now, and you will see, God will help us through Sunday too.' All day yesterday they were preparing the chapel, it made my heart ache to think of the victim, for I never doubted what would be the outcome of the election. . . . Most of these preparations were going on while our dear Reverend Mother was kneeling in her stall.

This morning at Mass they sang *Benedictus qui venit* ; it made the tears start to my eyes. She was in the chapel before five-thirty, and went to Holy Communion with all of us at the seven-fifteen Mass. The Bishop's Mass was at eight-thirty, and then the election. I shall never forget it—all so solemn, and Reverend Mother so calm and selfless. Dear Reverend Mother Borget was so joyful that she almost recovered her voice when reading out that Reverend Mother was '*élue par une majorité absolue.*' I think there is in every heart grateful joy—or perhaps joyful gratitude expresses more what I mean. The Bishop congratulated us, and said the result of the election would give personal pleasure to the Cardinal.

Reverend Mother was so bright at recreation, and yet one knows what it all means to her. . . . God alone knows what her poor heart goes through : she herself will never show it. I thought of poor Roehampton, and of how lovely the chapel will have looked to-day. Everything the same and yet such a void !

From henceforth Mother Stuart belonged to the whole Society, and for life. Though Roehampton would still have the largest share of her love, the very reason which secured this privilege would necessitate that it should have the smallest share of her presence. Her message had been given there : she had now to carry it to others. On August 28 she wrote :

. . . Whatever happens, my first letter must be to you. The spirited—and, more than that, heavenly-minded—telegram signed Roehampton was the first that reached me at five-forty yesterday,

and I thanked God and you for it. . . . It was worthy of all
that everyone has shown herself at Roehampton through these
three months; and now I commit its dear future to God. . . .
Yesterday, when I watched the last flicker of the voting papers
which were burnt, it seemed like the closing of a great chapter
in all our lives; and then we went off processionally to the chapel
saying the *Benedictus*, which linked it for always in my mind
with that perfect *Benedictus* in the cemetery at Roehampton,
which I hear without having heard—' *ad dirigendos pedes nostros
in viam pacis.*' I told you that the Cardinal is at Beuron re-
cruiting and preparing his new book (his telegram came in second
after yours), so it was Monsignor Legrève who presided . . . he
was immensely impressed and consoled to see how things were
done. . . . The ritual of ours . . . is so solemn and strong,
and one realises the great independence of the Society and our
immediate dependence on God, each one standing by her own
conscience without human interference. The result may be
personally dreadful, but in themselves the principles are very
grand, and carried out with such ' quietness and confidence '
that, in spite of all it means to me, the remains of my spirit go
out in admiration of it. . . . I must not take much of this
recreation of writing to you, but to-day I had to. . . .

On September 21 Mother Stuart wrote her first circular
letter to the Society: in it she announced that she was about
to return to Roehampton for a few days, to be present at the
' second funeral service ' for Mother Digby. The vault had been
prepared for her reception in the chapel of the Sacred Heart.
She proposed at the same time to visit all the houses that lay
on her way. This was the first of many ' journeyings ' which
filled her short generalate and wore out her life.

On September 25 she was in Antwerp; and a few days later
she left Ostend in what she described as a wild wind—so wild
that it was with the greatest difficulty that the Ostend-Dover
mail was at last brought into the harbour some three hours
late on the evening of September 30.

The next few days passed all too quickly. On the night of
October 3, Mother Digby was laid in her new resting-place,
close to that Tabernacle which she too had loved best on earth.
A few days were spent in visiting the neighbouring houses,
and Mother Stuart finally left Roehampton in the early morning
of October 12: hearts were too full for words, and, blessing
her community in silence, she went. But what she could not
say, she had written the night before, and when she was gone
the letter spoke for her:

MY DEAR MOTHERS AND SISTERS,—

The last things one wants to say are better to write than to speak. I do not want to go away without telling everyone what a joy it has been to see them again, how I thank God for it, and what a happy memory it leaves me. We all felt rather choked, when the first ceremonies for our dearest Mother General took place, that I had to be absent—and God was all the time planning for us these beautiful days which were ten times more precious to us. Is not His Providence always better to us than our best thoughts! We have seen it once more—let us never forget it. For my own part I shall never forget September 30th— it was such a finished picture of our life on earth—the prolonged tossing and beating up against an angry sea ; the long, mysterious loss of time waiting at Dover, turned back to reflect still longer when we thought we were off—so like purgatory to our waiting souls—and then the arrival and the welcome, and all the dear faces that I had pictured appearing one after another as we shall see those who have gone before ; and then the heavenliness of the chapel and our moments of adoration and thanksgiving before the throne. Wasn't it perfect, a thing of beauty and joy to be ever remembered !

Another joy was to see how souls had grown in the months that have passed, and how convincingly they felt that it had been a great time in life—one that they would not for anything have missed—and they are without doubt stronger and greater for it. The pain of these things will pass, and all the rest will endure. We know God better and we are more His own by reason of all this.

And now we must go on again, each one to the duties which contain for us the Will of God and the means of growing in His service and love. It does not matter what, nor where—we will take it as it comes. And if the sea of life is angry and trouble-some for our navigation, we shall bear in mind that the harbour lights will surely appear one day, perhaps soon, and we shall be in port.

If I had to sum up what I chiefly want to say as to the future, to each one it would be, I think, this : *Think glorious thoughts of God, and serve Him with a quiet mind.* I think that includes my best wishes. May He bless you all.

The next day she wrote again : ' Yes, yesterday was beautiful, and will be a joy for us all, for I think we all gave some of this earth's best to God, and I felt that it was on all hands without a regret *in our wills.* Such moments are golden. . . .'

On reaching Belgium she visited the houses at Wetteren and Tournai, and arrived at the Mother House on October 17 to begin her new life. A few days later she wrote to Roehampton :

Last week I got through two such heavy pieces of work that I said to myself in Mother Maxwell's words, 'Well done, good and faithful servant. You need a little recreation: you may write to Mother ——; and this is indeed a recreation, dear Mother, just as reading your letters is a real recreation—they are almost as much alive as a talk with you. I shall complete the recreation by reading the last two over again.
We have All Saints weather, and if you have the same I know exactly how every single tree in the garden is looking. Here we have also a share of gold and brown leaves fainting on the ground on still days, and flying to my window when it is gusty, and in the air the autumn something—death with a subtle intuition of life to come, which says like a living voice,·' *Pretiosa in conspectu Domini mors sanctorum ejus.*' The realisation of what Roehampton looks like, within and without, and this autumn understanding of the shortness of life make one realise what small things are time and distance, and how great our human souls are in the midst of them. I thought so much between the last two bells at supper one day that it would take a whole book to expand it ! I wish I could write that book ! It would be on the love of God in our religious life, and the title would be ' *Domine, Domine, quis sustinebit !* ' I am in the third degree of resignation, if there is such a stage, about books. . . .
Did I tell you that at Tournai two French Jesuits came to see me ? One was Père de la Judie, who had danced with our Mother[1] when he was a light-hearted cavalry officer, before he became a private in the army of Ignatius. Now he is really frightening to see, so thin, as if one could take him to pieces at every joint, and with a voice completely gone . . . he sold his life dear in the great Cause, as our Mother did. Beautiful lives, and how little we know yet all that God has thought of them. I am so delighted at the news of Father Roche's book[2]—this is *my* book— and thirsting for it to be out, for I am sure that it will be a living word of joy and truth.
Did I tell you this story of one of our First Communicants at Vienna this year? A foolish and indiscreet person . . . asked her what Our Lord had said to her when she received Him. She answered . . . ' *Il ne m'a rien dit, mais Il m'a extraordinaire- ment réjoui.*' Was it not a glorious answer in a child's mouth, above all effort or pretence !
This afternoon we had a long and most pleasant visit from

---

[1] Mother Digby.   [2] *The House and Table of God.*

the Cardinal.[1] He came straight from the Bossuet festival at Meaux, and told the assembled household about it all; then turned to spiritual subjects and discoursed for the probanists on recollection most beautifully. What he said of the Cathedral of Meaux might be applied to his own words, for there is no adornment to them, but much directness and perfection (*il n'y a que des lignes mais de toute beauté*). He is intensely earnest, but very agile in his words—never oppressive in his earnestness. I must really say good-bye. . . . Will you tell the community that St. Eustachius has obtained my third intention ? So all are gained now : they will help me to thank.

Writing to Reverend Mother Rumbold at Cairo, she said :

Ixelles : October 21st, 1911.

. . . Your letters are always delightful and welcome. What a *contretemps* the outbreak of war was [Italian-Turkish war] which kept Reverend Mother C. prisoner ! To-day she sails, I hope, from Genoa—rather a thrilling sail, with the lights out all along the coast, but God will protect her. It takes one back to the Middle Ages to think of the Mediterranean with Turkish ships on the prowl. One can realise so little the condition of things, but I feel sure that all will be well. You will be glad to get her and her companions. . . .

It was beautiful at Roehampton, for they were all so good, drawn up to their full supernatural height and saluting the blessed Will of God. . . . Our Mother's sepulchre is glorious, so near the two altars and so reposeful under a marble flag with that beautiful inscription. I wonder if a copy has been sent to you : if not, it must be.

One other letter, written to Father Daignault, may fittingly close this chapter. It shows her as she stood on the threshold of a new world.

Ixelles : October 30th, 1911.

This is in a way your feast, though I believe your real patron is St. Alphonsus Ligouri; but I am sure you love this other Alphonsus too, your own lay-brother in religion, and practising so heroically the virtues which you particularly love. It sounds presumptuous to know this; yet, dear Father, in the course of years, thirteen years, I have learned to know a good many things about you, and often thank God for them. You know a good many things about me too. And I know that you will always keep me a place in your prayers, especially now when my responsibilities are so much increased, and my last hope of becoming a complete private has disappeared. One is riveted to this

[1] Cardinal Mercier.

charge for life, and that would be a dreadful thing if one allowed oneself to think of it.   But I am learning to walk *au jour le jour*, and to be blindly confident that God will never fail me, and if I pray and keep myself down in the dust before Him, He will not let me do harm to the Society in the course of my government.

I think often of death, which may be very near, although, humanly speaking, it is not, for God gives me health and endurance.   But the thought is cheering and stimulating all the same, and helps one to go on. . . .

In the depths of my soul, deeper than anything else, there is a well of joy.   God is so good to me.

It was to bear this joy to all her daughters that she now set out on her three years' ministry.

CHAPTER XX

1906 *to* 1914

> ' The thing that struck me most was the solitariness of a soul's inter-
> course with Our Lord. In that crowd they two (Our Lord and the
> good thief) were alone. The taking possession of each by the other is
> wonderful: Our Lord's new life in His penitent, and (more within the
> range of my understanding) his new life in Our Lord, who became every-
> thing to him. He suddenly came into possession of what he had never
> had, a real friend, and he gave himself away and must have been happy
> like a little child. I can realise a little how his eyes must have rested
> on Our Lord's face with great contentment and wanted no more.'
>
> *From Notes of a Meditation, J. Stuart.*

BEFORE following Mother Stuart to the close of her laborious
pilgrimage, we may pause here a moment to look once more
at the almost finished picture.

In a former chapter we have followed her, as we could,
through the earlier stages of her inner life, in the pages of a
correspondence with one whom she called ' the father of my
soul.' [1]

Interesting as the matter of those letters was, it has but
led us through ' the freer parts of the domain which border on
the closed garden. But the closed garden ! Who has the key
of the closed garden ? Nobody knows, except those who have
it and the one who gave it. And no one knows what lies
within it. But we guess at that.' [2] We can, however, do more
than merely guess.

Some records are available, from whence to draw the story
of these years—a story which she dared not submit to her
former process of analysis : ' a process too coarse,' she wrote,
' for anything so subtle and delicate as our inmost consciousness
of God.'

As in the earlier phases of her spiritual adventure God had

---

[1] See chap. xii, p. 156.   [2] *The Closed Garden*, J. Stuart, 1903.

sent her help and guidance, so again, in the moment of upheaval,
when the time had come for her soul to go forth :

> Pathways to find through perilous abyss
> Too deep for reason, not too deep for faith,
> Almost too broad for hope but not for love,[1]

He sent her what she needed even more than guidance and
direction—a spiritual friendship. ' We must always be more
or less lonely,' she wrote, ' but sometimes it is given to spirit
to touch spirit . . . then we understand and are understood.'
And so it was now.

Through the medium of this friendship we can trace the
history of her inner life in the following passages which we are
allowed to quote from a correspondence. They will be found
to supply a key to all that follows.

Mother Stuart played her part in life so perfectly [says the
writer] that, with a kind of refined instinct, she hid from everyone
the things she suffered. It would have been unfitting had any
association with her led to breaking down the wall that made
her ' a garden enclosed ' for God alone. . . . Her wonderful
power of self-obliteration helped her to this ; her fixed determination to live a perfect life, no matter what she might be
feeling within ; her meeting of others *always on their own* ground,
as every letter she wrote illustrates. At the same time no one
can read the story of her conversion, nor detect the quickness of
her intuition, nor feel the gentleness of her correcting hand,
without concluding that in her own soul everything could not
have been so smooth and even, as appeared on the surface. That
she was unable to reveal herself, she hints at in the beginning
of her life.

With this opening word of warning as to the impossibility
of penetrating to that solitude where ' God speaks to the heart,'
we may pass on to the story ' of her attainment to that higher
freedom in prayer which came to her during her last years at
Roehampton.'

The magic word that opened the way may seem elementary
enough [continues the writer], but all understanding of prayer
is based on very simple elements ; ' unless you become as little
children ' refers even more to the kingdom of prayer than to
anything else. A meditation during a retreat in 1907, on the
Personality of Our Lord, led to conversations which, originating
thus, turned naturally on prayer and on the value of living

---

[1] From verses, 1904, J. Stuart.

with Our Lord during it, even if one did no more. . . .   Mother
Stuart's loyalty to her directors was very marked.   While her
soul had from the beginning peeped round the corners, and
longed for what lay beyond, she had thought that *for her* the
rigid dry path of intellectual effort was the right one ; that
this was the true discipline, and that she must make this daily
sacrifice and penance as the price of spiritual strength.[1]   Without authority she would not allow herself to go any further ;
but she confessed she found this prayer growing more severe,
more penitential, the older she became.   One day, and many
times after that, the conversation turned on what writers like
Poulain call the Prayer of Simplicity . . . in which the scaffolding of meditation is allowed to look after itself : should the
first rung of the ladder, say, the act of the Presence of God,
satisfy the soul, then there is no need to proceed further, for,
as Saint Ignatius says, ' *Non enim abundantia scientiæ satiat
animam sed sentire et gustare res interne.*'

This thought, neither new in itself and certainly not new
to her, came this time as a summons and a revelation.   As often
happens, words which have fallen times innumerable on our ears
spring suddenly to life, illumined by an inward fire, and then we
know that we know and that the message is for us.   So now
' it seemed to make all the difference to her.   She at once began
living with God, living with Our Lord in prayer ; and her quick
sympathy, which made her so easily enter into the minds of
others, made her no less easily dwell in the mind of Our Lord.
She became extraordinarily happy in her prayer, like a bird let
loose from its cage.'

There is a passage in ' The Society of the Sacred Heart,'
written in 1914, in which she appears to refer to this experience.
Speaking of the training and direction given to prayer and the
interior life in the Order, she says :

The Methods of Prayer . . . when explained by masters with
experimental knowledge, do not constrain . . . but set at liberty,
with the liberty that comes of looking beyond the letter to reach
the spirit and the real intention—*what must have been meant*—
and with the liberty that comes of not being afraid to be oneself,
most of all in prayer.

Then there came upon her sooner than might have been
expected [continues the letters from which we are quoting] that

[1] It must be said, however, that this only regarded the daily morning
hour of meditation, at other times she had never considered herself so
constrained, but had held that ' a silent joy in the sight of God was all-
sufficient.'

sure sign of God's invitation to the higher paths of prayer, what
St. John of the Cross calls ' the dark night of the soul ' . . .
She feared to continue in the way begun . . . in which ' in a
mysterious manner all natural experience, and she herself, was
being altered and transfigured.'

In a letter written at this time she said :

Everything that has to do with prayer seems to have given
way and become a complete blank. . . . [And it ends with the
words] : If it is to change for the better, God will have to make
the next move, for I cannot. . . . I must only wait and see what
happens.

But humiliation in prayer [it was explained to her] is no
reason for abandoning it ; on the contrary, this painful realisation
is what St. Ignatius includes under consolation as much as, perhaps
more than, spiritual joy.   But even had she wanted it . . . she
could not have kept herself from prayer ; she had ' tasted and
seen how sweet was the Lord,' and she could not, *being what she
was*, help hunting after Him, no matter what it might cost.
About this time the pressure of outward events became very great.
There was the Beatification of Mother Barat, the transfer of
her body and the examination of the relics at Jette, the death
of Sister Violet Ashton Case—I never saw anyone so triumphantly happy as Mother Stuart on the day of her funeral—the
preliminary illness of Reverend Mother Digby in 1910, the
elevation of Cardinal Bourne, and a number of other things ;
all these seemed to take her out of herself and to provide her with
matter for prayer suited to her breadth of mind.   Then came
the death of Reverend Mother General, followed by her own
election ; and from that time her journeys, her enormous
correspondence, and her interest in life generally, without in the
least diminishing her spiritual vision, yet ' directed her life of
prayer into that channel in which contemplation and action are
united without prejudice one to the other.'

For God [as she said] never gives a work to do and then takes
away the means of doing it.   It may be, indeed, that as she wrote
of Blessed Mother Barat ' she had thus to sacrifice some favours
to which her soul seemed so well attuned. . . . Favours which
might have carried her into regions where the sounds of this
world would hardly have reached her, and so would have made
her less fit for the demands made upon her in directing the
complex organisation . . . in her hands.'

But the greater number of men are sent forth by God to
labour ' until the evening,' and yet no honest work of man can

hold him from the divine tryst. 'Every friendship with God,' wrote Mother Stuart, 'and every love between Him and a soul is the *only one* of its kind,' and so her own. While harnessed to a burden of duties which would take no denial, she found the home of her soul in that state described by Tauler as one in which the soul is so perfectly disciplined that the exterior and interior lives, far from hindering each other, are in harmony . . . and the entire life is a prayer.

In some notes of a meditation written at this time (1909) on 'Mary in the Public Life,' she said, and the words seem to be an avowal of her own way in the last crowded years :

The thing I dwelt upon most was the new aspect of the Hidden Life, and its further development, hiding more and more deeply in His crowded life ; the true current of her life flowing now underground. There was perhaps no longer direct intercourse, or very little ; there were even barriers to it in the crowds which surrounded Him, their constant claims and needs had to pass first. He was everybody's except hers, yet, she was more than content, and they were still all in all to each other. He could trust so entirely to her love and understanding that He could put others before her, to the extent of being misunderstood, and it did not matter to Him or to her, because they understood so perfectly. . . . It seems possible to attain to something of this kind of hidden life in one's own circumstances, so that nothing should come across the truth of the inner life and the friendship of perfect understanding and perfect trust.

During all this time [continues the writer quoted above] it became easier and easier for her to spend long hours in prayer. After the 'dark night' she seemed to *sail into sunlight*, became very quiet, and was as one who is certain without troubling any more about doubts. . . . Mother Stuart, during these last years when I knew her, lived a supernatural life in and beneath all her activities ; she could with ease make the outer machinery stand still ; in a sense, nothing had hold of her, especially after she became Mother General ; the unconcern with which she faced her last illness and death is to me one of the most striking revelations of her spiritual state. She could pray for long hours without interruption, and she could find consolation in a glance through the chapel door. She made much use of hymns as a means of prayer. . . . As ever, she was extraordinarily docile. When she found the delights of freedom in prayer, and was warned, as St. Teresa warns her daughters, not to presume on that, but carefully to prepare her points of meditation, she obeyed implicitly, and kept up this practice till her death.

In the strength of this ' highest friendship . . . she had
dared then to let the contemplative spirit, which she had so long
crushed, live again,' and she found, she said, that to do so was
' to sail with the wind and no longer against it.'

In speaking to those who could understand, she described
this inner life in picturesque phrase, but this was in her last
years, when she looked back from the heights attained on the
long line of march.   ' It was, as it were, a narrow mountain path
which seemed to vanish and lead nowhere, but where there were
flashes of light from time to time to show that way had been
made.'

Turning now to the second record, we find in it many illustrations of the facts brought out in the passages quoted above—
the hiddenness of this inner life—the depths that lay behind the
outward serenity—the pain of the long waiting—the yearning
for what ' lay beyond ' realised as it had been at least in moments
—and finally the rise of her true *Dies Domini*, when she at
last ' held in one hand the supreme substantial vision, and in the
other created loveliness and was friends with both.' [1]

This second record was that which she herself committed to
the leaves of her poems, in verse or prose.

Through their medium she caught and fixed for a moment in
quivering flashes, glimpses of the inner life, where *Dieu donne
rendez-vous à la créature*.

This method of self-expression served a double purpose ; it
relieved the imperious pressure of thought escaping from the
bounds of words, and yet kept sacred the ' secret of the King.'
This record is perhaps even truer than that confided to her earlier
letters ; truer, in the sense that a poet sees deeper things than
reason can discover, and reveals truths that no analysis can lay
bare.

These writings, then, to which we may turn to complete the
picture of her inner life, were in reality parables ; the intimate
revelation of her own soul, told in language of great beauty and
often under the guise of some simple story ; told through symbol
and image, which, as she said, ' often serve to express what the
soul has lived through in prayer.'   And so it happens that what
seems ' a description of natural beauty leading the thought to
God, is a bit of soul history.'

Read in this light, all the writings of the last fifteen or sixteen
years of her life would repay study.   The change that gradually

[1] C. C. Martindale, S.J., on ' Saint John of the Cross,' in *Upon God's
Holy Hills*.

took place in them is very marked. Interesting as the earlier papers were, through the later ones there breathes a spirit not of this world. In the first we feel that she ' believes,' in the latter that she has ' seen.'

' There are day-lilies growing in the closed garden,' she wrote in the essay already quoted above, ' holy, lovely thoughts, born of God, given for a day only, for delight, and for a foreshadowing of what the lilies shall be that will never fade away. And there are immortelles . . . thoughts that even now are everlasting, that time and age and change can never touch.' In the pages that follow some of the flowers from the secret garden have been gathered together.

The first chosen is from the Christmas poem for 1897 : ' Long the ages rolled and slowly to the coming of the Word.' Having pictured the weary waiting of the world for Christ in the opening verses, she continues :

> So they prayed, and through the ages so the faithful singers sang,
> Sighing for the great appearing, sighs that like their harp-strings rang.
> Dreaming that they heard the music of the High Priest's bells of gold
> Ring among his silken fringes in the glory known of old.
> Dreaming that they felt Him coming, that the blessed time was near . . .

Then turning to the similar longing in the individual soul :

> Long the waiting, long the sighing of the spirit in distress
> Groping after type and figure in the pathless wilderness . . .

For a moment she draws aside the veil of the Holy Place and pictures in three verses ' the great burst of music which,' as she said, from time to time swept through her soul.[1]

> Then a moment when the thoughts, even longings, all are still,
> All the mind, the soul in silence, of His Presence, drink their fill,
> Past and future, all are blended in a present so complete,
> That eternity could only such another moment meet.
>
> .   .   .   .
>
> Hold Him not, the vision passes, not for earth such moments blessed,
> Time is all too frail to hold them, in eternity is rest.

[1] Letter quoted in chap. xii (1900), p. 165.

' Here is true poetry, can I have it ? ' said a visitor as he
came out of a chapel of one of the London convents, showing as
he spoke a paper on which this Christmas hymn was printed.
But more beautiful as ' Songs of Another World ' were, perhaps,
the poems written in 1900 and 1901.   They not only show the
vividness of her inmost consciousness of God, the ' Music within
the soul and mystery,' but they appear to tell something also of
all that He was to her.   In the first, ' To whom, Lord, shall we
go ? ' the thought, pouring out in words of praise and homage,
rises to a climax of triumphant joy.

Thou the Creator of created ways,
Poet and maker of the length of days,
The uncreated Word, that ever says
        ' I am the Way.'

Thou the eternal answer of the mind,
Thou the strong chain of truth, our fears to bind,
The hidden key to all that lies behind,
        Thou art the Truth.

Thou art the love that ever maketh life,
And in its struggles with contention rife,
Thou the resolving chord that ends the strife,
        Thyself the Life indeed.

Thou art the utterance of all unsaid,
The hidden name revealed, but never read,
The Word returning living from the dead,
        Sanctus immortalis.

Thou art the opal of the sevenfold light,
The marriage ring for ever to unite
The nothing with the loving Infinite,
        Sponsus animæ.

Thou, when our hearts are full with inward stress,
To breaking or to brimming, dost express
The words that die in utter helplessness,
        Unsaid through tears.

The joy of the Christmas mysteries is felt in the opening verse
of ' *Apparuit*,' the second poem referred to above :

As a Flower, in our land winter-white,
Frost-stricken, with woods standing sere,
        Fair Flower unfolding,
        Fair Mother beholding,
Creation awakes—He is here.

In verses written in April 1902, under the heading of ' Eternal Thoughts,' we read :

> Burning as adamant in light,
>   Clear as angels interchange,
> In undivided words of fire
>   Through inward firmaments they range.
>
> Beyond all deep astonishment
>   They bear the soul's vibrating cry,
> Beyond emotion's utterance
>   They fathom deeper unity.

Such words seem to bear witness that, though in time of prayer, from self-diffidence and humility, she still hesitated to follow the leading of desire, transporting her ' to the limitless Presence of God,' and still, though against the grain, reasoned about what He had done for her, and she should do for Him ; yet, at other times, ' God's felt presence in the soul ' overcame all such re-sistance. And we realise too, that the very magnitude of the struggle to restrain her soul from following its great attraction gave a wonderful impetus to her ascent, when the flame of love was at length set free. Nothing had in reality been lost. In a few years she ' fulfilled a long time.'

Of two extracts chosen from poems written in 1904, the first, from which the influence of Francis Thompson is not remote, recalls the joy she always found in the Easter feasts : ' Between the Easter glory and the Fire of Pentecost,' when—

> . . . liquid praise of Alleluias long
> Rolls through the long aisles from the lofty choir,
>
> Like the full-flowing waters after frost
>   And upward borne by force of hidden springs,
>   So, in this time, exult all living things,
> And over all the Church rejoices most.
>
> While Nature, shy as a child-acolyte
>   Flings up its incense, and its wood-notes long,
>   Like a boy-chorister's half-conscious song,
> A hymn of life, a worship of delight.

While the second, written for the opening of Armagh Cathe-dral, is wholly occupied with the description of the spiritual temple : ' The wondrously created heart of man ' :

The living altar of the mystic Mass
Where the High God His wonders brings to pass.

.   .   .   .   .

Then, without herald, without warning note
        Thou speakest Thy word,
Thy temple holds Thee, and the soul of man
        Embraces Thee,
The heart that Thou hast deigned to love
        Is one with Thee.

Sweet, sudden is Thy coming, blest be Thou
        That passest by,
In breaking of the Sacred Bread of Life
        I know Thee nigh,
I see Thee in the trans-illumined light
        Of dying eyes,
I own Thee in the separating joys
        Of sacrifice.

The next year, 1905, in ' *Obiter Dicta* ' already referred to,
she spoke of the *Dies Domini*, when ' the soul gives all for all,
the world and heaven and earth become its own ; there dies
desire, for possession is attained.'   Reading it, it is impossible
not to be convinced that the glorious *dawn* of her own day had
risen.   When Cædmon sings his inspired song before the Abbess
Hilda, she exclaims :

Yes [the *Dies Domini*] came to him as song, and his trouble
has vanished for ever, because the God of consolation and
sweetness and of song has shown him a glimpse of His loveliness
and made Him hear the oracles that speak behind the lowly
works of this world.

But ' weariness is also law, the ebb-tide of the spirit's powers,'
she wrote the following year, 1906, in a poem which drew its
inspiration from the words ' *Jesus fatigatus ex itinere.*'   It
seems to have been written in one of those moments when, in
face of the sufferings of those she loved, filled as she said with
weariness at the uncertainties and perplexities of life, she ' longed
to tear the veil aside, and see how everything was to come
straight.'   A note of sorrow, or as she herself expressed it, ' a
question like a cry of pain ' rings through the verses.

        Lord, art Thou weary ? scarcely yet
        The sun has touched the mid-day line

> Above the morning of Thy life,
>   The heaven of that youth of Thine,
>   And scarcely in Thy strength appears
>   The fullness of Thy thirty years.
>
> Lord, art Thou weary ?   Is the work
>   The Father trusted to Thy care,
> His ruined temple to restore,
>   Beyond Thy mortal strength to bear ?
>   Is Thy Omnipotence indeed
>   Too sorely pressed in this our need ?
>
> Lord, art Thou weary ?   Has the road
>   So soon worn out Thy sandalled feet ?
> And must Thou slacken in the way
>   Before the journey is complete ?
>   Must evil weary out the saint ?
>   And Godhead in the strife grow faint ?

Then, having pictured in two verses the weary struggle of the Church and the Saints through the centuries, she answers what she calls the 'faithless questioning.'

> . . . no redemption has been wrought
>   But by the pain of One who loved . . .
>
> And weariness is also law,
>   The ebb-tide of the spirit's powers,
> The pause of winter, while the earth
>   Slowly prepares her fairest flowers
>   Regenerated from decay
>   To meet creation's newest day.
>
> Then welcome be the weary hour,
>   The pause between the beats of time
> When every oracle is dumb
>   And silent every distant chime ;
>   In stillness, then the attentive ear
>   Can hear His footsteps drawing near.

But 1907 dawned at last, when, as we have seen at the word of 'authority,' her soul was set free to seek God as she would in prayer ; no longer 'thoughts about God, but God' would fill her soul.

In the summer of that year she wrote the 'Fable of the Ugly Duckling' and in it told her own adventure. It shows, she wrote on the first page, 'how the soul, which is an ugly duckling, by adversity and experience, and the abhorrence of

Y

worldliness, may attain to true life.' And it reveals in a vivid flash something of what that ' true life ' was, as lived by her.

The ' Ugly Duckling ' ' thrown out from among its brethren ' from the security of the farm-yard, finds itself alone in the marsh. ' It is all over,' it exclaims, ' my life is a failure ! I have come out into the marsh to die alone.'

But on the marsh lives the ' wild duck,' the one who knows. It appears on the scene, asking what is the matter, and, hearing the trouble, says for all consolation : ' Well, who cares if the old maids titter, aren't you born for the water ? I will give you a bit of advice. Believe in your own destiny. . . . You will live to see.'

' What ? ' asks the Ugly Duckling.

' To *see*,' replies the other ; ' that is more than seeing *something*. It does not matter what you see, so long as you *see*.'

And to the question : ' How do you live on the marsh ? Who takes care of you ? ' he replies :

' God, and our own good sense ! God sends the food and we look for it ourselves. When the wind goes to the north we find shelter if we can ; if not, we turn our heads to it and endure, till it changes. If it freezes we work hard together to keep a hole open for drinking. We listen to the wind among the reeds and it tells us many things. But nobody says " cluck " to us, no one talks about our lovely green heads, but when they glint in the sunlight we think God is pleased to see them,—we think so, He never said it in so many words to us, but we believe it—so we don't pine for the goose-girl and the hen-wife . . . to stroke them. We have very few wants indeed.'

' I think it is a lovely lovely life,' exclaims the Ugly Duckling.

' You don't understand a bit about it. " Lovely " is quite a weak word, a wretched word—a pond word—this is quite a different place—wild and grave and free. We want nothing but what we have. Hark to the sweep of the gale ! I am off . . . *Trust your destiny !* '

Then the Ugly Duckling goes on his way, meeting the wild geese and passing through the cottage in the wood. And finally comes out upon the fens, where he reviews his year's education, and concludes : ' The wise Wild Duck told me to believe in my destiny. . . . Only one thing I am certain of, that I am made for the water, so to the broad deep water I will go.'

Then there break upon his vision three swans coming through the reeds : ' Oh ! the beautiful birds ! I never saw the like of them. How splendidly they swim ! If I could be like them, so

white, so strong, so royal! They would kill me if they knew I
thought such things; but I will go to them, better to be killed
by them than to live among the lower creatures.' And as he
goes, a child's voice says: ' They are four! See the fourth one
coming through the reeds.' And the piece ends with the song
of the swans.

Spirit seeking light and beauty,
  Heart that longest for thy rest,
Soul that askest understanding,
  Only thus can ye be blest.

All the joy and all the fairness
  Fade away from earth's delight
By the steadfast contemplation
  Of the glory out of sight.

Through the vastness of creation
  Though your restless thought may roam,
God is all that you can long for,
  God is all His creature's home.

Taste and see Him, feel and hear Him,
  Hope and clasp His unseen hand.
Though the darkness seem to hide Him
  Faith and love can understand.

In 1909 she gives another glimpse of her ' life on the marsh '
in 'Comfort for the Faint-hearted,' where her own soul speaks
through the mouth of Paula, the friend of Saint Hyacintha.
' Do you ever think you find God? ' asks Hyacintha, and Paula
answers:

Now and then, when we are poorer and have to do without
more things, and when things are a little harder, then I know
He is nearer, and when things fall out just across my will, then
I can laugh to myself and say, ' Now! just for a moment I have
caught Him up! And He laughs back to me and hides Himself
again. . . .'
How do you know where to seek Him?
My heart always tells me which way it is.
It is a terrible detachment . . . you have to let go so much.
No, it goes the other way. I have to hold more than I
can hold, and receive more than I can receive. I have too much
and not too little. . . .
And so everything else drops off, just of itself?
You don't want both—it must go.

. . . But that is not the place to begin.

You begin every day, just where you are, no matter where. It is always *here* and always *now*.

And in an essay already referred to, called ' Highways and By-ways in the Spiritual Life,' written also in 1909, the following beautiful passage pictures the home of her soul :

But straight across this track [the Highway] comes another current of travellers, that of the by-ways, who go . . . because go they must, and it is not evident where they are going.

There pass the inspired people, the seers, poets in contemplation, shepherds and sons of the soil, who hide under irresponsive faces strange gleams of the unseen world, shadows of inarticulate fears, and hopes still more unutterable; there pass . . . all the uncounted seekers after that which can never be known, and lovers of that which always lies beyond.   The people of the other world are attracted by the by-ways, where the mysteries call them onward, and the shy nightingales sing, and the stress of life is lifted off, and the ticking of time is still.   Where it is no longer the chronometer that divides the seconds, but the sun that rules the day, and the moon and stars that govern the night ; where life seems larger because of silence and calm, where the soul may be invaded and taken captive unresisting by the powers of the world to come ; where the mind learns to rest in the Lord and wait patiently for the heart's desire, where the conviction grows that at long last all things come home to their God, *Ad Te omnis caro veniet.*

The peace of attainment and of possession is felt in these words, and writing of her at this time, the Archbishop of Bombay says :

And so in the latter years of her life did she exult as a giant to run her course, revelling in the sunlight of heaven.   Kindling to white heat in the burning fire of the Heart of Jesus Christ, and resting her head for hours, that seemed to her as minutes, on the breast of her Beloved in the Blessed Sacrament.

Turning from these poems of the inner life, we find one more record in some notes on prayer written in the spring of 1909, and in the last Notes of Retreat, those of the early days of December 1911.

In the Lent of 1909 Mother Stuart wrote a short daily summary of the impressions gathered from her morning's meditation. The following are a few extracts chosen from these papers :

Compassion.—The impression which the sight of suffering makes upon me is, that it is that which makes me understand union with other souls, and so with the soul of Our Lord.   When one sees anyone suffering there is an impetuous movement to become one with them, to give them in some way all that one has of strength and life. . . . The impossibility of doing more than this comes back upon one as a pain, and this if one could feel it with Our Lord would be the most real compassion, I suppose. . . . But there is another aspect of the Passion which stops me here. . . . The beautiful part of the Passion, if it is not merely natural tragic beauty, is the light of the Godhead shining through it, and the resignation, and greatness, and sweetness, and collectedness of soul in Our Lord throughout all that came after the Agony.   In thinking of this the most spontaneous affections are adoration and admiration. . . . I thought perhaps it would be better to keep these two aspects apart and meditate only on one of them—say—through the whole of one Lent.   But the Church seems to put one aspect suddenly opposite to the other, as in the Mass of the Crown of Thorns, in the sudden transition from the splendour of the Tract to the terribly short harsh words of the Gospel—perhaps she means us to feel it the more from the shock of that change.

The Agony.—I have made it three times over, concentrated realisation and no more. ' The heart speaks not reflectively to itself, but affectively to God '; mine does not speak at all, I am quite dumb.   Perhaps the Divinity gives the overpowering impression that makes me dumb ; and yet I think I should be dumb with the most intimate friend in a great moment.   But though it is nothing, I think this very dumbness is prayer, for all that is in me goes out to Him without reflecting on itself, and that must be prayer.   It is almost an agony, but better than most kinds of quietness. . . .

Even with a great wave of compassion sweeping me away, I don't think I should have anything better to offer than silent companionship.   I can quite understand Job's three friends until they begin to speak.

Judas.—I tried to lose sight of, or keep my thoughts from, the Divinity of Our Lord in this meditation, and was startled at the way in which the physical horror of the scene stood out, it makes the whole impression to be of another kind, and terrible. . . . When one has kept the thought of the Godhead in the foreground there is too much solace in it ; its sovereignty, and untouched, untroubled life certainly takes away from the desolate horror of realising what Our Lord as man is going through. . . . When one thinks of Him only as a man among men, not as directing it but going through it and being quite passive, the whole set of the current of one's mind changes and the wish to be with Him and to be passive with Him comes to the front.

Pilate.—This is always to me a meditation in which the Divinity stands out—even now I cannot keep back the thought of it. God shines through the broken human life. Pilate, with the air *dominateur* of Rome . . . so studied in carelessness and ease ; it can be so offensive—the real world. And the Truth looked it in the eyes and made it quail. ' I have overcome the world.'

The Women.—There are two scenes that I can really enter into and feel that I have some understanding of them ; one is the anointing of Our Lord by St. Mary Magdalen before His Passion ' for His burial,' the other the act of St. Veronica. They both seem to be complete in themselves . . . and I think I can understand something of what they meant to those who offered these courtesies to Our Lord ; they were *only* courtesies, not useful, that is part of their beauty. I have a great devotion to things that are meant intensely, and are, or turn out to be, of no use. These had no meaning except love and sympathy, they would not be understood by anyone except Our Lord and themselves, and they must have felt they had said all they had to say, and not a word was uttered . . . I can almost feel the great sweep of understanding and sympathy that must have gone over St. Mary Magdalen . . . and for St. Veronica, I can almost feel what it must have been of pain and consolation together to do for Him what was so very little in itself, but meant so much.

Companions of Jesus.—The price of companionship was what made me think most. And the crucified life that one sees in some and guesses at in others, a crucifixion hidden away under the appearance of an ordinary life. . . .

Behold Thy Son.—Loves and sorrows that one cannot analyse (I cannot). The separation of life from life without the slightest resistance, the stillness of it all, the perfect worship and submission to God. How it came upon St. John, for he could not have foreseen it, and it is his point of view that helps me most to understand, because it was so far above and beyond him, he must have felt it to be so, and have been overwhelmed at being brought into it, into the very heart of it all.

The Death.—The actual moment of His death is one which I can almost always dwell upon, the actual moment of one of our own deaths helps me to realise it. I have seen so many and love them so much. All one's very deepest convictions and affections and sympathies seem to meet there, and

everything seems so true, and Our Lord so near, remembering
His own experience of death. And the mysteries in a dead
face appeal to me, and most of all the thought of His dead face.
I do not think much about it but only dwell on the fact, and
look.

The Anointing.—Everyone understood, probably no one
spoke, but all had the same thought of what they wanted to do,
and did it. . . . These last services, full of unspeakable tenderness and devotion, with no meaning except devotion, are among
those into which I can best enter. It seems possible . . . to be
right in the heart of what is going on. . . . The less event and
action there is in a scene the more I can enter into it. I do not
see why this should be, but it is so, and the same is true for me
in ordinary life. The greater things that happen do not make
their full impression until long after, when I have got to some
distance from them; but the very slightest incident, a mere
word, or tone, or gesture, or effect of light, seems sometimes so
full of meaning that it brings tears to my eyes, and I could get
lost in it if I were not constantly rousing myself. And yet there
is nothing to say about it. . . .

In the May following she again wrote her impressions of ' a
month of meditation on Our Lady.' In her notes on the fifth
day she said :

The effect of these meditations so far is more general than
particular. They make in my mind an atmosphere of Mary,
full of wonder, at moments overwhelming in beauty, and I like
to stay there with a consciousness that somehow this atmosphere
is altering the quality of my soul. . . . It changes one somehow,
though one could not quite put it into words, as beauty subdues
restlessness and silences one's soul.

And on the 17th we read :

Cana.—I have always had devotion to this scene, for its
gracious human side, I love to see Our Lady and Our Lord
coming into touch with every side of our life. This time (my
thoughts turned upon) how they were *in* everything and yet
outside it all, and all in all to each other. And all their unspoken
intercourse and the understanding that needed no words carried
the hidden life into this beginning of His public life, and it was
the real life still.

The last Notes of Retreat of 1911 are more scrappy half-
sentences than the orderly paragraphs she had written before,

but one who can read between the lines will see in these few
sentences another light and shadow on Mother Stuart's life.
They illustrate, too, what she wrote :

The Saints were ' passable like ourselves,' theirs was not a
far-away life, but a life very like our own. They never sat
down to rest flushed with success ; their fighting and failures
and fears and experiments went on to the day of their death.
. . . We are apt to think childish thoughts . . . to think
they knew they were saints, and that this made all things
comparatively easy. . . . We see the saintly attitudes in their
pictures and the aureole round their heads, and we do not see
the dust of every day. . . . They did not escape, but they
endured ; and in the end, after trying and failing over and over
again, they ' overcame and persevered to the end,' not dejected,
not despairing, but standing with an even mind, resigned to
the will of God, and to bear for the glory of God whatever might
befall them.

Notes of Retreat, 1911.

(1) Let my soul sink into solitude, for that is its home, and
there I shall find God. I want no reasoning, nothing convincing ;
I am convinced. I want the barest, deepest facts. My soul
face to face with God, as it will be, alone, at death.

(2) The ministry of things, the comfort of things (friendship,
etc.), use but not lean on, *ut migraturus habita.*

(3) As the Superior is, so is the house. I see it more and
more. Bound all the more to try for truth and love and sanctity,
for their sakes . . . six thousand five hundred people depending
much on me. And I am their servant.

(5) Death. ' Give an account of thy stewardship, thou
canst be steward no longer.' Sixth Superior General of the
Society of the Sacred Heart : fifth in line from our *Beata.* What
record will there be, before God, of my stewardship ? What
account to be given ? Of how long ? Perhaps very short.

Beyond all human reason I hope in God that He will receive
me to Himself. I affirm it. I believe it. I almost know it.

(8) St. Joseph governing with the authority given to him,
but with what humility, self-abasement, sweetness. . . .

(12) I think the key to all for me is ' less rather than more.'
So, to deny myself, efface myself, be silent, listen, think of the
presence of God, be faithful in least things, diligent in things
of the inward life. All things of that kind.

(16) Apparition to St. Mary Magdalen. Her Master making
Himself so natural that she took Him for the gardener ! He
is not altered, only more than ever true and faithful and good
to His friends.

Conclusion:

To strengthen the inner life, to live in a spirit of solitude, a life hidden with Christ in God.

It is better to say less rather than more, and to have less and to desire less, and even to do less rather than more. And in place of that; to be attentive to the presence of God, to be faithful to grace in the least things, to self-effacement, self-denial, diligence in all the things of the soul.

I shall always fail, and fail again, but it is better for me to fail and be humbled and ashamed, than to do glorious things and be pleased.

In the last year or two of her life she sometimes lifted the veil a little, for those whom she felt were walking a similar way in prayer, to help them over the difficult moments. ' God comes and carries off my soul into a far land,' she said to one, ' it is no longer its own master, but it is all in God's power.' ' In our mixed life God always leaves the soul free enough to do its work, although all that is not *He* is weariness to the spirit. . . . He gives in a short moment of intense prayer as much as could be gained in a long contemplation.' And again : ' Sometimes I must turn my soul away, because I feel my spirit would fly like a wild bird far beyond earth. . . . In prayer God gives me His own wine, old and new, and lovely surprises. Perfect trust and surrender are necessary, but God plays no tricks on the soul.' And to another, ' Sanctity is the progress of the soul towards liberty, and when the drawing of God becomes so great that the soul can no longer be kept from Him, its full liberty is reached, and He takes it to Himself.' In these few words she tells her own story.

Three months before her death, speaking of the life of the spirit that for some would blossom into contemplation, she said that ' symbols and images given by God in prayer are one of His ways of teaching ' : and she added, ' why be afraid of what God offers ? Even if these things were solely from the imagination, why should He not teach by the way He chooses ? Don't be suspicious of them ; these are His graces ; delicate exotic things that we must not handle. Take them with reverent gratitude, and if He takes them from us, learn to live without them. . . . God takes them away by degrees, they do their work in our soul. But these flashes of His presence are only the road to contemplation and not the goal itself.'

And when that goal had been reached, we can only say in her own words written in 1913 :

And then what ? We cannot answer or know. Beyond what we can see or hear, or feel or get security for, 'there lies the land.' In that direction we turn our heads when we speak of sanctity. There walk the saints. There pass those whom we guess at as having their lives hidden with Christ in God. There are all the secrets which God longs to show us, of what He would do in us and through us if we would let Him be free in us.

In her public teaching she never directly mentioned the higher paths of prayer. But for any who could understand and read between the lines its spirit was all-pervading. She taught rather what she herself never failed to practise, the faithful daily preparation of meditation. ' In that,' she wrote, ' and in colloquies (hateful word) is I believe the secret of success.'

Writing to one who shrank from the graces offered to her in prayer, fearing her unworthiness, Mother Stuart said :

Your ' reasons against ' seem to me to be founded on an error, that the particular kind of prayer to which you feel a call is given as a reward to those who have already acquired virtue. I do not at all think it is so, nor does the teaching of spiritual authorities point that way. So, without deciding your question, which of course I cannot do . . . I advise you to follow the clue ; preparing, yes, you must not risk going unprepared, but if the presence of God takes hold of your soul, or if you can keep thus in His presence, do not force yourself to do anything else. . . . The best thing for you is to go on quite simply and not ask yourself whether the way is ordinary or extraordinary, there is so much border-land in these things, and really in practice and to you it does not matter much what one would call it. You have only to go on quite simply, *pre-paring faithfully*, keeping your head in the dust, for you know whatever grace God gives you is His gift and not your own deserving.

When asked why she was thus reticent in public, she answered :

God must lead the soul Himself into this land, we cannot do so. It is His gift, coming sometimes at the end of a life of heroic struggle, sometimes in unspoiled souls at the dawn, but always a free gift. . . . No one can put others on this road, nor know with certainty that they are meant to enter on it. Some who reach the border-land are artist souls, who may mistake it for what God is not offering them ; others there are who meant to enter, delay on the border-land, and fearing the pain go no further.

In the last year of her life, when the Society lay before her as a whole, when she had found in it as she wrote, ' a hunger and thirst for God,' she said : ' I am convinced now, that many of our young nuns could be more contemplative if we initiated them more into the secrets of the interior life.' And to the question : ' Does our vocation *include* a call to be among *les parfaites amies* of Our Lord, of whom Blessed Margaret Mary speaks, or do we need for that a call within our call ? ' she answered : ' Our Lord calls those in the Society *who have an understanding* of their vocation to a degree of intimacy and friendship far above any that they can imagine or desire.'

In the last conference she ever gave at Roehampton in July 1914, on her return from her long journey, standing almost on the threshold of heaven, she said :

We shall not fully know what it means to have been called to religious life until we get to heaven. God has called us to the fullest spiritual life of which we are capable. The stop will always be put by ourselves. It will always be what Our Lord Himself said over Jerusalem, ' I would . . . but thou wouldst not,' and the finish of understanding that God looks for in those who profit by His training is liberty of spirit, freedom in the House of God.

If she did not speak of the stranger or more intimate pheno-mena of the spiritual life, yet she showed that life in its essence as the desired goal, and like Dante in the ' Paradiso ' might have said :

> *Now* if my words have not been faint,
> *If* thy listening hath been attent,
> *If* thou call back to mind what I have said.

In the Essay on Colour already alluded to in an earlier chapter, Mother Stuart described, under the symbol of ' the seven bands of monochromatic light, the seven stages of seven years that will have comprised my life when I reach the golden year of fifty.' She ended her paper with the words, ' after that we shall have, not coloured but white light, complete, unbroken, collected, the very light of eternity.' And it was, in fact, about her fiftieth year, that, as has been said above, ' her soul sailed into the sun-light,' and in the radiance of this white light the last few years of her life were spent ; in that ' simplicity . . in which . . .

all our spiritual life is unified into the one desire of union with God and His Will. It is for this union that we were made.' [1]

It may not be amiss to note that high as her aspiration soared, intense as was her spirit of prayer, perfect as was her life in each detail, yet we can close this story with the simple affirmation that she sought no perfection beyond the bounds of the Society which she had chosen. But within these bounds she had realised that there were limitless possibilities for sanctity.

There is no common mould in which the saints are fashioned. Each one is in a sense unique. But though this is so, there are certain great traditions in the Church embodied in the Religious Orders, each of which is first and foremost a ' school for saints.' Within each of these schools is to be found the ideal ' shown to its Founder on the mount,' in the framework of which all true sanctity of its members should find expression. The ideal of sanctity for each Religious Order is then a type apart.

In the pages of her Constitutions, Blessed Mother Barat has drawn the portrait of her religious *ainsi que je les avais rêvées*. Had the description there given been written as a life-sketch of Mother Stuart, its striking truthfulness would have been at once apparent, so completely did she embody its principles in her life.

Entering the Society of the Sacred Heart she had found that ' it was to the school of His own Heart that God had called her . . . that though consecrated and set apart to work for the salvation of others . . . yet she was bound henceforth to make it her most sacred duty and·sweet occupation to contemplate, study and know intimately the Heart of Our Lord.' For no human model, however perfect, would be proposed to her, no spiritual treatise by which to fashion the conduct of her life, but ' His Heart was to be an open book ' in which all was to be read.

She learnt that her ' charity was to be modelled on that Divine Heart' and to make its sole rule, the commands ' Love one another as I have loved you' and ' Let this mind be in you which was also in Christ Jesus.' The depth and extent and detailed graciousness of her charity, which filled people with amazement, were in her eyes but the logical outcome of these words.

' From the Divine Heart ' she was bidden ' draw that spirit of humility, meekness, gentleness, simplicity and obedience which should (and did) characterise her.' She was directed to

[1] ' Contemplative Prayer.' Extract from the August number of *Pax*, 1913, by Dom J. Chapman.

learn from it ' the value and importance of little things in the service of God . . . thus to establish herself in fidelity to all details of the Rule. . . .' Her exterior moreover was to be so regulated that the ' gentleness and peace observed in it ' should witness to the indwelling of God in her soul.

Mother Stuart took these words literally. She sometimes said that she believed sanctity consisted in taking the words of Our Lord literally. Her daily study of them revealed depths of meaning, hidden from the less diligent student. The character-sketch of her Order, which she wrote in the last year of her life, was her commentary on the Constitutions, and was the outcome and fruit of some thirty years of study. Her faith in the Constitutions as God's instrument for sanctification was unbounded, and her trust in their power was a stay and solace throughout life.

Her final judgment of religious life as found within her own Order was :

If *really lived*, our life has nothing to envy any other. But it must be so anchored in the land of faith and hope, so faithful in renunciation, so full of prayer, and washed daily by contrition.

CHAPTER XXI

SUPERIOR GENERAL

First Journeys: Italy, Sicily, Malta, Holland, 1911 and 1912

'God gave me an opportunity to launch my spirit more than ever upon His power, and He also gave me the assurance that His hand would trace my path. My answer was: " Behold, I come to do Thy Will." Then certain glorious words became realities, and I learnt the meaning of a spirit crucified, as never before, and kept a spiritual birthday.'

Written by Mother Stuart after she became Superior General.

MOTHER STUART stood on the threshold of a new life. A great work lay before her, and with the full power of her trained mind and loving heart she prepared to devote herself wholly to it. She might count, it seemed, on many years. She entered on her new post younger than most of her predecessors, and her power of work and of endurance was tremendous. And so she laid her plans for the future in perfect peace, while trusting all to God.

Her first desire was to be, if possible, as true a ' mother ' to the six thousand five hundred Religious now given to her keeping as she had been to the five hundred in the English Vicariate. She wished the Mother House to be to all the true home of their souls, to which they would turn naturally in any difficulty.

But for this the first requirement was to know all, and that as soon as possible. And so she planned her many journeys. Time would be short in each house, for she gave herself six years to visit the whole, that by the meeting of the next General Congregation she might, in council with the heads of the Society gathered from all parts of the world, be able to bring personal, first-hand knowledge to bear on the many questions which arise in the organisation and development of a great body designed to take a leading part in the work of education.

To be a witness to the fact that God is love, and to share with all this secret of her own joy ; to strengthen the spirit of prayer, ' the whole foundation and support of the Society,' as the Rule calls it ; to make its educational work keep pace with modern needs, while sacrificing nothing of its strong foundation, these were among her aims and ideals. How fundamentally right this education has been is gradually gaining recognition in the thinking world. Character is now seen to be of more value than specialisation in learning, and the demand is that schools should teach 'how to learn and how to live, rather than how to gain a living.' ' You give values and you give anchorage,' was an estimate of the educational work of the Society much appreciated by Mother Stuart.

Wherever she went she noted all that concerned the needs of the Religious and the welfare of the children, and this in no narrow spirit. She tried to see from the point of view of the people with whom she was, and she was far from imagining that in details there could be an ' ideally best ' which would suit the children of every nation. ' I have a plan in the back of my head for education here in Holland,' she said to the Superior of Bennebroek ; ' your children are capable of solid work,' and so in many other places. As she went round the world she gathered stores for future use, and her schemes grew and matured.

It was an overwhelming programme, but nothing daunted her ; and no one seemingly was more fitted to accomplish it.

But, though she little knew it, only three years and eight weeks remained of her working day, and of this she spent six hundred and seventy-two days in visiting the houses in Belgium, Holland, Alsace-Lorraine, Austria, Hungary, Poland, Italy, Sicily, Malta, Spain, the Balearic Isles, Egypt, Australia, New Zealand, Japan, Canada, and some in the States and the United Kingdom. One hundred days were spent on sea, and one hundred and one convents were visited. She saw individually some four thousand seven hundred Religious, also many Bishops, priests, educational authorities, as well as countless friends of the Order. ' In many places,' writes one who accompanied her on her journeys, ' she met discouraged and troubled souls, then her solicitude was extreme. She multiplied the most loving little attentions towards them, and gave back joy to their hearts, and left them strengthened and encouraged by that joy to go on their way again. "You will let me hear how you get on," she would say to such when leaving, and these letters were always answered by her own hand. . . .' Thus many new ʻriendships were formed, and her already enormous correspondence grew rapidly.

She gave at least one conference in every house, some ten

in the last visited : never, it is said, repeating herself. She
saw something of all the works established in the different
convents, and made a point of talking with the elder children.
Confidence was quickly established everywhere, and even little
children who knew no language but their own, as in Poland,
loved her at once. One little one meeting her on the staircase
at Leopol [Lemberg] stopped, looked a moment, then threw
her arms round Mother Stuart's neck to give her the tightest
hug she could. It was returned warmly, no words could be
exchanged, but they parted satisfied.

The remaining year and sixteen weeks were spent in her
new home, the Mother House at Ixelles, where she returned
after each long journey for two or three months.

As she had previously visited some forty houses with, or
as the delegate of, Mother Digby, when her short period of
government ended there were, perhaps, five or six convents in
which she had never been.

But in 1911 the end seemed still far off, and the 'Alleluia'
of the telegram from Roehampton was re-echoed throughout
the Society : for by reputation at least she was already well
known and valued. It was with the greatest hope and love
on her part that she set out to accomplish her mission.

God had quite other designs, it is true ; her mission was
not what she imagined. As someone well expressed it, it
seems rather that ' having fashioned a perfect thing, God took
it out of its obscurity to show it to all as an ideal. And so He
led her, as it were, through the world, and she won the hearts
of all to believe in her ideals, in her type of sanctity, in her
spirit.'

Her travelling was no pleasure trip, but the hardest work.
Long nights in the train were followed by days filled with receptions and visits. There were new surroundings every few days,
and never a moment's rest. And yet no one was allowed to
realise, or to be inconvenienced by her great fatigue. No one
was allowed to see anything but the gracious charm of a unique
personality which no weariness had the power to alter.

The first journey was to Italy and Malta. She announced
it in a letter to the Society dated October 20, 1911. ' It is a
great joy to me to go to Rome as soon as possible to ask the
blessing of the Holy Father.' On the way she proposed to
stop at Lyons and Marseilles to see the faithful Children of
Mary, whom no laws against Religious could drive from their
old attachment to the Society of the Sacred Heart.

She left Ixelles on the evening of November 13th, and reached Rome on the 24th, having visited the houses at San Remo and Sartorio. On the way she wrote:

For the love of God no more books while I am on the march, I have taken only a small portmanteau for two persons and it is like the omnibus, ' full inside.' . . .

And a little later:

I should love to have you all here to show you the loveliness of God's work at San Remo. Some of the woods and hill-sides between Marseilles and Cannes were covered with a beautiful pink heath in full bloom. Not the heath with wicked-looking little bells close together that we call Mediterranean heath, but the heads were much looser, and the bells larger and lighter, real pink. I should so like to know the name of the variety.

A great pleasure awaited her in Rome, for the Consistory was being held, in which the Archbishop of Westminster was to receive the Cardinal's hat.

The story of her journeys will be best told in her own letters. For, as someone wrote very truly:

Her wonderful powers of observation, her affection for little details, her love of dramatic language, make the descriptions far more real and personal than any chronicle could do.

Nearly all the letters which will be given in the next chapters were written to the Superior and Councillors at Roehampton.

Villa Lante: November 25th, 1911.

. . . We had an excellent journey from San Remo; between the Catholic abstention[1], and the war, and cholera scare, few people go to Rome at present, so there was no crowd, and beautiful weather; 'a quiet night and a perfect end,' for contrary to the usual custom the train was only a quarter of an hour late, and they had kept a priest ready to say Mass for us. I was very keen to hear the Italian side about the war, and of course it presents quite another point of view; of course, too, there must be some truth in it. Seven years' ' insupportable insolence ' of Turkish authorities to Italian residents and officials, determined neglect of diplomatic remonstrances (so very Turkish), neither apology nor amendment, and finally

___

[1] From the celebrations in connection with the fiftieth anniversary of Italian Unity.

an Italian girl carried off, and in reply to all representations, the maiden not restored, and no apology even ; one can understand that ' in their meditation the fire was kindled.' There was the greatest enthusiasm at first, and the Italian soldiers thought in their simplicity that they were going on a Crusade ! and they went to Confession and armed themselves with scapulars as good Christian men, and they write such touching letters to their families of how they were hours standing in the trenches saying the Rosary all the time. . . .

The Cardinals are not suffered to go out before the Consistory, so the Archbishop is hiding away in the English College and preparing his discourses. Mgr. Jackman says the Archbishop wishes that I should be at the three ceremonies, so I suppose I shall go to all. To-morrow is for the giving of the *biglietto*, and the time is quite uncertain as the same messenger has to carry it to all the Cardinals ! They have simplified it as much as possible by getting some of them together, but in any case he has thirteen journeys to make. The Archbishop is very much pleased about his title. I suppose you heard it is S. Pudentiana, the very nicest they could have chosen because of the antiquity of the Church, and also on account of Cardinal Wiseman, so I no longer regret that SS. Andrew and George is not free. I had written so far, when the Cardinal Protector came. . . .

I am back from the English College, where the Cardinal received the *biglietto*. It was brought by the Chamberlain of the Cardinal Secretary of State who made his way through the crowd, mostly the English colony, but some of all nations, and a host of ecclesiastics. At the appointed moment the Archbishop appeared at a curtained door and met him, received the *biglietto* and handed it to—I think—Bishop Stanley to read aloud, received congratulations and returned thanks in Italian; then the messenger sped away in his hurried flight for the rest of the thirteen visits, and [the Cardinal] made his way to the top of the reception room, where, standing very suitably under a statue of Our Lady and a painting of St. George on horseback, he made his discourse in English, and one could have heard a pin drop. It was very grave and strong and clear, but he was much moved and had difficulty in mastering his voice, he spoke beautifully and with deep affection of England, but I need not tell you this as, of course, you will have all in the *Tablet*, and then the *pieuse cohue* crowded up to kiss his ring, a great squash but orderly ; he said as I passed that he was glad I had come and he would say Mass for me on Saturday if I would make arrangements about it with Mgr. Jackman. They gave three English cheers for him *reverberating* ; and then I went to see all I had always wished, and never hoped to see—the church of the College, St. Thomas of Canterbury, and the pictures of the English Martyrs that carried their Cause of Beatification through, and the old English College chapel, now the Beda ; and the nice English student who opened its door for us and ran about for keys was kind and simple enough to show us the refectory.

Villa Lante : December 1911.

. . . The days at the Trinità were simply breathless so I could not write at all. There are forty-two choir nuns, and big *œuvres* and quantities of outside visits, and then at least one Cardinal every day, and I had to go out three times, to the Vatican, to the German College, and to the Villa Lante to meet Cardinal Vincenzo Vanutelli, and by that I lost the visit of Cardinal de Azevedo ; so you see why I got behindhand with correspondence.

Cardinal Farley[1] made a great effort to come to the Trinità the day I left as he heard that I was going into retreat ; it was very nice of him, for he had a terribly heavy day before him, with his own *Possesso* as one of its items.   He created a sensation by his rapidity of movement—they are accustomed to Roman prelates, and threw up their hands :   ' *Mon Dieu qu'il est prompt.*'   As he got down from the carriage he said : ' Is this Mother General ?   Mother General, I have read your book ; it is very good,' and so he sailed on to the sacristy ; he came to say Mass.   At breakfast he showed me with great pleasure a beautiful ruby ring, set in diamonds, which the children of Manhattanville[2] had given him.   He was accompanied by a very young American Monsignor and his nephew, Father Farley, S.J., both very much in spirits and refreshingly youthful !

Villa Lante : 19th December, 1911.

MY DEAR MOTHERS AND SISTERS,—

There will be quantities of letters from you I know which it will be a delight to read, but as I am going further away it seems better to thank you for them by anticipation, and, as I cannot answer them individually, to write as long a collective letter as circumstances will allow.   It will not be cut short by want of materials.

But to begin with a question, which seems obvious at first sight ; which do you think gives you a better knowledge of a saint, his biography or his autobiography, if you cannot have both ?   I do not think the answer is so obvious as it looks. The biography of the Venerable Anne of St. Bartholomew puts

---

[1] Cardinal Farley, Archbishop of New York, died September 19, 1918.
[2] Manhattanville, Convent of the Sacred Heart, New York.

this into my mind. After a question—a reflection—isn't it wonderful that two of the most sacred and symbolic plants, the olive and the vine, live upon almost nothing, a terrace of limestone, sun and rain—that is all, and then we have wine and oil. And on the flat lowlands we have beet-root and colza ! Is there not a great deal in this, about the oil and wine of prayer, they don't want *circumstances,* indeed they are better off without them. After a reflection—a *bouquet spirituel* for a treat, you know I do not abound in them ! But Our Lord said this to the Venerable Anne of St. Bartholomew when she was going into France and was dreading the difficulties and sufferings that were before her, He said : ' those who take the honey from the hive get stung but they carry off the honey.' After a *bouquet spirituel* I will come down to news of what I see and hear. The Cardinal Protector was here to-day and he was perfectly charming, and he sends you all his blessing. . . . I have had a visit from one of the Judges of my Commission last year, the light-hearted Bishop of Memphis. . . . He told me that the saintly Mgr. Lazzareschi still spends all his free time poking about his old parish of San Lorenzo in Damaso, and falls a victim to the old beggar women who prey upon him, and that he is still called by the other Canons the peacock of the Chapter of St. Peter's, because his robes are so old and poor that they scarcely hold together. . . .

Cardinal X. is the only Cardinal who will not allow himself to be accompanied down the great staircase here, he takes it in one swoop by himself. We look over the landing at the top. ' *Regardez, regardez !* ' said Reverend Mother de——— under her breath, and he passed like a flash, and as he was in ceremonial dress even the red hat (not the Hat, of course), it was all scarlet and lace and gold—a gorgeous sight. He went down in what an air-man would call a ' *vol plané,*' and his secretary, young and slim though he was, could not catch him up.

This is enough of news and nonsense. I will end with a thought for the New Year. I don't know where it comes from, but it is nice : ' Behind the dim unknown standeth God, within the shadow, keeping watch.'

Good-bye to everyone for 1911, and a happy New Year for 1912. I do not remember the latitude of Rome but at a guess I should say the sun was fifteen degrees higher here than at Roehampton, it makes a wonderful difference in the December days, morning, mid-day and evening. I salute the green slate on the chapel roof at Roehampton, which the shadow reached two days ago. . . .

Two remarks which I forgot : (1) Having lived a little with Mater Admirabilis it seems to me that she is especially an

Advent Madonna, with that dawn creeping up in the sky behind her. It *might* be her last day in the temple, and just a few days before the Incarnation. (2) Looking round from a high tribune on the Consistory I realised what strength and heavenliness there is in the Fifth Rule of Modesty (each one must express joy on her countenance . . .). I also realised that it is mental austerities which really wear the human frame, more than vegetable diet and night vigils.

Palermo : December 31st, 1911.

. . . I have been wishing so much to write but could not, you will have known how my spirit walked through Christmas Eve and Christmas night and stood among you at the Kiss of Peace which I gave this morning—here in the flesh, with you in the spirit, and I thought of many New Year's Eves, and of our annual walk to the cemetery in the twilight, after the last 'points' of the day's retreat. Perhaps you went down as usual. I can't tell you what a treat the Roehampton letters are, all so full of life and D.G. of God and His Kingdom. No phrases, all most refreshing. . . . We are leaving for Rome to-morrow night, by sea to Naples, it looks as though it would be quite a good crossing. Not like the last two (to and from Malta) which were records for my experience. I have met far worse weather, but never such pitching and rolling. But Malta itself was a huge Christmas holiday of which I must tell you more when I can. It was well worth the bad journeys and the broken connections at Syracuse which gave us another night in the train.

This is a nice house and a good school of one hundred and thirty, in two departments, boarders and day children. They are naïve, friendly, violent creatures, very fond of their school, very fond of their Sicily. They say that when God had finished the creation and pronounced it very good, He smiled at it, and that smile was Sicily ! . . .

Florence : Feast of the Epiphany, 1912.

Now I will go back a little, and if I go over ground covered by Mère le Baïl's letters it will be from a different point of view. . . . To go back to Malta of which I have not told you. Those four days were a Christmas holiday indeed. The fact of Reverend Mother R. being at the head of the community and Mother D. of the school tells you that all was simplicity and spontaneity and breeziness ! And the community so spiritual at recreation, nothing else comes up—but all with a freshness of open air, their thoughts undisguised ; 'thinking aloud' to a degree that is rare, and scarcely possible elsewhere. Our work there is good, it is greatly appreciated too, and Mother D. is immensely looked up to by the parents as by

the children, and loved in the nicest and most respectful way.
Imagine Reverend Mother R. after the last Sacraments in
August, and that long illness since, being on foot at three A.M. to
receive us at the door, again at midnight to see us off, and in
between at the three Masses in the night at Christmas.   The
spirit flings the body over its shoulder and carries it off!   She
is not a bit changed in appearance, perhaps she walks a little
more slowly, that is all. . . .   You know we had bad weather
coming and going.   Mother M. will know that I can realise
the joys of a ' dysa ' bouncing in a rough harbour.   It was
delightful the first night under stars, but in returning we rowed
out to the *Carola* in a real squall of wind and rain, carrying
umbrellas at our risk until they turned inside out.   Then we
made for Syracuse, the way St. Paul knew and saw what he
saw, Syracuse beautiful from the sea ; but arriving two hours
late all our connections were lost, and we were received with
hospitable joy by two old children of the Trinità, now married.
Delightful beings, really our own children, bearing the best
stamp of our education, so brave in their troubles which
each separately came out with in the simplest way, and
living for their children.   We went to the beautiful *palazzo*
of one of them (such Sicilian marbles everywhere !) and saw
four of the dearest children, most beautifully brought up.   Two
boys who carried about tea and biscuits with perfect little
manners, and then sat two together in an armchair, a real
picture.   Two little girls neither shy nor forward ; astonished
and delighted to see the kind of nun that is to bring them up
hereafter.   And the mother brought out her treasures from
sacred boxes (pink, green and blue ribbons, all the congregation
medals), and showed us all her prize books, dearly loved ; and
in a reserved book-shelf all her text-books.   The thought of
those happy years at school and the things learnt there keeps
up her troubled life at a very high level of courage and accomplishment of duty, and even light-heartedness.   The eldest
child is already at the Trinità dei Monti.

I think it is very good and helpful to see from time to time
such instances as I saw here of our education, it makes one
realise that *inter omnes viae et vitae hujus variationes*, the
Society has a great educational secret of its own.

The Cathedral is exactly opposite her door, so I thought
we would go and make our adoration there, and we found the
Forty Hours going on, alas without any pomp, but the Archbishop is labouring hard to ' restore all things in Christ,' and
at least the Seminarists in adoration were very devout.   The
Archbishop is stripping the stucco off the columns and exposing
the beautiful massive columns of the temple of Minerva which
the nave of the church was originally.   It was something,

to look at the very columns that St. Paul must have seen, and pass one's hand over what he had perhaps touched. Various earthquakes have disturbed them from their centres, but the Archbishop means in time to straighten them all up again. Talking of Archbishops, I saw at Naples, Cardinal P.—who never appears at all, so that the portress arrived to call me, as white as if she had seen a ghost. . . . He came in the twilight which made him seem still more mysterious, and was gone in ten minutes. At Palermo there is a delightful Cardinal, who is quite a daylight apparition, he has to do the visitation of the outlying posts of his diocese riding on a donkey, as nothing else could get there. He has his hands full in trying to restore all things in Christ in Palermo, and being Milanese he received some shocks at first, for instance, to find that his flock celebrated the Feast of Our Lady of Sorrows by donkey races. . . . The donkeys race by themselves without any riders, tasselled and ribboned and plumed in great glory, they are handsome things and carry themselves with pride. There are always people killed by accidents in the crowd, and the Cardinal tried to put it down, but did not succeed. . . .

The last Cardinal I saw was Cardinal X., at the Villa Lante. He was kind enough to give an instruction to the novices, and I think for one happy half-hour forgot that he was a Cardinal. . . . He seems to have an extremely scholastic mind, which never loses its elaborate minuet steps even in the warmth of discourse ! One day he gave Benediction and then, of course, he had to be in Cardinal's robes, but as soon as he came back from the chapel, as one of the Mothers said '*il a procédé à une spoliation violente*,' tearing off one thing after another and flinging it from him, even the red sash which the Cardinals never take off, and tearing a large hole in the sleeve of his rochet in the desire to get it off ! At last he stood there black and thin . . . not even a red button-hole appeared, then he was content. He does not fill an arm-chair as a Cardinal does, there is, as Mother N. said, ' no amplitude anywhere,' he sits on the edge of it looking meagre and stooping. I must really stop, a happy accident let me run on as far as this, but it must come to an end. I lived through the ceremony of the 27th with you and the three happy novices, thanking God for them. I asked that one might excel in faith, one in hope, and one in charity, they will know which was which, please tell them their letters were a great joy to me.

Padua: 18th January, 1912.

I have read all the ' green book ' with immense interest [a book in which each member of the Roehampton community had written a page on any subject she liked]. Do you know the page I liked the best of all was yours, and I think it is so true, and it tells me how much you are learning of the mind and heart of Our Lord, this is a great joy. . . . But they were all full of interest and of things one would like to discuss with those who think about such things. There has been, as Mother Stonor says, ' a deal of thinking ' going on while the ' green book ' was being written.

This is such a nice community and atmosphere. It is not a city of pleasure like Venice and Naples, but the University gives tone and a certain seriousness to it, and studies are in honour, the children simple, the nuns not worried by follies and flightiness downstairs. There is a group of precious old Mothers, between seventy-nine and eighty-five years old, really very holy I think, and it is beautiful to walk with them in the quiet gardens of their souls. Some were received by our Blessed Mother herself. One was kept a week at the Mother House *pour la consoler de Papa et de Maman,* and saw our Blessed Mother *une bonne demi-heure chaque jour.* I assure you it gives one quite a feeling of awe to give advice to those who have received it from our *Beata* herself. It is very nice to hear them glowing in their appreciation of what life has been, and the Society, and above all God. I remark in this journey that the really choice and holy souls (and I have met several) are *very old,* this is encouraging to those who are afraid of growing old ! They are also distinguished by a wonderfully grateful spirit, and they think very meanly, but in no way gloomily of themselves. These things they have in common, for the rest they differ very much. This is all just as it should be, and as one ought to expect it, but it is good to see it in the concrete.

Did I tell you that I went to see our burial place at Venice, a strange cemetery, an island of the dead, thickly populated; a beautiful monastery, beautiful only in its plan and arrangement, for it was fit for the Franciscans who live there and serve the cemetery: there is nothing ornate—all is most poor. The silence can be felt, it is so deep; one could have spent a long meditation listening to it and looking at the cypresses; and, stranger still, all over the little cupola of the church tower the grass has grown up and withered. I suppose it is green and flowery in spring, but this was the season of frost, and wonderfully impressive—*exsiccatum est fœnum, et cecidit flos,* an emblem of the death all around it.

Sister Lisa Morris is buried there. How little she thought, when she ran about as a child at Roscrea, where would be her last resting-place ! I must come to an end now, for I am off again this morning to Peschiera.[1]

---

[1] Peschiera—Bergamo.

Peschiera : 20th January, 1912.

. . . This place is in the depths of the country, a beautiful property and a very nice house. . . . This morning I looked out of my window, between the dark and the light, on a beautiful snow scene, the more beautiful because there are both cedars and palms and a little plantation of spruce. I saw an old Mother come cautiously out of the house and look to the right and the left, exactly as a fox does with one pad lifted when he does not like the look of things, and then she trotted off along the snowy path looking quite sporting, and adding the human element to the snow scene. I felt inclined to cheer her from my window, for I thought they would be afraid of the snow ! They are nice and simple people in the village; the curate and some of the inhabitants let off squibs when I arrived, as an expression of their affectionate regard for the Society. But for all the charm of their simplicity I shall save up my letters to post in passing Turin on Tuesday, for they fairly often get lost in these parts. I always forgot to tell you a tiny but nice detail during the days at Malta. The Cardinal said he would give solemn Benediction one day, and we asked Mgr. Jackman whether His Eminence would do as the Cardinals in Rome do, and only come in for the *Tantum ergo*. He thought very hard, and then said : ' We'll do exactly as we do at Roehampton.' Wasn't it nice ? . . . It was so interesting at Padua and Venice to hear of the Holy Father in his early days as a young parish priest, Canon, and Bishop.[1] Of course all the old women of Venice in our congregations for the poor knew him personally, and the children in the elementary schools told sweet stories of his goodness to their mothers and grandmothers when he was Patriarch; but some of the Sisters knew him in his first parish when he was quite young, and so did the Superior of Padua. One of the Sisters there told me that when she was nine·years old she went one Sunday to Catechism with a little blue ribbon in her hair. The watchful shepherd caught sight of the vanity and came down to inspect the lamb at close quarters. ' What is this little midge doing here in such attire ? ' he asked, and he took off the ribbon and put it in his pocket. ' And he never gave it back to me,' added the Sister with some feeling still in her voice about that blue ribbon !

Trinità presso Fossano : 24th January, 1912.

Here at the very end of the world the current of life is less rapid than elsewhere, and this gives me an excuse for the recreation of sending you a little news of things in general. . . . At Peschiera I thought it was the very end of creation, but find that this is much more so ! Peschiera is very pretty indeed, even under the half-melted snow, and it must be charming in spring.

[1] Pius X.

The farm stands Italian fashion, on the high point of the property. We went up there on Sunday afternoon, all the community, by thymy terraces which must be lovely in summer—at present, of course, the wild thyme is almost scentless—and from the top we had a fine view of a wide valley and mountains all around, and the towers of many churches, one of which is a place of pilgrimage to Our Lady, much frequented when the silkworms are ill. Then cocoons are brought as *ex votos*, and palms for her adornment.

On Monday we left very early in great darkness, enhanced by rain and fog. Someone had kindly lent us an excellent motor to go direct to Milan, so we avoided many changes in little local trains. As it grew light and we went through sleepy villages, it was touching to see men and women waiting in the rain at the church doors until the Arch-priest should come at his good pleasure to say Mass. We went through the park at Monza, and passed the Chapel of Expiation where King Humbert was assassinated. At Turin we surprised the community by a visit between trains, as the motor promised to go on with failed us by the illness of the chauffeur, so we took the local train, which seemed to deposit us at the end of the world, and made our way on here by carriage about six miles further.

This was of old partly hunting-lodge, partly farm-house, partly an agent's house belonging to the ' di Trinità ' family, of whom two members are with us; one is the *économe* here. The family take their name from the place, not the place from the family : they are, as we should say in Scotland, ' Trinità of that ilk ' ; and the origin of the place goes back to the earliest records of Christianity. It is so out of the way that socialism, etc., have as yet little entrance. For us, of course, it is only a refuge, and we have it for the two lives of the Mothers di Trinità. It is primitive and old-world. The church bells regulate everything, from the morning rising onwards. The Angelus gives this signal and it is beautifully rung, first on one bell, then on two, and finishing again on one. After the Angelus the weather is announced : nothing if it is fine, one stroke if it is overcast, two if there is rain, and three if it is snowing—in which case the prudent villagers put off the hour of rising—as there is nothing to do. There was a heavy fall of snow last night, and as we are very high up, on a little peak rising from a high tableland, we see a great expanse of snow, the Maritime Alps on one side of us, and the great Alps on the other—but so far these have been invisible. Some people, however, got up in spite of the snow, for I could hear from my room a High Mass in full solemnity at six-thirty. There are two very old Confraternities here : the ' Red Flagellants,' for men— they do not scourge themselves now, but wear red and say Office in their chapel on certain occasions; the *Humiliate*, for women—their robe is of a canary yellow, and they too say Office, but how much further than that they persevere in pursuit of humility I do not know.

At processions, which are frequent, the young men of the confraternity of St. Aloysius walk in long white tunics, and the maidens in white with blue sashes; they all give each other much devotion. Our nuns have Catechism and needlework classes, and a Guard of Honour of the Sacred Heart. The clergy say they do much good. . . .

Rivoli : 2nd February, 1912.

Here I am at the last stage but one, only one more *Magnificat* to hear. . . . Turin was very nice, though Piedmont always seems neither one thing nor the other. But there are interesting recollections of the old foundation. The most interesting visit I had there was from Don Albera, the Superior General of the Salesians, who had been designated by Don Bosco in the spirit of prophecy years before as the second who would succeed him, and the paper was only found after his election ! He has the reputation of being a saint, as his two predecessors were, and I can believe it.

He has white hair, and keeps his eyes mostly shut, but when he suddenly opens them he sees a great deal ! I asked his blessing at the end, and after a moment he said, ' Let us say an *Ave Maria*, that the blessing may be a success'; so he standing, with his eyes tightly shut, and I kneeling, with my eyes wide open, said an *Ave Maria* together. I hope after this that the blessing was indeed a success !

I want to tell you about the school entertainment at Turin, because I was thinking all the time what an exquisite thing you could make of a similar one for the Prizes, and in preparation, for Reverend Mother's feast. . . . They had five scenes from Dante. The first was the opening scene with the three wild beasts, then Virgil. The beasts were beautifully made by one of the nuns: the lion and leopard rolled in on invisible wheels, and the leopard was never still for a moment; the wolf came in with a bound, and was horrible to see, so lean and fierce. Dante had a perfect profile and voice and gestures, dressed all in crimson. Virgil was in white and less good. The second scene was Hell, where Dante and Virgil are refused admittance: very well done, and two little windows were cut in the wall, at which appeared red-habited demons with black claws—this I am sure we should modify, for it makes people laugh to see devils ! and the door with the inscription would be more impressive to our minds. The third was quite lovely . . . it was the arrival of the barque-load of souls in Purgatory, with the ' Bird of God,' who standing facing the souls in the stern of the ship, looked grand. They make moving waters beautifully, and the barque was very beautiful, and the white-robed souls with angelic faces, singing *In exitu Israel* in the Gregorian chant, were exceedingly touching. Dante represented most wonderfully the efforts to embrace Casella, finding nothing to embrace, and the look of wonder on the faces of the souls was a beautiful discourse in itself. The fourth scene was the earthly Paradise with Matilda ; the procession of Angels and Virtues and the great chariot with the gryphon all came in the same scene. The Angels danced and the Virtues, after the manner of Fra Angelico's Angels, slow minuet steps and turning under their raised arms. The fifth scene was the rose of Paradise, beautifully arranged with the saints of the Old and New Testaments, and the little Innocents waving golden palm-branches in front ; Our Lady very stately and beautiful ; Dante and St. Bernard stood in the foreground, a crimson and white figure ; and the end of all was St. Bernard's prayer to Our Lady. The recitation throughout was beautiful and full of understanding ; of course it would be less beautiful in English, but still something quite superlative. They gave me at the end a really beautiful rose, made in silver gilt, to be laid at the tomb of our Blessed Mother Foundress. . . .

. . . Yesterday I had just got up to the highest and furthest point of the property at Turin, a vineyard on a hill, when one of the farm-men came running full speed, being lighter of foot than the portress, to say that Cardinal Richelmy was there. I am so glad to have seen him. . . .

A few days later Mother Stuart was back in Ixelles in time for the ceremonies of profession. She wrote from there a last number of her journal.

Ixelles : 9th February, 1912.

. . . It seems so very long since I wrote to you that I have simply stolen a little time this evening, the first profession day, to have a few lines to send you by the young professed. . . . I have a delightful letter to thank you for—more than one indeed, but the last one was particularly full of juice—facts—that are above all interesting. . . . I am delighted that the Queen of Portugal's visit and the Cardinal's visit went off well. Thank you so much for sending me the address and the details of the illumination ; it all interested me intensely. . . . I do not think I told you anything of my last stations, Avigliana, Grenoble, Paris. Avigliana had a breath of spring about it in spite of the snow. . . . This fact I commend to the consideration of the community : in Paris I was given most beautiful violets, large bunches of Parma and Czar and others, as large as small pansies ; at Avigliana they brought me, almost from under the snow, three wild violets, pinched and shivering and very small ; the gorgeous ones could scarcely be perceived in the room—the three wild, struggling ones filled the place with fragrance.

We have at Grenoble a part of an orphanage reserved for our Children of Mary, and we are lent a tribune in the chapel : rather a pathetic establishment, eight sisters struggling to maintain forty orphans—and they seem to bring them up very sensibly. The little creatures sang unaccompanied all through Mass, up to the Consecration, a swinging ballad of Christian life and warfare, of an indefinite number of verses sung by three or four cantors with a chorus of tender appeal after each.

I thought if I had to bring up orphans I would make them sing a great deal by way of devotion—unending ballads of holy living and holy dying with uplifting refrains.

The President of the Enfants de Marie is eighty-eight years old—an indomitable old lady—and she was there for the Mass at eight o'clock : a chapel packed so that they could hardly move, and she looking round with the air of a commander-in-chief, seeing them all going up to Communion. I thought she was not going at all herself, but when the very last was at the altar rails, and the struggle for access was over, she solemnly walked up behind them all: I could only think of Ulysses ! Grenoble was rather unconventional and nice, and the chains of mountains round it magnificent. I met ever so many of the old Duchesne stock, and from their appearance I should say they have the fine old Duchesne temper.

Paris was, of course, very different, and the procession of visitors outside the general meetings was endless. I saw eight Jesuits and two secular priests the last morning beginning at eight A.M. At the general meeting I don't know what we should have done without Comtesse d'Alsace, whose great stature and commanding presence and old habits of ' adjutricing ' made her an invaluable policeman. . . . Now good-bye. I am thinking of all the questions I want to ask you. . . .

Towards the end of March, Mother Stuart left Ixelles to visit the houses at The Hague, Bennebroek, and Nimeguen. She wrote from Holland :

The Hague : 23rd March, 1912.

. . . When we crossed an arm of the sea yesterday by the ' Mooldyke '—that is how it is pronounced—a bridge of arches one hundred metres each !—I felt quite near England. This inlet of the sea, when it came, swallowed up fifty villages. What a strange country, battling for life with the sea, sometimes worsted, sometimes victorious, occasionally swallowed alive ! It is just as one imagines it, so staid, so clean, so grave, such straight blue eyes, such determined faces: no wonder with their seaboard that

their motto is '*Je maintiendrai.*' There are more than five hundred children in the school, fair clean things and very friendly,
innocent-looking too. They have boys up to nine years old,
and they teach them as we do to sing very softly, which civilises
the young Hollanders much. The school is built for one thousand,
and we inhabit the unused part, for the community building does
not yet exist. More requirements are made according to law
than even by our authorities in England. In Belgium the
authorities seem not yet to make any 'requirements,' so the
Elementary Schools are very poor. The *Mijnheers* and
Mevrouwens are just as one imagines them, and the houses likewise. The whole of Saturday is devoted to cleaning, and carpets
are beaten every week at the hour regulated by law, nine to
eleven A.M.—at no other time.

I send you a photograph of Princess Juliana. They say that
when she was born it was not joy but *delirium* which took possession of the Hollanders. The Queen . . . says the Catholics
are her best subjects, and is on friendly terms with them ; she is
also nice to the poor. A poor family came from one of the
remoter provinces and without any intervention went to the
palace and said they wanted so much to see the baby ! and
Princess Juliana was sent down at once. She is said to have a
will of iron, or rather a will of *Orange*, and as the Queen has the
same I dare say there will be trouble when the education of the
Royal Infant has to be seriously taken in hand, and both will
say : ' *Je maintiendrai.*'

This community is not numerous, so I hope to get on to
Bennebroek on Monday : a kind friend of the house is going to
lend his motor, so we shall get there in one and a half hours. . . .

Ixelles : Holy Saturday, 1912.

. . . It is near the hour when the blessing of the house
begins at Roehampton, and I know exactly how everything is
looking. But what is most vividly in my mind is Easter Sunday
of last year, a day as near to heaven as anything on this earth
could be. I think none of us will ever forget it, for in the light
of all that followed we understand it even better than we did then.
I can see every bit of it still, and the only thing to compare it
with is that picture of Fra Angelico's, where the Blessed are
executing heavenly dances with their Angels guardian. Everyone's cup of happiness seemed to be full to the brim. God
was good to give us so much of it. I kept with many memories
too the anniversary of the Saturday [Passion Saturday, April 1st]
on which the book [1] was finished last year, and I received
the congratulations of the community on the terrace. Those
Thursday and Saturday recreations make me laugh when I

[1] *The Education of Catholic Girls.*

remember them. They were so considerate in their enquiries as to the morning's work and so cordial in their congratulations when it was a good record of pages ! But these are reminiscences.

I will come to what I have been wishing to tell you about— our houses in Holland. They are most interesting, and the Dutch, many of them, singularly charming, very full of life and capable of taking it seriously, and full of spirits too. It was extraordinary that my wish, which seemed quite out of the question, to see the hyacinths was almost completely fulfilled, for they came out between three and four weeks earlier than usual, and they were in full glory, without the first hint of overfullness or decline, the very, very perfect moment, in all its glory. And nothing that they say in reporting these things is exaggerated ; that is all I can say about it. The clearness of the colours and their variety, the perfection of the culture, the sort of grandeur about the individual flowers is not to be described. And one sees in all the fields, walking in the narrow spaces between the ridges of hyacinths, solemn growers in deepest contemplation of their bulbs, with a transplanter in one hand and a basket on their arm ; now and then they make a dive with the transplanter and lift out with one touch some bulb that departs from the type and is not quite worthy of its compeers, and it is flung as refuse into the basket. They throw away glorious specimens which we should look up to with awe and plant in bottles. The tulips were just coming out, and I am glad to see that the little old *Van Tholl* of our youth is still grown and loved. It makes beautiful patches of deep crimson, otherwise I do not think the tulip is interesting.

Bennebroek is charming, but, alas ! too far in the country ; one of those charming places that we ought not to possess. But in the early morning it was quite a picture when one looked out far across the fields of hyacinths, and saw what seemed to be boats of considerable size apparently sailing along side of them on dry land ; it is because the canals are so narrow that one only sees the big sails and the boat : the water is invisible. I liked the Bennebroek children very much ; they are silent, determined, stand-off creatures, but they grow quite tame and friendly. I suppose there is a kinship of race without antagonism which they feel.

I saw two types of clergy, one pastoral, the other intellectual. The pastoral type kindness itself, with heads smooth and oval as eggs : one was occupied in his leisure moments [at Bennebroek] in translating the Canticle of Canticles into Dutch ! The other was deep in the concerns of his parish, in which we have nearly six hundred children in an Elementary School [at The Hague], all stubborn Catholics. The intellectual type was very different from these—it was lean, eager, fiery, and most interesting.   One of these was a secular priest D.D. wearing a quaint costume ; no cassock, but knee-breeches and fine stockings, heavy shoes, and a frock-coat with skirts down to the ground—rather like pictures of the Vicar of Wakefield.   He was most interesting to talk to, and all fire and flame for what we could do for Holland.   It was *our* book which brought him over from Utrecht to talk to me ! Another was a Jesuit from Amsterdam, also as keen and interesting as the Society can make them ! At Nimeguen we are among the Dominicans, but they are very quiet and reposeful, as one might expect in Guelderland.

I made a little expedition into Germany to reconnoitre, and had an hour and a half to wait at Cleves.   There was a church close by, so we went to make our adoration.   I had a little shiver at the thought that at any moment G. might spring upon me ! I had never been at Cleves, and was very much interested to find myself in the heart of the Lohengrin country, the old castle of Schwanenburg still standing in its pride with the swan on the top *ad perpetuam rei memoriam.*   We crossed the Rhine in most primitive fashion, our carriage, and a smart dog-cart, and a heavy-going waggon all on a ferry-boat together. . . .

The ecclesiastic here referred to was Dr. Ariens, surnamed the Manning of Holland.   He had read Mother Stuart's book on ' The Education of Catholic Girls,' knowing nothing of her, and declared it was the best thing he had ever read on education.   He no sooner heard that its author was in Holland than he wrote asking for an interview, and for two hours discussed problems of education.   He said he had found in the plan of education established in the Society of the Sacred Heart the realisation of his ideal for women, an education which ' would fit them for the mission which awaits every Christian woman in the world.'

On April 2 Mother Stuart returned to Ixelles.   Two months later, in a letter to the Society in which she thanked all for their good wishes for her feast, she announced that in pursuance of her desire to get to know, little by little, all the members of the ' great family,' she was about to set out once more on her travels ; this time to visit the houses of the Austrian Vicariate.

CHAPTER XXII

Journey through the Austrian Vicariate, 1912

'May peace be your gift to all who come near or depend on you. . . .
May God's presence be ever your living joy and the central fact in your
life, from which will flow patience, calmness, and an unquenchable joy,
with that in your soul you can meet anything and each trial will be a
small treasure to offer Him, the secret of the sanctuary.'

From a letter, J. Stuart.

ON her way to the houses of the Austrian Vicariate, which
then included those of Alsace-Lorraine, Hungary, and Poland,
Mother Stuart stopped at Blumenthal, which stands on the
frontier line between Holland and Germany, on the outskirts
of the village of Vaals.

In this 'valley of flowers' the Convent of the Sacred Heart
had been established since 1848. Burnt down in 1862 and
rebuilt on a larger scale, in addition to the usual works of
education it has a great field of apostolate, in retreats for the
working classes; these are sometimes attended by over a
thousand girls and women. To the hard-working factory
hands these few days of rest and prayer at the convent are
the most refreshing holiday of the year. Mother Stuart wrote
from there:

Blumenthal: May 11th, 1912.

. . . It is a most interesting thing to be in this great
Blumenthal of which one has heard so much. It is a large
community, fifty choir nuns, one hundred and sixty children in
the school, and an elementary school of four hundred. There
is a very nice element in the school of the old Westphalian and
Rhine-province families: dear simple children with nice manners
and that look of reflected light in their eyes which makes one
think that the baptismal candle is still shining in them.
Among these are three young Droste-zu-Vischering, nieces of

2 A

Sister Mary of the Divine Heart.[1] It must be strange to have an aunt on her way to beatification. The Ordinary Process has been introduced, but with the state of things at present existing in Portugal, no doubt it will be delayed.   The mistress general is first cousin to Sister Mary.   They went to school at Riedenburg the same day, and were companions in class there, six weeks apart in age.   She says it was for threatening of chest trouble that Sister Mary of the Divine Heart was refused by us, a wonderful story !   Probably with us she would not have reached the first stage of Beatification, but have lived unknown and most happy !   God has His own ways with us.

This is a house of wonderful extent in its activities and has simple country ways. The Saint Cæcilia Society of Vaals asked to come and sing the High Mass for my devotion yesterday: they say ' Our Mother ' like the nuns, and they said afterwards that I had wept with devotion, which was unfortunately not true !   They sing wonderfully well, with great finish and execution, but the very simplest expression, no subtleties of feeling ; but, when they let out their voices, the volume of sound is sheer joy to them, and probably to God also ; to His creatures it seemed that the chapel was not quite large enough to contain it.   They came again in the evening *en grande tenue*, the frock-coats and, as they call them, ' cylinder hats,' which make them feel so good and look so ugly ; the village band came too, in full dress also, and they grouped themselves in front of our high steps, and sang and played alternately, and, when they sang songs of the home-land in German, there was real feeling. They speak German much more than Dutch in the village. We stood on the steps, and the children hung out of all the windows, and the police stood across the open gate with all Vaals drawn up behind them ; with a setting of young foliage and the stillness of a Sunday evening in May over it all, it was a scene that one could not forget. We are so near to the German frontier that I think one could reach it in two or three minutes on foot, and it is so insignificant that Wilhelm and Wilhelmina could shake hands across it, each standing in their own domains, and Princess Juliana in a year or two would be able to jump it.

We have just come from a Rogation procession before Mass, with larks singing around us, hawthorn scents in the air, and everything looking pleased to be blessed and prayed over.

Mother Stuart was delighted with Blumenthal. She found there one of those hard-working people, leading the strenuous life that she was for ever setting before those around her.

[1] Sister Mary of the Divine Heart (*née* Droste-zu-Vischering), a nun of the Good Shepherd, 1863–1899. At the command of Our Lord she asked Pope Leo XIII to consecrate the whole world to the Sacred Heart. He did so on June 11, 1899.

. . . One more thing on the subject of work and I must stop. At Blumenthal the Confessor came to see me—a professor from the Seminary at Aix-la-Chapelle—and, like Alice in Wonderland, I said : 'Come, tell me how you live!' And this is what he told me. Twenty-one classes a week in the Seminary, with necessary preparation and correction. Three sermons on most Sundays. The confession of one hundred and fifty nuns, of whom we are ninety. On his free day he takes six hours at a stretch, of voluntary work in the confessional, just to keep his hand in, then an instruction here, a spiritual conference there, etc., etc. Then his face lighted up. 'Once a week,' he said, 'on Thursday evenings, I have recreation for an hour.' 'And what do you do for recreation?' He beamed all over. 'We meet together, five priests, and practise Italian, French, and English!' I made him at once give me a specimen of his English and it was quite *blooming*. . . .

Instances of such lives were always stored up in her mind. From Blumenthal she went by Hanover, Magdeburg, and Dresden to Prague. 'I am glad to go this way,' she wrote, 'it is two hours shorter than by Cologne and Frankfurt, and, besides, there is a bit that I do not know.' From Prague she wrote to the community at Roehampton for the first anniversary of Reverend Mother Digby's death :

Prague :[1] May 17th, 1912.

. . . These days are full for us, and I am sure that each one is living over again each one of them as the anniversary of last year comes back—the last time of this and of that as it came to our Mother and to us. And now the 21st is coming, and though there is no need for it, I want to tell you how I shall live through it with you all, as it was last year when the shadow crept over the dial hour by hour and we waited for the answer to our telegram, and what we had not expected so soon came upon us at the moment God willed.

I cannot forget any minute of that day, up to the last walk with the aspirants on an afternoon that was so lovely, a perfect May—and then on through the hours that followed that meant for us so much more than we knew. It was all very perfect. One could not have wished it otherwise, and I think God has it whole-heartedly from every one of us. He 'put out the lamp of Israel' as the Paschal candle was put out yesterday, but it was to light it again for us in heaven where it will never more go out, and we will carry our processional candles steadily

[1] This convent no longer exists. The nuns were driven from it seven years later, 1919, in the course of the revolutionary movement which followed the Great War.

until we get there too.   Do you know what is the symbol to me
of that afternoon, connected for all time with it ?   It is of all
things, *pink may*.   Because it was the flower at Roehampton
and the flower at Ixelles, in a *great* flower—the first thing I saw
when Reverend Mother de Pichon whispered ' *vous êtes Vicaire
Générale*' and I turned into that stall.   So pink may will
have a meaning for us and I like it, for it is so full of hope
and fragrance, and it belongs to our Lady's May.

And so earth and heaven are blended together in our minds,
and we will go through each day as our Mother went through
her last day of ordinary life the 15th, until the evening, knowing
so little that it would be the last, a little more gay than usual
they say, and doing every little thing as she always did it, and as
it always should be done.   So we never know our last common
day, but we must always be ' as men that wait for their Lord
when He shall return from the wedding, that when He comes
and knocks we may immediately open to Him.'

May God bless every one and give them on our Mother's
first birthday all they most need and long for. . . .

You will never guess what visitor I am expecting this afternoon, the Holy Child of Prague !   The Carmelite parish priest
allows it as a very great favour, now scarcely ever granted, so
I must make the most of it, for the Society. . . .

On May 20 she reached Vienna, but only to spend one night
there.   As the centre of the Vicariate she had chosen that
convent for the anniversary Mass for Reverend Mother Digby.
The old house in the Rennweg has, moreover, a special place
in the annals of the Society of the Sacred Heart.   Père de
Tournély is buried in the vault of the church, having found a
last resting-place in a house of the Order which he had planned
but had not lived to see in existence.

Vienna : 21st May, 1912.

. . . I know you will like to have a line to say what the
anniversary was like here, you do not need to be told where my
thoughts were !   All our ceremonies were over before yours
began as our Mass was at nine-thirty which was eight-thirty
with you.

I arrived yesterday afternoon and we had Office in the evening
six-thirty to seven-thirty.   The chapel is very nice, well proportioned and good for sound. . . . The verses were Père de
Tournély's *Calme du ciel* applied to our Mother, and they very
sweetly gave me, instead of the conventional basket or bouquet of
flowers, a beautiful cross of bay leaves to put on the catafalque
with lilies and roses and lilies of the valley, a nice thought.   The
chapel was very dark this morning during first Mass, except that
the sun streamed on the catafalque which was surrounded with

palms and lilies. The Mass was devotional. . . . The Children of
Mary of the world of the great congregation of the *Immaculata*
were there, and I saw them afterwards, that is as many of them
as are still in Vienna, but most of them had left early to be back
for the Eucharistic Congress.

We saw the great wooden construction that is being made
for the Mass and Benediction of the last day, and the great space
between the two museums where the faithful will be massed.
The Emperor says he is going to the Mass and the procession . . .
he is eighty-two, and though he is proud and vigorous, he
could not walk in the procession ; he did so up to two years
ago.

To-morrow we go to Gora—real country. . . .

The next day she left for Poland, where there were two
houses to be visited—one in Leopol and the other four miles
from the Russian frontier at Zbylitowska Gora. Her first halt
was at the latter house. By June 14 she was again in Vienna,
having visited Budapest and Graz on the return journey.
The following letters speak of all these visits.

Gora : 25th May, 1912.

. . . I know Mère le Baïl has written to Reverend Mother
an account of our most picturesque arrival here, but I shall have
to tell it all over again to you because things sound so different
in English—especially horses. But to begin with Poland
itself. It is a great surprise, for I had imagined Poland a little
dishevelled in her mourning ! but find the country so gay in its
colouring, so carefully cultivated and so brilliantly clean ; the
houses are limewashed with bright colours in the country parts,
and the colours are not glaring, so the effect is very pleasant.
The long tracts of woodland are delightful, mostly spruce and
birch and what we call Austrian pine, we have a bit of ' forest '
of our own which I shall see to-day if it does not rain.

It takes nine hours to get here from Vienna. A charming
group of old children with flowers were at the station, but this
is tame, it always happens. As soon as we got outside it ceased
to be tame. A ferocious-looking coachman drove up at a canter
with a little open carriage driving the haughtiest-looking little
pair that you could see anywhere, he had withdrawn to a distance
to make this evolution handsomely. He was dressed in white
linen, laced and tasselled with crimson, crimson cap turned up
with astrakan fur and three tall peacock feathers in aigrette at
the side. One ' old child ' got in with us, the others followed
behind, and at the turn of the road where it leaves the town we
found our escort drawn up—farmers' sons who work on our
property and have horses of their own—such horses ! They
would be a credit in any hunting-field, rather small, half-breed I

should think, only about fifteen hands high, but full of spirit and
beautifully groomed. The riders were all in national costume,
long white linen coats with red or blue scarfs and caps like the
coachman's with erect peacock feathers. They wheeled into
position with great precision and quickness. We did not stop
a moment, but with seven in front and six behind and one on
each side we went at a splendid pace over a good road. There
is an old covered bridge to be crossed, and down went every
peacock's feather with a loving look up at Our Lady whose
statue guards it. Our house stands a little high and quite
by itself, but, though in a solitude, it has not the usual fate of
such picturesque places, but is full of children, some from great
distances, even from Moscow and Odessa, sent here at the cost
of many vexations and great expense to their parents, and
responding well to it, a real school of ours. And the children
are dear, mostly of the fair type, and many have the shape of
upper lip that Saint Stanislaus has in the old portrait of him as
a boy, of which we had prints a few years ago.

They are very like ours in some ways, only there is less backbone, but life teaches them, and they do gallantly later on.
They are delightfully spontaneous, one day a company of the
mounted farmers that escorted me came here to present themselves after some procession, and were taken into the house
by the *économe* to have some mild refreshment. The horses
stayed by themselves on their honour, for they trust them as
Arabs trust their horses. The first division of recreation were
playing near, and in one second, without a word, they left their
ground, the mistress and the game, mounted the horses and
galloped off down the road to the forest. Imagine the consternation of the *surveillante* ! They ride from their babyhood.

We had a very dear ceremony the first day I was here, the
clothing of a novice and the first Communion of her little
sister, two white prie-dieu side by side. Two little sisters of the
novice in white wreaths and veils carried the basket. Grandmother and mother, for whose sake the postulantship was allowed
here, went to Communion with the remaining sister ; a great
family party, but all the men are dead ! The Jesuit looked as a
Polish Jesuit might be expected to look, young, a little stern,
very highly strung, and ready for great endurance ; they say the
sermon was beautiful, on what our Blessed Mother had woven
into her habit beyond what she laid down in the Constitutions.
But it was in Polish; so I knew no more. The novice is a real
novice, so happy and ready for anything ; she goes to Jette
almost immediately. There is a charming group of *old ones*
staying here for the retreat, the consecration of the church,
and my visit, mostly *very young*, and they have been working
like sisters, doing dormitories and scullery, and replacing the

nuns in the school to let them be with me, and all wearing the blue ribbons which they had won at school and having commandeered all the medallions not in use if they had a right to them. But among the very young was a grey-headed countess, whose name I dare not spell, the mother of many children, and grandmother of more, who in the course of years has grown to very considerable proportions. Imagine the impression when she walked up to Communion yesterday with her blue ribbon, as simply and proudly as if she had won it yesterday! Most of them speak English very fairly. I asked one, who was telling me about her home in the Carpathians and the forests, whether there were wolves. 'Yes,' she answered, and after a pause, 'and *beers*.' This brought one very near to the primitive conditions of life ! . . .

Leopol : 29th May, 1912.

. . . This was meant to be an 'Educational Supplement' for this very Wednesday morning, only it has come too late. But that does not matter, it will do for another time. And no doubt as usual the criticism lesson furnished more than enough hares for the coursing. But these are my reflections.

At Gora the manner of dealing with children and teaching them is more like ours than anything I have seen, therefore keenly interesting! and their old children are curiously like ours (even their shoes and curtsies are like ours). But here comes the interesting point—of course I could not judge of the Polish studies, but in drawing and perspective and design and brush-work of the little ones they beat us off the field. Their drawing is on the best lines, all from the object, nothing from copies, and the drawings of chairs and tables in perspective by children of ten and eleven were wonderfully workmanlike. The best teaching is by our nuns, the division taught by a master was quite inferior as to originality and independent work. They are evidently gifted children for drawing, some of their designs from plant form would do credit to grown-ups. They do a good many useful exercises in rendering the structure of particular plants in diagram, the placing of buds, branches of trees, venation of leaves, etc., and this helps them very much in designing. I saw their gymnastics : they do far more dazzling and brilliant feats of writhing and climbing than ours, but they do not pay nearly so much attention to the elementary and fundamental things of life—walking, breathing, etc., so the clever feats do not move me to envy. . . .

. Here I saw a lion rampant worked on canvas by a Junior School child, and it made me think many things which I only suggest for consideration. It is such a pity that all trace of Heraldry should disappear from education. Would it not be rather

a nice kind of 'free work' for Third Division or Junior School to do
a few heraldic things on canvas, nothing so elaborate as the arms
of England, but simple elements, so that they should at least
know the tinctures and principal charges? And would not 'the
flags of all nations' be a very interesting and useful thing to do in
chalks for the Third Division, and it would also save them from
doing and saying ignorant things about flags? In our own
enclosure in Roehampton, I have seen the Union Jack upside
down ! . . . These things made me reflect, and hence the
suggestion. . . .

*Back numbers of my journey for Reverend Mother's
holiday.* How many things there are which I should like to tell
you all, and I have to let them go for want of time to write them.
But these are a few gathered at random.

Leopol. A charming exhibition of a Polish harvest festival
was given me in the school, too long to write, but a good deal
would be found in ' Poland, the Knight among Nations,' by Van
Norman, an American book of impressions, which comes as near
the realities of Poland as any book can without the essential
point of the faith of the Poles. Their faith and patriotism
together are the soul of their life. The harvest festival ended
in dances of course—most interesting, and some beautiful.
Their strong point is their figures rather than their steps, and of
course figures in themselves are less interesting. The peasant
dances are delightfully naïve and childlike, the sort of things that
might have been danced by Cain and Abel if the earthly paradise
had been prolonged—only (and this is like the fun of children)
they make their turning on themselves mostly backwards. The
dance of the nobles is very different, mostly complex figures,
with a curious strain of romance through it all, and many things
besides too long to tell. I feel as if I could write a thin book on
the Elements, the Ethics, and the Æsthetics of Dancing ! The
last day I was there the principal families of the neighbouring
village came to see me in the most brilliant and elaborate
costumes, dear souls bringing wild flowers and cream cheeses.
An old man driving a long wicker chariot with two beautiful
horses asked me to drive round the grounds with him. I had
to refuse from want of time, but sent the children instead. Two
of the farmers had fiddles, and all of a sudden someone said
' dance,' and without a second's delay the men led off the
maidens and the courtyard was alive with dancers. The girls
had such beautiful innocent faces and thin fair hair plaited in
crowns, they danced with their eyes shut ! Fra Angelico would
have loved them as models for a Paradise.

Budapest. Beautiful things in the school—scenes from the
life of St. Elizabeth of Hungary ; they were taken from a great

series prepared by the Archduchess Valerie for the Hungarian
Millenary celebration, and first acted by little archdukes and
archduchesses. There were ten scenes, not long of course, but
perfect ; and what is, alas! so rare in our entertainments, every
gesture was thoughtful and expressive. Staging, scenery, and
costumes all very good.

Reflections on Budapest. Clergy were more characteristic
than laity of the type of the country. . . . Here for the first
time I received an address in Latin, from the Premonstratensian
director of a Congregation of Elementary School Teachers. He
stood in front of them in a white alpaca habit and watered silk
sash like a bishop's, white also, but called blue! and—white
kid gloves! all new, such an apparition of white backed against
the variety of colours of the congregation ; the address was very
pretty, fortunately the whole thing was *standing up*!

I met another prelate there whose working powers made me
reflect much. He has enough ordinary work to fill a good man's
day in the University; he is also on the senate, and, as the University is autonomous, the senate has to judge all cases that
come up, so that he has to get up in his free time complicated
cases of law, medicine, etc., to be able to judge them. And for
ten years in his odd moments he has been writing a book on the
apocryphal tradition of the Jews up to the time of Our Lord.
The first volume is just finished. When the days are too full,
there remain the nights, he said.

The riots were just over when I arrived at Budapest; they
were announced again for the day after I left, but all I saw were
the troops of cavalry keeping the streets clear. And Reverend
Mother de S. was having the window-frames taken out to save
her plate-glass! Some years ago when she was first Superior
a most quaint thing happened. All the city was draped in black
for the death of Kossuth, and we hung out no black flag. It was
Holy Thursday, and at ten P.M. the nuns were all praying at the
altar of repose when the roar of a mob was heard round the
house; they were clamouring for the black flag. Reverend Mother
. . . flew up to the top-floor dormitories, took a black petticoat,
tied it to a broom head, and held it out at arm's length from
the window! That makes a picture in one's mind. . . . The
crowd yelled ' *By-thian*,' which is *Salve*, and dispersed to work
elsewhere. She was advised then to hang out a black flag that
the house might not be sacked, and did so. And of course there
was a sequel. The Archduke Ladislas, then a small boy, had
leave to come and take his spiritual refection at the children's
Sunday sermon. So the next time he came he saw the black
flag! ' *Comment! les Religieuses du Sacré Cœur arborent le
drapeau noir, c'est anti-dynastique!* ' The tutor replied with
that promptitude of spirit which tutors of princes acquire (and

require) : '*La Supérieure Générale vient de mourir !*' It was true, Reverend Mother Lehon had just died. And the soul of the infant Hapsburg was soothed.

I will end with a suggestion of a mental occupation for those who are anxious to improve their minds! Take a book like Cardinal Newman's ' Idea of a University,' and to every sentence in which he lays down a principle, or suggests one (and that is nearly every sentence), add an illustration from history, or science, or experience, or an example in point. It will be more or less difficult according to the book chosen, and of course to be worth while it must be a book of value. This is especially recommended to those who have time only to read a sentence or so !

This is really the end. I wanted to have my share in the holiday. I hope there will be visitors from the other houses !

Graz : June, 1912.

. . . The children here acted the two most important scenes from Grillparzer's *König Ottokar's Glück und Ende* exceedingly well, and the thing that struck me most was the understanding of the *grandeur of moderation* in the child who acted Rudolf of Hapsburg. It was beyond the usual understanding of children, or even of those to whom I have preached it until ' they could no more ' . . . .

From Vienna she went to Pressbaum, where a convent had been built in a beautiful property given by the old Emperor Francis Joseph in compensation for the injury he had unwittingly inflicted on the convent in the Rennweg, when he had allowed the enormous buildings of the State printing-houses to be erected so as completely to overshadow the house and gardens. With great generosity he had told the nuns to choose a part of the crown lands in the beautiful pine forests which surround the capital. Mother Stuart gives her impressions of these places in a letter from Riedenburg, Bregenz, the next halting-place in her journey.

Riedenburg : 23rd June, 1912.

. . . Here I am again with 'travellers' tales' and impressions . . . but from a house of noviceship there is double reason for writing to you. It is very nice to see novices again, and they are curiously like ours in many ways ; not so numerous as one could wish, but there are four nice postulants, and they are all alive and know where they are going to, and have no airs. There is a great charm about all these Austrian houses, and about the real Austrians. I have been looking about to find the characteristic feature in Austria, as one looks for noses in Rome and eyes in Ireland, and there is no doubt about it, that the characteristic thing in Austria is the smile; it is kind and courteous and goes all over the face, 'a smile like sunshine, a silent anthem,' as was said of a certain Cardinal. Nuns and priests have it, and railway guards and children, all classes, and a certain graciousness of manner goes with it. The fault of the children is that they are almost too easy to manage, not enough resistance. The little Archduchesses give out sparks sometimes! I passed through a class-room in Vienna and found the *haute bourgeoisie* with perfect plaits of hair and dimpled faces listening, rapt, to the primeval tragedy of Adam and Eve, and in a corner was an Archduchess of eight, snorting and chafing, with face to the enemy and dishevelled curls. Her Imperial Highness had troubled the public peace and been—to use Mother Oddie's scriptural expression—'put away' by the gentle aspirant, who did not like scenes! The Archduchesses are delightfully simple, in and out of school, no 'hobble skirts' or big hats, their only distinguishing mark is their simplicity.

The little Archdukes are all made to learn a trade—really learn it, not to play at it; the two youngest at present are gold-smiths, and astonished the workmen in a gun-foundry by their intelligent handling of things. The Archduchesses have every-thing like the others, school dormitories, school benches (literally), school fare without extras. A certain high severity of the simple life comes down from the old Emperor, may it last after him! The women are very prominent in manual labour in Austria—the trains carry a housemaid, there are women masons in short skirts. I saw a signal-woman once on the line, and several times gangs of women plate-layers. In the cemetery at Vienna, where I went to inspect our burial place, I saw a band of women mowers, mowing the grass most cleverly and smoothly, but with sickles instead of scythes, and a whole staff of women gardeners bedding out for the summer, very choice bedding plants and beautiful patterns. They did it with a quickness and a finish that Kew might envy.

The most interesting visitor I saw in Vienna was our old lawyer, who has been called the Austrian Windthorst and the second Mallinckrodt;[1] he has been kissed on the forehead by Leo XIII and hugged in the arms of Pius X for his services to the Church; and he told me thrilling stories of how he fought the Emperor, and the Ministry, and the Cardinal himself, and proved right in the end, all on Church matters. On one occasion he obliged the coadjutor Bishop to go up to the late Cardinal's[2] room at midnight, the Cardinal being then very old and feeble, to insist on his making up his mind to fight in the Courts in

---

[1] Hermann von Mallinckrodt, 1821–1874, was leader with Windthorst, 1812–1891, of the German Centre Party.
[2] Cardinal Gruscha died in 1911.

defence of a priest who was attacked on political grounds ; ' tell him that I will do it, but it will be my death,' said the old Cardinal, but they won.

The reason I tell you about him especially is because of his devotion to our Society. He works like a slave for us and never takes a fee. His wife says he is more espoused to the Society than to her. You will see from the above that he is not the *premier venu*, so it gave me great pleasure when he wound up his visit of one and a half hours by such a panegyric of the influence of nuns in the world, and the beauty of a nun's life. I wished that everyone could hear him, of those who sometimes wonder, in a phase of bewilderment, whether our life is of such great consequence and worth, after all, to God or the Church.

The journey from Vienna to Bregenz is very beautiful, but I had to put the best part of it into the night so as not to miss Holy Communion. Towards morning God illuminated it Himself with most beautiful lightning, but of course too dazzling to see much by. In some places we were only fifty feet below the snow. I had always imagined that Riedenburg was on the lake, but it is a considerable distance away ; we only see it, and we have a watercourse that goes down to it, quite a river in winter, now one of these blue-green streams that come straight from the snow.

The day after I arrived Mother Jacqman died ; she was quite well up to last Sunday week, and then had a stroke and lost speech, if not consciousness, before I came. She was seventy, but now, after death, has a look of the youth of immortality about her. She is a great loss, for she was one of those people who have an extraordinary tact for souls, and in retreats and even among mere visitors, she reaped great harvests. In the community she was the very perfection of cordial charity, at everyone's service, flattered at being called upon in and out of season, and offering herself if she was not called for. Riedenburg has quite a charm of its own ; of course it has memories of our Blessed Mother, and now these houses that she has seen are rare, besides that it has a simplicity and breeziness which you can well imagine, and as a house it has a family likeness with Jette and Roscrea. The way to the refectory is extraordinarily like Roscrea, but of course much larger, as the household is between ninety and one hundred. . . .

A little later, in another letter, speaking of Riedenburg, she wrote :

. . . I sent you from Riedenburg some lovely Alpine flowers, but I fear they will be dead : such a variety ! All the musical staff of Riedenburg went up six thousand or seven thousand feet high, a whole Sunday, to collect them for me. Wasn't it nice of them, four gallant lady professors. . . . I don't want the names, I only send them for delight for you. . . .

Towards the end of June she was in Kientzheim. The house stands in a valley of the Vosges, not far from Colmar. Seven red-roofed villages are seen from its high terrace; they are the favourite resorts of storks. And each is built round a picturesque spired church. This has earned for it the name of the valley of the bells.

The beautiful background of hills all around remind one of Bavaria [she wrote], the country itself . . . is like a garden, the prettiest parts of Kent perhaps. . . . It is very thickly dotted with tiny villages—Kientzheim, Ingelsheim, etc., and each has some special distinction of its own : one a great monastery of Capucins, another a chapel and shrine of a miraculous Our Lady of Sorrows, one the great dignity of a stork's nest on its church roof and so on. Our own garden is so pretty and laid out with such taste and judgment. . . . It is carpeted, literally carpeted, wherever there is grass, with violets (sweet ones), anemones, periwinkle, and wild thyme. . . .

' Be sure,' she said a few months later to one who was passing that way, ' be sure to go out alone as I did on Sunday morning on the terrace when they ring for Mass, and again for Vespers, and listen to those lovely chimes ringing down the valley.'

Montigny and Metz were next visited. Full of memories of the earlier days of the Society, their schools had been closed when the May Laws had turned the Religious of the Sacred Heart out of Germany.[1]

Montigny : 3rd July, 1912.

. . . This Montigny is full of the thought of Reverend Mother Desoudin, and yesterday, in a gathering of old pupils from many houses, there were nieces and cousins and grand-nieces of hers ; none of them had one spark of likeness to her. The chapel is very pretty, but the house is to me not at all attractive ; the timber is very fine, but the property very tame compared with Kientzheim, which is laid out for beauty by a master hand. The house at Kientzheim is badly built, having almost every fault one can imagine.

The Bishop auxiliary of Strassburg, Monsignor Zorn de Bulach,

---

[1] These schools were reopened when Alsace-Lorraine was restored to France in 1919.

whom you will remember at the Eucharistic Congress, came to
see me there. He arrived at eleven, and said as he got down
from the carriage, that he would leave at five. For me, it was
really a great holiday and pause to walk and sit under great
trees with a bishop. . . .

Bois l'Evêque, Liège : 12th July, 1912.

. . . The Bishop of Liège, who is reputed punctual, is already
three quarters of an hour behind time, and it has given me such
an advance in my work that I feel justified in beginning a letter
to you, the last of my travelling notes for a time. This house
is very full of life and charm, and its *œuvres* are wonderful. I
saw them altogether the first day, men and women, boys and
girls ; all, after having been dispersed by a thunderstorm and
gathered together again, performed and declaimed and made
speeches under a great broad avenue of limes. Then we had a
simple household procession of the Blessed Sacrament and an
open-air Benediction. I am sure they will send an account,
so I say nothing of the festivities of the household, but will tell
you of my visit to Flône[1] and Strée. The Comte de Liederkerke,
brother of one of our nuns, motored us down there in an hour.
Flône is quite unique and very charming. Until the Revolution it was an Abbey of Regular Canons ; we have a little oratory
and the Blessed Sacrament in the house, but otherwise the old
Abbey church is the Parish church and our church at the same
time. We are placed as at the Trinità dei Monti, but there is no
screen, and the choir is formed partly of men in the organ gallery
and partly of our children below ; the two choirs answer one
another on Sundays ' in blissful antiphons ' at the High Mass.
We are in the spacious and massive stalls of the late Canons in
the choir, and in the transepts are very handsome black marble
tablets with full-length effigies of the Abbots in relief. There
is a French school of about seventy children, very nice indeed,
as of course only the nicest will take the trouble to expatriate
their children for the education of the Society. Some of them
come twenty-four hours' journey from Brittany and the centre
of France. . . . There is an elementary school and infant
school—boys and girls with heads like cherubs and, of course,
the usual ' patronage ' and ' Christian Mothers.' All these
elect souls and the community were in the avenue and escorted
me to the church. At the church door was the Parish Priest
in cotta and stole !—Imagine the situation !—attended by altar
boys. He made a gracious discourse and then gave me his
blessing and, what was still better, Benediction. And after
that, things were as usual—receptions, etc. ; charming in the
infant school, for they all brought flowers from their gardens

<hr>

[1] Closed in 1921.

which the boys waved vaguely round their heads. Little girls brought jugs of whortleberries gathered in the woods, and mushrooms, and one a live hen, holding it down in the basket. Two angelic-looking boys in white smocks staggered up carrying a pail of water between them in which were six live minnows; and one brought a huge carp which had just breathed its last, his father had caught it for an offering !

Flône Abbey stands beautifully on a bend of the Meuse, a rather narrow garden behind it, and behind that the lime-stone crags rise up almost straight, I should think two hundred feet, the lower part has gathered wood in the course of years, small trees and undergrowth of hazels, but the beautiful rocks are bare at the top. We went up in the afternoon, community and school together to the highest crags, by winding paths and steps, and from there had a beautiful view over the course of the Meuse, and the wooded low hills beyond, and cornfields stained with poppies —a glory and a scandal in one. The children ran before us, and halted here and there and sang hymns to entertain us and talked a little and scampered away to meet us again further on. We had another motor to take us back and as we were told (it turned out false, for very few people tell the truth or know the truth about distances) that it was scarcely farther to go by Strée, I thought I would surprise them there. It was a great success, though one dear old Mother had prophesied it, and all the community had extinguished her idea, and another, bed-ridden and very near to God, aged eighty, hugged herself when I came in, and said that she knew I would come, she was listening for the bell. Then we had a long run (long for Belgium) back to Liège. Imagine the thrill of going through the village of Quatre Bras, along the great paved *chaussée* to Liège, over which the armies tramped 'in those days.' That is the end of my travels. The Bishop has telephoned that he will come to-morrow at nine. So God meant to give me time to write to you. . . .

Just a year later Reverend Mother Stuart visited Flône again, and this time for several days. Her letter may, perhaps, best find its place here.

Flône : July 6th, 1913.

. . . Now I am writing from what has been the cell of a Canon Regular of St. Augustine in this old Abbey of Flône. Perhaps the Provost's cell (I see they call him Abbot), for it is a rather solemn one. They were here from A.D. 1000 to 1793 ! There is a great charm about it, I think I told you last year how beautiful the position is. . . . we face, across the river, the infirmary of the Abbey, to which the Canons Regular were transported in their sicknesses by a sub-way under the Meuse. This sub-way no longer exists.

I was met at the station yesterday by two medallions of the school—dear creatures! '*Depuis ce matin nos Mères ne vivent plus*,' they said. They were escorted by the house carpenter, who is also the confidential factotum, head-gardener, and the village organist. He does very well, as I will tell you presently. The Abbey church is the Parish church also . . . and the whole church has the masculine touch of massiveness and repose which one often misses in our chapels. The stalls are of very massive oak, with a twisted column between each, and round it a trail of vine and cherry, the two local fruits; and all sorts of quaint heads, human, animal and fiendish, no two alike form the necessary knobs and finials. It is all such genuine, simple, human work, no machine has touched it, every tool mark is visible.

The vaults under the church are full of canonical bones. Monsieur le Curé made an expressive gesture to convey to me how many, and after nearly eight hundred years of Canons Regular living and dying here one cannot wonder at it. . . .

The children are charming in their blend of spontaneity and *tenue*. They have such high, clear, untrained voices, with a natural bird-like trill in them; they sing the late Mass on Sundays, alternating with the village choir of men and boys in the organ loft. It is plain chant. On Sunday it was the *Missa de Angelis*. The carpenter accompanies out of his head, in the real soulful Gregorian style, and with wonderful skill keeps in with the two elements of his choir, though the children are so far off; and gives a lift to Monsieur le Curé in the dangerous parts of the Preface. He has a bass voice of great power himself, and fills the church with great reposeful notes that seem to come from very far away. M. le Curé preached at both Masses a sermon of seven minutes on 'Thou shalt not kill!' He is going through the Decalogue, it was very fundamental and plain and ought to correct the parishioners of homicide. We had a procession of the Blessed Sacrament after Benediction, but, as it came on to rain, we only went round the Abbey and in again at a quick pace, which I thought very devotional indeed—though it does not sound so! The Sisters have a beautiful transept to themselves, where they are in real pews and look most dignified, and see a great deal more of parochial life than we do from the choir! Of course this is only for the public Masses. At other times they go where they like. The *last* devotion of the Sunday afternoon function was the Asperges, quite a surprise, and very abundant in its diffusion of holy water. It was altogether a unique Sunday for me.

I am ending on the 7th and need not tell you that I have been in spirit at Roehampton, and kept the feast of the Translation of St. Thomas in summer, in the side-chapel, with much devotion and many memories while making my adoration in this beautiful church. It is wonderful in the afternoons for very few people go then, they prefer the oratory, and if they do go they are lost in the large space; the afternoon sun falls on the face in a great painting of real value, which is over the High Altar, a very Flemish Descent from the Cross. The bells of the clock are very soft and church-like, and the whole place steeps the soul in silence.

On July 15 she was once more at Ixelles, where she remained till October, with short visits to Fontaine l'Evêque and to Jette for her retreat.

Ixelles : 11th August, 1912.

If I can finish this in time it will go by Mrs. L., if not it can travel by itself. I have been meaning to tell you what *perfect joy* I had in the letters from Roehampton ; when you can, I know you will tell them so from me; it was like walking in a garden of roses in June, all aglow with sun and fragrance, like the wonderful rose terraces at Potsdam, that is what I thought in reading them. . . . You cannot think how sweet the English lavender is, I like it almost better than any growing thing in its way. Sister Richardson has made me a lavender bag and it is under the lid of my desk, and makes me say often ' take and receive, O Lord, that precious England.' Monsignor Croke Robinson came over for three days, and between him and Mother P. and Mother M. I have been hearing some English, which is sweet and flowing, *super mel et favum*. Monsignor has gone now; we had some long talks after his Mass, *extremely* English and interesting and quaint. His beloved Father Tubbs was his travelling companion, and when he begins ' Tubbie ' says it is as if the law and the prophets have uttered, and such utterances ! Father Tubbs is a great theologian and at the same time English to the very extremist limit of that word. Another thing which made me laugh, speaking of Dr. Meynell's Oscott sermons which he is going to send me, Mgr. C. R. said with his eyes tightly shut, ' My *dear* Mother, he was the only man—I don't say *living*—but the only man who *has ever lived*—who ' (you would expect something fine after this, something on predestination or free-will—not at all, he went on to say) ' the only man who has ever existed who has succeeded in taming a wild rabbit after it was grown up ' !

To-day I am going to Jette for the examinations of the second juniorate, and on the 15th and 16th are the professions. We have two Jesuit preachers, no Bishop this time. . . . After that will come the dispersions and very soon the reassembling of another probation.

2 B

Ixelles : Feast of Immaculate Heart, 1912.

. . . What a date ! One can hardly count all the memories
that hold on to it . . . Our Very Reverend Mother Lehon's
two jubilees made it a marked day, too—then my obedience as
Vicar was dated on this Feast in 1894, and the year afterwards
our dearest Mother's election, and last year mine; just as
August 17th had been a date for both ! These things are not
by chance, God means and wills them, and even so we only see
the beginnings of them ! I meant in any case to write to you
for this Feast, more than ever dear to you since you are again
with the novices, and that, too, dates from this blessed Feast.
Last year you and I took up our new charges together, it is
all woven very closely together. But upon my intentions to
write come another reason—that beautiful, *beautiful* Russian
Madonna (I think it must be Russian, and I should so much
like to know its history). The faces are beautiful, the calmness,
the clearness of the eyes and likeness of the Son to the Mother
are all wonderful. And the beautiful work in which they are
set adds a sort of strangeness that comes from far and makes
me think of so many things spiritual. . . .

Jette : September 7th, 1912.

. . . There is a ceremony of nine between clothing and vows
and one hundred and forty-two guests for breakfast ! What
patriarchal families. The father who gave the retreat will
officiate. I wonder how he will look after a retreat to one
hundred and seventy-eight and only the ordinary confessor
to help with the confessions. However, he seemed to go
cheerfully and briskly, and he seemed buoyant with energy to
the last to judge by his step. I have never heard a priest walk
so fast, it was like the step of one of our Sisters !

I had an incomparable retreat. I have never once since
my profession had one so uninterrupted. Except to go over
and take back a letter from Mère le Baïl I did not see a single
creature. I had thought of following the community retreat,
but decided not to.

Do you remember all the trouble we took, and unsuccessfully,
to find an English equivalent for the word *arrière-pensée* ? I
think I have it now ' reticences,' not reticence, for that is often
becoming and necessary and in some spheres of activity beautiful.
But reticences expresses to my mind thoughts withheld and
silences not altogether normal, a little uncanny. What do you
think ? And what will the community think of the suggestion ?

Ixelles : 22nd September, 1912.

. . . Another letter from you this morning, you are too good.
It is always a joy to see your handwriting. Letters from
Roehampton are always put down at the bottom of the pile and

I tell myself after the fashion of the nursery, ' When you have eaten the rice pudding you shall have the strawberries.' My next letter of ' general information ' will be from Spain, imagine ! But to-day I must try to write a little about Fontaine l'Evêque and Waterloo. The mother of one of our nuns at Fontaine lent her motor, so we went by road, and thus my unrealisable dream was realised and I saw the field of Waterloo, but better on the return journey than in the first, as we took another road. To begin with Fontaine l'Evêque—I meant to bring back some post-cards to send you, but forgot them. It is a typical mediæval castle, combining the picturesque and the utterly inconvenient in equal proportions ; but, pressed as she was to find anything at the time of the expulsion from France, Reverend Mother Nieuwland was obliged to take what she could find, and fortu-nately this is only rented. The moat still exists half way round the house, full of water, and with a pretty island. The old gateway still has all the grooves and channels in which the port-cullis worked. There are seven towers, of which two are separate from the house, the others incorporated, but these towers out-side have to be used as dormitories. There is a very pretty Gothic chapel—thirteenth century—but the new façade on the courtyard is of the date and style of Louis XIV. The name of the place comes from a certain wicked Seigneur Nicholas of the Fountains (there are many) whose life did not bear looking into. But one day when he came home tired from hunting he threw himself down by the side of one of these springs, and leaning over to drink, he read the records of his soul through the water, in letters of blood at the bottom. He hardened his heart for three days, but the mysterious letters remained, and in the end he yielded. I suppose as a matter of fact the legend means that a moment of grace came upon him at the fountain, and instead of finding his conscience when ' he entered into himself ' the bright still pool that it ought to have been, he found it troubled with bloodshed and many crimes. This time, however, he so fully repented of them, that he gave himself to the service of the Church and became Bishop of Cambrai, to which that part of Hainault belonged, and built the pretty chapel, and hence it is Fontaine l'Evêque. The spring is still there, very shallow and clear, white at the bottom, it never freezes and the ducks use it for bathing in winter ! It steams a little in cold weather, so I asked them to test the temperature.

Now as to Waterloo, it was impressive beyond what I could tell you, but you can imagine it. We went out of Brussels by the very same *chaussée* that Wellington must have gone by when he slipped away in the early hours of the morning from the Duchess of Richmond's ball, and leaving the Forest of Soigne on our left (knowing that he had noted it as a position

from which it would have been almost impossible to drive out
infantry if he had to fall back on Brussels) we went straight
through Waterloo—the village—and the smaller one of Mont
Saint Jean where he had his headquarters. I think I made out
the house. We passed close to the lion, but he says nothing
at all to one, since his pyramid and himself only stand as a
memorial and neither Wellington nor ' Bony ' ever saw them,
though it is true that the lion is made of the metal of the guns
taken in the battle. Coming back we took a worse road for the
motor but better for the memory, and though, of course, we could
not get down and go to the actual places, yet ' I saw with my eyes '
the back of the farm of Hougomont where such hundreds of
ours fell and are buried, and at a little distance La Haye Sainte
which was so often taken and retaken, and La Belle Alliance
where ' Bony ' spent nearly all the day with the great kitchen
table of the farm house before him and his plans on it, and where
Wellington and Blücher met and congratulated each other in
the evening.

The *chaussée* had been taken up for repairs so we could not
pass the door but had to turn back and get into another road,
but I saw the white buildings, and we passed between the two
monuments which are close to the road, the Gordon Highlanders
on one side and the Hanoverians on the other ; and at every
cross-road (there are many in that bit of rolling country), the
names are thrilling when one thinks of the battle—Planchenois,
Papelotte, Genappe, Wavre, Ohain. One would have liked to
say to everything—please stop—and keep silence, and let me
think. It passed almost like a flash—with unspeakable feelings
and realisation, and to one's memory it is something better than
it was at the moment itself. . . .

Ixelles : 26th September, 1912.

. . . I am sending you in this, a little MS. book to examine.
It is meditations that I have made and found helpful, and so
wrote them out to use again. I want you please to read it
through and see whether you think it would be worth while
to get Mother K. to do them, as she did the little books of conferences, under the title of ' Occasional Meditations,' as people
so often ask me how to prepare a meditation for themselves
without a book. There are some, perhaps, that would not be
suitable, for instance that are obviously for Superiors—in that
case you would mark the page ' omit ' in pencil. *If* you think
it worth while perhaps you would instruct her to do it as a job—
of course with Reverend Mother's leave. I should like to have
the little old book back when it is done with, as it is stuffed
with precious things and ' of no use except to the owner.'

I am sending back to you two packets of those little books

of conferences, for your friends and mine, you will do what you
think best with them. . . .

Thank you for telling me about the new things in the house,
and the inauguration of the Sisters' room. I hope it will be a
citadel of silence, and of holy recreations, and of joy, and of
singing. Good-bye for to-day, a letter from you makes a red-
letter day for me. May God bless you! . . . Of course the
meditations should be put in some sort of order. I made
Sister C. index them, but there are more since then. Those
according to the second Method of Prayer would come at the
end, as I have put them. . . .

As can well be imagined, the little manuscript book was
published ' for private circulation ' without delay. Meanwhile
Mother Stuart set out on her third long journey.

CHAPTER XXIII

Spanish Journey, 1912

' One realises in constant travelling that He remains and He is all,
the rest passes away, and how soon it will be all over and we shall look
wondering back from the other side and be amazed to see how He has
loved us.'—*From a letter, J. Stuart.*

TELEGRAMS kept pouring into Ixelles. The Spanish journey is
impossible. Barcelona is in a state of revolution. The railways
are on strike. No one can cross the frontier.

But Mother Stuart having considered the matter, telegraphed back that she was still ' coming on,' and she left the
Mother House as she had planned on October 1, 1912. Her
intention was, as she wrote, ' beginning by the Barcelona side,
to take in Mallorca, but leave out the Canaries,' as she wished
to be back in Brussels for Christmas.

Perhaps no place she visited gave her ' such happy memories '
as Spain. ' It was a delight,' she said, and the affection was
reciprocal. ' *Si vous entendiez ce que disent d'elle les dames du
monde, ma bonne Mère!*' wrote her companion from Seville.
' *Tout se résume en* muy simpatica, *elles sont ravies. Les
communautés disent d'autres choses, que je vous dirai cet été.*'
' *Tiene una cara santissima,*' said a priest at Granada as he
came from an interview with Mother Stuart.

But the state of the country, at no time an easy one for
travellers, made the journey very fatiguing. ' We have had
twenty-eight and even twenty-nine hours in the train between
Valencia and Granada, with two changes and interminable
stops . . . At eleven-thirty P.M. we reached Granada, to find,
however, the ever-faithful Children of Mary still waiting for us.'

Mother Stuart always appreciated what she called ' local
glories,' and every house vied in showing her its own. These
were naturally very varied in Austria where so many different
nations were united in the one Vicariate. But within the four

walls of Spain there was an equal if more unexpected variety, north, east and south are in fact so many different countries.

On the way to Barcelona, Mother Stuart had arranged to stop for a few hours at both Toulouse and Perpignan to see the Children of Mary and other faithful friends of the Society. She speaks of this visit and of the journey to Barcelona in a long letter written from there on October 4.

. . . When we passed close to the ' Vernet ' in coming into Perpignan, I thought I must write to you from there, since my only living link with it was the remembrance of your winter (such a winter) there. I did not think then that I should ever see the ' Vernet,' but I did as you will see. To begin with we had telegrams from Barcelona warning us that the strikes were making travelling very difficult, but I thought I would go as far as Perpignan, and see whether it was not possible by one means or another to get across the frontier into Spain. At Paris, in the station, a telegram message reached me to say it was really impossible, and that the Mothers from Barcelona who visit the Enfant de Marie congregation could not come to meet us at Perpignan as arranged. I thought if the worst came to the worst I would go on to San Sebastian, and reverse my order of visits, and telegraphed to Barcelona that we were—as they say in America, ' coming on.' We had two hours' wait at Toulouse to see the few members of the congregation who had returned from the country, but most of them were still there, finishing the direction of the belated *vendange*. We got to Perpignan at two P.M. and found at the station the Bishop and the heads of the Children of Mary congregation. Do you know the Bishop ? he is a delightful type of Bishop, poor but not ' needy,' full of life, a convinced optimist, and most spiritual. (I believe that for our times one has to be optimist to enter into the best spiritual tendencies of the day. I think this more and more.) He and his chancellor and Mère le Ball and I went in his carriage, and the E. de M., very *méridionales* in their high spirits, took possession of our *mince bagage*, and left us behind triumphantly. We went to the Convent of the Blessed Sacrament, and there, as soon as they were gathered together, had a very cordial meeting presided by the Bishop and adorned with two Canons. And then came a telegram to say that the Mothers from Barcelona had actually started. Reverend Mother V. had decided that as I had not stopped my journey they *must come*. So she sent them under an excellent escort, Señor Diaz, father of one of our children here ; one of those typical pupils of the Jesuits that one sometimes meets. He defended their college in the revolution of 1909, and called his baby boy

and girl Ignacio and Ignacia ; so he very kindly undertook the
journey ; it would not have been possible to travel without a
man in the unsettled state of everything. The journey from
Barcelona to Perpignan takes six hours—it took them thirty-
three ! The soldiers are turned into engine drivers and take one
train backwards and forwards each day for the mails.

Being inexperienced and having a very heavy train they
broke down two engines, and landed themselves about midnight
at a wayside station without light or provisions, and tele-
graphing to the frontier for an engine, heard that perhaps they
could have one by the afternoon of the following day ! Señor
Diaz went off in a thick fog to see if he could get some provisions
for his charges in a neighbouring village, and came back about
an hour after, two P.M., bringing bread and an omelette. Mère V.
had a blessed candle end with her, and by its light they refreshed
themselves. Señor Diaz had waked up the local barber and
promising him good pay had sent him on a cycle to a friend two
miles off to see if he could borrow his motor. The friend was
in the country ! nothing to do but to wait. A passenger from
Marseilles, and returning there, began to get restive and proposed
to set the train on fire, *afin qu'on s'occupe de nous.* The civil
guard in charge of the train (they are an admirable body of
police) took out his revolver to explain to him he must not do
it ! Señor Diaz thought the big baby was starving and gave
him a share of his bread and omelette, after which he ceased to
rail at the Spaniards ! The engine arrived after all in the course
of the morning, and eventually they reached us—twenty-four
hours late. You can imagine that we were not happy about
them, since no telegrams are allowed along the line except those
of the military authorities. We were glad to see them, and Señor
Diaz was as proud as he had a right to be. The next day we
left with him and the two nuns, and were told at the station that
if all went very well we might get through in twenty-two hours, as
we had the best engine and driver on the temporary staff. It was
really a wonderful journey, for we got through in eleven hours,
not a stone thrown, not an obstacle on the line—I am sure it was
all the prayers—and so here we are. Barcelona is quite quiet.
The military governor has a wrist of iron, and several regiments
have been called in. He sent word to those who were beginning
to riot a little that they need not worry about whether he would
put them in prison, he would take them straight to the *cemetery*
if they gave trouble, so they are over-awed and going carefully
on tiptoe like naughty little boys ' not to wake papa.'

To come back to Perpignan. The Bishop asked me to go
and see our house ' au Vernet ' as he considered his seminaries,
higher and lower, as only tenants at will keeping the hearth
alight for our return, and to see our Elementary School, now

carried on by three secularised nuns, I do not know of what
Order, poor things, pictures of melancholy, sad to see. The
Bishop and his chancellor came with us and it was delightful to
see him among the children, they crowded round him and glowed
in his sunshine. I wish that some well-meaning but untruthful
moralists could have been with him ; some that I have seen (and
really good people) stop in front of a beautiful child and say by
way of doing her good ' what an ugly little girl, what deplorable
hair ! ' to take down her vanity. The Bishop did the contrary,
he stopped in front of a beautiful child of six or seven, and said
with real gladness in his voice : ' *Mon enfant, quel beaux cheveux le
bon Dieu vous a donnés. Voyez donc,*' and he took up a handful
of silky curls, ' *remerciez-Le bien,*' and I am sure she was the
better for it, and thought more of God and less of herself than
those that are ' taken down,' but must inevitably find out the
moralist in the end. Then we saw the house which you know,
and I thought of you in every place and especially in the chapel
where you saw the breath of the nuns rise up in a pillar of cloud
before each, from the cold, and the lonely little brazier was
brought in for the honour of heating the chapel. I wondered
so much which was your room. I saw Manrèse, where Père
Poncelet must have lived, opposite to the Chaplain's quarters, and
I saw the Canigou and the *Jordan*! and thought of the washing
done there at two o'clock in the morning! The nicest thing is
the square with intersecting walks of plane trees, I suppose they
were used as playgrounds. They are beautiful walks for the
priests to say their office in. . . . Did you know—perhaps
you have actually seen it—that Perpignan has one of the most
wonderful relics of the world, the hand of St. John the Baptist!
The Bishop showed it to me because St. John is my patron.
It has been at Perpignan since the tenth century—and the
authentication begins in Hebrew, continues in Greek, only
the stages of the last ten centuries are in Latin. It looks
incorrupt, certainly the skin is over it ; they say it is supple,
but of course the reliquary is not opened now. It is a beautiful
hand, very young looking, just the right look for thirty-two or
thirty-three years, beautifully shaped, long and thin, with very
small joints, the sort of hand you would expect from a desert-
dweller, active looking, but untouched by hardening work. It
is the left hand, therefore not the hand that baptised our Lord,
but the hand that must have held His, to lead Him into the
Jordan. . . .

(Saturday night.) We have just heard that the strike is
over, a great blessing, and on a secondary plane a great simplifica-
tion for me, as it was thought all the railway men would join,
but it has not spread beyond Catalonia, so my movements
will not be hampered. I have changed dates on account of

steamers to Mallorca, and go there on Tuesday, 8th, after a day
at Sarriá, returning to finish the visit there afterwards.

We had a very good gathering of E. de M. to-day, a little
broken up as the Bishop arrived in the middle of it, and I had
to leave the congregation and go to him. I tried to get him
to come to them, but he would not, so they waited. He is
a great friend to the Society. . . . There have been no posts
since I left the Mother House, until to-day, so I had odd minutes
and kept this under my blotting paper to write little bits. The
school here is two hundred and fifty—very nice—but not easy,
they have wills of iron, splendid if they turn well, but if they
won't, nobody can turn them. . . . I hope to spend St. Teresa's
feast at Sarriá with great pomp, as it is their patronal feast,
I think. . . .

Mallorca : October 10th, 1912.

. . . I had hoped to get back from here by the boat on
Friday night, 11th, but there is no boat. There are only two
excellent boats in the week, in one of which I came over on
Tuesday night. There are also second-rate boats, one of which
I must take on Saturday, as it would take too long to wait for
a good one. These carry cargoes of live pork, and, if the weather
is very bad, the boat does not start, as the live pork suffer
so much in transit, that the quality is lost or spoilt. The
Christians on board could manage very well, but the little pigs
would be too seriously affected, so the risk must not be run.
The island is very pretty, and its memories of St. Alphonsus
Rodriguez and St. Peter Claver are very holy; they say that
from the upper windows one can see a corner of the house in
which they lived and grew holy—one finishing and the other
beginning his career as a saint.

Mallorca : October 12th.

. . . This is only to give you a little news from the very
ends of the earth, for this island seems like, and is indeed, a
terminus. One goes from here to nowhere except back to the
mainland, and this I hope to do to-night and shall not post
until I get there, in case there is anything at Sarriá requiring an
answer. This island is a great deal more beautiful than I thought.
It is like Malta in its best features ; rather an Eastern look and
gleaming white stone, but it is beautifully wooded and very
fertile. The three chaplains very kindly prepared for me a
reception of their own, in which I learnt that it was rich in
fruit. They collected specimens of the produce of the island,
and the senior chaplain (who looks about thirty) discoursed on the
Promised Land, and the visit of the Israelites, Caleb and Josue,
and the fruits which they brought back. The land flowed with
milk and honey, of course. There was milk, and honey from

his own bees on the table, and twenty different kinds of beautiful
fruit; twenty other kinds were not represented because they were
out of season, which gives the measure of their wealth in fruit.
They showed me also the spiritual fruits of the island, pictures
of its saints and wise men; and they little knew what a picture
they made themselves, standing round the map of Mallorca by
the side of their beautiful fruits in the Spanish cloak that falls
so gracefully round them.

From the top of the house we can see the roof of the chapel,
erected on the spot where Our Lady wiped the face of St.
Alphonsus Rodriguez, as he panted up the hill after the light-
footed Father whom he had to accompany. . . . Now I am
going back to Sarriá, where I have spent one day, and on the
18th I go to Valencia, and so get back into the track proposed
as to dates. . . .

In Mallorca a somewhat unusual ' good work ' is carried on
in the convent. The men of the Apostleship of Prayer meet
there every first Sunday of the month for Mass and Communion
in the convent chapel.   ' A miracle of the Sacred Heart,' said
one of the chaplains ; ' greater, I think, than to raise the dead,
seeing the want of faith among these men before the foundation
of the convent in their midst.'   They were presented to Mother
Stuart.

The enthusiasm at Sarriá was very great. ' We have *seen*
the ideal Religious of the Sacred Heart,' they wrote ; ' we are all
inflamed with the desire to follow such a Mother in the service
of God.'

From Sarriá she went on to Godella, a village near Valencia.
Writing from there, Mother Stuart's secretary said: ' The community and the children of the different schools, and numbers
of women and young girls were assembled in the beautiful
garden to meet our Mother General (at five-thirty) on October 17.
And a great crowd "of the uninvited " was massed outside the
walls—all Godella, in fact, was on its feet. The women had
taken the precaution to make their husbands' supper in the early
morning, so as to be quite free for the reception, and when Mother
Stuart got down from the motor they obtained for themselves the
better part.   In their eyes she was their guest as much as ours.'

In the course of the next few days the glories of Valencia
were shown to Mother Stuart. In the school the drama of the
taking of the city from the Moors by the Cid was played ; and
the girls of the Sunday and night schools gave a delightful
festa, with dances and songs, in national costume ; gilt combs

shining in their dark hair, long ribbons floating in the wind, and dresses of every bright colour delighted the eye. Between the dances the legends of the country were represented in picture or recitation, none prettier perhaps than that of the curé of Alboraya in the fourteenth century. Thrown from his horse by a violent wind, while carrying the Blessed Sacrament to a dying parishioner, the ciborium fell into a torrent. The fall caused it to open and three consecrated Hosts were lost. Full of sorrow, the curé called his people to the spot, and while all united in prayer three small fish appeared, each bearing one of the lost Hosts in its mouth.

But perhaps the most charming of all receptions, in its simplicity, was that of the ' Alcalde ' of the village and his councillors. The Superior presented each to Mother Stuart with suitable words of commendation. But before one gentle-man she paused in surprise. ' I have not the honour to know Monsieur,' she said with assurance. ' Oh yes, Mother, you know me well,' he answered. ' I am the well-cleaner.' The Superior was profuse in apologies, not able to explain that the metamorphosis operated by the change of dress made recognition impossible. But it was true she knew well the strong workman who, almost at the risk of his life, had cleaned out the old Moorish well on the property. Friendship was quickly established in these simple and beautiful surroundings, and it was with real sorrow that the parting came on the evening of the 21st, when Mother Stuart left for Granada.

The name of Granada is a spell in itself.

Beautiful relics of the Moorish domination were lent by friends and adorned a long cloister near the chapel. The bishop sent the treasures of the cathedral to show to Mother Stuart : the sword of Ferdinand the Catholic ; the crown and sceptre of Isabella ; a magnificent vestment which she had worked with her ladies ; a bronze and gold box in which she had sent jewels to Columbus to help to pay the expenses of his journeys ; and a wonderful Missal which had belonged to the Royal chapel of the great sovereigns.

From Granada Mother Stuart sent the following long letter to Roehampton :

. . . These are disconnected notes, and ' Travellers' Tales,' in no order but that in which they come into my mind, and intended for recreation.

Begun at Granada, October 23rd. It was nearly midnight when we arrived here yesterday, having left Godella at seven the evening before. The strike is only just over, so that all railway matters have fallen in arrears. But at Alcazar I was thankful for the delay, because at the moment we ought to have left there arrived two of the incomparable ' old children ' who love the Society in all parts of the world. They had left Madrid at seven A.M. in a motor, because the train would have brought them to Alcazar at the same time that we arrived, and they wanted to be there before us. It was then one P.M. They had sometimes lost the way and sometimes found no way at all, and motored straight over the stubbles, their only anxiety being to be ' in time,' and for this when they appeared desperate, they promised to have a High Mass sung in honour of Our Blessed Mother Foundress. And they came simply to bring the salutations of Reverend Mother M. and the three houses of Madrid, with flowers and the 'Foundations of St. Teresa' for railway reading ! It is devotedness like this that makes one reflect in silence on the education given in the Sacred Heart Schools, and the work of our Blessed Mother Foundress. We had half an hour's talk by the fortunate delay, and then they went to have luncheon and motor back to Madrid ! Such a dear pair ! One a widow with two children, but with spirits enough for a girl of twenty. . . .

It is a wonderful thing to say to oneself that one is in Granada, with the Alhambra just behind the crest of the hill. We can see two of its towers, only prisons, and I believe the way to the cemetery passes before it, so that I shall see the front in going to look at our new vault. In driving from the station last night they showed me something very impressive—a way-side cross of white marble marking the place of St. Francis Borgia's conversion. The *cortège* of the funeral stopped there, and the face of the sovereign was uncovered for him to swear to her identity, and then we know the rest. And then they pointed up to the top of a hill to a large house with many lights, formerly a Carthusian monastery, now a Jesuit house, where many Fathers were ' burning the unblest oil of midnight,' but as it is an observatory, I suppose, in their case, the oil is not ' unblest,' and night is the time for work.

I cannot tell you how kind and good and delightful (there is no other word) the Spanish Jesuits are to us, really Fathers and Brothers. Did I tell you that in Barcelona they sent St. Ignatius' sword, and the crucifix which St. Aloysius received at his vows and with which he died, for me to see. They came carried by a very young scholastic, who was simply sparkling with life and joy of being a Jesuit, and evidently loved handling the holy relics, he was attended by a deferential brother of his own age ; one felt they were both such as St. Ignatius would have loved. The scholastic looking lovingly at the sword, reminded us how nearly it had run through the heart of the Moor who spoke against the honour of Our Lady. Two young Fathers came to the station at Tortosa where we passed, having sisters in our Society, they came as brothers, and though there was only a five minutes' stop, they sat down in the carriage, bringing postcards and photographs and reports of the work of the observatory at Tortosa, both looking such holy men—angelic in countenance and freshly come from their first Mass, they too brimmed over and glowed with joy. The thing that strikes me so much about them is that one would think they were born, not made, Jesuits, it is so natural to them. . . . At Valencia, the Rector of the College and the Superior of the Residence were actually waiting at the station to give a welcome, with the children in blue ribbons and Children of Mary ; and as to the Jesuits of the novitiate at Gandia, when they were asked for a little information to facilitate tableaux of St. Francis Borgia, they sent a whole ready-made play, written by one of the Fathers for the use of one of the colleges, with the music they had composed, the songs, everything ! Are they not indeed perfect as Fathers and Brothers to us. . . .

Our house at Godella is unique in its way ; for Godella is a village and we are the centre and life of it, and Reverend Mother A.'s word is law and her opinion life. The popular works simply overflow. We have to build an elementary school, for the present one is unworthy of the numbers that want to flock in. The property is lovely; there is a wild part which might be miles from human habitation, wooded with very old pines, and undergrown with a wonderful variety of precious and aromatic things. And set like a jewel in this exuberant village life is the school, very small as to numbers, but very choice. I was there for the feast of Mater Admirabilis, the patronal feast of the house, and therefore there was great amplitude of devotions. The Bishop of Urgel, who is Valencian by birth, was staying there and had promised to say our community Mass at seven, but as his coachman lost the way he arrived half an hour late, and spoke with so much eloquence and devotion at the time of Communion, that it was nearly nine when he had finished. The High Mass was to begin at nine, but it was spaciously removed till ten. He paid a short visit to the school, who were drawn up in white under the trees—and this was a perfect picture—for they are beautiful children, they looked like a herd of antelopes, and he, glorious in purple, made such a centre. They were invited to come up and kiss his ring, and they came up two by two looking just becomingly timid ; they did not kneel, but each little head was put out exactly like a fawn's to feed out of a trusted hand, and the little ones rose on tip-toe to reach it. It must really be a great holiday to a Bishop to see such children. His own diocese is cast in rougher surroundings: it is cross-shaped, made up of lonely valleys, and he makes his visitations on horseback. Andorra is in his diocese, and there he is temporal as well as spiritual ruler, and I should think he wields the two swords in a masterly manner. I forgot to tell you that when the village heard that a Bishop would say Mass, the poor women and children came flocking in to receive Holy Communion from his hand. The chapel was packed, so that it was hard to move. It was most devotional. We had High Mass at ten—sermon, Rosary, Benediction, extra devotions in the afternoon. We saw the village procession singing the Rosary in the evening. The clergy were there in copes; Our Lady was carried, a huge statue; blissful little boys ran about with torches.

Among the countless visits of that Sunday afternoon was a formal one from the 'Alcalde,' with his councillors, *i.e.* the Mayor and the Corporation of the village, delightful people, shrewd and faithful farmers and tradespeople, looking up to Reverend Mother A. as, I imagine, the inhabitants of the village of Andorra look up to their prince Bishop. I do not tell you the various things done in the schools. . . . I only aim at telling you my own impressions and observations and the things which other people will not say. For instance, that at Valencia there are grapes of the colour of pink topaz, truly beautiful. . . . I am staying here [Granada] an extra day to avoid travelling on Sunday, so it will help me to get my correspondence afloat. The Archbishop has been so kind as to send me up some of the treasures of the cathedral to see, as I could not go there to see them. A glorious chasuble embroidered in some of the first gold from America, by Isabella the Catholic, with her own hands. An illuminated Missal used in her chapel, priceless, and other things. . . .

[To] come back to a dear little detail of Monsignor de C., the Bishop of Perpignan. You remember how cordially we have often disliked being called 'the good Sisters.' I dislike '*mes bonnes Mères*' just as much. Mgr. de C. says '*mes pauvres dames*,' '*ma pauvre Mère*,' not with condolence about any particular trouble, or the expulsions from France, but with a general patient and happy sense that all human things are put together in a very temporary way, and all the conditions of life upon earth rather calling for endurance than exultation : there is a tone of the Blessed Curé of Ars about it ; he loved the word *pauvre*, and it made one feel almost like the 'Poor Ladies of St. Clare.' The same tone pervades the Hymn for Vespers of All Saints, '*Placare Christe*,' which I have been considering since the novena of All Saints began.

I love its brave and reticent wistfulness, . . . and recommend it to your meditations. This will only reach you after the Feast, I suppose, but all the same I wish you a happy and lovely feast in which heaven and earth meet, *lacrimarum gaudium* !

I have just had such an amusing letter from Reverend Mother de S. She tells me that the new Hungarian Provincial S.J., and his Socius, both know seven thousand different species of flies ! and she adds with a pathetic questioning, ' As we are not of this race will he care for us ? ' . . . Thank you for all letters, sometimes there are such beautiful things in them, bits from Father G.'s sermons, and wild flowers out of your own hedges, that I long to keep them all. They are refreshment by the way, but as I have very little space they have to be sooner or later torn up, though often I cut out a shred to keep. . . .

From Granada she went on to Seville, and from there to Puerto de Santa Maria, near Cadiz, from whence she wrote on November 4 :

. . . I am now at the very limit of distance from you all, and to-morrow shall go a stage nearer, back to Seville for one night, and to Madrid (Caballero de Gracia) on Wednesday 6th, then letters will take much less time. It was only a three hours' journey down here from Seville. At Xeres there was a large group of old children from various houses . . . so glad to speak of their school and friends. The most interesting things (at least the strangest) I saw on the journey here, were the herds of cattle among which run the real wild bulls which they use for bull-fights; the best are black Andalusians, and are, as an English fellow-traveller told me, to other bulls as English race-horses are to hacks, most beautiful. I cannot transport myself into a frame of mind that would like to see a bull-fight; but it is the overpowering interest here, where the bull-ring is the first in Andalusia and the third in Spain. . . . I have seen a holy old Jesuit here, Padre Labrador, who was in prison when our Mother [Digby] was in Mexico (in 1899). We could see from the hills over Guanajuato the tower where he was. It was on account of the number of conversions he had obtained in a mission, that the Government was enraged and shut him up. I got him to tell me all about it, and he told it so simply and delightfully. He did not lose his time in prison, for he repeated the misdemeanour for which he had been locked up, and gave a little mission to his fellow-prisoners. . . . His remedy for all things is spiritual joy, and his own laugh is a short discourse on the subject. He brought me a little book which he had just written on St. Paschal Baylon, not wrapped up, but tied with a bit of blue ribbon to look

festive, the blue ribbon he had evidently begged from the
brother who represents Sister Beha at the Jesuit College, ribbon
off a little boy's chocolate box, and as evidently tied by his
own venerable hands, one would feel disposed to keep it as
a relic.

The same day she wrote to the novices at Roehampton for
their feast :

. . . This evening I know the novena to St. Stanislaus will
begin, and I am beginning it with you for all the novices of
the Society whose thoughts are turning to that wonderful
Brother, who has set the pace for you all. May no one of you
lag behind, and still less look behind you, on this wonderful
race-course of our life, which gives such opportunities for ' distinguished service' under such inconspicuous circumstances.
It is only afterwards that you will realise how the unseen
heroism has been beside you all the time, great persons incognito,
great dispatches communicated in cypher, the whole thing
going on all round you, and so much more intensely real than
it seems.

Someone said, speaking of St. Gertrude—I think it was
Aubrey de Vere—' The Saints are always believing what we
profess to believe' : *there* is a short cut out of many complicated
situations, to believe in real earnest what I profess to believe.
It may startle you at first to think that there is a discrepancy,
it will startle you more to see how great that discrepancy is,
and it will astonish you most when you experience the results
of bringing the two together. I am watching these blessed
results often. Pray that I may not be left behind in carrying
out my own share.

May God bless you all, and make the new novices a real
reinforcement. Your increased numbers are a great joy, for
the Society wants you all, and all of the right sort,· please.

Madrid was reached on November 6. Here two houses in
the town and the noviceship at Chamartin were eagerly awaiting their turns. As Mother Stuart passed from house to house
her reputation grew and sped before her, so that, if possible,
each reception increased in warmth. The discovery that she
knew Spanish and ' could be talked to in their own language '
cemented the growing friendship.

At Caballero de Gracia, Queen Victoria and the Infantas
Isabel and Paz came to see her, and the succession of visits
was so unending that she wrote: ' Madrid was tremendous as
to work ! I felt as if I had had almost enough, but this is
only for your ear.' Such a confession meant much. It was

2 C

the only ' complaint ' of any sort that escaped her in the overwhelming rush.

Here she found a work which always won her sympathy
and interest, a Training College for Elementary School Teachers.
She spoke to these girls of their ' great mission ' and asked to
be introduced to each one. But of all these things she speaks
in delightful letters from Madrid St. Denis, where the convent
is established in the old Palace of the Dukes of Pastrana, and
from Saragossa, which she reached on November 21, and where
she found herself in the ' holy place ' of Spain, the city of
pilgrimage, the favoured city of Our Lady del Pilar.

Madrid St. Denis : 20th November, 1912.

. . . You have written me so many letters which I valued
very much and I seem to have written nothing to you for a
long time. This is a beginning, I do not know what fortune
it will have ! . . . There are so many things I should like
to tell you, but when I arrived in Madrid two waves, one of
visitors, the other of correspondence, met me, like an inexperienced swimmer, full in the mouth, and I have not got back
my breath since, so things have accumulated, and to-morrow
I leave Madrid.

The Jesuits continue to be incomparably kind and most interesting. I saw Padre Astrain who is writing the monumental
History of the Spanish Assistancy, we have three volumes
already at Roehampton, and the fourth is just coming out,
this contains the great question *de auxiliis*, so the Dominicans
are waiting with bated breath for its appearance. In fact it
is rather like the *hounds* at the meet, *nosing* about, and when
the fox gets away from covert all the *Domini Canes* will be
in full cry after him ! But I am sure they will not catch him !
Padre Astrain entered the Society with the permission of Father
Beckx when he was thirteen and a half ! so now he is just fifty-
four and forty years a Jesuit. He has the kindness of Father
Walmesley, the eyes of Father Porter, and the instincts and
learning of Father Thurston ! He thinks, and I am delighted
to repeat it, that the majority of people have not the faintest
idea of how much they could do and understand because they
do not work their minds, and he is particularly insistent on the
marvellous development *in all orders of things—of mediocrities*,
if they will only be faithful to grace.

I must tell you another delightful Jesuit story told me by
one of the nuns. In the last retreat she confided to the Father
her earnest longing to die young, and she paused thinking he
would say something about the death of St. Aloysius and
of being prepared, etc. Instead of which the man of God

murmured under his breath with a sigh : ' the precipitous flight
of the slothful'; the yearnings of the soul found no further
utterance. This was certainly not characteristic of Sister
Agnes' departure; what a soldierly death, fighting to the last.
I think that last stand she made to look out with Mother B.
over the scene she had known so long, and out of eyes that
could scarcely see was wonderful, and the story of the pillow
and carpet [refused on the day before her death as immortified].
She would cordially have approved of ' Bonnie Dundee,' when
with one kick he dispersed from under a sleeping trooper's
head the little pillow of snow which he had rolled for himself.
I like that last tray of folded handkerchiefs, she was at her
service to the last.

I must stop, for we are going in a few minutes to Saragossa.

By the time Mother Stuart reached Saragossa the enthusiasm
had become so great that the two autos which had met her
at Barcelona had grown to thirty, which stood in rows outside
the station. Unfortunately twenty-nine had to be satisfied with
preceding her processionally to the convent ! More and more
they found her *muy simpatica, una cara santissima*, to
which the Chaplain at St. Denis had added, ' *c'est l'humilité*.'
She had scarcely reached the house when the Archbishop
arrived. ' I wished to welcome you at once,' he said, ' and
to-morrow I expect you at Pilar.' With great kindness he had
arranged that one of the priests should say Mass for her in the
chapel of the miraculous Madonna, after which he would say
his own Mass at the high altar, with the cathedral illuminated
as for a great feast. His first decision had been that this
should be a private Mass, and no one should be admitted. But
he confided the secret of his preparations to too many people
and it met with the fate described in the ' Imitation,' with the
result that crowds besieged the palace begging for admission.
So many ' particular favours ' had to be granted that in the
end the great church was crammed. After Mass His Grace
invited Mother Stuart to follow him to the sacristies, the crowd
rose *en masse* to accompany her, but this time he held firm.
' No one but the children of the Sacred Heart.' Then, setting
Mother Stuart in the episcopal throne and standing before her,
he brought out the treasures of the place. ' It was a painful
position,' she said afterwards, ' but good to have such an
occasion of obeying.'

Saragossa : 24th November, 1912.

. . . There are many things of interest accumulated in my
memory, shall I ever get through them ? This is a beginning,

and I will begin with the Queen. . . . She had been ill with influenza for a fortnight, and I believe in the end her coming was a little touch of independence which the doctor had to put up with. . . . The Queen came in a little victoria with a pair of brown bays—very pretty, rather small—and two outriders. The community had assembled in the hall, all those who were free, that is the aged and infirm, which made a wonderful contrast when the Queen came in. I caught one moment when a saintly old mother of eighty or more, with dark complexion and very dark Spanish eyes, had to look up so high to see the very fair radiance of the Queen's face before kissing her hand. It was beautiful and made one think of many things.

Then I saw the Queen alone, and I cannot say how charming and simple she was . . . her laugh is delightful. . . .

Canalejas'[1] murder came the very next day, and the King set off alone at once and prayed beside the body, but very thoughtfully forbade that the Queen should be told until he came back. His appearance again at the funeral called out a greater ovation than he has had before, they almost carried the motor in which he was, but one never knows what may happen from day to day.

The Queen had just the little tension in her voice that must come from a constant effort to face and bear things that are difficult and anxious. But it has not spoilt her youth. It is a beautiful face, *very* English. . . . She works a great deal for the poor, and has three things going at once, so that in whatever part of the palace she is there may be something at hand. The hall was packed full when the Queen went out, not only with the community. I again saw the light in Mother R.'s eyes glow when the Queen passed her. She gave her hand to all those within reach to be kissed, so prettily, almost as if she were shy of giving it. . . . The rest of the space was packed with the families of the nuns and children, whom I was to see that morning. . . .

I saw the Infantas, not the Queen Mother, for since the death of the Infanta Marie Thérèse, she has seen no one except the Royal Family, and does not leave her room; she sent a gracious message and a lady-in-waiting. The Infanta Isabel was one of those I saw, and I can quite understand the enthusiasm of the people for her; she is so good to the poor and has a frank simple manner that would bewitch them. A characteristic touch was that when the bad party wanted to have a bull-fight during the Eucharistic Congress to draw off the people from the procession, the Infanta bought up all the tickets, thousands, so

---

[1] Señor Canalejas, Prime Minister from 1910, was shot on the way to a Cabinet meeting.

that there could be no performance, and on the following Sunday
she gave all the tickets to the army, imagine the joy ! . . .

The Jesuits continue to be wonderfully kind and cordial.
I have met several who have been in England and liked it so
much that they were quite sorry to leave! Among these
Padre Pagasartundua, a name I should not venture to spell if
I had not his card. He is at Seville now, and as the dear Andalusians do not like laborious works they find his name too much
for them, and both Fathers and faithful call him Padre Paga !
His father is still living and is a Jesuit too. In Madrid the Bishop
of Sion is particularly good to us, he is the Bishop of the Court
and the Army, and performed the ceremony at Chamartin on
the Feast of St. Stanislaus. He spoke beautifully of the religious
life but did not mention the Saint. It was just after Canalejas'
death, and when I saw him afterwards he let out his oratorical
powers which are not small, and spoke with very great vehemence,
and as he went away he whispered to Reverend Mother, '. . .
Tell the Mother General not to think that all Spanish Bishops
are like me,' which I thought a very pretty, unconscious act
of humility. It seems it is not etiquette, or at all events not
customary, for Spanish Bishops to have horses. I have seen one
in a motor, but otherwise they have mules, often very smart,
sometimes very wicked looking, and occasionally the hair on
their backs is ingeniously clipped into patterns like stamped
brocade ; it is most quaint and very pretty. . . .

Three more houses remained to be seen at Larrauri, Bilbao,
and San Sebastian, and Mother Stuart speaks of them in the
following letters:

Larrauri : November 29th, 1912.
. . . It is so pleasant to write to you at Roehampton, that
I have tightened up my lines to give a little space and tell you
of my last journey here from Saragossa. It is a broken journey
by train, so the Marquesa X. lent her motor car, and the two
hundred and fifty miles were very pleasantly done in twelve
hours without stops. The Marquesa also lent her eldest son to
sit beside the chauffeur, for deference in case of a good journey,
and service in case of an accident. We left at six A.M. by moonlight, in white frost and fog, without lamps, anywhere else the
fine would have been formidable. A good margin is left for
the care of the Angels guardian, ' Ces heureux gentils-hommes
du Roi Céleste' as St. Francis of Sales calls them. (How well
that would sound in English, ' the merry gentlemen of God's
Household.') Anyhow we met only donkeys with fuel and
market-carts before sunrise ; and donkeys, with their soft ears
cocked and heads well up, said they knew all about motors
in the dark as well as in the light.

The road is said to be the worst in all Spain for motors, and I am glad to think there is not a worse, in one part we went straight across country without a road at all. And here, in a lonely place, we came upon about a hundred people, men and women, with horses, mules and donkeys. I suppose they were going to the hills to cut fuel, but these were country animals and thought the motor a most shocking sight, so with horror in their eyes they bolted, if they could, and scrambled and plunged and kicked in the general panic, all except one mule, and he, in sheer defiance and spite, lay down and rolled in front of the motor, four hoofs in the air. I suppose it was a challenge to the car, 'which of the twain is king of the causeway?' The chauffeur threaded his way through very cleverly, and the company were most sweet and patient and did not utter a word —only they held on to the heads of their animals as hard as they could. I noticed that the donkeys had much more self-control and remained more collected than either horses or mules. We stopped an hour in one town for the Marquesito and the chauffeur to refresh themselves, while we made our adoration in a beautiful old collegiate church, and then we began a long climb up into the mountains from which the view grew wider and wider over the plain, most beautiful to see, and very lonely; on the crest we stopped some little time as the car had something wrong, but once over it, we came shooting down the steep descents from the 'high places' of God at a pace that was perfectly delightful. At the end the roads grew better, and at sunset we did light the lamps, then we met ox-waggons, their drivers lit torches of twisted straw and waved them over the bullocks' heads, so that we saw a gleam of quiet eyes and great horns as we went by, and they never stirred. I only saw an ox start yesterday when a rocket was let off just under his nose.

This place is a village and the village life is so good, so peaceful and unspoiled that it has quite a charm of its own. The people scarcely speak anything but Basque, so they cannot be spoiled by the bad newspapers. The whole village came yesterday afternoon, and boys and girls in the costume for dancing showed off the national dances. The parish priest and the curate were in the thick of it all, enjoying proudly the per-formances of their lambs, while a tertiary of St. Francis whipped them into their places with a kind but not a light hand. The children of the boarding school also danced the 'fandango' under the trees for us to the accompaniment of drum and fife from the village, and the villagers with their ox-carts stood 'at gaze' and clapped. The local clergy have just been to see me, eight together! but it is very nice when they come together. At Madrid I was receiving the visit of the Chaplains and the Con-fessor when all of a sudden the electric light went out all over

the house. We sat still awaiting a light, as I did not know a
step of the house, having just arrived. After a minute Don
Thomas, the senior Chaplain, took wax matches out of his pocket
and began to light them up, and I said to myself, 'O, Sirs, how
Rembrandt would love to paint these three Spanish Ecclesiastical
faces in the soft light of a wax match!' And then the nuns
arrived like wise virgins with candles and tapers shaded by their
hands, such a picture of light and shadow on black and white
and dark eyes. I have wandered on so long that I must stop. . . .

                                     Bilbao : 3rd December, 1912.
    . . . This is only a few lines to keep you up to date. I go
to San Sebastian to-morrow the 4th, and leave on the 9th, from
that date until the 13th I shall be at Bordeaux, Poitiers, Paris,
Amiens, on the 13th back at the Mother House, so perhaps
from the time that this reaches you it would be better to address
to Ixelles. . . . Here they have in the *œuvres* over three thousand souls ; a Sunday school of seven hundred children taught
by forty 'old children' with great zeal and regularity. It is a
beautiful sight to see each one with her own group of children.
There are endless 'Consolers of Mary,' about one thousand
seven hundred I think, but of course all cannot come every
Sunday. A Jesuit spends almost all Sunday here amongst all
these works. He 'presented' the Sunday School, the apple of
his eye ; he led and conducted the chorus, which he had himself taught and rehearsed up to the last moment, and walked
about among the seven hundred as they sang, in Basque and
Spanish, to steady the parts and support the chorus and wave
on the laggards, and tone down the erratic, and they all looked
at him with obedient unquestioning eyes, as if he were God's
Providence itself; then he came and insisted on handing to me
himself each picture as I gave it to them, and returned thanks
for me (the thanks were due to himself) and returned thanks for
them and conducted me out—in fact, he was the soul of the
situation with Mother M. In the evening he was there again
for the Consolers of Mary, half of the one thousand seven
hundred, and showed off to them, for my benefit, a cinemato-
graph of which he is very proud, given by a lady for this
congregation. It was very broad comedy, though of course
most innocent, the girls were enchanted, and I was lost in
admiration of the Father, his kindness, his earnestness, and
his catching laugh like a boy's. It also came home to me
very powerfully what a *child* human nature is all over the
world when it is in its natural state; these were just the sort
of adventures that make Punch and Judy and Jack the
Giant Killer, only modernised by the introduction of telephone
and motor-car and aeroplane, but the joy is the same—to

see people knocked down and beaten and punished for wrong-doing, stealing, etc., and to see physical force overcome by wits! Padre Lumarraga had just sat down breathless and very hot after showing the last film, when there came a telephone message from the Residence, which is across the street, ' Would he please come home as quickly as possible and preach to replace a Father who could not come,' and forgetting his cloak in his obedient and joyful haste, he *flew*, leaving me one more subject for reflection!

I have seen the room where Reverend Mother Burke died. It said many things to me. I have prayed at her grave and left a bit of wild heather for auld lang syne. .   .

Two months later the following letter, written from Ixelles, completed the picture of the days in Spain.

Ixelles (finished February 13th), 1913.

. . . Here is at last the beginning of my last letter from Spain. I meant to write it at San Sebastian, and it has been two months and more waiting. But here it is at last, for I want to tell you my last impressions and *whole* impression of that most lovable country. San Sebastian itself was to me a half-way house that did not seem like Spain at all, for it is one of our frontier schools, a transplanted French house with the very minimum of Spanish elements, except the congregation of the Children of Mary, which is properly Spanish, and, as they told me, the real life of San Sebastian is Spanish; but there is a floating cosmopolitan element beside it like a tourist world, or a sea-bathing world which is not San Sebastian properly speaking. . . .

The position is quite beautiful. But to go back to what was more really Spain to me; the country and the people. The country in the parts I saw is more striking as God's architecture than as His finished pictures. Because in so many parts the dryness checks vegetation, and one goes sometimes almost a day without seeing green except by the watercourses, a day's meditation on the 1st Psalm and Jeremias' reflections on the heath in the desert (by which I believe he meant *tamarisk*). Of course there are exceptions, even in what I have seen, trees of great beauty, but in general the vegetation is austere rather than luxuriant. And in the austere conditions of growth there are *marvels* of cultivation, of vine, olive, and orange, triumphs of patient labour. The labour is so patient and so hard that one stands amazed at it; the implements are so primitive, and they will have no others in some parts. In the North the farm-ing is much more progressive, but about Saragossa it is still as it must have been centuries ago; for instance, the plough has no ploughshare, only a coulter, and perfectly straight handles making the work mechanically as resisting and heavy as it can be to man and horse, and with all that they sing! I watched one man ploughing at Saragossa a stiff soil, with one horse and one of those ploughs. One would have supposed that one turn of the field would exhaust him, but he sang as he worked to cheer the horse, and in the end the horse was so cheered that, being unharnessed, he bolted and careered about in the attitudes Velasquez gives to his horses, the one on which the little Prince Balthasar Carlos sits so calmly,—he was that make of horse. It left one 'with many things passing through one's head.'

As to the people, the little moments of insight that one had here and there into the life of all classes, rich, poor, and clergy, are unlike anything I have seen elsewhere, and carry one's thoughts back to their wonderful past. Life must have been simply intoxicating in Spain at the end of the fifteenth century. I saw high above us, in driving to the station at Granada, the very windows of the ' Hall of the Ambassadors ' in the Alhambra in which Isabella the Catholic received Columbus on his return from America, so short a time after it was taken from the Moors. When one thinks of the two currents of life and thought and action that met there on that day, it simply goes beyond words and imagination. And these things do not die. And Father Luis of Granada's mother was a washerwoman in the Alhambra! There is another avenue of thought that takes one far. Such memories meet one at every turn and they live in the life of to-day, but then one has to think and catch the impression of them here and there, very fleeting (sometimes) perhaps, but they catch one's breath and fill one's horizon for those moments, in a way that one cannot forget.

Then I loved their expressive words and the grand ways of their devotion, and the faith and reverence that makes their religion so great and true. The hateful fault of flippancy does not seem to exist, and that in itself is a joy.

To come to another order of things, I think there is a very close kinship, or at all events a very straight understanding, between their point of view and ours on educational matters, and I quite understand their liking to send their children to school in England, and the ease with which the children get accustomed to our ways. I think their vitality, both physical and mental, is of the same genus as ours, though not, evidently, of the same species. But we are made to understand each other very well.

One more thing, the community were a little worried last year that I could only report that I had found singular sanctity among the very old in my visits! Let them take heart again! I found some very choice souls indeed among the young and early middle-aged in Spain!

Here ends my Spanish volume, but I left the country hoping to see it again some day!

CHAPTER XXIV

THE MOTHER HOUSE

Journey to Rome and England, 1913

'Please tell the professed that the thing which stands out more clearly every day as the problems of the Society come up before me is that our life is Paradise on earth to those who give themselves in the spirit we promise at our profession, that circumstances simply *do not count*, because we came to give rather than to receive. With God we make our own life, within, and if we don't do this, our life is a great disappointment because its centre is self.'—*From a letter, J. Stuart.*

THE next nine months were spent chiefly at Ixelles, with short visits to neighbouring houses, a month in Rome in April 1913, and a visit to the British Isles in June.

It was the last moment of comparative rest in her life; the last pause in the long journey.

From words spoken here and there it is clear that Mother Stuart looked on these visits to the Houses of the Society as the most important part of her mission as Superior General. She saw, as everyone must see, the advantages to be gained administratively: the possibilities they afforded for understanding the needs and considering the real good of each soul more effectively; but above all she saw in them 'her mission given to her by God,' her vocation within her vocation 'to carry afar her message of hope and confidence,' and to cement still more strongly the *cor unum et anima una* in the Society.

This was the secret of these three years of apostolic journeys, in which she was wearied out for God and the souls He had trusted to her.

> '. . . He is Peace, and where He is is Peace,
> And all along the way where He has trod
> The thorny earth itself has blossomed Peace,'

she wrote in 1883, in the first verses written as a novice, and the words paint her own passage.

The strong bond of union in the Order owes much to the

constant 'visitations' of Blessed Mother Barat to her foundations. From very early days she had foreseen the spread of
her Society throughout the world, and unity amid diversity
had become her ideal. To attain this she had planned a single
noviceship, and constant intercourse with the centre, as the
chief means. The former soon passed beyond the realm of
possibility, but the latter remained, and has even increased in
power with the developments of modern life. As long as it had
been possible, she herself had passed from house to house in
Europe, and would have gladly followed her daughters when
they went out, in the first decades of the nineteenth century,
to then remote America. We can well believe that had she
lived in our time, she too would have extended her apostolic
journeys so as to encircle the world.

Her instructions to those carrying on the work of foundations bear witness to her breadth of view, and were the basis
of Mother Stuart's action, and a source of strength and consolation to her. No one could have been more emphatic than
Blessed Mother Barat in insisting on the necessity of studying
the needs of each country, and of adapting her Institute to
them, while holding fast to its great central principles of
education. 'We cannot hide from ourselves,' she had written,
'that time brings many changes and necessitates modifications,
which must be examined and weighed with care. The Rules
and Constitutions must remain intact ; but we *can* and even
must narrow or widen their application. If we hold strictly
to the letter we shall put obstacles to the progress of the Society
and hinder the good which it can do.'

Mother Stuart had, in a wonderful degree, the power of
seizing at a glance the possibilities and needs of places, times
and persons. She suggested her ideas when an opening occurred,
but she never imposed them. 'I have planted a seed there,'
she sometimes said, 'but I do not know if it will bear fruit.'
Her influence was in reality all the greater that it was so
impersonal and discreet. Her words and actions suggested the
presence of some hidden force, of some secret to be learnt,
some discovery to be made, and very few escaped their im-
pelling power. Her influence was like that of the 'by-way' so
beautifully described in the essay already quoted : 'The elusive,
silent, solitary by-way is a master, and by it we go . . . because
we must.'

Some who did not know her, thought that English methods
of education would be imposed throughout the Society. But

this was far from being her ideal. ' Our things (all things) need native soil for growth,' she wrote, ' when transplanted they die, and what is worse they decompose after death.'

' The best education, the most solid instruction *according to our time and the country where we are*, but always essentially based on our principles, that is what our Blessed Mother would have desired if she had been called to found a house here,' she said, speaking in a new foundation in the last year of her life. And in her instructions to the assembled Superiors at Manhattanville, she reminded them of the words of Montalembert : ' It is not for us to do what our fathers did, but to do what our fathers would do if they were here,' and she added : ' Not as our Blessed Mother *did in her time*, but as she would do here to-day . . . must be our guide.'

' To aim at the best and to remain essentially ourselves is one and the same thing,' she said on another occasion, encouraging some who perhaps feared the inevitable changes and struggles of a restless age.

' Of all the Superiors General, she is the one who most resembles the Foundress,' was said of Mother Stuart more than once during these years. ' *Une autre Mère Barat*,' was the Cardinal Protector's delighted comment. In the very dissimilar and typical settings of their own races, they possessed many gifts in common. In both there was a great wealth of natural endowment, breadth of view, womanly intuition, attractive humility, winning gentleness and horror of inflicting pain, unwearying patience, and a strong common sense.

Mother Stuart's understanding of the spirit of the Blessed Foundress, as written in her Institute and impressed on its traditions, was profound. She had made it the matter of serious study during the long years she was Superior at Roehampton, beginning under the guidance of Mother Digby, who was herself the child of Blessed Mother Barat and of Mother Gœtz, and had been personally trained by them. In answer to the question, ' On what subject could you pass an unprepared examination any day ? ' ' I think,' said Mother Stuart, ' on Scripture and our Constitutions and Decrees.'

In the trials and occasional misunderstandings which were inevitable in her new position, she found consolation and support in more than one episode in the life of the Foundress. ' Suffering and contradiction belong to and befit those who consecrate themselves to the Heart of Jesus,' wrote Father Varin in the early days of the Society. That such things should be is in no way surprising. Opposition seems to be a law inherent to development, as it is also a source of security, testing the permanence of our desires, and insuring slow growth to those in which there is a germ of life.

Left alone to face grave decisions, her confidence in God grew more deep-rooted. 'Now that I am at the centre,' she wrote, 'I see more clearly that He does all . . . I am convinced that it is He who sends people from one place to another, and plans their circumstances. . . . Remember . . . the depressing side is never the true side, but only the hopeful, beautiful view of His love and Providence.'

As Superior General, Mother Stuart considered that more than ever each moment of her time belonged to the Society, and was to be used for its good. She still read and studied when she could. Her conferences were an instance of the care she put into all her work. 'You do not know what a conference means to me,' she said. With her wealth of thought and imagery, it might have been supposed that she could speak with little preparation, but that was not her view. 'We must try to give the cream of the cream of excellent thought to each soul. . . . Who is there of us of whom bread might be asked to satisfy soul hunger, and who would offer a platitude ? ' This same principle made her always shrink from giving mottos and *mots d'ordre* constantly asked for by children and communities. 'It is too serious, I must think,' was her invariable answer, instead of giving the first pious thought that came to her.

'I read the "Paradiso" twice a day for three minutes. My five minutes' reading at another time, I can sometimes lengthen into ten, and get through a good deal,' she wrote shortly after her arrival at Ixelles. Books were constantly sent to her, and she generally commented on them.

Welton's 'Psychology of Education' is *v.g.* Perhaps I think so because there is an extraordinary likeness between his views and those I have expressed in my book ! You will notice it, I am sure, in particular in the chapter on General Mental Endowment, and also Development of Interests.

I read Stevenson's defence of Father Damien. It is a fine, fair, and loyal defence, but of course he has very little insight into what is to me the soul of Father Damien's life. I find it very hard to like anything that Stevenson writes as to style. (Of course, that was not the point for which this was sent.) His depth seems to me that of a swimming-bath, carefully graded for children, never deep enough to drown in. The texture of his prose is like a bedroom carpet, and his horizon like that of houses called ' Heath View,' where there is neither heath nor view.

But this, is cantankerous criticism I ' Then up an' spake the auld gude-wife. And wow I but she was grim I ' I forget the rest, but that is enough. . . .

I have returned (1) ' Craftsmanship in Education,' which is quite good, and might be used among the method books; (2) ' What is and might be,' which is quite bad, and does not deserve to exist. . . . (3) ' Ford Maddox Hueffer,' which is charmingly written, but not of any worth; (4) ' Dean Hole on Roses,' which might go to the children. A charming little book, and will interest them in rose-growing. . . . Mgr. Croke Robinson could write exactly the same kind of book, in exactly the same style, on birds. I wish he would, but he wouldn't, perhaps now he couldn't. . . .

Read two things in Father Faber's Hymns; they are neither of them hymns nor yet poems, but full of good sense and truth: one is ' Peevishness,' the other is ' The Right must Win.'

. . . X. gave me A. C. Benson's ' A Thread of Gold.' I shall send it back by an opportunity. Not a safe book to lend to anyone in general, but ' The Secret ' is good to read. It expresses exactly what I think on Milton and the other point. And the last two things in the book are also good. But ' The Secret ' is the best thing. . . . ' Village Life in America ' is a real disappointment. It betrays itself as one of those made-up things like ' William Walshe.' It is not of the period 1852 to the war, in any way—language, manners, thoughts, institutions —no value at all. I cannot understand whether the reviewer and the writer of the preface are taken in by it, or whether they are all in the plot together. . . . How from any point of view the preface writer can speak of it as fascinating is hard to understand. . . .

Each return to Ixelles found Mother Stuart more 'alive,' if such a thing were possible. Her interests grew daily larger. Those who lived with her there, and those who from time to time came from her old Vicariate felt this, and felt how truly she had given herself to the whole Society.

' There is no harmony like that of the *Cor unum*,' she said one day at recreation, *nous sommes si bien ensemble*. As she walked quickly through the house, the smile with which she invariably greeted those she met ' made us feel,' wrote one, ' that it was a joy to her to see us.' Simple and retiring as ever, she seemed to slip into her place in the general recreations : and

passed in the long files of community and probanists without
being seen. At recreation her attitude was the sweetest and
humblest that could be imagined. Alive to everything, her
interest was always real and spontaneous, and never gave the
feeling of being kept up.

By her kindness [wrote Mère le Bail], she obtained everything from those she met, correction of faults, sustained efforts
for perfection. If anyone spoke to her of a book they longed
for, it was immediately procured. . . . 'Address it to so-and-
so,' she would say, ' so that it may not get lost on the way on
another writing-table.' . . . It gave her real pleasure to see
us interested in any study. . . . She never hesitated to procure
the means of study, books, journeys, professors, especially
for her nuns, for whom she looked on all this work as a great
means of progress in the spiritual life. . . .
    She never complained of anything, nor of anyone. Some-
times I tried to discover her preferences with regard to more
or less air, heat or cold, but it was impossible. ' I don't notice
those things,' she said, and it was true. She never asked for
doors or windows to be shut or opened. She left all these
things as she found them, unless there was some inconvenience
for another, then she was immediately alive to all.
    Her little attentions to others were constant, and what was
even more gracious was the gratitude with which she accepted
those offered her. She never refused what she was offered,
unless it was really wholly out of place. She always liked to
travel with as little as possible. Once on a journey she said
to me : ' You brought this shawl, it was not necessary.' She
must have feared that there was some want of graciousness
in this, for the next day she came and asked me to give it to
her.
    It seemed almost as if she had made a vow to obey her
subjects, having no superiors over her. For she did immediately
what they asked her to do, even in the smallest details.
    She never refused to give pleasure to others when it was
in the least possible to do so. At Peschiera, for example, she
had given, as usual, a picture to each of the Children of Mary.
One of these ladies followed her after the meeting and begged
her to sign the picture. This seemed a brilliant idea to all
there assembled, and they immediately followed suit. Mother
Stuart showed not the least annoyance, though she was greatly
pressed for time, and taking back all the pictures, she went
off obediently to sign them. No *contretemps* ever disturbed
her. . . .
    Even strangers felt something indefinable after a short

moment of interview with her. The Bishop of Avignon could
not be drawn away from his conversation with her. . . .

Mortification had become as a second nature to her. For
it is no little thing to accept without even one of those in-
voluntary signs of surprise or impatience, interruptions of every
sort, requests often wanting in discretion, perpetual changes
of country. . . .

Her discretion was so perfect that it was impossible to
find out when speaking to her, if she already knew anything
of the matter in question. If she asked for information about
unknown people, at the first word which seemed wanting in
appreciation she would cut the conversation short, saying
' *Bien* ' and one understood ' That will do.'

The smallest details, not only of our Rules, but of our customs
were kept by her with absolute fidelity. In nothing was she
more remarkable than in her invariable punctuality. And if
obliged to be absent from a community exercise she always
sent word beforehand, ' Lest you think I am dead, if I am not in
my place with you ! ' she wrote on a note apologising for being
absent. Wherever she went it was the same thing. In every
convent in the Society five-fifteen A.M. found her in her place
for prayer, even on the mornings after long and tiring journeys.

As the strangeness of the new surroundings gradually wore
off, she was as fertile as ever with questions and suggestions to
set people thinking, and she found a ready response in her new
home-circle. ' When she left for her long journey,' wrote one
of the community at Ixelles, ' she had given an *élan* to our
desire to read and study.'

' Does it seem to you that you are reading or writing your
life ? ' she asked one day, and gave as her own answer :

' Until forty I wrote a great deal, now I read.' And then
she explained that she thought that ordinarily youth wrote—
that is to say, gave more to personal action—later, this
diminishes, and we read, or watch the action of God and *nous
nous laissons faire.*

Another day, discussing the value of self-contempt and
self-respect in ' our own daily life and in the education of
children,' she said :

In education of children I think contempt of self has no
place except in those extremely rare cases of arrogant natures,
overpoweringly selfish. But in general childhood is so frail,
so astonished at the novelty of life, and with a rebound so easily
broken that a feeling of personal dignity is of far greater help
for good and should be first awakened. . . .

She interested herself also in the house and garden, beauti-
fying Our Lady's chapel ; redecorating the church ; planning
improvements with the gardener, persuading him to grow her
favourite roses in the narrow precincts of the town garden.

All categories in the four houses of her Vicariate received
special attention—the novices and juniors at Jette, and the
probanists at the Mother House. But to write about what
she was to them would be to repeat what has already been
written. As ever, she made those who were ill or in difficulty
or suffering of any sort her chief care.

One writes :

She seemed to us a perfect example of her own words, ' When
we come to have our minds so filled with the thought of God,
that the difficulty is to keep ourselves from being absorbed by
it, then we shall not be far from that heroic love which makes
Saints.' A whole new horizon was opened out to me by seeing
her, and it seemed that even if the blessed opportunity should
never come again, she had imparted to me a lasting gift, a certain
radiant peace and satisfaction which nothing could take away.
It was as though at last . . . my ideal stood up perfectly
revealed. Having known her, I am convinced we could never
be the same again.

Another says :

Probation made a complete change in me which under
God was due to Mother Stuart. I arrived at Ixelles still ' very
proud ! ' and some months passed without bringing any real
change. One day when I had spoken to Reverend Mother
with pride, and even almost rudely, I heard her say gently :
' What means are there to make you feel at home, dear child,
I should so like to know them.' These humble words, said so
gently, triumphed over my resistance. I was completely won.
I told her of all my cowardice. ' It is easy to repair,' she said,
' but if you wish to be a Religious of the Sacred Heart you must
humble yourself.' I took her words *literally*, and how she
helped me ! Words of reproach were always followed by
words of tenderness and encouragement, which made me feel
ready for everything. And when she saw me trying to be
faithful to grace, she herself found excuses for all my faults.
' God is good to you,' she said one day, ' you can hardly as yet
understand the magnitude of the grace you have received.'
When my profession day came, and with it none of that feeling
of fervour so desired, she consoled me saying ' Our Lord has
many ways of giving Himself, you have the reality.' And
then I left her, but she followed me still by word or letter until
her death.

2 D

This loving charity was extended to all the families of her children. ' She asked after all my relations,' writes a young American nun, ' as if they had been her own, and when I told her of a dear brother then very ill and thought to be dying, she said quickly : " Should he die, is there any income ? " " I do not think so," I replied. " Then I shall educate their little girls, tell them so." '

And another, also an American, says : ' Walking with our Mother General in the garden of Ixelles, I told her of a letter I had just received from my brother (in which he spoke of many troubles), saying how it grieved me, especially as I was seven thousand or eight thousand miles away from him. She took the letter from my hand, saying " Let me read it." It was twelve closely written pages. That same afternoon she sent it back and with it a paper on which she had written : " He must be the dearest and best of brothers so full of faith and ideals. Trust him and all of them to God who loves them better than you do." The way in which she seemed to care brought comfort with its human touch.'

In the midst of all she had to do, no details seemed to escape her. A probanist asked her one day ' to suggest a few books, " good for a young religious to read." Taking a paper she wrote several—one was " The Practice of Mental Prayer." As she wrote the title she said : " You spelt that incorrectly the other day, the substantive has *c* and the verb an *s*." She was referring to a paper which I had given in several days before along with those of many others.'

The professions in the summer of 1913 were made at Jette. When there Mother Stuart loved to kneel in the still dim chapel, by the shrine of Blessed Mother Barat. ' I never saw a more perfect expression of peace than that which shone on her face as she knelt there on the eve of our profession day. . . . The next day, when saying good-bye to us, her only words were : " Be simple, faithful, fervent. Don't forget anything ! " '

The following letters were written during these months :

To the Roehampton Community : Christmas, 1912.

. . . I have a Christmas present for you, it is what you like better than anything—an *idea*. The idea is that each one who is so disposed should write or compile, at all events prepare, her own Meditation book. We know there are excellent books of Meditation, but would not our own work gathered and prepared have a special value for us, as we know what suits us ? —and those who have given a real trial to personal preparation say that meditation is quite a different thing to them, and they would not willingly go back. It would be a very considerable work and no one should undertake it who does not feel that it would be a comfort and an inspiration to their inner life, and that they would persist in it and carry it through.

This is how I imagine it. First one would write one's introduction, that would be a short collection or arrangement of principles that experience has taught us would be useful for *ourselves*, anything concerning aspects of prayer, or methods, or applications of principles or results of experience, or soul-like thoughts that are ours by possession or acquisition ; things regarding meditation, contemplation ; second or third methods of prayer as it suits us *personally*. Perhaps in detail things concerning preludes, composition of place, management of meditation.

There would be a good deal of collecting and preparation to do, before one could write in the meditations ; for instance, the choice of titles which are certainly helpful in giving a key-note to the meditation—compositions of place which give atmosphere instead of imaginary locality. Father Blount suggested this. Petitions well grouped, which can be repeated as prayers if the meditation goes heavily, and as antiphons caught up after Psalms if it goes well.

Then there is endless work to be done in enriching the vein of one's own thoughts from which the substance of the meditation is to be drawn, by really assiduous devotional study of Holy Scripture and of books that are fundamental, such as the Fathers of the Church and the greater spiritual writers, as Father Balthazar Alvarez. . . . And there would be divisions to make in one's book counting out the proportionate pages, so much for the Christmas season, so much for Lent and for Paschal time, so much for the long afternoon of the year from the Sacred Heart to Advent ; and perhaps a special section for Feasts, and one for *exercises* such as recollection days, preparation for death, exercises on the second method of prayer, etc.

I do not suppose that one would write a meditation straight off into the book, but draft it first and make it, and then write it, modified or enriched with the result of that morning's experiment ; and of course, there might be many days that would give nothing for the book, for it would be only one's best meditations—and I think it would be an advantage not to put two meditations on the same page—but if there were some lines left to leave them for further development of the subject, new lights or jewels to be set in later.

You see I write as one in the middle of an experiment, and that is true. I am doing it for myself, and have a certain amount of material ready. I am at present working at my introduction

and find it so interesting that it occurred to me to hand on the
happy thought to you, and if it is successful there—then to
other elect and enterprising souls—this time, at least, it is not
experimentum in corpore vili !

I wonder if it will appeal to the many or the few. In any
case I should like to give you the books. Mother B. will supply
them for me. What should you think of certain fat note-books
that exist at the shop and cost 1s. ? I should like that if I were
stationary, but being so often on the move I must have it in
smaller sections. At the beginning I suggest there should
be a picture, and if you like Mother B. will supply these too
for me—mine is a post-card of Mantegna's ' *Ecce Homo* ' which
is in the Louvre.

What do you think of the undertaking ? Happy the eyes
that may be invited (for of course one could not ask it) to see
round the precincts of a neighbour's Introduction, and the
hands allowed to gather an apricot off a neighbour's wall.
Perhaps this will be one of the delights of that diversion that
you have had this year on holidays, ' spiritual trios.' And
the green books of last Autumn have been an excellent remote
preparation, if you undertake this great work.

Perhaps some, who do not feel they could face the work of
writing their own meditations, could collect and compile from
their favourite authors what they have found most helpful,
and I am sure that in whatever way it is taken up you will adapt
and plan and improve on the method suggested so as to make
it really *your own* which is the chief point.

December 20th, 1912.—This letter was written ready for
Christmas before I went to Spain ! So now it only needs
finishing off with the wish that Christmas may be happy and
heavenly, and the holidays glow with the gifts of the inner life
that God will give to each one.

10th February, 1913.

. . . I am sending you by the young professed a few pictures
which some people may like for their meditation frontispiece,
they are the Purgative, Illuminative, and Unitive Way. I
shall be interested to hear who chooses them and *which*. (I tell
you, not them, so as not to interfere with their taste, that I
think the Illuminative Way quite inferior to the other two
which I like very much.) They need not be shy of choosing
the Unitive Way, it will not be taken as a label that they are
supposed to be advanced in it. . . . I shall enclose here, if
I have time to copy it, a contribution to your Lenten fare at
silent suppers ! Mother M. and those who remember him will
be interested to hear that I had a surprise visit from Monsieur
l'Abbé (now Monsignor) S., to whom we owe the expression

for accumulated disasters, *Ah ! si vous saviez la septième partie de mes épreuves !*

'Enclosed. *Savoury dishes for Lenten suppers !*

'1. What kind of souls require forcing, and what kind require pruning to make them give their best ? (I do not think it is a case of bridle and spur.) What circumstances are forcing, and what are pruning circumstances for the soul ?

'2. People of many kinds ask questions, but few and rare people listen to answers. Why ?

'3. What gives *balance* to our religious life ?

'4. Is it more helpful to speak of actions or of motives for actions ? '

February 14th, 1913.

. . . I must tell you now, as I promised, the impression that Abbot Marmion made on me. I was *immensely* struck by him, and have not met anyone so interesting for a long time. He seems to me exactly like what the early Irish abbots who founded St. Galls must have been—a great-hearted and great-souled monk. And a typical Benedictine Abbot, Irish Benedictine too, brimming over with wit and pathos. He preached a sermon of rare beauty, on Romans xii. 1, all scripture and the Fathers of the Church (the Latin rolled richly off his tongue), and so condensed that a word could hardly have been cut off without loss to the sense. If the taking down has been successful I shall send you a copy of the notes. . . . Our Chaplain was struck to the depths of his spirit by the Abbot's discourse. He is going to give a retreat to the monks of St. Joseph's next January and has promised to go and see Roscrea. . . .

Do ask the community some time whether they work their lives in crimson and gold or blue and silver, if they do not mind confiding their names to a list it would be most interesting to know !

Writing to another she said :

[It was] a real Benedictine sermon, large and spacious . . . one thing I liked was [the Abbot's] insistence that we should *love the world*, because God so loved the world ; we are to love the Father first, but after Him the world, and live intensely to God, and for God to the world, to give what we receive to it. . . .

Ixelles : February 27th, 1913.

. . . This will be crowded and badly written, such a long list of things before me to say to you. . . . To begin with thanks. I send so many and such grateful ones for all the letters, and for the lovely flowers and for the meditation books, so exactly what I wanted, and paged all ready. . . . I love

to hear the domestic details from the kitchen to the ends of the
house and garden.

Personally, it interests me more to hear of actions than of
motives—of course *ordinary actions* of every day that everyone
knows are not worth talking about, but actions in difficult
circumstances, in crisis, in moments of peril and emergency,
in carrying out plans, in laying out work, in all these sometimes small but often thrilling points of decision in our lives,
I think it is immensely instructive and interesting to know what
people *do* and *did* and *would do.*

Ixelles : March 11th, 1913.

I have only just this morning been able to formulate to
myself something of which we talked once in community, what
it is to be facetious and why it is so detestable. I think it is
a tone in the voice, and in the mind which says 'Your
difficulties are to me the easiest things in the world, merely
amusing. I have outlived your age, solved your problems,
outgrown your ideals, seen to the bottom of your illusions; it
is most curious and interesting to me to see you struggling
with them.' So—a boy of six to one of four takes a facetious
tone, a brother of sixteen to a sister of fourteen, the brother
who comes of age to the struggling boy of nineteen, and especially
the successful uncle to the shy nephew—dreadful ! . . . .

On March 31st Reverend Mother Stuart left for Rome, taking
a look, as she said, at Turin, Avigliana, and Rivoli on the
way. A week later, on April 8th, a child died at Roehampton ;
as soon as she heard of her illness she wrote :

. . . Indeed I do live with you, thinking of that precious
Mary who is costing so much. · I hope God will not give this
sorrow to her parents and my M., but if He does He will
give the grace to all to bear it, and Mary will go off with the
' brighter crown.'

> Of the hero who falls early in the strife,
> Not a leaf withered, not a flower fallen.

God will do the best, but one aches for everyone concerned.

A few days later, on hearing the news of the death, she
wrote again :

My poor dear X., I have had your letter this minute
and read it with tears, for it is all so beautiful, and they may
well say that Roehampton is ' heaven on earth ' to live and die
in; it is passing from the vestibule (as Father Purbrick called
it, *i.e.* the very vestibule of heaven) to the unveiled splendour

within. I can see it all, the before and the after, and you
will tell me exactly where she rests. R.I.P. And may Our
Lord be to you *lacrimarum gaudium*, your Paschal-tide joy,
only more heavenly, because God has accepted your pearl and
let you prepare her for Him.

Writing of it again, she said :

The only regret I have is that the children were not there.
To see and hear of such a death, and be in the presence of it,
would give them, as Sister Ashton Case's did, true thoughts
about our passing from this world to God. . . .

In Rome, Mother Stuart stayed at the Villa Lante, the house
of noviceship, and writing from there on April 8th she said :

The novices are not numerous—only fourteen, and three
postulants. But they make up by containing persons of interest. One of them has an uncle—her father's brother—
already Venerable ; he died a Capucin novice, aged twenty-one.
Another has been all over the world with a ' scientific caravan,'
of which her father was a member. The only place she missed
was Central Africa ! which was to have taken three years, so
she would not keep her vocation waiting. She has ridden on
horses, mules, elephants, camels, everything that can be
mounted, and has had from time to time, as she quaintly said,
des aventures macabres ! She is Costa Rican, the only one in
the Society, and she told me some things about the languages
spoken there, before which my mind stops.
Another has made special studies, chiefly in Hebrew and
Sanskrit. These languages appeared for the first time in my
experience at a reception in the noviceship on Sunday. There
were ten languages [represented] : Sanskrit, Hebrew, Greek,
Latin, Italian, German, French, Spanish, English, and
Russian. . . .

This cosmopolite composition of the noviceship was typical
of those of the Society of the Sacred Heart, and was a point
which appealed very strongly, for its formative influence, to
Mother Stuart. ' The mingling of nationalities, there have
been as many as twelve or more in one novitiate,' she wrote
in ' The Society of the Sacred Heart,' ' tends to bring out the
best in each, to make for mutual understanding, for seeing the
good in all, for tact, for a right reticence. . . .'

To THE ROEHAMPTON COMMUNITY,—
Villa Lante : April 29th, 1913.
. . . This is written by anticipation, that I may sit
under the plane tree with you, weather permitting, on the

holiday for my feast, and talk of various things which I have been keeping for this reunion.

Some of your papers on pruning and forcing reached me, and delighted me, there was so much thought in them and also careful expression. And a ' nice person ' also sent me a list of the community *colours* [referring to the question in her letter of February 14th quoted above]. I was astonished at their aptness (all except one or two about which I should have thought otherwise) and enjoyed them very much, they even gave me lights on new members of the community of whom I have little first-hand knowledge.

I am leaving Rome of course without seeing the Holy Father, but one's thankfulness that he is recovering makes up for everything else. I think that in England you had mostly the cautious notes of the *Osservatore*, which were, I believe, always nearest to the truth, but it said the minimum and was determined to be hopeful. It was quite true that the Holy Father fainted after the audience of the Bishops from Lombardy, he fell *in deliquio*—what an expressive word—he melted or *liquidified* (like David whose ' heart melted like wax ') with a temperature of 102°. No wonder there was consternation. After some days the three servants, who habitually wait upon him and had to go in and out in silence, were allowed to kneel round his bed and receive his blessing, and they too *liquidified*, but into tears, and only then the Holy Father knew how ill he had been, from their emotion ; and a few days afterwards his brother came and was admitted and hugged him and called him *Beppo mio* and wept over him, and the Holy Father wept too, and they were both comforted by the interview and the Holy Father was the better for it. Was there ever such a *human* and loving and beloved ' Christ upon earth ' ?

I only spent a day at Albano this time, but the *going there* was a great holiday, for an American ' child,' or rather *old* child, Lucy D., sister of a child at Roehampton, took us down by motor, and got a permit to go through the Aldobrandini property instead of by the high road, and this way goes by Tusculum and Cicero's villa ! ' Not at all, not at all,' would say any Jesuit commentator, ' Cicero's villa was on the site of our College on our property at Mondragone,' but in this case no one can tell, so I believe what I saw. This road is usually followed by riders on horses, and chiefly on donkeys, and occasionally by carts, but never, said the guide whom we picked up in the square at Frascati, by motor cars. However, the chauffeur had the courage to try, and made his car climb like a cat and turn like a snake, and moved the guide to admiration and awe. ' *Che macchina !* ' he exclaimed, ' *e che macchinista !* ' However, in the end, fortunately, we had to walk, and there was

Cicero's villa ! and if we had climbed the hill for five minutes there would have been the theatre ! However, 'the straightest and most obvious line of conduct' seemed the line of duty, and we followed it. But we saw the villa, the very tiles on which he had walked, the very mosaics against which his robes had rubbed as he passed by, a lovely site, looking across a wide valley at Rocca di Papa and Monte Cavo, and round it are grassy banks and slopes with wild thyme in flower, just as he must have seen it, and then one forgets wicked old Mommsen's spiteful view that he was nothing but a gossipy solicitor, and remembers only what he has been to all Europe through the centuries since then—and is still, although Mommsen has 'rediscovered' him with the evil eye. It was very silent and lovely in the solitude up there, and a nightingale sang in a low tree just over our heads, quite indifferent to us, and even to the smell of petrol, and only careful that his lady on her nest should be comforted by his best notes. I thought of contemplative souls set in the midst of distracting duties and wished them well ! I send you a wild anemone (*Anemone Pulsatilla*, I think) picked under this tree.

Cicero's villa speaks to one's *imagination*, but when I was at the Vatican I saw something that spoke to one's *soul* among the relics which are not often shown ; but the Augustinian domestic chaplain of the Vatican took us—where perhaps some of you have been, into a little sanctum beside the 'Matilda' oratory—there behind a curtain, which the obliging sacristan drew back with triumphant jerk, was the *burnt head* of St. Lawrence ! wonderful to see, one would say preserved by fire with the skin and flesh on it, the lip caught up with an expression of anguish that made one feel that it had come from a real and not a story-book martyrdom. And what is it to him now, 'of whom the world was not worthy,' it was good for a meditation, though perhaps the cautious Bollandists would say, 'Be careful, it is possibly, probably, almost certainly not the head of St. Lawrence, one should bear in mind, etc., etc.' No one of course can tell, but I prefer to think it was the head of St. Lawrence.

The Chaplain of the Swiss Guards came to see me at the Trinità, Monsignor C., the third of a very united trio ; Mgr. Zorn von Bulach, who also came as far as Rome, but was not fit to go on to Malta, and the unforgettable Mgr. de Croy. He lives at an hour's distance from us in Belgium, but I have to come to Rome to see him. Anyhow, the chaplain of the Swiss Guards told me his own story, and the dream of his life shown to him and withdrawn in a moment ! As a young priest he served at Whitechapel, and simply loved it, and was absorbed in his work, and one day Cardinal Vaughan sent for him and said :

' I was going to-day to name you German confessor at the Cathedral, and the Secretary of State writes that he wants you back at once in Rome as Chaplain to the Swiss Guards.' To slave in London had been his dream, and behold the awakening !

San Remo : May 6th, 1913.

. . . One thing about this book [' The Education of Catholic Girls '], the most impressive testimonial that it has received : Bishop Donelly, auxiliary of Dublin, came to see me in Rome, and told me that he takes it about with him to prepare sermons and addresses for Confirmation ! I felt very much honoured . . .

To go back to Rome, I am laughing at myself now for thinking that it would be a time of leisure, and for all the things I took with me to do : germs of circular letters to develop, the introduction of my meditation book to write, Italian grammar for leisure moments. I saw visions of quiet mornings, even if the afternoons were full. A vain illusion, even correspondence fell into arrears.

I counted, on the last afternoon, as a curiosity, that I was called fourteen times to the parlour, the climax being at seven P.M. when, coming out from conference, I was told that two Bishops were waiting. . . . At the same time the Trinità has its beautiful moments of solitude, in the afternoon when one is in the church . . . there are times when one cannot hear a sound, and the world seems very remote indeed.

A nice vision appeared in the parlour one day, two young English Benedictine monks from San Anselmo, Brother Cuthbert X. and another, immense boys with innocent faces, *non Angli sed Angeli*, looking real monks. I thought of the ' elegance ' of Brother Cuthbert's ' style ' in boxing of old days, and all that was hidden behind his angelic smile ; truly a religious vocation taming all that strength and lifting those young lives so high, is a thing of beauty and wonder. . . .

Ixelles : May 15th, 1913.

. . . Think of this day two years ago and of to-morrow two years ago when you called me to the telephone during examen to read that telegram [telling of Reverend Mother Digby's stroke]. I can hear the sound of your voice still, dried up with anguish. How one remembers every moment of those days. ' In the sight of the unwise they seemed to die, but they are at peace ' ; perhaps you will sing that on the 21st. . . .

A few days later, on May 24, a letter from Mother Stuart announced that she would pay a ' flying visit to Roehampton ' before setting out for Australia. June 3 was the day named for this happy and wholly unexpected meeting, of which she

speaks in the following letter, written to the community at
Roehampton after her return to the Mother House.

Ixelles : 22nd June, 1913.

. . . Yesterday evening when I was back at the Mother
House and remembered that it was just a month's mind of the
first idea of that journey to England it seemed to me that it
was a month of months for all that God had given us in
it, and yet it was all like one long June day—a midsummer
day that has no night and a foreshadowing on earth of a great
Dies Domini that will have no night for ever. There are two
kinds of ' days which the Lord hath made '; days such as
May 21, 1911, and days such as June 3, 1913, both days that
never could be in any other state of existence than this border-
land of ours, the home where joys and sorrows live together as
brothers and sisters in contrasts and changes and paradoxes
so unaccountable now, and so wonderfully precious for ever
and ever, we would not be without one of them. There are
two kinds of tears also, one kind for each of those days, and both
precious before God and also to us. Some people would say
I was writing nonsense, but you will all understand it and
agree with me that what remains of it is inexpressible thankfulness, and the feeling that God could not have done better
for us and that nothing was wanting. A very nice person at
Roehampton wrote to me just before I came over, and the
remark struck me very much, that ' there comes a time when
the fact that a thing is fleeting does not detract from its value.
It is a quite true remark, but there must ' come a time ' for this,
it is not a beginner's remark. It was a joy to find you all so
grown—like the trees, and so intensely alive—(no one too fat
except Llewellyn [1]—all in perfect condition !) It was quite
ideal that nothing should have stopped where I left it, but all
have gone on to something better. I could go on a long time
talking of this and other things, but these things, too, must
be fleeting without detracting from their value ! I had plenty
of time to think them all over, on a calm sea and a too calm
Scheldt with so low a tide that we did not get into Antwerp
until a quarter to ten. They had prepared the laying of the
foundation stone for the following day, so we laid it in an
interval between two showers. There was no Bishop, but a
Canon delegated by the Cardinal. It was all very nice, and I
have informally and hopefully accepted an invitation for the
Consecration on the Feast of the Sacred Heart next year, so
the Architect will be racing me with the cock on his beloved
petit clocher while I am going round the world. It seems to
me that I am more likely to be back than he is to be ready.

[1] A pony.

Now good-bye, and let us live in grateful remembrance and full of hope that even the best things that are behind us have no proportion with what is still before us, since God will always be better to us than He has been yet, and in all the vicissitudes of life we shall always know Him better and have to lean more upon Him. I am with all the love you know, your Mother in C. J. M.

Ixelles : June 23rd, 1913.

. . . I meant to come back with the community on the subject of the introduction to their meditation books. I am inclined to think (and the best beginnings I have seen bear me out in this) that the introduction would be best made from the minds of the great masters of prayer and of the spiritual life, arranged in such order as would suit our personal tastes and needs. Some which I read were the expression of their personal experiences, and read like a letter which they might have written to me. I do not think that in the long run this would be helpful, because if one is going on, it is always to outgrow one's past experience, and that is why so many cannot bear (and rightly) to read again what they have written themselves in the past, because even in a short time they have outgrown it. It is therefore an encouraging sign rather than otherwise. For the introduction it is well to have something that will remain true. I am sure they will agree. We should have talked of this again and many other things if there had been time. God bless you *all*.

P.S.—Please ask the community to draw up a list (drawn up and agreed to by the majority) and send it to me, of those minds in which light dominated over heat, and those in which heat dominated over light. Saints or geniuses or merely human beings worth talking about, and do not let anyone say that the subject divides on the lines of St. Peter and St. John, for this controversy ought never to be opened again ! Where would Shakespeare be, and Napoleon and Dr. Arnold of Rugby, and St. John Chrysostom and St. Ignatius ?

The beginning of July was spent in visiting Flône, Strée, and Bois l'Evêque, and on the 14th she returned to Ixelles for three months. On August 3 a great sorrow befell the Mother House in the sudden death of one of the Assistants General, Reverend Mother de Pichon. Mother Stuart wrote : ' Her example was for all of us a perfect model of holiness. God grant we may inherit her spirit, for it was of rare religious perfection in its utter loyalty, obedience, and submission . . . and the perfection of charity which made intercourse with her full of sweetness and harmony.'

To be at home meant no diminution, but only a change
of work. ' Alas, my dear child ! ' she wrote on September 12th,
' I know I am dreadfully in arrears in thanking X. and you,
her faithful commissioner, and my unwearying agent, for
all I have received. But my life has overflowed its banks
these last days, with comers and goers and official visits, and
the souls of saintly maidens in retreat, swarms and swarms,
so you must make allowances ! ' And again : ' You can imagine
what these last days are like, with letters pouring in for a " last
word," and people coming for the same, as if I were going to
the red planet Mars.'

A few days later she wrote to the community at Roehampton.
The school had just reopened.

Maison Mère : September 28th, 1913.

. . . The *Dimbula* has left the harbour and my boat is
ready for its cruise of nearly the same length, so between the
two sailings I must write you one word to wish you a happy
passage, and I am sure that God's blessing will be upon the
year, all the more that its beginnings had something of the unexpected about them, and that there are gaps in the community
circle that leave great aches.

These are two happy expressions that I have preserved
for you, ' our times call for workmen that are valiant, humble
of heart, and patient in work,' and even our small and hidden
sphere of work calls out for these apostolic virtues ; courage
to keep up against the daily pressure within and without, to
rise above emergencies, and to keep each other's courage up,
the most apostolic duty of all ; humility of heart to make us
magnanimous and impersonal ; I am more and more struck
by the beauty and efficacious influence of impersonality as an
apostolic virtue : and patience in work, this is so specially
wanted in our work which is nearly all a work of preparation
that does not show its results. These are the apostolic virtues
that I wish you for this year, but most of all I wish the
' apostles ' themselves growth in religious virtues and perfect
union with God. It looks very daring to write the word
' apostles,' but since Leo XIII called us by that magnificent
name, there is no reason why we should not lift ourselves up
by the thought of it to become more and more worthy of
bearing it.

The other happy expression I hoarded up for you was an
admonition of Blessed Angela of Foligno to her ' sons ' in Christ.
I gather that these were stirring personalities of the Franciscan
Order, tertiaries at least, perhaps real Friars. She tells them
to be ' shining examples of splendid gentleness ' ; is not that very
fine ? Such a light on the splendour of community life.

Nice people write as though I were certain to come by Roehampton on the way back from round the world. It is not so certain as all that. They must please arrange it with our dearest Mother General in the chapel of the Sacred Heart, that as she gave us (so evidently) the surprise visit of June this year, she may dispose of all things to make right and possible a very flying visit in July 1914. May God be with everyone, at all times and in every place where we are scattered, but still more than ever one in C. J. M.

The blessing of the Holy Father had been solicited for the coming journey. In a paper, written by his own hand and dated June 8, 1913, he said :

We gladly bestow the Apostolic blessing on our beloved daughter the Mother General of the Society of the Sacred Heart, and We pray that the Archangel Raphael may be with her in her journeys. She will carry Our blessing to all the Religious she visits, teaching them to recognise the hand of Providence in all the vicissitudes of life, whether joyous or sorrowful, and to repeat at all times *Dominus est.*

PIUS PP. X.

The following beautiful appreciation of Mother Stuart, from the pen of Père Charles, S.J., picturing her as she was when setting out on her last journey, finds its fitting place here :

Vers la fin du mois de Septembre 1913, j'ai donné la retraite à la communauté du Sacré Cœur à Ixelles. La Révérende Mère Stuart, qui s'apprêtait à ' faire son tour du monde,' comme elle disait, est venue me voir plusieurs fois et m'a parlé, avec beaucoup de confiance et d'abandon, de ses principes et de ses attraits spirituels.

Je me borne à consigner ici le souvenir très net que j'ai conservé de ces entretiens.

S'il est vrai de dire que tout le travail de la perfection consiste à revenir, par le moyen de la grâce, à l'état de bienheureuse liberté qui précéda la chute originelle, on peut affirmer que la Mother Stuart était entrée dans la perfection. A force de docilité déférente vis-à-vis de l'action divine ; à force de pureté d'intention et de parfaite candeur de désirs, elle en était arrivée à se mouvoir en Dieu aussi aisément que si elle n'avait jamais pu faire autre chose. Comme dans les œuvres des véritables artistes, la trace de l'effort pénible semblait avoir disparu de sa vertu : il n'en restait que le résultat visible et harmonieux d'une perfection devenue ' naturelle.'

J'ai parlé de ' ses attraits spirituels.' Le mot est inexact.

. Au fond elle n'avait qu'un attrait, et n'aimait pas à se perdre dans la multiplicité et dans les complications. Très proche du Principe, elle voyait tout de Son point de vue, et gardait donc une estime souveraine, un respect total et filial pour tous les dons et pour toutes les œuvres de Dieu. Elle avait une capacité d'admiration—que la prière et le contact avec Dieu grandissait chaque jour—mais c'était une admiration sans étonnement, sans la surprise naïve de ceux qui ne ' connaissent pas la richesse divine.' Aussi cette admiration ravie pour tout ce que Dieu aime et opère lui laissait l'âme très libre. C'était une source de joie sans bouillonnement et sans écume, toute de limpidité et de calme.

Possédant Dieu, elle se sentait chez elle dans toute œuvre de Dieu. Elle m'a dit en souriant que faire son tour du monde ne lui donnait pas l'impression d'un déplacement. Elle faisait aussi, très volontiers, crédit à la Providence divine. Sa patience était le résultat immédiat, le fruit spontané de cette conviction surnaturelle que nous n'avons pas à précéder Dieu, mais à Le suivre. Je n'ai pas connu d'âme plus sereine dans son abandon.

Elle avait même renoncé—sans effort—à porter ce que j'appellerais la toilette de ses vertus. Incapable de se préoccuper de paraître ; elle ne songeait qu'à être. Ses grandes qualités portaient l'uniforme. Sa seule élégance surnaturelle était l'élégance native de ceux qui n'en cherchent point.

D'après ce qu'elle m'a dit, j'ai compris que, pendant ses premières années de vie religieuse, elle avait donné dans un ascéticisme violent, et qu'elle avait—comme beaucoup—cherché Dieu dans les décombres. Une très haute idée de renoncement lui avait vite fait comprendre que la forme parfaite de la vertu c'est de ' recevoir Dieu,' et que la béatitude des vrais pauvres est de tout posséder. Le cœur et l'esprit libres, calmes, doux ; sûre des promesses du temps et de l'éternité, elle servait fidèlement ayant banni tout sentiment d'esclave.

Elle croyait à l'amour de Dieu, et s'y reposait, et là encore, avec une simplicité si franche qu'on la sentait ' de la famille divine.' Vivant avec son Maître, elle ne pensait pas qu'il fût nécessaire, pour Lui plaire, de fermer les yeux devant les merveilles qu'Il opère ; elle savait que la Beauté est céleste comme le Vrai, et que ces deux mots signifient Dieu seul. Aussi son âme était-elle infiniment accueillante, et son horizon large comme l'Esprit divin. Elle n'a jamais dit ' non ' qu'au mal ; et elle n'appelait mal que la destruction de l'œuvre éternelle. Si je devais résumer en une formule ses pensées les plus intimes, je crois que je choisirais l'affirmation vigoureuse et totale de St. Paul : *Omnia vestra sunt, vos autem Christi.* Puisque vous êtes au Christ, toutes choses vous appartiennent. N'est-ce pas le royaume du ciel ?

CHAPTER XXV

JOURNEY ROUND THE WORLD, 1913–1914

Egypt, Australia, New Zealand

' You will find him perfect in sweetness and patience, in greatness of soul and consideration for all. No one will complain of having him for a neighbour, no one will ever shrink from him as a *foreigner*, but everyone will treat him as a fellow countryman, as a brother and a friend. For he carries the whole human race in his heart and loves all men with the love of perfect charity.'—*St. Hugh of Lincoln.* H. Thurston, S.J.

THE journey of 1913–1914 was, some have said, the crowning work of Mother Stuart's life. She seems to have looked on it in this light herself. ' What a solemn moment ! ' she said, as she stepped on board the *Orsova* at Port Said.

When it was all over, and she was about to leave New York, one of those who could measure something of its effects wrote :

The mere sight of her simple and lovely holiness has done more to raise and encourage souls spiritually than any other influence that has come into their lives. This impression has been made, not only on Religious who saw her within the family circle, but on people of the world as well, whom she met perhaps once for a few moments, and with whom she hardly had time, it would have seemed, to do more than exchange greetings. The universal approval and even affection shown to her, an English woman, wherever she went is more remarkable as we live so often among those who though friendly are critical, especially when a ' foreigner ' is concerned

This same verdict was given by all the houses which she visited. Each community and each individual seems to have gathered a like impression of sweet charity and of deep personal understanding, which ripened into friendship at the first meeting. This feeling of having a personal friend seems to have taken hold even of people who never met her, but whose hearts were warmed by her words and actions, written or repeated to them by others. ' Those who saw her can never forget what they have seen,' continues the writer quoted above. ' If this is the grace she left behind her, then it is not difficult to see how this journey round the world was a fitting climax to her apostolic activity. "A long time fulfilled in a short space." She gave herself utterly to and for us, but nothing else, no written word, could have had the same spiritual results as this personal intercourse ; and those who realise something of its effects can scarcely dare regret that it was so that *tradidit seipsam.*'

From the day of her election as Superior General Mother Stuart had been entreated to visit the houses of the Order in the Australian Vicariate. No Superior General had as yet seen them, nor had they received any ' visitor ' from the Mother House.

Far away as they were, the life of these houses was so bound up with that of the English Vicariate, that Mother Digby had felt she knew them as her own. Their founders had nearly all gone out from Roehampton, and the postulants from the new country had all returned there for their noviceship. These facts gave a special colour to the visit of Mother Stuart. Of the one hundred and twelve choir Religious in the vicariate she knew at least ninety personally. All the younger generations had been her novices, and the older, her companions in the first days of her religious life. She was going to her own. This in part explains the enthusiasm with which she was welcomed everywhere. An enthusiasm which had nothing of officialdom or formality in it. The nuns who knew her inspired the children and even their parents and friends with their own joy, and it seemed as if no one could do enough to interest and please her.

On October 4, 1913, she left Ixelles *en route* for Trieste, where she was to embark for Alexandria on the 17th. On the way she spent a few days at Kientzheim, and thence went on to Riedenburg by motor. The promise of thus shortening the journey—unfortunately not fulfilled—attracted her as much as the beauty of the way. Leaving Kientzheim in the early morning, she reached Bregenz late that evening. The strain of some of the mountain roads had been too much for the motor. But the periods of repair gave the travellers the pleasure of walking, as one wrote, ' just in the loveliest parts of the Black Forest . . . where, though it was late in the year, wild flowers were still abundant.'

Venice was next visited and Lovrana. This was the only

house in Europe which she did not know. Founded in the
previous April on a lovely site on the Adriatic, with Fiume to
the north-east, and the coastline and mountains of Dalmatia
appearing on the horizon, it was destined to be short-lived, as
the events of 1914 necessitated its abandonment. The following
letters speak of this part of her journey :

Riedenburg (begun October 10th, 1913).

. . . I know that all ' inquiring friends ' have news through
you, so I am going to begin the story of my wanderings, without
regard to what my two companions or Mother C. may write.

I was glad when the setting out from the Mother House was
finished . . . and was more than thankful that God had called
away dear Reverend Mother de Pichon before. Now I hope
Reverend Mother Borget is at Strée or Flône, and that will
make a change in the current of her thoughts.

Kientzheim was looking lovely in a wistful October mood,
with the last flowers of its myrtles and pomegranates, and the
last winged insects taking the last joy of their lives in warm still
air ; and the beautiful groups of trees, partly stripped and partly
golden, reminded one of All Saints at Roehampton. I had two
days there, one for the community and one for the Bishop of
Erythrae (Auxiliary Bishop of Strassburg).

Mother W.'s brother sent us his motor from Kientzheim
to Riedenburg . . . he sent his young nephew with the chauffeur,
and a hamper of provisions that would have lasted us as far as
Rome *easily*. .

The Black Forest was in great beauty. I had never been
through it except by night, when one smells but does not see.
And travelling by motor, there are not the envious tunnels to
cover up the views, and besides on one excuse or another, when
the motor had to stop for a repair, for petrol and for the chauffeur's
dinner, we were able to get out and walk in all that beauty, and
among the late gentians and wild thyme and other things that
hold on until October. We were about five hours longer than we
were supposed to be on account of the state of the roads ; though
through the Black Forest they are beautifully made, and I don't
know what more any chauffeur could wish ; after the roads
about Saragossa, these seem like polished marble galleries.

I have told Reverend Mother how we passed through
Donaueschingen, and how I thought of Sister Beha in her native
place, and how, though we could not see the source of the Danube,
yet we saw the Danube at its source, a few yards below ; the
source must be almost under the church. We did not see snow
until we got to Lake Constance. It is, as Mother de S. says,
all the winter we shall have until Japan. . . .

This is continued at Venice. The journey from Bregenz was

beautiful over the Arlberg and Brenner passes; they told us it was the way that both Saint Francis Xavier and Saint Stanislaus had gone to Venice and Rome, one from Paris, the other in his flight from Vienna. It gave me devotion to think of it, and of what must have been in their minds and their glorious souls as they looked at those mountains. It made me ashamed, too, to think of their hardships on foot and our well-appointed second-class compartment. There was no night nor day train to go straight through, so, as we had to stop the night somewhere, I said I would stop at Trent—another impossible dream of my life realised ! We chose an hotel close to the church of the Council, Sta. Maria Maggiore, and went in a clear darkness at five-fifteen to the first Mass there. It is quite a small church, with no aisles and little character, but what memories ! You can imagine what devotion it gave me to recite that paragraph on the Blessed Eucharist, from the Creed of Pope Pius IV, within the very walls in which it was formulated. One could have stayed for hours, but we had to make an early start. (We had rooms and food for seven francs, three of us, and breakfast for three for eighty-four centimes, which shows you how quietly Trent lies off the beaten track of travellers.) There are statues of Fathers Laynez and Salmeron, one on each side of the church door. Many of the houses look as if they might have existed in their time, and one as if it might have been a hospital in those days. Opposite to our hotel was an old *palazzo* with beautifully carved wood doors; in every alternate panel was Matilda of Tuscany wonderfully carved, with a face the same at different ages, holding up a mitre high above her head. There seemed to be no such thing as a carriage in Trent, or cab, or fly, or even a cart, so we went on foot from and to the station, following our bags on a hand-cart: thus we saw Matilda. We asked to whom the *palazzo* belonged, and were told *a un principe*, but his name was not known, and he lived in Vienna, so no one cared about him. The rest of the journey was not remarkable after we got down to the plain. We saw a Zeppelin airship floating over Verona, but nothing else of note. To-day I spent half a day at Padua, and saw among the old living relics there a Mother of seventy-six who gets up every day at four-thirty, and makes the visit of the meditation ! She is very deaf . . . she has just finished a piece of lace-work containing one thousand eight hundred stars of lace joined together ; each took her one and a half hours—imagine the total. It is for a rochet, and at Padua a rochet has two laces, one above the other. She says she cannot imagine anyone happier than herself ; she cannot hear a word, cannot understand a word of Italian, but loves everyone, thinks them all saints, much too good to her, is edified at everything she sees. What a blessing for old age to have such a nice mind and such clever fingers.

I must end ; these are only traveller's tales for everyone, and one word of thanks for your letter of the 10th. . . .

Trieste : 17th October, 1913.

. . . A little word before leaving Europe : we go on board at twelve, it is now eight. We had to come up yesterday from Lovrana as no morning train would have brought us up in time. Lovrana is certainly beautiful, on a landlocked bay, with its back to Italy and its face to the East. The full moon gave us a beautiful outdoor evening recreation, and afterwards I watched its broad track on the water, and three fishing boats that sailed slowly across it—such a picture. One could open the window wide all night, for we are so high that no one could see in. We climbed the limestone terraces above the house in the afternoon, looking at Fiume and other white places all round the coast. This morning we heard five Masses in the church close by here, in compensation for those we shall miss between this and Alexandria. There were quantities of Communions—such a study of little boys ! We had been to Communion at five-thirty, so we could pay attention to their devotions. It was a whole college of creatures from ten to twelve, real sons of the Kingdom—not in any drilled order, but going up each as he chose in his fine independence, and coming back rapt and wondering ; the kindest of priests wandered about without fussing them, but whispering here and there *willst du beichten*, and they said ' yes ' or ' no ' quite freely as they chose. Father Roche would have loved it.

Now good-bye, this is ' the day that the Lord hath made ' the real beginning of the long absence. God will guard us all on both sides of the world ! and bring us all together again on the other day which He has made, and of which He knows the date.

The days on sea were not to be wasted. Before she left Brussels a friend had asked Mother Stuart to write a book on ' The Society of the Sacred Heart.' It was destined to be one of a series treating of the spirit and work of Religious Orders of men and women, and was to form part of a new Catholic Library. To find time for such a work seemed, even to Mother Stuart, to be beyond the limits of possibility, and she had at first hesitated to accept. She promised, however, to do what she could in the long sea voyages now before her. She had planned to give her days to reading ' books I could never hope to read at home,' calling for leisure for thought, and for this end she had chosen a small library and arranged to have it refilled or ex-changed at the end of each journey. But this occupation had now to be given up, and her days were passed as ever in strenuous work. She began at once, and planned what she afterwards called ' my little book of the sea ' on the Adriatic. It was destined not for the Catholic Library, which was brought to a sudden end in the following year by the dispersion of writers and editors, but to be her last gift to her own Order. The first copies were printed the day after her death.

On October 20 she reached Alexandria, and the next fortnight was spent between the houses at Ramleh, Cairo, and Heliopolis.

The fascination of the East appealed to her strongly, and she was delighted with all her surroundings. ' I loved Egypt and go back to it in thought with joy,' she wrote a few months later. And again : ' The remembrance of Egypt is like a gorgeous pageant in my memory, full of consolation on the spiritual side, and a pageant of ages in the historical side of one's mind. I feel that I have seen Moses and Joseph and Jacob and almost Pharaoh and the Holy Family and Origen and Athanasius and the monks of the Lybian and Nitrian desert. I cannot stop when I begin to reminisce.'

Cairo : 25th October, 1913.

. . . I shall only be able to write a little to-day, so I will tell you about the greatest personage I have seen—the Greek Patriarch—his full title is Cyril VIII, Patriarch of Antioch, Jerusalem, Alexandria and all the East.

They wrote to him to tell him that I was coming, and His Beatitude sent word that he would receive me the next morning at ten. It was obviously a duty to go, as they said he never went out. He was staying with his Bishop Auxiliary, who has charge of Alexandria, but the Patriarch is the Ordinary in all these Sees. He is a beautiful sight to see, a very Syrian face with a long white beard, grave, serene and kind to look at— dressed in red and wearing most glorious jewels in his cross. He was very kind and interested in all things. We had to drink tiny cups of Turkish coffee with him, it is against etiquette to go until this ceremony has taken place. The Bishop Auxiliary was there too, and took us afterwards to see the private chapel and the great date-palms in the garden, in all their beauty, for, the dates are not yet gathered and are most beautiful in colour, deep gold, pale gold and coppery brown. As we went out the Bishop whispered that His Beatitude would return the visit in the afternoon ! . . . It makes quite an impression when a noise-less portress comes in and says ' His Beatitude.' It makes it all feel so old and venerable, as if he might just have returned from one of the early Councils, and have come to tell us that the heresy was crushed. He was wrapped over the red in a great black cloak and veil, and the Auxiliary and chaplain likewise.

All very kind and charming, a mace bearer went before him,
but it was most curious to see this majesty drive off in a little
open victoria like a lady's, with a pretty pair of little Arabs,
perhaps fifteen hands high ! . . .

Heliopolis : October 27th.

. . . Now to come to news of the journey. I have just come
from the last wonder, receiving Holy Communion under both
kinds at the Greek Mass. The Holy Father has allowed this
within the last few months, one of his own wonderful *motu
proprio* actions, which have cut so many knots and silenced so
many dissensions. A dear old Greek Archimandrite came last
night to prepare everything, and laid out his lovely vestments ;
the chasuble was like a small cope, without lining and therefore
very graceful, closed in front which must have been very embarrassing to the hands. I wish I could tell you the little I can tell
after hearing it once, of the beautiful ceremonial and prayers.
He had a cantor who sang without ceasing endless *Kyrie Eleison*
and *Alleluia* and other responses, with the strangest intervals,
and notes so low that I did not know how voice could utter or
ear hear them. He prepared the particles for Communion
before the Mass, cutting them from a leavened loaf ; mine was
cut in honour of Our Lady, Mother de S.'s was cut in honour
of Jesse and David and the Three Holy Children in the furnace
and others, I think Mother X.'s was in honour of St. John
Chrysostom, etc. For Communion he put them all in the chalice
in the Precious Blood, and then gave Communion with a spoon,
and said aloud ' the slave of God . . .' (naming if he knew their
name), to me he said ' the slave of God Joanna receives the Holy
and Precious Body and Blood of Christ our God for the remission
of sins and life everlasting.' As Mother de S. said, it was like
a new First Communion ! a wonderful joy. At Cairo our first
Mass every day is said by a Maronite, the Ordinary of the Mass
is in Syro-Chaldaic, the Proper in Arabic. There are five solemn
incensings ; in the first before Mass begins, he holds the chalice
reversed over the thurible and fills it with smoke, then covers it,
and when he uncovers it again the incense goes up in a cloud.
At the end of all things after the Mass he kisses the altar saying
' Abide in peace, O holy altar, and I shall return to thee in peace,'
but after a few other words he adds : ' And yet I know not
whether I shall ever return to offer sacrifice again upon thee.'
It is very touching indeed. To-morrow we shall have a Coptic
Mass, but the priest will give us Communion out of the tabernacle,
and not consecrate for us. The Greek children at Cairo go to
Communion twice a week with their own rite. The Archimandrite brings the particles in a chalice in the Precious Blood,
and gives them Communion when the Imperial Romans have
passed. The other days they go according to the Latin Rite.

This Heliopolis is a marvellous place, but not at all attractive in itself. It is like a mirage city risen out of the sand, and I wonder whether it is destined in part to return sand to sand as 'dust to dust.' They make bricks of the sand by hydraulic pressure. There came one of their very rare cyclones with rain some time ago and six houses collapsed, smart new houses; nothing is more than eight years old in Heliopolis. It was literally the Gospel story of the house built on sand. The rain descended and floods came and winds blew and it beat upon the house and it fell. . . . I do not think we shall come down, because we laid our foundations in concrete, and so built our house upon a rock. We are just on the racecourse, and beautiful horses are galloping there at exercise in the early morning. Sometimes there are camel and dromedary races. I hope to see a camel gallop before I go ! The children are interesting, and very fond of the house already. . . . We have five Catholic Rites in the school, three Orthodox Rites, Mussulman, and Jews ! and one Protestant. Now I must say good-bye for to-day and write to the dear Cardinal Protector who is anxious to have news of the Egyptian houses. The desert is fascinating.

Cairo : All Saints Day, 1913.

Yesterday we had a beautiful High Mass of the Greek-Melchite Rite. Imagine the charity and imagine the pious latitude of the rubrics. The Archbishop Auxiliary whom I had seen at Alexandria came up to sing it himself, and, for my devotion, sang it in Greek, as they do at Constantinople, whereas here they sing it in Arabic. Of course the Proper was in Arabic. It was very wonderful, there were two con-celebrants, who consecrated with the Archbishop and two other assistant priests. The Archbishop's mitre is like the Russian Imperial crown; there were five boy servers in gold and white tunics, almost like dalmatics, with crossed stoles, slim dark creatures such as might have served St. John Chrysostom whose Liturgy was used, and a choir of six boys with a cantor whose bass voice was magnificent; none of them had a note or a book before them, but they sang away by heart the beautiful responses and antiphons as if they were doing it every day. A personage of about thirteen read the Epistle, his joy extended almost palpably round him in waves, his little brother aged four was baptised here by the Archimandrite last week, another *festa* prepared for me ! And the two sisters were godmothers. They were also only lately baptised. . . . they are in the school. I don't know when I have had anything so beautiful as that Greek Mass. The Baptism was beautiful too. The catechumen arrived barefoot in a nightgown, conducted by his mother ; a round bath was prepared, draped in white and wreathed in oleander flowers like a pool of Jordan.

He went through the unction with great steadiness, then the
water in the bath was solemnly blessed with the oil of cate-
chumens only, and a short prayer.   After his profession of faith,
made for him by a priest, his mother lifted him into the bath,
he curled up his toes with a little apprehension, but stood it like
a man, he stood upright in the bath, and three great bowlfuls
of water were poured over his head and whole person—'George,
servant of God, I baptise thee, etc.'   He never winced, but his
anxious mother came with a large dry sheet and snatched him
up and was carrying him off, when the Archimandrite called out
for him to be brought back and he was confirmed while still
dripping !   Then she was allowed to have him, and when he
came back white-robed and radiant, the Archimandrite kissed
him on the forehead and formed a procession with lighted candles,
of the servant of God and his sisters !   They went three times
round the table (it was in a class room) to express the joy of the
newly baptised, the Archimandrite following and the school and
community looking on. . . .

4th.   This has been laid aside for two days and must be
finished off quickly.   We have just had a telegram from Watson
Bey that we need not sleep at Port Said but can leave here
to-morrow (5th) at eleven A.M., and join the *Orsova* at four.
That closes a very pleasant stage of the journey, about which I
have a great deal more to say but it must wait. . . .

Cairo : November 4th, 1913.

. . . To-day would have been our dearest Mother Digby's
golden jubilee, if God had not taken her to where all these things
are uncounted though not forgotten, in the ' day that has no
evening.'   And this evening you will begin the novena to St.
Stanislaus.   I make it with you from far off, and thinking this
morning what I should ask St. Stanislaus for his Sisters, I resolved
to ask for the pilgrim spirit in which he went on foot from Vienna
to Rome, so intent on the end that no difficulty could stop him,
with joy in his spirit that made impossible things possible, and
that single-heartedness which set him so steadfastly in the way
of perfection, that the work was begun and carried through and
ended in the time that it takes many of us to look about and
get our bearings in the religious life.   We shall be satisfied with
a slower maturity for ours, so long as they manage to get there,
and so long as they walk their pilgrim way without stopping or
looking back, and without letting good or evil delay them on
the way.   I see so well how a little thing, in the beginning, which
is not wholly given to God, cripples the soul as life goes on, and
makes its step less free. . . . God be with you. . . . we start
to-morrow for the first long journey.

On the same day she wrote to another :

One line before I join the *Orsova* at Port Said to-morrow.
There is a Bishop on board, Bishop Grimes of Christchurch, so
good and so friendly. It was for the sake of his Mass that I
chose his steamer.

You wondered what books I have. I have taken the minimum of luggage, only a small Willesden canvas bag for each of
us, and a hand-bag, and mine is mostly full of books, and I have
ordered a fresh relay from England to meet me at Sydney.
I have Saintsbury's ' History of English Prose Rhythm,' Morley's
' Life of Gladstone,' both books which will take a little time;
Tacitus, Cicero and Virgil, some German classics which I want
to read again; some of St. Augustine; Druzbicki's 'Tribunal of
Conscience ' (probably the seventh reading of it)—I forget the
rest. They are now all packed up for to-morrow.

Egypt is full of dreams, mysteries, memories. The desert is
a joy, so is all that is old. It makes me hot and cold with shame
to think how Europeans dress (men and women) ; so vulgar and
graceless are our best costumes of the European mould.

An old Aunt of mine who died last year, said to a friend :
' My dear, I have seen women dressed in various ways, but the
best dressed women I have ever seen are Janet's nuns ! ! '

From Cairo Mother Stuart addressed her last circular letter
to the Society. It was dated the Feast of All Saints, but destined
to be her New Year's greeting for 1914. ' May the year which
is about to open,' she wrote, ' be for each member of the Society
the best of her religious life, by the completeness of the gift of
all her faculties to the service of God, and by her correspondence
to the abundant graces which He gives.' She then recalled the
life and death of Reverend Mother de Pichon ' a perfect model
for youth, middle life and old age.' Developing this thought she
dwelt on the dangers, difficulties and hopes of each period. For
youth she signalised the chief danger as that of want of personal
formation.

Overflowing with good will, devotedness, activity, we let
ourselves too often be carried by the current. . . . We do not
think, learn, ripen, take responsibility to heart, and remaining
children we reach the ' high seas ' of mature life without sufficient
preparation for its more difficult navigation. . . . In the second
period the principles and virtues which ought to have been
acquired are put to the test. . . it is *in middle age that the interest
of a life attains its highest point.* The opposing forces, long prepared, are brought face to face in a decisive struggle . . . and
the result establishes our life in holiness or in mediocrity. . . .
When this last triumphs the cause has generally been discourage-

ment, which lowers the ideal, and makes one ' lose the faith '
of religious life . . . then follows sadness, bitterness, inaction.
. . . Yet this is a time of great power of good, of magnificent
second conversions.   It is the age of great awakenings, of new
beginnings, strong in their foundation on truth, humility and self-
knowledge, of sanctity hastened by the thought that time is
passing.   It is the time when courage is drawn from the simple
thought of God . . . and not from the eagerness of our own good
will. . . .   Finally it is the time when we learn that questionings
and arguments must be dropped in which ' it has not pleased
God to save His people.'

Many years before speaking on this subject Mother Stuart
had written :

Why have so many been found to sing the glories of youth
and the praises of old age ? and so few to speak of the grace
of middle life ?   Perhaps youth and age have more to say for
themselves and more freedom in saying it.   Perhaps it is good
to keep silence on what no one can know until they reach it.
And yet for once it might be well to speak and say that it
is a stage which those who have reached would not exchange
against anything that has gone before.   Now that life consists
more of answers than of questions, more of appreciation than of
criticism, more of fruit than of flower, more room in the retrospect, more of the vision of the end.

This was written when she was about forty-three.   It was in
a special way her period of life, the one which she was to sanctify
and enlighten for others, the one in which she herself was to
attain the goal.   It had no aftermath for her.   In it she found
her destined completeness.

As all that she writes is steeped in personal experience and
observation, it is but natural that in speaking of the third period
' old age ' she had far less to say.   She ended her letter on a note
of hope, drawn from the thought of the triumph of the unnamed
Saints, that is, the triumph of those who were not a race apart,
nor privileged beings ' but a *great* crowd whom no man could
number of all nations, and tribes, and peoples, and tongues,'
who have worked and wept as we have, and as we, have fallen
and risen again, and having ' washed their robes and made them
white in the Blood of the Lamb . . . are before the throne of
God.'

On November 5 Mother Stuart embarked at Port Said on the
Orsova.

From the outset she established an order of day, which she

and her companions followed regularly in all sea voyages. The mornings till nine were given to prayer. Then followed work—reading, study, writing; from two to five interesting reading aloud in English, French, and German. Then the evening was given to prayer and recreation.

It was during these mornings of quiet work that Mother Stuart wrote the greater part of her book. Its first chapter was begun in the Red Sea. In the following letters she speaks of it and of life on board.

Red Sea : November 9th, 1913.
R.M.S. Orsova.

There is a whole week to wait before this can be posted at Colombo next Sunday, but at least it may be begun to diminish the feeling of distance, and talk to you as we should be glad to do in this dear novena of St. Stanislaus. We are getting on perfectly with the protection of all the prayers, nothing could be better, even the Red Sea has never been so cool they say at this time of year, the highest temperature we have reached is eighty-seven degrees. This evening or to-morrow we shall be in the Indian Ocean, that will probably be cooler, because of the greater ocean spaces. The Red Sea is like a basin of hot water, and as from both sides the wind is warmed up by the desert, it is not the fault of the sea if it is not cool, the water was ninety-three degrees yesterday.

Bishop Grimes says Mass every day in the music room, but to-day for the sake of the third class passengers it was on deck, he had tried to get the Italians in the third class to come and sing, but, alas! they did not even turn up at the Mass, but a swarm of dear Irish passengers came, with their rosaries in hand, and the light of their baptismal candle in their eyes, and that rapt look which comes over their faces at Mass. It was good to see them. There were a few Communions. The Bishop only, says Mass, the other priests go to Communion. He is very kind, delighted to be asked to do anything . . . he calls upon us once a day for friendship.

Think of it. . . . We have seen Mount Sinai! They told us it was nearly impossible. One of the officers said he had only once seen it, because it is so far inland, and there was one disappointment first, a great black mass, announced as Sinai, and then ' not Sinai,' but in the evening it stood out unmistakably to those who knew it—rocky, bare, black, and forbidding, quite an Old Testament mountain, but it is a very impressive sight, I am glad we did not miss it. I do not think I told you of another joy of this journey, which was the sight of Greece, the mountains of the Peloponnesus; one whole morning after we left Brindisi, we went along in sight of them. I need not tell you the impression of that, it was a day to note in one's mind for all time. Of course we saw Corfu and Cephalonia, but the Greek Islands are not Greece itself, and by comparison they say nothing at all.

. . . I write badly, the wind is very strong, but the sea calm, and the *Orsova* is a very steady boat, I think it would take a good deal to put her out; twelve thousand tons, I think, and fourteen thousand horse power, it would be beneath her dignity to make much of trifles.

I know you will be glad to have news of the book, and as it seems possible that I may be able to do it, I should be glad if you would tell the nuns, so as to get their prayers, which used to lift me through chapter by chapter in the last enterprise. I have planned out the whole book, and written one chapter, but—what will be its quality! If it is fit to live it will be God's book and the fruit of prayer, for the circumstances are not favourable to writing. The boat is very crowded indeed, and the passengers have not the delight in silent mornings that we have. So they are talking all round me the whole time. There is an American whose slow and careful utterance makes me think she must be from Philadelphia, she is giving an interesting and detailed account of her travels to an appreciative Englishman. There are groups discussing the sports that take place on the upper deck about every three days, and the bridge tournament, and how well someone looked as the Duchess of Devonshire in the fancy ball. And then a Scotch family comes upstairs and plays all my favourite Jacobite airs on the piano; and Bishop Grimes looks in for a canonical or uncanonical visitation; and there is a man who comes up to practise every morning at eleven, and exercises himself in a song about 'these blooming flowers,' in which I can remark no perceptible progress from day to day, so I hope the concert at which he is to produce it will soon take place. And then there comes a gust of wind and most things blow away, and everyone runs to help everyone else to pick them up, so you see it is an exercise in concentration of attention, if it is nothing else; and as usual I feel that I cannot form any opinion as to the quality of what I have written. But I put a great deal of good-will and prayer into it.

14th. We are coming near to Colombo, to-morrow we shall probably be there, but as no one knows, not even the captain, how long we may be obliged to stay for cargo and passengers, beyond the coaling which will take twelve hours, we do not know what we shall do, perhaps we shall go to the Little Sisters of the Poor, where we have been hospitably invited, and spend half a Sunday there, but I can only tell you about it all when we are on board again. The weather is still beautiful, and not excessively hot. We have seen the first signs of approaching land, two islands covered with palm trees—palms out of a tropical sea, with surf breaking on the reef all round them are a thing of beauty.

I must end . . . as there are many letters to write for to-morrow. My hours for private work at the book are from nine to twelve; in the longitude where we are now that is five to eight A.M. with you, but when this gets to you how much further off we shall be.

R.M.S. *Orsova* : November 21st, 1913.
(To the Roehampton Community.)
MY DEAR MOTHERS AND SISTERS—EVERYONE,—

This is supposed to be a Christmas number of travellers' tales though in fact on sea there are not many stories to tell, and I feel that Egypt is too big to be attempted. If I could tell you about it some day it would be different.

It is such an extraordinary thing on this boat crowded with passengers to think that, while scarcely any of them know it, God comes down and stays amongst them in the music-room for twenty-five minutes or so every day. If they could only know and believe it, what an awakening! It is very devotional for Mass. He takes His walk amongst us, not as in Paradise ' in the afternoon air,' but in the early morning, seven-fifteen. Only we and three priests are there. The Bishop says Mass. The Consecration is a wonderful moment, here in the middle of the Indian Ocean. The Bishop is not very certain of himself, so he is not liberal at the Elevation, and I often think of our rude but devout forefathers calling out during Mass, ' Hold up, Sir John, hold up! Heave Him a little higher! ' Mother Stonor wrote that it was ' difficult to imagine me with nothing particular to do.' She need not try, for I have many most particular things to do, and my only trouble is that there is not time for all. You know I have what the catalogue calls ' *un travail particulier* ' on hand, and even without that, which took me by surprise, I had brought many other particular things. She also wants me to tell you about sunsets, but so many people have written about sunsets that the subject is not tempting. I will only tell you of one. We have got into a trade-wind, the S.E., and it makes a strong head wind which has searched out the sea-worthiness of my companions. This trade-wind has a curious trick of blowing round holes through the clouds, through which one sees blue or stars by night. One evening there was a great mass of grey clouds driving westward, and driven into all sorts of shapes, and at one moment part of it rose up with the shape of an immense monstrance of old silver of the latest renaissance type, blown out into a crown of cherubs and clouds, and the wind blew a round hole right in the middle of it, and—think of it!—the setting sun came down exactly there, and seemed to rest in that towering monstrance over the horizon, with the foot of the monstrance on the sea. It was a splendid

Benediction ! Does Mother Stonor know Francis Thompson's
Orient Ode ? It was just like that, only on that day ours was
not a ' flaming monstrance ' but, as I have said, old grey silver.
. . . A question for the community: ' Are democracy and
poetry exclusive of one another and, if so, why ? '

R.M.S. *Orsova* : 21st November, 1913.
Will you please tell those who wrote to me at Colombo, that
I got their letters with great joy. The Bishop came out of the
saloon almost wringing his hands with sympathy. ' I pity you,
there's such an awful budget waiting for you in there ! ' Most of
it was Australian letters of welcome, some in French from the
children, apparently uncorrected and very good. The rest was
—good to read ! We went ashore during the coaling, but we
took the Bishop with us, so could not go in rickshaws. But
I hope to do so in Japan. The Little Sisters of the Poor came
to meet us at the boat, one of them an old child of Poitiers, so
delighted to see the habit again after twenty-three years. We
saw their convent and their little old men, all Singalese; they
nearly all come into the Church before they die. We saw a
man one hundred and five years old sitting on the edge of his
bed finishing an evening meal of bananas. The sisters look
so sweet and good, very much worn by the climate. We
expected to find great heat on land at Colombo, and it turned
out to be the coolest day that Colombo had had during twenty
years. We called on the Bishop. I wanted very much to see
the delegate, Sister Zaleska's uncle, but he lives at Kandy,
too far off. The Bishop is French, Franciscan, and looks as
if his charge were a heavy one. We came back to the port
through the cinnamon gardens from the Bishop's house. The
Bishop (ours, Bishop Grimes) said that this was essential, it
was so wonderful, the scent of the cinnamon came in wafts
to an immense distance. We sniffed and sniffed, and at each
turn of the road someone said : ' I smell cinnamon.' When
we got there the chauffeur told us that the cinnamon trees
were all dead, and the other precious things too, so there was
neither balsam nor spice in the air, but only a sort of Battersea
Park in which the British, undaunted by the heat, were playing
football and cricket !
I recommend myself to the prayers of the ' Brethren,' and
always to yours—I know they do not fail me !

On December 1st Mother Stuart landed at Melbourne. It was
a true Australian day, cloudless, blue, and sunlit, ' such as we
wished to have to welcome her to our southern home.' Knowing her love for local glories, in every house, things typical of
the country had been gathered together. Not only rare and

beautiful plants and flowers, but the children brought as pets young Australian bears, ' grey and fluffy,' one of whom they had killed with kindness before her arrival, kangaroos, laughing jackass, opossum, parrots, etc., all of which took up their abode within the convent grounds.   Native work and weapons had also been collected, and the service of a ' native ' was secured to exhibit the use of the latter.

Four houses had to be visited in Australia, two in Melbourne and two in Sydney.   The latter stand on two of the most beautiful bays in Port Jackson, Rose Bay and Elizabeth Bay.

At Rose Bay the convent property stretches down to the water by rocky terraces, and there Mother Stuart delighted to spend the evenings with the community, watching the life in the great harbour below.   The swiftly moving ferry-boats with their brilliant lights alone visible recalled, she said, the vessel in the *Purgatorio*, 'a light coming o'er the sea so swiftly that no flight is equal to its motion . . . and on the stern the celestial pilot.'

The other property at Kincoppal, with its adjoining stretches of real Australian bush, offered attractions of another sort.   A long day was spent in the quiet of the country, in the unused property at Kenthurst.   ' Though it is not of much use to the Society, it has given us a delightful day,' she said on her return, looking at the quantities of wild flowers she had herself gathered in the woods.   The following letters were written from Australia:

Melbourne : 3rd December, 1913.

. . . Imagine my surprise when a letter from *you* came out of an envelope with a kangaroo stamp at Fremantle !   It was forwarded by Sister E.   Then I saw two thousand mail-bags laid out on the deck of the *Orsova* for landing at Adelaide, and in one of them was a second letter from you, which was delivered two hours after my arrival, both great delights to read. . . .   But how far off I am, one realises it in reading the date of the last news, October 27th.   Our journey ended as well as it had begun, not one ' trip ' out of twenty, the captain said, was anything like it.   Even the Australian Bight, which is the ' wickedest place,' the Bay of Biscay of these parts, lay for one day like the sea of glass in the new Jerusalem, and the other day was correct but very cold, the remains of a gale from the Antarctic regions ; we wondered what it must be in winter since it is so cold in summer.   We arrived, as foreseen, on the 1st December ; Mother Kerr's anniversary and the transferred feast of S. Andrew, as in 1884.   Happily we had Mass early on board, so the usual ceremonial of deputations and welcomes was not what it sometimes is! The Archbishop kindly sent his carriage down to the port for me, and I am now waiting to say good-bye to him while he has tea with the Children of Mary. Reverend Mother S. was here, and Reverend Mother F. and her councillors came over from the other house. It is an astonishment to me to find ·the faces so little changed; the fact of having always the same setting of the religious habit must account for it. . . . The Australians look more flourishing under their own sun. . . . Reverend Mother F. told me that, coming back to Melbourne after eleven years at Sydney, she was walking in the garden and for the first time after these eleven years she heard a thrush sing. There are real thrushes and blackbirds here. She stood still and listened to it with joy beyond words, almost in a trance like that of the Monk Felix, for she had no idea how long she stood there until she heard laughing and voices behind her and turned to face the Archbishop and the Dean, who declared that they had been a long time enjoying the spectacle. There is also a ring-dove here, whether wild or captive I do not know, but he gives out his note during medita- tion, and I am divided between a new realisation of what is meant by *meditabor ut columba* it is so insistent, and so ' affective ' in that repeated note—and—the thought of Mother Stonor as she will be among her chosen joys in heaven ; hands full of bluebells and face absorbed in the notes of heavenly ring- doves. As she is curious about sunsets I will tell you of another unusual one I saw in the Indian Ocean one evening at eight o'clock when we came up on deck. The sea was still white from the reflection ; there was still a band of pale red, and above it a white sky, which I can only describe as having a look of astonishment and a look of worship that one sometimes sees in the eyes of the dying, ' life's smile through death's eclipse,' the sky was astonished, and so was the ocean, and so was I. . .

Rose Bay, Sydney : December 21st, 1913.

. . . This is the shortest day with you, a day that I always had a special liking for, with us it is the longest day and it seems most strange. There is no great heat yet, it is just like an English June as to temperature, but very dry ; of course (as wherever I go) ' such a summer has not been known before ' so cool ! Thank you all for your letters. I was not at all surprised to get the cable of Mother Oddie's death, for the mail of that week had brought me all the bad news, and it was only the following week that brought news of improvement and some idea that she might get well, and this was a surprise to me ; perhaps the end was quite sudden as she so often thought it would be, like her father, all this I can only hear in New Zealand.

They say the strike is at last over; we have tickets for the

American steamer *Tahti*, and there is every hope that it will start on the 27th but it goes to Wellington, so I have to go from there to Auckland and back by train. To come back to Mother Oddie, what sweet letters from the Junior School; they really have right thoughts of God and of death and how wonderfully her death was arranged to suit her tastes exactly. . . .

I have had a little opportunity of seeing more of the country in Australia since I wrote last, but everyone tells me I have come at the wrong time! We have still a property outside Sydney, real bush, one hundred and twenty acres, which I have been to see. It gave us a beautiful walk, with handfuls of unknown flowers, only the shadows of their real selves on account of the season and the drought, but very good to see and gather with one's own hands, just as it is very good to see with one's own eyes flocks of parrots flying wild!

I should like to tell you many nice things about the Church in Australia, but it would be too long for this mail. I must say a word about Rose Bay. I assure you there are scenes worthy of Assisi! . . . Dear Mother N. whom I have had photographed by the side of Mother Smith's grave to send to Roehampton, is a great friend of the cockatoo; she says that God, the Father of All, gave us 'these toys' and she does not think it is nice not to show gratitude and appreciation of them. The cockatoo got away out of the aviary and there was great lamentation in the whole Assisi household, the school were all out, and with every blandishment tried in vain to get him back. Then they sent for Mother N. to pray to St. Anthony. When she appeared and prayed the cockatoo came down and stood just out of reach, put his head on one side and looked fixedly at her for a few moments. Then he drawled out condescendingly, 'poor old darling' and let himself be taken!

Now a lovely story to finish with. A native Australian of the race that is considered so stupid was seen in one of the country churches praying, absorbed to all appearances, for two unbroken hours. Then the priest went and asked him what prayers he was saying and he said, 'Jesus, Mary'; it was all he knew. Think what a prayer.

23rd. Two days to Christmas! What Christmases we have had in times past, what a delightful New Year time we had last year when you were at the Mother House. Blessed be God for all He gave us and all He took away. May he bless your New Year, dearest Mother . . . and draw us both more and more close to Him in mind and soul and affections in the coming year.

On December 27 she left for New Zealand on board the *Manuka*. They reached Wellington on December 31. During these three days she finished the book begun in the Red Sea.

S.S. *Manuka* : 31st December, 1913.

. . . In two or three hours we shall land at Wellington. Things were so disorganised by the strike which is only just ended, that we could not get a boat to Auckland, and had to be very glad to get to Wellington at all. But I do not change the proposed order of visits. I shall go on to Auckland and then back to Wellington for the real visit, then to Timaru as arranged. This is an incredible last day of the year, just steaming into a New Zealand port, but I hope there will be Benediction this evening, and the *Miserere* and *Te Deum* will balance us on the solemn frontier line of the old year and the new. God has been so good to us in 1913. What a joy there was set like a jewel in the middle of it.[1] He will be better still in 1914, though we cannot guess how. I used to quarrel with Father Faber for his ecstatic, ' On, on, Our Lord is sweeter far to-day than yesterday,' until I realised that He is so because we know Him to be so, better to-day than yesterday, and we shall know it still better to-morrow. May He grant all I ask Him to-day for you and everyone *there*, and what I know you ask for me. To-day, as far as I am concerned, I have the joy of saying, ' Go, little book,' go to Mother X. for I have written the last word, the Introduction. It is quite a little book of the sea, for it was planned on the Adriatic, begun on the Red Sea on the First Friday of November, mostly written on the Indian Ocean, and finished in the South Pacific on the feast that is one of my great days, Saint Thomas of Canterbury, full of associations and memories. Mother de S. will finish typing it in New Zealand, but I shall only post the second half when I get back to Sydney in the first days of February, as I have not much confidence in the New Zealand post, whereas the letters generally go right from Sydney.

Good-bye for to-day. . . . I send my love quicker than this can go to everyone.

I have left so much *sous-entendu* between the lines of the book that it seems to me like two books, one outside for the ' neighbour that won't understand,' and the other inside for those who do !

I have much more to say but it must wait for another letter.

The first sight of New Zealand on entering Cook Strait is bleak and dreary in the extreme. ' I concluded,' said Mother Stuart, ' that the beauty must be as that of the King's daughter within,' and so it proved. Island Bay, where the convent at Wellington has been built, is surrounded by cone-shaped hills, and in the distance the snow-capped Kaikoura Mountains of the Southern Island can be clearly seen. The next day

[1] Her visit to Roehampton in June.

(January 1st, 1914) she left for Auckland, a journey of nineteen hours. Much that is typical of the scenery and life of the country is passed on this journey. The cultivated lands and great sheep runs of the south give place in the north to forest, mountain and plain still in that almost primeval solitude which shows the trees and flowers in their undisputed ownership of the earth. On the January 9th, 1914, she returned to Wellington, leaving it again ten days later to visit Timaru, near Christchurch, the only convent in the South Island.

As in Australia, so now in New Zealand the 'old children' came in numbers, even from the most remote places, to welcome her. 'You have ideal old children,' said Mother Stuart at Timaru, 'jewels of old children.' Here as always she gave herself wholly to each house in turn, and especially to the communities; 'It is for you that I have come.' The happiness of those days can only be realised by those who shared it.

Auckland : 5th January, 1914.

. . . The country is very different from the parts of Australia that we have seen, but they were not the best ! This is a land of forest and mountain and water, which one misses so much in the Australian landscape, and a very paradise of ferns. There are splendid tree-ferns in quantities, and lesser ones in great and beautiful variety. Some parts of the railway route reminded me very much of Scotland, only that in the glens and along the hill-sides are Pampas grass in great beauty, and New Zealand flax, which is rather like a yucca, and grows as high as the top of the railway carriages. Parts of it again remind me of Switzerland, and in the high meadows (there is real grass here, very fine and close crops) there is the scent of newly-cut grass, sweet and summer-like, in the foreground, and in the background—(if there is a background of smells—and I think so)—the wonderful air that comes straight down from snow, with an austere purity that is almost a special scent of its own, by its clearness from every other. Along part of the railway is a laborious spiral which, with the rest, took thirty years to make, and in this we circled round and round a great snow-covered volcano, most beautiful to see, and another a little lower, with a trail of steam from its cone: it was active last year. I dare not spell the name of either ! The Maori names are very soft and beautiful, nearly all vowel sounds, scarcely any sibilants; but they are so much alike, and so deprived of consonant features, that I should not like to have to keep them in my head and do a blank-map study briskly with a class. The names in Australia suffer from other difficulties, in the confusion of times and places—(as in America when Troy, Athens, and Versailles may meet in half an hour's journey)—but some Australian names one could not forget, such as ' Come-by-chance !' or ' Never-tire!' They allow one to imagine how and in what frame of mind people arrived there.

This place is quite beautiful; no one said too much about it! Dear Mother Smith is so living here; one sees her thought in every detail. . . .

Island Bay, Wellington : January 14th, 1914.

. . . If this catches the Vancouver mail, it will reach you in a month instead of six weeks, but this is only a mail for once a month. Yesterday brought me the news in detail of Mother Oddie's death—R.I.P.—from you and Reverend Mother and Mother G., etc., so I had a feast, and thank everyone who spread the banquet.

I think of her every day, she makes a great gap in that circle at Roehampton, and will be sorely missed by many. She was one of the people who are an institution. I must try to get my ideas together about her and send a little contribution for her circular. . . .

I have seen very few Maories and all were in the ugly un-characteristic costume that white men wear, only their faces were rather picturesque, heads and features not at all bad. It seems they can ' civilise ' and ' educate ' (so calling it) up to a certain point, but they always return. There is a certain Maori lady, ' Bella ' is her name, no other, it is enough, who studied at the University and got her B.A. But ' the call of the wild ' came back into her soul, and she left the University to return to her village and her Maori life. She is the hereditary chieftainess, so the village has the advantage of the enlightened rule of Bella, B.A. I doubt whether her government will have gained by it. The Maori are dying out—a great pity, and one cannot help thinking a great wrong done to them ; if only they could be in ' reductions ' under Jesuits they might have little Paradises on earth and antichambers of heaven.

One thing that I hear from bishops and priests is immensely consoling, and that is the value to Australia and New Zealand of nuns. The wonderful Sisters of St. Joseph[1] do untold good, they go by twos and threes into the neglected parishes and even in the bush, from station to station, preparing the way for the priests and keeping up faith, hope and charity and the elements of Christian Doctrine. They devote themselves so far as to settle in places where they can most rarely have Mass and the Sacraments, in other places they make the parochial life. One Jesuit told me that he had often been ' on supply ' to the parishes along the coast near Sydney for the Sundays. In some, even if there was a resident priest, there would be ten or twelve at

---

[1] An Order founded in 1866 at Penola, South Australia, by Father Woods and Mary MacKillop.

Mass and no one for Confession. But in the parishes where the Sisters are, the church would be crowded, and the confessional besieged . . . and a most wonderful innocence. The nuns teach boys and girls and have a wonderful hold on the boys, even when they grow up, which confirms me in the idea that nuns are ideal teachers for little boys. The Bishop of Auckland[1] told me that he wanted to reclaim an island called the ' Barrier,' where there were a number of Catholics, all lapsed. He sent a good priest to spend six or seven weeks there, and he came back without having been able to effect anything. Then the Bishop thought he would try nuns, and he sent two Sisters of St. Joseph, and some time afterwards sent the priest again, and it was all alive—a harvest ready to be cut, and now he has been able to put a resident priest, and he has a steady congregation of one hundred, and Protestants creeping up more and more for instruction. These things are a joy to hear of.

The Bishop of Auckland is wonderful. He is going round all the diocese in a motor, absolutely alone, no chauffeur, or chaplain, or servant. He takes an axe and blocks and chains to get himself out, for he is often stuck fast in river beds or heavy clay. Once he dug himself out three times in a hundred yards. He goes where no motor has ever been seen ; cutting down trees sometimes to get through, and often cutting shrubs, ' tea-tree ' (not real tea, the native) shrub, to throw before the motor and carry it over a place in which it would sink : he says these are in general four feet wide by six deep, there are no roads at all, and almost all that part is clay, so imagine it. Sometimes he finds himself on one of those clay roads in heavy rain, with a drop of three hundred feet down into a gully on one side, and the slope of the road outwards, only just the width of the car ; then he goes on in front and digs a groove for the inside wheel, and so gets past in safety. You can imagine all the good that is done by such an adventurous Bishop so set upon his pastoral care. When he gets upon a real road he exceeds in speed and goes along perhaps thirty miles an hour. He is so much respected that the police instead of 'running him in ' say ' it's his Lordship,' and look the other way. Such is the New Zealand Bishop. They are rather afraid he may be taken for Adelaide.

At the other end of the scale I must tell you of a deplorable contrast, a New Zealand bird called the ' Ki-wi,' a collateral survival from the gigantic and now extinct moa. This wretched bird is said to have had wings once, and never using them, they atrophied and disappeared. It has only two lappets where they used to be. It has a round body, apparently no tail, and an

---

[1] The Reverend Henry W. Cleary, Bishop of Auckland.

enormously long bill, apparently it never raises its head . . .
The impressive lessons conveyed by the Ki-wi I leave to each
one's reflections. . . . To-morrow we go on anothers tage,
to the last limit of distance (Timaru). I have missed the
Vancouver mail, it caught me at the first page.

The Bishop here referred to was the first in the world to visit
his flock by hydroplane. He began to do this during the Great
War, thus reaching the most unattainable parts of his vast
diocese.

Timaru : 21st January, 1914.

. . . The first primrose in spring is not more welcome than
the first letters that came by Vancouver ! The first suggestion
of another way round the world, through which lies the track
of return. When I thought of January in New Zealand, before
setting out it seemed so far and remote that one could never get
there, and now it is actually true, and I am here writing to you
from this extreme outer rim of the world, and saying that this day
next week is, strictly speaking, the first step of the return journey !
though with relapses among the islands on the way to Japan.
The name of the steamer which takes us there is the *Coblentz*,
North German Lloyd. I think it stops at Brisbane, Friedrich
Wilhelmshafen, Manila, and Hong Kong . . . I am looking
forward to the great freshness of the news that will reach me in
Japan, only sixteen days old. I wrote last from Wellington, and
the day we left it was blowing a gale; we thought it would have
been a very bad journey, but every mile we went southward it
grew calmer, and we got into Lyttelton in very good weather.
Wellington is built on a point that collects all the winds of
heaven, the south-east, which is the dreadful wind, blows straight
upon it from Cape Campbell; the south-west works itself round
into a funnel through the Straits and comes in with a shriek ;
the north-east comes in a shy way round a corner with high
piping, and the north-west eddies round Mount Egmont until
it gets quite giddy, and seems to come in from every quarter
at once. They say that a Wellington man is known everywhere
because he always holds his hat on at a corner.

I had to see Bishop Grimes at Christchurch, so we had a whole
morning there, waiting for the second train. He kept a priest
to say Mass for us, as we arrived too late for the Synodal Mass,
which was that morning. . . . It was the last day of the clergy
retreat too, so the whole diocese was there. When the Bishop
went to the Synod meeting he left us in his museum, where he has
all sorts of curious things from the South Sea Islands, and afterwards he took us to the top of the cathedral, and I understand
why it was called Christchurch. It is really like Christchurch

in Hampshire, and its Avon winds slowly through it in the same quiet way.   The site was first offered to the Irish bishops to make an Irish colony, and I cannot imagine why they refused it ; then it was offered to the Church of England, and they sat down and called it Christchurch.   All the way along the ' Canterbury ' plains I said to myself ' it is just the little more that would make it England,' and as we got near Timaru ' it is just the little more that would make it Roscrea.'   In the long plantations round Emo Park there are places where one sees nothing but islands of spruce fir in a sea of grass.

This house is very charming.   At first sight it reminded me of St. Michael's, Louisiana, both inside and out, and I learned afterwards that Reverend Mother Boudreaux had actually brought with her the plans of St. Michael to inspire the architect ! Imagine that within a month of her setting foot in the country the foundation stone was laid by the Bishop.   She caught cold at the ceremony and was dead in a week !   But she left a true spirit in the house, and Mother Gartland and Mother Sharman cemented it in.   The garden is so pretty with a lawn like English grass and all our annual flowers and beautiful roses. . . .

Among the curiosities shown by the Bishop to his guests were the wooden forks of the cannibals !   ' I do not generally give these things,' he said, turning to Mother Stuart, ' but I should like you to take one as a souvenir ! '

Timaru : 26th January, 1914.

. . . Your letter of December 11th and those that came with it made me feel that we had made connections again across a great space of time and distance, because you had just had my letter from Colombo . . . Yesterday, 25th January, was the last Sunday Mass that we expect to hear until March 15th, unless some chance of a port on Sunday gives us this. . . .

This is a very nice house ; it has a quite old-fashioned charm in the buildings and garden.   Shaven lawns, such as one rarely sees out of England, old-fashioned borders full of annuals and really choice roses.   The roses are modern, but I think the lawns and annuals and half-hardy borders and herbaceous plants must be relics of the mind and tastes of Mother Sharman. One of the real beauties of the garden is the clipped cypress hedges—*Cupressus macrocarpa*, so green that one could not even think of anything greener, and so close that the small birds hop on them as on a lawn, and so strong that a whole band of hide-and-seek lay flat on the level top of one of them.   They were not found, nor was the hedge injured.

Mother Stuart felt greatly leaving those far-off convents, the homes of so many she had known and followed from the

opening days of their religious life, and with little likelihood of
seeing them again. She arranged, however, that in future the
young nuns should go to the Mother House for the six months
of their probation before profession, a privilege which had
been long enjoyed by all others, even those in the remotest
parts of South America. Before leaving, she invited all the
Superiors to meet her in the following summer at a retreat to
be given in Ixelles.

On leaving Timaru, Mother Stuart returned to Wellington
for a few days, while waiting for a boat to Sydney, which she
reached on the evening of February 3rd. ' It is delightful to
come back to Rose Bay,' she said, ' it is such a home-like place ;
I felt it on entering the Heads.' But the time was short.
The *Coblentz* was to leave for Japan on the 7th. The evening
before, the First Friday of February, at the moment of the
Consecration to the Sacred Heart, instead of reading the usual
one, Mother Stuart read another, in which there was a special
prayer for ' her amongst us who will be the first to die.'
Intentionally or not, no one knew ; but it was for herself that
she was praying.

As usual she had gained almost as many friends as there
were people whom she had seen. ' I look on it as one of the
greatest privileges of my life to have met her,' wrote an
Australian priest some two years later. ' In a few moments, by
her mere presence, she taught me many lessons, which I have
not forgotten. . . . She was undoubtedly the most remarkable
woman I ever met. . . . Here is a Saint, was my inward comment. . . . Her conversation was in heaven . . . but she was
by no means a dreamer ; on the contrary most observant, most
interesting in conversation, and yet it seemed to me continually
in the presence of God. Though her responsibilities were so
great, there was no trace of worry or anxiety—her face expressed
only calm and peace.'

But though this was so, to those who knew her it was too
evident that the strain of the long journey and of the overwhelming work of the last two years was beginning to tell
heavily. All noted her fatigue on her arrival in each house, a
fatigue which indeed appeared to pass off, and which was never
allowed to interfere with any official programme, but which
none the less was surely and quickly wearing out her life.

CHAPTER XXVI

JOURNEY ROUND THE WORLD (*continued*)—1914

Japan, America

' It is always a great and solemn moment when we turn the page of a new year. It must be the best we have ever spent, since it adds one more to our experience of God, and subtracts one from the way that is yet to be walked before we reach Jerusalem. . . .'

From a letter written for the New Year of 1914, *J. Stuart.*

THE *Coblentz*, the smallest and oldest vessel of the North German Lloyd, left Sydney for Tokyo on February 7, 1914, with a Chinese crew officered by Germans. It was neither a fast nor a punctual line, and long delays at the ports of call kept the travellers on sea till March 10.

The first stop was at Pinkenbar, the port of Brisbane. Reverend Mother Stuart took advantage of it to visit the Coadjutor Bishop, who wished to arrange for a foundation in his diocese.[1]

Leaving Pinkenbar, the *Coblentz* wound its slow way through the coral reefs for some hours, emerging at last into a sea like oil, through which it went north towards the ' Bismarck Archipelago.' Here the first halt was at Rabaul, on the Gazelle Peninsula, in the Island of New Mecklenburg. A rumour of small-pox led to a formal prohibition to all passengers to land. The three days' stay was to be spent on board. Great was the consternation of the Sisters of the Sacred Heart of Issoudun. They had come a two hours' journey from the Mission enclosure at Vanupope to bring Mother Stuart back with them. For six weeks, they said, her room had been prepared. A traveller met at Melbourne had announced her passage by this route. At first the authorities were inflexible, the Sisters must return alone. But they were not to be daunted, and tried the art of

---

[1] The foundation was made at Stuartholme, Brisbane (a lovely solitude on the crest of a high hill, with a magnificent view), in 1917. The property had belonged to Mother Stuart's brother Richard.

persuasion so successfully that at length leave was given to the nuns alone to disembark, on condition that they visited no place but the Mission.

This Mission belonged to the Fathers of the Sacred Heart, and within its great enclosure were two convents of nuns. They had orphanages and schools, and taught both boys and girls. Nothing could exceed the cordiality of their welcome. ' Had it been their own Superior General they could not have done more for her,' wrote Mother Stuart's secretary. After two days at Vanupope, the nuns returned to the *Coblentz*, accompanied by a priest and two brothers who were on their way to Europe.

On February 21 the steamer reached Friedrich Wilhelms-hafen, ' a gayer port than Rabaul.' No town was visible from the boat, but the passengers alighted to walk in the beautiful alleys of cocoa palm, with houses scattered at intervals along the road. It led, they were told, to the interior, a place not to be rashly ventured into.

A group of coral islands was next visited, and on the 28th the *Coblentz* passed through the Caroline Islands and stopped at Yap. A rough sea made any near approach to the island impossible, but a coastal steamer, bringing European settlers, arrived, and among them one white-clad Sister. Coming on board, she made straight for Mother Stuart, and implored her to land and stay a fortnight with her, the time between two steamers : she was alone on the island, she explained, her fellow missionaries had been called off to other work, and their successors had not arrived ; she had to supply unaided for all the needs of the mission schools. Three days a week she taught in one district, and three days in another in the ' interior.' She seemed to see nothing heroic in her solitary life of labour—it was all in the day's work. To stay with her was unfortunately impossible.

A few days later the *Coblentz* entered the magnificent approach to Manila, through the ' thousand islands ' of the Philippines. There an old child of the Boulevard des Invalides (Paris) awaited Mother Stuart. She placed her house at her disposal, and took her to visit properties in the neighbourhood where it was hoped that a Convent of the Sacred Heart might be established.

A forty-eight hours' stay at Hong Kong was the last pause on the road to Japan. On March 10, Kobe was reached, and Tokyo the following day.

S.S. *Coblentz* : 21st February, 1914.

. . . Since I wrote this we have, alas! lost time—we are now two days behind owing to adverse winds and other delays, with a probability of more.

It cannot be helped, and now that I am obliged to take a later steamer from Tokyo it does not so much matter. We spent two days at Rabaul. . . . It seems that Bismarck was strongly opposed to the purchase of these islands by Germany, so it was rather a doubtful compliment that they were named in his honour the Bismarck Archipelago. There are two hundred white inhabitants, of whom one hundred and twenty are officials . . . the rest are cocoa-planters, missionaries, and nuns.

The Company had telegraphed to the missionaries that we were on board, so there were two nice German nuns in white waiting to receive us and take us off in the Mission motor boat, with the Father of the Mission who had travelled with us, but without Mass requisites. But the Imperial authorities said ' NO.' There were reported to be two cases of black small-pox on the island, so they all said ' NO ' as loudly and officially as they possibly could, and we asked the Father not to think of us but to go on. We could have persuaded him, but the nuns were animated with a spirit of heroic obstinacy and would not let go. They went themselves to the Governor and explained to him that all the doctors who had seen the patients said it was not small-pox, and only those who had not seen them said it was. That their Mission was above suspicion, etc., etc. What could the poor Governor do ? He spent twenty minutes writing a document with the most awe-inspiring formulas that he could think of, letting us out on our promise to go straight to the Mission station and straight back to the boat, and not to set foot anywhere else.

So we set out. Two hours in the motor boat, managed by the natives, took us to Vanupope. Incidentally as we happened to be there we took the mails for the district, and to make it known one of the natives blew beautiful notes on a great shell fifteen inches long (a univalve like a great whelk) in which a hole had been cut. They say the sound of it carries ever so far. We met numbers of natives in their canoes, burnt and cut out of tree trunks, carrying for balance a heavy bamboo frame, and generally paddled, but one had an immense green palm branch, perhaps twenty feet long and holding it up used it as a sail. It was beautiful to see, especially as the canoe was full of green palm branches, I suppose to make his hut. On the landing-stage all the German community came down to receive us, and a few minutes afterwards the Bishop arrived and then the Father Superior. They have in the same great enclosure the church all made of zinc, the Bishop's house where the Fathers live

with him, and their lay Brothers. They are Fathers of the
Sacred Heart, all German except the Bishop, who is French.

They have great workshops and cocoa plantations. There
are German Sisters of the Sacred Heart with whom we stayed
who have the half-caste schools of girls, and for the present the
half-caste boys, and a dispensary, etc., and a Convent of the
Sisters of the Immaculate Heart of Mary who are French, Dutch,
Australian, etc. They have the native school for girls, one hundred
and thirty boarders, the youngest sixteen months old! They stay
till they are married. They are most sensibly managed, for they
make them live as much as possible in the native style, no beds,
only a blanket to roll up in on the floor, their food mostly cocoa-
nuts and bananas, so that they are not unfitted for the life before
them. They are not at all like Australian natives, but a much
finer race, perhaps Malay, but no one quite knows. Their build
and walk and attitudes full of dignity, but unfortunately all
who are not Christians are cannibals. There are four native
novices and postulants! dear things with shy novice-like ways
and smiles. The Bishop gives them some instruction on a
possible rule not yet determined. The lay Brothers teach the
boys their trades, and they have in fact built all the houses and
schools for the Mission. The Brothers are all German, and
quite excellent, two of them are now travelling with us and a
priest, so we had Mass this morning.

We went to Mass in the Mission Church and it was very
beautiful. We heard five Masses and so made up for some of
our lost ones. The servers looked so devout with long brown
fingers joined, and a little ceremonial *stoop* as those one sees
in the pictures serving St. Peter Claver. They serve in their
usual dress, only adding a white jersey without sleeves. In their
work dress they are bare to the waist, and have a yard and a half
of turkey red stuff wrapped round them like a kilt and belted
up; the girls have the same, only they wear a short red tunic
over it. The red suits their beautiful brown colour perfectly.

The children look perfectly happy and are most friendly.
The big ones can speak a little German. They bathe in the
sea every day and we went to see the performance. Such a
sight! When the Sister clapped her hands, one hundred and
twenty of them dashed into the surf with a shout and were soon
swimming out ever so far and waving back to us, diving, floating,
and enjoying it hugely. The one hundred and twenty black
heads were a sight to see! They had a *Visitatrix* sent from the
Mother House last year, and when she arrived the whole school
swam out to meet her! The big ones teach the little ones to
swim, and they all swim like dogs, not as we do. It is astonishing how long they can stay under water. They are perfectly
obedient. The Sister clapped her hands and they came out

of the water directly and walked up in procession, dripping, and ten minutes after they had changed back into their turkey red clothes and were singing vociferously from a modulator. We had a day and a half there and then a very rough return in the motor boat, with the two Brothers and picking up a Father on the way. The whole school came down to the landing-stage and lifted up their voices and howled to see the Brothers go, though it is only for a year.

The German Government are doing all they can to put down cannibalism, but of course they cannot get at the people in the interior of the islands, and twenty miles from the Mission it goes on as before. As they go through the wood from station to station the Fathers are always in danger. The Bishop told us that he happened to ask his favourite altar boy, ' Angelo ' by name and disposition, how long it was since he had tasted human flesh, and he said quite simply ' Yesterday.' The Bishop did not believe it, but found it was quite true. The chief had returned unexpectedly from a raid and brought victims, and Angelo had been of the invited guests at the banquet. It is so natural to them that it is hard to make them realise that they must not do it. The Bishop said he looked grave at Angelo, who kept away for some days and then returned with a little reserved air which gave the impression that he had been warned at home not to speak of such things to people who could not understand them !

March 3rd.—We hope to be at Hong Kong to-morrow, and these will be posted there and go to you very quickly *via* Siberia . . . We had eight Masses on board, but the Fathers and Brothers left us at Manila. The Brothers were delightful people to talk to, so simple and ready to do or say anything that might be of service. They had shot crocodiles (and cooked and eaten them, too) and slain sharks, just as they have felled trees and built houses—all in the day's work as if it were nothing at all. They had the childlike laugh of Rhinelanders and a look of such deep happiness. . . .

In Japan Mother Stuart found many of her former novices, and those who had worked under her in England. They had left her, not so many years before, scarcely daring to hope to meet again. The joy of the reunion was all the greater that by their position they were so far removed from all they held dearest, and surrounded by a spiritual atmosphere which Mother Stuart described as ' oppressive ' with the weight of paganism.

Her arrival awakened interest outside the convent walls, and the education authorities asked her to visit the State establishments. She did so, having in view the more perfect adaptation of the educational scheme of the Order to the needs of the country. Referring to her reception, she wrote :

It is an indication of the interest felt in education that foreigners, keen on the same subject, should receive so cordial and courteous a welcome as was given to visitors staying at the *Seishin Jochi Gakuin* (Convent of the Sacred Heart) in the course of a journey round the world.

She saw in this way the High School, the Women's University, the Higher Normal School and that of the Peeresses. When she was about to leave Japan, Dr. Mikami, Professor of History, and the Historian of Japan, asked her to write an article on what she had seen, to be published in some English magazine. The result was an article in the *Month* for July 1914, entitled 'How Japan Educates Women.' In the course of the paper she wrote :

The idea of the foundation of the Women's University originated in the mind of its present President, Mr. Naruse, who in 1875, when quite a young man, spent a sleepless night in a hotel in Kobe, listening to the sounds of revelry overhead, and pursued by the problem of what was amiss with his country. By morning he had reached the conclusion that the evil lay in women's ignorance, inefficiency, and inability to perform their duties, and he said to himself, ' If women are contented with this, how can their nation be great and this people happy ? ' He was convinced that woman's influence lies at the centre of a nation's life and is the foundation of its strength. The education of girls did not satisfy Mr. Naruse's aspirations : he aimed at higher education—to reach the young women of Japan by the foundation of a University *specially organised for them.*

This last point appealed very particularly to Mother Stuart. She questioned if Japanese women were not on wiser lines than their English sisters, establishing their own University and University system, instead of attempting to graft themselves on to those systems especially designed for men. The University offered Collegiate and Post-graduate Courses. Among the former the ' Domestic Science Course ' was of special interest : it ' included all things favourable for the making of an intelligent home.'

Speaking of the children of Japan, Mother Stuart touched on a point the importance of which she has emphasised in all that she has written on education ;

Their manners . . . are most carefully trained and perfected
from infancy ·to the University, where lessons in Japanese
etiquette are given all through the course. Even tiny boys
and almost babies learn to bow—the ceremonial Japanese bow
with open palms sliding down to the knees—a very dignified
salutation when it is given·in the beautiful Japanese dress, and
quaintly pretty when the baby of eighteen months, in brilliant
satin brocade, attempts it on a slippery floor and ends in a
prostration—a perfect little Japanese lily with all its petals
outspread.

The fortnight in Japan passed all too quickly for those
who had so long looked forward to it, and on March 27
Mother Stuart left for ·Vancouver on the *Empress of Russia*.
Two days before leaving she wrote to Roehampton :

Tokyo : March 25th, 1914.
You have written me such splendid letters, and I don't seem
to have written to you for ages and ages. . . . There were
three drawers full of letters waiting for me here; quantities
required a personal answer : so I have been working downwards
through that heap, promising myself a letter to you when I
got to the bottom of it. This has just been reached, and I
deserve the promised holiday. To begin with, I have always
forgotten to tell you for Sister K. that I saw (of course) her
brother at Sydney, so curiously like her when he smiles ! Such
a good man and faithful member of the household, devoted
to it and to the Mothers, but very lonely since the death of his
wife. . . .
This morning we had the distribution of certificates. There
are no prizes. . . . It was in the Japanese School first—very
solemn, all standing, with the reading of the Imperial Rescript
addressed to schools in general on the value of education, etc.,
and singing of the Japanese National Anthem. . . .
I have seen some things for education's sake, to understand
the needs of the country—for instance, the Women's University
and the High School attached to it. The School was more
interesting than the University. They were having what we
would call a general assembly before classes opened—with us
it would have been for prayers ; with them, they said, ' to quiet
their hearts '—standing in a body and singing in presence of the
Head Master . . . and in the four corners of the room were
colossal figures of some heroes of Japanese mythology—in
particular, ' Momotaro ' (' son of a peach '), accompanied by his
preternatural monkey whose wisdom helped him. It is sad
beyond words to see such bright children surrounded with
such horrors in place of Our Lady and the Saints. In another

room little boys and girls were sitting at low single desks—very
quiet, the boys' heads buried in their hands—and this was five
minutes' meditation to quiet their hearts, said the Principal,
stroking the region where the heart is symbolically, and, I think,
the bronchial tube in reality.   To judge from the faces that the
little boys cautiously lifted up, their meditation was not without consolation : they were brimming over with merriment.
I asked what they meditated upon, but the Principal could not
or would not understand.

I also saw Kamakura, which is the Riviera of Japan, in case
we should have to get a villa there later on for the summer.
The father of one of the children took me there in his motor
from Yokohama, which is only an hour from here by train.
It is a pretty bit of coast, but not quite the Riviera, only one
gets a splendid view of the sacred mountain, Fuji-San, which
appears in almost all Japanese landscapes ; and on the way we
saw the gigantic Buddha of Kamakura, whose temple was
entirely carried away by a tidal wave ; but as Buddha is colossal
and all of bronze, he 'sat tight,' and now remains exposed to
view, as one often sees him in pictures.   Poor lepers were
praying at the gate.   They are not isolated here unless they
choose to go in for treatment, and the poor cannot.

. . . A tiny little Marchioness came to meet me at the
station in her motor, glorious in blue silk brocade and gold.
The dresses are beautiful.   She looks like a child of ten years
old, but is twenty-three.   She was the only daughter of the
last of the Shoguns, the dynasty who persecuted the Christians
so cruelly for three hundred years. . . .   Her title has gone
to her husband that a new line of this exalted race may be
begun, and she has three children already.   Things are changing
even in Japan.   Up to 1868, when the restoration of the Emperor
took place and the power of the Shoguns was broken, when the
carriage of this family appeared in the streets every man, woman
and child was obliged to prostrate with face on the ground, and
any head that dared to lift itself up to look was immediately
chopped off by the outrunners of the carriage.

I have never told you about Manila.   We spent half a day
there and went about with an ' old child ' to inspect, who, since
her parents' death, lives alone, giving herself to good works,
having collected in her house her god-children, six, I think, a
professor to teach them, an old and courteous man ; a controller ·
of the household, various servants, and four dogs, who rushed
out baying to receive us.   The house was very much illuminated,
and the gramophone sang Gounod's *Ave Maria* while we dined,
each fanned by one of the god-children, the professor looking
on and bowing, the controller directing the service, the dogs
sniffing round, and C. herself beyond all bounds in excited

happiness to have three Mothers of the Sacred Heart under
her roof. It was a scene indescribable, never to be forgotten,
especially coming after the interviews with the Delegate
Apostolic, the Jesuits, some nuns of the Assumption, of whom
the Superior delighted me, one of those shrewd Irish nuns that
one sometimes meets who hold both worlds in their minds,
straight and true in a land of lies. Then back to the *Coblentz*
in the dark across the harbour, and all of a sudden it broke
into phosphorescence. . . . Good-bye, I must really stop ; the
next letters will be at Vancouver, the next posted will come
to you from the West. . . .

The cold was intense in the North Pacific, and added much
to the sufferings of the journey. On the evening of April 5 the
steamer reached Victoria, and the next day arrived at the port
of Vancouver. The spring sun lit up a scene of wonderful
beauty. The snow-covered Canadian Rockies towered above
the forest-clad slopes of the hills, which stretched down to the
waters of the bay, out of which rose innumerable little islands
covered with giant trees. ' One of the most beautiful spots in
the world,' was the comment of the travellers. But Mother
Stuart had not come to rest, nor to enjoy beautiful scenery.
On reaching Point Grey, the Convent of the Sacred Heart, she
heard that all had been prepared to take her to Seattle by the
night train, and she accepted the proposal. It was three o'clock,
she had five and a half hours before her, as the departure was
fixed for eight-thirty. During this time, quite forgetful of her
fatigue, she first saw the assembled community, then went immediately to the school for the official reception. On leaving
the hall she found the Archbishop awaiting her. She left him to
receive the Children of Mary, assembled in great numbers. This
interview over, she returned once more to the school for a
literary meeting. She had scarcely re-entered her room, where
she found two hundred letters on her bureau, then she was again
called to see the Archbishop. Leaving him, she sought a little
quiet in the chapel, then, having again assembled the community,
she left the house to pass a sleepless night in the train. Referring
to this afternoon, she wrote a few days later from Seattle : ' We
came here by night, having spent an afternoon at Vancouver, and
got through all the receptions in that space—three-thirty to
eight-thirty—Alleluia ! '

It was not wonderful that some who already knew her were
filled with dismay at the sight of her fatigue when she reached
Seattle the following morning at nine o'clock, still fasting, in the

hope of being able to receive Holy Communion, and gain strength for more strenuous days.

The situation of Seattle was as lovely as that of Vancouver, the Interlaken of the States, it has been called. The convent itself is in a forest, where clearings have been made and a park and garden laid out. It was only three years old, and yet, as Mother Stuart told the children, ' it had all the marks of a school of the Sacred Heart.'

On Holy Saturday Mother Stuart returned to Vancouver, where, in the absence of the school, the community was able to enjoy her visit to the full. The only ' ceremony ' of those days was the planting of a cedar to commemorate her passage. Long walks were taken in the forest, and excursions into the no-man's land around them.

On Thursday, the 16th, she left for Montreal. The long journey of four days and five nights was broken at Winnipeg, where an old child of Manhattanville was awaiting her. The visit had been announced in the local papers, so that all former pupils in the neighbourhood might come to meet her. A great number appeared, all with one request, that a school of the Sacred Heart might be opened without delay in the town. Many future pupils were presented, their ages varying from sixteen months to six years. The following letter was written *en route* for the East :

Medicine Hat : April 18th, 1914.
This will be an experiment in writing on the Canadian Pacific Railway. We are about half-way to Winnipeg, having left Vancouver on the 16th. . . . It is a wonderful railway to have built, especially the Western part through the mountains. We spent all yesterday going through the Rockies and Selkirk Range, beautiful indeed, but I fancy the most beautiful part, which they call fifty Switzerlands in one, was passed during the night. . . . I saw nothing more beautiful than—for instance—the Semmering Pass or the Swiss Alps, but still there were great glories of God's creation, but very lonely. One eagle was the only remarkable wild living thing we saw. And now we are on a plain bounded only by the horizon. Soon we are coming to the great grain country. . . .

One thing I have learned this morning and it made me laugh. Instead of ' No admittance except on business ' or ' You are humbly requested not to enter ' or ' Please do not knock,' they put briefly and impressively on office doors ' Keep out.'

The Sault and Montreal were already known to Mother Stuart, and when she left, wrote one of the community, ' not one of us but felt her departure as a personal loss. Her very manner of coming up the steps to greet us on her arrival had such a winning appeal in it that it went straight to each heart.' In both houses there were large communities and many works, all of which had to be presented to her. One day, speaking of Indian customs, she said she liked the name the Indians had given to their Black-robe, Father Brébeuf, ' *Echon*,' or ' the one who carries the burden.' ' Afterwards when I saw her,' writes the nun quoted above, ' she asked me to write this word for her. Looking up and seeing the tired look in her dear eyes, I said, " You are our *Echon*," and she answered so gravely and earnestly, " Yes, I am *Echon*." '

The long strain was telling more and more upon her. She had been, as Father Gallwey had said he feared she would be, ' too willing,' and had never known what it meant to spare herself. ' Looking at the programme and seeing " Reception of the Children of Mary of the World " marked, she turned to me,' continues the above writer, ' and said, " What are they going to do with me ? " This pathetic question gave as it were a keynote to her life.' She had surrendered herself to God, and to all the instruments of His choice.

Many visitors came to her at Montreal, among them some Christian Iriquois, one of whom spoke to Mother Stuart of Katherine Tegawithka, the Lily of the Mohawks, and showed a relic which she said she always wore round her neck. Its appearance bore witness to the truth of the statement; without a moment's hesitation Mother Stuart kissed it reverently.

A priest who met her on this occasion wrote later :

I regretted very much not having been present when she received the Iriquois of Caugnawauga, and won their hearts by kissing all their babies. Indeed, it is the motherliness of Reverend Mother Stuart that struck me as her most charac-teristic trait. . . .

Naturally she spoke of the new book she was about to publish, and which by some extraordinary economy of time and an unexplainable control of surroundings, she had succeeded in writing during her journey round the world. ' Would I like to have a copy of it when it appeared ? ' Of course I was more than delighted, but soon afterwards she left Montreal, and then came the distressing news of her death. This sudden termina-tion of her earthly career naturally banished all hope of ever receiving the promised volume. To my great astonishment, the book arrived a few months later, before it was announced

in the public press. Inside was a card which informed me that
just before her death Mother Stuart had left a list of those to
whom she wished the book to be sent, and that my name was
on it. This extraordinary solicitude for even a casual acquaintance made me understand how Mother Stuart had such a deep
hold on the affections of those who knew her intimately.

On May 4th Mother Stuart left Canada for the States. The
date fixed for her return to Europe was June 20th. In these
seven weeks she visited her convents at Kenwood, Maplehurst,
Eden Hall, Madison Avenue, Elmhurst, and Manhattanville.

Everywhere it was the same story, ' her state of suffering
combined with such patience and sweetness, and such lavish
spending of self for souls was a silent but forcible witness to her
finished holiness. We felt she was all unconsciously painting
herself line by line in the conferences given at Manhattanville,'
wrote one of the community at Maplehurst.

In the Vicariate House of Manhattanville she spent four
weeks; fully occupied weeks. In one she gathered together all
the Head Mistresses of the Schools and Mistresses of Studies in
America and discussed with them their important work. They
had scarcely gone when the house refilled, this time with all the
Superiors in the States and Canada.

In the days which followed, in the closest intimacy, she
spoke to them as to her most trusted auxiliaries, of her desires
and hopes for them and for the Society. ' The lantern of the
Shepherd is the light of the Flock,' she said, quoting the words
of St. Gregory of Nazianzen. And in a daily conference for
eight days she set before their eyes the ' ideal Superior ' in her
relations to the central authority of the Order, to the house
under her care, to the souls entrusted to her, and finally and
above all to God.

' We have reached the very heart of things,' she said, when
we came to speak of the spiritual life of the Superior. . . . ' She
is the soul of the house, its spiritual well-being depends upon
her as to the whole. . . . If she is the soul of the house, it is
just as true to say that her spirit of prayer is the soul of her
soul.'

It is not possible, nor necessary, to give a complete analysis
of these conferences here. They have already been printed for
those for whom they were intended. In them as in her little
book on ' The Society of the Sacred Heart,' she insisted on the
Mother's love of every true Superior.

There is no one among them all [the community] who has
not a claim, a real right to our best devotedness, our prayers,
intense study, our patience, the use of our experience, as far as
we have it . . . we must not be too bad copies of what a Mother
should be. . . .

While outlining the 'ideal Superior' she was careful to
insist on the personal equation.   Copies, she insisted, were always
deplorable.   'God never meant us to be copies: no two flowers
are alike, no two leaves, so no two souls, and no two houses.
Each must give what she has got, and God's gifts are divided
as He pleases.'

In the midst of these important occupations she never forgot
the needs of any around her.   During these weeks she daily
visited the infirmary to read to a Sister, who was very ill, less so
indeed than her visitor, whom she survived.

She was always trying to give pleasure by little acts of
courtesy.   'Whenever she wanted a book from the library or
wished to return one, she sent for the librarian.'   It would have
been easier and quicker for her to have given the books to her
secretary, but she knew the great joy it gave another to have
these frequent opportunities of saying a word to her, and on
these occasions she was never in a hurry, but always had time
at her disposal !

During her long journey her clothes had become much worn ;
she said nothing, but her gratitude and pleasure when anything
was mended or replaced was overwhelming.   When a new habit
was given to her, she sent for the Sister who had made it, to give
her the pleasure of seeing it was all right, and to thank her for
making it.

Her fidelity to Rule and exactitude never failed.   On her
way to recreation one day she passed a room in which a number
of specimens of creatures native to American waters had been
gathered for her inspection.   One of those with her begged her
to go in and look at them.   'But I should be late for recreation,'
she answered in surprise.   Had she been so, it would have been
for the first time in her life.

She always wished to be treated as the rest of the community,
and was unwilling that more should be given to her than to her
daughters.   Wherever she went it was the same, and she gently
refused many little attentions dictated by love, and by the wish
to alleviate her sufferings.

When in New York a doctor was at last called in, he was

amazed to find her working in such a condition. ' But this cannot go on,' he said : ' you will kill her.' He declared—as, indeed, was too evident—that rest was absolutely necessary. But for her, at the moment, it was practically impossible. Each day had its allotted task, and until all had been accomplished ' rest ' was out of the question. Half an hour daily in an arm-chair was all she could find time for ; and the first day that she gave herself this slight relief she said, with something of surprise, ' It is the first time I have ever sat in an arm-chair.'

When people spoke of her return to America for the centenary of the establishment of the Society of the Sacred Heart in Louisiana by Mother Duchesne, she answered : ' It is possible, but for the moment my only plan is to return to the Mother House. The curtain falls after July 4.'

This memorable visit and retreat at Manhattanville closed, as perhaps was fitting, on the Feast of the Sacred Heart, June 19. ' We felt that day the full joy of our *Cor unum*,' said one present. And Mother Stuart too had her heart overflowing with consolation. ' It was a heavenly day,' she said, ' scarcely for earth.'

The separation came all too quickly. The next morning she left for Europe on the *Olympic*. Writing, while on her way to England, to Monsignor Zorn de Bulach, she said :

The last stage in America has left me full of thankfulness and consolation. We had a gathering at Manhattanville of sixty-four Superiors and possible Superiors, for a retreat of eight days. On the Feast of the Sacred Heart one hundred and sixty-three of us renewed our vows, and we spent a day that was like heaven, feeling in its fullness the strength of our motto, *Cor unum*. We sailed the following morning, and there is no room in my soul for any feeling except thanksgiving for God's help and protection on this long absence.

The long journey had been accomplished. Its fruits she trusted to the hands of God. She had given of her best, good measure, pressed down and running over, and she had received in return a love which it has been given to few to receive. A bond of sympathy united her to her Society, so strong that from henceforth it seemed that all she had dreamt of for its good would be possible to her.

CHAPTER XXVII

' He Himself knew what He would do.'

AND so she returned home—ready, it would seem, if anyone ever had been so, for her life's work. She had seen all, studied all at first hand. Her nuns were no mere names to her, but living personalities !

> . . . one thing with me
> My cross, my consolation and my crown.

The wearying details of her life were as nothing to her, for the hope that burned strong within. In a letter written during these years we read :

> I don't think the conventionalities are using me up ! I live my inner life apart, and very happily. I am getting accustomed to the conventional and ceremonial part. It is wearisome, but it now impresses me so little that it is not exhausting. It is like the jingling harness of a Neapolitan mule, and, like the mule, I shake my ears and go on my way. What is exhausting is the hours of listening to personal difficulties, and trying to straighten them out. But that has to be : it is one of my most useful fields of work (I hope) when I am visiting.
>
> My head is full of plans and dreams of what might be done, but I must be patient : people are not ready yet.

Her ' ideals ' for her nuns were among these dreams, and her ' ideals ' for the education of the children—dreams apparently about to be realised. All the threads were in her hands. For this her previous life had been but a preparation ! So all thought, and perhaps she herself.

But ' the moment we are most fit to live is the moment God will call us to die,' she had said once ; and so it was to be now.

On the evening of June 26, 1914, she reached Roehampton. The joy of her return was clouded by anxiety, for her suffering was too evident. The light had died out of her eyes : they were

sunken, and so weary. ' For the first time in my life, entering
her room, I found her leaning back against her chair, and not
working.' It was indeed an ominous change. A fortnight of
complete rest was ordered, and she was to take it at Roehampton. She seemed to revive in the old loved surroundings.

But it was evident to those who knew her best that her
interest, even in all that was most beautiful on earth, was fading.
God only had a place in her soul. It was more and more of an
effort to turn from that heavenly attraction. ' When I looked
up last evening, during recreation [on the terrace at Roehampton],
to the oratory,' she said, ' I had to turn away quickly, otherwise
I should no longer have been free.' From her place among the
community she could see the red lamp burning before the
Blessed Sacrament. ' In prayer one gets nearer and nearer to
something, and then the faculties can no more : it is the vision
of God to which we are approaching. To pierce the veil is
not for this life, but oh, the joy and bliss of being allowed to
approach it ! '

It was in truth the dawn of the vision of God ; but, before
the full sun should rise, a way of sorrow had yet to be traversed.

On June 28 the first mutterings of the world-storm were
heard from then almost unknown Serajevo. A month of alternating hopes and fears was to pass before it burst forth in all its
fury, and on July 9 Mother Stuart returned to Ixelles, rested,
so she said, but still far from well.

She immediately settled down to her usual life of labour :
to escape from it was impossible ; but all was done that could
be to lessen the burden and obtain for her the still much-needed
rest.

There were twenty-four aspirants in the Mother House, come
together from all parts of the world, ' chosen and brought here
by God Himself,' she said to them, ' in circumstances most un-
foreseen by us, but foreseen and provided for from the beginning
by His Providence.' They had arrived the previous February,
and she seemed determined now to make up to them for anything
they had lost by her absence. In the ten days before the opening
of their retreat, she saw them all in private, and went frequently
to their recreations. They questioned her one day as to the
most beautiful thing she had seen in her journey. ' In the realm
of souls or of nature ? ' she asked, and then answered : ' I have
seen at least a great variety of souls. No two alike, and their
study is more interesting in age than in youth, as the type is
firmer, the characteristics more marked ; there is less apparent

variety among younger souls. . . . As to the most beautiful thing in nature, I think it was the entrance to the port of Vancouver.'

On July 23 the following letter was written—the last—to the community at Roehampton:

It is a fortnight to-day since I left Roehampton, and I have been wishing to write a line in remembrance and in thanksgiving for the joy that God gave us all of being together again for so many unexpected days. So He gives us surprises in our life from time to time, all intended to shorten the way of our pilgrimage, and carry us forward, braced up by joy, towards our heavenly country. I often think of the many things we touched upon at recreation, and how much one would like to say further upon these and a hundred others still untouched. The spiritual world is so rich, tropically rich, and one longs to explore it, and speak of it to those who care, and that is all of us.

I found the beatitude of hunger and thirst for the things of God all through the Society, and to come back to an old refrain that you well know; I am quite sure that we must work in the vein of spiritual things, and especially spiritual conversations, to get something for our own hunger and thirst, and something to give to others; and also that there is a corollary of special beatitude for those who have helped to spread the spiritual banquet before others.

Talking of thoughts and spiritual things, I have not ceased to think about blind obedience, have you? And the more one thinks of it, the more splendid it seems, for if one comes to think of it, the blindness is not from darkness but from light, the light that is beyond us still, which we may gain in flashes, 'the flash of one trembling glance,' as St. Augustine says, in the most trivial moments and things, and the more we look, the more the blindness will be light, dazzling and incomprehensible, but unmistakably from heaven.

And so we can see with wide-open eyes that God is nearer to us than we thought, in school-books, and details, and end-of-term occupations, and all sorts of things that are not as we should choose for ourselves: because obedience is there, and the more we walk in that way, the brighter the light of God's presence shines: and the least little following after self-will or personal choice dims it, and chills our joy.

I was at Jette yesterday for a clothing, and it was supposed also to be my belated feast, so I reaped a great bouquet of all the charitable prayers of nine months from each category, and gave my account of her houses round the world to our Blessed Mother Foundress, and recommended you all to her. . . .

The last week in July opened, one of the most momentous in the history of the world. On July 28 the die was cast. Austria declared war, rejecting Serbia's apology. Mother Stuart announced the evil tidings to the community, and begged for earnest prayers that a world disaster might be averted. But it was not to be, and a few days later Europe was aflame.

On August 2 Belgium in her turn received an ultimatum, and having refused to betray her trust, saw armies pouring over her frontiers. For ten days her little army gallantly resisted the violation of her territory : but Liège fell on the 15th, and on the 20th Brussels was occupied.

It would be impossible to describe Mother Stuart's sorrow and anxiety. Her days were spent in prayer, and in the immediate duty of trying to organise for the safety of her Religious. Her first thought was for the novices at Jette and the aspirants awaiting their profession.

' I was one of the Americans whom she did not know how to dispose of, whether to keep or risk sending to England, if passports were available,' writes one of these who was a probanist at the time. ' Our little party spent hours in the streets of Brussels, looking for passports, going from American to British consulates. I can still see Reverend Mother sitting in her room as we gathered round her on the evening of our long day. . . . Her face was very careworn. We said we were not a bit afraid, and that it had seemed to us the most natural thing in the world to be walking in the city on business. She brightened up visibly. " That is right," she said, " the unexpected ought to be natural to you." '

The professions made in such circumstances had a special solemnity. Instead of the usual affluence of guests, two only could be present. All the aspirants had left the Mother House in safety, if not without adventure, before the ' doors closed between Belgium and the outer world.' Writing on August 14, Mother Stuart said :

. . . In these times specially, when all human landmarks are wrenched away and we are sailing, as they have to sail now, ' all lights out ' the one thing to which we can thrill is hope in God, an utter trust without understanding, that He will bring the best out of our lives. I loved a thing they read in the refectory yesterday, from the sermon of a Jesuit at a profession, ' *les événements sont les sacrements de la volonté de Dieu.*' And to-morrow is Our Lady's Assumption, good to think of, isn't it ? When we get there, beyond all the troubles of this

life, how glad we shall be to look back on hard days, how ashamed
we should feel if our lives had passed without being tried ! And
certainly it is a time to learn to go beyond ourselves, and forget
our own little unit, so as to grow into the spirit of the great
whole. . . .

How great a consolation to know that our whole Empire,
united in heart, is at war in a noble cause ! I could not have
dreamed of anything so wholly satisfying for England, after
years of scolding for her inertness and love of play had fallen
on unheeding ears. It takes reality to rouse the British Lion,
but what a fine lion cub we are fighting for in this little Belgium.

The departure of the British and Americans is hastened
lest communications should be cut with Ostend, so I must
finish. . . .

No sooner had war been declared than Mother Stuart
organised an ambulance in the house. All were set to work
to prepare the necessary linen for its occupants. She came
herself to these busy meetings, bringing delightful books, and
proposing questions for discussion as if no great burden pressed
upon her.

At two o'clock in the morning of August 6 the house was roused
by prolonged ringing of the bell. When the doors were opened,
some fifteen or twenty nuns entered. They had left the house at
Liège, for on account of its commanding position overlooking
the town, it was exposed to heavy fire. Not all had come, the
old and infirm and the young had been sent on to seek a safer
shelter ; when the town fell, the convent was occupied for a time
by the invading army, and its lawful inmates, with the exception
of three or four guardians, sought shelter among their friends
at Liège. These fugitives were taken to the ambulance in the
Mother House, of which they were the first inmates.

Mother Stuart's health had seemed to improve after her
return to Ixelles, and the doctor held out hopes of a complete
recovery. But the anxieties of these days were too much for
her, and a bad relapse soon reduced her to a state of great
exhaustion.

The Mother House was cut off, not only from the outer world,
but even from the Belgian convents. No communication was
allowed. ' We are, as it were, in a prison cell with high walls and
no windows,' she said, ' having only a dormer-window looking
to the sky. Each morning the sun penetrates by it—Our Lord's
presence in the Mass.' The prayer that seemed to her best
suited to those days, and which was constantly on her lips, was
that of Josophat when confronted, as the Scripture tells us, ' by

a multitude, which cometh violently upon us : '' Lord, as we
know not what to do, we can only turn our eyes to Thee.'' '

Rare messengers appeared from time to time, risking much
to bring a few words from the isolated houses, many of which
were at the moment in the firing line. After days of silence, a
messenger arrived from Tournai, but only to announce that in
the street fighting, which had accompanied the taking of the
town, two of the nuns had met their death ; one of them the
Superior of the house. No certain details were available. The
situation of the convent had exposed its inmates to peril. Many
of them were old and infirm, for the house had been a ' refuge '
for the French exiles, and in barricading the windows looking
on the streets, to protect her community, the Superior and her
companion had met their death. One bullet had killed both.
It was a moment of great sorrow to Mother Stuart, all the more
that she was unable to do anything to help this sorely tried house.
The messenger dared not take more than a few words of loving
sympathy written in haste. The letter which she wrote later
never found a bearer. This news redoubled her anxiety as to
the fate of the other convents.

Presently rumours were spread abroad that Pius X was dead.
No confirmation of the report could be had, and for long the
uncertainty remained. The following letters were written
during these trying days, in the hope, she said, that some chance
might bring them to their destinations. They reached Roehampton on September 4, brought by a Belgian who escaped
with his family, a few hours before her own arrival :

. . . Yesterday evening the door closed between us and the
outer world, by the entrance of the Germans into Brussels, but
in the later evening I had the happy surprise of a letter from
England, the last for the present. . . . Now, on the chance of
some opportunity, or re-opening of the door, I will begin to write,
and tell you what happens, if anything happens, and if the letter
breaks off without ending you will know that an opportunity
came. On the 19th I saw the Vice-President of the *Chambre*,
who thought, as all the papers, that even the expectation of a
raid on Brussels was over for the moment or altogether. However,
in the night there was a great panic, and the Civil Guard, all we
had in the city, had to be disarmed, and I suppose they faced
then the German occupation as probable. Then the news came
nearer and nearer during the day, and after various details that I
need not go into, we heard yesterday, the 20th, at five-thirty, that
the capital had surrendered. Of course it could not fight, being
an open town ; there was no question of siege or bombardment,

but simply of entering. The little army is no doubt concentrated to defend Antwerp, which is looked upon as more important, and may and probably will be besieged.

Now we are under German government. A force of three thousand occupies Brussels, the staff established at the Hôtel de Ville, and the soldiers in the barracks. Yesterday we expected an occupation here in the house, but as things have turned out, I think it improbable, as they have placed themselves more at the centre. I know I have your prayers. How beautiful to have that daily ' nightly adoration.' We could not have our usual Thursday-night exposition last night, as the Chaplain warned us that it would not be wise, as our chapel windows are so much in view. The new inhabitants spent the night in setting telephone wires round our walls; we do not know where they communicate. In fact we know nothing at all excepting that God is directing everything, and says ' thus far and no farther ' when He pleases. It teaches one as nothing else could do, what detachment and confidence in God means.

24th.—This morning I had a visit from the new military Governor of Brussels, new since the day before yesterday, for Count von Armin went on with the army. This is a German Pole, also a Catholic, by name Jarosky. He came in answer to a request which I sent to him to be allowed to communicate with our houses in Austria, to tell them that all is well here. I have tried, through the Spanish and American Legations, to send a word to other parts of the world, but it is out of the question; they can do nothing. He tried to be as nice as he could, and will send a telegram himself to Vienna to say that our houses are untouched. . . . He said that England had not wanted the war, but that it was inevitable. How much of his news is true remains to be seen. It will be ancient history when this reaches you, and we shall know the truth or error of what he reported : that it is all over with Russia ; that the troops were throwing down their arms and coming over in masses to Germany ! . . . I begin to doubt more and more about the Pope's death. The Nuncio is in Antwerp, but at the nunciature they know nothing, so we held no service for him. How oddly this will read to you, that we should have been in such complete ignorance. It is something to live through it. I think for all of us, these are some of the greatest days and grandest opportunities of our life; may they not be lost by any one of us, for they are chances that will not come again.

27th.—No doubt left now about the Holy Father. At least his death is believed at the nunciature. We pray for the repose of his soul, and the election of a new Pope. What a moment for a Conclave. . . .

We get very little news of the great movements. The

Comte de Vauzelle comes every two or three days to tell us
what he has been able to gather. And Reverend Mother
Nerincx gets faint echoes through her family at Hal. One of
them walks in by the canal, a quiet way, nine miles, and he has
not been molested once so far. Reverend Mother Nerincx's
brother is Vice-President of the *Chambre*, and with the Doyen
and Burgomaster is carried off every evening at nine by the
police, and let go in the morning. It is as a hostage for the
quiet of the inhabitants of Hal. These three notables would be
promptly shot if there were any disturbance, or if the passage
of troops was impeded. . . .

To another she wrote :

This is written without knowing when or how it can be
sent, but it will tell you that I have thought of you while we
are cut off from all the outer world. I know how hard these
times will be for you, and I pray daily to God to remind you
that you are a professed of the Providence of God, and therefore by right and duty more bound to see and hope for the
best. . . . How lovely it will be to look back at it all from
heaven.

Though few if any foresaw, or believed then, that a long
war was possible, yet the inconvenience of having the Superior
General and her council shut up in Brussels, and cut off from
communication with all but half a dozen of her houses, was very
evident. It was thought that she should do as Reverend Mother
Gœtz had done in similar circumstances in 1870, and take
refuge for a time in another house. England appeared to be
the most convenient place. The Superior of Ostend appealed
to Canon Camerlynck, Dean of the Chapter, asking him how it
would be possible to get the Superior General out of Brussels.
After some delay, he announced that he had found a friend able
and willing to undertake the adventure—M. Maurice Elleboudt,
nephew of an alderman of the town. It was not without danger
that he set out for the occupied zone. Passports were not given,
entrance was prohibited, and he knew he must trust to the
Providence of God to get him in by some unguarded spot. His
faith was rewarded, and he entered Brussels unmolested on
September 2. Going immediately to the Mother House, he
explained his mission to Mother Stuart and her council. All
urged her to avail herself of this chance, the last possibly, and
to go where she could watch over the welfare of the Society.
She yielded reluctantly, for it was not possible to take her

assistants with her. .She felt deeply leaving them and her
Belgian houses exposed to such difficulties.

Those who so bravely bade her go where duty seemed to call
had another anxiety, for they knew that she was quite unfit for
the fatigue and uncertainties of the journey. To reach Ostend,
an affair of two hours in normal times, now twelve or fourteen
hours were needed. She was at the moment on the way to
recovery, so the doctors said, and with rest and care might yet
be well. But in the gathering gloom of the spreading war-
cloud, with the uncertainty as to its end and meaning, it seemed
best to let her go.

Leaving the Mother House, Monsieur Elleboudt attempted
to get passports. He was told by the German officials that he
was too late, he might try the following day. From the manner
of his reception, and the rumours in the town, he was convinced
that none would be issued, and determined to risk an escape
without them.

Early the next morning he called at the *Chaussée de Waterloo*.
Mother Stuart was ready, and accompanied by her secretary and
a Sister set out on her last journey.

The parting was sorrowful in the extreme : the hasty farewell,
which was in reality the last, the empty place, and the great
silence that must follow. It was made endurable only by the
hope that at no distant date they would be reunited.

The travellers could take no luggage, as they had to avoid
attracting attention. A wonderful Providence watched over
this ' flight into England.' No questions were asked as they
made their way by a succession of trams to Ninove and then to
Denderleeuw on the frontier of Brabant. But where they had
hoped to find a train they discovered that the line was no longer
in Belgian hands; it had been lost since the previous evening,
and no trains were running. A countryman passed in his cart
' with a grey mare,' as Mother Stuart did not fail to note. Monsieur Elleboudt asked him to convey the party to another station
some twenty miles further on. He willingly agreed, and a long
drive of two-and-a-half hours landed them at Sotteghem, outside
the occupied territory. From here they made their way to
Ghent, where there was a long wait for a train, and in the station
they learnt the name of the new Pope. That evening they
reached Ostend. A day later they could not have left Brussels
by that road : as they passed, the waves of the invading flood
had closed up behind them. The convent servant, who had
accompanied them half-way, brought back reassuring news to

Brussels and a few lines from Mother Stuart; they spoke of the
sorrow of the parting, and ended ' it was for God and the Society.'
Ostend was besieged by Belgians seeking to take refuge in
England : to get a place on the overcrowded boats, Mother
Stuart had to stand next day for some two or three hours in a
long queue, waiting her turn.   It was cold and damp, and when
she reached Roehampton late that evening she was utterly
exhausted.

The return was indeed unlike anything one could have
imagined.   It was a revelation of the way God's ever busy
Providence loses sight of no thread in the lives of any one of His
creatures, in the midst of even world-wide calamities.   Had
Mother Stuart been told to express a desire, or choose a spot on
earth in which to die, she might have wondered at the question,
like St. Monica, or she might have said, in the words of the Jesuit,
which she quoted in a letter,[1] ' May I pass from *that* very vestibule
of heaven to the unveiled splendour within.'   But that it should
ever have been so had seemed to her, and indeed to all, to have
gone beyond the realm of the possible in 1911.   But now, the
onflowing tide of war had carried her boat into that very haven.

She found there all the Superiors from Australia, Japan, and
Egypt.   They had arrived for the retreat in the Mother House,
planned so lovingly and destined never to be given.

For four days she tried to take up her old life with the community.   She even assisted at a ceremony on September 8,
but the next day she confessed that she ' could no more.'   On
the following Saturday the doctors decided that an operation
should be attempted, as the only means of saving her life.   It
was to take place the next afternoon, and at eleven o'clock on
Sunday she received the Last Sacraments.   In the absence of her
assistants, she herself wrote a circular to the Society telling of her
illness; it ended with the words, ' Let me take this opportunity
to ask pardon of the Society for . . . all that I have omitted or
done badly, or which may have caused suffering to you.   But
let me also assure you of my real love for all and for each.
Knowing it, you will, I know, forgive the rest to your poor
Mother. . . .'

To the last moment she continued to work, answering letters
and reading all she received, even seeing those whom she feared
were in some need.   ' We heard of the doctors' decision on
Saturday evening,' writes an American then passing through

[1] See chap. xxiv, p. 406.

Roehampton. ' I abandoned all thought of seeing her, but I had not fathomed her charity. On Sunday morning, shortly before receiving the Last Sacraments, she sent for me. My letter, in which I had told her all I wished to say, was in her hand, and she answered it fully. . . . The following Friday I was to leave for Glasgow. . . . She sent for me again that morning, reminded me of what she had said the previous Sunday, and as I left the room she added : " Give my love to them in America. You know I love America." '

It had been said of her more than twelve years before, by an acute observer, ' she has finished with herself long ago.' And so now it appeared in reality. ' Her unconcern regarding her bodily needs was like that of a child, resting in the arms of its mother. She gave herself into the hands of those who nursed her, as if she felt them to be the very sure and safe hands of God Himself.'[1]

For a time she seemed to rally, but the results hoped for from the operation had not been obtained, and the doctors, called in for further consultation, while disclaiming to give up hope, declared her recovery would be very slow. Great patience is needed, they said ; but of that and of prayer there was an abundance all around her. No length of waiting would have been too great to obtain the desired end.

The story of these last days is gathered from those who were in constant attendance on her.

' During her illness, she was at all times serene and undisturbed,' writes the assistant, ' in spite of the news from without, and all the variations of her own state. She was ready for everything as it came, and all was accepted with a radiant simplicity which gave the impression of one living in a world beyond the vicissitudes of human life.

' Yet she was present to all that went on around her. She asked for news of the war every day up to October 17 ; and was full of thought for everyone, especially her nurses. . . . She looked upon all treatment, however repugnant, as part of God's Providence, and submitted whole-heartedly to all that was prescribed. When told to say what she thought might do her good, she did so. " It is as much an act of obedience as anything else," she would say, but she was glad to leave everything to others. When she had been for days unable to take any food, she said to one who was with her : " You will tell me in all simplicity

---

[1] Father Roche, S.J.

if I seek comfort too much." A smile of welcome always greeted those who entered her room, and thanks followed them as they left her.'

Fresh flowers were brought to her every morning, and in the earlier days of her illness she would take them in her hands and look at them with joy, then keep them for a little by her that she might, she said, ' Praise God for all their beauty.'

A special blessing sent to her by the Holy Father filled her with consolation. She kept it on the altar in her room, and often asked for it that she might kiss the writing. Here, from this little altar, she received Communion almost daily. At the end of her silent thanksgiving she sometimes asked that a hymn —generally from the Liturgy—might be read aloud. Her choice fell on *Jam sol recedit igneus*, the Vesper hymn for Trinity Sunday, which she said she loved ; the ' triumphant ' songs of the Feast of the Holy Rosary, and the Hymn of St. Bernard, *Jesu dulcis memoria*. The last she had asked to hear was *Cælestis urbs Jerusalem, beata pacis visio.*

On Sundays she asked that the Sisters might sing to her from the cloister outside her room, she herself choosing the hymn or motet she wished to hear. For a time it was possible to read to her daily, a short quarter of an hour morning and evening. For the morning she chose ' The House and Table of God,' of which she had written to its author[1] two years before : ' The book is before me, a daily joy now. I foresee that it will become my prayer-book as well as my book. The two chapters on death said a great deal to me, and I hope they will to other people too. We have got so hopelessly wrong in our manners as to death, between the world and the doctors and the undertakers, that it is quite refreshing to see the truth in print, as we ought to think it without sentimentality.'

For her afternoon reading she asked for something ' spiritual to be followed by poetry of her own choice.' And her choice fell on Rutherford's ' Last Words,' which she had loved since childhood, and now listened to with ever fresh delight. It was read to her some twenty times. The approaching reality filled her with joy ; each day with fuller truth she could repeat :

> The sands of time are sinking,
> The dawn of heaven breaks,
> The summer morn I've sighed for,
> The fair sweet morn awakes.

[1] Father W. Roche, S.J. (Longmans.)

She looked as if heaven were already in her possession as she listened to the glowing words. 'They are all gone into a world of light' of Vaughan was also a great favourite, and on Sundays she asked for Herbert's poems 'Sweet day so cool, so calm, so bright' and 'Sondayes.' Her choice also fell on the nineteenth chapter of the Apocalypse, where 'the voice of much people in heaven' are heard saying '*Alleluia*,' and the Apostle is bidden write, 'Blessed are they that are called to the marriage supper of the Lamb.' 'My idea of heaven,' she had said once, 'is " and passing He will minister unto them."' [1]

She did not confine her choice to sacred writings and poems. Kipling's 'Recessional' was asked for 'that she might recall a line she had forgotten.' His 'Kitchener's School' and 'Said England unto Pharaoh, I must make a man of you,' were also on the list, as well as Tennyson's 'Ulysses,' and even the 'Lay of the Last Minstrel.' When asking for this she said : 'I will go back to the days of my youth.'

Such signs of life and vigour of mind were deceptive. On October 17 the fever returned with violence, and the doctors knew that she was lost. She herself did not at once feel the end approaching. But knowing that it could not be far off perhaps, and giving as it were one last look on the many souls she had so loved, and on the great work she had planned to do, bowing to the incomprehensible designs of Providence, she said to the assistant, 'God knows all about it.' It was the last incomparable act of submission to things as they were for the love of God, which she had so often encouraged others to make.

Gradually her power of speech began to fail, and her sentences were finished by signs. But as the things of earth faded, her vision of the other world became more and more a reality. That she was intensely happy was impressed on all who approached her. 'I never saw such peace ; it is all beyond my comprehension,' said the nurse, as she listened to the words that from time to time broke forth, revealing a complete inward contentment. 'Very happy for you, Reverend Mother,' whispered one of the nuns kneeling by her side. 'Very happy, oh so happy,' she repeated ; then there was a pause, it seemed the thought had passed, when again the whisper came, 'Oh so happy.' 'You are going to God.' 'Yes, to God,' and she dwelt with love on the word, which years before she had said it was her 'rest' to say.

To love all with the love of perfect charity, as the friends

[1] St. Luke xii. 37.

on whom God had set His Heart, had been her aim and endeavour. On one of the last nights of her life she said to one who was watching by her, showing where her thoughts were travelling, ' I have over six thousand daughters and I love them all.' It was true, no exaggeration, no mere words, no empty boast. Each had a home in her heart ; she had made her own all the sorrows, joys, and interests of these thousands, and indeed of many more besides. The miracle of her life was its so great love. Its meaning, to shadow forth the love of the human Heart of Christ.

It has been said that to every Christian, called by that title to be a saint, some portion of the life and character of Our Lord has as it were been entrusted, that they may show it forth in their own lives, and a continual representation of His life on earth may be found in the Church, His living Body. To some it has been given to show forth His Passion, in others the Poverty of Christ is resplendent. In Mother Stuart's life we see perhaps an image of the *love* of Christ for man. From old, from the beginning, the commandment had been given, ' Thou shalt love the Lord thy God,' that had been taught from heaven, and given forth amid the thunders of Sinai. But ' thou shalt love thy neighbour as thyself ' was taught by the human life of Christ, spoken as He, ' meek and humble of Heart,' stood among the suffering multitudes of men, one with them in all but sin. He Himself, knowing what He said, called it a ' new commandment.' ' A new commandment I give unto you, that you love one another as I have loved you.' As Father Nieremberg says, in his treatise on Divine Grace : ' The whole object of our Saviour's life on earth may be said to have been devoted . . . to teach us by word and example the love of our neighbour. He put before us a height of self-devotion such as no patriarch or prophet had dreamed of, no pagan philosopher imagined.' And it was this ideal that Mother Stuart had striven to attain. ' To pour myself out in love ' was, she had said, the glorious opportunity of her life. Father Nieremberg was one of her favourite authors, and she had grasped fully what the same writer calls ' the two all-important facts : that the seat of this love is in the heart and its expression in personal service of our neighbour.' Such had been Christ's love in His earthly life, and following in the divine footsteps, of such sort was hers. ' God is charity,' says St. Paul, and patiently bearing the limitations of her nature, she too strove to become charity. And that she succeeded, the word-picture of the same Apostle makes abundantly clear.   She too ' was patient, was kind, envied not . . . sought not her own . . . was not provoked to anger, thought no evil. . . .   She bore all things, believed all things, hoped all things, endured all things.'

' If we love well and much, we shall need no other prepara- tion for death,' she had said, ' squandering ourselves and what we have on God and on our neighbour, that is the best way to prepare for it.'   So now she was ready.

But such a friend could not be given up without a struggle ; one last effort was made to win from God the prolongation of her life.   On October 18th and 20th two great novenas were made through Our Lady's intercession, an appeal to the love of a Mother to spare a loved Mother to her children.   Every hour the whole household assembled in the chapel, a great cry mounted to the throne of God, a cry for mercy, and it was re-echoed in many hundred hearts in all parts of the world.

On the afternoon of the first day the prayers for the dying were recited by her side.   At their close Father Roche, a friend of many years, spoke to her, interpreting the sorrow round him.   He asked her ' would she not come back to them, would she not be glad to stay, if God so willed it.'   She had seemed unconscious, but suddenly as if awakened she laughed gently, and said ' Yes, yes,' so sweetly ; then making a sign for her spectacles, she put them on, and tried to look at the kneeling figures round the bed.

It was but for a moment ;   the last in which she turned her thoughts to earth.   During the few hours still left of her pilgrimage, she spoke only to God, or of Him, quite unmindful of those around her ;   sometimes in loving converse, as to one present with her, and sometimes as if still at her daily work, encouraging others to love and trust Him as she did.   ' God is good.   Don't be afraid of God. . . .   I would not be afraid of God.'

On Tuesday, the 20th, Communion was brought to her, and when she was told of the approach of the Blessed Sacrament her face became radiant.   ' He knows, He comes. . . .   He knows what I am,' she whispered to herself.   The priest[1] gave her her last Viaticum, and moved slowly back to the little altar, as he did so, she spoke aloud, the words breaking forth from the fullness of her loving heart.   ' Dear Lord . . . *dear, dear* Lord . . . dear Jesus.'   And she lingered caressingly on the words.   ' How lovely . . . lovely. . . .   What a change ! . . .   Oh, how He

[1] Father Roche, S.J.

loves me !   Oh, *how He longs for me !* ' and then her voice died
away.   Her face was radiant ; it seemed to those around her
' that she had then and there discovered the intensity of the
Divine Love, and was marvelling at its manner.   " *How He
longs for me,*" not as might have been expected " How I long
for Him." ' [1]

God wanting her, longing for her : the words and the
thought hushed earthly sorrow and brought peace to those who
heard them.   It was clear she was no longer theirs.   The
Creator had appeared to claim His own.

That evening again, a wonderful moment revealed to all
that the gates of heaven were open, and they were standing on
its very threshold.   ' Opening her eyes,' writes the nun who
was watching by her, ' she looked up steadfastly, not with the
fixed gaze of the dying, but with eyes beautiful beyond words.'
She appeared as if not more than twenty, her face glowed with
colour, light streamed from her eyes, and a smile of intense
happiness transfigured her.   She spoke to God as to her Father,
there followed an interval of intense silence, while she still gazed
at something seen ·by her alone, then as if exhausted she
repeated several times, " *Ich kann nicht mehr.*"   For over half
an hour she remained in this state of rapture, and then the
light died out ; but throughout the evening from time to time
she broke forth into words of love.   " If you only knew . . . if
you only knew. . .   He is so bright . . . so beautiful . . . so
very beautiful.   My God ! " '

Early in the morning of Wednesday, the 21st, the assistant
entered the room, and going over to her said : ' *Haec dies quam
fecit Dominus, exultemus et laetemur in ea.   Alleluia.*' She
turned her head ; it was clear that she had understood.

The Blessed Sacrament was brought to the room, but she
was unable to receive Communion.   The priest [2] held the Sacred
Host above her head and blessed her.   For some two hours the
watchers knelt in prayer.   Then suddenly, to her listening mind
alone, came the longed-for midnight cry : ' Behold, the Bridegroom cometh,' she opened her eyes, fixing them on some distant
place, and in great silence passed from earth.

Writing of death she had said : ' To us it is a glorified
sorrow, purple with hope and tears, not a sunset but a dawn.'

The public Requiem took place ten days later, on Friday,
October 30.   The Bishop of Southwark, Dr. Amigo, sang the

[1] From a paper written by Father Roche, S.J.
[2] Father Roche, S.J.

CHAPEL OF THE SACRED HEART, ROEHAMPTON

FATHER VARIN, S.J.   MOTHER STUART.   MOTHER DIGBY.

High Mass, and Cardinal Bourne, Archbishop of Westminster, assisted at the throne, and afterwards performed the funeral rites. Numbers of priests were present at the ceremony, while from all parts of the world testimony of grief and veneration reached Roehampton. The world-agony of the war, while accentuating rather than diminishing the personal sorrow, made her death appear, as one wrote: 'a loss which at this time of crisis seems to be a disaster not only to your Order, but to the cause of religious education and the Catholic Church.' 'This is more than a private loss,' wrote another, 'it is a public calamity.'

'Your grief will be shared by many,' wrote the Bishop of Waterford, 'who will never forget her gentle ways and her overflowing kindness. I am one of these.'

From Strassburg, through Italy, Monsignor Zorn de Bulach wrote: 'I have seldom met with such a union of goodness, gentleness, high-mindedness, and keenness of intellect. With her death I have lost a precious friendship, which had brought me both comfort and strength. My deep sorrow is only lessened by the thought that in heaven, where she now sees God, she will pray for me.' And writing later, he said again: 'Her death has been one of the greatest sorrows of my life.'

'For the Order her death is a calamity,' wrote Monsignor Brown, 'for ourselves it is a personal sorrow that lies too deep for words.'

'Personally I feel it as I have felt few deaths,' wrote Father Peter Finlay, S.J.; 'I had come to know her intimately and to entertain feelings of great veneration and affection for her wonderful qualities of mind and heart; and I looked forward to years of friendship, and to great things which I expected her to do for religion. I had hoped the long journey would have compelled her to rest, at any rate on sea, and I fear she worked as hard there as at any other time.

'But it was a wonderful year: I am sure it did more for the advancement of religion, and for the Society of the Sacred Heart, than many quiet years of government at home. I can think of few greater blessings than that so many should have come to see her, and know her personally, and love her.'

She was buried in the chapel she had loved so much, whose walls she had once seen 'flooded with light.' A vault had to be prepared where she might rest, as indeed she would have chosen, at the foot of the altar of the Sacred Heart, and near to the Mother who had guided her in religious life.

While the coffin waited covered with flowers, a robin was its constant companion. He took up his abode in the chapel, and sang his most beautiful songs, sometimes perched high over the Tabernacle, sometimes inspecting the newly-made vault, sometimes feeding among the flowers. He joined his voice with the Office of the nuns, and it was heard through the rolling of the organ. Nothing daunted him, neither numbers of people, nor noise, nor lights, nor incense, and it seemed to his hearers that God had sent him, ' missing on earth the song of hope ' which had never failed to rise to Him from the heart of Mother Stuart.

Thus the poem of her life was finished, its last line written ; the first among the woods and flower-strewn fields of childhood, the last on the threshold of a fairer life, and between lay an ocean of understanding and love.

LETTERS ON THE SPIRITUAL LIFE

' The best we hear in English spirituality of our own day is distilled, drop by drop, from much thought. It does not flow, but it is like the real Turkish attar of roses, distilled from an acre of flowers and priced at £1 a drop ! '—*From a letter, J. Stuart.*

THESE letters are given without comment, except in the rare cases where the owner has supplied it. The grouping under the letters of the alphabet is merely for convenience, and has no other signification.

Letters to ' A.'

March, 1908.

Many thanks for the beautiful spoonbill, who will be stuffed for the glory of God who made him, and the honour of J. who shot him, and the delight of the museum which will possess him, and the memory of A. who sent him, *ad perpetuam rei memoriam.*

Look up, my dear child, look up, not down or backwards.

> Onward and upward
>   Time will restore us,
> Light is above us,
>   Rest is before us.

If you put ' God ' or ' hope ' instead of ' time,' it will be truer and more Christian. Now God bless you. . . . Think of God and He is all yours.

June, 1908.

. . . The little one is very sweet; she has the family eyes, I think, and looks capable of riding a donkey and following the animated traces of B. Thank you for sending her to pay me a visit; I send her back to play with you and to remind her Aunt that as our heart goes out to the weakness and babyhood and trustfulness of such a small creature, and we would *do anything for it*, so and much more God looks at us lovingly and tenderly to dry our tears, to foresee [for] and take care of us, to animate us to mount on our donkey and to gallop without fear ! God is guiding our life always for the best, and everything that comes to us is from Him and must turn out well. He has sent you this great sorrow, my dear child, but great consolation with it, is it not true ? The sorrow will pass, the joy will endure, 'weeping may endure for a night, but joy *cometh in the morning.*'

November, 1908.

My dear, you have just come to a hard place where the two currents meet, and you could let yourself be beaten back towards the shore ; but you can, instead, bend your back to the oars and pull the boat for all you are worth across that rough bit, and it will be better when you get out of the cross-currents. Hold on and let nothing dismay you. You may have to change your means; don't change your purpose. Remember you are doing God's work and God is with you, and all His Saints are looking on, 'a great cloud of witnesses,' while you fight in the arena, and they too have fought and overcome, so they know what they say when they say ' Well done, A.' God bless you always.

December, 1908.

Ever so many thanks for the precious *intense Memorares.* I cannot say how grateful I am for these prayers, and for your recommending me to *holy* people *poor*: what lovely adjectives. How nice if you and I could deserve them both ! But it is better not to think of the adjectives one deserves, but to admire them in others and be lowly and trustful before God. . . .

February, 1909.

God, who looks after the robins and the chaffinches, will surely not forget our dear N., and He who clothes the flowers of the field so that Solomon in all His glory was not arrayed like one of them, will surely not neglect the poppies, but His A. must blindly trust Him and not let the cares of this world pre-occupy her, and keep her anxious and restless. God knows and loves you all, and He knows better than anyone what each of you needs and He will provide. Your work is pleasing to Him, and one of its most precious qualities is that it *constantly* calls on your patience and devotedness. We seem to be *giving* in those things, but we are really receiving, and the most precious opportunities of all are those which seem to give no return for your trouble. But all the same I cannot help being very glad when, now and then, God shows you that He is blessing and loving the work. . . .

May, 1909.

Only a line to tell you that I *love* to think of your ' making a cheerful noise to God.' Joy is splendid, the joy that admits of no half measures, but *will* be glad because its joy is in God, and God and heaven and Our Lady and all that is lovely belong to it. That joy is queenly, and moves in a realm above the huff and the squeeze, so I shall love a banquet of it for my feast. . . .

August, 1909.

Thank you for all, but the news of the soul was the best. You have lived through the first gale after the retreat and kept your rudder firm, *Deo gratias*, a good beginning. It is as you say a critical moment when the first head-wind comes against us after the retreat, and, alas! many let go the rudder, and then follows a great tempest of discouragement. . . . The year will have—as every year has—its trials and temptations, but if you keep the very heart of your life right with our Lord, not a shade between you and Him, all will be well, and I shall find an athlete of Christ in good fighting form when I see you! One that He is proud of: ' Hast thou seen my servant A. ? '

How I should love to hear J. [a little nephew] singing alone *Panem de cælo praestitisti eis* and see their two sweet faces open-mouthed with song to God. They must be sweet little choristers with the organ. I can imagine B.'s rapt look singing *Gloria in excelsis* and thinking of God knows what—very far away—his dead goose perhaps (is it dead ? or was it the antelope ?).

October, 1909.

Courage, my soul! God has all in His hands! We are all very small, very blind, very stupid; when things are going well we are just like little boys, trying some experiment to make them go better, and set the whole nursery screaming (as our dear N. is doing now with the best will in the world, only you must not tell her so), and when we have set it all wrong, we roar to our ever patient Father and Lord to come and set it right again, and He does, though sometimes He waits, as when He knew that the whole family at Bethany was in trouble.

It will come right somehow. You can do little but pray. It is not good to give one's advice unasked. Pray and be patient and nestle closer than ever to the Sacred Heart of Our Lord, where I hope to find you safe—*laughing, soon.*

November, 1909.

You wrote me a good letter, but there is one point on which I should love to see you more free and independent, and that is with regard to responsibility and things which you look upon as ' trust.' Do you know that whatever one may call it to oneself, that is a *little* bit out of tune with the Heart of Our Lord, and a little remains of dancing to the world's fiddle! There! Is that a very hard thing to say ? Not to you, my dear child, who want to be absolutely His. You must go even as far as His tastes,

inclinations, feelings, and He loved best the hidden years of
Nazareth, a heaven on earth. So I think that in employments
that have no show one can, if one will, make the truest heaven
on earth ; and if one will pay the price the *richest* life, morally
and even intellectually, but it is at the condition of the price,
looking upward, heavenward, not stooping to look down, keeping
free from absorption in the work, labouring to make one's mind
think, repeat, observe, compare, treasure up. So much wealth
goes through our hands every day, it is such a pity if it goes to
waste. *Don't let it.* Live a life that, in the midst of material
details, is quiet, rich, thoughtful and progressive. These are the
years to ripen your judgment and give you balance; the first
condition is contentment and quiet. There is a long sermon !
God bless you. I shall pray for you in the procession this morning at the end of the Forty Hours. . . .

                                        November, 1909.

   I am determined to be in time for St. X.'s day to wish you
all the joys of a saint's day with a special meaning, and what
else ? The strong faith and heavenly-mindedness, the fortitude
of your Queen patron, and all our Lord's best blessings at her
intercession. God has been very good to you this last year and
taught you many things. Each year He turns over a new page
for us, and we have a picture to study and a page to read, and at
the end He says : ' Have you understood ? ' and if you can say
' Yes,' then He turns over another, with great pleasure having
a willing and apt scholar ; and then He gives you nature study
lessons Himself between times from your gallant hard-pressed
robins who come in the last extremity, and happy, careless tits
who come at all times, and He makes you understand how all
are welcome so long as they come to Him and are willing to be
tame and confiding. May you be one of His dearest birds. . . .

                                        March, 1911.

   . . . Do not lose a particle of your spiritual joy for any
failure that you find in yourself to come up to your aspirations
and to all that God has done for you. He is not disappointed,
for He knows exactly what we are like, how sensitive, how easily
wounded, how too easily discouraged. He minds nothing in
the way of follies and failures if we only run back quickly to
Him to tell Him the story of our fall and be comforted and run
again. And so we get home in the end. He is very good and
sweet to you and you love Him very much, and with that you
are rich ! . . .

   Thank you for the bird article, most interesting. No
defence for the magpies ! and yet they, too, are God's birds.
God's own magpies, what a problem ! May He bless you
always.

Turin : February 1st, 1912.

Poor N. I feel for her, because it is none the less hard when it might have been avoided, and even harder if she realised it. But often it is not realised in those cases and the onlookers suffer most. I will pray with and for you and her to-morrow, when Our Lady offers the first snowdrop of the world to God, and for His sake and hers, God loves all of us poor little things who can only shiver and tremble and wait for the sun. Keep on looking towards it, looking to heaven and as little as possible to the troubles of earth. The more you trust them all to the Sacred Heart the more faithful Our Lord will be to His trust. . . .

September, 1912.

I do not want your heart to be saddened by my being away. In the thought of Our Lord, in the presence of the Blessed Sacrament, distance is annihilated. He is our link and we live in Him, one heart and one soul beating through and ruling us all. Sing to yourself the Twenty-second Psalm in the Hebrew version, ' The Lord is my Shepherd, I shall not want.' The less anyone else can help us at the time the more He will do Himself. So lift up your soul again and sing.

Letters to ' B.'

The following letters refer directly or indirectly to prayer, and were all written after 1910 :

I think God has given you His two best gifts, light and peace. The first letter filled me with gratitude to Him, for until His light, and He only can give it, shines into that inner stronghold of our unconscious self-love, all other work is only provisional and will require to be re-arranged. Now you have reached bedrock, that truth will not move from under you, and the proof that it comes from God was that the sense of humiliation came with an inward joy. That is God's gift. That was the great thing of that most blessed retreat, something which, please God, you will never lose or cease to be grateful for. Thank God for all.

How glad I am, my dear child, that you have come across that chapter of Père Poulain's (the Prayer of Simplicity) which the C.T.S. have been so well inspired to publish by itself. I think and hope it will disperse all the hesitations and ' preconceptions ' of your noviceship days. The ' light of the latter days ' to your soul is that it is made for God and God made it, and it is unique to Him and must go by the way He calls it, simple and true and confident, using all things as means and letting none be an end but Himself. So go with a free step and a glad heart, despising all that would hamper the movement of your soul towards Him. May He bless you.

You could do without this answer I know, only because the principle is so important, I call your attention to it ; that is, the principle that the framework of aids to prayer is made up of means ; they must be used if useful, not imposed.   You must find the best way of attaining the end, you, yourself, the end for *you*.

You did quite right.   It is well known that Our Lord likes daring prayers when the thought and courage for them come as they did to you.   The *before* and the *after* both seem to indicate that the thought and invitation came from Him, and the joy of that minute, though the feeling of it may go, will ever remain with you as a gift from Our Lord's own love.

Your soul is going through a time of transition and a very blessed one, for you are entering into possession, by degrees, of what He really means for you, and all your whole-hearted endeavours in a wrong direction will not have been lost because they were meant for Him, and they have given you experience of ' how not to do it.'   It is quite true that violence is not God's way *for us* at least.   I know there are heroic examples as of Dom Mus the Trappist, but these ways are not for us, and the best way to God is the straightest and easiest that we can find, not approaching Him like an acrobat, walking on our head, and turning our heart upside down, but running and bounding like a child in its own home, *which He is* to all of us, a home as well as Father and all the rest.

I don't think there is any ground for fear in your ' spectre ' as to prayer, that it may be simply day-dreaming.   You prepare your meditation, which preparation is the homage and service of your mind ; in the morning you set a light to the offering prepared on your altar, and let it burn quietly.   That is all good, and an excellent way of praying.   When God wants anything else He will let you know.   Remember that what He does for you in prayer is ninety-nine hundredths, and what you do is only one hundredth ; it is essential, but you must not fidget about it. Holy fear is good and great, it makes silence and childlike awe in your soul, but frights and panics and spectres are not like God.   As to the folds and folds of self-love ! accept beforehand peacefully, that it will be a progressive revelation perhaps all your life long, but nothing to lose your peace of mind about, and the sun of God's presence is what melts away these folds and mists better than anything. . . . In the sunlight of His presence we live and grow.

How I thank God for every word you write about the retreat ; it is all true and good, and just what ought to be, full of God's gifts and His leading, and scarcely anything for sensible delight, but peace and assurance of God's presence and delight in the will that He should work out His Will in you. Is not that precious beyond everything? So let your soul overflow with thankfulness and let nothing make you afraid.

You are perfectly right, a thousand times right in your feeling about, for instance, newspapers! All these things are weariness of spirit ; ' there is nothing in the whole world to compare with God,' as St. John of the Cross says ; and so I cordially approve and think you have the right thing in your particular examen. And if God sends you any other attraction, then you will follow it. . . .

Letters to ' C.'

. . . I cannot help hoping that you will find the retreat a very great help. In the solitude and silence you will be able to look back better over all that God has done for you, and realise things a little. Don't think that anything very extraordinary will happen or ought to happen. . . . God's words are creative in their power and they live.

Another *don't*. Don't get impatient with yourself, one is so tempted in the beginning to want to be a saint all at once, and to scold one's soul for not being saintly. It would be just as sensible to overwhelm a baby with reproaches for not being six foot high. He will be six foot high if one gives him time; but it takes one-third of his lifetime to do it, and if the growth is hurried it is spoiled, and he grows, as they say of horses, ' weedy.'

. . . You made one great discovery that I was very glad of . . . that to say bad things against yourself is often a ' foolish *nervous* desire,' exactly that, to make people see what you really are. And it does not answer this purpose, because you don't know yourself yet, what you really are. I believe the best way to make oneself known for what one really is, is to be quiet about it, and say nothing at all if one feels excited, either very much up or very much down, for in these moods one is certain not to be true to one's real self. And one's real self is so deep down, that only God knows it now, and we come to the knowledge of it ourselves by degrees. . . . To keep quiet and not get excited or savage with oneself is a great step towards seeing clearly. . . .

. . . ' If one only knew that one would come out safe the other side ! '—Yes, I know, but that can't be, when one is trying for such high things as we are, the higher we want to fly the greater the risk, but that is the glorious part of it ; and the great uncertainties in which we trust God, the breathless risks we run— with no assurance *but* our trust in Him,—that seems to me to be of the essence of our life and its beauty. This will grow upon you,

you will get your balance in the risks, and get to love them. That is faith and hope. One can trot along on the earth in great safety, but it is not so well worth while.

You ' feel your grasp of the spiritual life is utterly gone,' yes, that is part of it. It has to be so—and the last stanza of Matthew Arnold's ' The Journey,' or rather the whole poem, ' A wanderer is man from his birth,' has a curious suggestion of this passing out of sight of known landmarks, but the thing is, *to be glad of it*, because it means learning something of what God wants to teach us.

Letters to ' D.'

August, 1911.

Thank you for your letter out of retreat and for remembering my love for the heavenly feast of the Assumption, the most perfect blending of joy and wistfulness that one can have, with the Ascension and All Saints ; and I am sure that Our Lady looks with a certain wistfulness back on earth, as we shall ever do to the home of our childhood. May she draw our thoughts and longings more and more to heavenly things. How happy you are to have the ' Saint of the Province ' for your retreat ! It does good to be in touch with God's intimate friends. . . .

Your letters do not fall into the abyss, my dear . . . they are always welcome and full of interest, though I cannot always answer you ; but you must admit, it is not the silence of the grave, I give a faint squeak from time to time. Never mind having nothing to write about, your thoughts are the most interesting part to me, others can give me the events of the day ' over there.' Let us keep on going, giving to Our Lord what we can day by day, especially in giving ourselves to others and keeping our hearts in His ' in sure and perfect hope.' I have not any time for reading except the oddest of odd moments, but in these I get through something. In November one goes back to Bernard of Morlaix and the Dream of Gerontius and Catherine of Genoa's beautiful little book on Purgatory. God bless you.

Thank you for your letters, which are refreshingly interesting, even when you are in a phase of depression. We are surrounded with things incomprehensible, and that often cannot be helped ; the only rule for all the cases is the Benedictine (or is it the Franciscan) summing up, ' *et enfin chacun fera ce qu'il pourra.*' It is easy to see the problem, but the solution is hard to find. No, I do not see processions of strange faces at night [an allusion to Cardinal Manning, who, when he lay down to rest at night, remembered the past day only as a river of faces flowing by]. The transom of my window makes a cross against the sky, the right shape, and there is always light enough to see it by, and I know our Mother [Mother Digby] looked at it night after night, so it is rather dear, and when I am away I see what there is to be seen, no faces D.G. unless I go back to the Islands where they are all dear and well known. Have you read 'Heroic Spain,' by Miss Boyle O'Reilly, an old child of Eden Hall?—it is really very pleasant reading.

. . . Many thanks for your interesting letter full of all sorts of things, and a few echoes from the retreat. I envied you your preacher; to me it is a joy to 'sit under Father Roche,' as the Non-Conformists say. Thank you for the harebells and the growth on the rose-bush; I used to know its name, but forget it. If I remember right there is a tiny white grub in it. God has in us the oddest family that ever was, taken in with so little, a little salt and water, taken *off* with even less; but He understands and *likes* as well as *loves* us, and that is all that matters. May He give us all a quiet night and a perfect end.

March, 1912.
. . . No, you don't leak out of my mind, although this life is so different that it seems like another phase of existence, and I ask myself sometimes: 'Is it really I?' It is just as well not to realise it always, as it is easier to walk on a plank across a stream without looking, and just as you say the living things at this time of year make one lonely for what is gone! but that loneliness must really make us look forward. 'We shall be there the day after to-morrow,' as Father Morris [1] said, and the few buds I see and the few blackbirds I hear say the same thing.

To-morrow I go into Holland, or rather towards Holland, staying two nights at Antwerp on the way, so think of me among tulips and hyacinths and strange clean people, 'who scrub their streets with soap and water,' but I do not know if it is their friends or foes who told me this.

. . . Hold on to the *Nunc coepi* until the Compline bell rings for the *Nunc dimittis*, and try to prepare for that happy hour by silence when the storms are rising, words so often leave us deep regrets, and remember that we can do deep harm to others by unguarded words, *not in the least meant*. You know all are not skilled in the 'discernment of spirits,' and a remark from D. that I might easily understand to be only a groan from the Cynic tub, might be taken otherwise by the young and inexperienced, and they might say it, meaning more, or it might rankle as a shaft of temptation to bad spirit. You

[1] Father John Morris, S.J.

2 I

do well in a hot moment, as that day [at X.], to keep
silence on the points where you feel strongly. . . . Let nothing
move you from that citadel of silence, you are safe there.   And
then don't judge your superiors, but believe what they say.
Mother X. could no more say what she did not mean than
she could fly to Jerusalem, and God is very strict on the
judgment of His anointed, as strict as He is lenient on other
things.   Anyhow *courage et confiance*; don't get tired of beginning again.   God bless you.

A good deal of the difficulty is physical—you always get
fagged at this end of the year. *God takes all that into account*,
and you must take patience for your companion.

. . . Christina Rossetti says truly that the road winds
uphill all the way, yes, to the very end.

I am more and more convinced that life is meant to be
burdensome and toilsome and extraordinarily like travelling
with an ox waggon in South Africa at the rate of about two
miles a day ; sometimes the waggon turns clean over, often it sticks
fast in a drift, sometimes they have even to take it to pieces
in the mud of the drift, and reconstruct it on the further shore.
So I am more doubtful about things that go smoothly than
when they are troublesome from morning till night.   Never
mind, the arrival will be worth it all, and it is not so far now—
to see Our Lord's overflowing gladness of welcome as each
poor battered heart-sick child comes home for the everlasting
home-coming, and to see all that He thought of the struggles
and troubles and accidents of the way.   In moments when one
can realise this, one understands that nothing else matters,
except that we should keep our eyes on Him, and try to be
submissive and patient for love of Him.   It is all worth while,
that is the thing to bear in mind.   Thank you so much for
the extracts; I am keeping them for my walk to the cemetery,
which, in retreat time, I have at four o'clock.

Letters to ' E.'

. . . Yes, there is balm in Gilead ! but I have been too long
in writing to speak of it to you.   Yet every day the ' jeremiade,'
as you call it, has been before my mind, and I have asked Our
Lord often to give you strength to fight and courage steadily
to hope on.   In spiritual warfare, unlike the temporal battle,
effort is success, though often it does not seem so; but the very
effort shows that the will is unconquered, has not given in.   Even
if it has rolled in the dust with the adversary, it has not bitten
the dust.   The desire of better things is the pledge and earnest
of them, and the all-important thing is to keep hope. . . .

Above all remember that you are the cherished object of
Our Lord's most tender love. May He convince you of this.

I approve fully of the aftermath of your retreat as embodied in the words: ' I can give something to God to-day,
whatever I may do later on.' Better still without the latter
part of the sentence! Will not God who keeps you to-day
keep you to-morrow and so on, a day at a time, the ' now ' that
is our only possession, and in which God is ours. May he bless
you each day, ' now and at the hour of death.'

Do not ratiocinate about St. John of the Cross's ' nothing.'
Each soul must speak its own language, and of course we are
first cousins to nothing on the father's side! But there are
ways and ways of taking it up, and if they don't suit one, better
leave the subject alone, since by all our endowments we are
obviously a very living something. . . .

That very little fraction of will you call your own is not
so very small after all, for it is capable of indefinite growth,
not a fraction at all but a living thing. A ' grain of mustard
seed,' if you like, with latent growing powers, and it will grow,
indeed it has already grown much. Yes, it is ' dogged as does
it,' and I will say, as Father Bernard says : ' persevere,' says
he. God bless you.

Yes, my dear child, life is a solitude, and yet as Our Lord
Himself said : ' I am not alone, for the Father is with Me,'
though perhaps three hundred and sixty-four days out of the
year we cannot feel it. But you know that beyond your own
erratic guidance, and the plunging of the chariot, a hand has
guided your life, and kept you safe through many a storm,
beyond what you could do for yourself, and that same guidance
will bring you into port at last.

One can never see a thing exactly as it is, if one looks too
closely at it. It loses all proportion. So I think you judge
yourself as worse than you are, and no one can judge themselves quite fairly, God alone can do this; but the judgment
of others on us is in most cases truer than our own, because
not disturbed by the thought of what ought to be or the pursuit
of an ideal self. But what I wish for you is the modesty of
mind that knows its own littleness in the face of overwhelming
truths and does not try with its foot-rule to measure them
out. . . .

. . . We are to walk by faith, not by sight. The *realisation*
that you wish for so much is not necessary for us, nor would

it be good, or it would be granted. Conscious communion with God is reserved for heaven, and *snatches* of it come to help us here. But we can walk without it, ' stepping fearless through the night.' Do not look for a magic word, a magic hour or thought which will change all this, it cannot be, and it need not be ; the law of our life is struggle, and often struggle in the dark, but God is always near you, and I think if you could see things in daylight for a moment you would be surprised to see His joy in the efforts that seem to you so poor. So all I can say is ' patience. . . . And be not weary in well-doing, for in due season we shall reap if we do not faint.'

Your good sense has come to the rescue in a difficult moment, thank God for it, and as the screws said to the rivets when the *Dimbula* was creaking and straining in a gale, ' in case of doubt, hold on ! ' The time will pass, and with it all of the difficulty that depends upon the body. . . . The rest is the usual share of fighting that belongs to every member of the Church militant while ' seeking that which is to come.'

There must be pain and darkness and unsearchable mysteries, and insoluble problems ; but there again, ' in case of doubt, hold on.' Wait for God to explain Himself in eternity. It would be childish to think that we could understand in time. But never let go of the belief that He is the *All-Good*.

I have torn off a bit of your letter and send it back to you. It is the thing I have been so long wanting you to see, and I am glad that you have seen it. Do hold on to this. We believe in God so utterly that all that could be said and ' proved to the hilt ' against Him, against our high and loving conception of Him, would find us quite unconcerned and indifferent.

Think your best thoughts of Him, and they will ever fall short of His Fatherhood and love, and the sum of our words must be ' He is all.' And for the rest follow the authoritative voice within, without asking it to disclose too much the secret of the *voice production*. God teaches thus, no matter what we call it, and it makes for what is best.

. . . I was not at all surprised on receiving your second letter, though I should have been unspeakably delighted if you had received a sensible grace. You will think me incorrigibly hopeful, but I cannot say that I feel discouraged, though full of the deepest sympathy for all you are going through. I believe in your faith, although it is hidden away underground, as entirely hidden as the bracken-roots in winter, and as full of life.

I think you are making two mistakes, one is looking for

realisation and finality, a spiritual barometer that will not
vary, in reality for sense, to which realisation belongs ; secondly
you are not perfect in patience ! It is impossible for God not
to hear your prayer, to hear every prayer of His creatures,
but, being God, He must hear it in His own way, and not in
the way of His creature. But let us go no further than that,
' Thou wilt call, and I will answer Thee ; to the work of Thy
hands Thou wilt stretch out Thy right hand.' And waiting
His call, you will pray, but don't analyse.   Analysis is a
process too coarse for anything so subtle and delicate as our
inmost consciousness of God ; only pray, and in its own time
all will be well. . . . Pray humbly, ' God is in heaven and
thou art on earth, therefore let thy words be few.' Don't let
us forget we are all blind grubs at present, ' it does not yet
appear what we shall be.'

I should like to think that you prayed especially every day
for light to know God's truth. ' *Emitte lucem tuam et veritatem
tuam*,' for I feel so sure of the end of the verse—' *ipsa me
deduxerunt et adduxerunt in montem sanctum tuum et in taber-
nacula tua*.'

As to personal sorrow, I will be very frank with you. The
deep personal sorrow to me, for I have a very special affection
for you, is that your mind should be as it is, so obscured and
over-clouded in all those things that are to me the light of light,
and life of life.

The next extract given was written after a considerable
period had elapsed.

You can have no idea of the joy of reading your letter and
your notes, my dear child. You could only measure it, if you
could measure the sorrow I often had in my soul about you,
though I never ceased to hope. But in these there is the voice
of the resurrection. You are alive, in the best sense of the
inward life. You will trust in God now day by day, never let
yourself look back, nor pull your life to pieces in self-analysis,
but take it whole, uncomprehended, but entirely trusted to
God's loving keeping. This is a joy with a seed of immortality
in it.

' I may add,' writes the person who received these letters,
' that all she ever asked for me in prayer, all she hoped for me,
all she had ever been urging upon me, was given me while I
was kneeling by her side in Our Lady's chapel at Roehampton,
on the afternoon of the day she died.'

Letters to ' F.'

You must not let slip, in a moment of flatness and difficulty, what you have battled for with such blessed results, for your life is quite on a different plane from what it was. The remedy is to be found in prayer only. We need to be constantly in touch with God, drinking deep of His grace, to lead a life such as ours must be, and you know if our life is run on wrong lines ' up in arms, criticising, intolerant of others,' it is the poorest sort of life on earth, *manquée* for both worlds.

God touches the very springs of our life, and the very springs of our life hold on to God, and nothing matters except that. I would, if I were you, have a very solemn half-hour down in the very heart of things; 'wherefore camest thou hither ? ' and whither goest thou ? and then make one of those acts of faith and truth, external penance or humility, which have always seemed to have like a sacramental efficacy in your life, and so start again. Do not lose heart, there may be an occasional waver in the line of battle, but you must not really run having got so far.

To every life must come its days of trial and peril and weariness, unless the life is quite without dignity or value ; but the truest of all true things is that God is all to us, will never leave us in the lurch, but will guide, sustain, surround, uphold us, do everything for us. Can we not trust Him ? Could our own best providence and prudence, planning our life for the best, ever approach to His for us ? And in your heart of hearts I am sure you would not have it otherwise, and would not wish to find yourself in the religious life *vouée* to the perambulator, and the sunny side of the road, a smooth and happy baby. . . .

After a great sacrifice had been asked :

. . . So it has come ! Just what you had dreamt for a moment of asking. It is one more proof that God makes the organisations and not the Superior Vicar, or even the Superior General, for it is the last thing anyone thought of for you. So you will go with all the more courage, taking it, cross as it is for you, from His hand and making it your proof of love for the year. ' As I can't shed my blood, I give the best I can,' and that with a great heart. No, I did not think it was good-bye either, but it is better so, and as you say better to rush a hard thing through ; and God will have His own time and way of letting us say ' how do you do ' again. I am going to quote for you one of Saint Jeanne de Chantal's vigorous calls to the supernatural spirit of faith : ' Jésus ! que j'ai d'aversion à cette recherche inquiète que les Sœurs font d'avoir des Supérieures capables et de grande expérience.   Voyez-vous, cette imaginaire croyance des grandes capacités nécessaires à une Supérieure, ruine entièrement la pureté de l'obéissance!'   (Jésus! there is, I am afraid, a little *swear!* not a prayer!)

There is nothing worth living for but God and heaven and the kingdom of God in the souls of those who love Him— our own soul first.   So let us say welcome, without looking further, to anything which detaches us and makes us have less of this world that we may have more of Him.   He is leading and ruling and blessing you—let yourself be led and ruled and blessed—'and thou shalt see it thyself that all manner of things shall be well.'

The next few letters were written during a time of difficult exterior circumstance and interior trial.

. . . I take it that the last half-sheet of your letter was really the one that counted.   Your *fixed mind* in fact, that came then to anchor in the thought of God's will.   In a storm things always loom larger than life.   But when things calm down again and one remembers that God's action is always there, unerring and all-powerful, and that He can make people walk on the water and feed five thousand with five barley loaves, then one understands how 'love complains not of impossibilities and faith moves mountains. . . .'

. . . Whenever you go back to the human side of things it sooner or later gets to be too much for you. . . . I do not think there is any use in discussing things from their human side (I mean from me to you here and now).   I think and I know that the only thing is for you to look straight through them and beyond them to Our Lord, who says to you ' What is this or that to thee, follow thou Me.'   And then follow on; follow Him who has the threads of all things in His hands, without Whom ' not a sparrow falls to the ground,' how much more without Whom no tiny thing or big thing happens to you.   Hold on to Him, hold His hand, and He will keep you up, and make all things clear and well in His own time.   He means every one of the things that happen to you, they are not accidents, but it will be done to you according to your faith ; so have faith, ask for it, get it, exercise it, hold to it in all things.

. . . Disregard *natural* confidence or attraction and the human views of things and walk by *faith,* you can and you know the way.   Humble yourself and pray.   If you can't take a big penance you can by the side of your bed at night lay your

forehead in the dust and say: ' O God, Thou knowest all,
I put myself and all I have and wish and feel into Thy hands,
do with me what Thou wilt and I will love and bear it.'

'As soon as you forsake yourself, resign yourself, you will
enjoy much inward peace,' so says the ' Imitation ' and so truly.

. . . Lessons are being learnt and you must thank God
for them. . . . Reverend Mother Desoudin used to say to her
probanists, ' *Je vous souhaite une Supérieure qui n'est pas
de votre couleur* '; because then our religious life was thrown
out of its depths into the supernatural and learned to swim ;
in one way or another it is a necessary lesson and I don't see
how you would have learnt it otherwise than as at present. . . .
At the same time there is a natural side, from which I want
you to learn, and which you must not lose sight of.

Don't make *too much* of what you are doing. It is exactly
what in every great department, army, navy, law or Church is
happening every day without men thinking themselves heroes
for it, but merely by loyalty to chief and cause, and sometimes
entirely out of sympathy with their chief, and with very good
reason. Sometimes the chief is a mere figure-head, and all
the trouble and blame and responsibility is borne by a second
in command, loyal, silent, patient, respectful, and never thinking himself heroic ; and yet that is only the world. We have
far more, the great cause, the great Master, the great stakes,
children's souls and lives—who would not throw themselves
into the breach to do for God and for them what they can ?

In the Society it is God's work and His success that matters,
not us ; just as in the army and navy, with the true men it is
' the service ' that matters, not the individual. . . .

. . . What a misfortune it would be, religiously speaking
and educationally speaking, if we could only work happily with
those who saw things as we do. You know ' there are nine and
sixty ways, etc.,' and it is our part always to play up, loyally and
impersonally, to the views of those whom God now sets over
us. . . . Do not throw away the precious real things of the
moment for ideals of work that God does not want from you *now*.

He wants *now* humility, conformity, faith and abnegation.
You have chances now that may not come again. I heard
Mother W. say to a sister in somewhat similar circumstances,
one who ' knew her way was best, etc.,' and materially it was :
' You have thrown away the good thing of religious life—giving
in. So-and-so has picked it up and I cannot ask her now to give
it back to you, things must remain as they are.' Isn't that sad,
a lost opportunity, and all that God had meant to give one
through it. . . .

. . . I send all my sympathy to the young hound for whom life, at moments, is inexpressible. Never mind, God is at the back of it all. . . . It may be, it probably will be, that in years to come you will look back on this hard flat bit of road as being *the* time of your life that was really developing you, when God set you down on your feet and carried you no longer (sensibly), and bid you walk in faith and trust ; and you will remember with a smile how you squealed and looked back to where I stood with the perambulator, and God said : ' No, no, walk on, child, and grow strong.' You think your mental development is going to seed, but it is not, only the will side is getting more attention now, and it is of even greater price. . . . You need the hard things, the plain, common things, the lowly every-day realities of life to put that knowledge of realities into you, from which you have been too much shielded. Those cubs at X. are doing more for you than you know, and the more experience you get of low classes and low minds and mental gutter-snipes the better. These are your apprentice years, make the most of them, leave the future to God, nothing is lost, and if your soul wants a satisfying answer, say to yourself : ' Nazareth ; eighteen years of hidden life, three of the ministry.'

. . . I should be inclined, if I were you, to leave all entirely in God's hands and strike no stroke for yourself. You know your tendency is too much to look at the human side of things ; this is a case to react against it. I said *leave* it in God's hands, but I mean *put* it there, positively, explicitly and every day. ' Thou *knowest*, Thou *canst*, therefore do what is best for me in this.' And you will learn how true it is. And this refers to great things and small down to the tiniest detail. *Expertus potest credere*, and it is always done to us according to our faith.

. . . You are indeed hard pressed, and I am sure in many ways and on many days you have made a gallant fight. But you must win again, and let the soul besieged in Lucknow hear the sound of the pipes, which mean relief to the garrison—' The Campbells are comin' ' ; but the Campbells are obviously not me but *you*. You must conquer if you die of it ! But as a matter of fact you won't die but live ten times as much. It would never do to give back your hard-won results and capitulate to the rebel ; and you can command it. I like what Henry Martyn writes of his experience when in bad health : ' I resolved to lead a life of more self-denial, and the tone and vigour of my mind rose rapidly.' You see, you let yourself get panic-struck twice, as if God could not, and would not, carry you through. But we won't look back but rather forward. ' It was our fault, our very great fault,' and now we must turn it to use.

We had forty million reasons for failure, but not a single excuse ! So, my dear . . . laugh up to God and try again. . . .

. . . We walk on a height and cannot either stop or look down. If we keep *going on* and look straight up to God we can cross the bad places without our heads turning. The opening word of to-day's Collect ought to be always in the accompaniment of our thoughts, while we *soar* in the melody and try for glorious things, impossible and possible. ' O God, who seest that we trust not in anything that we ourselves can do,' all the rest comes after that. But when we come quite down to the depths, as we all do from time to time, the prayer is ' *De profundis clamavi ad Te Domine, Domine exaudi vocem meam,*' and God always *does* hear and help. And we must leave the future *all* to Him, and be each of us intent only on living up to His wonderful graces to us and to the Society. He will not be less good in the future than He has been in the past, and if each one is faithful to light, and to live the life of faith—for reason falls far short of what we want to attain—God will be with us.

Yes, let us humble ourselves down to the dust before God, there only—experience has tested it—do we find light and breadth and horizons of hope. . . . Give a long level look at God across the wolds and fens of this world. God all, and everything else nothing ; make your act of absolute trust again.

Letters to ' G.'

October, 1900.

. . . I was glad to get your letter. While you are in retreat, think over these things. The thing you are most wanting in is, I believe, the fear of God, the sense of His Holiness, and of your duty to Him.

After a fault I miss three notes in you : the spirit of truth to own it without excusing, cloaking, justifying yourself.

The spirit of humiliation ; you will do all in your power to keep up appearances and ' save the situation.'

The spirit of reparation and expiation ; to get out of it as easily as possible and have it blotted off your records seems the one desirable thing in your eyes. Doing penance and expiating does not seem to come in.

This is a passage of Cardinal Manning's which sorrowfully reminds me of you : ' There is a moral and intellectual blindness which hides the light of faith and of nature from such minds (those stricken with folly) . . . in such men there is also a strange levity, a want of moral earnestness which nothing can arouse, a want of reverence which nothing can impress, a want of self-chastisement which nothing can awaken from its self-indulgence.'

But I will still hope for better things if you make a great effort for a thorough conversion in this retreat : a definite resolution, and determination to keep everything open and straight with X., who makes it so easy for everyone. This is your only safety.

October 23rd, 1907.

. . . That was a bad moment, wasn't it ! Hold on though, ' after the storm cometh a calm, after the night day returns,' and you know Whom you have believed. So give your soul, your whole self entirely into His hands, by ' an incomparable act of resignation ' ; you cannot be tossed away out of His keeping. Here is a nice passage from Cardinal Newman to the point : ' I will trust my God . . . wherever I am, I can never be thrown away. If I am in sickness, my sickness may serve Him. If I am in sorrow, my sorrow may serve Him. My sickness or perplexity or sorrow may be necessary causes of some great end which is quite beyond us. He does nothing in vain ; He may prolong my life, He may shorten it ; He knows what He is about. He may take away my friends, He may throw me among strangers. He may make me feel desolate, make my spirits sink, hide the future from me, still, He knows what He is about.' Is that not rather comforting even for blue hours ! Never mind . . . it will have a tremendous explanation hereafter ; it will not explain itself, as you say, but God will explain it when He wipes all tears from their eyes. So hold on.   ' Grip fast gin the buckle bide,' so said Bartholomew the Hungarian to Saint Margaret of Scotland when her horse was plunging in a deep and dangerous ford.

February, 1908.

. . . How quickly time goes, and you find you are not out of the struggle ! And am I surprised, horrified ? Neither, only surprised that you should think it possible to be surprised at this. Life's work is done in a lifetime, not in a day. I wonder whether your ideas of work are grave enough, and strenuous enough, for the very strict and urgent kind of work you have to do, in which there is nothing for nature, nothing for leisure, and nothing for dilettantism ! Anyhow, seek first the Kingdom of God and His justice. God first and everything else nowhere !

December 22nd, 1908.

. . . Christmas must not come without my wishing you God's best blessings, and that your mind and thoughts and affections may be filled with Him and nothing else. ' Get thee on with thy dying,' and try not to seek solace by the way, except in Him on whom you can pour out all that you have to give, and from whom you can receive all that you crave for. ' If thou knewest the gift of God ' once, you would see that nothing else matters,

JANET ERSKINE STUART

and nothing else is worth turning your eyes upon for a moment. So don't look back, and be abjectly humble and dependent and contrite and God will be with you.

. . . It sounds heartless to say it, but, I am very glad ! It is a proof that God has you in hand and is teaching you and following you up. It is just what you need, to have the harriers constantly after you in one way or another ! Otherwise you sit down in gardens and nibble the herbage sweet and poisonous. Isn't it true ? You need to be running with the hounds to keep you in good running form ; so welcome be the hounds of God that goad you to run, and when you are hard pressed you know where to run to, poor hunted leveret, to God, ' the hiding place of His vexed creatures ! ' N. was created for you.

. . . Somebody worded a resolution rather simply and nicely in saying : ' I must keep to the way òf the Cross in the little things of life.' There is a great deal in it, and as you say, there is always a foundation of truth ; when the chisel gets hold of you there is something to chisel. What does anything matter ! Try to learn to

> ' Welcome each rebuff
> That turns earth's smoothness rough.'

God chooses each for you, and if you want life and truth and religious freedom it must come so and no otherwise, do not doubt it.

. . . Try to see in every circumstance the special, not general Will of God ; the smallest comes to you with its precious power of humbling, purifying and expiating, and there is so much to be done. Look no further. But if you cannot help looking further, believe on the human side that there must be another view to the view you take, that there are two sides to every question ; that perhaps you misunderstood or exaggerated, unconsciously, much which would look different if you could see that other side. . . .

Sister N.'s death was a great instruction, the moment may come so quickly, and now we must always be ready . . . not lounging among the pleasant things but watchful. . . . If you want to be holy you must submit and humble yourself utterly and utterly. A critical spirit has a very low crouch down to make before it can pass through the low door into the Kingdom of heaven.

December, 1910.

I got all your letters and pray for you as I hope you do for me. As far as we are concerned God means things to be just as they are, what does happen and what does not happen. So never wish them otherwise by a hair's breadth. All our raw material for sanctity is in the *now* just as it is ; and if it had not the two elements, the one that we do not understand and the one that we should not choose, it would not be what it is to us. I hope that for Christmastide you will pasture on the great thoughts that help you. Why should you take anything less satisfying ?

February, 1912.

I think your news is good. *Everything* lies for you in keeping down in the dust before God, in the spirit of contrition, self-blame, submission. The slightest self-justification or comparison or human judgment is a note of danger. *Humiliate capita vestra Domino.* To our Master we stand or fall, and He sees to the depths of our being. It is good to live in His presence, ashamed but not afraid. That solitariness is what you meant and chose, though without knowing all it meant, when you said God was to be the God of your heart and your portion for eternity. You will not be surprised at it now, for you know what bitter fruit grows from trying to people and plant that solitude. We are strangers and pilgrims on the earth. No *home* for us until heaven, but yet a home by anticipation and faith wherever the Blessed Sacrament is.

June, 1912.

. . . To judge by your letter I am quite sure I should find you better, but it is true you must never leave off wariness even when temptation does not appear for a long time.

Down in the foundations, in the Purgative way, in the First Week, the Penitential Psalms, the great salt sea of contrition, one is so safe and blest. And there the soul can grow hardy and wait God's time, and if He ever means to make a real saint of it there is no time lost ; no illusions to disperse, nothing to undo. Whereas dreaming of great sanctity and expecting the great day on which the soul will assist in white tunic and golden girdle at its own transformation, or to picture the ' doing good to souls ' whether with the trumpet and drum or the whisper of private direction—all this is nothing !

> ' Passing soon and little worth
>   Are the things that tempt on earth ;
>   Heavenward lift thy soul's regard,
>   God Himself is thy reward.'

I don't remember where that comes, but it is true.

August, 1913.

Your letter was very good to read. Don't envy the quiet, undistracted Carmelite life ; but thank God that he has called you to a life which shows nothing, but asks for all and gives *all*. Give all for All, leave desires and thou shalt find rest. I think you are leaving desires, and the ' finding rest ' is a question of realisation and constancy in the arduous way. Trust God and do not fear, you have the *best*.

Red Sea : November, 1913.

Your letter was very good, and I think things are going well. Yes, I do believe that your way of praying is good and is to be followed. You need not ask yourself if you are worthy of it, of course not ! But it does not go by that. It is not a criterion of virtue but a grace that God gives, and I do not think that you *could* be so silly as to be vain of it or look down on others who with discourses and considerations climb their laborious road to God. It should tend to make you more humble and more ready *in will* to give yourself to hiddenness, submission, service, to be thwarted in your wishes and tied to uninspiring duties, all these things will make the spirit of prayer grow, will make Christ Himself grow in you and set you free from desires.

Try not to look forward. Each day is sufficient for itself, both good and evil. One often heard, ' sufficient for the day is the evil thereof ' ; I have seen it once not *translated* but quoted as ' sufficient is the day for the evil,' and I liked that better.

We are about there where the Israelites must have passed through the narrow arm of the Red Sea, wide enough indeed, and yesterday we must have cut the line at some unknown point where the Holy Family crossed the Isthmus of Suez. These two flights, out of Egypt and into Egypt, are full of many thoughts.

Letters to ' H.'

Roehampton : February, 1907.

. . . You did quite right in sending me the uttered thoughts that had been worrying you, even though in theory you know something of how to answer them as the end of your letter showed. It is a very natural form for a fit of discouragement in work and depression to take. Every teacher knows it, every priest knows it, every monk knows it, every Bishop knows it ; I have often thought the Pope must know it best of all, having to spend hours in the day giving audience to people to whom he *dare* not say more than a platitude.

God's work is done thus. The one thing that matters is what we *are*, not what we say or teach. It is the being with people devoted to God and united to His Will that tells more than you could imagine or believe on the thickest-hided pupil in the dullest scheme of work. Keep close to God—your will in His, your heart in His; accept all without understanding and you will have an awe-stricken surprise when death comes, and you will see what He thought of it all and He says 'You did it unto Me.' So make once more the incomparable act of resignation and be content to walk by faith, ' *ad firmandum cor sincerum, sola fides sufficit.*'

Roehampton : April, 1907.

. . . You answered yourself, do you know, in stating your question, ' How to get the maturity that comes from selflessness?' *There* is just the answer about being one-sided, narrow, and incomplete. It is not the study or teaching that does it, it is not their life that is one-sided, but if they [nuns] are one-sided it is their living of the life that is at fault. It is only Saints that are not one-sided, because their centre is in God and their equilibrium is stable there. If nuns are one-sided it is their own most grievous fault, because they do not live their own most beautiful life fully ; it is sanctity that is wanting. We are all trying for it, we have none of us attained it, we shall die fighting, please God.

August, 1908.

. . . Life alone with God does not mean the life of the Miller of the Dee . . . it simply means facing the truth that love consists in giving, not so much in receiving, while we are here. The receiving will be so superabundant even in this life when we have learnt to give, that we shall feel small and ' confused ' at our little gift. It is more love for others, not less, more feeling for them, and not less that we want—only to find our joy in giving ' me last ' . . .

August, 1909.

. . . It is all good, my dear child; it shows how utterly you must count on God, how slippery and treacherous are our best resolutions. Be true and try to be quiet in the retreat, the Good Shepherd will come by and pick up the lamb straying again. Nestle up to Him to love and to be loved. . . .

Make it a point of honour with God that you let go the instant you have made reparation (after a fault), and turn to Him quickly for His blessing and *further orders.*

1910.

. . . I know you have a very rough bit of road to go over, but you are going in the right direction, and that is much, and there has been much more progress than you can probably realise in the last year. You will make up your mind to bear patiently what is hard and to hope and hope and hope, and trust God

utterly; that is the thing that sustains when all else fails, and
it is called upon by the very idea and name of God, so go on—
'though He slay me, yet will I trust in Him.' Do you pray
every day to Our Lady ? Except the prayers of Rule ? Ask
her to be a Mother and a guide always at hand. . . .

Letters to ' I.'

. . . To think that we are going to win an easy victory, and
walk with bands playing and banners flying on the ruins of
where our faults have been, that is an illusion that has to come
down. But to expect to conquer is our duty, understanding
that we shall be dusty, travel-stained, and have to fight up to
our last breath. But why not ? Surely Heaven is long enough
for rest, and we must not grudge the short working or fighting
hours of the day. *Courage, mon âme.*

. . . I am convinced that your faults of charity are chiefly
manner, but as you say, faults of manner rest on something
deeper, which is a fault of character, and that—what is it ?
I think a little touch of pride and a little touch of hardness in
the *grain* ; probably at home you all took each other very much
as you were, understood each other quite well, made every
allowance in one sense, no allowance in another, and were very
outspoken. This I *suppose.* It is the old English race that
made martyrs for the faith or Ironsides, according to circumstances ; *excellent* and most precious—but being called to a
Society that has such a high supernatural standard of charity,
the rougher sides of this must be smoothed away.

Keep the downrightness, but clothe it with Our Lord's own
patience and sweetness, and above all *judge kindly*, that is the
heart of everything.

You know that we all have a character fault that we break
our hearts in trying to cure. You are not a solitary instance ;
and everyone thinks her own the most hopeless and heart-
breaking of all, but they are none of them hopeless, and Our Lord
must have what he wants.

Writing of work that seemed wasted :

When a thing like that happens, and it is curious how often
it does, take it as a most special gift from Our Lord. He has
accepted your whole basket of fruit for Himself, and only you
and He know about it. I call that lovely, and as to the poor
human side that smarts, you must make it give a little laugh to
itself and say, ' Come along, my soul, let us try again.'

God bless you, my dear child, and help you every day. Try
to look over the heads of all circumstances and troubles that

grow around your path. They are only the needles and thistles of the path, made to give us a little chance of being brave. You must look higher.

> ' *Jamais les moyens, mais la fin,*
> *Jamais l'instrument, mais la main qui le meut,*
> *Jamais la terre, mais le ciel.*'

Now to answer your questions. It is not hard.

1. What I should like to see never, never again.—The least touch of bitterness.

2. What I should like to see always and ever growing.— Imperturbable confidence in God. The conviction that He will do the best in all things, and that nothing can go wrong because it is surrendered into His hands, even yourself, though of yourself you might often go wrong. But *Dominus regit me, et nihil mihi deerit.*

Letters to ' J.'

Roehampton : May 11th, 1907.

. . . I have been thinking of you and meaning to write since your last letter. I think you are forgetting one thing, and that is ' personal equation.' Give everyone's words the weight which they have in that person's own voice and mind and intonation, discount all that, and take the rest very quietly indeed, as Our Lord means you to do.

You must not let yourself get too sensitive, nor take things unduly to heart, because it defeats His ends. You must be quite impersonal (by degrees) about your work, remembering that it is God's and not yours. So by prayer and will, make yourself a quiet mind, and do things as they come, trusting in God to make all things right. Humble yourself, which means quiet yourself every day under God's hand, and when you find fright invading your soul, or resentment or agitation, trust God and let go of all else. Is He not more than able to keep all right, or set it right? Don't say that you do not deserve that He should do this, of course you do not, but He will do it, because He is God, not because you have deserved well of Him. . . .

Roehampton : February 6th, 1908.

. . . Please establish firmly in your mind, that to abandon yourself to the Providence of God and the Love of the Sacred Heart is no myth or illusion, but the humblest, truest, and most worshipful stand that your soul can make against every temptation, difficulty, or danger. If you let go of all else, and *drop*, you will find God's love and strength ' circling ' you round, and sooner or later a great calm, in what St. Catherine of Siena so beautifully calls ' the Sea Pacific ' of the Divinity. Where could

God's creature be better or more at home ! Nothing matters except that. . . . But you must give up your own self-will in little things and great. If you get your way, you get a hideous little idol to nurse ; if you give it up, you have God. God loving you, bearing you up, and taking the responsibility Himself of all that happens to you.

Brighton : March 12th, 1908.

. . . I think there is only one way to meet trouble such as that which sometimes invades your soul at the thought of present disabilities from your health, and the fear of the future ; and it is an utter abandonment of yourself to God, a complete and blind resignation to His will.

Our Lord Himself has passed through all that *for you*, in the Garden of Olives, that when the time came for you, you might know from His example how to take it. He feared, He was sick of it all, He was overwhelmed, He was flattened to the ground, He felt that He *could not* go through it, but He prayed and then He made His complete resignation, ' Not as I will, but as Thou wilt.' And then He went through it all, ' and the third day He rose again from the dead.' Do not think otherwise than thus about it all. To work for the Society is a very second-rate thing ; to love God, and to be united to God, and to resign yourself to God, that is what the Society cares about. Expense and trouble and you being unable to do anything visible, all that is *nothing*, remember that.

Roehampton : March 17th, 1909.

. . . I am not in the least surprised or distressed at any thoughts or temptations to distaste, disgust, weariness in well-doing that may come to you. After all, it is obvious that it must be so from time to time. ' Thou art man and not an angel,' flesh and not yet altogether spirit, and you may say to yourself with entire conviction that everyone in their own way goes through the same thing. We have given up for the love of God the best we had in the world, we *meant* to carry the cross, we *meant* hard things, and we meant to feel them and to suffer them. We did not seek the things that were to be easy, congenial, cultivating, enriching, but to follow Our Lord in the way of sorrows and of hardships. He gives us the hundred fold often and often by the way, and our nature calls out for it still more often, but that *means* no more than it *means* to be hungry on a fast day, or to be thirsty in hot weather ! So pay no heed to the ' doubts and fears of what it all means,' for it does not mean much ! The real things lie deeper down and the real love lies far deeper than that, and the things that are ' too strong to be reasoned with ' had better not be reasoned with, but left to Our Lord, who can manage them and command and quiet them just when and as He chooses. . . .

Go on without looking too closely at things, bear with perplexities and temptations, and do not think you can drive them
away, for you can't. God can, and when He chooses, He will.
Pray and leave all the rest to Him.

Villa Lante : April, 1910.

. . . I have been waiting and hoping to know that you would
be able to read a few lines yourself, but now I really can wait no
longer, to tell you how much I have entered into your feelings,
and into each day's offering as you make it to God. He knows
best what is good for us, and if He seems to close the avenues
through which you would willingly have gone, devoting yourself
to His service, it can be only to give you what is much better, a
shorter way to Him and a more excellent way, than any which
one could have dreamed of for you, or you for yourself. He is
bringing home to you, whether you feel it or not, that He Himself is more than His gifts, and that to love Him is more than to
serve Him, that to be submissive to Him is the greatest of all
worship.   So try to do the one thing worth doing, abandon
yourself to His care and His love and let Him love you in His
own way, and try to agree with all that He does, that is best.

Ixelles : January, 1912.

. . . That was a beautiful letter and a great recreation for
me. There is an immense amount of thought condensed in that
view you reported of Mother N. on the ' Companion of His
Cares.' How people draw their own portraits without knowing
it. You do too, to my reading which knows you so well. My
dear child, however solitary and lonely the way may seem to you,
God is there with you—you want Him. Could He possibly fail
or forget ? He will send you help or give it to you Himself,
always in the moment of need, and the very uncertainty of the
supplies is the glory of the thing. You live on trust and hope
and love. Do not be violent in your efforts to give an account
of yourself—or even to be conformed and resigned. Be a daughter with God as you were with your Father. Take all that is
best for granted, and leave all best things, even a retreat alone,
to God. He will give you the best.

Ixelles : September, 1912.

. . . These things that come home to us and hurt our self-love
and humble us in the dust, these are some of God's best graces,
full, full of promise, and never think that you are at the end of
them. There will come more revelations ever more humbling,
ever more intimate and ever more true. But never let them cast
you down. Remember that they are birthdays, the putting
away of the things of a child. And your vocation beaten by
storms, will come out all the truer,

Chamartin : November 15th, 1912.

. . . I think all is well, really well with regard to your prayer. Those plunges into frights and darknesses are just what you must expect, and to be often puzzled and not know where you are, or where God is, the thing to do is never to lose confidence. God will see you through somehow, not for your goodness or merits, but for His own great Name's and Love's sake, because He is God and loves you. That is enough ground for hope and the best ; and the more you find to humble you, the more glad you must be, because it is only God that could give you these lights, and His light has the power of healing. So contrition always, hope always, prayer as you can, in the way that is easiest at the moment. Be very flexible, don't want to have it this way or that, but tend to what is simple and quiet, and persevere in hard times. One moment of realisation is worth days and weeks of waiting and God will always give you what is best. Active minds are meant for that kind of prayer if God calls them to it.

The thought of all that God is in Himself, and of all that He has done for you, must not lead you to fear, but to love and confidence. The thought that you could ever find in yourself even a respectable, proportionate correspondence would be simple arrogance, take it all from Him. You are nothing in it except a happy recipient. . . . The first part of your letter which needed no answer was so delightful, that I had to tear it up without reading it a second time, as an offering to Our Lady.

Ixelles : March, 1913.

. . . Do not for a moment think that God loves you less, but believe that He loves you more in the troubles and because of them. He lets you be near Him, and in some way that we cannot understand, it comforts Him that you should be there, suffering with Him, though He makes no sign and you can scarcely make any. . . .

Sydney : December, 1913.

. . . I am so far off . . . that I will not wait for the next promised letter before I send you a word lest it should seem very long. How I thank God for all you tell me; the greater peace of soul, the sort of distance that is coming between you and things that 'happen or do not happen,' so that they have lost much of their power to torment or distract you from the one need of your life which is God. I like the new manner of preparation, so that meditation either in preparation or in retrospect goes on all day ; that is good. Let God be your sun penetrating you with His own life, while you do in His sight all the small duties that make up your life and are nothing in themselves but everything to Him—as Father Faber says, ' Like the faces of babies, unmeaning, except to their mothers.'

N.G.L. S.S. *Coblents* : February 13th, 1914.

. . . Yes, I believe that you will find more and more that surrender in daily life is the solution of the great problem, 'How is my soul to get to God ? ' We are so earthly-minded in our measurements that we are a long time before we stop looking for something great ; yet see God's choice of means to His great ends, the matter of the Sacraments ; the trivial, apparent chances of word or act that make a hinge, and turn the direction of whole lives. We must train ourselves to see that great side, or at least believe it firmly, and set great store by the little things that are so much more than symbols. . . .

Vancouver : April 14th, 1914.

. . . I *am* glad that you have laid aside that restless fear of deterioration of mind through want of intellectual work. Nothing can deteriorate it if its willed tendency is towards God, the light and the life of the mind. He teaches it and makes it grow, and enlightens it, as He wills. Yours is gaining, not falling off ; the mind only deteriorates through wicked neglect or bad food in its reading. . . .

God is stern, or seems to be, with you. Take it for granted that it is all His love for you ; to put it very humanly, His ambitious love for you, just like a father who overlooks nothing. But the revelation of His love for you at your death, will be something surpassing. Believe it. The first verse of the Psalm six or five, I forget which, is a lawful cry of the soul, ' O Lord, correct me but with judgment.' I forget how it is in our English translation— also very human, a legitimate howl. . . . I understand so well about being two persons ; it is almost necessarily so, but it is not untrue. . . . Don't make the mistake which many make of thinking that intimate union with God in prayer comes as a gift to those that are worthy of it. The ' Spirit breatheth where He will ' . . . Perhaps He gives it not because you are worthy, but to make you so. Anyhow persist in prayer in spite of all disinclination, not violently but patiently and silently and even *dumbly*. Don't seek to be contented with your efforts, or to be assured within that all is well, balance yourself on the tremulous outer edge of hope, over the abyss, trembling sometimes, but self-surrendered to God's loving care.

Letters to ' K.'

The following letters were written to a nun with whom Reverend Mother Stuart had a lifelong friendship. The first was a little note written the day she left Roehampton to take up her work in another house :

My Very Dear X.,—

'All the birds of the air fell a-sighing and a-sobbing when they heard the bell tolling for poor Cock Robin.' And I was thinking so much of my poor Cock Robin that I began the Consecration by blessing myself 'In the name of the Father, and of the Son, and of the Sacred Heart. Amen.' I hope you had a good afternoon, and a dear and lovely Benediction.

22nd December, 1900.

. . . One word of happy Christmas to you and all. Your soul just out of retreat will ' delight itself in the Lord ' and have some moments of *causeries divines* that will console you for the ups of Daughter X., and the downs of Daughter W., and the rights of Daughter Y., and the lefts of Daughter Z.! For He is our life, and they, the daughters, are only the accidents of the way, though we are to answer *âme pour âme et vie pour vie* for them, according to the terrible *bouquet spirituel* you gave me from Père Judde (not an improvised ditty this time). Well, be a mongrel, and fly after the cats, but keep one eye on the Master, and may He bless you always in your work and in your prayer, in your going out and coming in, in your life and in your death, and may the last be a very remote joy !

14th February, 1904.

. . . What a nice thing to gather our old Wandsworth students together for meetings. I think a letter must have gone astray, for you wrote as if I had already had this good news, and I don't think I had. Please tell them how glad I am to hear of their meetings and how we count on their help ; that no one is so dear to us as an ' old child ' doing God's work in her own line as they are ; that their work is one of the most beautiful that the Church entrusts to the laity ; and that they are preparing a good future for the Church in Malta by trying to train a faithful people ; and they are training souls for heaven. Are they not privileged ?—but it must be themselves that they train first ; since we can only give what we ourselves have, one sees that daily more.

Roehampton : June 8th, 1904.

. . . You will have known that it was Paris that prevented me from writing in time for the Feast, but also you will know how very present in spirit I shall be at the first Feast of the Sacred Heart that we spend in Malta, the first professed renovation of vows. It will be a great day. I am sure Monsignor de B. will be melting with devotion, for no doubt he will spend some part of the day with you. They will all be in great fervour and you the most of all, my dear, having wound them up in the triduum ! We have Father Considine for ours and

it is really very excellent, insisting much on devotion to the
Sacred Heart being an inward not an outward devotion, tending
to perfection of motive, not publicity . . . and also insisting on
generosity in a nice way, as being highly bred ways and liberal
manners towards Our Lord, not petty, not stingy, not
punctilious, and having great, noble, trustful, generous thoughts
of God, and even being generous to our poor selves! not
hitting ourselves when we are down ; rather nice, isn't it ?
I wish them all great hearts and noble thoughts in that wonderful little island of yours and all that is most truly the spirit
of the Society. . . .

The price of your Church land excites much admiration and
some amusement ! Tell me how much land you got for the
price.

Roehampton : 18th June, 1905.

Thank you so much for your dear letter received this
morning; but oh ! how badly you treat me—how unsisterly, how
unnatural, how unkind not to tell me your own self that you
had been ill and even obliged to keep your room, which shows
you must have been in all extremities ! But it was all found
out. It oozed to me through Reverend Mother de L. and Mrs.
Pollen and D. and everyone except your own self.

Do be nice and tell me ' the truth, the whole truth, and
nothing but the truth ' for the sake of our lifelong intimacy,
and especially as my fangs are drawn and I can do nothing to
you !

I love everything that comes from little Paul, or rather
from you. I wonder when we shall meet again! Perhaps *Ma
Mère* will send for us both at the same time, and then won't
we talk ? . . . I shall be so glad to see Father Rector ; I love
him very much because he is kind to you.

Roehampton : November 27th, 1905.

. . . This envelope of scraps must hold one scrap from me
to thank you for letting me eavesdrop a moment at your
causeries divines and say how nice I thought them, and how
sure I am that they were Our Lord's own *causeries*. He would
not know you, would He, if you went in for ways and methods
and pigeon-holed your soul. He would say, ' Who or what is
this ? This is not the H. of Malta, but some stuck-up H. of
outre-mer ! ' Oh, my dear Reverend Mother, what unspeakable days we should have if we went sailing in a boat together !
I will not let myself think of it. The Lord will provide. I
think we should talk without stopping. But these are castles
in the Mediterranean. . . .

October 31st, 1910.

. . . To-morrow is All Saints, and we will go to heaven in
mind and hopes and meet there with heavenly people who know

what it is to have lived on earth and loved God, and are inclined almost to envy us our little troubles; and then we will come down to earth again and love them all the more, because they give us chances of loving Him more.

I often think of you and always love you.

Roehampton : 23rd January, 1911.

. . . I suppose yesterday was kept as Cairo's patronal feast, the Holy Family. It is a nice one, and how touching the Collect is about the ' unspeakable virtues ' of family life, so true ! and they are becoming rare, alas ! and must take refuge to grow in the enclosed gardens of religious families, where I think the soil ought to befriend them more than it does ! How necessary to teach the young generation *les mœurs antiques* in the sense of manners, and how deep the root of these goes ! I am rambling, dear Reverend Mother, but this is a letter written only for love, and neither for an occasion nor any business.

How very true it is, as you say, that souls cannot be pushed along any path, however good, but Our Lord, in His own way and time, must lead them. ' His sheep hear His voice, and He knows them, and they follow Him.' How I should love to have your Syrian probanist to look at for two or three months before she goes back to you. I would do all I could for her ! Next to *Ma Mère's* there is no envelope in the post which I love as much as yours.

San Remo : 24th November, 1911.

Where do you think I gathered these two flowers for you this morning ? On X.'s grave. I went to inspect our ' concession ' with very little hope of finding X., and yet it was almost the first grave I saw, with its reclining cross, and ivy and these little roses and stag-horn geranium growing on it. I said a prayer such as I thought you would have said, and told him to be sure to pray always for you, but I could not stay more than a moment because I had three with me and it was pelting with rain. And do you know I saw E. too ; she kindly came to see me at Victoria. How young and bonny she looks ! She gave me a kiss ' to be sure to give it to you,' so it is laid up in lavender in my soul until we meet. May God bless you and keep you safe.

Ixelles : 15th December, 1912.

This is my Christmas letter. I nearly wrote it from Spain feeling so far off, but now I feel pretty sure that it will reach you in time. Last year we spent Christmas together. How lovely and wonderful ; perhaps we never shall again, and yet in reality we shall never spend it apart, for ' where the heart loves, there it lives,' first of all in Our Dear Lord and Master and then in all those whom we love in His love, and Holy Communion makes us all so one that all else matters little; the shadows dance on the wall and the people sit round the hearth and are all together. Dear *Ma Mère* seems to transcend it all now, and look at us with eternity in her eyes, so gloriously at rest after the great battles of her generalship. And we too, one day, *mine* dear Reverend Mother, after our little battles, we shall see it all and know and love what we have believed. . . .

Ixelles: 27th February, 1913.

. . . What lovely views you have sent me, tied, I think, with your own fingers. I long to see those sands and palms and that pyramid with you. I dream of next November—but that is a thing I have breathed only to you ! And then we will talk of God and His creatures, and how Our Blessed Lord walked with the feet of a child in those sands and gazed on the stars and stretches of desert that He had made with His own mind, and at the toy pyramids which the Pharaohs had made to bury themselves in dead, and perhaps to adore themselves in living. And He knew at that time that H. of Cairo and I would one day walk and talk of Him together. He is so near, is He not ? and, as life goes on, nearer still, and all things rather less and less except to know what He wants and to do it, or want it, too.

Ixelles: September, 1913.

. . . Your illness makes my heart ill. The evening post brought me very poor news of you and made me sad; but ' joy cometh in the morning '—this morning's post was much more hopeful. God has blessed the remedies for all the prayers, so many and so loving, that were said.

You are very precious to us, my dear Reverend Mother, much more than you know, and the thought of you is such a heart's comfort to me that I don't know that I could spare you yet, so I say, like Sister X., when she had a little interior movement of a detachment from some beloved book, ' I am sure you don't want it, dear Lord.' So I like to tell Him that I am sure He wants me to have the joy of finding H. of Cairo as I want to find her when I come. May His love be round you and in you and give you not only strength of soul, but of body too, that we may thank Him together. I am longing to get to you. . . .

Dear, dear Reverend Mother, how often my thoughts are with you, and I say to Our Lord: ' Lord, H. of Cairo whom Thou lovest is sick,' and He answers that He knows and that He is looking after her.

You know you must not risk giving yourself a relapse by coming to Alexandria if it is not wise. I shall love to have you if it is wise, but otherwise I would much rather wait to see you than run any risks.

I have just seen a picture in a fairy-book of Tom Thumb, ' Hop o' my Thumb,' as a baby lying in his father's hand, and I think you are just like that now. May Our Lord bless and love and lift you up.

Seishin Gakuin, Tokyo : 17th March, 1914.

From far Japan my soul salutes your soul, and thanks Our Lord for keeping His eye on it. He will not let you forget the sight of the turbid current, nor yet the joyful assurance that, in spite of *le mélange de la vie*, you are one of His dearest, redeemed with His precious blood, and daily fed with It. . . . I loved Egypt, and go back to it in thought with joy . . . indeed, I visited you more than anyone else on the 12th [the anniversary of their profession]. I wrote a letter to our survivors that will be typed and sent from the Mother House.

Letters to ' L.'

March, 1902.

It [a letter] referred to two classes of spiritual difficulties, one general, the Creation and Redemption, light and darkness in meditation ; the other particular, X.'s affairs. . . . The last is the group that is easier dealt with ; at the most they are mosquito bites, and if we want *God* we *must* learn to keep our souls free, to attach little importance to these things, and in general to allow ourselves no voluntary reflexions on what concerns us personally : It is the Lord, let Him do what seemeth good in His sight.

The other calls for a still more reverent silence. How can we know or see, and if we could, where would our faith be. Faith lives on the things that are most dark, as hope lives best on the elements of despair. It is because the whole thing seems out of joint, and out of tune to our human eyes (and it is childish to pretend that it does not), therefore we believe that its solution, the last Apocalypse of all, will be more glorious, more overpoweringly beautiful and satisfying than we can even imagine.

I wish I could find a worthy translation or make one, of a few lines of Schiller's that often come back to me on this subject, or perhaps you read enough German. Tell me in your next.

Enclosed in a lost note was the translation :

April, 1902.

Ah ! would that I could find the exit from
the hollows of this valley oppressed with chill
mists. How blessed would be my lot !

LETTERS ON THE SPIRITUAL LIFE

There I behold hills, ever young
and ever verdant.   Had I wings !   Had I pinions
I would take flight to those hills.

Harmony rings in my ears, the tones of heaven's
rest ; and the light breeze brings to me
the sweet odour of balm.

Golden grows the fruit among the dark foliage,
and the flowers that blossom there fall not a prey
to any winter.

Ah ! how beautiful must the days be in that eternal
sunlight, and the air upon those heights how
invigorating must it be.

Yet I am kept afar by the sweep of the wrathful
river current, its surges rise so high that my
soul sinks within me.

I see a skiff rocking on the water, but alas !
no pilot.   Dare it !   Doubt not, falter not.
Its sails are ensouled.
(I have seen this word in a good, if not a ' grave,' author !)

Thou *must believe*, thou *must dare*, for
the gods give no pledge, and nought but a
miracle can carry thee to the land of wonder.
(Schiller ' Sehnsucht ' *Longing*.)

On first reading, the opening verses will perhaps strike you
like the Christmas-tree notion of heaven that the English Martyr
wrote of in his cell, where the pears and peaches were ' exceeding
good and wondrous big,' but I do not at all think Schiller's
German idealistic mind meant it thus !   What I like is ' *the gods
give no pledge*.'   My translation is v. poor.—J. S.

January, 1906.

Now your letter is spread before me, for I am taking a letter
afternoon to get through the formation of stratified letters that
have accumulated.   And this is the thesis that I open upon,
that ' wholeness seems to you inseparable from detachment to
an uncommon degree.'   (Bless you ! that is the beauty of your
ferret ; he won't leave go.)   I think *it is so*, but why not ?   Don't
you think God asks of you such detachment ?   Read ' wholeness '
or ' simplicity of spirit ' as an erratum when you find ' detachment,' and I think you will find that all three make the same
sense.

As to ' loving many people,' I think the point of the problem comes in the question : ' From loving many people shall I not rise to loving God ? ' And I think the answer is *no* ; very few people can manage it that way. St. John seemed to think we ought, but we seem to be stupid about it somehow. The inductive method in these things breaks down ! But from loving God alone, can I get intuitions of Him in everyone and therefore love them, and ' have them in my heart ' and not only in my eclectic head, with a very high-priced ticket of admission ! But this I find expressed in other words on your next page, so I need not have said it at all. . . .

What are you changing in most ? and what are you going to invest this year in ? These are not conundrums.

August, 1906.

■ . . . There are as many varieties of humility as there are of St. John's wort, of which I believe there are twelve British varieties. In the case of humility, not one British. Wicked persons say that one was discovered, but it created such a surprise that the discoverer took it to the British Museum.

So long as you have any of the varieties I shall be glad, though *défaillance inouïe* is the one that pleases me best of all, and next to it the unobtrusive kind that flowers from that variety of temperance or product of temperance, which I call natural humility, *i.e.* modesty of mind, a very moderate estimate of oneself. . . .

June, 1907.

My dear, in solitude you meet God, and if you call it the sands of the desert, and see yourself an Arab in it with your sullen camel, the body, to carry you, you will love it better than if you think of it as snow. Snow paralyses all but the cheerful Arctic explorer and the Eskimo (and he has to live on whale fat), but the desert has vibratory lights and wonderful adumbration of things that are not seen, but divined, and many other things as well.

July, 1907.

. . . B. sailed on the Feast of the Epiphany. He is ' growing rubber ' in the Straits Settlements, and ' rather likes it.' I often reflect with wonder upon the number of lives given to rubber-growing, tea-planting, char-womaning (what is the verb ? Choring is American), fowl-keeping, etc., and God means it thus; it is all a problem and a tangle, all the more call for faith and hope. . . .

Why ask of the thought or the light which helps you, to show its passport or even its pedigree. If true it is of God, to be used, whether it be a farthing rush-light of earth or a meteor from the seventh heaven.

[No date.]

. . . I am amused at your weariness of the Samaritan woman !
Yet there is so much that you must love in the story, ' wearied
with His journey ' as He might be when he reaches our low
depths—coming to us in Communion from the journeyings of
His eternity—and *sedebat sic* and the *naïveté* of ' Sir, thou
hast nothing to draw with, and the well is deep,' and the ' meat '
of the Father's will, and the fields white for the harvest. All
that must appeal to you as well as what you mention.

Dublin : October, 1907.

Many thanks for those most interesting enclosures which I
retain.

Father D. writes to me that he travelled over to New York
in company with an Armenian priest who could not speak a
word of English, and had twenty-seven martyrs in his own
family, beginning with his grandfather, and had himself the face
of a man who had lived expecting martyrdom. These things
make us feel somewhat behind the times and ' out of the running,'
but God knows best, and we must do what we can in our circumstances. ' Not degrees of growth in holiness makes saints,' so
said an S.J. lately, but to ' take on us the mind of Christ.'

I think the rest of our soul in the simple thought of God is
one of the best things for it. ' God the refuge for His vexed
creatures,' who alone can understand and satisfy us. . . .

August, 1908.

. . . This will be but a shabby answer to all your interesting
' holiday letters,' and the one before them and the notes—all so
interesting ; but the pearl to me is what I have always thought,
but never knew that anyone had said, still less Bossuet, ' *Le ciel
est un Ah ! éternel.*' *Ah* says everything to my mind, an eternal
assent, an unspeakable joy, an astonishment utterly satisfied.

Your letter went out walking in forbidden places, an *oubliette*,
from which I have just rescued it after a momentary fear that
I had enclosed it to Mr. Witham !

1. I meant the patience that bides ; the work is God's. He
must have His time and we can do little more than wish and
wish and dispose ourselves, live with our souls *aux écoutes*.

2. I think the detachment, too, is more passive than active,
laissez faire Dieu. . . . Most things worth anything (after the
heroics of the noviceship) are more passive than active. . . .

3. I don't know exactly, but if I said it (be ready in any
way He likes to come) at this minute I should mean—sacra-
mentally—or by His will—or by the inspiration of the Holy Ghost,
or by those lowly human messengers to whom he entrusts His

messages to you, in fact again to be *aux écoutes* for the word of God.

I do not see any risks in self-surrender *to God*, but rather in keeping back anything from its completeness.

What wonderful things human lives are. Pray for two whom I am watching with much interest and admiration. One has plunged into a heroic marriage to save a girl's faith and character ; the other is struggling through the roughest possible waters to religious life. I think there will be many more martyrs and confessors than we expect.

September, 1908.

. . . I was very much interested in your first water-coloured sketch from nature. People's unbiassed instinctive colouring of landscape is to me one of the most telling things about them ! It strikes one at first sight that another mind has touched the trees in your sketch. I suppose to those who know enough about it, the way in which we sew on a button is as full of character as anything else, but to me at present, movements and colouring in painting are about the most characteristic things I know. . . . I have small intelligence and small time and many letters this afternoon.

June, 1909.

The thought that ' it might have been ' may be either bad or good ; bad if it lets the inward vigour of the mind slacken through the thought that one has missed the line and may never see the hounds again ; good if it works out into that beautiful permanent contrition (Father Faber calls it ' abiding sorrow for sin ') which rose to such heights of sanctity in the saints—say St. Francis of Assisi or St. Catherine of Siena. It is so often thus, is it not ? *vide, paris sumptionis quam sit dispar exitus*, true of the reception of the Truth as well as of the Life.

And for the rest . . . ' having God as not all have Him,' it is worse than useless to look at the ' all,' the thing is ' God and I.' It is for each one a unique relationship—love, friendship, prayer or union—whatever you choose to call it, and in that unique relationship *quis nos separabit*? The more you believe in it and hope in it the more you take possession of it ; and you *must* be ' His absolutely,' no matter in what way as compared with others. We know so little of what each one's secret is— ours to ourselves is everything. . . .

September, 1910.

I have just turned over the pages of your letter again, and must send a small word in answer. I don't think I could write a treatise or even a page on religious spirit. But I think it is fundamentally an act of faith, recognising that all things which come to one in religious life are very good, and that ' *it is well* ' because God works through them *thus* and *now*, whatever may be their own drawbacks, the limitations of the creatures are the sides where God's action comes in—so all is well.

If you can get '*Le Cœur de St. Gertrude*,' by Père Gros, it has some beautiful passages, showing the incredible tenderness of God for His creatures—sinners or just. There is in it the words about Our Lord appearing to sinners who have done some little thing for Him, on the extreme frontier of life ; ' on the low dark verge of life,' showing Himself to them and infusing His love into their souls.

March, 1912.

. . . I think in the abstract a good case could be made out for singularities, but in the concrete it seems otherwise. The mind of the saints is against them unless unavoidable, especially the mind of more modern complex saints, and there is always the danger of setting oneself a little above others as more enlightened, more *elect*, more fervent, more desirous of the Sacraments, and so on. I spare you what I read and laughed over in Father Nieremberg on ' a singular beast or a beast of singularity.' I forget what is the Latin in the psalm on which he is gravely playing, Spaniard and German in one ! I am quite sure that in going down, being submissive, effacing yourself you will get deeper draughts of *La communion au Christ* even with the sacrifice of a sacramental Communion.

Letters to ' M.'

July, 1911.

You should not make phantoms to yourself of ' terrible thoughts.' . . . On the same principle no one who has much to do ought ever to say to themselves how much I have to do, and how little time to do it in, because as the old women in the Midlands say, it ' vapours them,' and then they can do nothing. There is a good deal in that piece of advice if you meditate it ! Also listen to the end of things and you will not be vapoured by them. . . .

August, 1911.

Oh, yes, I do indeed understand. Arguments and reasons and explanations, plentiful as blackberries, do not really touch the question. We know this, that we have given God our very best, and staked our lives on it, and we are trying to spend every breath of life and every power of soul in His service, cut off from what we might have enjoyed, to pour out more before Him.

Could He be insensible to this ? Could He be God and not be touched to the heart by it ? I think He would be Moloch ! But He is our own God and knows that failing often and blundering daily we are trying to give Him of our best, and the result is the best worship that earth can give Him, the fullest music, the most heavenly thought. The more we pray and give ourselves into His hands the better we shall see, the more we reason and struggle to see the darker it grows. . . .

July, 1912.

. . . All that is the matter . . . is the stress of end of term, examinations, the pull of the term, and everything. You are all weary and haggard with your nerves too near the surface, and that makes some depressed, and others contradictory, some irritable, and others ready to howl ! Bear it and keep quiet. Go to the inside oratory, how glad I am you have it, and say ' Ah ! God, nobody knows all there is between you and me.' And then you will feel better and remember that heaven is not far off. And you will get a nice letter from me almost directly if you have not got it yet, which is an answer to one that I told you I would answer. But I did not invent the answer to suit the letter, it just turned out that way. God understands, and blesses all, and you too. . . .

September, 1912.

. . . I must write you a few lines to say a few things which I left unsaid for want of time when there was so much to say. It was this, and your letter brings it to my mind again, that when one gets into quite new circumstances and surroundings, among complete strangers, there is necessarily a moment—a period— of very great loneliness, before there is any new interest or stimulus on the human side or any new ties.

This is hard to go through, but precious supernaturally, it is the spiritual leisure which is more important for your soul's life. It is soul first, and everything that is not as you would wish or plan is to the good on that side; renunciation, disengagement from self, all the real ' spiritual exercises ' on which our life is strengthened. And in that solitude your friendship with God must ripen, and your soul grow strong.

So do not fret at the thousand and one things that will be contrary, but enter into them and learn *through* them, if not *from* them. . . . Pray quietly and constantly ; now you know God better you must keep very close to Him, talk to Him of every trouble or joy or aspiration or knock-down, and be very sweet to everyone.

September, 1912.

. . . Your letter made me laugh very much. The story of X., I could quite see her smooth round face convulsed with emotion, and your charitable consolation ; then the horror of the discovery that she was fifty-five ! ! . . . Tell me especially how your meditation gets on. Take trouble and a little time for the preparation of it. I am more and more convinced that the secret of progress in prayer is *there*, and in colloquies (hateful word) more than in reflections. . . . God bless you . . . all the hard things will be ' the making of the pup.' Try to take them lightly as God likes us to do, and the great and glorious things ' mightily ' as He also likes, terribly glad, terribly in earnest about them. All the rest is nothing.

September, 1912.

. . . Your account of X. was delightful and the rest of the letter also, the meeting with H. R. and finding her thus, one of God's own by-ways, where He walks with souls. . . . God has taken you out of the rush of life to set you in quiet for Himself for awhile, and teach you what He only can teach. . . . Try to be—to use the old English word—' inward,' living silent and content, and He will teach you without your knowing how, and you will hardly know *what* until afterwards. . . .

You are doing a great deal for me by getting nearer to God . . . the best of joys for you and for me! You have a good chance of mortification, but how good it is thus to rough it, and be poor. All sorts of spiritual gifts come through privations, if they are accepted.

Do you know I went to Fontaine l'Evêque *across the field of Waterloo*! God bless my dear child, be brave and laugh at the funny things. It will often save you from crying. . . .

October, 1912.

. . . I have been meaning to send you this letter to read, it is so human and suffering underneath the bravery that I think it is good reading and will sound to you like when ' a comrade's voice comes floating on the mountain air.' . . . I don't want you to lose one day of the good gift, but to go singing through it, singing in God's arms, where you take refuge, and where I like to think of you, the child of His Providence—a young swallow learning to fly and not rest. . . .

You are quite right, often there is not enough prayer. Clasp your God tight to your soul, and let the home of your thoughts be in Him. Bless you.

October, 1912.

. . . I send you a little pattern of a meditation which I often apply to any scene in the Passion, it is very easy. All prayer and no discourse. I send you also the last splendid bell of the heather here, which waited for me. Is it not a great and beautiful kind? I wonder what its name is?

An easy pattern for a meditation on the Passion. I often use it. Based on Cardinal Manning's Prayer for Fortitude.

Composition of Place. The particular point.

Petition. Give me light to contemplate the Love and Passion of Jesus, that I may be changed into love and patience.

(1) Take from me by the contemplation of this mystery of . .
　　　All selfishness.
　　　Take from me all softness.
　　　Take from me all self-love.
　　　Take from me all delicacy.
　　　Take from me all cowardice and fear.

(2) Give me by the contemplation of this mystery of . . .
　　　A spirit of endurance.
　　　Give me a love of labour.
　　　Give me a love of the Cross.
　　　Give me a love of hardship.
　　　Give me a spirit of courage.

(3) That I may be willing
　　　To spend myself
　　　And to be spent
　　　For the sake of the elect.

COLL. : Passion of Christ, strengthen me.
　　　O good Jesus, hear me, etc. . . .

October, 1912.

. . . Ah ! isn't it good ! isn't it hard for you in the *beginning*, but *cella continuata dulcescit*, that is true of the interior cell as well as of the religious solitude of the cell. You can only learn to pray by praying ; it must be hard at first, because you have let yourself be overrun with things that don't matter, and now they do matter, because they overrun you ; like the rabbit, harmless in England, a plague in Australia. Try to remember that all that is behind the veil is the realest thing of all, and all the best things that faith knows and hope reaches out to, and love loves are there, and will be ours soon. God bless you.

November, 1912.

. . . Happy Feast of All Saints, let it be a second birthday for your beautiful resolution, which only had a fall into a little pool of trouble, like a young thing in a white frock. Give it a clean frock to-morrow, set it on its feet again and bid it go on.

Do you know Rudyard Kipling's ' If ' ? I am sending it to you as soon as an opportunity comes, hoping you don't know it. I like it. . . .

You are right in saying that in some things we expect more than God does of some people, and of ourselves. Only we will go on trying to get there even if we fail, and we will love God and our neighbour and sing even when there are tears in our heart. . . . Your after-life, my dear child, will be just what you will it to be. . . . The past is God's, the future is His, the present is His and yours together. Be joyful for His sake, inside as well as outside. . . .

February, 1913.

. . . There are valleys and woods where the shadows are rather gruesome and weird, but your soul will come out of them again, and walk at large where great thoughts live, and you see the skirts of God's glory trailing. It is all good, be patient . . . as Dante said : ' Can I not, from any corner of the earth behold the sun and stars. . . .'

What you wrote about charity was balm to my spirit . . . it is as true as truth, and it is the key of our life. In the ' rush of life ' so few understand it, and yet by the side of this the ' rush of life ' and the most stirring work and perfect success is less than nothing. . . .

Go on very quietly, trusting God absolutely for all things great and little—God ' who ne'er betrayed man's trust.' . . .

March, 1913.

. . . My thoughts go often to you, and I am glad you liked some of Thomas of Jesus. Yes, it is quite true you go more by reason and common sense where you used to walk by enthusiasm. The second, in many cases (most cases) cannot last, I mean enthusiasm. The first (reason and common sense) is mortally hard in our life ; but there is a ' more excellent way,' the way of faith and hope. This is what I wish you with all my heart. It is an Easter Spirit, an Easter joy, but not without its tears— tears of the right sort are good for this life. I love the lines ' *sis lacrimarum gaudium, sis dulce vitae praemium*,' and they belong to Paschal-tide hymns.

Love and trust, and live in the great mansion that is your home, the Providence of God.

December, 1913.

. . . You said in a letter a few weeks ago that sometimes you thought you would almost forego ' special chances of sanctification ' than go through the difficulties.

Don't admit that thought, ever. You cannot think what a special chance of sanctification implies. Think, for a few acts of patience and forbearance and holding up against difficulties, you can be nearer to God for the whole of eternity, look more deeply into His unveiled face, and drink deeper of His know-ledge and love ! What does a little more trouble and pain matter, here, so soon to end, in comparison with all that. . . . Perhaps God lets you march through this flat dry place for a time, that your love and thoughts may rise more freely to those things which alone really matter. . . .

I don't in the least mind you copying what you want from my circulars, the only object in writing them is the hope that they will help somebody, and it is a keen joy to me when they do.

Your letters are always good to read and joyful to get.

God bless you and us all—'*quoniam bonus et in aeternum miseri-cordia e-e-e-jus.*' I got all the books. My own little book has prevented me from reading half of what I wanted to read. . . .

Letters to Different People.

Yes, the first year after Profession is often very hard, and your experience is that of many others. I will answer your letter in a very plain and matter-of-fact way. It is possible for every sensitive and artistic temperament to let itself go to such an extent as to become unbalanced, the slave of its impressions and ideas. But you have a great safeguard in yourself, your keen and intelligent interest in a thousand things, and so I say quite plainly : you are to a great extent responsible for your own health of mind, and quite capable of leading a full, rich, intelligent, inward life. I do not for a moment think that you will come down from this high place, where God means you to live, and become the slave of moods and emotions, but I owe it to you, as you have asked me the question straight out, to say that you could do so, as hundreds of others could, who by grace and effort keep themselves straight and true. So with you. God bless you.

To Another.

. . . I see you have been going through a special course of training, one of those necessary, but rather excruciating ones, so bad to go through at the time, so precious to look back on afterwards, though for a long time one cannot look back on them without getting red to the roots of one's hair. How ashamed one feels about being half-hearted with Our Lord, and when ' much has been given ' all the more; but the self-knowledge, and one hopes self-contempt, which comes out of it is worth it all.

I have come across lately two very different ideas of humility, both so full of teaching on their different sides. One is from Ruysbroeck, ' *Nous avons à obtenir de nous-même quelque défaillance inouïe, non quant à l'essence, mais quant à l'estime.*' That puts so perfectly in a nutshell the difference between the many bad *défaillances* and the few good ones. We are so apt to faint away ' *quant à l'essence*' just at the wrong moment, when heart, courage, generosity, or perseverance are wanted, when we ought to be at our best in real earnest, *contrariis non obstantibus*, with wind and tide against, and the ' *défaillance quant à l'essence*' takes such insidious forms, like Jonas, ' I am angry, with reason, even unto death,' and all the time it was the '*défaillance de l'estime*,' a fainting away of pride and vanity, and self-contempt that was wanted to pull us through.

It seems to me that the means, and the missing link between the two, to lift us from one to the other, from the wrong to the right, is St. Thomas's little word about the heart : ' *Te contemplans totum deficit.*' What do you think ?

The other idea of humility was in very great contrast, coming from the calm and balanced big Benedictine mind of Bishop Hedley. 'Humility is rather truth than abasement, rather filial trust than destitution.' What do you think of that ? If you take the two together there is a great deal of matter for meditation.

To Another.

. . . The right way in the Society is to settle down as a matter of faith and a matter of course where obedience places us, making from the first moment the interests, joys and sorrows of that house our own, not waiting as if settling down were a thing that should happen of itself. Is not the Society all over the world our home, its people our people, and above all its tabernacle our own God ? As long as you lean on circumstances, dear child, you will only live your life half and half. You must launch out into the deep and plunge in much deeper.

To Another.

. . . Life is for us all doing the will of God as it is made known to us moment by moment ; we cannot make a scheme of life like an architect's plan, this for the ground floor, and that for the first floor, and the staircase here ; the great Saints were made by the other method as Cardinal Newman says : ' I do not ask to see the distant scene, one step enough for me.'

To a Girl who wished to enter the Order.

July 3rd, 1912.

. . . It did not make me laugh at all, as you thought it would, but it made me very happy for you. Because if God has really given you a vocation to the Society of the Sacred Heart, then, I think, He has looked through all His treasures and given you the best, because He has called you to a life that is both hard and beautiful—very like His own, and based on friendship with Him, the very most beautiful thing in all life. May He give you the grace to be always faithful.

INDEX

Printed in England at THE BALLANTYNE PRESS
SPOTTISWOODE, BALLANTYNE & CO. LTD.
Colchester, London & Eton

CPSIA information can be obtained
at www.ICGtesting.com
Printed in the USA
LVHW051237200221
679497LV00007B/127